BRONZE AND IRON AGES IN SOUTH ASIA

ARCHAEOLOGY OF SOUTH ASIA – II

BRONZE AND IRON AGES IN SOUTH ASIA

D.P. AGRAWAL and J.S. KHARAKWAL

ARYAN BOOKS INTERNATIONAL
NEW DELHI

BRONZE AND IRON AGES IN SOUTH ASIA
(*Archaeology of South Asia – II*)

ISBN-81-7305-252-2

First published in **2003** by
ARYAN BOOKS INTERNATIONAL
Pooja Apts., 4B, Ansari Road, Darya Ganj, New Delhi-110 002 (India)
Tel. : 23287589, 23255799; Fax : 91-11-23270385; E-mail : aryanbooks@vsnl.com

Computer Typeset at ABI Prints & Publishing Co., New Delhi
Printed in India at B.B.N. Printers, New Delhi

For
Sheela & Vibha

PREFACE

A summary account of Indian Archaeology entitled, *The Archaeology of India*, was published two decades back (D.P. Agrawal 1982). Its revision was postponed again and again and in the meanwhile archaeological data kept on accumulating. Gradually we realized that to do justice to this vast data, one will have to produce two volumes. We therefore brought out the first volume, *South Asian Prehistory* (Agrawal & Kharakwal 2002) last year. The Bronze and Iron Ages have been covered in this volume. We have given an interdisciplinary survey of Indian archaeology giving due emphasis to technology as also environmental changes. As there has been some controversy about environmental changes, we have devoted a complete chapter to it. The Indus civilization required a much fuller treatment and therefore it has been dealt with in Chapter 3 in detail. The Copper Hoard culture has been included in Chapter 4, under the Chalcolithic culture. Of course the Iron Age is dealt with in a separate chapter.

Most of the general books on Indian archaeology have become out of date now, except for some on the Indus civilization. We have therefore tried to cater to the much felt need for a comprehensive book covering both the Bronze and Iron Ages. The book is addressed to the students, scholars and the interested laymen alike. We only hope that we have succeeded in this mission to satisfy such diverse demands.

The senior author has been associated with radiocarbon dating for a long time. We therefore wanted to give all uniformly calibrated ^{14}C dates, but soon we realized that the details required for this exercise (like their exact value on 5568 yr half life, stratigraphic association, etc.) were simply not available within the time frame of our book projects. We are however happy to note that Dr Sheela Kusumgar, long associated with ^{14}C dating lab, has taken this big task as a project sponsored by ICHR.

In any such ambitious venture one needs the help and cooperation of several friends and colleagues, which we were very fortunate to get in abundance. Both the authors got an opportunity of extended stay at the International Research Centre at Kyoto, which provided excellent library, computer facilities and a very congenial milieu.

Archaeological Survey of India and the Deccan College, Pune have been very kind and very liberal in allowing us in the use of their photographs and illustrations. We have acknowledged the help given by various individuals and institutions separately. Here we would like to record our gratitude to R.C. Agrawal, R.S. Bisht, J.P. Joshi, Janki Kandpal, Sheela Kusumgar, Richard Meadow, Heather Miller, V.N. Misra, Gregory Possehl, Hideo Tabata, Rakesh Tiwari, Vibha Tripathi, Y. Yasuda and a host for their help and cooperation. Finally, we owe our thanks to our young and quality conscious publisher, Vikas Arya.

D.P. Agrawal
J.S. Kharakwal

PREFACE

CONTENTS

ACKNOWLEDGEMENTS

The authors are grateful to the following for their help.

S.K. Aruni, R.S. Barhat, Piyush Bhatt, Harsh Chilwal, Govinda Dasila, A. Dikshit, P.S. Dobal , K.S. Gupta, K.C. Gyani, Tripta Jain, S.N. Joshi, A. Kadar, J. Kitagawa, Rajiv Lohani, J. Meena, Madan Meena, Rabi Mohanty, T. Nakagawa, Vinod Negi, Neha, L.C. Patel, Madhu Purti, Manikant Shah, D.D. Sharma, V.S. Shinde, Lalit Tiwari, S. Kanwar, M. Yadava, Azusa Yano.

LIST OF ILLUSTRATIONS

FIGURES

PLATES

TABLES

LIST OF ABBREVIATIONS

B-&-R W	:	Black-and-Red Ware
HARP	:	Harappa Archaeological Research Project
Kyr	:	Thousand years
LGM	:	Last Glacial Maximum
LRW	:	Lustrous Red Ware
NBPW	:	Northern Black Polished Ware
Pd	:	Period
PGW	:	Painted Grey Ware
TAP	:	Thailand Archaeometallurgy Project

Chapter 1

INTRODUCTION

Last year when we were thinking of revising the senior author's (DPA) *The Archaeology of India* (1982), we thought that we would be able to produce a handy volume, but soon realized that we cannot accommodate the whole range of new data right from the Stone Age to the Iron Age in one volume. Eventually we decided to bring out two different volumes, one each on Prehistory (Agrawal and Kharakwal 2002) and Bronze and Iron Ages of South Asia. This book deals with the Indus valley civilization and other cultures of Bronze and Iron Ages.

In this chapter we have highlighted only the challenging aspects that are discussed in greater detail in the following chapters, incorporating latest results of research on Bronze and Iron Ages.

The changing river channels, mainly in response to neo-tectonic movements of lineaments in Rajasthan have resulted in changes in the courses of the Satluj, Ghaggar and Drishadvati rivers as indicated by both the distribution of archaeological sites and satellite imageries (Agrawal and Sood 1993; for a detailed historical summary of such studies see Possehl 1999). As a result of these tectonic changes, the Satluj joined the Indus system and the Drishadvati, the Yamuna drainage. The ancient Harappan settlements of Kalibangan and other smaller sites were on the banks of the Ghaggar (old Sarasvati), which eventually dried as its main tributary joined the Indus system.

Remarkable progress has been made in the last few decades, in multidisciplinary studies towards reconstruction of past environment and climate. We have ourselves (DPA) carried out extensive projects in Kashmir, Rajasthan and Kumaun towards environmental reconstruction. In the marginal areas like Kashmir and Rajasthan, a little change in temperature or precipitation can result in flourishing of cultures or being forced out to look for greener pastures. Japanese and Indian teams have also carried out recently, high-resolution studies in the Sambhar and Lunkaranasar relict lakes to reconstruct palaeoclimate. We have explained the complexity of the situation as several ecological factors superimpose on each other. For example, in Rajasthan, besides the Holocene climatic changes, neo-tectonics has resulted in changing the loyalties of the rivers like the Satluj and the Yamuna. Nor are semi-arid ecologies suited for large sedentary populations for long periods of time. Despite the mid-Holocene climatic amelioration, Rajasthan remained a semi-arid ecology. The ecology had to give way once a threshold was crossed, till it regenerated again. This phenomenon is seen in Rajasthan as the Harappans appear around 2500 BC and wither away around 1800 BC, the Painted Grey Ware culture appears around 800 BC and disappears a few centuries later. So also the Rangmahal culture, which appears around 2nd-3rd centuries AD and withers away in a couple of centuries. We have discussed such issues under Chapter 2, Environmental Changes.

Thanks to the monumental efforts of Jarrige and others focussed on the north-western part of the Indian subcontinent, a gradual process of cultural development has been worked out, particularly at Mehrgarh, right from the 6th millennium BC.

The Indus civilization represents a glorious chapter in India's past and we have to bow to the Harappans for what they achieved in the 4th-3rd Millennia BC in a semi-arid ecology and for the rich cultural legacy they bequeathed. By what label we call them today does not really matter. McIntosh (2002: 205) says that unlike the Mesopotamian and Egyptian civilizations, the Indus had a brief moment of glory and was gone. However, the second urbanization was achieved in the mid-1st millennium BC (1500 years later) in an entirely different ecological zone (in the Ganga valley) "where civilizations continued to rise and fall for the rest of the South Asian history".

The urbanized Harappans are well-known for uniformity and standardization in weights, measures, ceramics, architecture, town-planning and in other arts and crafts, though there is variation in ceramics and town plans. Their metropolitan towns might have had an interesting and intricate network of trade. Each Harappan town seems to represent not only an economic interest, but also a system of beliefs and language. Regional variation in the material culture appears to be an important feature. We have tried to understand complex processes involved in the building up and also in the decline of the great Indus tradition. We may not be able to answer a large number of questions unless we decipher their script, though recently some scholars have claimed that their script is non-linguistic in nature (Chapter 3).

The Harappan legacy is not only its city life, but rural technologies or peasant science, knowledge that was within the control and experience of the ordinary household or village elements of culture that had been internalized and passed down generations within the family and the community (Ratnagar 2000: 126-128). These processes require a logical examination of the data. We would address these questions regionwise.

One important evidence, which is seldom discussed in the context of the break of the Harappan tradition, is in the area of agriculture.

It is interesting to note that Meadow identifies two early farming transformations in South Asia: One after the Indus civilization declined and the other in the Neolithic times. When viewed on a broad basis, two distinct agricultural revolutions can be identified for the north-western region of South Asia during the pre- and proto-historic period. The first involved the establishment by the 6th millennium BC of a farming complex based principally on the rabi (winter sown, spring harvested) crops of wheat and barley and on certain domestic bovids including zebu cattle, sheep and goats.

The second transformation saw the addition during the early 2nd millennium BC of *kharif* (summer sown, fall harvested) cereals including sorghum, various types of millets and rice along with new domestic animals including the camel, horse and donkey. These agricultural innovations might partly explain the obvious changes in settlement patterns. Meadow suggests that the introduction of the summer-sown cereal crops, when combined with the new means of animal-based traction, transport and communication, facilitated widespread settlement in areas previously marginal to food production as well as realignment of settlement in already occupied areas of north-western South Asia.

The glamour of archaeology of the rich Indus civilization, led to neglect of less prosperous cultures. Transition from Mesolithic to village-based agricultural societies to urban centres was not an exclusive Indus valley phenomenon, but a universal process, which is now traceable in Gujarat, Rajasthan, etc. Hence, Chapter 4 is devoted to all the non-urban rural Bronze Age cultures such as Ganeshwar-Jodhpura, Ahar or Banas, Anarta, Malwa, Savalda, Jorwe, Black-and-Red Ware of the Ganga valley and Copper Hoard people. Some of these, e.g. Anarta, Ganeshwar-Jodhpura and Ahar complexes now appear to be contemporary to Early/Mature and Late Harappan stages. All these have regional character and a gradual development is visible in respective regions. In recent years, some important sites like Balathal, Gilund and others have been studied, which have yielded interesting evidence of structural complexes.

The problem of the Copper Hoards culture is quite challenging, not only for dating but to identify their authors too. Why do we find them in caches? Even the recent discovery of a hoard of Harappan jewellery at Mandi is also enigmatic. Presence of arsenic in Copper Hoard artefacts, though common, does not appear deliberate but is perhaps an artefact of ore-impurities. These Copper Hoards have been circumstantially associated with the OCP, but as the hoards are themselves accidental finds, any definite association at this stage can only be conjectural. Besides, some waterlogged potsherds of Red Ware were termed Ochre Coloured Ware. The identities of different claimants of the term OCP have yet to be defined. The new discoveries from Pithoragarh and Madarpur have also been discussed in Chapter 4.

We also need to address issues like the symbiosis between hunter-gatherers and early farming communities, cultural and technological exchange, hinterland trade mechanisms and emergence of rank society, etc., in the Bronze Age societies as Levy (1998) and others have done for West Asia.

Chapter 5 deals with Iron Age cultures of South Asia. It has been divided into two sections. The first part incorporates description of various Iron Age cultures, e.g. Gandhar Grave, Painted Grey Ware, Megalithic and others, though not strictly in chronological order. The second section deals with literary evidence of iron, technical studies, ethnographic studies and early iron from Bronze Age sites. There is circumstantial evidence of diffusion of iron technology from Caucasus to north-western region of the subcontinent and then to the Himalayan region. Some scholars argue that iron was introduced in South Asia by the Indo-Aryans. However, in recent years, various independent centres have been advocated for indigenous origin of iron in South Asia, e.g., Central India, Central Himalayas, South India, Rajasthan and others. Some new sites like Raja-Nal-ka-Tila, Malhar have been discovered which date back to mid-2nd millennium BC. Apart from these, we have also added a discussion on wootz steel.

We need to address the following outstanding issues to understand the South Asian Iron Age and its technology:

- If iron technology is indigenous to India what and where are the technological stages?
- Where are the early examples of the production of the accidental iron during copper smelting.
- Did we use meteoritic iron in India?
- Why cast-iron making was so late in India? What are the stages of steel making? Was there an ornamental stage of iron use in India too when it was valued as a precious metal?
- What are the developmental stages of making wootz iron and how extensive was its use?
- In what way iron contributed to the socio-economic processes associated with the second urbanization?
- When does iron effectively replace bronze and stone?

- What role the Central Himalayas played in providing iron and its technology to the Ganga valley?
- Did early iron technology come with some Indo-Aryan groups?
- How are the multiple foci of early iron technology related to each other, if at all?
- What is the absolute chronological framework of early Iron Age based on calibrated radiocarbon and TL dates? Now that AMS dating is going to be available at the Institute of Physics at Bhubaneshwar, we should be able to date the actual iron artefacts and slag so that there is no ambiguity about relating the age of an iron artefact and the date based on charcoal.

Chapter 6 deals with the Central Himalayas, which appear to have played an important role in the expansion of agriculture and metal technology. The archaeological, linguistics and also genetic studies indicate that rice technology was perhaps introduced from south China, via South-East Asia, Brahmaputra valley and the Himalayan corridors to North India. We have emphasized that we need to look at the eastern contacts both for copper technology and rice agriculture, if we do not find their early beginning in Rajasthan and Ganga valley respectively. On the other hand, we also propose to examine the scenario that the MonKhmer speaking people brought rice technology with them. This would require a paradigm shift in our thinking, hence the need of interpolating this chapter, which deals with the role of the Central Himalayas in the archaeology of North India.

In the last and concluding chapter we summarize the evidence and point towards the lacunae to be filled and the new directions of research.

Chapter 2

ENVIRONMENTAL CHANGES

Contents:

- INTRODUCTION
- ENVIRONMENTAL CHANGES AND CIVILIZATIONAL PROCESSES

INTRODUCTION

The effect of environment on humans is a hotly debated subject. In sensitive zones, it assumes special importance. When, for example, it became too cold in Kashmir, or too arid in Rajasthan, humans had to migrate elsewhere. To explain the effect of environment on humans, we would like to quote a long but a very telling extract from Diamond, as it is very germane to our discussion of environment.

Jared Diamond (1997: 400-424) in his famous book *Guns, Germs & Steel* tries to reply to Yali, an aborigine of New Guinea, that :

> The striking differences between the long-term histories of peoples of the different continents have been due not to innate differences in the peoples themselves but to differences in their environments. I expect that if the populations of Aboriginal Australia and Eurasia could have been interchanged during the Late Pleistocene, the original Aboriginal Australians would now be the ones occupying most of the Americas and Australia, as well as Eurasia, while the original Aboriginal Eurasians would be the ones now reduced to downtrodden population fragments in Australia. One might at first be inclined to dismiss this assertion as meaningless, because the experiment is imaginary and my claim about its outcome cannot be verified. But historians are nevertheless able to evaluate related hypotheses by retrospective tests. For instance, one can examine what did happen when European farmers were transplanted to Greenland or the U.S. Great Plains and when farmers stemming ultimately from China emigrated to the Chatham Islands, the rain forests of Borneo, or the volcanic soils of Java or Hawaii. These tests confirm that the same ancestral peoples either ended up extinct, or returned to living as hunter-gatherers, or went on to build complex states, depending on their environments. Similarly, Aboriginal Australian hunter-gatherers, variously transplanted to Flinders Island, Tasmania, or south-eastern Australia, ended up extinct, or as hunter-gatherers with the modern world's simplest technology, or as canal builders intensively managing a productive fishery, depending on their environments.... Of course, the continents differ in innumerable environmental features affecting trajectories of human societies. But a mere laundry list of every possible difference does not constitute an answer to Yali's question. Just four sets of differences appear to me to be the most important ones.... The first set consists of continental differences in the wild plant and animal species available as starting materials for domestication. That's because food production was critical for the accumulation of food surpluses that could feed non-food-producing specialists and for the build-up of large populations enjoying a military advantage through mere numbers even before they had developed any technological or political advantage.... For both of those reasons, all developments of economically complex, socially

stratified, politically centralized societies beyond the level of small nascent chiefdoms were based on food production.... But most wild animal and plant species have proved unsuitable for domestication: food production has been based on relatively few species of livestock and crops. It turns out that the number of wild candidate species for domestication varied greatly among the continents, because of differences in continental areas and also (in the case of big mammals) in Late Pleistocene extinction. These extinctions were much more severe in Australia and the Americas than in Eurasia or Africa. As a result, Africa ended up biologically somewhat less well endowed than the much larger Eurasia, the Americas still less so and Australia even less so, as did Yali's New Guinea (with one-seventieth of Eurasia's area and with all of its original big mammals extinct in the Late Pleistocene).... On each continent, animal and plant domestication was concentrated in a few especially favourable homelands accounting for only a small fraction of the continent's total area. In the case of technological innovations and political institutions as well, most societies acquire much more from other societies than they invent themselves. Thus, diffusion and migration within a continent contribute importantly to the development of its societies, which tend in the long run to share each other's developments (insofar as environments permit) because of the processes illustrated in such simple form by Maori New Zealand's Musket Wars. That is, societies initially lacking an advantage either acquire it from societies possessing it or (if they fail to do so) are replaced by those other societies.... Hence a second set of factors consists of those affecting rates of diffusion and migration, which differed greatly among continents. They were most rapid in Eurasia, because of its east-west major axis and its relatively modest ecological and geographical barriers. The reasoning is straightforward for movements of crops and livestock, which depend strongly on climate and hence on latitude. But similar reasoning also applies to the diffusion of technological innovations, insofar as they are best suited without modification to specific environments. Diffusion was slower in Africa and especially in the Americas, because of those continents" north-south major axes and geographic and ecological barriers. It was also difficult in traditional New Guinea, where rugged terrain and the long backbone of high mountains prevented any significant progress toward political and linguistic unification.... Related to these factors affecting diffusion within continents is a third set of factors influencing diffusion between continents, which may also help build-up a local pool of domesticates and technology. Ease of intercontinental diffusion has varied, because some continents are more isolated than others. Within the last 6,000 years it has been easiest from Eurasia to sub-Saharan Africa, supplying most of Africa's species of livestock. But inter-hemispheric diffusion made no contribution to Native America's complex societies, isolated from Eurasia at low latitudes by broad oceans and at high latitudes by geography and by a climate suitable just for hunting-gathering. To Aboriginal Australia, isolated from Eurasia by the water barriers of the Indonesian Archipelago, Eurasia's sole proven contribution was the dingo.... The fourth and last set of factors consists of continental differences in area or total population size. A larger area or population means more potential inventors, more competing societies, more innovations available to adopt and more pressure to adopt and retain innovations, because societies failing to do so will tend to be eliminated by competing societies.

Those four sets of factors constitute big environmental differences that can be quantified objectively and that are not subject to dispute. While one can contest my subjective impression that New Guineans are on the average smarter than Eurasians, one cannot deny that New Guinea has a much smaller area and far fewer big animal species than Eurasia. But mention of these environmental differences invites among historians the label "geographic determinism," which raises hackles. The label seems to have unpleasant connotations, such as that human creativity counts for nothing, or that we humans are passive robots helplessly programmed by climate, fauna and flora. Of course, these fears are misplaced. Without human inventiveness, all of us today would still be cutting our meat with stone tools and eating it raw, like our ancestors of a million years ago. All human societies contain inventive people. It is just that some environments provide more starting materials and more favourable conditions for utilising inventions, than do other environments (Diamond 1997: 410-424).

We think that Diamond's profound observations provide a fitting prelude to our discussion of climatic and environmental changes in South Asia.

We have, however, to enter a caveat here. Diamond seems to take climate and environment as constants, though they are subject to short and long-term fluctuations. We have taken a dynamic view of these parameters.

During the last two million years, climate has been changing with 100 Kyr long cold periods alternating with 10-12 Kyr long warm ones. The Earth has already enjoyed this period of sunshine. So if this trend is right, the planet should be slipping into another glacial period. But the global warming due to higher emissions of Greenhouse gases (CO_2, CH_4, CFCs) may have reached a point where it could reverse the natural trends. It has therefore, become all the more important to know accurately the past trends and periodicities of climatic change so that we have a better understanding of the climate machine. It may alone enable us to predict the effects of anthropogenic factors on global climatic change.

The past global changes have been recorded in a variety of natural archives like ocean sediments (Fig. 2-1), lake deposits, wind-borne loess, ice sheets and glaciers, tree-rings, etc. Unlike the sea and ice cores, which generally provide uninterrupted sequences, on the land there are often disturbances and gaps due to various geomorphic processes. The continental records, however, provide higher spatial and temporal resolution. For example, the marine oxygen isotope record from 1.2 to 2.4 Myr shows a relatively monotonous 40 Kyr oscillation with an even amplitude, while on land at least four and possibly six, exceptionally intense and/or prolonged glacial climate episodes spaced some 200-300 Kyr apart took place during the same time (Kukla 1989). Here lies the importance of the land archives and hence of the Kashmir Karewas. Research on climatic and environmental changes in the past is being carried out in different parts of the Indian subcontinent by different institutions using a variety of techniques. The more definitive type of proxy climatic data, however, are available only from the transect, which runs from south-west to north-east, from the Arabian Sea to the Kashmir Himalayas. We have been associated with major interdisciplinary palaeoclimatic research projects in Rajasthan (Agrawal 1992; Singh *et al.* 1990) and Kashmir, besides our initial work on the sea level changes on the western coasts (Agrawal and Guzder 1972). Here we are highlighting our work on the Kashmir Himalayas and western India, which was carried out under an interdisciplinary project for about a decade in the background of the other work done in India but in a global perspective. We are trying to present a review of the work done so far, as also a summary of more recent findings so that this body of recent proxy climatic data, based on the natural archives located in continental South Asia, are available for regional and global correlation. The work on Kashmir has now been published in the form of two monographs (Agrawal *et al.* 1985, 1988) and a number of papers. The present review, however, gives the latest position regarding the palaeoclimatic evidence obtained from Kashmir along with its comparison with other parts of South Asia including the role of the Tibetan plateau in forcing climatic change.

With this backdrop, we would now take a brief look at the palaeoenvironment of the subcontinent.

ENVIRONMENTAL CHANGES AND CIVILIZATIONAL PROCESSES

In marginal areas, the environmental changes have played almost a deterministic role in affecting human settlements. As two case studies, of Kashmir and Rajasthan, we will examine in retrospect.

The earliest evidence of humans in Kashmir seemed to be the discovery of some pebble tools. Later on, their association with the earlier Neolithic levels of the valley ruled out their Palaeolithic association. The next culture is marked by the presence of stone blades and burins of the Upper Palaeolithic vintage. Though stratigraphic evidence is not conclusive, they appear

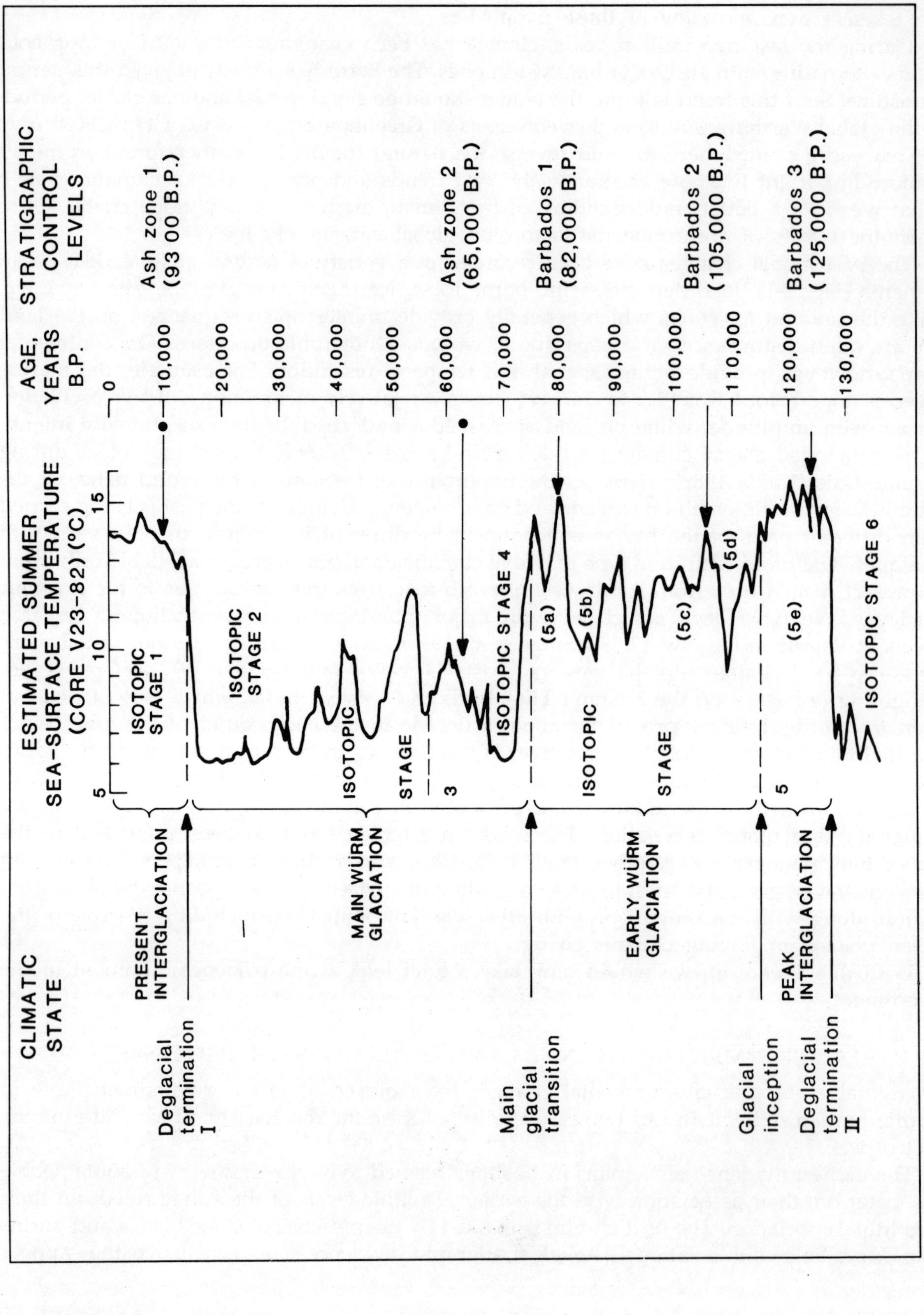

Fig. 2-1. Climatic changes during the last 1,30,000 years reconstructed from the analyses of a sea sediment core.

to be associated with the second palaeosol dateable to *c.* 18,000 BP in the valley. Thus we see that there is evidence of climatic amelioration as manifested by soil development, $\delta^{13}C$ values of the humus, dominance of thermophilous plants over conifers, etc., at this time. The next climatic amelioration is of mid-Holocene date and is evidenced by both pollen spectra and the development of the topmost palaeosol in the valley. This warm temperate climate is associated with large-scale Neolithic settlements all over the valley. Again we have evidence of climatic amelioration at about 1800 BP and 1000 BP. The warm climate of *c.* 1800 BP is marked by a large number of Kushana sites in the valley. The medieval warming was a global phenomenon. Even Iceland was colonized by the Vikings during this period. In Kashmir this period is marked by the famous Hindu dynasty represented by such illustrious kings as Lalitaditya, Avantivarman and others. The Kashmir valley is literally strewn with the monumental remains of this period both secular and religious. The famous temples of Martanda near Pahalgam and near Srinagar belong to this period.

On the one hand, the periods of climatic amelioration are marked by significant palaeodemographic increases, on the other, the intervening cold, arid periods do not seem to show any significant human activity. In such marginal areas, a drop of few degrees in the average annual temperature would result in large ice sheets covering not only the cultivable area, but also the lakes. During cold periods, therefore, the possibilities of economically surviving in the valley must be bleak indeed and humans must have migrated to greener and warmer pastures during such periods. The other remarkable development was that for the first time, the alluvial plains were colonized during the Kushana period. The earlier settlements were on the top of the Karewa plateaus. This only means that during this period, the alluvial plains were drained out of the remaining water bodies or swamps.

A similar picture emerges from Rajasthan. In this area also, large settlements appear only during periods of higher rainfall. The Upper Palaeolithic, the Mesolithic and the Harappa cultures are associated with relatively wetter periods. During the Harappan period, the rainfall was much higher than even today.

Superimposed on a gradual trend towards aridity were other factors, which made life difficult for early humans. Neo-tectonic movements led to changes in the loyalties of older tributaries of the Saraswati.

The Palaeo-Satluj joined the Indus and the Palaeo-Yamuna, the Ganga. The Saraswati river became an ephemeral river. In fact, one can trace the movement of cultures as palaeo-Yamuna was shifting towards the Ganga. Besides the environmental causes, there was the intrinsic constraint of the semi-arid ecology, which could not sustain very large sedentary populations of towns and urban centres. Besides these there may have been invasions/ migrations from the west. Though the case of Rajasthan appears to be a bit more complex, it is obvious that here too environmental changes were playing a deterministic role.

We also note that due to aridity, at the turn of the 2nd millennium BC, the Harappans started migrating towards the monsoon ecology of the Ganga doab. But they were not equipped to cope up with a higher rainfall environment, which was covered with dense forests and big swamps. The Doab could be colonized only with the advent of iron technology, which could provide an abundance of cheap iron tools.

Early humans had to face environmental crises too, as humankind is facing today. When in the Indus region water tables arose, or salinity of the lakes increased, or the rivers became dry, early humans had to move towards more congenial environments. Iron technology, as explained above, allowed them to colonize even monsoon forests. Early humans had faced other environmental crises even in the early Stone Age for which they had found a technological solution. In the early Stone Age humans could match neither the strength nor the speed of the animals and had to resort to wasteful mass killing of large herds of animals by stampeding them across cliffs and precipices. This resulted in a large-scale extinction of mammals. The Middle Palaeolithic humans, therefore, invented the first missiles in the form of spearheads and arrowheads. With this new technology they not only could pick and choose the animal they wanted to kill but it was ecologically less wasteful too.

With our concern for the future of this planet, we may perhaps draw some lessons from the past. Early humans resolved the economic crisis either by moving into more congenial environments or by developing new technologies to face new environmental challenges. Today the American prosperity is based on the exploitation of 45 per cent mineral wealth of the world. If the whole world, including the largely populated developing countries, want to attain that sort of prosperity, there are no more worlds left to exploit. With a better understanding of the world now, we also know that large-scale denudation of the tropical forests or melting of snow-covered polar areas in the north and south will lead to devastating damage to the overall ecology of the planet. By developing new technologies humans could live under the sea or colonize other planets. But is this the answer to the environmental crisis that we are facing today mainly because of the exorbitantly rich standard of living and impossible levels of consumption of the people of the north. The north now wants to put a moratorium on the developmental activities of the south on the plea that the south would further pollute the Earth by burning its coal, by growing paddy and with its large cattle population. Today the north seems to have forgotten that they have polluted the Earth so much during the last 200 years to raise their levels of consumption to impossible heights. If we want to maintain ecological balance today and leave a healthy environment for posterity, the only way is by reducing our wants by following Gandhian ideals of modest living and symbiosis with nature.

Let us now discuss the palaeoenvironmental evidence of different regions of the subcontinent.

Kashmir

The Kashmir valley is one of the intermontane basin-fills in the midst of the Himalayan ranges, like the Kathmandu and other valley-fills in Nepal. The Kashmir valley is situated between 33°-34°33' north latitude and 74°10'-75°30' east longitude. Today, the Jhelum river drains the valley and joins the Indus system in Pakistan. Kashmir provides almost a 1.2 km thick fluvio-lacustrine deposit covering the last 4 Myr. Various scholars have discussed the orogenic processes associated with the Himalayan uplift, basically the upthrusting of the Pir Panjal ranges (Agrawal *et al.* 1989; Burbank and Reynolds 1984). Thus from the northern-most part of South Asia, we have almost an uninterrupted fluvio-lacustrine archive preserving the signatures of climatic change.

In brief, the previous Himalayan drainage debouched directly into the Punjab, i.e. north-east to south-west before 4 Myr ago. About that time, the upthrusting of the Pir Panjals created a boat-shaped valley, impounding the Himalayan drainage, thus giving rise to a large lake of about 5,000 sq. km. As the Pir Panjals continued to rise, the lake was shifted to the Himalayan side, thus exposing the lower lacustrine sediments for aeolian deposition on the south-western flank of the valley. Eventually the Jhelum emerged *c.* 85,000 years BP and drained out the remaining primeval lake and provided a surface for aeolian deposition of loess on the Himalayan flank also. Subsequent upheavals and erosion by the Jhelum and its tributaries have exposed several geological sections, which made sampling of the total fluvio-lacustrine deposits easier. We could manage without recourse to expensive drilling operations. About 50 per cent of the valley is still covered by these fluvio-lacustrine sediments, topped by a mantle of loess giving rise to a flat plateau like surface which is called "Karewa" in the local language, a term now used by geologists to represent these fluvio-lacustrine deposits of Kashmir of Plio-Pleistocene age.

As mentioned above, around *c.* 18 Kyr, thermophilous (warmth loving) plants like Corylus, Juglans, etc., start appearing at the expense of the conifers. A palaeosol develops. In the valley an Upper Palaeolithic culture appears at this time. Again by the mid-Holocene climatic amelioration, there is a proliferation of Neolithic sites. Kushan Period (*c.* 1800 BP) is also a period of warming up accompanied by increase in population. The medieval warming, a global phenomenon, is also marked in the valley by the historical towns of Lalitaditya and others of his dynasty.

We did try to achieve, wherever possible, concordance between different parameters to verify the definite occurrence of a specific climatic event, e.g. the loess profile showed a well developed palaeosol at *c.* 18,000 years BP which itself is an indication of climatic amelioration; the humus from the palaeosol gave $\delta^{13}C$ value of 25 per cent (indicating C-3 type of plants), hence climatic amelioration as explained above. Around this time, a significant presence of the Upper Palaeolithic humans in the valley is evident, a sure sign of better climate. On the other hand, the Butapathri pollen profile shows a clear dominance of thermophilous plants like Alnus, Juglans, Carpinus, etc., at about the same time, at the cost of the conifers. Thus we find that there is convergence among four different parameters showing climatic amelioration at *c.* 18,000 years BP, a time when in the northern latitudes, it was still the Last Glacial Maximum.

At about 10,000 years BP, the bogs of Kashmir show cool temperate conditions changing to warmer conditions of the Hypsithermal period around 7,000-4,000 years BP. At the top of the profile, a cooler climate sets in again. The Anchar pollen profile again shows (Agrawal 1992, Figs. 5.4, 5.5) a mid-Holocene warming. The Hokarsar profile records a warming at *c.* 1000 years BP.

There are ten soils developed in the loess profile indicating warmer and more humid conditions. Out of these ten soils, only three appear to be fairly well developed. The valley starts warming up, indicating the onset of deglaciation around 18,000 BP, which was the time of the last glacial maximum elsewhere. During this time, the Arabian Sea shows glacial conditions and Rajasthan an arid climate. There seems to be an anti-correlation between Kashmir and Rajasthan. In Kashmir, the north-west monsoon probably became stronger at about *c.* 18,000 years when the south-west monsoon was very weak. This is now confirmed by Sarkar *et al.*'s (1990) work on the Arabian Sea cores. During the last 10,000 years, Kashmir shows a distinct cool-warm-cool oscillation which is confirmed by the Nepalese pollen diagrams. In Rajasthan between 13,000 and 6,000 BP, the lakes record violent fluctuations between hypersalinity and sweet water. During mid-Holocene both Kashmir and Rajasthan were warmer and wetter (Wasson *et al.* 1984). Minor and high-resolution changes in climate were monitored through a study of modern lake sediments from Kashmir, e.g. the Manasbal Lake seems to fluctuate between oligotrophic and eutrophic conditions with distinct cooler periods during which pigments were better preserved. About 1000 BP, the pollen diagrams, magnetic susceptibility data, etc., show a warmer and more humid climate, in tune with the global medieval warming.

Western India: Rajasthan and Gujarat

There have been various theories about the origin of the Thar Desert. Now we have worked out an outline of the Quaternary climatic history of Rajasthan and we know that the Thar Desert came into existence about 200 Kyr. The loessic deposit of Kashmir also dates to the same period. Here we will confine our discussion to the Holocene period.

We think that human-environment relationship in Rajasthan is determined by three main factors:

1. Change in rainfall
2. Change in palaeo-channels caused by neo-tectonics (Fig. 2-2)
3. Limited capacity of semi-arid ecology to sustain large sedentary populations. Singh *et al.* (1973, 1990) had carried out pollen studies on the cores raised from the saline lakes of Didwana, Lunkaransar and Sambhar in Rajasthan (Fig. 2-3). There have been mainly four theories about the origin of their salinity, as summarized by Possehl (1999c: 263-265):

(a) It is marine and results from the regression of the Tethys Sea; (b) the salt derives from brine springs in the region; (c) it is wind-borne, from the Arabian Sea and the Rann of Kachchh; and (d) G. Singh's hypothesis that it results from the concentration of salt through the evaporation of lake water with dissolved salt in it.

For periods younger than 20,000 BP, the palaeoecological data derived from pollen and the physical and geochemical evidence of Wasson *et al.* (1984) from the Didwana lake (Rajasthan) profile show independent, but converging, trends that clearly reflect the history of past changes in climate and the vegetation response in the semi-arid region of the Thar Desert (Figs. 2-3, 2-4).

The evidence for tree-less steppe environments, the extremely low values of wetland taxa and the simultaneous deposition of halites together with low sedimentation of clastics in the lake basin, from about the time of the Last Glacial Maximum to *c.* 13,000 BP, indicate hyper-arid conditions. As *Artemisia* (a winter rain taxon) values are much higher in pollen Zone Dl than those at present, it appears that hyperaridity was probably caused by a decline in summer monsoon precipitation and that winter precipitation was probably higher than that at present. For this rainfall pattern to exist, the westerly circulation must be farther south and the summer monsoon circulation must be weaker. The evidence of increased aridity during the Last Glacial Maximum and the Late Pleistocene, in the Thar Desert, has many parallels in other parts of the world (Sarnthein 1978). That the monsoon circulation had weakened during the Last Glacial Maximum is also amply supported by pollen, oxygen isotope and faunal analyses of deep sea cores from the Arabian Sea (Van Campo *et al.* 1982).

The change in a shrub savanna grassland, about 13,000 years BP, corresponds closely with the transformation of the lake basin to a fluctuating, saline to deep freshwater regime, in Zone D2. Both these developments, together with the rise in the values of freshwater wetland taxa in the later part of the zone, are indicative of a rise in precipitation, presumably through reinvigoration of summer monsoon circulation, about 13,000 years BP (cf. Van Campo 1986). That the winter precipitation was not adversely affected was shown by the fact that *Artemisia* values remained high, increasing towards the top of the zone, dating about 9400 years BP. It is possible that with the rise in sea level and increasing sea surface temperatures, during the terminal Pleistocene and early Holocene, both summer and winter atmospheric circulation carried greater moisture than before.

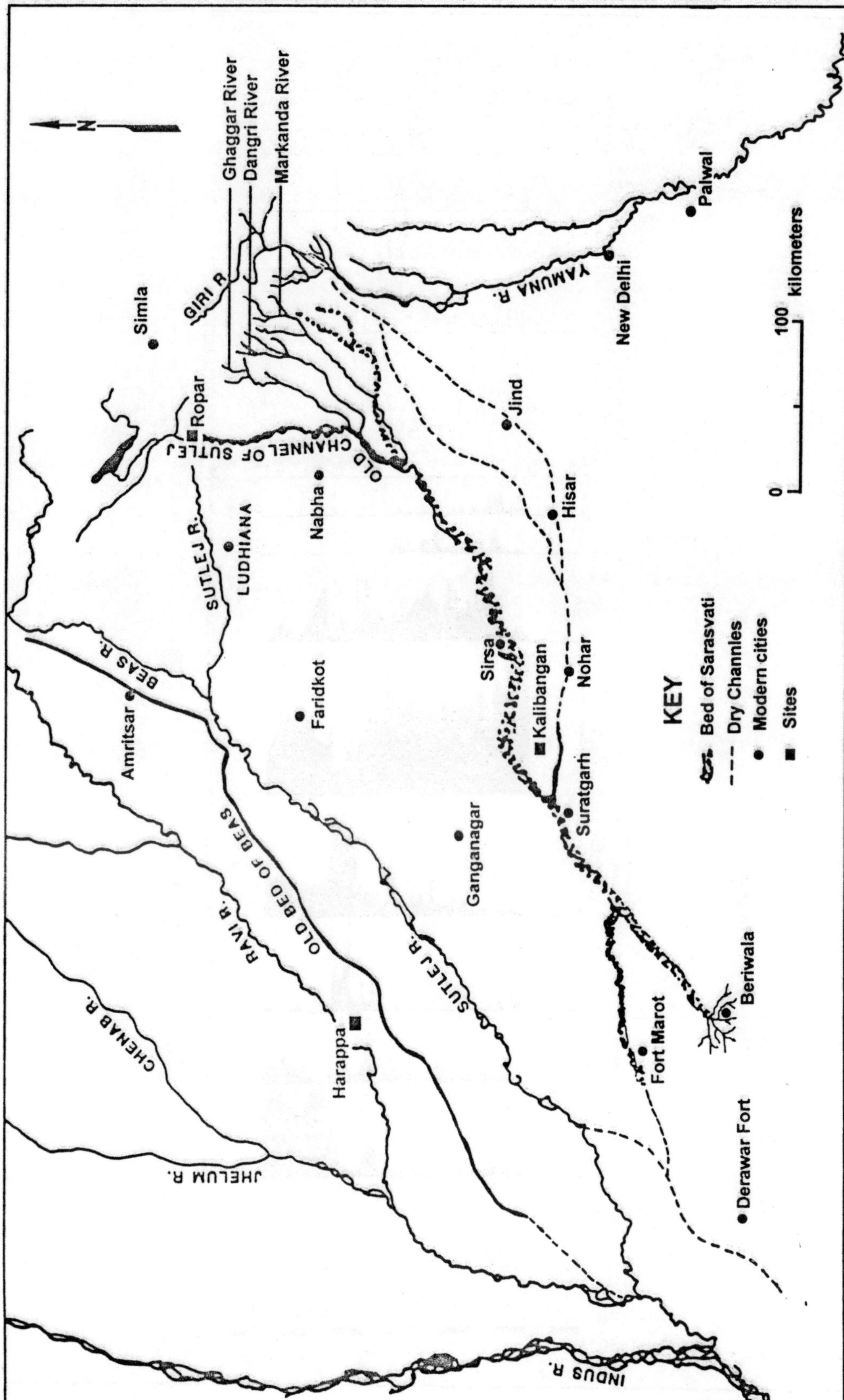

Fig. 2-2. Palaeo-channels in Rajasthan and main archaeological sites. The ancient Sarasvati has been identified with modern ephemeral River Ghaggar.

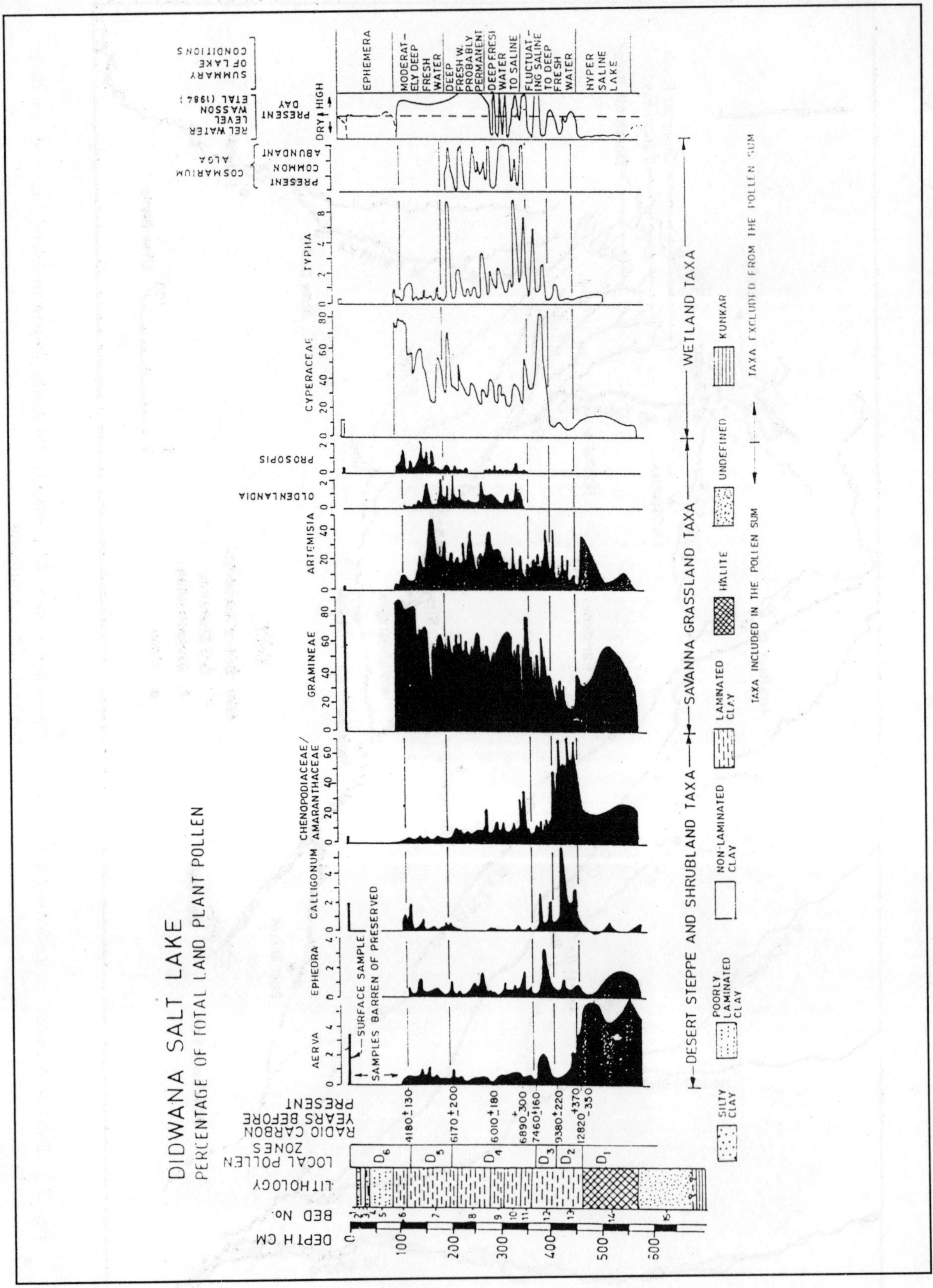

Fig. 2-3. Climatic reconstruction based on palynological and salinity data on the Didwana Salt Lake sediments.

In Zone D3 (*c.* 9300-7500 years BP) and Zone D4 (*c.* 7500-6000 years BP), the trend continued towards increasing precipitation (cf. Singh *et al.* 1990, Swain *et al.* 1983). The establishment of a tree savanna in Zone D4 correlates with a sustained deep, freshwater lake condition around 6000 years BP. Precipitation levels were considerably higher than at present. As taxa from the sub-humid and humid zones (with almost twice the present rainfall at Didwana), comprising both summer (*Oldenlandia*) and winter (*Artemisia*) precipitation, reached their highest values in Zone D4, it would appear that the total mean annual precipitation during the mid-Holocene between *c.* 7500 and 6000 years BP was about twice the modern value. It seems likely that the doubling was largely due to an increase in summer precipitation and that winter precipitation had remained as during the early Holocene (Figs. 2-3, 2-4 & 2-5).

After *c.* 6000 years BP, the change to moderately deep freshwater conditions, in Zone D5 (*c.* 6000-4200 BP), corresponds with the return of *Calligonum* shrubs on dunes in the region. By about 5000 years BP, both *Oldenlandia* and *Artemisia* show decline indicating that both summer and winter precipitation had started to decline, a trend which appears to have intensified further from *c.* 4000 years BP to the present-day. The evidence for intensification comes from the change in the lake to an ephemeral regime, from *c.* 4200 years BP and from the quality of the surface pollen spectrum in which *Aerva, Calligonum* and *Gramineae* pollen is shown to dominate the present-day sedimentary record. As *Artemisia* values are at their lowest level and *Oldenlandia* practically non-existent at either end of Zone D6, it is likely that both summer and winter precipitation fell to present levels at or soon after *c.* 4200 yr. BP.

The Singh *et al.* (1973) hypothesis has been recently questioned, most seriously from the following observations. The salt lakes are all grouped together within a very small region of Rajasthan. They are under one climatic regime. On the other hand, there are freshwater lakes in this same region, flourishing under the same climatic conditions that produced the hypersalinity in the lakes that have been studied by the geoclimatologists. The freshwater bodies are Pushkar Lake near Ajmer and the lesser-known Lake Gajner 30 km south of Bikaner city.

The salinity of the lake water is a function of the balance between rainfall and surface drainage on the one hand and subsurface conditions on the other. A change in total average annual rainfall, surface drainage or subsurface drainage will change the halite content of these bodies of water. As indicated by the changing palaeo-channels of the Satluj, Yamuna, Drishadvati, etc., the area is riddled with lineaments and fault lines caused by neo-tectonics. These changing lineaments could change both surface run-off and also subsurface drainage, affecting the salinity of the lakes. There is no doubt that Pushkar and some other lakes have access to subsurface water which more than neutralizes evaporation. But that does not mean that the lakes of Sambhar, Lunkaransar and Didwana, separated from each other by a few hundred km, could have remained unaffected by severe changes in precipitation. Swain *et al.* (1983: 1-17) used precipitation sensitive species to calculate quantitative changes in precipitation in Rajasthan. They estimated greatly increased summer precipitation of about 480 mm/yr, from 10.5 to 3.5 Kyr. The interval from 5-3.5 Kyr had the highest winter rainfall. Bryson (1988: 233) also remarks, "In northern India, summers during the mid-Holocene were much wetter. Now the summer monsoon is essentially the only rain in northern India, but in mid-Holocene time there was also considerable winter rainfall". One has therefore, to note that not only the summer monsoon but also the winter rainfall was significantly higher during the mid-Holocene, which brought down the salinity of the lakes in question. These climatic

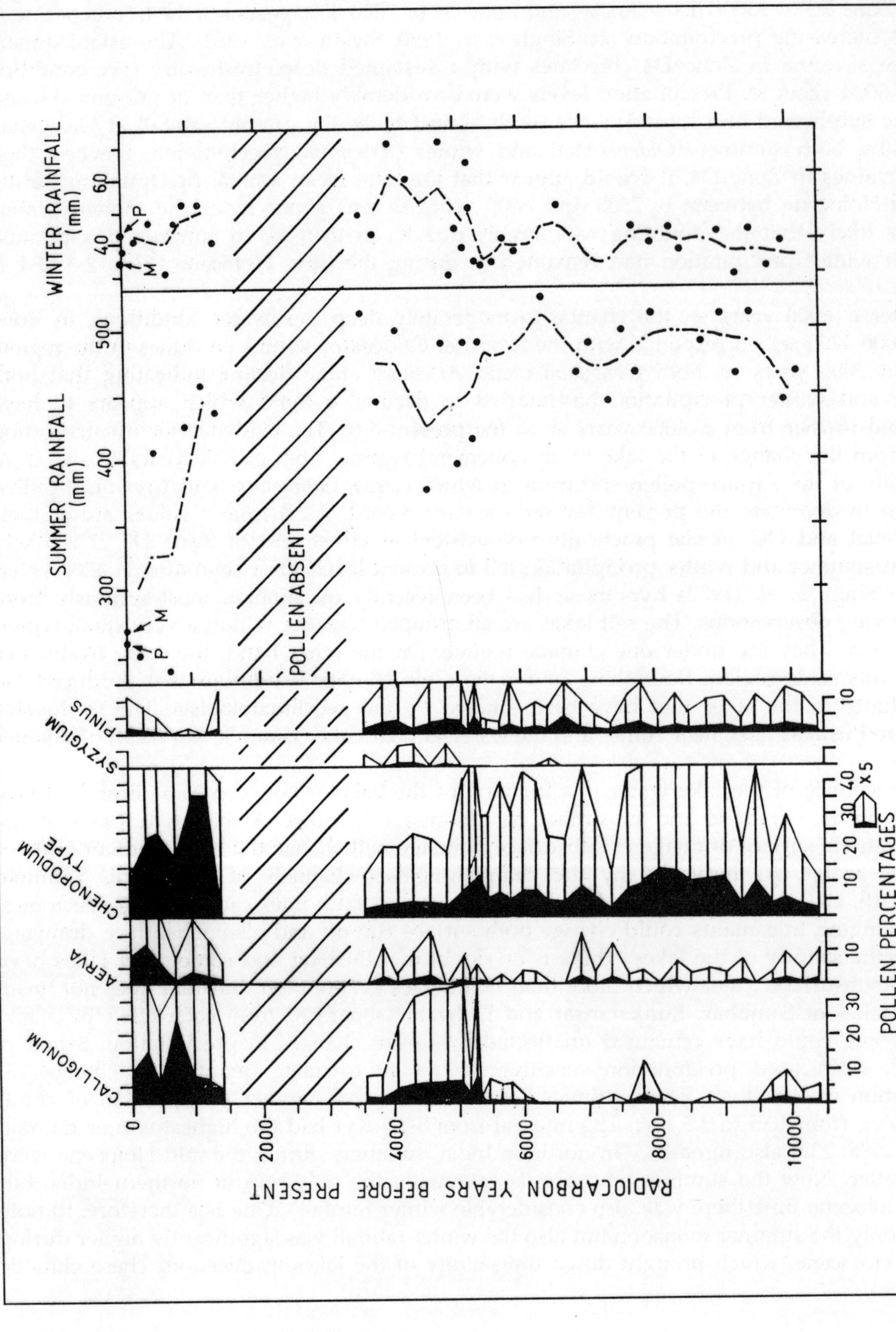

Fig. 2-4. Climatic reconstruction based on climate sensitive species from Rajasthan. Note the decrease in summer after 5000 BP and increase in winter precipitation rainfall.

inferences were based on rain-sensitive pollen spectra. Wasson *et al.* (1984) carried out extensive geochemical and sedimentological studies at Didwana. They inferred that the deepest water conditions in the entire sequence were indicated soon after 6 Kyr, thus confirming the climatic pattern indicated by pollen studies. Recently, a Japanese team in collaboration with the Deccan College, Pune, has again raised cores from Didwana for high-resolution work. Their detailed results are awaited.

Bryson (1988: 233) emphasizes the importance of the fact that there was "the long dry period from 3500 to 2000 BP". Recent work on the cores taken from the "oxygen minimum zone off Karachi at water depth of 700 m contains continuously laminated sediments with a sedimentation rate of 1.2 mm/yr and a unique record of monsoon climatic variability covering the last 5000 years (Rad *et al.* 1999: 39-53)". They further notice that the period from 3900 BP is marked by varve thickness minima and low turbite activity, which they interpret as indicators of low precipitation and decreased river run-off.

Prasad *et al.* (1997) carried out multidisciplinary studies in the Nal Sarovar in Gujarat involving sedimentological, faunal, $\delta^{13}C$, C/N in organic matter, magnetic susceptibility and measurement of crystalline index of clay minerals. Their study concludes that this period (6-4.8 Kyr) "showed the highest value of C/N indicative of higher proportion of terrestrial plants in association with enriched $\delta^{13}C$, shallow water loving *Bittium* and land snails". The overall climate was dry but evenly spaced with wet spells. During 4.8-3 Kyr the climate was wet. Thus we see that the Rajasthan climatic data, though admittedly not of high-resolution quality, do show convergence not only between different indicators but also agree with the multidisciplinary studies carried out by Gupta and Prasad (Prasad *et al.* 1997) in nearby Gujarat. We have also to note that the whole of northern hemisphere shows mid-Holocene warming and wetter conditions (Bryson 1988, Figs. 10 & 11).

A recent study by Thomas *et al.* (1999: 192) supports the findings of Singh *et al.* This study concludes: "(1) The present study provides evidence that during the Holocene the Thar Desert experienced multiple episodes of aeolian accumulation of short duration. These are spaced by periods of 1.5—2.0 ka of low accumulation/quiescence. These results also pose new questions that would require further work to consider: i) the role of winter precipitation changes in regulating aeolian dynamism; and ii) the implication of monsoonal teleconnections and phase lag in dune accretion. (2) The study also indicates that the earlier phase of desertification in the Thar ended at 0.6-0.8 ka ago. This may be an important input for land use planning of the region. (3) Evidence of increased sand mobilization/accretion is seen during the past 0.3 ka, suggesting anthropogenic effects".

Bryson (1988: 234-235), Singh (1971: 177-189), Singh *et al.* (1990: 351-358) and Agrawal (1992) all have emphasized the role of climate and environment in affecting habitations, especially the Harappa culture. But one has to admit that in Rajasthan the situation is more complex.

The changing river channels, mainly in response to neo-tectonic movement of lineaments in Rajasthan, have resulted in changes in the courses of Satluj, Ghaggar and Drishadvati as indicated by both the distribution of archaeological sites and satellite imageries (Agrawal and Sood 1982; for a detailed historical summary of such studies see Possehl 1999c). As a result of these tectonic changes, the Satluj joined the Indus system and the Drishadvati, the Yamuna drainage. The ancient Harappan settlements of Kalibangan and other smaller sites were on the banks of the Ghaggar, which eventually dried as its main tributary joined the Indus system.

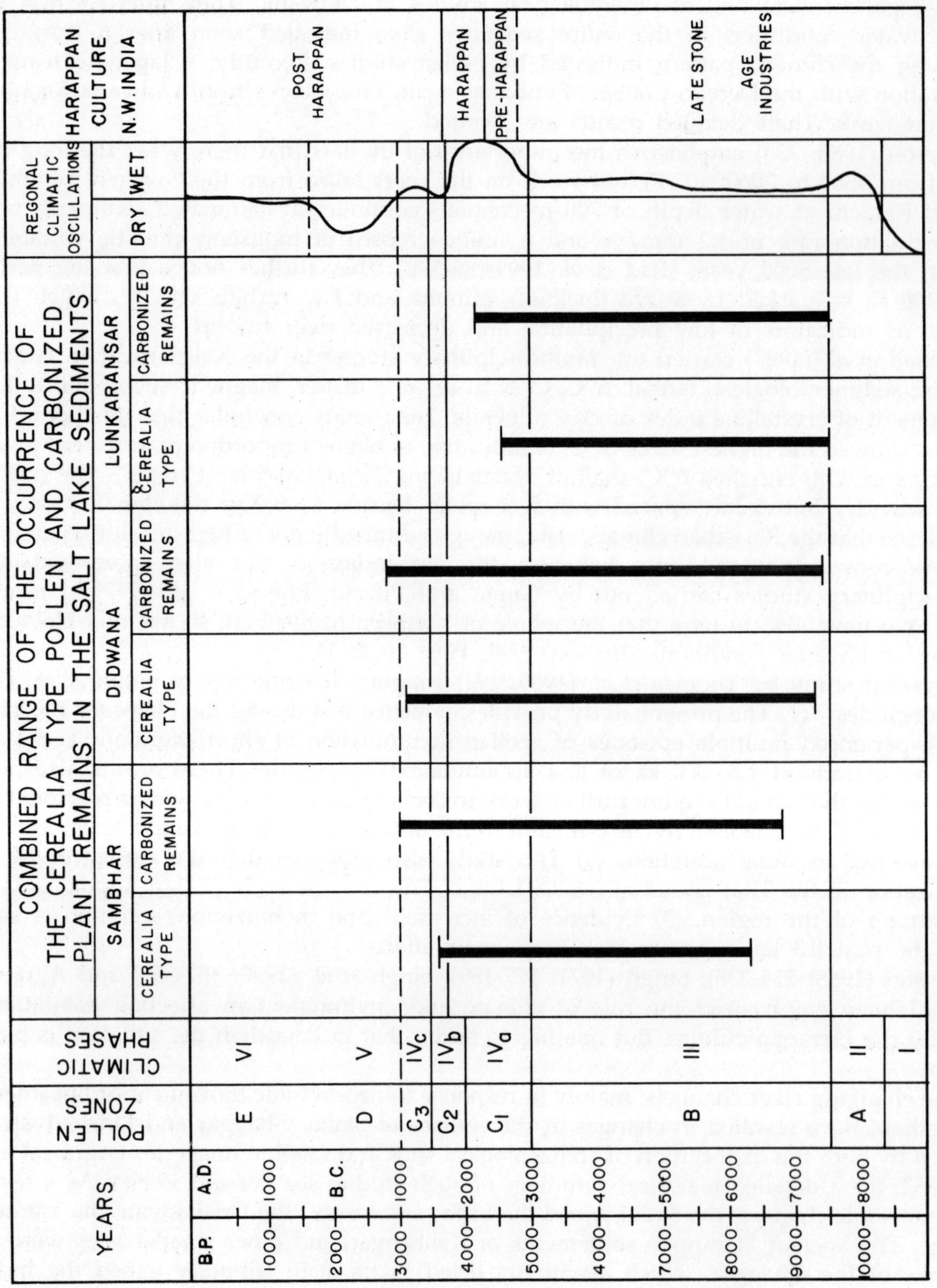

Fig. 2-5. Integrated climatic reconstruction of the Rajasthan lakes. Notice the occurrence of *Cerealia* type pollen, (a precursor of cultigens) and carbonized remains indicating forest clearance.

The third factor one has to take into account is the limited sustainability of semi-arid ecology for large sedentary populations. Despite the mid-Holocene climatic amelioration, Rajasthan remained a semi-arid ecology. It could not sustain large towns for any length of time. The ecology had to give way once a threshold was crossed, till it regenerated again. We see this phenomenon in Rajasthan. The Harappans appear around 2500 BC and wither away around 1800 BC (uncal.). The Painted Grey Ware culture again appears around 800 BC and disappears a few centuries later. So also the Rangmahal culture, which appears around 2nd-3rd centuries AD and withers away in a couple of centuries.

We thus see that in Rajasthan, it is not only the changing precipitation that affects habitation but also the changing loyalties of the rivers and the sustainability thresholds of semi-arid ecology to allow large sedentary populations for long periods of time. All these trends are superimposed on each other in Rajasthan.

More recent work of Singhvi *et al.* (1998) has shown that the main dune building activity is dateable to *c.* 14 Kyr, just before the onset of the strengthening of the monsoon. Our studies also have brought out the vital role of the Tibetan plateau in forcing climatic change (Agrawal and Yadava 1998: 55-58).

Other Areas

Acheulian sites are particularly densely concentrated and are richer in Central India and the southern eastern Ghats. Both these regions today receive adequate rainfall, have a thick vegetation cover and are rich in wild plant and animal food resources.

Further east, recently some studies have been carried out on the lagoons of the Pulicat lake in Orissa. The evidence is relevant to the climatic changes during mid-Holocene as it reflects the sea level changes in this area (Farooqui and Vaz 2000). They report,

> Monsoon appears to have increased in strength abruptly since the last deglaciation, firstly, between 13 to 12.5 ka and 10 to 9.5 ka and secondly, between 9.5 and 5.5 ka (ref. 21). The latter may have been punctuated by centuries-long periods of weaker monsoon circulation. Records of maximum monsoon from the Arabian Sea and terrestrial sites in the adjacent areas of Africa and Asia and north Atlantic warmth were thus coincident with each other between 9.5 and 5.5 ka and after 5.5 ka, the monsoon weakened more gradually in concert with slowly decreasing summer insolation in the northern Hemisphere. However, the records of maximum winter precipitation in north-western India during the Indus Culture period of 5000 to 3500 yrs BP have also been reported.... It was during this period that the northern Hemisphere summer monsoon strengthened over the African-Eurasian land. Reduction of monsoon rainfall indicated by the decay of mangroves after 11,000 yrs BP and a drier period in Central India, from 4500 to 3000 yrs BP and in Rajasthan from 4000 to 2000 yrs BP have also been reported. The dynamics of the South-West Indian monsoon and related sea level over the last 18,000 years conforms with the changes recorded in the present study. The above records indicate that the transgression and strong monsoon should also have favoured the establishment of mangrove vegetation along this part of the Indian coast during Early Holocene. But the drier period coupled with intermittent sea regression during late Holocene rendered the ecosystem not favourable for mangroves.

Farooqui and Vaz further say, "The post- LGM sea level rise reached its maximum around 6650 yrs BP at Sulurpet and after this, the area experienced regression and desiccation with the decelerating mangrove line too".

Ganga Valley

The Ganga valley has hardly much scientific palaeoclimatic data. H.P. Gupta collected a pollen sequence from an oxbow lake in Pratapgarh district of Uttar Pradesh in Ganga valley. He has concluded, "The climatic sequence, as determined from the biostratigraphy of the lake-basin has been grouped into four phases (I-IV). The general vegetation pattern is rather uniform and is tipped more towards open savannah forest with vast stretches of grasslands and a few scattered stands of arboreal vegetation". Gupta's chronology has poor controls and is not of much use in the present context. But in the Ganga valley, which is a monsoonal area with 100-150 cm/per year rainfall even today, finding savannah grasslands in the ameliorated climatic conditions of mid-Holocene looks highly improbable. The University of Allahabad is now making fresh attempts at raising cores and getting them analysed in collaboration with the Japanese team.

Development of morphology and soils of the study area in the Ganga plains, according to a more recent study by Kumar *et al.* (1996) can be considered to have taken place in the following stages:

Stage I (10000-8000 BP) : Large areas of the Indo-Ganga plains experienced a long spell of dry and cold climate during the last glaciation, effects of which were felt till about 6000 yrs (Fig. 11 a). The study area, however, has surficial soil deposits that are no older than *ca.* 10000 yrs. During the period starting from the Early Holocene, vegetation was scant, rivers had braided nature over vast stretches due to low and variable discharge and high sediment load. Soils developed with concentration of salts near the surface and precipitation of pedogenic calcite in the subsurface over only small upland areas in the east and north-east.

Stage II (8000-5000 BP) : This stage started with uplift of the Lower Ganga-Yamuna Block and corresponding activity along Ganga, Yamuna and Meerut Faults. Till about 6000 BP, climate continued to be cold and dry and later climate was warmer and wetter. This led to higher vegetation in the area and higher discharge and low sediment load of the streams.

Stage III (5000-2500 BP) : At the start of this stage, the Upper Ganga-Yamuna Block subsided and became a site of deposition. Also, the Yamuna river, which was flowing in Haryana (west of the present area) and was a part of the Indus system, shifted to south and became a tributary of the Ganga river. Both the Yamuna and Ganga rivers deposited sediments in the Gn-YP. Lateral erosion by the two rivers modified the northern boundary of the Lower Ganga-Yamuna Block and changed it to V-shaped with end pointing to the north. These plains were also the hub of activity of the Ochre Coloured Pottery (3900-3000 BP) and Painted Grey Ware (3000-2600 BP) cultures.

An increase in rainfall and improved drainage led to some regressive pedogenesis in Gn-Y1 (NSA) adjoining to the Ganga and Yamuna rivers and the Gn-Rgl. Salts and pedogenic calcrete were washed down partially to completely to the deeper levels (Kumar *et al.* 1996: 307).

This study by Kumar *et al.* also is in conformity with the general pattern of climatic amelioration during mid-Holocene in all the three regions of Kashmir, Rajasthan and the Ganga valley.

But it is obvious that in the Ganga valley, the urbanization processes had to wait till the middle of the 1st millennium BC. The monsoon forests, mentioned in the epics as *mahavana*, which were dark even in the day, could be cleared only after the mass-production of iron artefacts which alone made it possible to drain the swamps and clear the dense forests to produce the requisite agricultural surplus which could sustain towns and cities. The Harappans, who were only equipped to deal with the semi-arid ecology of Rajasthan and Sindh, simply withered away on the fringes of the Ganga valley.

For pre-Iron Age settlements, Murty (1981: 65-81) has given a detailed account of the South Indian ecology. This is one of the few papers dealing with the South Indian evidence.

This summary indicates that a lot remains to be done in the area of palaeoclimatic and palaeoenvironmental reconstruction in South Asia. Except for Kashmir and Rajasthan where multidisciplinary research has been carried out, in other regions there is hardly any work worth the name.

Chapter 3

INDUS CIVILIZATION OR HARAPPA CULTURE

Contents:

- PREAMBLE
- ORIGINS
- REGIONAL VARIATION AND MAIN TOWNS
- CRAFTS
- TRADE AND ECONOMY
- RELIGION
- BURIALS
- SCRIPT
- DECLINE AND LEGACY: LATE HARAPPANS

PREAMBLE

Besides the classical reports by Mackay, Marshall and Vats on Mohenjodaro and Harappa excavations, recent years have seen a plethora of books on Indus civilization (Wheeler 1968; Lal and Gupta 1984; Rao 1985; Chakrabarti 1990; Mughal 1997; Kenoyer 1998; Possehl 1980, 1993, 1999c; Possehl and Raval 1989, etc.). Unfortunately, the reports on the major excavations in India at Banawali, Dholavira, Kalibangan, Rakhigarhi, etc., are yet to see the light of the day. Possehl's *Indus Age* is encyclopaedic in its range and is most thorough in its documentation, though it covers only the antecedent phases of the Mature Harappa culture. More interesting, however, is Kenoyer's *Ancient Cities of the Indus Civilization* (1998), from which we have drawn a good deal for this chapter. In this book, the author has made bold interpretations of the archaeological data and put flesh on the archaeological bones. Kenoyer's childhood was spent in India, which has given him a unique advantage of being deeply steeped in the Indian folklore and rituals. May be not all his inferences are strictly warranted by the evidence but there is no harm at all in suggesting such interpretations and reconstructions.

The Indus civilization or Harappa culture (named after the first discovered site, Harappa) is remarkable for its uniformity and standardization in weights, measures, ceramics, architecture and in other arts and crafts, though there is variation in ceramics and town plans. This uniformity appears all the more imposing when one considers that the culture extended over more than a million sq. km, an area more than that of Pakistan today. What this uniformity reflects, whether it was an empire or a trading zone, can only be a speculation. But such uniformity, almost amounting to monotony, in a 3rd millennium BC context is indeed

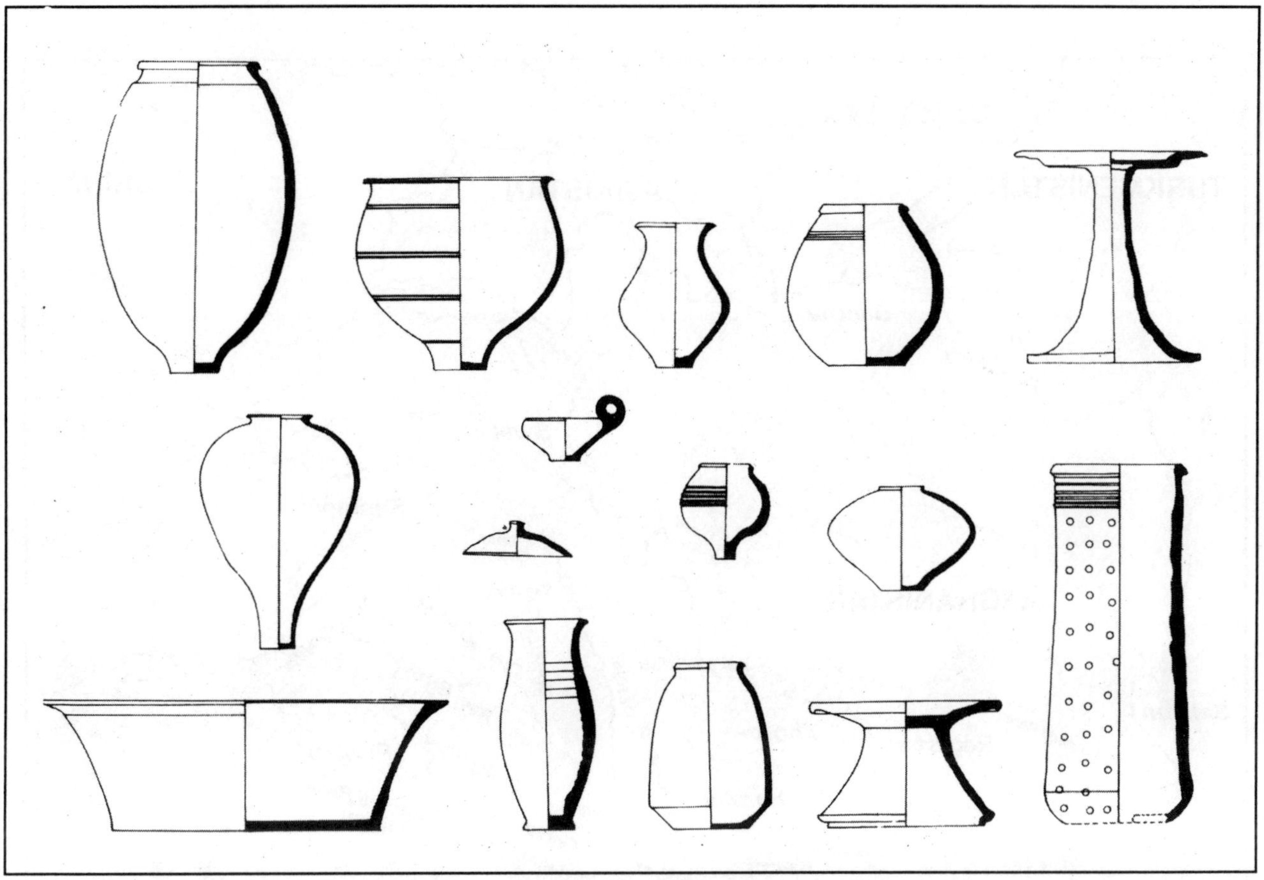

Fig. 3-1. Main Harappan pottery types.

unique. Recent studies, however, are revealing numerous regional variation.

To define the Harappa culture is not an easy task. The traits that originated earlier and the regional variations complicate the definition. Wheeler tried to define the culture by the alternative or accumulative presence of: (i) Indus seals; (ii) Indus script; (iii) motifs like intersecting circles; (iv) ceramic forms like goblets with pointed base, cylindrical pots with multiple perforations, jars with S-profile and dishes-on-stand (Fig. 3-1); (v) triangular terracotta cakes; (vi) kidney-shaped inlays of shell or faience; and (vii) certain beads, notably discoid with tubular holes. To these one may add town-planning (streets in grids, underground drains, fortified townships); brick dimensions in the ratio of 1: 2: 4; and typical shapes of copper artefacts like bent-bladed knives, double-edged razors, barbed triangular arrowheads with holes, etc.

The hallmark of the Harappa culture is town-planning, though fortifications and some amount of planning are also evident both at Kot Diji and Kalibangan in the Pre-Harappan levels. The Citadel, whether fortified with the lower town, or separately, was located in the west (except at Lothal). Houses, with rooms opening from three sides into a central courtyard, provision for water, drains and latrines, are characteristic of the Harappans.

In the outlying areas, the classical Harappan tradition absorbed some local traits also. The mother-goddess figurines and phalli of the Sindh are absent in Rajasthan and Gujarat. At Lothal there are fire-altars, but they are different from those of Kalibangan. At Kalibangan, the tower platforms with fire-altars, approachable only through a staircase, are unique in

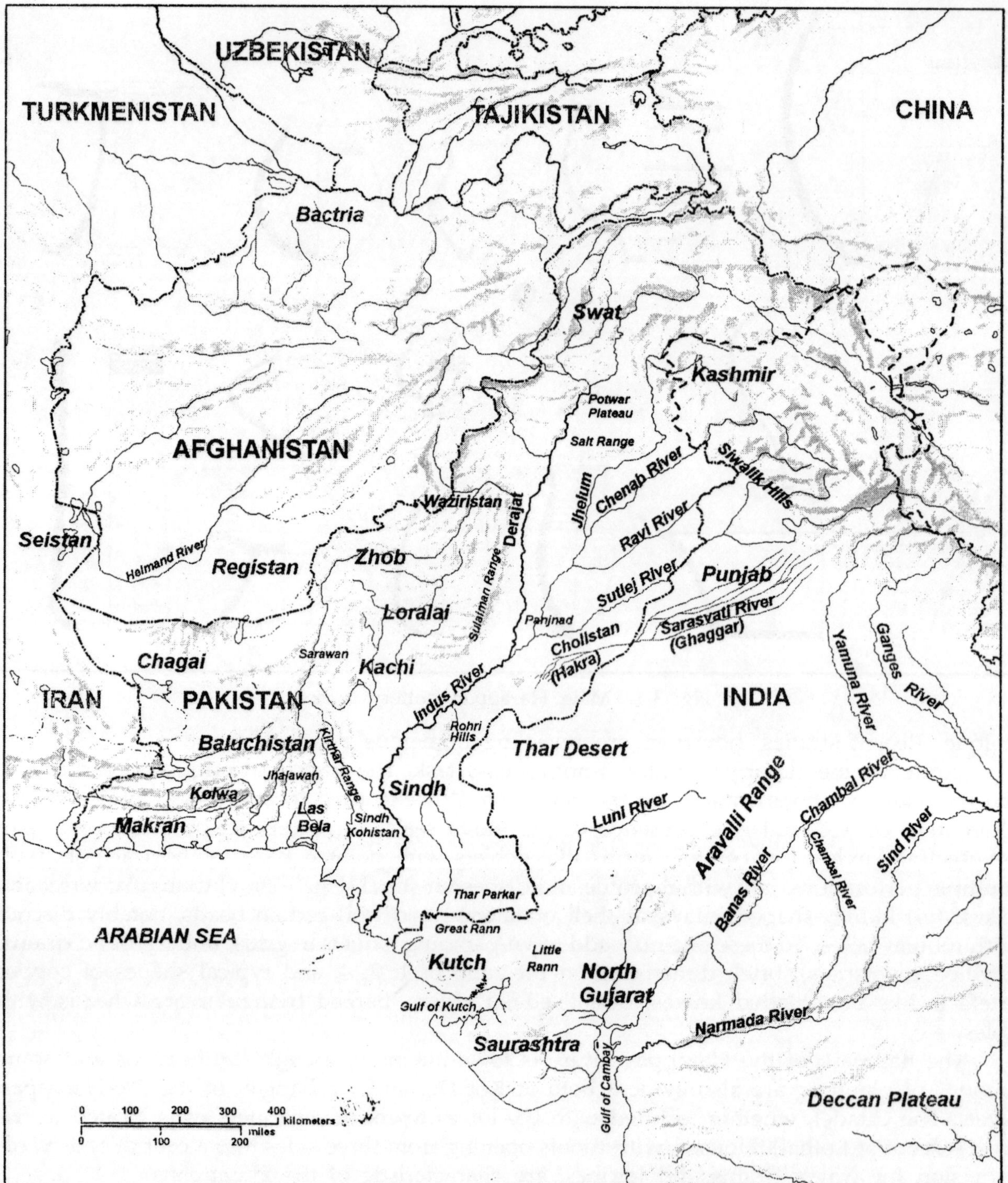

Fig. 3-2. Map of north-west South Asia, Iran and Afghanistan, showing main rivers and mountain ranges.

the whole of the Harappan "empire". It seems that though uniform standards were imposed over artefacts of mass consumption and trade, local differences in culture and religion were not interfered with. The script and the language too may have shown regional variations, but nobody has looked into it so far. These local differences will come to the fore in the course of our discussion of individual sites.

The Harappa culture was spread over 1.25 million sq. km. In the west Sutkagendor (Makran), in the east Alamgirpur (UP), Manda in the north and Bhagatrav in south Gujarat represent the outer limits of the culture (Fig. 3-2; Pl. 3-1). The uplands of Baluchistan, most of Uttar Pradesh and the south were out of its purview. Even the Indo-Gangetic divide does not have the Mature Harappan culture as such but only an amalgam of Pre-Harappan, the Harappan and local elements. The culture is mainly confined to the Indus valley and Saurashtra, including Kachchh. There are, a large number of Harappan sites on the dry Ghaggar-Hakra system, which probably joined the Indus or the Nara in the past.

The Harappan towns present a contrast to the Mesopotamian and Egyptian towns. Mark Kenoyer (1998) thinks that the Indus rulers governed their cities through the control of trade and religion rather than with armies. No monuments were erected to glorify their power. The stamp seals of the elite with symbols of wealth and power separated them from common people. Large buildings of the elite were not located in a single area of the town, but were spread all over the different mounds, unlike the layout of the Mesopotamian cities. He thinks that the seal has a name or title represented by the totemic animal which may have represented a clan or political office. These seals appear from the very beginning of the Indus civilization and linger on even in the Late Harappan phase. He notes that at Harappa mound E, the walls were rebuilt at least three times between 2600 and 1900 BC. He thinks that such phases of rebuilding and growth may denote the rise of new rulers who had gained the support of powerful communities living in the cities and suburbs.

Kenoyer contrasts Mesopotamia and Egypt where stone sculptures and relief of kings were made, unlike in South Asia. Ashoka built more than 115 stone columns but none of them had the portrait of the king.

Renfrew also echoes the same views about the character of the Harappa culture. He says,

> I have often thought how singular the Indus valley civilization is in this respect. For it possesses very large urban centres with a rectangular layout more impressive than any in Early Dynastic Mesopotamia and worthy of comparison with Teotihuacan. The centres have Citadels with large granaries, which were clearly the hub of a complex re-distributive exchange system. A range of traded materials is seen. Yet nowhere, on the basis of archaeological record at present available, is the superabundant personal wealth so characteristic of the early civilizations of Egypt, Mesopotamia and China. Nor has there been found the exceedingly complex and monumental religious symbolism characteristic of the Mesoamerican early state modules. Nor yet, despite the existence of a script, is there the vainglorious assertion of personal power, expressed in colossal monuments and inscriptions that we see in Egypt and Mesopotamia. The Harappan civilization does not reveal to the world any Ramses, any Hammurabi, nor yet any Gudea of Lagash. Indus exchange evidently functioned without such emphatically assertive statements about the prestige and power of the central person. (Renfrew 1984: 106).

It has been suggested that stamp seals with animal motifs carried messages understandable to all the different communities. As totemic symbols, the animals represented a specific clan or an official. The totemic animals represent at least ten clans: unicorn, humped bull, elephant, rhino, buffalo, hump-less bull, goat, antelope, crocodile and hare. It is to be noted that zebu bull is found only at Mohenjodaro and Harappa. The unicorn motif is most

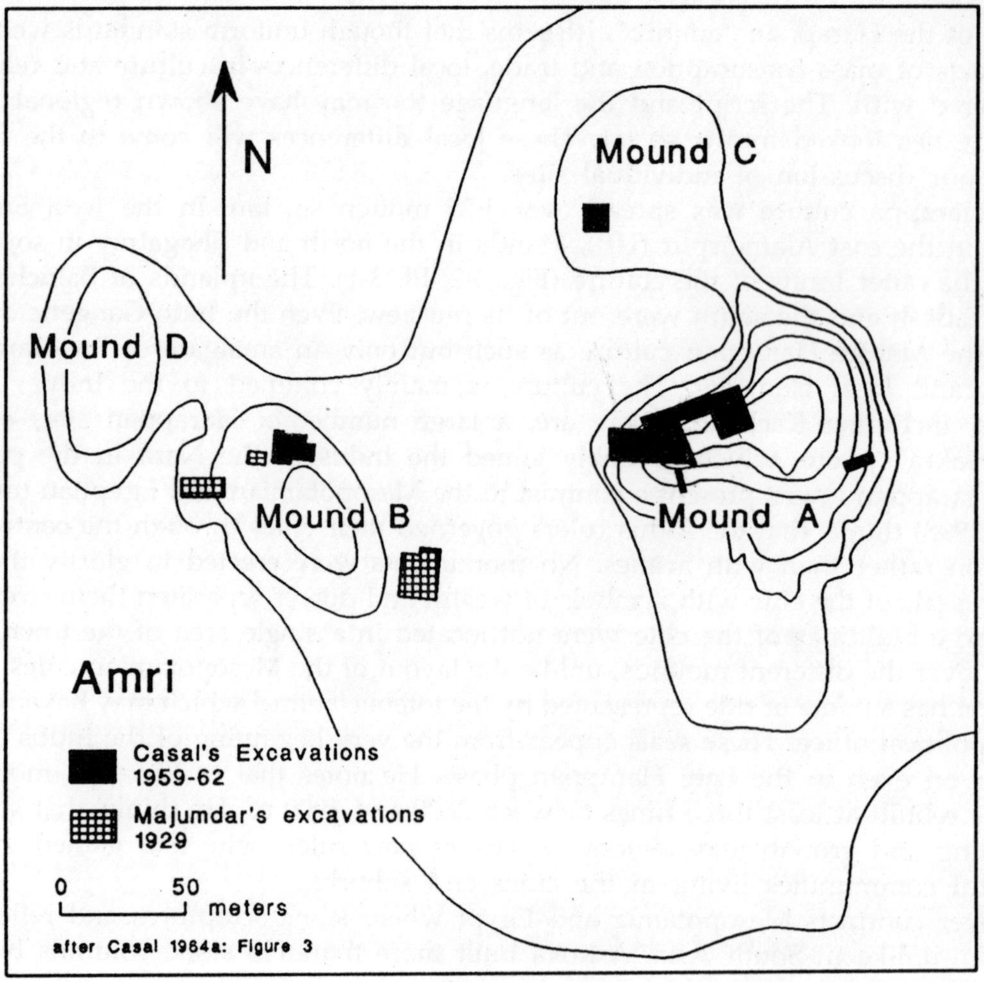

Fig. 3-3. Site plan of Amri. The areas excavated by Majumdar and Casal are shown separately.

popular (Pls. 3-2, -18). At Mohenjodaro 60 per cent seals have this motif. Unicorn probably represents the aristocracy and merchants directly involved in governing the different settlements. Of course, seals were also used to verify the contents of the parcel to be sent. From Lothal more than 100 impressed clay lumps have been found. Many other common animals like cobra, peacock, monkey and mongoose are seen in the narratives but never on stamps seals (Kenoyer 1998).

Although the Mature Harappa culture appears in a fully-developed form, a closer look at it reveals that it had, in fact, derived a great deal from the antecedent cultures, so much so that Mughal terms the so-called Pre-Harappan cultures, "Early Harappan".

Let us analyse the traits that the Harappan culture inherited from the preceding cultures.

It is seldom realized that the fortified sites of the Pre-Harappan cultures equal the Harappan ones. The Pre-Harappan people had fairly permanent settlements in the riverine environment indicating that they had learnt to exploit such ecology and some centres had developed, or were capable of executing large-scale communal works of elaborate fortification. It appears that the Harappans learnt fortifying the towns from the Pre-Harappans.

Many important industries were already developed by the Pre-Harappans. The blade technology had a uniformity, irrespective of the material uses, in the whole region. Copper was being exploited and used for ornaments and artefacts. Copper artefacts are also reported from Amri, Kot Diji, Saraikhola, Ghazishah and Kalibangan Period I. Steatite disc beads were manufactured at Kalibangan I and Pandi Wahi and lapis lazuli beads at Saraikhola. All these industries, which were later to become an integral part of the Harappa culture, were already established in the Pre-Harappan times.

The Pre-Harappan brick sizes were standardized (30 x 20 x 10 cm) and bricks were laid in the English bond. The Harappan ratio of 1: 2: 4 for the bricks, compared to 1: 2: 3 of the Pre-Harappans, marks only a preference, the concept of standardization remaining a borrowed one. The same English bond was also used by the Harappans. Terracotta cakes, whatever be their function, are a contribution of the Pre-Harappans to the Harappa culture. Even typical Harappan motifs of fish-scale pattern and intersecting circles had already been employed by the Kot Dijians (Fig. 3-11) and the Amrians.

The Pre-Harappans were already employing bullock carts for trade and communication as the toy-cart models indicate (Pl. 3-3).

So the contributions of the Pre-Harappans to the make-up of the Harappa culture in the fields of architecture, town-planning, transport, stone and metal industries, pottery motifs etc., are quite significant. It is therefore, quite logical that this stage of the Amrian, the Kot Dijian and other cultures of the Indus valley was defined by Mughal as "Early Harappan".

As discussed earlier, the contributions and connections of the upland cultures of Baluchistan with the Harappans are also quite significant. The nomads have been coming seasonally to the plains since time immemorial. At some stage, the limited fertile land available to the uplanders may have forced the increasing population to settle down in the riverine ecology. The crafts, the technology to build gabarbands, etc., and the necessary organizational system had already developed at the Pre-Harappan stage of the uplands.

The riverine milieu drew on these skills as well as on the communal effort. Rivers did not have dams, but bunds to protect the settlements. Architects, masons, stone fabricators and smiths had a greater role to play now, which they did. The new social hierarchy had to decide how much and in what form were these technicians to be provided for from the agricultural surplus of the society. A central authority was perhaps necessitated to look after the interests in balance and demands of different classes of people.

The Harappa culture was not a transplant from Sumer. The Sumerian art forms and society were change-prone whereas the Indus civilization shows all the marks of stability and a very slow change. The Sumerian civilization, which was a thousand years older than the Indus, did spread out its influence through Iran, Bampur, Makran and Kulli sites. So the idea of city life and its innovations was already in the air to have influenced the Pre-Harappans and the Harappans too.

At the village level, religion was a private, family concern. But now the Citadels have a special system for communal jobs. This required a priest class, which not only controlled religion, but perhaps also the relationships between the craftsmen, peasants and other classes of society. Such concurrent developments in many segments of the society could have led to urbanization.

There is another aspect of the problem: the Pre-Harappans and the Harappans need not be time-exclusive cultures. Ghosh once pointed out that it is of great interest to note that the pottery of Kalibangan Period I occurs in mound-2 from the bottom to about the mid-height of the Harappan. This shows that the Harappans not only co-lived with the local population (the Pre-Harappans), but possibly in the same houses, for the two sets of pottery are found mixed up.

Kunal (in Haryana) Period IC represents a transitional phase between the Early Harappan and Mature Harappan culture. The dwellings changed from the semi-subterranean huts to regular square rectangular houses built of standardized mud bricks on the ground level which was further raised at various points to provide height and stability. The brick sizes are in two ratios 1: 2: 3 and 1: 2: 4 (9 x 18 x 36; 13 x 26 x 39;11 x 22 x 33 cm), both used simultaneously. It is common knowledge that 1: 2: 3 ratio bricks cannot always produce the so-called "English Bond". The houses, though modest in size compared to those of the Mature Harappan period, developed drainage systems also.

To explain this paradox of part-contemporaneity of the Pre-Harappan and Harappan traits, the first author had proposed that Harappa culture was an urban, artificially standardized and selectively Indianized form, which derived from, yet continued to be coeval with, the so-called Pre-Harappan cultures. The two cultures existed as the present-day planned city of Chandigarh exists in the matrix of a rural Punjab. The Pre-Harappan and the Harappan cultures are not two disparate entities but urban and rural aspects of the same cultural phenomenon. The Harappa culture did not supplant the Pre-Harappan cultures, except where cities were built, but had a bilateral relationship with them. The regimentation and commercial uniformity of the Harappan industries stands starkly against the diversity and delicacy of the regional idioms of the Pre-Harappan cultures. The Harappan abruptness was deliberate and a process of natural growth. The apparently eclectic assortment of traits that comprise the Harappa culture has a conscious bias to local chauvinism, for example, the depiction of the flora and fauna on the pottery like the Brahma bull, cobras, peacock and fish. The Harappan phases of Kot Diji, Amri and Kalibangan therefore, should not be understood as one culture supplanting another, but like a city corporation taking over a suburban village to urbanize it.

ORIGINS

Though the Harappan cities are abrupt in appearance, the process of urbanization in the area was not so. Several recent studies (Dales, 1965; Fairservis, 1967; Kenoyer 1998) have shown that the Indus basin and its adjoining regions (Fig. 3-2) were on the threshold of urbanization even before *c.* 2500 BC. Larger villages were growing into towns: a "Palace" and a rampart were built in Mundigak Pd IV; Kot Diji Pd I and Kalibangan Pd I settlements were fortified. This process of incipient urbanization can be discerned in Phases D and E of Dales (1965) and Stages III and IV of Fairservis (1967).

Perhaps the increase in the agricultural produce of the villages forced the need of markets and hence a merchant class. Recurrent floods required the building of trading centres at elevated grounds—a regular feature of the Harappan Citadel. This merchant class not only planned the Harappan cities, but also deliberately standardized the cultural traits of these city centres.

The Pre-Harappan cultures, on the other hand, betray a natural growth. They show their regional idioms, as also the Iranian affinities, as has been emphasized by several authors. The process of the Iranian influences can be traced to the so-called Chalcolithic cultures, e.g. Malwa and Jorwe cultures. Sankalia has traced a large body of traits and motifs common between the Indian Chalcolithic and West Asiatic cultures, as also between the Chalcolithic and the Pre-Harappan cultures (Sankalia 1969). All these facts betray a gradual cultural diffusion from West Asia into India.

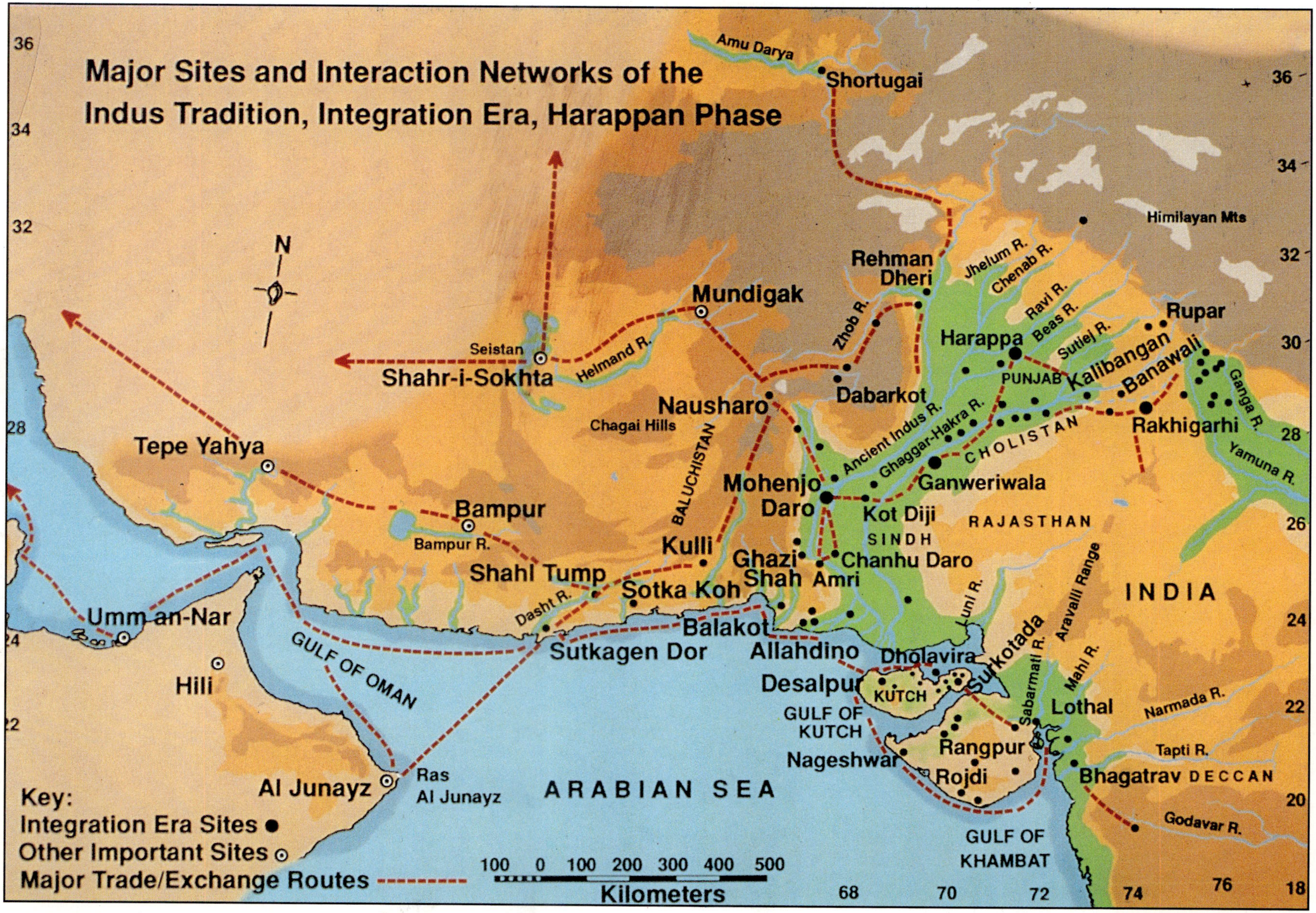

Pl. 3-1. Map showing main Harappan sites.

Pl. 3-2. Steatite unicorn pendent, Mohenjodaro.

Pl. 3-3. Terracotta model of ox-carts from Nausharo.

Pl. 3-5. Clay tablet showing a person holding two tigers, an elephant below, and a wheel above, reminding one of the Gilgamesh myth.

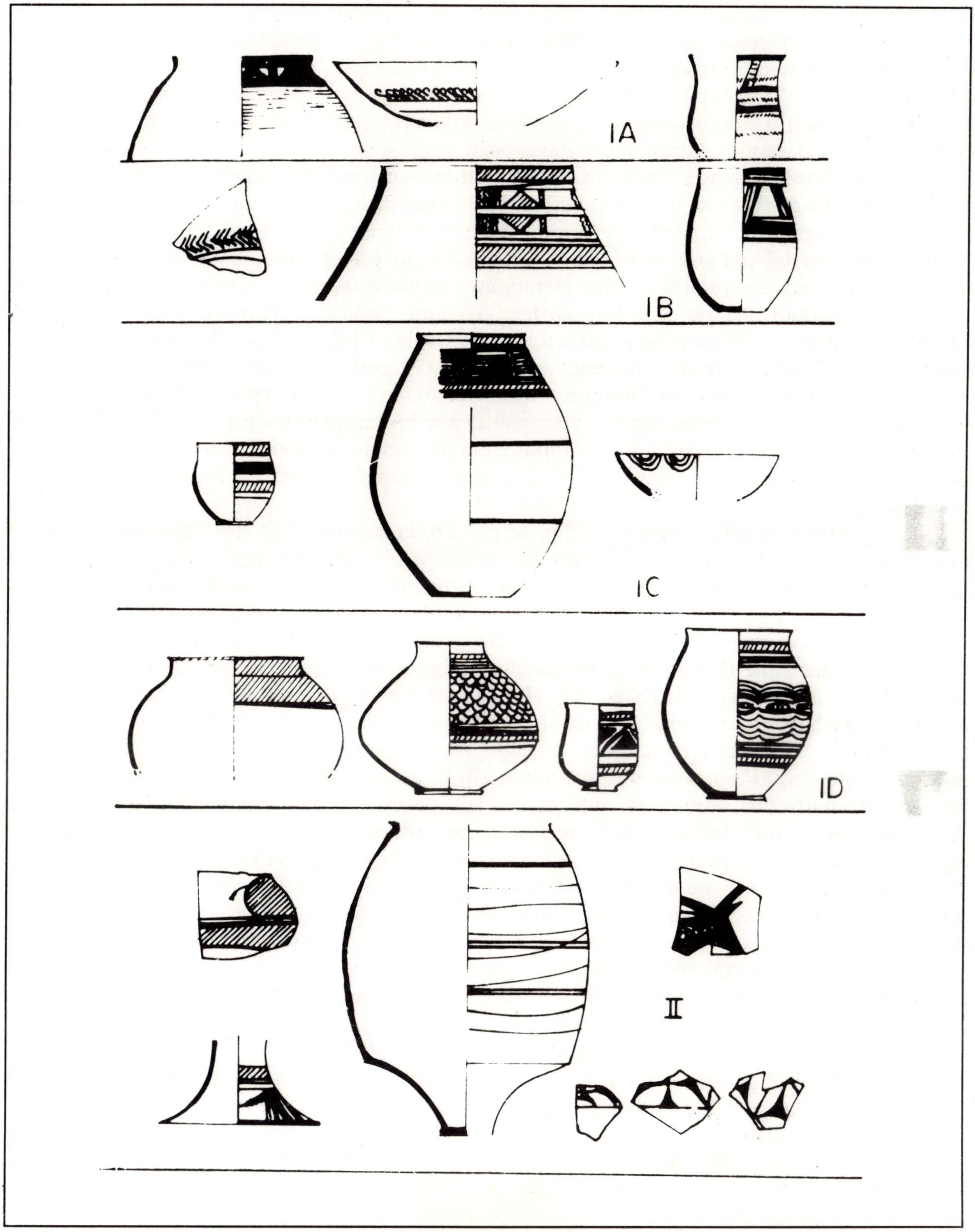

Fig. 3-4. Amrian pottery assemblage of different periods.

But the Harappa culture stands apart from this cultural stream, though a number of Pre-Harappan elements go into its make-up. So, while the village cultures (the so-called Pre-Harappan) continued to absorb foreign influences and develop the diversity of their regional idioms, the Mature Harappa culture seems to be quite selective and regimented in its choice, which imparted it a uniqueness. And if it was deliberate, the time involved in the genesis of the Mature Harappa culture must have been very short.

The requisite evidence comes from the cultures of northern Sindh and the Kachchhi plains, which Fairservis has, in fact, called an Early Harappan Stage. One can trace the Mature Harappan elements of unpainted terracotta bangles, female and animal figurines, terracotta "cakes" and overall patterns with floral dominance in pottery motifs in these cultures.

Even the monumentality of the Harappan architecture is not unique. We noted the ramparts of Mundigak and Kot Diji earlier; at Damb Sadaat a platform with drains was situated at the top of the site; large structures like those of Edith Shahar complex are known from Kolwa, Drakalo, Ornach, as well as Zhob and Loralai (Possehl 1999c).

It is significant to note that though the secular items, like pottery and the size of bricks, were standardized, the religious practices could not be tempered with. This is reflected in the ritualistic remains recovered, for example, from Mohenjodaro and Kalibangan. The mother-goddess figurines of Mohenjodaro give way to the so-called fire-altars with phallic (?) objects at Kalibangan.

In southern Sindh, however, the large Pre-Harappan villages maintained their individuality for quite sometime, despite the appearance of the Harappan culture. This alone explains the Harappan pottery at the Kulli sites and in Amri Pd ID and the Pre-Harappan ceramics in the early Mohenjodaro levels. At Kalibangan, the coexistence of the two is unmistakably documented. Finally, the nearby Pre-Harappans did succumb to the urban fashions, perhaps like the present-day satellite villages of the cities. The Harappan phases at Kot Diji, Amri correlation (Figs. 3-3, -4, -5) and Kalibangan should not be understood as one culture supplanting another, but like a city corporation taking over a suburban village to urbanize it. The Harappa culture, though essentially derived from the Pre-Harappan cultures, continued to be coeval with the latter. The cities as trading centres had vital economic relationship with the numerous villages, which produced the agricultural surplus. The Harappa culture and the so-called Pre-Harappan cultures (obviously a misnomer in the context) are in fact, urban and folk (rural) faces respectively of the same cultural phenomenon.

It should, however, be emphasized that the presence of the Pre-Harappan elements in the composition of the Harappa culture does not underestimate—much less deny—the large number of innovations that were part of the Harappan urbanization.

The Mature Harappa culture seems to appear on the scene with a deceptive abruptness and is thought to have succeeded the so-called Pre-Harappan cultures. The monumentality of its city architecture and the regimented and standardized (and also commercialized) cultural traits aggravate its uniqueness and hence the problems of its genesis. In recent years, Dales (1965), Wheeler (1968), Fairservis (1967), Ghosh (1965) and the first author (Agrawal 1971), have put up theories to explain the Harappan origins. Fairservis has given a very comprehensive and a stimulating discussion of this subject (1967). The evidence is re-evaluated here in a new perspective and an unorthodox hypothesis is suggested to explain the data.

As most of the excavations were confined to the Harappan cities (Pl. 3-1), which were planned to a large extent and thus had an in-built abruptness. The recent evidence of Kalibangan excavations and, a large number of ^{14}C dates that are available help us to understand this genesis in a proper perspective now. If we take into account the total matrix

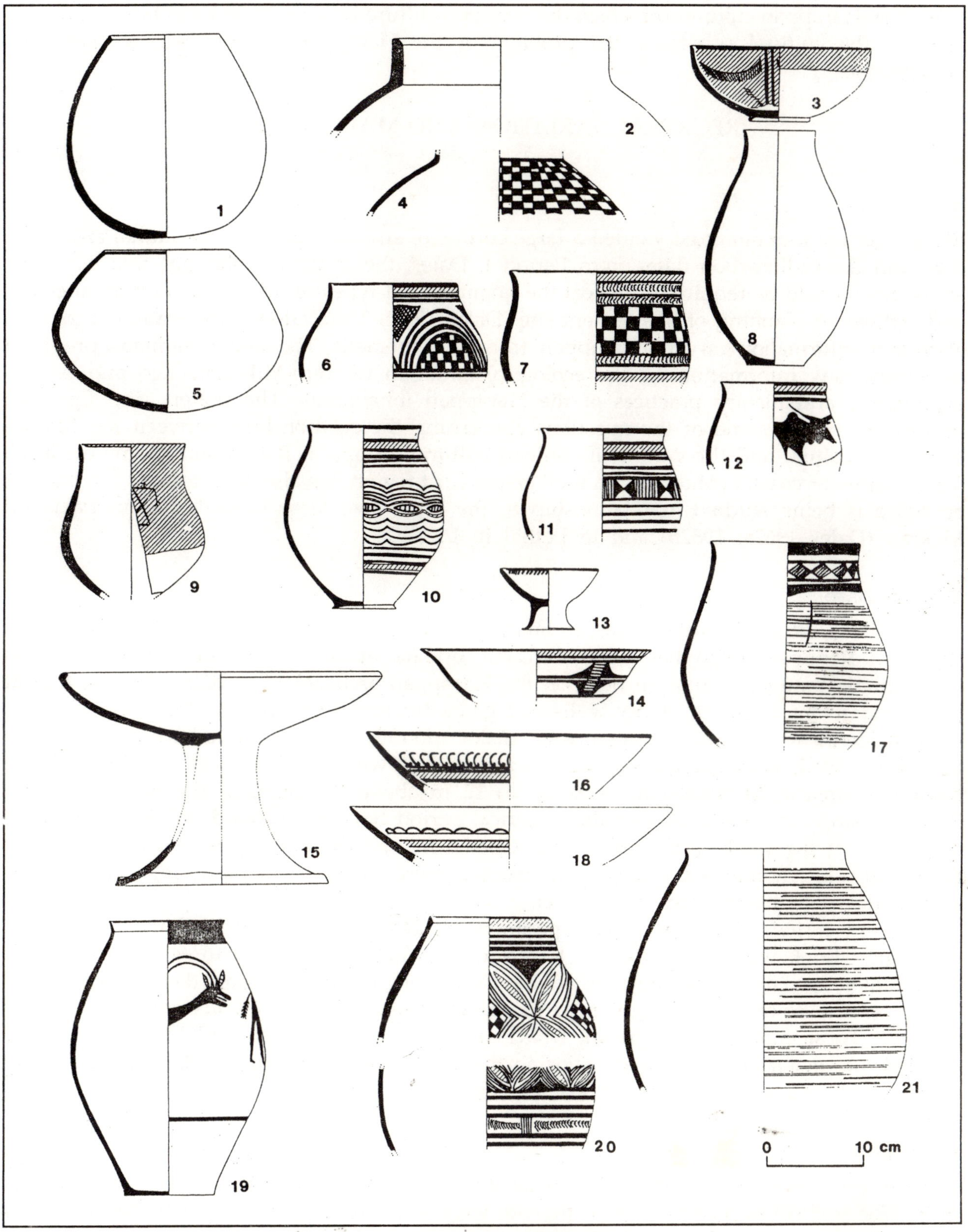

Fig. 3-5. Pottery from Amri.

of the Pre-Harappan cultures on which the Harappa culture was implanted and take a dynamic view of the cultural processes, the problem of the Harappan origins becomes easier to understand.

REGIONAL VARIATION AND MAIN TOWNS

Pakistan

Balakot

Balakot on the Makran coast yielded a large corpus of stratified pottery, the faunal and floral data and the radiocarbon dates from Period I. Dales, the excavator, thought that extensive excavation would be required to reveal the quantity and types of information on architecture and settlement planning of this ancient site (Dales 1979). The Period II excavations provided abundant information on this Harappan frontier settlement. The faunal remains provided important new information on the ecological situation of four Millennia ago and on the exploitative and dietary practices of the Harappan inhabitants. The pottery and figurines promise to clarify some of the questions concerning the relationships between the Mature Harappan culture and the various ill-defined cultural groups in Baluchistan. Some evidence for maritime or coastal contacts with the Persian Gulf region has also been found. The Balakot evidence is being studied in relationship to the other two large coastal sites in Pakistani Makran (Dales 1962a; 1962b) and to Lothal in India.

Mohenjodaro

Mohenjodaro, situated on the Indus, in Sindh, is one of the oldest excavated Harappan sites (Pl. 3-1). Kenoyer (1998) has done a recent update of the excavations and has given considerable thought to putting flesh on the Harappan archaeological data. He says that at Mohenjodaro the presence of city walls and gateways has been doubted, but recent studies seem to confirm that like Harappa, each major mound was surrounded by an enormous mud brick wall, with gateways at key locations. The western Citadel mound, the highest habitation area at Mohenjodaro, rises up to 12 m above the plain in the north, where a Buddhist stupa and monastery of the historical period have been found. Wheeler identified a gateway at the south-east corner of the Citadel mound, though he never fully published his report. This mound is encircled by a massive mud brick wall or platform, which is now eroded down to the modern plain level.

Recent corings along the eroded perimeter of HR area have revealed the presence of great mud brick walls or platforms. Kenoyer says that if these structures indeed are the foundations for city walls, they would be even more impressive than those recovered at Harappa. The so-called lower town to the east consists of low mounds covering over 80 hectares. These mounds (comprising DK-G area, VS area, HR area and Moneer area) are divided into major blocks by four major north-south streets and four equally wide east-west streets, with numerous smaller streets and alleyways.

Harappa

The site extended over a circuit of 6 km on the left bank of the Ravi. It is sad to note that from 1856 to 1919 burnt bricks from the site were removed to provide ballast for a railway line, resulting in considerable devastation of the site.

There is a lower town and a Citadel in the form of a parallelogram. From mound F were excavated the "coolie-lines", the granary, etc. In a pit, in area G, was found a tightly-packed mass of human skulls and bones. The Harappan Cemetery (R-37) and the Post-Harappan Cemetery H were located south of the Citadel. The Red Ware associates of the Cemetery H have no affinity with the Harappan wares and shows signs of being an intrusive culture. Stylized birds and plants and bulls with slim waists comprise the painted motifs.

The following account of Harappa is mainly based on the HARP team's several years' work at Harappa (Meadow 1991; Meadow and Kenoyer 1993; Meadow and Kenoyer 1995; Kenoyer 1998).

It seems that at Harappa, the different walled areas were spread around a central depression that may have been a large reservoir. Each major mound was surrounded by a massive mud brick wall, with brick gateways and bastions located at intervals along each face. Mound E, oriented along an east-west axis, is one of the oldest parts of the ancient city that grew up on top of the early village settlement. This mound is surrounded by a large mud brick wall, which was partly faced with baked brick. A major gateway was constructed along the south wall. At the gateway itself, the mud brick city wall is over 9 m wide and may have had additional bastions making it up to 11 m wide. The gate itself is made of baked brick with one metre thick walls firmly bonded to the mud brick city wall. A small projection on the inner eastern edge of the brick gate (2.8 m wide and perhaps 4 m high) may indicate stairs leading to the top of the wall.

It is suggested that the large open area inside the gateway may have been used as a market or checkpoint for taxing goods being brought into the city. To the east of the gateway there is evidence for shell and agate workshops and on the west for copper working. Outside the city wall and only some 30 m due south of the gateway, is a small mound dating to the Harappan phase, with houses, drains, bathing platforms and possibly a well. This cluster of houses may represent a temporary resting place or caravanserai.

Kenoyer thinks that the modern road, which runs along the southern edge of the mound past this gateway, probably belongs to the Harappan period. The small mound outside the ancient gateway of mound E was used earlier as a caravanserai and a stable for horses used in postal relays between Lahore and Multan. The well in the centre of the caravanserai was probably a reused Harappan well.

The actual opening of the second gate is only about 2.6 m wide, but the gate pylons and side rooms cover an area over 25 m across and some 15 m deep. This gate is the second major gateway of mound E and is much more complex. It is located some 200 m to the east, at the juncture between the corner of the old city wall of mound E and a new wall that encircled the suburb on mound ET. The main function of this gateway seems to be to control access into the new suburb of the city, where numerous workshops were producing ornaments and trade goods. Outside of this gateway and about 50 m to the south there was perhaps another caravanserai for merchants.

Kenoyer suggests that the other mounds at Harappa probably had their own walls and separate gates, but only the wall around the mound AB has been excavated. This wall, much larger and higher than the wall around mound E, was up to 14 m wide at the base and faced on the exterior with baked bricks, gently tapering to the top, more than 11 m above the plain level. Wheeler had found three small gateways built at different periods along the western face of the wall and in the north was the larger gate with a ramp leading down to a lower suburb (mound F) in the north. A mud brick wall enclosed the area of mound

F, which was like the suburb of mound ET in the east. This northern suburb was probably a craftsmen's quarter as it had numerous house structures associated with craft manufacturing debris and a series of circular working platforms. To the north of this area was probably a palace or storehouse, which is an extremely large building with twelve sections.

Probably the different mounds or walled neighbourhoods at Harappa were established at different times as the city grew, but belonged to the same culture. The excavators admit that it still is not clear why the different mounds continued to be walled or how they were politically united into a single city. Characteristic styles of painted ceramics, clay figurines, inscribed seals and ornaments have been recovered from all the excavated mounds and there is evidence for the movement of goods from one sector to the other.

Though most scholars have assumed that the walls were constructed for military defence, Kenoyer thinks that it is impractical to have so many separate walled areas next to each other, nor did the HARP team found any evidence of damage from battles. It seems that none of the gateways found at Harappa was constructed for defence from frontal military attack. Generally in the later historical cities, major city gateways had a sharp turn just inside the gate to expose attackers to the defenders on the top of the gate. A fortified city also had a moat and double or triple walls like those seen at Dholavira. Kenoyer therefore infers that the lack of such defensive planning suggests that the gates and walls of Harappa were never intended to withstand battle, but were more symbolic in nature and intended to control the trade and commerce, which was the life blood of the city. Whatever the precise function of the walls and gateways, they demonstrate the high level of architectural skills and civic control in the Indus cities. And their presence made the city stand out from other smaller settlements (Kenoyer 1998).

Buildings and Houses

It is noteworthy that in the Indus cities there is a remarkable uniformity in both the raw materials used and the style of construction, in contrast to the historical houses built by people from different communities, which show considerable variation in the raw materials used and the style of construction. Because most Indus settlements were located in the alluvial plains, the most common building materials were mud bricks and baked bricks, wood and reeds. However, in the rocky foothills and on the islands of Kachchh and in Saurashtra where stone is commonly available, dressed stone replaced baked brick.

Standard sized mud bricks and baked bricks (7 x 14 x 28 cm) were used in house construction, but for the city walls a different size (10 x 20 x 40 cm) was used. Both sizes of brick have identical proportions—thickness (=1), width (=2 x 1) and length (= 4 x 1). This ratio is commonly expressed as 1: 2: 4; both sizes of bricks appeared during the Early Harappan Kot Diji phase and became standard at all of the settlements during the Harappan phase. Kenoyer makes an interesting suggestion that the uniformity is probably not the result of a state decree or federal building codes, but rather the rise of a class of brick makers whose craft tradition spreads to all of the different settlements.

As a guild of craftsmen, on the pattern of Early Historic period, the brick makers may have also branched out as masons and architects, filling an important niche in the rapidly growing urban centres. The result is a fairly uniform building tradition with variations depending on the availability of materials and the plot of land on which a house was being built. Mud brick and baked brick or stone were used for the foundations and walls of the houses; the doors and windows were made with wood and mats. Very few actual roof fragments have been recovered, but they were probably made of wooden beams covered with reeds and packed clay. The house floors were generally made of hard-packed earth that was often replastered or covered with clean sand. Some rooms were paved with bricks or fired terracotta cakes. Bathing areas and drains were made with baked brick or stone.

Kenoyer surmises that the wooden components in the Indus houses would have been made by a different set of artisans who used totally different techniques and tools. The Harappan pottery replicas of houses with carved and painted windows and doorways attest to the beginnings of the embellishments of the protective designs and decorative carvings on door-frames, which designated status and wealth in the cities.

Perhaps another guild specialized in woodwork. Tropical hard woods and aromatic cedar were used for buildings and furniture. One locally available hard wood that became famous in trade with Mesopotamia is known as shisham (*Dalbergia sisoo*). The dark heartwood is termite proof and used extensively today for making doors, windows and furniture. A type of cedar, deodar (*Cedrus deodara)*, was also used by the Indus artisans, but it is a Himalayan timber. The Himalaya traders may have intentionally floated down some cedar from the hilly hinterland, but landslides and storms in the mountains could have tumbled many trees into the river naturally. To fashion wood, copper and bronze axes, adzes, chisels, drills and saws were used. Stone tools were used for drilling, scraping and finishing. Some of the largest public buildings at Mohenjodaro and Harappa appear to have been made entirely of wood and specialized tools would have been needed to shape and fit the huge timbers for gateways and columns.

Yet another guild seems to have specialized in stonework. Hammer stones and chisels were used to shape the large discs and square blocks. Abrasive drills were used for hollowing out the centre of the ring-stones and for making the dowel holes. Fine-grained quartzite and sandstone were used for grinding and polishing the carefully finished surfaces. Large ring-stones and square column bases reflect a much more refined stone-working tradition. All these techniques were used on a much finer scale to produce polished alabaster grill-work that would have been set into windows or dividing walls. Dressed stone blocks and architectural components represent a third major craft associated with the architecture of cities.

Enclosed within massive city walls, many different social and economic classes were able to live in close proximity and still maintain their status and identity. Thus a variety of specialized craftsmen created a unique living environment.

In villages and small towns, houses were made almost entirely of mud brick with occasional burnt bricks or stone used in the foundations or drains. Although a few houses in the larger urban centres were made in the same manner, most buildings in the cities were constructed either entirely or partially with baked brick.

Kenoyer groups most of the architecture into three categories.

Category 1. Private houses with rooms were arranged around a central courtyard that offered privacy from the public passing along the city streets. Doorways and windows rarely opened out onto the main street, but faced side lanes. We would like to mention here that both the plan of an open shaft in the centre of the house and the street opening into the narrow lanes had air-conditioning effect. The former arrangement set up an air-circulation, which allowed cooler air to sink and warmer air to escape. The narrow lanes kept temperatures cooler, as the sun could hardly beat down. The view into the house was blocked by a wall or a hallway, a custom still practised in traditional homes throughout the northern subcontinent. Several rooms were situated around the courtyard; stairs led up to the roof or second storey from one room or the courtyard. Many houses were at least two storeys high and based on the thickness of some house walls at Mohenjodaro, there may have been three-storied buildings as well. On the average, walls were 70 cm thick and most ceilings were probably over 3 m high.

The doors were made with wooden frames and a brick socket set in the threshold served as a door pivot. Clay models of houses show that some of the door frames were painted and possibly carved with simple ornamentation. A hole at the base of the doorframe may have allowed a rope to secure or lock the door. Two holes at the top of the doorframe may have been used to hang a curtain. The lock at the base of the door and a curtain to cover the doorway is still a common practice in cities and villages throughout the subcontinent.

Windows situated on both the first and second storeys had shutters with lattice-work grills above and below the shutters. The roots of the elegant marble screens of the Mughal period and the wooden screens on high-rise apartment buildings of modern Karachi perhaps lay in these Harappan houses. This allowed air and light into the room when the shutters were closed and maintained the privacy of the room from outsiders. The shutters and grill-work were probably made of wood, but some may have been made of reeds or matting. A few examples of carved alabaster and marble lattice-work have been found at Mohenjodaro and Harappa. Set into the red-fired brick walls these lattices may have adorned the houses of wealthy merchants or rulers.

Category 2. Buildings in this category include large houses surrounded by smaller units. Complex passageways gave access to interior rooms and numerous rebuilding phases indicate repeated reorganization of space. Outer units may have been the houses of relatives or service groups attached to the original house.

Category 3. This category of structures includes large public structures that have many access routes or provide a thoroughfare from one area of the site to another. Markets or public meetings may have been held in large open courtyards, while other buildings may have had specific administrative or religious functions.

Groups of houses or public buildings were built close together with shared walls and formed larger blocks that were bordered by wide streets. Most houses or groups of houses had private bathing areas and latrines as well as private wells.

Hydraulics

It seems that the Harappans were aware of the pollution caused by sewage water draining into the rivers. Therefore, they used wells and reservoirs or cisterns, which were built within the cities to ensure drinking and bathing water. At Mohenjodaro, numerous wells were dug throughout the city and maintained for hundreds of years. When the early excavators had cleared some of these wells, they once again began to fill with water, although much of the groundwater around the site today is quite brackish. These 10 to 15 metre deep wells were lined with specially made wedge-shaped bricks to form a structurally round cylinder that would not cave in under pressure from the surrounding soil. On the top edge of the well there are grooves on the bricks, which show that ropes were used to lift the water out, probably with leather or wooden buckets. The wells in private houses at Mohenjodaro and Harappa were probably built by people living in these houses and not by the state government. Kenoyer suggests that the abundance of private, as opposed to public wells, indicates that water purity and pollution had become an important issue in the increasingly congested urban setting of the town. There is no evidence for a highly stratified caste society in the Indus cities, but such perceptions about water do become an important feature of the caste divisions in the later Brahmanical Hinduism. The members of the higher castes will not drink water that has been touched or carried by individuals of a lower caste.

Many neighbourhoods had public wells along the main streets for animals and the general public. The drains for collecting rainwater were built separately from drains used to remove dirty sewage water. At Mohenjodaro, most houses had at least one private well. On the basis of the number of wells found in the excavated areas, Jansen *et al.* (1996) have calculated that the city may have had over 700 wells. In contrast, Harappa may have had as few as 30, since only eight wells have been discovered in the areas excavated so far. Kenoyer suggests that the difference between these two cities may be that Mohenjodaro had less winter rain and may have been situated far away from the Indus river. At Harappa, a large depression in the centre of the city may represent a large tank or reservoir accessible to the inhabitants from all the different neighbourhoods. Dholavira, in Kachchh, has only a few wells and most water for the city was collected during the rainy season in large stone-lined cisterns.

Bathing platforms with drains were often situated in rooms adjacent to the well. The floor of the bath was usually made of tightly fitted bricks, often set on edge, making a watertight floor. At Mohenjodaro and Harappa, tapered terracotta drainpipes were used to direct the water out to the street. In the Indus cities, the top of the well would have stood above the ground level with a small drain nearby to keep dirty water from running back into the well itself. There was a small drain cut through the house wall into the street, which carried the dirty water to a larger sewage drain. Much care was taken to ensure that water from the bathing area and latrines did not flow into the rest of the house. Drains and water chutes from the second storey were often built inside the wall with an exit opening just above the street drain.

HARP excavations at Harappa reveal latrines in almost every house, though it seems that the early excavators at both Mohenjodaro and Harappa did not pay much attention to this essential feature of the Indus cities. The commodes were made of large jars sunk into the floor and many of them contained a small jar similar to the modern water jar or *lota* used throughout Pakistan and India for washing after using the toilet. Sometimes these sump pots were connected to a drain to let sewage flow out and most had a tiny hole at the bottom to let water seep into the ground. Clean sand was scattered on the floor of the latrine and periodically an entire new floor was installed. These latrines must have been cleaned out quite regularly by a special class of labourers, like the present-day sweepers in small towns.

The baked brick drains connected the bathing platforms and latrines of private houses to medium-sized open drains in the side streets, which flowed into larger sewers in the main streets. The sewers were covered with bricks or dressed stone blocks. The well laid-out streets and side lanes equipped with drains are one of the most outstanding features of the Indus cities. The fact that even smaller towns and villages have impressive drainage systems indicates that removing polluted water and sewage was an important part of the daily concern of the Indus people.

At Harappa, a sequence of four drains, built one after the other, leave the city at the main gateway between mound E and mound ET. Some drains appear to have been provided with wooden sluice gates or perhaps a grill to keep people from secretly entering into the walled city. A well-preserved magnificent corbelled drain is 1.6 m high, 60 cm wide and extends for 6.5 m beneath a major city street. Corbelled arches allowed the larger drains to cut beneath streets or buildings until they finally exited under the city wall, draining out sewage and rainwater onto the outlying plain. At intervals along the main sewage drains were rectangular sump pits for collecting solid waste. These sump pits were cleaned out on a regular basis; otherwise the entire drainage system would be blocked. There were also garbage bins along the major streets. At Harappa there were periods when the city drain cleaners did not do their job, causing the drains throughout a part of the city to become totally clogged. It seems that fluctuations in street and drain maintenance resulted in the rapid build-up of street levels. Many doorways and walls had to be raised above the level of the street to keep sewage from flowing into the house. Gradually, entire rooms would be filled with dirt and a new house had to be built well above the street level.

Large Buildings

The important buildings were prominent enough to be visible from all parts of the city. Many of the largest and best-known buildings of the Harappan phase are located on the Citadel mound at Mohenjodaro. Three prominent large buildings, on the northern part of the mound, are the so-called Granary, the Great Bath and the College. At many places protruding fragments of walls indicate that other important buildings may be lying buried beneath the Buddhist stupa, which covers the eastern quarter of the mound. The southern part of this mound has a large building called the assembly hall, which has a double row of square columns and lines of bricks set into the floor like in the modern Buddhist monasteries and Brahmanical ashrams, for the monks or students often sit in lines on the floor. Perhaps this tradition can be traced to the Harappan times. Other important public buildings have been found in different neighbourhoods of the lower mounds. A large courtyard in the DKG area may have been a large market or public assembly area.

A Temple?

Located nearby is a large complex of houses, which the early excavators called the house of a chief. To the south at the other end of the lower mound in the HR area, another important building was discovered. This building, called House A1, may have been a temple or the house of an important person. Two doorways lead to a narrow courtyard at a lower level. A circle of bricks in the courtyard might have been the site of a sacred tree. A double staircase led to an upper courtyard surrounded by several rooms. This house had numerous seals and fragments of a stone sculpture depicting a seated man wearing a cloak over the left shoulder. Other pieces of this bearded figure were found scattered in nearby houses. This sculpture closely resembles the so-called priest-king image, which was found far to the north in the DK area (Pl. 3-4). Thus there are indications that it may have been a religious area, or a temple.

Great Bath

Mohenjodaro without doubt has the earliest public water tank in the ancient world, which is referred to as "Great Bath" in archaeological reports and books. It has been also claimed as the first swimming pool, though it is unlikely that it was ever used for swimming or diving. The tank's measurements are: 12 m north-south and 7 m wide, with a maximum depth of 2.4 m. Two wide staircases, one from the north and one from the south, lead down into

Pl. 3-4. The so-called priest-king in stone, Mohenjodaro.

Pl. 3-6. The Great Bath, Mohenjodaro.

Pl. 3-7. Mohenjodaro granary and Great Bath.

Pl. 3-8. Granary at Harappa.

the tank. Small sockets at the edges of the stairs could have held wooden planks or treads. There is a small ledge at the foot of the stairs running the entire width of the pool (Pl. 3-6).

The Great Bath is a fine example of waterproofing engineering. Both the floor of the tank and the side walls are made watertight with finely fitted bricks laid on edge with gypsum plaster. A thick layer of bitumen (natural tar) along the sides of the tank and perhaps also beneath the floor makes the Bath even more watertight. The floor slopes down to the south-west corner where a small outlet leads to a brick drain, which takes the water to the edge of the mound. On the basis of a detailed analysis of symmetry of the building and comparison with other buildings, Michael Jansen suggests that the architects who designed and constructed this building and water tank had severe constraints of space, as there was a very limited area available between the main north-south street and the granary. Except for the eroded western side, brick colonnades were discovered around all the edges. Marshall had also assumed that there would have been a collonnade running along the western edge. The preserved columns have stepped edges that may have held wooden screens or window frames. Two large doors led into the complex from the south, with additional access from the north and east. Rooms are located along the eastern edge of the building. There was a well in one of the rooms that may have supplied some of the water needed to fill the tank. Rainwater also may have been collected for this purpose.

Kenoyer thinks that it is unlikely that this elaborate building was used simply for public bathing, because just to the north is a substantial building containing eight small rooms with the more common bathing platforms. Most scholars agree that this tank was used for special religious functions where water was used to purify and renew the well being of the bathers.

Granary?

A large building at Mohenjodaro was first identified as a *hammam* or hot-air bath and later as the state granary. Initially excavated in the 1920s, the complete structure ("Granaries" or "Great Halls") was reinvestigated by Wheeler in 1950, whose imaginative reconstruction of this structure as a state granary was based on comparisons with Minoan Crete and Rome.

The foundation of this building appears to have been laid before the Great Bath, as its exit drain cuts across the north-east corner of the foundation. Built on top of a tapered brick platform, this building had a solid brick foundation that extended for 50 m east-west and 27 m north-south. The foundation was divided into 27 square and rectangular blocks by narrow passageways, two running east-west and eight running north-south (one additional north-south passageway was added at a later stage). Some of these blocks had square sockets for holding wooden beams or pillars. Kenoyer suggests that the entire superstructure may have been made of timber.

A brick-lined well was located at the foot of the stairs and a small bathing platform was found at the top of the stairs. Wheeler identified a brick-paved staircase 4.5 m wide, which led from the south-western edge of the structure to the plain level. Wheeler identified the terraced platform with numerous sockets for wooden beams and an alcove as a loading dock. To the north of the terrace was a low courtyard or open area and two additional wells.

One cannot accurately reconstruct the function of this structure as the entire structure was excavated without detailed recording of the types of pillars found in the passageways or nearby rooms. However, the earlier excavators did note the lack of charred grain and storage containers. Besides, the absence of sealings from bundles of goods and the unique nature of the structure all raise doubts as to the identification of this building as a state granary or storehouse. Kenoyer has suggested that a more general name "The great hall" may be more appropriate for this building with large and spacious wooden columns and many rooms.

A granary at Harappa was identified by M.S. Vats with a different type of building located on mound F. This structure is built on a massive mud brick foundation that is over 50 m north-south and 40 m east-west. Two rows of six rooms that appear to be foundations are arranged along a central passageway that is about 7 m wide and partly paved with baked bricks. Each room measures 15.2 by 6.1 m and has three sleeper walls with air space between them. Small triangular openings may have served as air ducts to allow the flow of fresh air beneath the hollow floors. A wooden superstructure supported in some places by large columns would have been built on top of the brick foundations, with stairs leading up from the central passage area.

Earlier excavators had suggested that the nearby circular brick platforms were used for husking grain. They did not find any special concentrations of burned grain or storage containers. In 1946, Wheeler reported a large wooden mortar placed in the centre of one of these circular brick platforms. Such wooden mortars are still popular in India and are used in many parts of the world to remove the husks or crush grain. Even though these circular platforms were found near the granary, Kenoyer cautions that it is important to note that they were constructed inside smaller buildings and that they belong to many different building phases. One has to admit that there is little to suggest a connection between the circular platforms and the so-called granary. In fact, the main argument for suggesting that this structure was a granary is again based on comparisons with Roman buildings and not because of parallels with any building tradition in South Asia. One has to note that traditionally grain in the north-western subcontinent is stored in large mud plastered bins raised above the ground on bricks or wooden platforms.

Advising caution, Kenoyer says that most scholars agree that there is little evidence for the construction of massive granaries at either Mohenjodaro or Harappa and that these structures should only be seen as evidence for large public buildings. Powerful rulers who were supported by generations of artisans, traders and farmers lived continuously in these cities for over 700 years. Many such large buildings may have been used for specific religious functions; rulers and state officials probably did meet in such public buildings. Nevertheless, the size and complexity of these buildings demonstrate the ability of the Indus architects to construct imposing architecture. With the gleaming red-brick gateways and grey mud brick walls, the city would have been a towering landmark (Kenoyer 1998).

India

Haryana

Banawali

Banawali lies essentially in the Ghaggar valley, about 120 km north-east of Kalibangan and 220 km north-west of Delhi, in district Hissar, Haryana. It was excavated by R.S. Bisht. He discovered interesting architectural features. The site has a diameter of about 400 m. The 8 m thick occupational debris is divided into three cultural periods: Period I is similar to Kalibangan Period I; Period II belongs to the Mature Harappan culture; and Period III is essentially the post-Mature phase (Bisht 1984, 1994).

Period I has been divided into sub-periods A, B and C. There was no fortification around the settlement in Pd IA; it came up in IB. By IC, the settlement was divided into a Citadel and a Lower Town. All through the houses were oriented along the cardinal directions. While in sub-periods IA and IB the bricks were made in the ratio of 3: 2: 1, in IC these were also made in the typical Mature Harappan ratio of 4:2:1. Thus by IC the stage had been set for the emergence of the Mature Harappan civilization.

Unlike Kalibangan, here the Citadel or Acropolis was not detached from the Lower Town. It lay within the overall fortified area within which the Lower Town was also located. Besides, the Citadel had its own fortifications, with a common wall on the southern side. Unlike Harappa and Kalibangan, here at Banawali, the Acropolis, with the common wall as the base, the surrounding wall formed a semi-ellipse. Having been built over the remains of Period I, the Acropolis occupied a level higher than that of the Lower Town. The thickness of the Citadel walls varied from 5.4 m to 7 m. Inside the Citadel, a few streets with flanking houses have been identified. These houses, with a roughly north-south and east-west orientation, formed a grid-pattern. One street also ran along the inner side of the Citadel wall, a counterpart of which existed on the outside, falling within the Lower Town. No major gateway to the Citadel has yet come to light since only a small part of the fortification-wall has been exposed. The fortification-wall was provided with a squarish bastion on the exterior. A similar bastion was also exposed along the southern part of the wall. A 1.5 m wide ramp was found near the apex of the ellipse, laid with burnt bricks, leading from the Lower Town into the Citadel.

In contrast to the Citadel, the Lower Town was quadrangular. It has been exposed in fair length on the eastern side, where squarish bastions on the exterior have been identified. Along a part of the exterior of the fortification wall, a moat has also been identified.

There was an entrance in the northern half of the above-mentioned eastern wall. On the inner side of this entrance, there was a wide "open" space at the western end of which three streets, one going southwards, another westwards and the third to the north-west, formed a tri-junction. The western street met a south-north street emanating from the Citadel ramp referred to above. Along the interior of the eastern fortification-wall of the Lower Town there was a north-south street, which passed through the eastern end of this open space. Thus, one could go in five different directions from this open space. The bigger streets measured 5.4 m in width, similar to the Kalibangan streets.

Banawali seems to be inhabited by rich people, as indicated by the size and contents of their houses. With a central courtyard, the houses had, a large number of rooms around it; sometimes the rooms were paved with mud bricks. In the case of one house, the toilet "was provided with a wash basin placed on a high place in a corner near the drain which carried off the waste water into a sullage jar placed outside the street". This particular house seems to have belonged to a rich merchant as it yielded seals and weights. Another big house may have been owned by a jeweller, as, a large number of beads of gold, lapis lazuli and etched carnelian were found from it. Tiny weights found in the same house may have been used for weighing these precious commodities. The discovery of a "touchstone bearing gold streaks of different hues" is of great interest since it indicates that gold was tested for its purity, as is done even today.

As in Kalibangan, many of the houses had fire-altars. Here they are also associated with an apsidal structure (Pl. 3-9). An interesting feature at Banawali was the presence of alcoves, varying from 1 x 1 m to 1 x 2 m, set within the walls. The use of kiln fired bricks was limited to wells, bath-pavements and drains. The residential houses as well as the fortifications were all made of mud bricks. The difference, however, was that in the former case the brick-sizes were relatively small, viz., 24 x 12 x 6 cm or 32 x 16 x 8 cm. The construction of platforms adjacent to the houses was a common feature. There were no encroachments on the roads throughout the occupation of the site, indicative of an efficient and well-organized civic administration. An interesting find is the stone-ware vase with the horned deity done in appliqué design.

The pottery from Period II was typically Mature Harappan, in spite of the continuity of some traits of Pd. I. The Bara-type pottery, which constitutes a noteworthy feature of the Harappan sites in the upper Ghaggar–Sarasvati and Sutlej basins, was also found in Pd.II at Banawali.

Bisht makes an interesting observation that at Banawali the seals have only come from the Lower Town and not the Citadel. Banawali is rich in antiquities – seals, sealings, weights, beads, bangles, etc. This evidence requires to be examined further to determine the role of the inhabitants of the Citadel, if they at all participated in trade or similar activities. The site has also yielded, a large number of weights in small denominations. Two of these weigh around 0.216 g and 0.072 g.

Amongst the terracotta objects, a complete model of a plough is an important find. The presence of female figurines at Banawali, relates the site to Harappa and Mohenjodaro, where also such mother-goddess figurines have been reported. In this context, it needs to be stressed that at Kalibangan, no female figurines were found.

A habitation deposit of about 4.5 m represents the Mature Harappan occupation at the site. The reasons for this termination of the Mature Harappan period are not known. The next occupation (Period III) came up after a gap of some time. By now all that characterized the Mature Harappan had disappeared: there was no town-planning, no fortification, no seals, no weights and no use of script. The new settlement came up initially against the eastern wall of the Mature Harappan defences, but later on it encroached to some extent on the eastern part of the mound itself. The houses in Pd III were now made not of bricks but of mere rammed clay, though still oriented along the cardinal directions. Within the houses were noted cornbins made of clay and lime, tandoors and underground cylindrical silos, the last two items recalling their counterparts of the pre-Mature Harappan times. This resurgence of some of the earlier features is also indicated by the pottery. However, a distinct feature of the ceramics was their oily touch and glossy appearance. The colour of the slip in most of the cases ranged from subdued plum-red to purple or from glowing buff to bright orange. There was also a marked change in the features or forms of the pottery. For example, in the case of the dish-on-stand, the rim curved out pronouncedly and showed even a distinctive droop. The presence of incised patterns on the exterior was another distinctive feature. It links up the Banawali pottery with that of Bara, a site on the upper Sutlej and not far off from the well-known Harappan site of Rupar. A kind of burnished grey ware was also included in the pottery repertory. Bisht also reports the presence of Cemetery H type pottery and designs in Period III. This evidence connects it to the desertion of the main Harappan towns in Pakistan where also Cemetery H type of pottery marks the end of Mature Harappan occupation.

It has to be noted that the faience ornaments – beads, rings, pipal-shaped earrings, bangles and anklets still occur in large numbers, indicating that this industry was still going strong. Attention may also be drawn to a terracotta object which has a square base and whose sides taper as they go upwards, finally to culminate in a two-pronged horn-like top. Examples of this peculiar object have been found at many other sites in the Upper Ghaggar–Sutlej basins, in a chronological horizon similar to that of Banawali.

Kunal

Khatri and Acharya (1994-95) have made some exciting discoveries from Kunal. The recently excavated site of Kunal (lat. 29°30″ N and 75°41″ E long.) is also in district Hissar, Haryana. It is located on the banks of now dried-up course of the Saraswati. The total occupational deposit is only around 3.10 m. Dwellings were semi-subterranean, usually 2 m in diameter and 1.10 m in depth.

Period IA. The pottery repertoire is dominated by the so-called Hakra Ware. It has also a handmade Black-and-Red Ware. A dull Red Ware of the Early Harappan vintage with wavy incised decorations on the outer surface was also found. The faunal and floral painted motifs are noteworthy, which include bull head and pipal leaf. The cultural assemblage includes, a large number of bone tools, micro beads of chalcedony and copper arrowheads (of Ganeshwar type) and fish-hooks.

Period IB. This phase represents the expansion of the settlement and elaboration of the semi-subterranean houses of round pits. The pits were now lined with finely moulded mud bricks of very special sizes such as 11 x 24 x 39 cm. The pottery repertoire of Pd. ID, mainly consists of the bichrome Red Ware with black and white paintings of faunal and floral designs, including the bull head, with highly curved horns marked with three parallel lines. The pipal leaf, beautifully hatched, or solidly filled, presents the most popular and perhaps the most sacred motif. In Pd. ID they report practically all the six Kalibangan I fabrics, including the Grey Ware and internally incised Red Ware pots. The Black-and-Red Ware continues to occur in small quantities and so also the plain dull chocolate coloured Burnished Ware.

The excavators claim that the Early Harappans at Kunal, did have round silos or pits plastered with chunam and clay mixture for storage of grains.

Period IC. It represents the real transitional phase between the Early Harappan and Mature Harappan culture. The dwellings changed from the semi-subterranean huts to regular square rectangular houses built of standardized mud bricks on the ground level which was further raised at various points to provide height and stability. The brick sizes are in two ratios 1: 2: 3 and 1: 2: 4 (9 x 18 x 36; 13 x 26 x 39;11 x 22 x 33 cm), both used simultaneously. It is common knowledge that 1: 2: 3 ratio bricks cannot always produce the so-called "English Bond". The houses, though modest in size compared to those of the Mature Harappan period, developed drainage systems also.

Period IC has been divided into three structural phases, IC (i, ii, iii). The houses, the drainage systems, the street, etc., did not change much except slightly larger and better built. The site remained a village throughout its existence.

Phase IC (i) is the most significant phase. In one of the rectangular brick houses, the excavators found a virtual treasure of gold and silver ornaments placed on a silver sheet and buried in a plain simple dull red globular pot of early Harappan fabric. The silver objects include two tiaras, one small and one large, each with a large fully opened flower having petals, topped with a decoration like the Greek letter alpha. Never before such magnificent objects were found at any Harappan site. Along with these two silver objects, one large silver armlet with horizontal mouldings was also found. This too is a unique object. The excavators claim, "The three together, it seems quite likely, belonged to some *raja* or king, else a socially distinguished elite because not only the forms of the objects but also because the metal silver are foreign to the region". The availability of silver does not appear to be a big issue but these finds do upset the concept of egalitarian nature of the Harappan society.

The following ^{14}C dates have been given for the Kunal samples:

TABLE 3.1 CALIBRATED DATES OF KUNAL, HARYANA (after Possehl 1994)

No.	*BETA No.*	*5568 Half-life*	*Calibrated date*
1.	BETA-77726	4040±70 BP	2837 (2568, 2519, 2504) 2466 cal. BC
2.	BETA-77727	4250±130 BP	3016 (2884) 2621 cal. BC
3.	BETA-77728	3990±70 BP	2577 (2473) 2409 cal. BC

From a different cache, found in another house of the same period, a large number of gold ornaments with disc beads, cup-shaped tubular beads, with facets all over the surface, etc., have also been found. Beads in terracotta but of shapes identical with the metal ones are also found from several houses. Similarly, large hoards of lapis lazuli micro-beads and 92 beads of agate make the whole gamut of luxury items as the "richest" when seen in the context of the rural nature of the settlement. Most of the shapes were similar to those found at Harappa and Mohenjodaro. The excavators claim that the Mature Harappan types of stone and metal beads were manufactured centuries before the emergence of Harappan cities at sites like Kunal. And this includes classical faience and carnelian beads too. Small chert blades were also found.

Significantly, copper objects included the so-called Mature Harappan types, e.g. coiled finger rings, coiled cones, a number of arrowheads identical to Ganeshwar type (two sides with marked curvature at the base) and inverted "V"-shaped ones with sides absolutely straight, flat axe and fish-hooks, spearheads, etc. It seems that copper melting was done at the site as a terracotta crucible with molten metal still sticking to the inner surface has also come to light. Undoubtedly, therefore, the copper ingots came from some other site but the objects were manufactured locally. One pottery kiln has also been reported. And above all, the discovery of as many as six steatite and one shell seals makes it absolutely clear that typical Mature Harappan square seals with knobbed back along with a hole were made centuries before the emergence of the urban centres in the Saraswati and the Indus basins, claim the excavators. The seals, however, bear only geometric designs, all of which are found in the Mature Harappan context. Thus, neither writing, nor human and animal motifs of the Mature Harappan type have been found here.

Rakhigarhi

Rakhigarhi (29°16' N and 76°10' E), located in Hissar district, Haryana, is one of the major Harappan centres in India. It was excavated by Suraj Bhan in 1963-64 and reopened in 1997-98 by the Archaeological Survey of India but no detailed reports are available yet. Fire-altars of the Banawali type have also been reported from this site. A cylindrical seal of faience with an alligator, two circular terracotta amulets with an elephant figure, gold fillet and beads, silver, copper and shell bangles constitute important finds. The remains of a pillared corridor, a granary, ritual places, a "shopping arcade" have also been reported.

Pl. 3-9. Fire-altar, Kalibangan, Rajasthan.

Pl. 3-10. A view of the Kalibangan streets, Rajasthan.

Pl. 3-11. The terracotta cake with a horned deity (obverse) and a sacrificial animal (reverse), Kalibangan, Rajasthan.

Pl. 3-12. Copper axe, ring and *parasu* from Kalibangan Period I.

Pl. 3-13. A pot burial without skeleton, Kalibangan, Rajasthan.

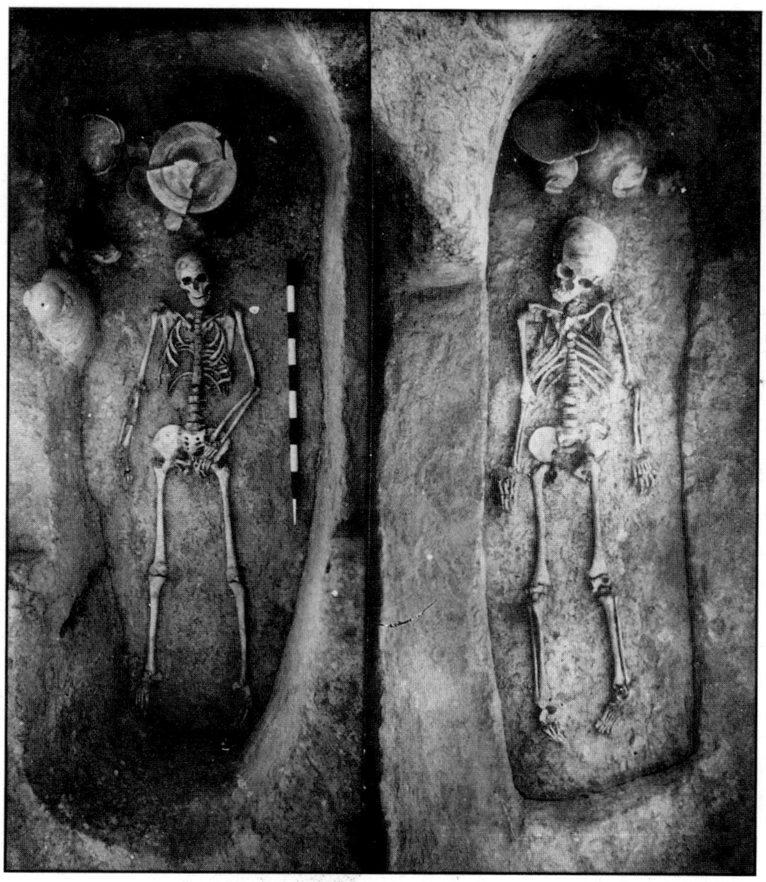

Pl. 3-14. Human burials, Kalibangan ,Harappan Period, Rajasthan.

Pl. 3-15. Copper objects from Dholavira excavations, Gujarat.

Pl. 3-16. Terracotta animals, Dholavira, Gujarat.

Punjab

Ropar

Ropar (also spelt as Rupar and now known as Rupnagar) is located on the left bank of the Sutlej in Punjab. It was the first Harappan site excavated in India after independence, the credit for which goes to Y.D. Sharma. At present, the site is divided into three mounds, but whether this was the case in antiquity also is difficult to say. Of these, the southern part is covered by the modern town and hence not much excavation could be carried out there. It is the northern mound, rising to a height of about 21 m, which has given the maximum information on the sequence of cultures. Underneath the western mound lay a cemetery of the Harappan times.

The excavation revealed six cultural periods: the Harappan (Period I); the Painted Grey Ware culture, Period II; continuing up to the medieval period (*c.* AD 1700). From the lower levels of Period I was discovered, besides the typical Mature Harappan material, pottery of the pre-Mature Harappan (or Early Harappan) vintage as found in Kalibangan, Banawali, etc. In Period I, the houses were usually made of mud bricks with occasional use of kiln-fired bricks. Sometimes *kankar*-stones, which are available from the natural deposits in the locality were also used. The bricks were irregular in size – a rather unusual feature for the Mature Harappan stage, but the thickness was uniformly 10 cm. The Harappan levels also yielded Bara type pottery, which is characterized by a variety of incised designs. Moreover, the site yielded the typical Mature Harappan antiquities, for example, a steatite seal, a terracotta sealing with impressions of three different seals, chert weights, a razor, arrowheads and spearheads of copper, beads of steatite paste and carnelian triangular "cakes" and toy-cart frames of terracotta.

Burials: The cemetery contained complete inhumation burials. The body was laid supine in an extended position but the head was towards the north-west instead of true north. The grave-articles included pottery, besides personal ornaments. One skeleton had a faience bangle on the left wrist; another had a copper ring on the middle finger of the right hand. There was also a burial of a dog, perhaps a pet, with a human skeleton.

Rajasthan

Kalibangan

The site is located on the dry river-bed of the Ghaggar, in Ganganagar district, Rajasthan. It was excavated by B.B. Lal and B.K. Thapar (1979) for a number of years, though no report has seen the light of the day so far.

The following account of the site is based mainly on Thapar (1979).

Period I. On the basis of the comparison of the material equipment of Kalibangan Period I with that of corresponding cultures at Harappa, Amri and Kot Diji, Thapar thinks that while these village-town cultures share a common level of economic subsistence, they are marked by regionalization with an uneven development and essentially differing ceramic traditions. However, one of the characteristic types of Fabric D of Kalibangan I is similar to Amri II B (Casal 1964a), thus providing a datable marker ceramics (Fig. 3-4) between the two cultures on a common timescale. On the strength of a radiocarbon date, Amri IC is dated to *c.* 2600 BC (cal. *c.* 3000 BC). Amri IIB, therefore, would fall around 2450 BC (cal. *c.* 2800 BC), which Thapar agrees with the date for the beginning of Kalibangan I. Confirmatory evidence is also forthcoming from layer 5 at Kot Diji, representing the late phase of the Kot Diji culture.

Another noteworthy analogue in both form and fabric is provided by the globular vase with short-neck and externally grooved body, found at Kalibangan I (Fabric C), Sarai Khola II, Pre-Defence Harappa and Kot Diji. (See tables for recalibrated ^{14}C dates by Kusumgar.)

Period II. In Period II the structural pattern of the settlement was changed. There were now two distinct parts: the Citadel on the west, represented by a smaller mound (KLB-I); and the lower city towards the east, represented by a fairly extensive mound (KLB-2). The former was situated atop the remains of the preceding occupation (Period I) to gain an eminence over the lower city which was laid out on the natural plain towards the east, leaving a gap of over 40 m.

The Citadel complex is roughly a parallelogram 240 m from north to south and 120 m from east to west and consists of two almost equal but separately patterned parts, rhomboid on plan. Both these parts were contained by a fortification wall 3 to 7 m in width (on the southern sides, the width was extended from 9 to 11 m) and reinforced at regular intervals with rectangular salients or bastions. The fortifications were built throughout of mud bricks; two sizes of bricks, 40 x 20 x 10 cm and 30 x 15 x 7.5 cm (ratio: 4:2:1), representing two principal structural phases, were used in the construction, the larger bricks in the earlier phase and smaller in the latter.

The southern half of the Citadel was more heavily fortified not only with corner bastions but also with rectangular salients along the northern and southern sides. While no complete plans of the corner bastions were available, the salients projected 8 to 9 m from the main face and were 13 to 17 m broad. The enclosed area contained some five to six massive platforms of mud bricks (40 x 20 x 10 cm for the earlier phase and 30 x 15 x 7.5 cm for the later), each separate from the other and intended to be used perhaps for a specific purpose by the community as a whole.

All these platforms were found to be oriented along cardinal directions. In the case of the fully exposed platform, the longer axis was east-west, for the remaining three it was north-south. The size of the platforms no less than the width of the passages separating them varied. At no point, however, were these platforms joined to or were integral with the fortifications. Access to the working floor of the platforms was by means of steps, which rose from the passage. Through the passages also ran baked-brick drains. Of the buildings, which stood upon these platforms, no intelligible plans are available as they had been obscured by depredations of brick robbers.

Nevertheless, the available remains do indicate that some of these might have been used for religious or ritual purposes. One had the complete outline, besides a well and a fire-altar (Pl. 3-9), a rectangular pit (1.24 x 1 m), lined with baked bricks containing bovine bones and antlers, representing perhaps a sacrifice, were found. On the top was noticed a row of seven rectangular "fire-altars" aligned beside a well. The entrances to this part of the Citadel were located on the south and north.

The passage was 2.65 m in width, which could have been stepped, fronting the main fortification wall. In this entrance complex again, two structural phases were recognized. The small-sized bricks, viz., 30 x 15 x 7.5 cm were used right from the beginning of the occupation for domestic structures. It was only in the fortifications and massive platforms that the large-sized bricks were employed in the earlier phases and smaller ones later. It is significant, however, that the ratio of both sets remained 4:2:1.

The northern half of the Citadel, which was also fortified, contained residential buildings perhaps of the elite. Although full details of the house plans could not be recovered, it was noticed that the houses were built away from the fortification walls of the Citadel, perhaps to give some privacy to these structures. The passage between the partition wall and the houses was paved with brick-on-edge, extending from the north-western corner bastion (of the partition fortification wall) to the easterly of the two central salients and perhaps reaching the entrance stairway. There was evidence to show that this pavement was renewed at least three times during the lifetime of the Citadel. The size of the bricks used in all these floorings was 30 x 15 x 7.5 cm.

A thoroughfare running north-south was partially explored to a length of 40 m. Starting from the easterly of the two salients of the partition fortification wall, it ran obliquely in the direction of the entrance on the north. There were three (one each on the eastern, northern and western sides) entrances to this part of the Citadel. The lower city was also a parallelogram, some 240 m from east to west and 360 m from north to south and lay to the east of the Citadel beyond a broad space of some 40 m. Involving three to four structural phases, the lower city was enclosed by a fortification wall ranging in width from 3.5 to 9 m. It was made of mud bricks of similar sizes to those used for the fortifications of the Citadel, viz., 40 x 20 x 10 cm for the lower phase and 30 x 15 x 7.5 cm for the upper. Within the walled city was a grid or planning of streets running north to south and east to west, dividing the area into blocks.

The excavations established the existence of four arterial thoroughfares, running north to south and three running east to west (Pl. 3-10). While the former were found to run unimpeded, the latter did not cross the former but were staggered on plan and possibly served as delivery or entrance lanes for certain house blocks. Again, while the former were not equally spaced, the latter were situated on an average of 7 m from each other. Besides, there were quite a few other streets, which served only one or two blocks and were not thoroughfares. The width ranged from 1.8 to 7.2 m. To avoid damage from the vehicular traffic, fender posts were provided at some street corners. The width of the thoroughfares seems to have been maintained throughout the occupation; the only structural encroachments into the streets were the rectangular platforms (of uncertain use) immediately outside some houses. The streets, except in the late phase, were unmetalled. House drains, which were either of wood or of baked brick, discharged into soakage jars buried under the street floor.

The layout plan of the city shows that the alignment of the streets is at variance with that of the fortification walls. Perhaps the alignment of the fortifications was conditioned by the Period I (Pre-Harappan) layout of the adjacent Citadel and by later modification by the Harappans as occupation advanced. Excavation has revealed that the fortification and the streets had been planned at, the same time, viz., the very beginning of Harappan occupation of the site. Interestingly enough, it was observed that the house walls near the fortification wall faithfully followed the alignment of the latter, while those nearer the streets followed the streets.

From the very beginning of the occupation, the houses were built of mud bricks (30 x 15 x 7.5 cm), the use of baked brick (of the same size and also the wedge-shaped type) being confined mostly to drains, wells, sills and bathing platforms. In the typical chessboard plan of the city, each house faced two, if not three, streets and consisted of a courtyard with six to seven rooms aligned on two or three sides. Entrance to the house, located usually on the lane side, was either through a courtyard or through a corridor running between sets of rooms.

The finds obtained from the occupation of Period II were all characteristic of the Indus civilization and need not be listed individually. The following finds deserve special mention: a cylinder seal; a terracotta cake, incised on the obverse with a horned human figure and on the reverse with a human figure pulling a sacrificial animal (?) (Pl. 3-11); a terracotta human head; a copper bull showing the dynamic mood of the animal and other copper objects (Pl. 3-12) including a pin; a terracotta feeding-cup with a cow's head on the rim; a terracotta graduated scale (incomplete) and an ivory comb. Both wheat and barley were found in the deposits of this period. No evidence of rice was obtained.

Besides the above two principal parts of the metropolis, there was also a third one – a modest structure situated upwards of 80 m east of the lower city. The structure, of which the complete outline could not be recovered, was built of mud bricks of the usual Harappan size, 30 x 15 x 7.5 cm and consisted of an impressive wall enclosing a room containing four to five "fire-altars" of the kind referred to above. No other building, residential or otherwise, existed on this small mound. The absence of normal occupation debris suggests that the lonely structure with the altars was used for ritual purposes.

Kalibangan Cemetery: The cemetery of the Harappan period was located 300 m to the west-south-west of the Citadel. Three types of burials (Pl. 3-13, -14) were attested: extended inhumation in rectangular or oval grave pot-burial in a circular pit; and rectangular or oval grave-pit containing only pottery and other funerary objects. The latter two methods were not associated with any skeletal remains. Of the first variety, the recurrent features were as follows: on the floor of the oblong pit, the body was laid in an extended position with the head towards the north; around the head area, the funerary furnishings comprising pots and such objects of personal jewellery as bronze mirrors, etc., were deposited. The pit was thereafter filled with the same soil. Three graves deserve special mention. In one of them, the body was lying face down with its head towards the south, quite contrary to normal Harappan interment and showed a crouching position with folded legs. The other grave was lined with mud bricks (40 x 20 x 10 cm) covered with approximately 2 cm-thick plaster.

The third grave showed evidence of two types of burial, one superimposed upon the other. The lower interment, consisting of pottery, was without any skeletal remains, while the upper contained the normal extended human body with pottery and one bead each of gold and carnelian around the neck. The grave in this case was quite large and had steps on the eastern side leading down to the grave floor.

Of the second variety, the grave pit was oval or circular and contained an urn and other pots including platters and dishes-on-stand clustered round the former. Besides pottery, some of the pits also contained objects such as shell bangles and steatite beads.

Of the third variety, the grave pit was rectangular or oval in plan, with the longer axis oriented north-south as in the case of the first variety, but it was marked by the absence of skeletal remains. The grave goods consisted of pottery and occasionally of personal ornaments like beads and bangles. The striking feature about these pits was the filling, which showed two stages: after the funerary deposit, the pit seems to have been left unfilled resulting in the accumulation of bands of fine sand and clay; at a later stage, the remaining part of the pit was filled in by human agency with cloddy clay.

Thapar recognizes that the occurrence of these three varieties of burial has posed problems of a sociological kind. Meanwhile, it may be affirmed that the grave goods obtained from each of these types are typically Indus. Graves of the first and second variety occur in separate defined areas, the latter lying to the north of the former, while the graves of the third variety are found largely in the area of the first but occasionally also in that of the second.

Thapar thinks that one of the compelling reasons for the abandonment of the site was the drying of the river Ghaggar and the consequent denudation of the watershed by over-grazing and deforestation. The settlement must have been seriously affected by the shortage of a perennial water supply for both agricultural and drinking purposes.

Uttar Pradesh

From Uttar Pradesh, Alamgirpur, a small Harappan site, was discovered in Meerut district in 1959. It was the first Harappan site to have been found into the Ganga-Yamuna Doab. It is a 60 x 50 m mound located on the bank of River Hindon. Period I here belongs to a late stage of Harappa culture, the other periods belong to PGW and later cultures. The brick sizes in Period I were either 30 x 15 x 7 or 35 x 20 x 10 cm. The main finds are: cubical dice, cart frames, terracotta animal figurines, miniature bowls of faience, etc. A small terracotta bead fragment seems to have been coated with gold.

Hulas, also in the Upper Ganga-Yamuna Doab, was excavated by Dikshit (1982). Like Alamgirpur, it is also a Late Harappan site. It did yield a sealing with some Harappan characters but no animals. A large mud platform was perhaps put up to guard against floods. Unlike Bhagwanpura, Hulas does not show any overlap with the subsequent PGW culture.

Most spectacular has been the recent discovery of a fabulous jewellery hoard from Mandi (29°26″10″ N, 77°34″35″ E), in district Muzaffarnagar. It was a chance find from a farm where local people were looting the precious Harappan hoard for several days, till somebody reported it to the police. Police was able to recover about 10 kg of jewellery. One can only imagine what has been lost to the local robbers.

The pottery from Mandi is of the same Late Harappan vintage as found at Hulas and Alamgirpur. The Archaeological Survey did a salvage digging at the site. Bricks measuring 8 x 22 x 31, 9 x 23 x 33 and 9 x 20 x 30 cm were found. The hoard, it is alleged, comprised, a large number of beads made of etched carnelian, gold, onyx and copper. The gold bead types are: spacer beads, circular beads, hollow terminal beads, bell-shaped beads and disc beads. Broken silver ornaments were also found. It is estimated that the Mandi hoard "is the most important and the largest amongst all" of the Harappan hoards so far. The circular wafer gold beads are generally found in small numbers in the Harappan sites, but at Mandi, the hoard has these as the main constituent. In fact, they are thousands in number and weigh a good 7 kg! The excavators estimate that the Mandi hoard might have contained at least three to four times the quantity recovered! (Sharma *et al.* 1999-2000: 36-41).

Gujarat

Gujarat constitutes three distinct zones: Kachchh, Saurashtra and mainland Gujarat. The narrow corridor, which connects the mainland of Gujarat with Kachchh bordered in the north-west by the Rann of Kachchh and in the south-east by the Sabarmati river, is known as north Gujarat; traditionally, the region was known as "Anarta". It is a semi-arid sandy plain, dotted with fossil sand-dunes. The region extends in the north up to the southern Rajasthan and gradually merges into the alluvial plains of Saurashtra and central Gujarat. The region is drained by the rivers Banas, Saraswati, Rupen and their tributaries, which flow into the Little Rann of Kachchh. Though none of these rivers are perennial, during monsoon they drain large volumes of water into the Rann. At present, these rivers contain brackish water for the major part of the year. The Banas and Saraswati, which flow in the northern part of the region, are heavily silted and have developed broad and shallow channels. But silting is not so evident in the Rupen, which forms a deep channel by cutting the alluvial plains (Sonawane in press).

The entire landscape is marked by a thick deposit of sandy loam and appears dead flat except for a few sand-dunes and attendant blow-outs. Such inter-dunal depressions accumulate rainwater and often retain water throughout the year. Since water in these village ponds remains potable, they are an important source of water for people as well as livestock.

The climate is characterized by hot summers and cold winters; a dry weather prevails in the region during most part of the year. Being situated in a climatic zone of 600 mm isohyte, rainfall in this region is sparse and irregular, gradually grading down from 80 cm to 40 cm from east to west. Because of the unpredictability and the uneven distribution of rainfall, drought in this region is a recurrent phenomenon. A major portion of the soil is sandy; however, the black cotton soil is also not uncommon in some parts. In many areas, the soil is poor and saline and subsoil water is brackish. As a result, most of the western part is marked by saline tree-less grassland, which is gradually transforming into a desert. The vegetation is characterized by tropical thorn forest. However, all along the eastern margin of the Little Rann of Kachchh, the riverbanks and large area of wastelands, locally known as Padthar, favour excellent growth of grasses including bokana (*Cressa cretica*), kharidhar (*Aeluropus flariddum*), lapdi (*Aristida redaets*), soma (*Enimochloe colonum*), jinko soma (*Panicum flaridum*), mancho (*Dhetyloclemium egyptium*), mano (*Chlarismonm*), dhaman (*Cenchrus ciliaris*), zinzvo (*Andropogan pumlis*), etc. These grasses are available immediately after the first monsoon showers and are exploited by the present-day pastoral communities for feeding their cattle (Bhan 1994: 73). This area also supports a large population of the Asiatic wild ass or onager and is an important source for the famous konkrej breed of cattle. Bajra (pearl millet) is the most predominant kharif crop of this region. It is drought resistant and also provides much needed fodder for the cattle (Patel 1997). Cotton also forms an important cash crop of the region. Likewise, a major food grain produced in the rabi season is wheat. However, its cultivation is restricted due to its dependence upon irrigation. It can, however, be grown without irrigation in the low-lying saline strips or in the filled up ancient inter-dunal depressions. These major crops have considerable influence on the subsistence activities of the people living in this area. Animal husbandry is another mode of subsistence, of which cattle, sheep, goat, camel and buffalo form the major component species. Nomadic or semi-nomadic pastoral communities such as Rabari and Bharvad make their living primarily out of breeding and/or herding of these animals. In fact, agriculture and pastoralism are the two important components of the economy of this region (Sonawane in press).

The archaeological research in Gujarat was somewhat overshadowed by the glamour of big Harappan sites like Mohenjodaro. The Harappan studies also dominated the archaeological research, as the local and independent development of Chalcolithic cultures was largely ignored. Now it is being recognized both in Rajasthan (e.g. at Balathal, Ahar, etc.) and Gujarat (Prabhas Patan, Rojdi, etc.) that there was an indigenous development from the Mesolithic cultures to Neolithic-Chalcolithic cultures on which the Harappa culture impinged at places. It is therefore, not surprising that sites, such as Rojdi, which had local roots did not get crippled, at the eclipse of the Harappa culture in the major Harappan towns.

Sonawane (2000: 137-146) points out that between the 4th and 2nd Millennia BC in Gujarat there existed a mosaic of different adaptations such as hunting and gathering, pastoralism, agriculture and various specialized craft production strategies. Hence we see not only regional diversity in the manifestations of the Harappan culture in Gujarat, but also the capacity of the Harappans to mobilize different subsistence systems by integrating them into their economic structure. In addition, the integration of the Harappan culture with indigenous counterparts offers an interesting situation in terms of the processes of cultural transformation. Regional diversity is now an accepted phenomenon of the Harappans, for which the role of the regional Chalcolithic traditions can be held responsible. Moreover, fresh data brought to light from recent studies have revealed that some of the non-Harappan indigenous settled communities emerged on the scene more than half a millennium prior to the beginning of Mature/Urban Harappan phase in Gujarat. However, in spite of the considerable overall advancement in Harappan studies, the information pertaining to the exploitation of plants for sustenance in this region is still inadequately addressed.

Herman (1997: 107-108) has made a very perceptive study of the Gujarat Harappan sites. He points out that the size estimates of settlements in Gujarat are built on very weak arguments, especially since the regional cultural differences within Gujarat (Sorath Harappan, Indus Harappan, Anarta tradition, Microlithic complex, etc.) have not been taken into account. Herman thinks that refined settlement sequences can indeed be produced, if based on, amongst others, reliable and (above all) independent pottery sequences. In this respect, Rojdi has a great potential, thanks to the detailed stratigraphic control over the pottery. The establishment of sound and detailed evolution in the many distinct pottery productions – Herman recorded over thirty-five different names of wares in Bronze Age Gujarat. This is an absolute must for a better chronological control. Herman suggests that if the excellent pottery sequence at Nageshwar could be complemented by one from, for example, Prabhas Patan, one from the northern Gujarat plains, one from Padri, one from the Sorath Harappan and Lustrous Red Ware (LRW) occupations at Dhevalio and also from Dholavira, the intra- and extra-regional variation may well show up to be less ephemeral. Such approach will prove more reliable than arguments based on isolated and often problematic ^{14}C dates (Herman 1997: 107-108).

Herman thinks that the relationship between Kachchh and Saurashtra during Early Harappan and Late Harappan times is in need of further exploration. Dholavira in Kachchh and the excavation of a site with a long history down to Post-Harappan times in Saurashtra and in the northern Gujarat plain will be useful.

Strongly pleading for a re-excavation of Rangpur, Herman points out that Rangpur, the first ever discovered "Harappan" settlement on Gujarat territory, still remains one of the best sites to return to. The de-urbanization process in the area is not only different in nature, but is also of a greater complexity. The apparent, quite distinctive cultural and trade networks as well as subsistence systems of Kachchh (including the Ranns), of the northern Gujarat plains and of Saurashtra, shed a different light on Rangpur as a settlement. Herman suggests that it should now be examined to what extent and at what stage Rangpur belonged to the Core/Periphery Interaction Zone, to the Sorath Harappan realm and/or to urbanized Harappan. The impact of the pastorals of the north Gujarat plains communities (Microlithic, Loteswar Anarta complexes) and Saurashtra should also be properly established. It should not be forgotten that Rangpur remains the largest settlement (between 50 and 100 ha) in Saurashtra, in the Mature, Late and Post-Harappan periods. With its more than 6 m of deposits, its period of occupation may well be much more extensive than is nowadays assumed. Sorath Harappan deposits (RGP IIA-B-C) have been found on the whole mound, showing more Harappan architecture in the north-western part. But the pre-structural levels with Micaceous Red Ware below the RGP IIA-architecture deposits may indeed belong to

Early Harappan times and date to the first half of the 3rd millennium BC cal. At the upper end, the Lustrous Red Ware (LRW) occupation may also have lasted much longer than presumed. The extensive deposits may well illustrate an internal evolution throughout the LRW occupation. However, to achieve this, the nature and shifts of lateral occupations need to be established. The excavations at Oriyo Timbo, Kanewal, Ratanpura, Nesadi, Jokha and elsewhere would receive new meaning for the relative chronology if a close re-analysis of the LRW-layers at Rangpur and Prabhas Patan is executed. The precise chronological relationship between the Late Sorath Harappan and LRW is crucial in this matter. Herman points to the puzzling stratigraphic interpretations of the LRW deposits at Rangpur, which show great disturbances in the RGP IIC layers, may lead to the question whether LRW does really belong to IIC or to III only? The fact that Rangpur, together with Prabhas Patan, is one of the few sites where LRW is associated with rectangular structures, instead of with round ones, is indeed of interest. We do also need the much awaited first radiocarbon dates for this key-site which, for instance, could illustrate the first occupation, the contact-phase or the crucial date of the introduction of LRW in Gujarat. In view of its overriding importance, Herman concludes that Rangpur would be a good candidate to receive on Indian territory full attention for further investigations as the other great cities of the Indus/Ghaggar-Hakra-Nara valley (Herman 1997: 107-108).

Lothal

Lothal, located on the head of Gulf of Cambay in Gujarat, is a small (4.8 ha) Mature Harappan site, excavated by S.R. Rao (1979, 1985) for seven consecutive seasons. Stratigraphically the site has been divided into five building levels each separated from the other by flood deposits. In the first four levels, numbered I-IV from bottom to top and designated Lothal A, were found ceramics and small finds of Mature Harappan character, while the fifth and final level (Lothal B) can be termed Late Harappan. Comparative typology and radiocarbon dates suggest that Lothal A can be dated between 2100 and 1850 BC (2550 to 2160 BC, cal.) and that Lothal B ends one-hundred to one-hundred and fifty years later. The following description of the site is mainly based on the comprehensive summary by Possehl (1979).

The first building level, with its limited architecture and no signs of settlement planning, suggests that Lothal was at that time a small "pioneer" settlement. Then in the succeeding three levels, the settlement expanded in size, with definite indications of community planning. In the fifth level, Lothal is once again reduced to a small settlement and the architecture suggests a "squatters" occupation just before the final abandonment of the site. The following discussion will be limited to the "mature" phase levels II, III and IV.

Lothal is basically a small town, approximately one-fourth the size of Mohenjodaro or Harappa with a population of about 1,000-2,000. Lothal has been divided into three architectural areas or "districts": the Citadel, the Lower Town and the Dockyard (Fig. 3-6). The Citadel is an imposing area artificially raised above the remainder of the settlement on a mud brick platform. This area occupies the south-east quadrant of the site and is 48.5 by 42.5 m in size. On the Citadel are streets at right angles to one another, which separate blocks of mud and baked brick structures. One of these blocks, with very thick mud brick foundations, has been interpreted as a warehouse.

The Lower Town is also divided into blocks separated by streets at right angles oriented to the cardinal directions. Only six of these blocks were excavated. The Lower Town was used both as residential and manufacturing purposes.

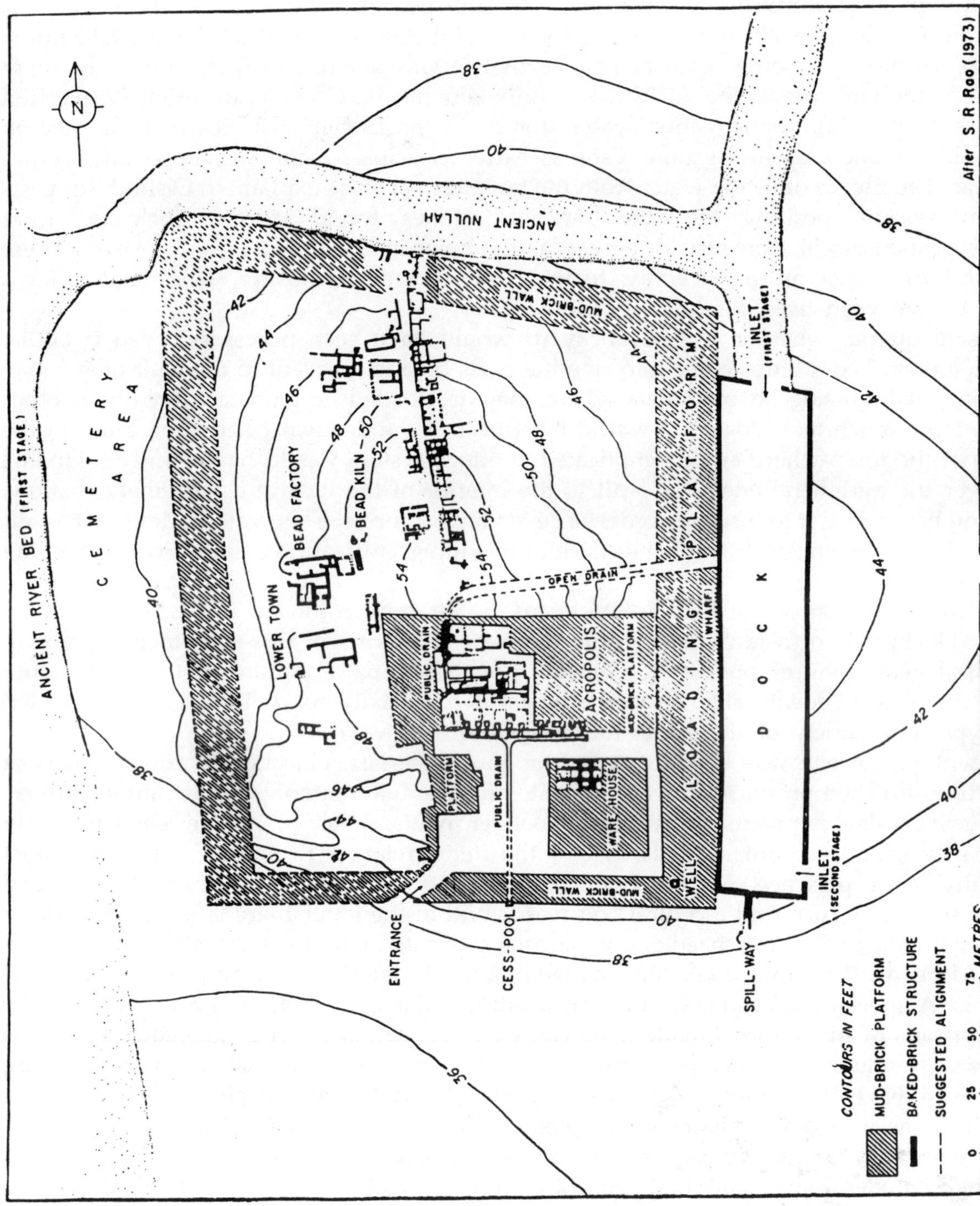

Fig. 3-6. The site plan of Lothal with its dockyard (courtesy ASI).

The so-called "Dockyard" is probably the most controversial feature at Lothal. This structure is located on the eastern side of the site. Constructed of baked brick, the "Dockyard" is nearly rectangular in shape, 219 by 37 m in size. The brick walls of the sunken enclosure are 4.5 m high. A platform borders the town side and permits easy access to the warehouse area on the Citadel. Possehl thinks that the precise function of this brick-lined enclosure is still open to question. Some scholars believe that it was a tank. In fact, neither of these alternatives, the tank versus the dockyard, is fully convincing. One has to seriously question the necessity of a tank for irrigation water storage in the Lothal area. Seasonal inundation is sufficient for one crop and groundwater is extremely close to the surface at other times of the year. The means of lifting water from the tank has yet to be explained. Leshnik suggests a shaduf system, positing that the "anchor" stones found in the enclosure were counterweights. Possehl, however, disagrees, as the holes in the anchors are too small. There are no stairs or other means of access to the interior of the enclosure. This means that it could not have been used for bathing and laundry.

Possehl queries whether a large dockyard would have been necessary, even if Lothal had been a port. Today ships come into riverine ports on and adjacent to the Gulf of Cambay and anchor at high tide on mud flats where they are loaded and unloaded without other facilities. How much more logical it would have been if the dockyard had been built on the riverside of the town where an uncomplicated entrance system would have sufficed. Finally, access over the peripheral enclosing wall to the interior of the facility is extremely shallow. Excavation has shown it to be of the order of seven brick courses. This would admit watercraft with less than a metre draft, probably excluding sailing craft appropriate for ocean going maritime trade.

The interpretation of the Lothal "Dockyard" is far from resolved. But whether it is or is not a "Dockyard" or a tank makes little difference in terms of this settlement's place in the cultural geography of prehistoric Gujarat. The differentiated nature of the architecture and the presence of identifiable districts suggest a complexity for Lothal. This is revealed in the type and variety of the artefactual assemblage as well.

Present at the site was a wide variety of raw materials, objects in various stages of manufacture, finished products as well as waste and residual materials. Stone anvils, bronze drills, crucibles, slag, remnants of conch shell, copper ingots, whole tusks from elephants (and others partly sawn) are but a partial list of the items relating to specialized crafts. Most noteworthy is the presence of a bead factory in the Lower Town. In this structure several rooms of small size surround a central courtyard. Within the latter there is a raised working platform with an anvil. The archaeological deposits associated with the factory contained many unfinished beads, drills and other tools as well as bead materials and hundreds of finished ornaments. A special furnace for heating carnelian to enhance its colour is also a part of the complex. Beads of many forms made from carnelian, crystal, jasper, opal, steatite, paste and the like were manufactured on a very large scale at Lothal, suggesting that this manufacturing process must have been one of the most important activities at the site.

Lothal was a carefully planned settlement, ordered into districts in a way, which led to an economy of space. There were areas, such as the bead factory, a smelter, a place within which shell bangles were made, that suggest craft specialization and an overall order to the layout of the town. It can be reasonably inferred that this diverse and evidently voluminous, specialized craft activity produced much more in the way of finished products than the settlement itself could have consumed. Lothal was not situated in a location particularly suited to resource extraction. Its immediate environs, in fact, produce almost none of the raw materials (copper and other ores, stones, shell, ivory, etc.), which played such a key role in the life of this settlement. The nearest copper comes from Rajasthan, as does steatite. Agate is found on the Narmada and in Saurashtra and Kachchh. Shell is found along the coast of the Arabian Sea. Ivory was undoubtedly available locally. Possehl emphasizes that Lothal should therefore, be seen as a hub of a complex and continuous exchange network. The nature of this exchange is not fully understood; however, it appears to have involved not only the inhabitants of this settlement but the other non-Harappan folk around them. Nevertheless, Possehl denies Lothal's role in external trade.

Seasonal hunting and gathering peoples inhabited the large north Gujarat plains, to the north and east of Lothal, at the same time as Lothal was occupied. This has been demonstrated by excavations at Langhnaj, a "microlithic" site 20 km north of Ahmedabad.

Of considerable importance is the occurrence of what appear to be trade items at Langhnaj. There is a 98.12 per cent pure copper knife, Black-and-Red Ware, which is typologically akin to a ware found at Lothal and disk beads of Harappan type. These items all suggest contact between the inhabitants of Langhnaj and the Harappan civilization. Langhnaj is probably not a unique site in north Gujarat since there were several hundred such hunting and gathering settlements. Possehl suggests that Lothal appears to have been a kind of "point interface" between the hunting and gathering peoples in north Gujarat and its parent Harappan hinterland.

Possehl argues that Lothal was an entrepot, a settlement of entrepreneurs interested in the procurement of raw materials demanded by the inhabitants of the cities and towns of Sindh and the Punjab. To facilitate this process of acquisition, they formed an alliance, an exchange relationship, with the hunting and gathering peoples on the south-eastern borderland of their civilization. Seasonal mobility plus an intimate knowledge of the resources available within the regional environment made these hunter-gatherers efficient partners in the overall acquisition process. But there is more than merely culture historical importance to this relationship. What it suggests is that within the late third and early 2nd Millennia BC a complex interlocking cultural mosaic was developing in South Asia. This mosaic is not one, which only portrays cultural diversity within simple geographic bounds and for which border phenomena and territoriality are particularly useful in terms of complete analysis. The mosaic is rather one, which suggests a growth of interdependence between socio-cultural groups with fundamentally different systems of settlement and subsistence, material culture and presumably diverse cultural traditions. This is a form of cultural integration still found in India as revealed by the ethnographic analogy employed for the hunter-gatherers. This interlocking relationship is also generally applicable to one of the essential aspects of caste organization if viewed as a total system. That is general economic integration of what are in deep historical terms ethnically diverse populations. Possehl makes an interesting observation, "Without making the undue claim that the discussion of the relationship between the Harappan civilization and hunter-gatherer groups in Gujarat charts the beginning of the caste system, it can nonetheless be suggested that the development of a complex and integrated cultural mosaic has its roots in prehistory and that such conditions are wholly congruent as a precondition to the growth of caste institutions in later historical contexts. This is, in fact, the larger significance of the discussion at hand and one, which deserves a greater attention in archaeological research" (Possehl 1979).

Dholavira

Dholavira, one of the five largest (60 ha), cities of the Harappans, is situated in the isolated island of Khadir in the Great Rann of Kachchh in Gujarat (India), which has been excavated for several seasons by Archaeological Survey of India (Bisht 1989a, b, 1991, 1994, 1999). Bisht (1999: 393-442) rightly claims that Dholavira has supplemented and complemented profusely to the database of the Harappa culture. For the first time, a full configuration, together with hitherto unknown elements of Harappan city planning, was laid bare here (Fig. 3-7). New evidence was added in respect of monumental and aesthetic architecture. An altogether new system of water harvesting and storage was brought to light. A congregation ground or stadium with seating arrangements for spectators was uncovered. In addition, fresh information bearing on funerary practices and structures is being gathered. A unique inscription made up of ten large-sized Harappan signs was discovered. Metal use though not too abundant was significant nevertheless (Pl. 3-15). Furthermore, an enormous accumulation of successive settlements of over a millennium has revealed seven significant cultural stages documenting the rise and fall of the first Indian urbanization known as the Harappan civilization. Arts and crafts show the typical Harappan virtuosity (Pl. 3-16).

All the seven cultural stages through which the settlement at Dholavira passed are encountered only in the castle of the Citadel (Pl. 3-17). The successive settlements containing residential structures and the habitation debris account for 11.30 metres of deposit. Bisht summarizes the features of the seven stages as follows.

Stage I: Right from the beginning, the first settlement was fortified by a massive wall. The occupational deposit, measuring 65-70 cm in thickness, has revealed a fairly developed state of culture. The first occupants at the site were familiar with diverse pottery traditions, copper metallurgy, stone-dressing, lithic tool technology, shell-working, use of steatite and the knowledge of definitive principles of planning and architecture, (Bisht claims) all datable to the beginning of the 3rd millennium BC. The fortification wall was made up of rubble-stones set in mud mortar. A strong cultural marker was the use of moulded mud bricks measuring about 36 x 18 x 9 cm (providing a ratio of 4: 2: 1). The presence of moulded bricks, monumental architecture, indication of formal planning, perforated jars, carinated dishes, basins, triangular terracotta cakes, long chert blades, steatite wafer beads, etc., from Stage I point to the beginning of the process which later blossomed into the Harappan civilization.

Stage II: The first visible evidence of the beginning of Stage II was found in the form of the widening of the pre-existing fortification wall. Resting on the antecedent deposit of Stage I, a 2.80 metre thick mud brick masonry was added against the inner face of the southern arm of the fortification. Most significantly, on the inner face of the defensive wall, there were at least 13 coats of plaster, each made of a white, off-white, grey, or one of the shades of pink clay which are available locally. Not only the fortification but also the house walls and floors were found respectively treated with and made of similar clays. It is the same trait, a part of the Harappan legacy, that shows the aesthetic sense of the contemporary society. During this stage, the settlement was extended towards the north and possibly to the east as well. This perhaps points to the introduction of a dichotomy in the settlement and thereby indicating an emerging stratification in the society or elevation of the political status of the establishment. Among antiquities, copper items, beads of chalcedony and steatite, bladelets of chalcedony and chert, bangles of shell and clay, industrial waste of stone and shell workings and triangular terracotta cakes increased in number. The shell bangles continued to be thin and elegant.

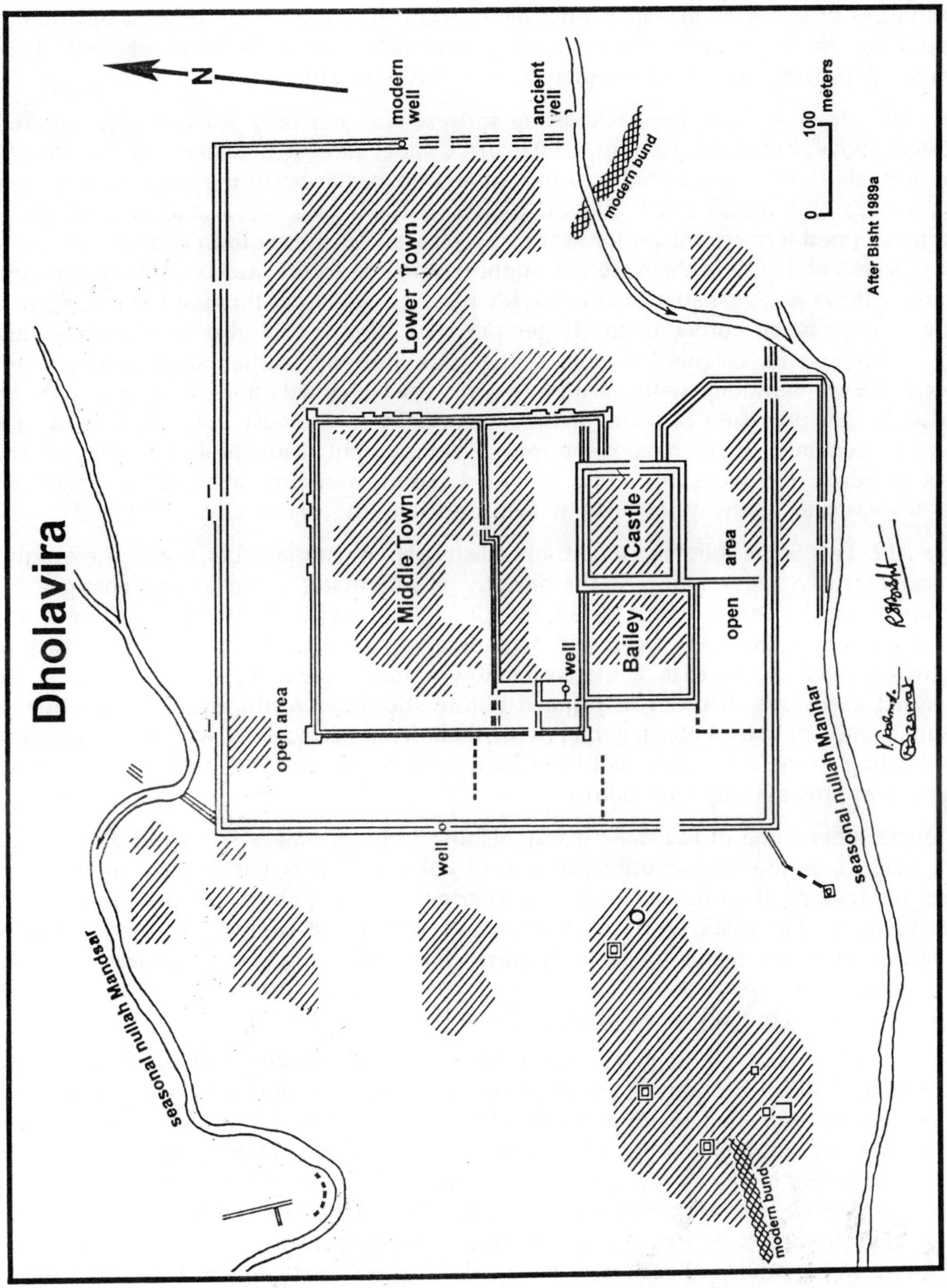

Fig. 3-7. The site plan of Dholavira.

Stage III: This was a very creative period at Dholavira. As in the case of Stage II, its beginning too was first recognized in the final widening of the southern wall by adding 4.40-4.50 metres broad brick masonry, once again from the inside. This stage is also denoted by six building phases contained in an occupational debris of 3.30-3.60 metres, which may be subdivided broadly into two sub-stages viz., IIIA and IIIB.

Stage IIIA: In this stage, the pre-existing fortress was not only substantially reinforced as indicated above, but enlarged into a bipartite Citadel having a castle and a bailey. The northern extension of the residential area that came into existence during Stage II was cleared of its structures and transformed into an extensive esplanade for a stadium, which was enclosed by stepped terraces meant for seating spectators. To the stadium's north, the general town was located and both of them were brought within one fortification with bastions, corner towers and gateways. A smaller stadium with massive walls on three sides was also laid out at the south-eastern corner of the larger one. An annexe was also in existence during this stage, although its origins, whether going back into the earlier stage remains to be ascertained. Reservoirs along with partition bunds, inlet channels and dams had also been provided although provision of some of them, especially in the east, south and west of the antecedent settlements, might have come into existence right from the beginning. All these reservoirs of Stage IIIA were, however, provided within a circumvallation, furnished with bastions, towers and gateways, which in fact, enclosed the entire city.

Stage IIIB: This Stage followed a natural catastrophe, most plausibly a severe earthquake that caused extensive devastation at the site. In its aftermath, some drastic changes were brought about in the inner layout of all the prevailing divisions, besides adding a third principal division, i.e., the lower town with well-defined streets and sectors. The newly added division was located to the east of the earlier town and, consequently, the city walls were also extended eastwards in order to bring it within the outer fortification. In addition, the monumental gates of the castle, together with their front terraces as well as a ceremonial pathway leading to the north gate had been built up by this sub-stage, which is represented by a deposit approximating 1.10 metres.

Amongst others, one of the most distinguishing traits of Stages II and III and, to some extent of Stage I, is the almost universal use of colourful clays particularly of white and pink hues for making floorings as well as plastering of both public and private structures. The broadway in the castle and the larger and smaller stadiums too were furnished successively with floors made up of such clays. The diagnostic Harappan elements, such as stamp seals, the script, weights and many typical pottery forms as well as decorative motifs, made their debut all along during Stage III.

Stage IV: The relics of Stage IV are represented by 4.40-4.60 metres of habitational accumulation revealing the mature urban phase of the culture which is well known from, a large number of excavated Harappan sites. The general planning and architecture of the preceeding stage was maintained but with a few minor alterations. During Stage IV, an overall phenomenal progress in the material culture is witnessed. Its manifestation may be seen in pottery, seals, writing, the weights and in a variety of ornamental and utilitarian artefacts made of metals, semiprecious stones, other stones, faience, steatite, shell, ivory, bone and clay, all found in abundance. Local mass production in each craft demonstrates that the city of Dholavira had become a great manufacturing centre to which raw materials were being brought from different sources for catering to the needs of the local manufactories as well

Although sheep, goat and cattle can be herded extensively and moved to new grazing areas as needed, water buffalo is dependent on better quality forage and water for soaking their hides. Thus, they are likely to have been kept in the city itself where the reservoirs of Dholavira would have provided a reliable source of water for daily bathing. It is possible that some of the sheep, goat and cattle needed for provisioning the city, could have been obtained from more mobile pastoral populations in exchange for agricultural products or other goods. Ideas such as these need to be systematically investigated by integrating faunal data with the results of architectural and artefactual studies. Individual kin groups or even households may have included both pastoral and agricultural elements, thus ensuring access to both animal and plant products. In addition, a particularly interesting study would be investigation of the relationship of Dholavira with its hinterland. Patel says that a large city like Dholavira would not have existed in isolation from surrounding communities, be they agricultural, pastoral, or even hunter-gatherer (Patel 1997).

Surkotada

Surkotada is located in Rapar *taluka* of Kachchh district, Gujarat. J.P. Joshi excavated Surkotada (Fig. 3-8) for a number of years in his usual meticulous way for which he is known (Joshi 1990). Describing the evidence, Joshi says Surkotada unfolded a sequence of three cultural periods dated to *c.* 2100 to 1700 BC (uncal.). The Harappans had a fortified Citadel and a residential annexe in Period IA and the same pattern of settlement had been maintained through the successive IB and IC periods. In later two periods, Coarse Red Ware and White Painted Black-and-Red Ware using folks respectively come to the site, yet the Harappan influence continues through the periods in a substantial way as evidenced by the pottery, chert blades, terracotta cakes, weights and measures, beads, terracotta cart frames and seals. Joshi points out that a remarkable feature is the coexistence of a non-Harappan element represented by Cream Slipped Ware, a Red Ware akin to Pre-Harappan traditions of Kot-Diji and Kalibangan and a Reserve Slipped Ware showing extraterritorial affinities with Ur, Mohenjodaro and Lothal.

The Citadel with bastions, elaborate gateway complex having guard-rooms, lanes and by-lanes and well-planned fortified residential area with a separate entrance and an intercommunicating passage between the Citadel and the residential area (Pl. 3-19) and a substantial quantity of the Harappan cultural-equipment shows full-fledged Mature Harappan influence even up to *c.* 1700 BC (uncal.), which Joshi thinks is itself a remarkable feature.

There is evidence of the Harappan script on potsherds. The copper objects found at Surkotada show that in Period IC, copper technology was popular and more copper objects are available in this period than in earlier periods. Joshi suggests that possibly the increase in the number of copper objects in later periods can be ascribed to the possible contact of Harappans of Surkotada with white painted Black-and-Red Ware using Banas culture people. Though Joshi claims that the Harappans knew Equus right from the time of their arrival at Surkotada, it is more likely that the bones are of onager. Joshi however, admits that the reserve slip ware and the cream slipped ware with its West Asian links and the find of Equus bones needs further comparative study. The Harappans at Surkotada were probably worshipping *linga*-type clay objects, which have been found from the mid-levels of Period IA. Neither mother-goddess figures nor fire-altars of Lothal and Kalibangan type have been found. However, terracotta triangular cakes are available all through.

It is rather strange that at Surkotada, there is a compact Citadel and a residential annexe

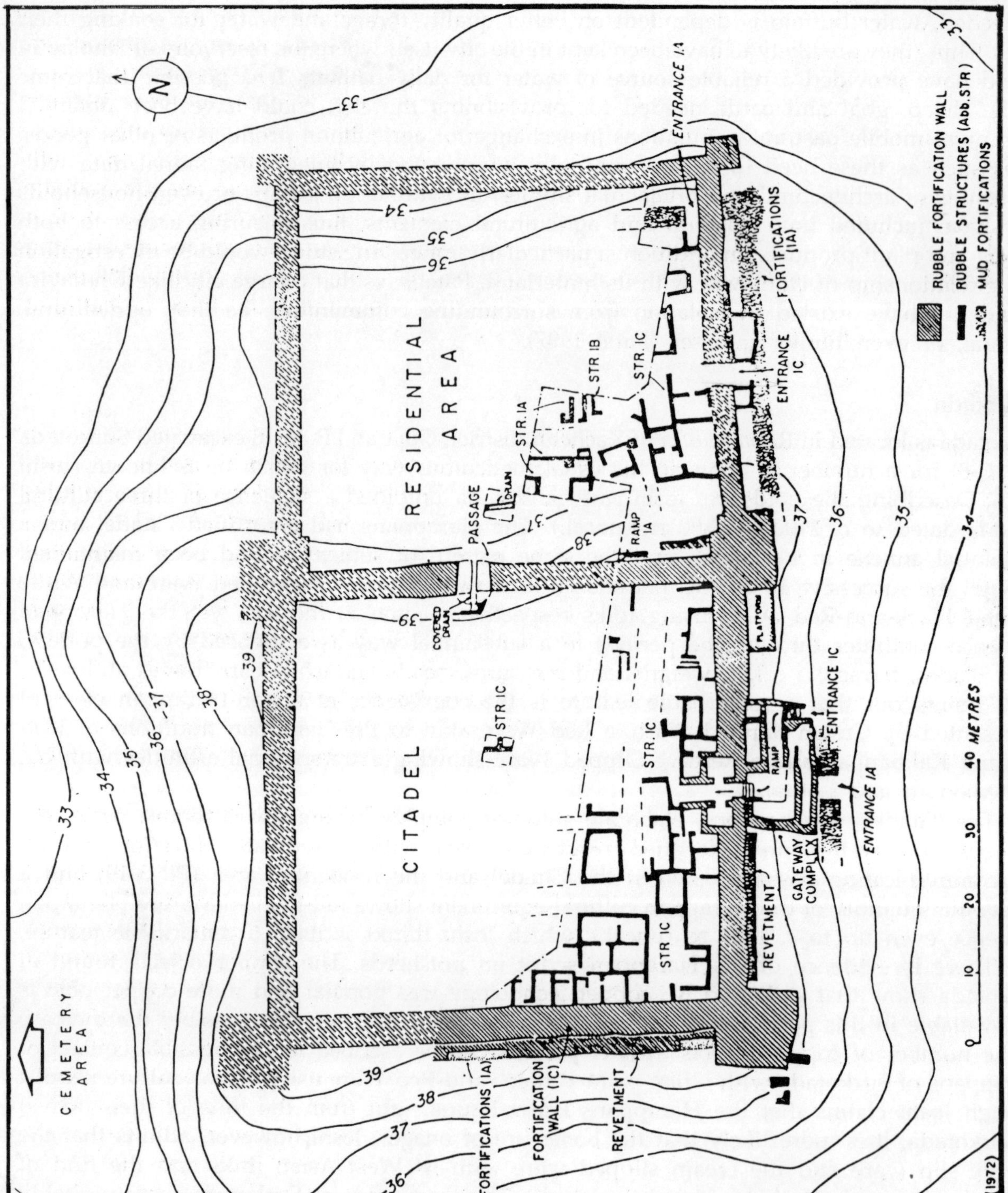

Fig. 3-8. The site plan of Surkotada.

but no city complex has been unearthed. Joshi thinks that most probably Surkotada was a garrison complex to control the eastward movement of Harappans. Possibility of the existence of a large settlement in the immediate vicinity is rather remote. The increased frequency of Harappan pottery from certain layers of the upper levels in Period IC shows a fresh lease of life, possibly indicating a fresh wave of Harappan immigrants.

It is significant to note that while the white painted Black-and-Red Ware is available at Lothal from the earliest levels of the Harappan culture (and also at Rangpur) and continues throughout, but this ware is available only in Period IC at Surkotada. At Desalpur too this ware occurs only in period IB. Joshi suggests a possible explanation that at Lothal along with the Harappans the white painted Black-and-Red Ware remained in a subservient form right from the beginning, but by *c.* 1700 BC (uncal.) with the decay of Harappan culture in Saurashtra, it got a fresh lease of life and rejuvenated and started moving to Kachchh where in Period IC at Surkotada it is available with the Harappan wares. It is also possible that with its remote connections with Banas valley, the white painted Black-and-Red Ware culture got fresh impetus in its movement and expansion. Joshi thinks that it may indicate the coming to power of a people represented by the white painted Black-and-Red Ware who remained in a subjugated state during the heydays of the Harappans and started a mass expansion by *c.* 1700 BC (uncal.) in western India (Joshi 1972).

Regarding the burial practices at Surkotada, the Harappans were sometimes burying the bones in pots and sometimes only pots in pits and covered them with a stone slab or a cairn. This is a most unusual form of burial tradition amongst the Harappans. The availability of the stone nearby might have tempted them to do so.

Migrations: The following is the summary of Joshi's views on migration of the Harappans. Joshi thinks that the Harappan expansion took place not as a sequel to a catastrophe but it was natural and constant waves of Harappans from their epicentres at Mohenjodaro and Harappa came in search of new lands and trade well within 2300 BC to 1750 BC (uncal.), possibly after that also. Economic pressure and man's natural urge for expansion in new areas were the prime factors. However, fleeing after a flood or invasion cannot be ruled out. One can doubt that flood and enemy attacks cannot solely be responsible for mass movements. From time immemorial, floods have been a constant feature in so many parts of India but people have hardly migrated *en masse* to safer regions forever. Temporarily they might move but again they come back and establish their own home at the original place or slightly removed from it. Hence on the basis of dates available, it is possible that during the lifetime of Mohenjodaro and Harappa, the Harappans with their best traditions moved towards south-east and north, which is attested to by the ^{14}C dates of Kalibangan, Lothal and Sutkotada. In Rajasthan and Punjab, land route and riverine routes of Indus, Sutlej and Ghaggar might have been used. Land routes were easy for migration when quite a large number of people move, may be in search of new lands or establishment of trade. After trading stations are fixed, riverine route is quicker for carrying merchandize and also keeping contact with the parent site with known land route assuring greater security and certainty.

It was Rao who first proclaimed that Harappans came to Saurashtra by a sea route. He envisaged coming of Harappans in two main streams one during the lifetime of Mohenjodaro and Harappa by sea and establishing the first settlement at Lothal for overseas trade and later on Desalpur in Kachchh and Bhagatrav on the Kim estuary and made several temporary settlements on the coastline. He further points out that, "The conspicuous absence of sites of Mature Harappa culture connecting the peninsula of Kachchh and Kathiawad with the mainland supports the view that the Harappans did not follow a land route". So Rao dismissed the theory of land route of the Harappan migrations. The suspicion of Raikes in 1964 that this part including Kachchh was under water during the Harappan times does not stand in the light of the discovery of so many sites of Mature Harappa culture by J.P. Joshi.

Joshi however, suggests that the following factors postulate a case for migration of Harappans to Kachchh by land routes and then to Saurashtra:

1. The geographical position of Kachchh is in between Sindh and Saurashtra. Kachchh could be easily accessible from Allahdino, Kot Diji or Mohenjodaro and is only about 400 kms from Kotada, a Harappan site in Kachchh. Coming regularly by boat following the coastline will involve a coverage of nearly about 1,300 km. Human instinct to follow the shorter route is a prime factor, which cannot be denied or overlooked.
2. At present, anybody can cross the Great or Little Rann of Kachchh from January to June on foot. Bombay Gazetteer clearly mentions, "Even when there is slight depth of water it does not make the Rann impassable on the contrary, camels move safer through water than over slippery mud". It is possible to think that the land routes were in vogue even in the 2nd-3rd Millennia BC. Luna, a Harappan site discovered by Rao himself does lie in the Banni area at a height of 3.6 m above sea level. Though the area around this site is flooded now during the rainy season, in ancient days this was not the condition, otherwise this habitation would not have been there or if at all it was there, the conditions could not be different from what we find at present. Today also the Rann between the mainland of Sindh and Khavada, Khadir and Kachchh as such is crossable at quite a few points except during the monsoon when the area in between is flooded to a depth of 1 to 2 metres. Even if the present position is taken then also the area is crossable at least for six months.
3. The Harappans being also agriculturists, it is but natural that they would move to explore fertile tracts available along the stream basins. In this pursuit, they could move along the available land routes, rather than taking journey by sea. Even in the present-day's geographical environment of Kachchh, there is abundant cultivable land and as such during the Harappan times, the condition could not have been vastly different when the population was also of smaller.
4. The Harappans made the first fortified establishment at Kotara near Kuran in Khavada. Here they could easily reach from Sindh crossing through Biar Bet, Gainda Bet, Kuvar Bet and then through the narrow valley between Kala Dungar and Gora Dungar. They could cross a strip of Rann at Amarapur (about 6 km) and reach Kotadi again, a big Harappan fortified establishment and from here cross the Rann and reach the present Rapar *taluka* where a cluster of Harappan sites is now available, besides Surkotada which is another fortified Harappan settlement.

The route from Sujwal, Jati, Musafir Khana in Sindh and Lakhpat led to Desalpur and the route from Rahim-ki-Bazar to Luna and then to Desalpur, were also in vogue besides many other land routes crossing through the Rann could have been also in use. The most popular land route preferred by the Harappans seems to be one from Allahdino to Kotara and then to Kotadi and to the various sites in Surkotada. Kotadi had a very strong Citadel to control and protect the eastward movements of the Harappans in Kachchh region. Thus it will be plausible to say that the Harappans used a land route and came to Kachchh and then also reached north Gujarat and Saurashtra from Surkotada after crossing the Little Rann (Joshi 1972).

Kuntasi

The ancient site at Kuntasi (lat. 22° 45' N, long. 70° 76' E), located about 2.5 km south-east of the present village in Rajkot district, was excavated jointly by Deccan College and State Department of Archaeology of Gujarat (Dhavalikar 1993, 1993a: 555-570 and 1996). The site is spread over an area of about 2 ha on the right bank of River Phulki. The maximum cultural deposit at the site is about 7 m of which the lower 5.50 m represents period I (the Mature Harappan phase) and is dated to *c.* 2200-1900 BC (uncal.), the remaining belonging to period II, Late Harappan, is assigned to *c.* 1900-1700 BC (uncal.). The excavators believe that this small Mature Harappan village was deeply engaged in inter-regional trade rather than agricultural activities.

Period I: A noteworthy discovery is that of a copper hoard in a small pot from one of the structures on the north (St 50). There were a few copper bangles, over a thousand micro-beads of steatite and two finger rings, which are unique as they have no parallel at any other Harappan site. Of the two rings, one is broken, but the other is intact. It has a large double spiral. The structure complex on the west consisted of several small and large rooms, some of them containing kilns and furnaces, storage areas and so on, clearly indicating that it was meant for manufacturing pottery, a variety of beads and possibly also copper artefacts.

Dhavalikar thinks that when the Harappans realized that there was a growing market in Mesopotamia for Indian luxury goods, such as carnelian and lapis beads, shell, ivory, etc., they soon started coming to Gujarat around 2200 BC for acquiring these raw materials, processing them into finished goods and exporting them to West Asia by sea. The calibrated dates for this phase are in the range of *c.* 2500-2300 BC (Possehl and Raval 1989: 10-11). There is evidence to suggest that Early Harappans had some trading contact with West Asia in the first half of the 3rd millennium, which was probably mainly confined to agricultural products (Asthana 1985). But sometime about 2300 BC, the enterprising Harappans found that there was also a sizable demand for other luxury items such as carnelian beads, ivory, copper, lapis lazuli, shell and so on. Most of this raw material was abundant in western India. The obvious course for the Harappan entrepreneurs was to travel to Saurashtra to procure the raw material and process it into finished products for export. The west coast also offered harbouring facilities, which gave a fillip to sea trade.

Padri

The village Padri Gohilni (lat 22°22' N, long. 72°95' E) lies hardly 2 km from the Gulf of Cambay. It is roughly 8 km to the west of Talaja and 50 km to the south of Bhavnagar town. Padri site is spread over an area of 7.15 ha. This area falls in the semi-arid zone.

Explaining the rationale of excavating Padri, Shinde says, "The reconstruction of the lifestyle of the Harappan civilization is based on excavations at sites like Harappa, Mohenjodaro, Kalibangan and Lothal. All these sites are large in extent and may be classified as Urban or Regional Centres. However, there were many sites belonging to other categories such as agricultural settlements, processing centres, farmsteads, etc. that are poorly understood, leading to a biased reconstruction of the nature of the Harappan lifestyle. It has been recognized for a long time that a number of small sites of different categories need to be excavated systematically in order to produce a more realistic picture of all aspects of the Harappan civilization" (Shinde 1992: 56-66).

Excavation at the ancient site revealed a twofold cultural sequence: Early Historic (1st century AD) and Harappan (*c.* 2200-1900 BC, uncal.). The total habitational deposit is 3.2 m of which the upper 1.2 m belongs to the Early Historic period.

Shinde thinks that there is a strong possibility that the main intention of occupying this site was the production of salt and its supply to other inland settlements. This hypothesis is based on two factors. First, a large section of the present population of Padri and the nearby villages are engaged in full-time manufacture of salt. The second factor that can be considered to support this theory is the presence of a large number of storage jars. These jars could have been made exclusively to store and transport salt to different places as their superior quality and sturdiness indicate.

Shinde assigned Padri to an intermediate phase, akin to Rojdi and Kuntasi in Saurashtra. The intermediate phase that precedes the post-urban seems to be economically as prosperous as the earlier Urban Harappan phase. The frequency of the perforated pots, leaf-shaped copper arrowheads with two perforations and the examples of Harappan script are on the decline and long parallel-sided chert blades (Pl. 3-20) which characterize the Urban Harappan phase are almost absent in this phase. The Sturdy Red Ware, which characterizes Padri, has also been referred to as the Sorath Harappan Fine Ware by Possehl (1989) in terms of the ceramic assemblage from Rojdi. The Sturdy Red Ware differentiates the Saurashtra Harappan ceramic tradition from that of Sindh and Punjab. From the mid-levels of the Harappan period, a considerable number of sherds of a new painted ceramic have been collected and named "Padri Ware" after the site. This ware is made of coarse clay and treated with a thick coating of red slip, which shows a tendency to develop cracks. It should be noted that there is a great deal of similarity between the Savalda Ware reported from such sites like Savalda (Sali 1964) and Kaothe (Dhavalikar *et al.* 1990) in the central Tapi basin and this ware from Padri. On the basis of a ceramic assemblage which is similar to that of Rojdi B and Kuntasi, Shinde dates Padri to 2200-1900 BC (uncal.).

Of the three intact painted storage jars recovered from Padri, two were found to be decorated with the motif of a horned deity. The largest jar in the Sturdy Red Ware is decorated with a linear human figure wearing a horned headdress. The other jar in Buff Ware bears three motifs of a horned headdress. Horned human figures and headdresses were earlier reported from other Harappan sites like Kalibangan, Mohenjodaro and Kot Diji, but for the first time Gujarat has produced some significant evidence in this respect. The discovery of the motif of the horned deity suggests an early date for the Harappan culture at Padri, but the ceramic assemblage resembles that of Rojdi B, which has been dated to 2200-2000 BC (uncal.). Perhaps the horned deity motif may be associated with the potter's religious beliefs.

Shinde reports two rectangular mud structures with low mud walls, possibly to prevent the rainwater from entering them. This is perhaps the first time that a rectangular mud structure has been uncovered in the Harappan levels anywhere in Gujarat. A number of other rural Harappan settlements like Kanewal, Zekda, Valabhi and Vagad in Saurashtra, subjected to small scale excavations by the M.S. University of Baroda, have produced evidence of circular mud huts. Two rectangular structures unearthed at Padri are similar to those found in the Chalcolithic levels in the Deccan, particularly in Inamgaon, in Pune district and Daimabad in Ahmednagar district, both in Maharashtra. Structure No. 1 was first noticed at a depth of 2.9 m in trench J2 beneath layer (7). It is rectangular on plan with low mud walls and post-holes on the periphery, obviously to support the superstructure.

Shinde concludes that Padri has produced very interesting evidence in the form of rectangular mud structures, three unusually large painted storage jars and a new ceramic. On the basis of ethnographic parallels and other factors, Shinde thinks that the main function of this site was the manufacture of salt. Rectangular mud houses, painted pottery and the restricted use of copper were some of the characteristic features of the Deccan Chalcolithic culture. The discovery of rectangular mud houses and a circular domestic hearth with a pillar in the centre in one of them at Padri is yet another piece of evidence supporting close contact between the two cultures. The discovery of a small globular jar with a beaded rim and decorated with a panel of hatched diamonds at Padri assumes great significance in the light of the predominance of the same type and design in the ceramic assemblage of the Deccan Chalcolithic culture. The ceramic assemblage from the excavations at Kaothe in Dhule district, Maharashtra has revealed a high percentage (nearly 50 per cent) of material of Harappan tradition. The Sturdy Red Ware of fine fabric found at Kaothe bears a strong resemblance to the Harappan Black-on-Red pottery from the adjoining Gujarat region. Shinde notes that the convex sided bowls and globular jars with either beaded or clubbed rims were predominant types at Padri and most of the vessels were provided with either flat or disc bases. Shinde points out that the same features also characterize the Sturdy Red Ware at Kaothe (Dhavalikar and Shinde 1989; Dhavalikar *et al.* 1990: 31-47). Kaothe being close to the border with Gujarat and almost falling in the peripheral zone of the Harappan empire, a considerable cultural influence is expected. Shinde therefore, surmises that the Harappans, after the decline of their prosperous period, began to migrate to the Deccan around the beginning of the 2nd millennium BC. The discovery of a new ware at Padri and its close similarity with the Savalda ware from the Deccan further points to close contact between the cultures of these two regions.

Maharashtra

Daimabad

Further south-east from Gujarat is Daimabad in the Godavari valley. In this valley, more than twenty Late Harappan settlements have so far been found in clusters; only Daimabad is an isolated site. Daimabad is famous for controversies. Earlier it was identified as a Chalcolithic site (we have briefly discussed it in the Chalcolithic Chapter 4); later on, it was branded a Late Harappan site, hence its inclusion here. Near the site has been discovered a hoard of massive images, which some scholars have also assigned to the Late Harappan, an identification we have contested (see Chapter 4). A hoard of massive copper animal figures of a rhinoceros, an elephant, a buffalo and bull chariot by a man, all mounted on wheeled platforms, was accidentally discovered at Daimabad, though not from the systematic excavation. Some scholars assign these bronzes to the Chalcolithic or Harappan phase. Each object, however, weighs several kilograms (up to 29 kg!) and to use such a quantity of metal for non-utilitarian artefacts seems unlikely for a Chalcolithic culture. Moreover, unlike the ornate and massive Chinese examples, the metal objects of the Harappans are small and entirely utilitarian. Therefore, it is quite doubtful whether they belong to any Chalcolithic or the Late Harappan culture of Daimabad and may be only of historical age.

The wheel-thrown Late Harappan ceramic assemblage at Daimabad is characterized by the Red and Grey Wares. The Red Ware is treated with dull or bright red slip, though the classical Harappan fabric and levigation of clay is absent. The common shapes include a variety of dish-on-stands, vases and storage jars. At Daimabad, three main wares have been identified: Sturdy Red Ware, Burnished Grey Ware and Thick Coarse Ware (Sali 1986: 221-47).

Their houses, made of mud and mud bricks and rectangular on plan, have mostly been found from Daimabad. A circular hearth from house no. 16 at Daimabad was 50 cm in diameter and 10 cm in depth. The discovery of terracotta seals from these levels is quite significant. Many houses were found interconnected and hence the excavator believes that this complex belongs to a merchant (Sali 1986: 25). The largest house was 6.3 x 6 m. An adult grave was found within the habitation area, which is alien to the Harappan tradition. However, this kind of disposal of dead was practiced by the Deccan Chalcolithic cultures. The grave pit was prepared by ramming brickbats and gravels. The entire pit was plastered with lime and clay and lined with bricks ranging from 32 x 16 x 8 to 28 x 14 x 7 cm (4: 2: 1 ratio). The male skeleton is oriented north-south, with head towards north.

The Late Harappans of Gujarat were forced to live a pastoral life due to sharp deterioration in climatic conditions around the beginning of the 2nd millennium BC. The pasture-lands of the Tapi and the Godavari valleys were perhaps ecologically more congenial, than Gujarat, to attract them to settle down. Possibly from Bhagtrav, a Harappan settlement on the Maharashtra border, they started moving towards the Tapi through Songarh pass (Dhavalikar 1979: 248), in Maharashtra. Two of their settlements, Shetgaon and Chikhali, are found on the banks of Nesu, a tributary of the Tapi. It appears that they were migratory camps. Shinde (1998: 20) writes, "From the Kan valley some people moved towards the north Dhule district and established large settlements at Prakashe, Khaparkheda, etc.". Most of the Late Harappan settlements in the Tapi basin have been identified on the basis of surface examination. The pottery generally resembles Rangpur IIC of Gujarat (Shinde 1998: 21). However, we do not know whether the Late Harappans really migrated to the valleys of the Tapi and the Godavari or the pottery at all these sites is a result of cultural contacts. The picture will remain obscure till most of the reported sites are re-examined.

The copper artefact repertory includes a fragmentary copper celt, a pinhead and a fragmentary knife. Also reported are terracotta animal figurines of dog and bull.

Because of its controversial significance, Daimabad has been discussed here; other Late Harappan sites would be dealt with towards the end of the chapter.

TABLE 3.2 CALIBRATED DATES OF HARAPPAN/PRE-HARAPPAN SITES (INDIA AND PAKISTAN) (after Possehl 1994)

(All BP ages are based on 5568 years half-life of radiocarbon. Calibrated ages are given in BC).

Site	*Sample No.*	*5568 Yrs.BP*	*Calib. Dates*	*Culture*	*Material*
Harappa	WIS-2145	4020±60 BP	2573,2535, 2506 cal. BC	Urban Harappan	Charcoal
Harappa	WIS-2074	3700±60 BP	2133,2067, 2047 cal. BC	Urban Harappan Hearth	Charcoal
Harappa	WIS-2142	4135±65 BP	2863,2812, 2742,2776, 2696,2677, 2666 cal. BC	Transitional Early Harappan/Urban Harappan Hearth	Carbonized wood
Harappa	QL-4380	3950±80 BP	2468 cal. BC	Transitional Early Urban Harappan Hearth	Charcoal

Cont. Table 3.2

Table 3.2 Cont.

Site	*Sample No.*	*5568 Yrs.*BP	*Calib. Dates*	*Culture*	*Material*
Harappa	QL-4377	3770±100 BP	2198,2151, 2149 cal. BC	Transitional Early/Urban Harappan Hearth	Charcoal
Harappa	QL-4378	3850±50 BP	2334 cal. BC	Urban Harappan Charcoal Kiln	Charcoal
Harappa	Ql-4372	3890±40 BP	2455,2416, 2405 cal. BC	Early Harappan Hearth/Pit	Charcoal
Harappa	QL-4374	3800±50 BP	2278,2234, 2209 cal. BC	Urban Harappan Charcoal in front of kiln	Charcoal
Harappa	WIS-2144	3720±100 BP	2138 cal. BC	Urban Harappan	
Harappa	WIS-2075	3830±60 BP	2299 cal. BC	Urban Harappan Floor Level	Charcoal
Harappa	QL-4376	3810±50 BP	2283 cal. BC	Urban Harappan Kiln	Charcoal
Harappa	QL-4373	3960±30 BP	2470 cal. BC	Early Harappan Kiln	Charcoal
Harappa	QL-4375	3920±40 BP	2462 cal. BC	Early Harappan Hearth Pit	Charcoal
Harappa	WIS-2043	3770±70 BP	2268,2263, 2203,2147, 2146 cal. BC	Urban Harappan Upper level	Charcoal wood
Harappa	WIS-2141	3920±70 BP	2462 cal. BC	Urban Harappan	Carbonized wood
Harappa	BETA-33873	4540±85 BP	3338,3213, 3203 cal. BC	Early Harappan	Charcoal
Harappa	WIS-2143	3825±60 BP	2293 cal. BC	Urban Harappan Hearth	Charcoal
Harappa	BETA-33874	4540±180 BP	3338,3213, 3203 cal. BC	Urban Harappan Charcoal in front of kiln	Charcoal
Harappa	WIS-2139	3820±60 BP	2288 cal. BC	Urban Harappan Heart	Carbonized wood
Harappa	WIS-2053	3920±210 BP	2469 cal. BC	Urban Harappan Upper level	Unknown
Harappa	WIS-2140	4290±70 BP	2913 cal. BC	Urban Harappan	Charcoal
Harappa	QL-4483	3784±30 BP	n.a.	Urban phase Harappan	Charcoal
Harappa	QL-4486	3785±45 BP	n.a.	Pre-urban/Urban phase Transition (late)	Charcoal
Harappa	QL-4485	3863±45 BP	n.a.	Pre-urban/Urban phase Transition (late)	Charcoal
Harappa	QL-4487	3816±25 BP	n.a.	Urban phase Harappan	Charcoal
Harappa	QL-4484	3730±30 BP	n.a.	Urban phase Harappan	Charcoal
Harappa	QL-4488	3750±40 BP	n.a.	Urban phase Harappan	Charcoal

Cont. Table 3.2

Table 3.2 Cont.

Site	*Sample No.*	*5568 Yrs.*BP	*Calib. Dates*	*Culture*	*Material*
Hathial west	BM-1949R	3980±140 BP	2554,2548, 2491 cal. BC	Late early Harappan Late Kot Dijian	Charcoal
Hathala	P-1813	4040±60 BP	2580 cal. BC	Early Harappan; Kot Dijian	Charcoal
Hathial west	BM-1948R	3820±120 BP	2288 cal. BC	Late early Harappan; Late Kot Dijian	Charcoal
Hisham	WIS-1703	3720±80 BP	2138 cal. BC	Mature Harappan	Unknown
Jhang	BM-2201R	4260±110 BP	2903 cal. BC	Early Kot Dijian	Charcoal
Jhang	BM-2200R	4010±250 BP	2569,2538, 2503 cal. BC	Late Kot Dijian	Charcoal
Islam Chowky	BM-2403	3840±110 BP	2315 cal. BC	Late Kot Dijian	Charcoal
Islam Chowky	BM-1941R	3910±460 BP	2459 cal. BC	Late Kot Dijian	Charcoal
Islam Chowky	OXA-1004	4010±120 BP	2569,2538, 2503 cal. BC	Late Kot Dijian	Charred goat-dung
Islam Chowky	OXA-1005	4160±100 BP	2870,2806, 2774,2720, 2702 cal. BC	Kot Dijian	Charcoal
Jhukar	P-2476	4630±300 BP	3371 cal. BC	Mature Harappan	Charcoal from an oven
Nausharo	BETA-18844	4010±80 BP	2569,2538, 2503 cal. BC	Period IC Mehrgarh VII	Unknown
Nausharo	BETA-18842	4030±70 BP	2576,2531, 2510 cal. BC	Period IC Mehrgarh VII	Unknown
Nausharo	BETA-18845	4040±70 BP	2580 cal. BC	Period III, Mature Harappan	Unknown
Nausharo	BETA-18843	4070±70 BP	2598 cal. BC	Period IB Merhgarh VII	Unknown
Niai Buthi	P-478	3740±64 BP	2181,2166, 2142 cal. BC	Period II, Kulli	Unknown
Nindowari	TF-862	3900±105 BP	2457 cal. BC	Period II, or III, Kulli	Charcoal
Nindowari	TF-862(BS)	3840±235 BP	2315 cal. BC	Period II or III, Kulli	Charcoal
Rana Ghundai	P-2149	4600±60 BP	3360 cal. BC	Period IIIA	Charcoal and burned seeds
Rana Ghundai	P-2148	5580±60 BP	4456,4417, 4403 cal. BC	Period I	Charcoal

Cont. Table 3.2

Table 3.2 Cont.

Site	*Sample No.*	*5568 Yrs.*BP	*Calib. Dates*	*Culture*	*Material*
Rehman Dheri	WIS-1699	4180±70 BP	2875,2802, 2778,2715, 2706 cal. BC	Early Harappan; Period II, Early Kot Dijian n.a	Unknown
Rehman Dheri	PRL-673	3900±130 BP	2475 cal. BC	Late early Harappan; Period III Late Kot Dijian	Charcoal
Rehman Dheri	BM-2062R	3810±150 BP	2283 cal. BC	Late early Harappan; Period III Late Kot Dijian	Charcoal
Rehman Dheri	BM-2062R	3960±110 BP	2470 cal. BC	Late early Harappan; Period III Late Kot Dijian	Charcoal
Rehman Dheri	PRL-674	4000±150 BP	2564,2541, 2499 cal. BC	Early Harappan; Period II, Early Kot Dijian	Charcoal
Rehman Dheri	WIS-1701	3850±70 BP	2334 cal. BC	Late early Harappan; Period III, Late Kot Dijian	Unknown
Rehman Dheri	WIS-1700	4070±90 BP	2598 cal. BC	Early Harappan; Period II, Early Kot Dijian	Unknown
Sarai Khola	BM-1946R	3920±130 BP	2462 cal. BC	Late Early Harappan; Period IB, Late Kot Dijian	Charcoal
Sarai Khola	BM-1945R	4020±120 BP	2573,2535, 2506 cal. BC	Late early Harappan; Period IB, Late Kot Dijian	Charcoal
Sarai Khola	BM-1936R	4120±250 BP	2860,2817, 2693,2684, 2662, 2626 cal. BC	Early Harappan; Period IIA, Early Kot Dijian	Charcoal
Sarai Khola	BM-1938R	4030±120 BP	2576,2531, 2510 cal. BC	Early Harappan Period IIA, Early Kot Dijian	Charcoal
Sarai Khola	BM-1944R	4270±220 BP	2909 cal. BC	Early Harappan Period IIA, Early Kot Dijian	Charcoal
Sarai Khola	BM-1943R	3920±120 BP	2576,2531, 2510 cal. BC	Early Harappan Period IIB, Late Kot Dijian	Charcoal
Sarai Khola	BM-1942R	4130±120 BP	2862,2814, 2738,2728, 2679, 2665, 2630 cal. BC	Early Harappan; Period IIA, Early Kot Dijian	Charcoal
Shahr-i-Sokhta	R-900	3730±50 BP	2140 cal. BC	Shahr-i-Sokhta IV, Phase 1, post-urban	Charcoal
Shahr-i-Sokhta	P-2073	3840±60 BP	2315 cal. BC	Shahr-i-Sokhta IV Phase 1, post-urban	Charcoal
Shahr-i-Sokhta	R-899A	3800±50 BP	2278,2234, 2209 cal. BC	Shahr-i-Sokhta III, IV Phase 1 post-urban	Charcoal

Cont. Table 3.2

Table 3.2 Cont.

Site	*Sample No.*	*5568 Yrs.*BP	*Calib. Dates*	*Culture*	*Material*
Shahr-i-Sokhta	P-2072	3750±60 BP	2191,2161, 2145 cal. BC	Shahr-i-Sokhta IV Phase 1, post-urban	Charcoal
Shahr-i-Sokhta	P-2070	4070±60 BP	2598 cal. BC	Shahr-i-Sokhta IV Phase 1, post-urban	Charcoal
Shahr-i-Sokhta	P-2082	4020±70 BP	2573,2535, 25066 cal. BC	Shahr-i-Sokhta II Phase 6, post-urban	Charcoal
Shahr-i-Sokhta	R-425	3950±50 BP	2468 cal. BC	Shahr-i-Sokhta IV Post-urban	Charcoal
Shahr-i-Sokhta	P-2068	4220±60 BP	2885,2794, 2786 cal. BC	Shahr-i-Sokhta IV Phase 1, post-urban	Charcoal
Shahr-i-Sokhta	P-2071	3970±60 BP	2483 cal. BC	Shahr-i-Sokhta IV Phase 0, post-urban	Charcoal
Tarakai Qila	BM-1691	3510±60 BP	1880,1830, 1829 cal. BC	Late early Harappan; Late Kot Dijian	Charcoal
Tarakai Qila	BM-1692	3680±50 BP	2123,2080, 2042 cal. BC	Late early Harappan; Late Kot Dijian	Charcoal
Tarakai Qila	BM-1694	3770±90 BP	2198,2151, 2149 cal. BC	Late early Harappan; Late Kot Dijian	Charcoal
Tarakai Qila	BM-1695	4060±120 BP	2587 cal. BC	Late early Harappan; Late Kot Dijian	Charcoal
Tarakai Qila	BM-1690	3640±80 BP	2032 cal. BC	Late early Harappan; Late Kot Dijian	Charcoal
Tarakai Qila	BM-1693	3810±60 BP	2283 cal. BC	Late early Harappan; Late Kot Dijian	Charcoal
Hulas	PRL-1031	3840±110 BP	2315 cal. BC	Early late Harappan	Charcoal
Hulas	PRL-1032	4380±150 BP	3028,2985, 2930 cal. BC	Early late Harappan	Charcoal
Kalibangan	TF-152	3615±85 BP	2014,2006, 1976 cal. BC	Period II, Urban Harappan	Charcoal
Kalibangan	TF-145	3895±100 BP	2456,2412, 2408 cal. BC	Period II, Urban Harappan	Charcoal
Kalibangan	TF-157	4120±110 BP	2860,2817, 2693,2684, 2662,2633, 2626 cal. BC	Period I, Early Harappan	Charcoal
Kalibangan	TF-161	3930±100 BP	2464 cal. BC	Period I, Early Harappan	Charcoal
Kalibangan	TF-147	3865±100 BP	2450,2348, cal. BC	Period II, Urban Harappan	Charcoal

Cont. Table 3.2

Table 3.2 Cont.

Site	*Sample No.*	*5568 Yrs.*BP	*Calib. Dates*	*Culture*	*Material*
Kalibangan	TF-143	3510±110 BP	1880,1830, 1829 cal. BC	Period II, Urban Harappan	Wood
Kalibangan	TF-163	3910±100 BP	2459 cal. BC	Period II, Urban Harappan	Charcoal
Kalibangan	TF-150	3740±100 BP	2181,2166, 2142 cal. BC	Period II, Urban Harappan	Charcoal
Kalibangan	TF-25	3930±110 BP	2464 cal. BC	Period II, Urban Harappan	Charcoal mixed with charred bone
Kalibangan	TF-244	3250±90 BP	1521 cal. BC	Period II, Urban Harappan	Charcoal
Kalibangan	TF-139	3775±100 BP	2200 cal. BC	Period II, Urban Harappan	Charcoal
Kalibangan	TF-151	3800±100 BP	2278,2234, 2209 cal. BC	Period II, Urban Harappan	Charcoal
Kalibangan	TF-241	4090±90 BP	2853,2882, 2655,2644, 2615 cal. BC	Period I, Early Harappan	Charcoal
Kalibangan	TF-155	4195±115 BP	2879,2799, 2781,2711, 2709 cal. BC	Period I, Early Harappan	Charcoal
Kalibangan	TF-947	3765±85 BP	2197,2154, 2148 cal. BC	Period II, Urban Harappan	Wood Charcoal
Kalibangan	TF-162	3940±100 BP	2466 cal. BC	Period I, Early Harappan	Charcoal
Kalibangan	TF-138	3075±100 BP	1391,1334, 1327 cal. BC	Pariod II, Urban Harappan	Charcoal
Kalibangan	TF-605	3810±105 BC	2283 cal. BC	Period II, Urban Harappan	Charcoal
Kalibangan	TF-153	3910±110 BP	2459 cal. BC	Period II, Urban Harappan	Charcoal
Kalibangan	TF-439	6507±125 BP	5475,5431, 5429 cal. BC	Period I, Early Harappan	Unknown
Kalibangan	TF-946	3605±100 BP	1968 cal. BC	Period II, Urban Harappan	Wood Charcoal
Kalibangan	TF-948	3815±100 BP	2286 cal. BC	Period II, Urban Harappan	Wood Charcoal
Kalibangan	TF-942	4055±110 BP	2586 cal. BC	Period II, Urban Harappan	Charcoal
Kalibangan	TF-142	3635±100 BP	2030,1990, cal. BC	Period II, Urban Harappan	Charcoal
Kalibangan	TF-141	3705±110 BP	2134,2059, 2048 cal. BC	Period II, Urban Harappan	Charcoal

Cont. Table 3.2

Table 3.2 Cont.

Site	*Sample No.*	*5568 Yrs.*BP	*Calib. Dates*	*Culture*	*Material*
Kalibangan	TF-160	4060±100 BP	2587 cal. BC	Period II, Urban Harappan	Charcoal
Kalibangan	TF-149	3675±140 BP	2118,2083, 2041 cal. BC	Period II, Urban Harappan	Charcoal
Kalibangan	TF-156	3740±105 BP	2181,2166, 2142 cal. BC	Period I, Early Harappan	Charcoal
Kalibangan	TF-152(BS)	3570±125 BP	1923 cal. BC	Period II, Urban Harappan	Charcoal
Kalibangan	TF-163(BS)	3925±125 BP	2462 cal. BC	Period II, Urban Harappan	Charcoal
Kalibangan	TF-439(BS)	6507±125 BP	5475,5431, 5429 cal. BC	Period I, Early Harappan	Unknown
Kalibangan	TF-240	3610±110 BP	2010,1973, cal. BC	Period I, Early Harappan	Charcoal
Kalibangan	P-481	3879±72 BP	2453,2424, 2398 cal. BC	Period II, Urban Harappan	Charcoal
Kalibangan	TF-165	3800±100 BP	2278,2334, 2209 cal. BC	Period I, Early Harappan	Charcoal
Kalibangan	TF-957	2355±200 BP	401 cal. BC	Period I, Early Harappan	Wood
Kalibangan	TF-607	3930±120 BP	2464 cal. BC	Period II, Urban Harappan	Charred wheat
Kalibangan	TF-156(BS)	4010±1665 BP	2570,2537, 2503 cal. BC	Period I, Early Harappan	Charcoal
Kalibangan	TF-154	3665±110 BP	2105,2088, 2038 cal. BC	Period I, Urban Harappan	Charcoal
Kalibangan	TF-608	3910±110 BP	2459 cal. BC	Period II, Urban Harappan	Charcoal Wheat
Kalibangan	TF-149(BS)	3585±120 BP	1942 cal. BC	Period II, Urban Harappan	Charcoal
Kalibangan	PRL-1282	3470±140 BP	1866,1846, 1772 cal. BC	Rojdi B,46L Harappan	Charcoal
Kuntasi	PRL-1371	3650±140 BP	2014 cal. BC	Sorath Harappan	Charcoal
Kuntasi	PRL-1370	3710±160 BP	2135,2052, 2050 cal. BC	Sorath Harappan	Charcoal
	TF-135	3405±125 BP	1735,1717, 1701 cal. BC	Period IIA, Lothal A, Urban Harappan	Charcoal
Lothal	TF-29	3740±110 BP	2181,2166, 2142 cal. BC	Period IVA Lothal A, Urban Harappan	Charcoal
Lothal	TF-23	3705±105 BP	2134,2059, 2048 cal. BC	Period VA, Lothal B, Post-urban Harappan	Charcoal

Cont. Table 3.2

Table 3.2 Cont.

Site	*Sample No.*	*5568 Yrs.*BP	*Calib. Dates*	*Culture*	*Material*
Lothal	TF-26	3830±120 BP	2299 cal. BC	Period IIIB, Lothal A, Urban Harappan	Charcoal
Lothal	TF-136	3915±130 BP	2461 cal. BC	Period IA, Lothal A, Urban Harappan	Charcoal
Lothal	TF-19	3650±135 BP	2034 cal. BC	Period VA, Lothal B, Post-urban, Harappan	Charcoal
Lothal	TF-133	3740±110 BP	2328 cal. BC	Period IIA, Lothal A, Urban Harappan	Charcoal
Lothal	TF-22	3845±110 BP	2328 cal. BC	Period IIIB, Lothal A, Urban Harappan	Charcoal
Lothal	TF-27	3840±110 BP	2315 cal. BC	Period IIIB, Lothal A, Urban Harappan	Charcoal
Malvan	TF-1084	2675±90 BP	826 cal. BC	Post-urban Harappan	Charcoal
Mitathal	PRL-290	3820±130 BP	2288 cal. BC	Period I, Urban phase	Charcoal
Mitathal	PRL-292	4210±210 BP	2883,2796, 2784 cal. BC	Period IIB, Punjab, post-urban Phase, BARA ware	Charcoal
Mitathal	PRL-291	3600±110 BP	1961 cal. BC	Period IIA, Urban phase	Charcoal
Nagwada	A-4555	3700±80 BP	2133,2067, 2047 cal. BC	Late Sorath Harappan	Unknown
Rojdi	PRL-1091	4150±110 BP	2867,2808, 2772,2723, 2699 cal. BC	Rojdi A, 45 K, Urban Harappan	Charcoal
Rojdi	TF-199	3590±100 BP	1947 cal. BC	Period I, Phase B, Harappan	Charcoal
Rojdi	PRL-1093	3920±110 BP	2462 cal. BC	Rojdi A, 45 K, Harappan	Charcoal
Rojdi	PRL-1083	3875±120 BP	2452,2427, 2395,2374, 2366 cal. BC	Rojdi B, 45 K, Harappan	Charcoal
Rojdi	PRL-1089	3870±120 BP	2451,2433, 2392,2384, 2356 cal. BC	Rojdi A, 45 K, Harappan	Charcoal
Rojdi	TF-200	3810±110 BP	2283 cal. BC	Period I, Phase B, Harappan	Unknown
Rojdi I	PRL-1081	2360±210 BP	402 cal. BC	Rojdi C, 78 J, Post-urban Harappan	Charcoal
Rojdi	PRL-1085	4020±110 BP	2573,2535, 2506 cal. BC	Rojdi A, 45 K, Harappan	Charcoal
Rojdi	PRL-1087	4010±110 BP	2569,2538, 2503 cal. BC	Rojdi A, 45 K, Harappan	Charcoal
Rojdi	PRL-1284	3810±100 BP	2283 cal. BC	Rojdi A, 46L, Harappan	Charcoal

Cont. Table 3.2

Table 3.2 Cont.

Site	*Sample No.*	*5568 Yrs.BP*	*Calib. Dates*	*Culture*	*Material*
Rojdi	BETA-61767	3570±60 BP	1973,1872, 1840,1811, 1809,1780; 2113,2087, 2038-1742 cal. BC	Late Sorath Harappan, Rojdi C	Charcoal
Rojdi	PRL-1281	3520±110 BP	1883 cal. BC	Rojdi B,46L Harappan	Charcoal
Rojdi	PRL-1084	3700±150 BP	2133,2067, 2047 cal. BC	Rojdi C, 761 Post-urban Harappan	Charcoal
Rojdi I	PRL-1088	3770±120 BP	2198,2151, 2149 cal. BC	Rojdi B,45 K Harappan	Charcoal
Rojdi I	PRL-1283	3980±100 BP	2554,2548, 2491 cal. BC	Rojdi A,46L Harappan	Charcoal
Rojdi	BETA-61768	3520±60 BP	1, 1913-1745, 2, 2013-2007, 1977-1682 cal. BC	Late Sorath Harappan Rojdi C	Charcoal
Sanghol	PRL-TL-10	None	None	Period I, Late Harappan	Soil in asssociation with Period I Pottery
Surkotada	TF-1295	3780±95 BP	2202 cal. BC	Period IB	Charcoal
Surkotada	TF-1311	3625±90 BP	2023,1998, 1983 cal. BC	Period IC, Urban Harappan	Charcoal
Surkotada	TF-1301	3840±130 BP	2315 cal. BC	Period IA	Charcoal
Surkotada	TF-1304/9	3645±90 BP	2033 cal. BC	Period IA	Charcoal
Surkotada	TF-1310	3810±95 BP	2283 cal. BC	Period IA, Upper level	Charcoal
Surkotada	TF-1305	3890±95 BP	2455,2416, 2405 cal. BC	Period IA, Earliest Levels	Charcoal
Surkotada	PRL-85	4140±130 BP 2747,2725,	2865,2810, 2697,2674, 2668 cal. BC	Period IA, Mid-Levels	Charcoal
Surkotada	TF-1307	3510±105 BP	1880,1830, 1829 cal. BC	Period IC, Urban Harappan	Charcoal
Surkotada	TF-1294	3620±95 BP	2018,2002, 1980 cal. BC	Period IC Urban Harappan	Charcoal
Surkotada	TF-1297	3635±95 BP	2030,1990, cal. BC	Period IC Urban Harappan	Charcoal

CRAFTS

Crafts create wealth and help differentiate the elite from the masses. As a preamble to the discussion of crafts, it may be useful to quote Kenoyer's interesting observations in this regard. He says,

> Generally speaking, a wealth item can be defined as an archaeologically preserved object that reflects relatively high levels of indirect or direct economic control of resources, labour, or technological knowledge. Archaeologically preserved objects, such as ornaments, architecture, or tools reflect other forms of wealth that are not preserved, for example, grain, foodstuffs, livestock, or even agricultural land. The relative value of preserved objects can be calculated on the basis of four major assumptions:
>
> i. Rare or exotic raw materials have relatively more value than locally available raw materials;
>
> ii. The overall wealth value of an object increases with the amount of labour required for production, where labour refers to time and/or number of artisans involved in production;
>
> iii. Technological processes involving numerous stages, high degrees of skill and/or specialized technical knowledge increase the value of an object;
>
> iv. Once an item has been accepted as a symbol of wealth within a society, elite will attempt to control the access to raw materials or knowledge in order to limit the production of specific wealth items and control their use.
>
> Within this framework it is possible to rank various craft products used in a society and estimate the relative value of specific types of objects. This ranking can then be compared with the actual distribution of objects throughout the site or their frequency over time.... These four assumptions can be further correlated with major groups of specialized crafts that are defined by two sets of variables: the accessibility of raw materials and the complexity of the technology required to process raw material into specific objects. In the geographical context of the Indus valley the craft technologies used to create objects can be divided into four major groups:
>
> i) Crafts processing from locally available materials using relatively simple technologies include woodworking, basket making, simple weaving, terracotta pottery production and house-building;
>
> ii) Crafts using imported materials with relatively simple technologies include stone-shaping for domestic purposes and chipped stone tool-making;
>
> iii) Crafts using local materials and complex technologies and production processes include stoneware bangle manufacture, elaborate painted and specialized pottery production, complex weaving and carpet making, inlaid woodwork production and construction of decorative architecture;
>
> iv) Crafts using imported materials and highly complex technologies include agate bead manufacture, seal production, copper/bronze metalworking, stone carving, precious metalworking, shell working and faience manufacture.
>
> The production and distribution of objects made by crafts in the last two categories are the most easily controlled. Consequently, these are the crafts that tend to be used in the creation of wealth items, a process that began with the earliest Neolithic communities and became modified with each subsequent phase of development (Kenoyer 1999: 90-112).

Let us have a look at the Harappan arts and crafts now.

Though the non-perishable art-remains of the Harappans appear poorer in comparison to the contemporary Egyptian or the Mesopotamian artefacts, the few surviving examples do show their mastery of plastic art. Perhaps wood-carving (an ancient Indian tradition) was a developed art though no remains have survived. Quite often, the stereotyped nature of stone statuary and terracotta figurines is emphasized but the naturalistic rendering of animals in terracotta and on seals, the bronze-dancing female, the stone male torsos (2. 3-54) indicate their sculptural virtuosity.

Quite a few stone statues (Pl. 3-4) represent perhaps the same person. Narrow eyes, stylized ears and hair, shaven upper lip, inlaid eyes and a hieratic rendering mark these statues. Two such pieces were discovered from a building, which Wheeler suspected to be a temple at Mohenjodaro. The plastic rendering of the Kalibangan terracotta head is livelier than that of the Mohenjodaro statues.

But the plastic modelling of the two male torsos in stone from Harappa is very naturalistic, almost sensuous. Perhaps one of the images was ithyphallic (with erect penis) probably connected with Shiva, the latter day Hindu god. The bronze dancing girl from Mohenjodaro is a very delicate representation in the round of a female nude. The ease of its stance, the graceful way of resting one hand on the hip and a slight tilt of the head enhance its voluptuous appeal.

Very naturalistic too is the rendering of animals, especially the bulls and rhinos and even of the mythical unicorn (Pls. 3-5, -18), on the steatite seals. Excellence in plastic art is reached in the rendering of terracotta bulls in the round. The examples from Mohenjodaro, though naturalistic, appear somewhat stiff. The best example of a charging bull comes from Kalibangan. The massiveness of the bull, the fury of the charge and the movement are eloquently expressed in the terracotta.

The female figurines in terracotta are very common in the Harappan sites of Sindh, but absent from Rajasthan and Gujarat. The more common type has an elaborate headdress, waist girdle, necklace and a lower garment. Breasts are big and the hips broad. The tradition of making such terracotta for worship still continues in the Indian villages and therefore, these figurines could as well have a religious function. Toy-carts (Pl. 3-22) with solid wheels, whistles, rattles, birds and animals, gamesmen and discs were also rendered in terracotta.

Ardeleanu-Jansen (1988) has made some interesting observations about the Harappan terracotta. She says that at present, we cannot draw a final picture of the significance the terracotta figurines had in the Harappa culture. With the help of the field inventories of the later excavators of Mohenjodaro and their photographic documentation of the artefacts, a considerable amount of terracotta figurines (Pl. 3-23) have already been re-evaluated and their archaeological association reconstructed. However, it has to be admitted at this point that even the most careful analysis of the field records runs the risk of failing to distinguish between a secondary trash deposit and an original setting of artefacts left behind by the inhabitants of that ancient town.

Yet the preliminary analysis seems to indicate that most of the figurines in Mohenjodaro were found smashed in secondary locations and that none was found in a context which could be interpreted as a shrine, altar or temple. The latter fact had already been mentioned by Marshall and Mackay (Marshall 1931: 340) and was most probably the reason for Marshall's assumption that they served as votive offerings rather than as cult images for household shrines (Marshall 1931: 50). Broken terracotta figurines were also in the majority throughout all periods of the Mehrgarh settlement (Pl. 3-24) (Jarrige, C. 1984: 133) and this could actually mean that the fragile models were only intended for short-term use after which, when accidentally broken, they were simply thrown away.

Some of the household rituals of Bihar and Uttar Pradesh, for example, require women devotees to prepare simple clay figurines for domestic worship, while the Bhils in Gujarat buy their votive terracotta idols from the potters after the harvest has been brought in and offer them to the gods through their deposition at the base of a tree. Also to drive out evil spirits and disease in a patient, a tribal priest or shaman called Bhagat performs a ceremony

Pl. 3-20. Harappan chert blades and cores.

Pl. 3-23. Terracotta female figurine, Mohenjodaro.

Pl. 3-22. Terracotta toy cart, Mohenjodaro.

Pl. 3-24. Terracotta female figurines, Mehrgarh.

Pl. 3-25. A typical Harappan pottery jar with intersecting circles, peacock and pipal leaf motif, Mohenjodaro.

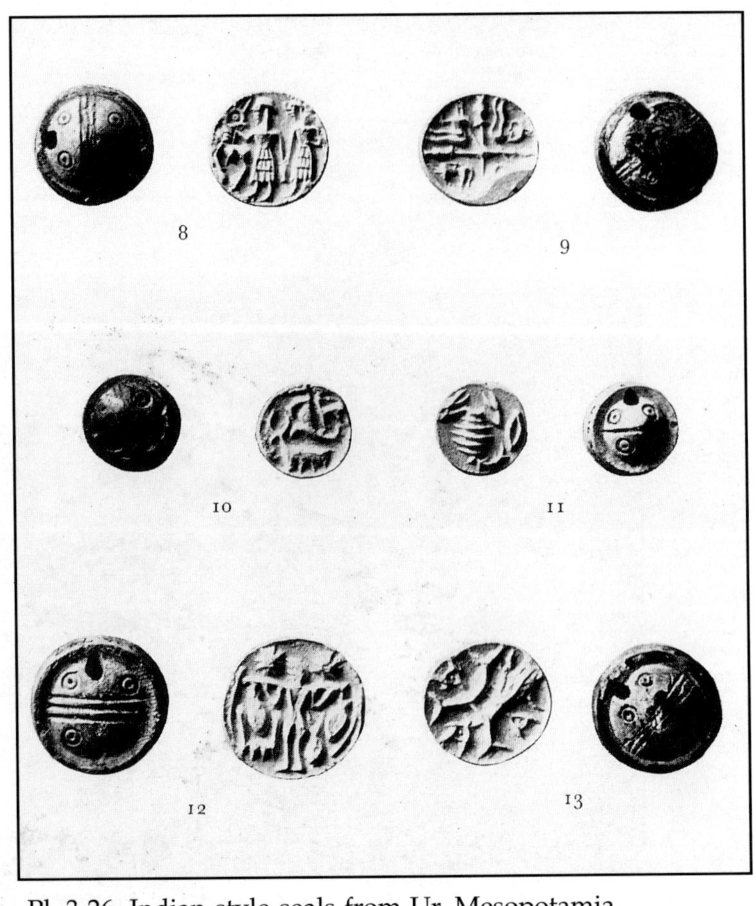

Pl. 3-26. Indian style seals from Ur, Mesopotamia.

and makes clay figurines, which are actually substitutes for the spirits and after food has been offered to them to placate the spirits, the figurines are deposited in a field far away from the village. Terracotta figurines are traditionally used in India as votive offerings and images representing deities.

Other Crafts

Faience was used to make bangles, rings, miniature animals and pots. A glazed ware from the earliest levels of Mohenjodaro is unique and anticipates a technique, which became popular only in the medieval times. Pottery is well fired and sturdy but the paintings look a bit stereotyped. Vegetal and geometrical motifs predominate. Animals hardly appear, peacocks was a favourite motif (Kenoyer 1998) (Pl. 3-25).

Stone: About rock material, Kenoyer (1998) thinks that most stones came into the Indus workshops as raw material, but there are rare examples of finished objects that were produced in the highlands to the west and brought to the cities by traders or visiting elite. Carved chlorite and green schist containers with distinctive woven mat designs were produced at sites such as Tepe-Yahya in southern Iran and possibly other workshops in Baluchistan. These vessels were traded throughout the Near east and the Persian Gulf and a few examples have been found at Mohenjodaro. Indus traders living in southern Baluchistan may have brought these exotic containers to the city along with copper and other highland raw materials.

One famous stone vessel found at Mohenjodaro is a tall glass with concave sides that is similar in shape to ritual columns found in Baluchistan and Afghanistan. This green stone, called fuchsite, is rare, but it can occur with quartzite, which is common throughout Baluchistan and Afghanistan. When this fuchsite vessel was first examined by a geologist in the 1930s, the only known source was in Mysore State, over 1,600 km south of the Indus valley. Early scholars suggested that the stone was brought to the Indus cities from the south along with gold and ivory, but both of these important raw materials were actually available from nearby sources. Herds of elephants lived in the thick forests of Gujarat or the eastern Punjab, so ivory could have been obtained by Indus hunters themselves or traded from tribal communities living at the edge of the Indus plain. Gold was easily obtained from the sands of the upper Indus river where it is still panned by itinerant miners. Another source of gold was along the Oxus river valley in northern Afghanistan where a trading colony of the Indus cities has been discovered at Shortughai. Situated far from the Indus valley itself, this settlement may have been established to obtain gold, copper, tin and lapis lazuli, as well as other exotic goods from Central Asia.

Beads: Vidale (in press) says that a good example is the development of talc-related industries from the Neolithic to the end of the Bronze Age. This reconstruction of the talc-related industries is largely possible due to the extensive research of the French mission at Mehrgarh and Nausharo. The technological and social evolution of these industries serves as an illustration of the type of research needed for each of the craft industries.

Vidale reports that during the 7th millennium BC, beads made from talcose rocks become progressively smaller in size; this is a trend, which continues until the 3rd millennium BC. (Vidale uses the terms "talc" or "talcose" and "steatite" interchangeably.) Pyrotechnological treatment of talcose rocks begins during the 6th millennium BC, then becomes more and more common, culminating at the beginning of the 4th millennium BC when more than 90 per cent of the steatite beads from Mehrgarh are fired white. The amount of talc working debris at the Indus sites becomes massive and data from the activity area of Mehrgarh 2

(5th millennium BC) are sufficient to suggest the possible presence of apprentices (Vanzetti and Vidale 1994). The application of blue-green glazes to steatite beads also begins in the 4th millennium BC. At the beginning of the 3rd millennium BC, artificial materials such as talc paste, steatite-faience and siliceous faience are introduced in the Indus bead repertory. The talc powder resulting from bead cutting is recycled as talc paste beads and this new technology culminates in the second-half of the 3rd millennium BC with the invention of the famous Harappan micro-beads (Vidale in press).

According to Kenoyer, technological studies of the manufacturing processes confirm that many long biconical carnelian beads as well as the decorated carnelian and green amazonite beads were actually made in distant Indus workshops. However, the long-faceted carnelian beads may have been made by Indus artisans in Mesopotamia. These beads are drilled with the unique technique of the Indus valley, yet, the faceted shape is a style that was never produced in the Indus workshops. The pear-shaped decorated carnelian bead is also a shape that was never produced in the Indus, but it is made using a technology that has only been documented in the Indus cities. These clues suggest that merchants or entrepreneurs from the Indus valley may have set up shops in cities such as Ur, to market their goods and also produce objects in local designs (Pl. 3-26). If this can be confirmed through further studies, it would be the earliest evidence for a pattern that came to be the norm in later historical times, when craftsmen and merchants from the subcontinent extended their trade networks throughout West Asia as well as South-East Asia (Kenoyer 1998).

Bead industry seems to be well developed as shown by the factories discovered at Chanhudaro and Lothal. Beads were made of agate, carnelian, faience, shell, terracotta, gold, silver and steatite. Inlay work and etchings on beads made them coveted objects both in India and West Asia and were probably exported. Lapis lazuli is comparatively rare, though unfinished examples from Chanhudaro indicate a local manufacture. Badakshan was the nearest source of lapis. It may, however, be noted that numerous so-called lapis objects have turned out to be azurite on analysis. Precious stones of all varieties were highly valued in the Indus cities and special designs and colours were sought after for making ornaments and utensils. Hard stones like agate and jasper that would hold a high lustre polish appear to have been more popular than the softer varieties, such as lapis lazuli and turquoise, that would quickly wear away to a dull lustre. Banded agate, variegated jasper and red-orange carnelian were among the most commonly used materials, obtained from distant sources in Kachchh and Gujarat, as well as widely distributed sources, one in the Chagai hills of southern Baluchistan and other in Badakhshan, northern Afghanistan. Turquoise also may have been obtained from southern Baluchistan or from the more distant regions of northern Iran, but neither of these stones was very popular with Indus city consumers. When worn as beads, these relatively soft stones become dull or change colour. This may have stimulated the production of glazed faience beads that could be coloured to look like turquoise or lapis lazuli. They also made beautiful gold ornaments and ivory objects (Pls. 3-27, -28, -29).

In contrast, the large gastropods *Turbinella pyrum* and *Chicoreus ramosus* were cut with a specialized bronze saw that would have been available only in the largest workshops. By studying the depth of each saw stroke on fragments of shell from the ancient workshops, we can reconstruct the basic shape of the saw. It had a very thin serrated edge that was long and curved, similar to the saws still used in shell bangle making in modern Bengal. Even more astounding is the fact that the Indus bronze saw was able to cut the shell as efficiently as the modern steel saws, which suggests that the Indus bronze workers were

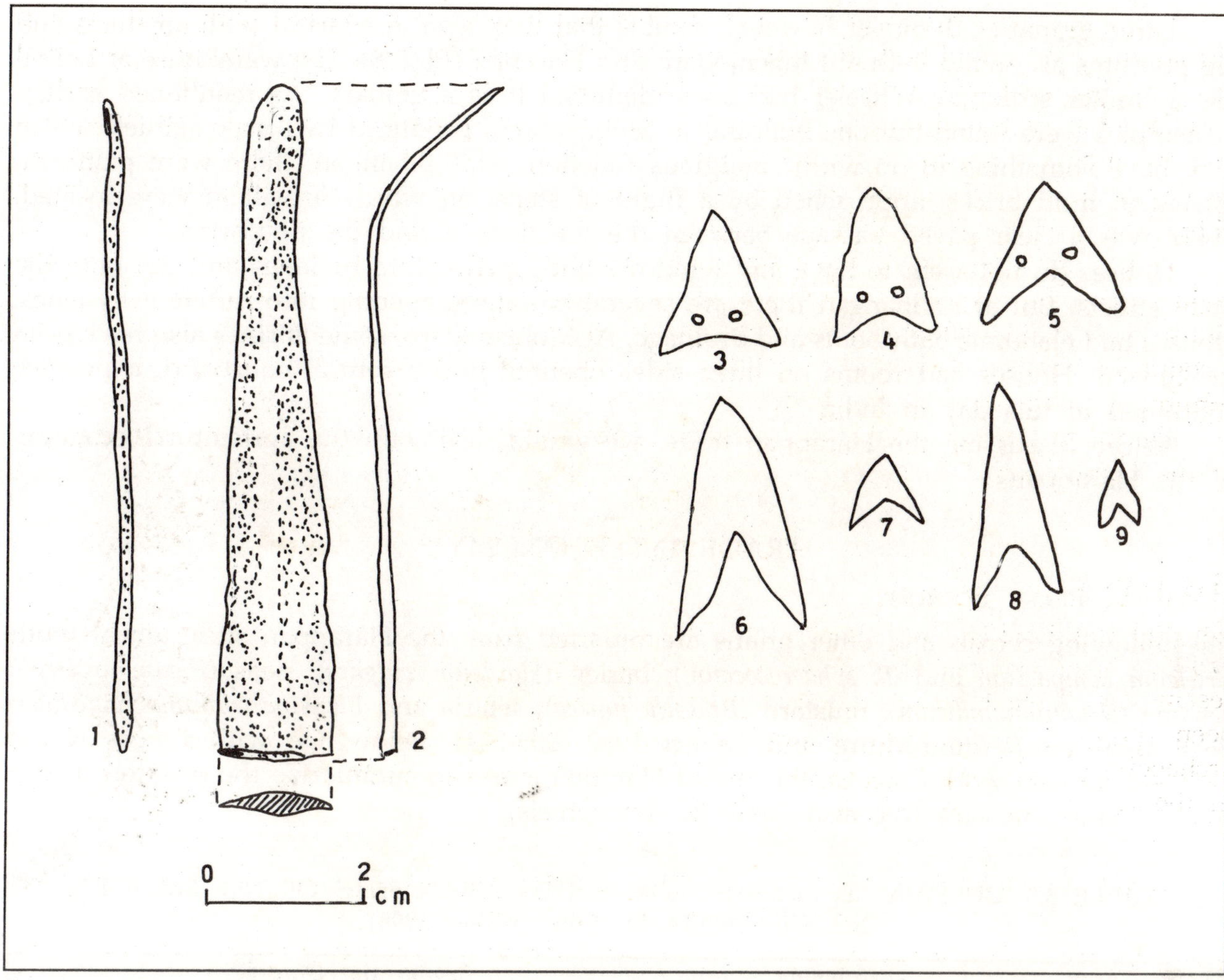

Fig. 3-10. Harappan copper tools. Bent blades (Nos. 1, 2) and arrowheads (Nos. 3 to 9).

Architecture: The Harappan cities are marked by a remarkable planning unheard of elsewhere in the 3rd millennium BC. The alignment of buildings and fortification walls was on cardinal directions. The streets were laid at right angles to each other. A well-designed system of drains leading from individual houses led to public soakage jars and underground drains below the streets. There must have been a civic staff to clean the sewage regularly.

As a protection against floods, the Citadels and the lower town buildings were built over raised mud brick platforms. The settlement was divided into a Citadel, which was on a higher ground, located in the west and the lower town towards the east. The Citadel was always fortified and so was often the lower town. Kalibangan and Harappa have a remarkable similarity of layout. Both the Citadels have fortifications, parallelogram on plan, west of the lower town. Mohenjodaro appears to have a similar layout, though flood-erosion has obscured the evidence. At Kalibangan, even the lower town had a fortification, a parallelogram in shape, but Lothal and Surkotada follow a different idiom. Here a common wall encloses both the Citadel and the lower town. At Surkotada, a wall separates the two, though the Citadel is still in the west. At Lothal, there is no wall separating the lower town from the Acropolis; the latter is situated on the south-east, a unique location (Fig. 3-6).

Large granaries (Kenoyer however, doubts that they were granaries) with air-ducts and big podiums are found both at Mohenjodaro and Harappa (Pl. 3-8). The warehouse at Lothal has a similar structure; Wheeler had once identified it as a granary. As mentioned earlier, no temples were found but one building in Mohenjodaro produced two male statues, which may have something to do with a religious function. At Kalibangan, there were platform-towers of mud bricks, approached by a flight of steps, on which fire-altars were located. There was a clear paved passage between the fortification and the platforms.

Houses do not seem to have any windows and opened into by-lanes and not onto the main streets. But at Kalibangan there are several entrances opening into different by-lanes. Houses had elaborate bathrooms and drainage. At Mohenjodaro, some latrines also have been recognized. Houses had rooms on three sides opening into a central courtyard, a practice continued to this day in India.

Before discussing the Harappan trade, we would deal with the agricultural economy of the Harappans.

TRADE AND ECONOMY

Harappan Plant Economy

The following cereals and other grains are reported from the Harappan sites: wheat (both *Triticum compactum* and *T. sphaerococcum*); barley (*Hordeum vulgare*); peas (*Pisum arvense*); sesame (*Sesamum indicum*); mustard (*Brassica juncea*); setaria and *Eleusine coracana* have also been reported (Vishnu-Mittre and Savitri 1982: 205-221). Below we will discuss recent archaeobotanical work done on the site of Harappa and also summarize the position of rice in the Harappan sites (see also Table 3.3 for cereals).

TABLE 3.3. CULTIVATED PLANTS FROM SOUTH ASIAN SITES OF THE 3rd AND 2nd MILLENNIA BC (after Weber 1998)

Plant Taxon	*Cropping Season*	*Region and Date* BC.		
		4000-2600	2520-2000	2000-1700
Cereals				
Wheat (*Triticum*)	W	R	R	R/K
Barley (*Hordeum*)	W	R	R/K	R/K
Rice (*Oryza*)	S		K	R/K
Millets	S	K	R/K	R/K
Pulses and Vegetables				
Pea (*Pisum*)	W	R	R/K	R/K
Chick pea (*Cicer*)	W		R	R/K
Grass pea (*Lathyrus*)	W	R	R/K	R/K
Lentil (*Lens*)	W	R	R/K	R/K
Horse gram (*Dolichos*)	S		K	R/K
Bean (*Phaseolus*)	S		K	R/K
Vigna	S		R/K	R/K
Medicago	S		K	R/K

Cont. Table 3.3

Table 3.3 Cont.

Plant Taxon	*Cropping Season*	*Region and Date* BC.		
		4000-2600	2520-2000	2000-1700
Oilseed and Fibre				
Lin (*Linum*)	W		R/K	R/K
Mustard (*Brassica*)	W		R/K	R/K
Sesame (*Sesamum*)	S		R/K	R/K
Cotton (*Gossypium*)	S	R (?)	R	R/K
Fruits				
Melon (*Cucumis*)	S		K	R/K
Date (*Phoenix*)	S	R	R	R
Jujube (*Zizyphus*)	W	R/K	R/K	R/K
Grape (*Vitis*)	W	R	R	R/K

(W=winter/spring harvest; S= summer/autumn harvest; R= rabi areas, with winter rain; K= kharif areas, with summer rain.

Evidence from Harappa: Weber thinks that a significant shift in agricultural strategies may have begun as early as 2200 BC. Though his data are based on only 3 per cent of the total samples, he thinks that his inferences may prove true for the total sample too (Weber 1998). New archaeobotanical data from the site of Harappa, though preliminary in nature, allow a glimpse into the potential of the plant database in Pakistan and how it might confirm, or challenge existing models of Indus valley subsistence. It may therefore be useful to quote his observations for the archaeobotanical material from the site of Harappa in detail. Weber (1997: 115-117) reports that:

The first characteristic and one of the most important, concerns preservation. Every sample so far examined has had good organic preservation. Seeds and seed fragments have been found in all samples. Although the seed density ranges from one carbonized seed per litre of soil up to 50, overall this represents a better than expected rate of recovery. Relatively speaking, this is a high rate of recovery for a South Asian site. From these 20 samples, nearly 3,000 seeds or identifiable seed fragments have been counted.... Associated with seed density is the sheer diversity of material being recovered. A minimum of three different taxa have been identified from each sample with a maximum of over 20 different species present. At least 30 different species are represented at Harappa, of which over half are cultivated varieties. This initial pattern suggests that an extensive agricultural system involving a great variety of plants existed at Harappa.... The second characteristic deals with form of the diet and the agricultural systems. On the whole, the data support the conventional view that there was a food producing economy involving domesticated plants and animals, with some hunting and plant gathering. However, I believe it is now possible to construct a more informative, three-tiered, hierarchical model of plant use. This hierarchy can be imagined as an inverted pyramid, with the topmost "layer" representing the species appearing in greatest abundance, as well as those most critical to subsistence. Relative abundance is a value that can be derived from the three principal means of measuring the archaeobotanical record: percentage of a given plant remains, its ubiquity and its density. At Harappa, wheat (*Triticum*) and barley (*Hordeum*) are the mainstay of the agricultural system and top the hierarchy. They occur in all samples, hence their high ubiquity. They occur in relatively high numbers, hence their high density. And finally, they make up the largest portion of each sample, hence, their high percentage.... The second level of the hierarchy includes cultivated crops of lesser importance, including lentils (*Lens*), gram (*Cicer*), pea (*Pisum*) and grass pea (*Lathyrus*). These taxa are found in about half the samples in numbers significantly below those of wheat and barley. Nonetheless, these do occur in significant numbers and are obviously a major part of the diet.... The third and final category consists of species which are found in very low numbers (low density and low percentage) and in only a few samples (low ubiquity). These include; *Zizphus, Trianthema, Chenopodium* and a variety of species found in the first two categories fit the suggested model of winter cultivation for the Mature Harappans. No evidence currently exists to suggest anything other than monocropping at Harappa prior to 2200 BC.... The third and final characteristic and the most speculative due to the limited sample size, concerns changes over time. The samples analysed for this paper belong to two general periods, Period 3B, dating from 2400 to 2350 BC and Period 3C, dating from 2180 to 2034 BC. The samples from the later Period (3C) are different from those of the earlier period. These later samples all contain greater variety of taxa, with a few new species including millet and possibly rice. Though wheat and barley remain prominent and there appears to be no abandonment of the existing agricultural strategy, new material is being introduced, suggesting a minor shift in both diet and cropping patterns. If this pattern holds up in other areas of the site and particularly in the late phases of occupation then it would represent the beginnings of a significant shift in agricultural practices (Weber 1997: 115-117).

Rice: Like the horse, the occurrence of rice at Harappan sites too has become controversial. The evidence of rice has been reported from the following Harappan sites (for detailed references mentioned below, see Kumar 1988), but it seems that rice did not play any major role in the Harappan plant economy. The evidence becomes widespread only in late Harappan times.

Rangpur

Rice and bajra were the cereals used at Rangpur. Rangpur Phase II a (Harappan, 2200-1700 BC) yielded the evidence of rice whereas in Phase III (Post-Harappan) remains of bajra were found. Rice (*Oryza sp.*) was discovered in Trench RGP-7 in the form of rice husk embedded in mud plaster. Though no grain or spikelet of rice has been observed, the manner of utilization of this by-product indicates the prevalence of rice in this region. Due to the highly deteriorated nature of specimens, determinations have to be confined to the generic levelof the plants (Ghosh and Lal 1962-63).

Lothal

At Lothal, on the coastal flats at the head of the Gulf of Cambay, rice remains have been reported in the form of impressions on three potsherds. Details are meagre, not finding more than a passing mention in S.R. Rao's report on *Lothal and the Indus Civilization* (1973). Vishnu-Mittre (1974: 17) retracted his earlier position and identified rice at Lothal as domesticated.

Kalibangan

Rice from Kalibangan has been reported (Kajale 1974), however, Vishnu-Mittre and R. Savithri (1973) contest this identification. They state that the carbonized food grains from this site were found to belong to barley, wheat, *Cicer arietinum* and *Pisum arvense*. The absence of rice in the carbonized plant remains from this site necessitated the reinvestigation of plant remains embedded in terracotta cakes from this site. The absence of chessboard pattern characteristic of rice on the husk remains in terracotta cakes ruled out their being rice. The identification of the sub-fossil cuticles derived from terracotta cakes and *pai* of wheat (*Triticum sp.*) establishes beyond doubt that the husk impression in terracotta cakes and *pai* do not belong to rice. It would appear that rice production at Kalibangan, therefore, is not proved.

Harappa

Fujiwara and others (1992) have found evidence of rice (*Oryza*) from Harappa, though belonging to the late Harappan phase. They have recovered the remains from soil and ash and terracotta objects like pottery and bricks and have carried out plant opal analysis (Fujiwara *et al.* 1992).

TRADE

Long distance trade had started much before the Harappa culture. Possehl (1999c: 680) points out that one of the distinguishing accomplishments of the Damb Sadaat Phase was the growth in connections between the Greater Indus Region and surrounding tracts. Even in Mehrgarh I, the aceramic period, there were abundant signs of long distance trade in luxury items such as lapis lazuli, turquoise and seashells. The ability of the people in the subcontinent to reach out and start economic relations with the neighbours, near and far, at the very beginning of the Indus Age, persists through the Mature Harappa stage. It is not something that builds slowly, or comes in fits and starts. Long distance trade begins with the development of villages and pastoral camps and persists right into the Mature Harappan. In the Indus case, it is not necessarily a distinctive marker of urbanization as suggested by V. Gordon Childe when he included this feature as one of his so-called "ten criteria for civilization" (Childe 1950).

The Baluchistan–Central Asia interaction sphere emerges in the archaeological record as one based on durable goods, mostly stone and metal. With the exception of turquoise, there are few durable products from Central Asia that might have been desired by the inhabitants of the Greater Indus Regions. Baluchistan might have supplied copper and Afghanistan tin. The recently reported source of lapis lazuli in the Chagai hills of Baluchistan would also have been important, as might have been the Badakshan source. But, viewed from a historical perspective it was not necessarily durables like these that played the predominant role in trade and exchange here. When we have written sources we learn that this kind of interaction is generally based on perishables, especially grain and textiles. These important commodities should not be neglected in our thought, in spite of the fact that there is virtually no archaeological record for these in the Indus Age (Possehl 1999c: 680).

The Early Harappan, Damb Sadaat Phase, Possehl remarks, marks a growth in inter-regional connections on the western side of the Indus area. This seems to have been on a large-scale, involved long distance travel and was enduring. It was also an important harbinger of developments that took place during the Mature Harappan, which was build on the foundation laid in Damb Sadaat and earlier interaction.

Many scholars like Rao, Chakrabarti and others believe that copper was one of the important material that were imported from Oman. The presence of nickel as a trace element in the ore of the Oman region and the high nickel content of the Indus copper bronze objects perhaps led Chakrabarti (1990: 143) to support this view. David Muhly writes that "nickel is so common that it cannot possibly be used to identify an ore from a specific source". Hence, unless we do extensive ore-artefact correlation studies on the Indus objects, we cannot put forward any final inference. As bun shaped ingots and large number of copper objects were found at Lothal, Rao (1986) thinks that copper ore was imported from Oman and purified at Lothal workshop and ingots were exported. The Oman copper ore is not arsenic-free! However, one of the ingots found at Lothal is of 99.8 per cent pure copper and it is arsenic-free unlike the Mohenjodaro ingot. Moreover, the analysis of as many as 300 copper objects from Lothal showed that none of them contained arsenic.

To support Rao's hypothesis, Chakrabarti (1990: 143) says that one has to explain an apparently widespread Harappan presence in the Omanese peninsula. Ras'al-Junayz, of course, is one of the well-known sites in Oman where an inscription with four Indus characters was found incised on the shoulder of a painted jar. And Tosi (1986) suggests that Oman was the base for Indus people for further voyage up to the Egyptian coast. He writes, "This locality occupies an even more strategic position on the coastal route from Karachi to the Horn of Africa". In fact, he gives more credit to the Indus people for their contribution in oceanic sea-craft than any other urban civilizations of the Middle east.

Chakrabarti (1990: 143-44) says,

> We have already drawn attention to the significance of Afghanistan as a positive source of Indus copper, lead and silver, although each of these metals is easily procurable in Baluchistan, Rajasthan and Gujarat. Ratnagar writes that there was no indigenous production of silver in India until a fairly late period and that the Harappan silver came from Mesopotamia. This statement does not appreciate the extent to which we have argentiferous galena in the lead-zinc deposits of Zawar and Agucha in Rajasthan. Besides, silver objects are found as early as Nal. The idea of Harappan tin coming from the relevant mines in the southern part of Central Asia is an acceptable one and we doubt very much if the Harappans could get all the tin they needed from any fluvial deposit. The nearest major source of tin in India is Bastar in the southernmost part of Madhya Pradesh and although tin is now commercially exploited in that region it is very doubtful if the Harappans were getting their tin from Bastar. On the other hand, Shortughai is conveniently located to receive Central Asian tin ores. The only snag in this hypothesis is that tin does not seem to be at all significant at Shortughai which does not even possess a significant amount of lapis, although its location is quite close to the lapis-bearing area. Tin has also been in Iran. Whatever the source of Harappan tin, Central Asia or/and Iran, it must have come, partly at least, from such an external source. A long-distance trade in raw materials, even bulky materials like ore, should no longer be considered a theoretical impossibility. A recent piece of pertinent research relates to the understanding of such trade in copper ore in the prehistoric Iranian plateau. It seems that from the Anarak mines, near Sialk, copper ore, in this case a natural arsenic alloy, was exported to Sialk I-III, Hissar I-II and Tepe-Yahya VI (end)-IVC. This distribution virtually covers a very large section of the Iranian plateau. There was local smelting of ore in each case, each site having its own technological process and distinctive artefacts. The trade was only in ore.

Regarding the Indus-Mesopotamian trade, David Muhly writes that judging from Ur texts the Mesopotamians imported lapis lazuli, carnelian, gold, silver, copper, ivory, tortoiseshell, a bird probably some sort of a chicken, peacock, dog, cat and monkey from Meluhha (Indus region) and exported raw wool, garments made of wool and silver in exchange. Some scholars also propose that Mesopotamians might have exported fish and grain to the Indus people! We, however, do not know if the Harappans actually received all these items as Chakrabarti also rightly points out (1990: 148).

But now the situation has changed. With the discovery of rich cassiterite bearing (up to 1.5 per cent tin) quartz-porphyry in the Tosham hills, near Bhiwani, Haryana (Kochhar *et al.* 1999) the possibility of bronze ingots being also supplied from Ganeshwar become more probable.

This new evidence requires a bit of a digression to evaluate the role of the Jodhpura Complex cultures in copper technology.

Relevance of Jodhpura Complex

The following are the salient features of this complex:

1. Jodhpura-Ganeshwar Complex has a distinct identity though surrounded by the Harappans.
2. Jodhpura-Ganeshwar Complex sites are spread over an area of about 200,000 sq.km.
3. Jodhpura site is a big settlement of 5-10 hectare size.
4. From this complex a large quantity and variety of copper artefacts have been found and a majority of them are of Harappan vintage though indicating a wide clientele.
5. The copper melting locations are on the periphery of the Harappan towns.
6. There are no smelting furnaces in any of the Harappan towns as pointed out by Chakrabarti and Lahiri (1996) and Miller.
7. Some burials have slag buried in them.
8. The tradition of itinerant smiths is still alive today.
9. The Mesopotamian texts mention Meluhha in the east from where copper was supplied.
10. The Jodhpura-Ganeshwar Complex sites are close to the 80 km long Khetri copper belt of Rajasthan and also to the Tusham hill (Haryana) tin resources.
11. The evidence from all over Asia of both copper and iron being produced by village-based non-urban societies.

Hooja and Kumar (1997) also emphasize, "Subsequent explorations and excavations at Ganeshwar brought to light over 5,000 copper objects.... The copper artefacts included arrowheads, beads, rings, bangles, fish-hooks, pins, spearheads, celts and balls.... Such a rich find of prehistoric copper objects from a single small site is very significant".

How do we explain the fact that the main metallurgical activity was not being done by the Harappan urban people but by non-urban communities like the Ganeshwar complex people. Here the Thai model may be more relevant to the Jodhpura-Ganeshwar Complex. To understand the Ganeshwar Complex Culture industries, Pigott's (1999) observations are very relevant,

> Early in the 2nd millennium BC the production of copper and bronze began in South-East Asia. The Thailand Archaeometallurgy project (TAP) had revealed the presence of major copper mining complexes and associated production settlements, the latter among the largest such sites known in Asia. The combined evidence from these sites comprises much of the primary production data by which the so-called "South-East Asian Metallurgical Tradition" can be characterized. Broadly speaking this "Tradition", defined in terms of the evidence from Thailand arose under somewhat unusual conditions. In contrast to most of the major culture areas of the Old World where large-scale production of metal, in particular bronze, is associated with complex societies and urban settings, in South-East Asia current evidence suggests that such metallurgy developed in village contexts. These villages were active in extensive network of inter-regional exchange, but exhibit only modest degrees of social ranking, at least during the early stages of metallurgy and development in the prehistoric period.... It is argued that production which will be reviewed for the sites of Non Pa Wai, Nil Kham Haeng and Non Mak La, was accomplished by a low investment "low-tech", very labour-intensive method, which was specialized only at the household-family level and which may have been only dry season industrial activity. Despite this level of production organization, the evidence suggests that prior to the appearance of chiefdom levels of social complexity and under conditions of economic decentralization, these village-based communities mined significant volumes of ores and produced large amounts of copper.

Ganeshwar Complex sites too are village-based but may have specialized in copper production.

The main copper source for the Harappans could be Rajasthan or Baluchisthan. In this connection Oman mines have also been mentioned. Heather Miller has pointed out that even copper rich prills were discarded at Harappa, which goes to show that there was an abundance of metal and that it was not a precious import. Even in the Mesopotamian texts, Meluhha is identified with the Indus and eastern region. We suggest that the Jodhpura-Ganeshwar Complex fits the bill better for being identified with Meluhha, with its rich 80 km long Khetri copper belt. It is estimated that in the Mardan-Kudan section there is a reserve of 28 million tons and in Dariba region 0.5 million tonnes. The main mineral is chalcopyrite ($CuFeS_2$). Therefore, import of copper from Oman does not make much sense unless marine transport was far cheaper than overland transport. There is every possibility of the Ganeshwar Complex itself being the much talked about Meluhha of the Mesopotamian texts!

They may also be producing copper ingots and exporting to the Harappan towns and further beyond into West Asia, though the evidence is not explicit on this point. But as smelting operations have spatial constraints of nearness to the old mines, these sites are naturally located close to the Rajasthan copper mineral occurrences. There is some evidence of sharpedged tools being made of bronze in the Harappan towns (Agrawal 1971; Miller 1999). Keeping in view the highly regulated nature of the Mature Harappan towns with their rules of town-planning, civic sanitation, standardization of weights and measures, we should not be surprised if some control was also exercised on the tin/arsenic content of the bronze ingots exported to the Harappan towns. With the discovery of Tusham tin mines nearby (Kochhar *et al.* 1999), it now becomes more probable.

Miller has emphatically said that none of the Harappan sites has any copper smelting evidence, though there is melting evidence. Heather Miller (1999) recognizes that there is some indication of crafts segregation related to semiprecious objects and metallurgy and ceramics. She says: "At Harappa, copper melting debris, the various bone-associated slags and to some extent pottery firing assemblages, tend to be isolated and not intermixed with debris from other crafts.... There are thus hints of differences in the organization of the pyrotechnological crafts vs the extractive-reductive crafts. This pattern seems to be somewhat true for Mohenjodaro, although it is perhaps not quite as clear".

It may be relevant to recall here that the locality for the metal smiths (Tamtyura, after *tamra* = copper) was kept outside the periphery of the main town of Almora (in Central Himalayas), the historical capital of Kumaun. King Kalyanchand shifted the capital to Almora in the 16th century from Champavat. So it was a deliberate act on the part of the king to keep the artisans away from the urban elite. Of course, metal was being smelted at the old mining sites only, as discussed elsewhere (Agrawal 2000).

On the other hand, we also need to keep in mind the recent thinking about the inappropriateness of modern concepts of production and technological management in ancient technological organization. Budd and Taylor make the following observation,

> Today, there is an ongoing discussion highlighting the inappropriateness of modern concept of production and technological development in conceptualising ancient metallurgical organization (Budd and Taylor 1995, Sherratt 1994). Sherratt (1994: 337-38) has attacked Childe's basic premise that metallurgy played the same role in urban and non-urban contexts in the European and Mediterranean Bronze Age. He highlights the diversity of patterns of use and consumption of, even closely similar metal artefacts and draws attention to the high, "chiefly" status of "smiths" burials suggesting that "... metallurgy was itself a prestige practice". And "prestige" itself is perhaps a modernist/ethnocentric term to convey the mystique that was involved" (Sherratt 1994: 338). The earliest metal making might thus have been associated with a politico-religious power and have a ritual or symbolic rather than purely economic component.... At present we understand

far too little about the social context of Bronze Age metal making or the role of metal objects in the societies that produced them. As a consequence we know little about how metals enter the archaeological record (Budd and Taylor 1995).

Moorey (1994) has also emphasized the contrast between Mesopotamia and highland neighbours.

> The contrast between Mesopotamia and her highland neighbours was not just one of unequal access to raw material, but also of unequal degrees of socio-economic organization and complexity. The urban crafts and industries of Mesopotamia were as dependent on the highly organized labour of those who produced but did not participate in the consumption of what was traded as they were on sustained access to foreign materials.... This is not the place to enter into the notoriously complex question of the relationship between centralized administrative system and individual entrepreneurship in the procurement of raw materials, their manufacture and the distribution of goods in historic Mesopotamia. But it is necessary to draw attention to it, if only to emphasize that they were not homogeneous at any time. The three modes of exchange conventionally distinguished as reciprocal, redistributive and commercial coexisted. They were not mutually exclusive, as is too often assumed.

We need to take into account the above examples to understand the metal trade of the Ganeshwar Complex. In the context of Jodhpura-Ganeshwar Complex, for production and export of metal artefacts and ingots to the Harappan towns and perhaps further beyond into Mesopotamia, what were they getting in exchange? Was it silver? Was it grain? Or something else? How do we explain the location of Kunal, a small village and Rakhigarhi, a large city, in close vicinity of Jodhpura-Ganeshwar Complex sites and their apparent prosperity? Was it a very unequal relationship where the economic benefits were largely appropriated by the Harappans? Kunal has yielded one of the richest hauls of silver and gold ornaments amongst the Harappan towns (see for site details of Kunal: Regional Variation and Main Towns).

Here we may take note of a refreshing ethnographic viewpoint. Lahiri (1993: 130) says,

> This (Harappa) 3rd millennium BC city, situated in the Sahawal region of Pakistan, was an important copper/bronze craft centre of its area although its immediate hinterland is minerally barren.... In the process of secondary manufacture, however, some slag and miscellaneous waste was generated and, as Vats's *Excavations at Harappa* (1940: 254ff) underline, these are primarily found in the post-cremation urns of its various mounds.... Slag was being produced at Harappa in the course of artisanal crafting and manufacture. However, its contextual association suggests that it was considered more than just a by-product of smelting and manufacture. When appropriated in funerary rites and rituals, it was divested of its technological meaning and reconstituted as a cultural signifier of beliefs which cannot be as clearly spelled out as at Sihi but are related to death and possible after-life.

She forcefully concludes,

> Generally, works on metallurgy in antiquity tend towards monolithic model made up of an evolutionary development of metal-craft with a unifunctional use of artefacts and raw materials, within which cognitive archaeology has no place. All those components that cannot be subsumed within this paradigm are dismissed as anomalous/discrepant products of technological/resource constraints/determinants and, hence, unworthy of interest in themselves. My purpose has been to show that some such elements of metal technology in India can, through the microcosm of ethnography and early literature, both rich sources of cognitive information, be located within historically documented cultural choices, an artisanal ecosystem that is based on resource conserving principles as well as folk traditions and historical events (Lahiri 1993: 130).

We have thus tried to make a case for identification of Meluhha of the Mesopotamian texts with the Jodhpura Complex area. With its rich copper and tin mineral hinterland and evidence of, a large number of Harappan vintage artefacts, Jodhpura Complex has a clear claim to such identification.

We have, however, to keep in mind the complexities involved. Both the role of metal technology in urbanization and the concomitant unilinear models of evolution and the relationship of metal producing village-based societies need a fresh evaluation of the evidence. The old axioms will not serve the purpose. Towards this end, we have quoted both ethnographic evidence as also the pan-Asian evidence of both copper and iron being produced by non-urban village communities. This means that we have to re-evaluate our assumptions of role of metal technology in the ancient societies.

Hunter-Gatherers and Cities

Relevant to this discussion is the economic relationship of the urban centres with the hunter-gatherers of the hinterland. Possehl has drawn our attention to this aspect in his interpretation of the Lothal evidence.

It seems that the economic relationship of the urban centres and the hinterland hunter-gatherers played a very important role in maintaining the stability. Probably a complex exchange system had emerged between the food producing groups, with sophisticated technologies and a demand for raw materials and the hunting and gathering group with a need for finished goods plus access to raw materials as a medium for exchange. It is pertinent here to quote significant observations made by Richard Fox (1969: 141-42) in a different context. He writes,

> ... that rather than being independent, primitive fossils, Indian hunters-and-gatherers represent occupationally specialized productive units similar to caste groups such as Carpenters, Shepherds, or Leather-workers. Their economic regimen is geared to trade and exchange with the more complex agricultural and caste communities within whose orbit they live. Hunting and gathering in the Indian context is not an economic response to a total, that undifferentiated environment. Rather, it is a highly specialized and selective orientation to the natural situation: where forest goods are collected and valued primarily for external barter or trade and where necessary subsistence or ceremonial items—such as iron tools, rice, arrowheads, etc.—are only obtainable in this way. Far from depending wholly on the forest for their own direct subsistence, the Indian hunters-and-gatherers are highly specialized exploiters of a marginal terrain from which they supply the larger society with desirable, but otherwise unobtainable, forest items such as honey, wax, rope and twine, baskets and deer meat. Unlike the Australian aborigines or the Paiutes, their economic process and well-being are dependent on the barter of these items for the crops and crafts of their more complexly organized plainsmen neighbours. The economic activity of Indian hunting-and-gathering groups is more akin to the specialization of caste hereditary occupation, than it is to the generalized environmental response of the Australian or Paiute (quoted by Possehl 1999c: 169).

Possehl suggests that the hunters and gatherers were the agents through whom the Harappan traders worked in the procurement of a broad range of raw materials useful to them in various manufacturing processes. The seasonal mobility of the hunter-gatherers would, through the course of a year, take them to or near the localities of materials such as steatite, shell, carnelian and other semiprecious stones. Copper ore may or may not have been procured in this fashion. It is difficult to believe that the hunter-gatherers themselves had a technology sufficiently sophisticated to take the ore and produce even crude, impure copper ingots. It is equally difficult to imagine them carrying the ore itself from the sources in southern Rajasthan. The exact nature of the procurement process utilized for this item is therefore, left somewhat open and a topic for future research. What is clear, however, is that the hunters and gatherers whose life was closely tied to seasonal movement and who would have possessed an intimate knowledge of the natural resources within their range of movement, can be envisioned as ideal groups with whom the Harappans could work.

Kenoyer (1998) states that as most of the basic raw materials needed by the Indus cities were available in the regions adjacent to the Indus valley, there was no reason for Indus traders to travel to far off lands. But, lured by untapped markets and the rewards for bringing back exotic items, some adventurous Indus traders travelled across the sea to Oman and far up the Persian Gulf to the cities of Mesopotamia. Scholars have argued that the long distance trade was carried out by intermediary communities or middlemen, but Kenoyer suggests that there is increasing evidence to suggest that at least a few Indus entrepreneurs travelled to these distant lands. Most trade was probably carried on by sea, although we have some evidence for limited overland trade through southern Iran.

Lamberg-Karlovsky, however, emphasizes the role of the sites like Tepe-Yahya in Iran in the Indus-Mesopotamian indirect land-route trade. He says,

> ... there was an established dialectic between these (Iranian) resource-rich areas with resource-poor Mesopotaia on the one hand and the Indus on the other, which brought about a mutually dependent parallel and contemporary process toward urbanization. As emphasized by Chakrabarti and Dales, for a clearer picture of the Indus trade, one needs: the distribution maps of natural resources and of ancient settlements; more data on the subsistence potential of different sub-regions; more excavations of the outposts and fringe sites; further data on the ecology and the ethnology of these regions; a firmer chronological framework; and of course, an interdisciplinary approach.

The trade with Oman was probably most heavy, although it was not critical to the Indus economy. Numerous Indus artefacts have been found in Oman and along southern coast of the Arabian Gulf and characteristic circular seals from the Gulf sites have been found in the Indus valley. Though Kenoyer thinks that the major imports from Oman were copper, shell and possibly mother-of-pearl, we doubt if the Oman copper had any market in the Indus in view of nearby abundant supplies in Rajasthan and Baluchistan. In historical times, the Arabian trade supplied the Indus valley primarily with dates, pearls, incense, dried fruits and slaves.

Exports to Oman would have included many perishable goods transported in large black-slipped storage jars. Numerous jar fragments, often with Indus script on the shoulder, have been found at many different Gulf sites. These vessels may have transported indigo or liquid foods such as clarified butter, pickled vegetables or fruits, honey or wine. The narrow base may have been designed to allow the jars to be placed along the bottom of the ships hold. At the site of Ras'al-Junayz in Oman, one of these large, black-slipped vessels with graffiti was found along with a bronze Indus stamp seal. Other exports may have included wood for boats (an unfired seal shows a typical Harappan boat, the type is still used in Sindh; Pl. 3-21), livestock, grain and fresh fruit, but the only preserved objects are Indus beads, cubical chert weights and ivory objects such as a comb. These items may have been left in Oman by Indus traders or brought to the region by intermediaries. Current evidence suggests that most trade with Oman took place during the height of the Indus cities between 2200 and 2100 BC (Kenoyer 1998).

Further to the west, in Mesopotamia, trade contacts with the Indus valley are reflected in artefacts such as terracotta sealings from bundles of goods that were being traded. The earliest contacts, dating to between 2600 and 2500 BC, are centered in southern Mesopotamia at the city of Ur. In the royal cemetery of Ur, kings and queens were buried with servants and livestock along with elaborate ornaments and personal objects. Lapis lazuli, shell and carnelian were used with gold, silver and bronze to create exquisite ornaments, utensils and weapons. Among the beads found with the kings, queens and serving ladies are distinctive long biconical carnelian beads and decorated carnelian beads that were produced by artisans from the Indus valley.

The Indus trade continued during the Akkadian period too. Textual references for Indus trade date to the period between 2300 and 1800 BC, beginning with the reign of Sargon of Akkad (2334-2279 BC). This famous ruler boasts of ships from Dilmun, Magan and Meluhha that are docked at his capital city, Akkad. Most scholars agree that in these texts, Dilmun refers to the modern island of Bahrain, Magan refers to modern Makran and Oman, while Meluhha refers to the general region of the Indus valley. Numerous texts describe the types of goods coming from Meluhha: hard woods, tin or lead, copper, gold, silver, carnelian, shell, pearls and ivory. Animals such as a red dogs, a cats, peacocks or black partridges and monkeys are also mentioned. Many of these items would not be preserved in the archaeological record, but Indus weights, seals and seal impressions (Pls. 3-33, -34, -35) attest to the presence of merchants and bundles of trade goods. The discovery of carnelian beads, shell bangles, ivory and shell inlay in temples or burials indicates that most of the trade objects from the Indus valley were destined for the gods and rulers of the Mesopotamian cities (Kenoyer 1998; Chakrabarti 1990).

It is strange that no items produced in Mesopotamia proper have been found in the Indus region. Mesopotamian texts list such exports as wool, incense and gold, which are perishable or would have been transformed into new objects in the Indus cities. The absence of Mesopotamian cylinder seals and sealings would indicate that Mesopotamian traders were not directly involved with the Indus trade and that no bundles of goods sealed by Mesopotamian merchants were being sent to the Indus cities. There is not enough evidence at present to argue for the exclusion of Mesopotamian traders from the Indus market, but the Indus cities were clearly involved in the import of raw materials and the export of finished goods. Thus perhaps the Indus people were trading both in exports and imports which may have been one of the factors that led to the rapid growth and spread of the Indus settlements throughout the north-western subcontinent.

This, however, required that the Indus traders control the movement of goods and be able to profit from the commercial transactions. Most trade was probably conducted through a common barter system and reciprocal exchange of goods for services. Both systems are well documented in traditional economies throughout the subcontinent and in the absence of a monetary standard would have been essential for supporting the Indus urban centres. A third system of exchange is seen in the highly standardized system of cubical stone weights that is common at all Indus settlements. Most scholars have assumed that this standardized weight system was used primarily for market exchange, but Kenoyer surmises that these weights could have been also used for taxation.

Weights and Measures

Though the standardized Indus weights were quite different from the weights used in Mesopotamia or Egypt, yet they were identical to those used by the first historical kingdoms of the Ganga valley (*c.* 300 BC) and are still in use in traditional markets throughout Pakistan and India. Till the introduction of the decimal weights (CGS System), a binary system of 1 seer (about 1 kg) = 16 *chhatacks* was used.

The Harappans had evolved a highly standardized system of weights and measures. For linear measures, two systems were in vogue: cubits and a long foot. A cubit was about 52 cm (52.5 to 52.8 cm) and the long foot 33.5 cm. Graduated scales have been reported from Mohenjodaro, Lothal and Kalibangan. The Lothal scale has divisions of 1.7 mm with decimal graduations. It may be pointed out that the *Arthasastra's angula* was 17.86 mm compared to 17.7 mm divisions on the Harappan scale. Rao reports a shell object (now also reported from other sites in Saurashtra) with four slits, which was probably used to measure angles.

The weights were made out of chalcedony, black stone, etc., and took cubical forms. They followed a binary system (1, 2, 4, 8, 16, 32 up to 12,800) in the lower denominations. The first seven Indus weights double in size from 1: 2: 4: 8: 16: 32: 64 and the most common weight is the 16th ratio, which is approximately 13.7 grams. The traditional Indian ratio of 1: 16 (1 seer =16 *chhattacks*) seems to derive from this. At this point, the weight increments change to a decimal system where the next largest weights have a ratio of 160, 200, 320 and 640. The next jump goes to 1600, 3200, 6400, 8000 and 12,800. The largest weight found at the site of Mohenjodaro weighs 10,865 grams (approximately 25 pounds) which is almost 100,000 times the weight of the "gunja" seed. The cubical stone weights, are thus based on a complex system of measurement that is calculated by both binary and decimal increments. The unit weighs 13.625 gm. Higher weights follow a decimal system with fractions in one-third. Accuracy of these weights all over the Harappan territory is remarkable indeed.

The base weight may have been a tiny black and red seed known as "gunja" (*Abrus precatorius*), which is still used by modern jewellers in Pakistan and India. However, it is possible that other grains such as barley or lentil seeds may have been used in the original calculation, because the "gunja" is equal to two mung bean seeds or two grains of barley. Scientific studies of the "gunja" seed show that the average weight is 0.109 gram and eight "gunja" equal the smallest known Indus weight of 0.871 gram. Lamberg-Karlovsky (2001) has presented an interesting paper, though short, on metrology in the Old World civilizations. He says that the ability to integrate different weight systems was crucial in developing both the scale and the nature of commercial exchange in the Near east and would have facilitated the emergence of the Ancient World System.

Most of the excavated sites of the Indus valley have yielded such cubical chert weights and all of the weights conform to the standard system established by the Indus rulers. Heavier weights have only been found at major trading centres such as Chanhudaro, or at the largest cities of Mohenjodaro and Harappa, but complete sets of the smaller weights are found at most of the rural settlements. In addition to the common cubical weights, many sites have truncated spherical weights that conform to the same weight system. Usually made from agate or coloured jaspers, these weights may reflect a regional style of weight manufacture or perhaps a competing class of merchants.

The larger weights could have been used for grain or large quantities of goods. This interpretation, however, does not fit well with the traditional trading practices of the subcontinent; there are not enough weights from the Indus sites for everyone to have been using them in commercial transactions. In market exchange, the smaller weights may have been used for precious stones and metals, perfumes and valuable medicines. A more plausible interpretation associates weights with taxation. In the recent excavations at Harappa, the highest concentration of weights has been found inside the city gateway, which is where goods coming into the city would have been weighed and taxed. Tax collectors or village elders in the smaller settlements would have needed only one or two sets of weights to collect tribute in precious commodities or produce. Finally, the large weights, which are found only at the urban centres would have been well suited for weighing tribute coming from all of the surrounding villages and towns (Kenoyer 1998).

Let us now try to locate the oft-mentioned sites of Dilmun, Magan and Meluhha.

Dilmun, Magan and Meluhha

The Mesopotamian texts refer to trading and supply centres like Dilmun, Magan and Meluhha. Where are these places to be located? There is still quite a bit of controversy about these. In this connection we would discuss the different views expressed by Chakrabarti, Thapar, Ratnagar, Shaffer and others.

Dilip Chakrabarti reviewing the literature on this problem says that the literature on this theme has grown steadily in recent years. The identification of Dilmun with Bahrain is perhaps universally accepted. In 1944, S.N. Kramer identified it "in all probability" with south-western Iran. Later on, he located it in the Indus valley. In 1946, P.B. Cornwall critically reviewed Kramer's opinion :

> ... it is essential to recognize at once that the cuneiform references to Dilmun fall into two distinct categories: 1. historical, commercial, epistolary, dedicatory and astrological inscriptions; 2. Sumerian literary compositions. In the former, Dilmun is a definite geographical locality—of that we may be certain. In the latter it is a fabulous land, a strange antechamber to the spirit world. That the two Dilmuns were thought of as being somehow identical is very likely; but I suggest that Dr. Kramer should not have decided the location of Dilmun merely on the basis of Sumerian literary compositions, especially since the evidence gleaned from the other class of source material points decidedly to the equation Dilmun = Bahrain.... In 1952 Cornwall re-formulated his earlier opinion: the identification with Bahrain island and part of the Saudi Arabian province of Hasa may be accepted without reservations...The Danish researchers in Bahrain and the adjacent areas in the Persian Gulf have clinched the issue in favour of Bahrain.

About Magan and Meluhha, Chakrabarti (1990: 148) says,

> Gelb's own inference is that Makan is the southern shore of the Persian Gulf and of the Arabian Sea; it denotes Arabia, extending east of ancient Sumer up to and including Oman. Meluhha, according to him, is the northern shore of the Persian Gulf and of the Arabian sea; it denotes Iran and India, extending east of ancient Elam and Ansan up to and including the Indus valley. In other words, Meluhha was a generic name standing for certain regions east of Mesopotamia, which also included the Indus valley.
>
> Regarding Meluhha this is a general conclusion to which we would like to adhere in the present stage of knowledge. Kinnier-Wilson suggests the following identification of Makkan, which has a bearing on the identification of Meluhha as well. He points out that the stone used in the Gudea statuary is not diorite but a substance, which occurs in the Tul-i-Marmar area in the general region of the Iranian oil-fields in the south-west corner of Iran. He does not seem to have any doubt about this identification, but the point is that if south-west Iran, or a part of it, stands for Makkan of the Mesopotamian literary sources, Meluhha will stand for regions further to the east, up to and including the Indus valley. This is very unlikely to stand for the Indus valley alone.

As Ratnagar's comments have much relevance to the problems related to this controversy, her views on trade are quoted below. Ratnagar's review of this problem appeared (1995: 115-127) much later than her book (1981). She writes,

> Harappan trade has been a popular subject for the last two decades. "Multi-national" excavations and explorations in Iraq, Iran and the countries of the Gulf have resulted in a voluminous literature on the cultural connections between various regions from the Euphrates to the Indus. An exhaustive discussion

is not possible here and we can only refer to an earlier monograph (Ratnagar 1981) and indicate the more important themes and emphases, or revisions of views that have emerged since then.

> Here we will deal only with the long distance overseas trade and situate this phenomenon in the wider framework of complex and multiple-stranded cross-cultural interactions which prevailed in the later third and earlier 2nd Millennia BC over an area much wider than that marked by Harappan trade routes...The inter-cultural trade embraced contrasting places and cultures, even though all regions are characterized as arid and semi-arid and the rainfall in all cases except Kachchh and Kathiawad and the relevant tracts of northern Afghanistan being below 300 mm per annum. Sumer and Seistan had relatively high agricultural potential, in contrast to the environs of Tepe-Yahya in south-west Iran or to northern Bahrain. The Upper Gulf could offer only dates and pearls for trade whereas in the Lower Gulf (the Peninsula of Oman) occur rich veins of copper and hard dark stones like gabbers and dolerites. Perhaps the Harappans were the only participants who had easy access to fine timbers. The largest of the culture areas, the Harappans incorporated areas with marine resources, others with forestry and yet others known to be agriculturally rich zones (Ratnagar 1995: 115-127).

Ratnagar (1995: 115-127) further notes that Mesopotamia and South Asia represent literate and urbanized societies, the "Bronze Age" in every sense of Gordon Childe's usage, but not so the Kulli, or groups at Yahya or in Oman. She finds it of interest that the various culture areas did not always exhibit the closest ties with those nearest them. It has long been appreciated that Mesopotamia, the agriculturally richest and the most populous area, had huge quantities of grain, oil and woollen textiles to offer. It was also perhaps the home of the most skilled metallurgists. But it was the largest importer of metals, stones and shells (having none of these locally), most of which came from South Asia, the eastern terminus of the trading circuit. Besides being procurers and suppliers of so many trade items, the Harappans may well have been the most accomplished seafarers, given their privileged access to the best boat-building timbers (these have up to recent times been imported by seafarers of the Gulf from India). It hardly bears repetition that the movement of heavy and bulk items like stone, metal and timber is immensely cheaper by water than by land. Ratnagar does not seem to concede to what Dilip Chakrabarti has said above,

> This point about the two urbanized termini of the trade comes across vividly when we consider the trade in silver. Little silver has been found in the intermediate areas of south-east Iran, Seistan, or the Gulf—except for two silver artefacts at Shahr-i-Sokhta in Seistan and two silver beads in an Oman grave. It had earlier been argued (Ratnagar 1981: 144-146) that the Harappans, the only people of proto-historic South Asia to have used silver on a substantial scale, imported this metal, most likely from Mesopotamia. A regular movement of silver from the Assyrian merchant colonies of Cappadocia to Mesopotamia is well documented for the period between 1920 and 1750 BC and texts from Ur which refer to silver being taken overseas by merchants to buy copper in Dilmun (clearly an entrepot) date to the time of Rim Sin of Larsa or 1822 to 1763 BC. It had also been pointed out that silver occurs in the two large Harappan settlements of Mohenjodaro and Harappa, but is almost totally absent at the other sites...Another argument for Mesopotamia as the source is that, even earlier, around 3500-3000 BC and also later, silver and lead were used on a substantial scale in Mesopotamia and Elam. One example is provided by the Early Dynastic III Royal Cemetery at Ur, with a truly exceptional amount of silver (Moorey 1985: 114 ff, 122 ff). Second, we now have a run of radiocarbon dates from the silver-lead bearing localities of Dariba, Agucha and Zawar, near Ajmer in Rajasthan, which testify to mining in the later 1st millennium BC rather than earlier (Craddock *et al.* 1989). The only earlier mining is attested to at Dariba, but these dates are Post-Harappan, viz. later 2nd millennium BC (Ratnagar 1995).

Ratnagar (1995) thinks that because in Dilmun (in the Bahrain archipelago), the Ubaid pottery was found in this region that was actually made in southern Mesopotamia (Oates *et al.* 1977, in Ratnagar 1995), Mesopotamian sea voyages had begun by 4000 BC.

All this evidence together prompts the adoption of a long chronology for the Barbar/Dilmun culture. The major argument for a short chronology has been the absence in the temples and settlements of Bahrain of carved chlorite containers of the early series (see Kohl 1986: 368), which date to Early Dynastic II-III. Such vessels do, however, occur on Tarut Island not far away and as grave goods. Carved as they are with intricate "mythological" elements, these containers in some cultures may well have been of exclusively funerary use.

Referring to the scale of the trade, Ratnagar (1995: 123) says,

> We have two glimpses of its scale from the cuneiform texts. The first concerns a trade transaction (see Roaf 1982) in which some 18,000 kg of copper were involved. In the second, consignment of 2,380 "gur" (a capacity measure) of barley goes to Magan (see Ratnagar 1981: 80). It, as is commonly accepted, a "gur" was 240 litres or 180 kg of grain, then 2,380 "gur" was a gigantic amount and its import requires careful thinking out.... Knowledge about metal ores and techniques and about pyro-technology appropriate for faience production may have spread wide, as Childe had often said. Yet the socketed spearhead of Oman does not appear to have influenced Harappan tools which lacked sockets and strengthening central midribs. Most intriguing is the use in Turkmenia of several kinds of alloys—copper-lead, copper-silver, silver-copper, copper-lead-arsenic/tin and copper-tin-arsenic—were in use (Masson 1988: 99) but in spite of "contacts" there appears to be no such experimentation with alloying in the Harappan civilization (where tin bronze was the alloy in general use, an alloy which apparently was scarce in Turkmenia!). Do we interpret this as a function of availability of metals, or as resistance to the spread of certain techniques?

This statement is however, difficult to understand in view of use of lead, tin and arsenic in Harappan coppers.

International trade of the Harappans is a controversial subject. On the one hand, Fairservis and Lamberg-Karlovsky deny its existence; Rao, on the other, lays great emphasis on it. During Caspers (1984) and Ratnagar (1981) have done a critical survey of the Harappan-Mesopotamian trade. There are frequent and consistent references in the Mesopotamian texts to Dilmun, Magan (Makkan) and Meluhha with which there was frequent commercial intercourse. And all these places could be approached by boat. Dilmun was located on the "Lower Sea", viz., the Arab-Persian sea. The early references to these places mainly come from the early Dynastic to Isin-Larsa periods. Dilmun used to export copper, carnelian, semiprecious stones, ivory and its artefacts, timber, silver, lapis lazuli, pearls, red gold, white corals, eye paint and dates. There is now a consensus to identify Dilmun with the Turant, Bahrain and Kuwait region. There are many evidences of contacts of Dilmun with Mesopotamia and the Indus. The weight system followed here is exactly the same as that of the Harappans. A Persian Gulf seal (typical of Dilmun region) has been reported as a surface find from Lothal. Dilmun, however, produced only pearls and dates; for other commodities it served as an entrepot. It is likely that the Harappans (and also the Pre-Harappans) traded with the Mesopotamians at the neutral sites of Dilmun.

Magan has been identified variously with Umm-an-Nar near Abu Dhabi; with the area around Minab or Tiz (Chah Bazar); and even with the inland region comprising Shahr-i-Sokhta and Tepe-Yahya in Iran. Gelb, however, identifies Magan as the southern shore of the Persian Gulf and of the Arabian Sea. Textual references mention reeds, onions, diorite, carnelian, red ochre, copper and ivory as the products received from Magan. Steatite vessels, probably produced at Tepe-Yahya and exported to both west and east may support identification of Magan with Tepe-Yahya region, but evidence for overland trade is lacking at the moment. Shahr-i-Sokhta was a large manufacturing and export centre for lapis lazuli objects.

Meluhha's identification is also controversial. Of course, in the later part of the 2nd millennium BC, Magan and Meluhha denoted Egypt and Nubia respectively, but before that perhaps they represented regions on the south-east. Chakrabarti, in his balanced review of the evidence, defines Meluhha as the northern shore of the Persian Gulf and of the Arabian Sea thus denoting Iran and India. Meluhha was thus perhaps a generic name standing for certain regions east of Mesopotamia, which also included the Indus valley. Meluhha, according to the texts, exported a variety of timbers, copper, gold dust, silver, ebony, lapis lazuli, carnelian and other stones and ivory figurines of birds and monkeys, etc.

Timber has been traditionally exported from the West Indian ports. Teak grows in Panch Mahal hills in Gujarat and has also been reported from Lothal. Placer gold is found in the streams of Punjab and Kashmir and may have provided the dust gold. Gold caps for stone beads, discoid beads with axial tubes and spherical beads joined together are exactly similar in both the Sumerian and the Harappan ornaments. Carnelian is known from Rajpipla mines and its beads were manufactured at Lothal and Chanhudaro. In fact, the stone-bead industry in Saurashtra is still alive and exporting. Etched beads of carnelian have been reported from most of the Harappan sites and in Mesopotamia at Ur, Kish, Al-Hiba and Tell Asmar.

Ivory objects mentioned in the texts include combs, figurines, boxes, inlay pieces, etc. Unworked and worked pieces of ivory have been reported from Surkotada, Lothal, Mohenjodaro and Chanhudaro. It is therefore likely that Meluhha may represent the north-west part of the Indian subcontinent, covering Jodhpura Complex area also, as already argued by us.

Quite a sizeable evidence of contact pertains to Early Dynastic III period and, as emphasized by Mughal, the international trade had started from the Pre-Harappan times and was not confined to the Harappan period only. The Ur texts mention that the commodities exported to the east were barley, flour, wool and woollen goods and silver. How much of it reached India is a matter of guess, as most of these items are perishable.

RELIGION

To reconstruct spiritual beliefs of people from the surviving material artefacts is risky indeed and the explanations given here can at best be only plausible. The main artefacts/symbols, which seem to have religious significance are trees (pipal, banyan) (Pl. 3-25), horned deities (Pl. 3-35), clay female figurines (Pl. 3-23) and fire-altars (Pl. 3-9). Symbols of tree worship and horned deities will be discussed in detail below, emphasizing the cultural continuity of the tradition.

The Indus seals seem to have served a variety of functions. Their discovery at the Lothal warehouses clearly suggests that they were used to seal grains or merchandize, but a majority depict scenes which can be interpreted only as religious. A well-known seal depicting a seated, three-faced, horned and ithyphallic figure surrounded by a number of animals recalls the *pasupata* nature of Shiva (Pl. 3-35). There is a terracotta cake from Kalibangan, which shows a standing figure (deity) with a horned headdress and on the reverse a man carrying a goat/bovine tied with a rope, perhaps for a sacrifice. In a lined pit, from the religious sector of the Citadel at Kalibangan, were discovered bovine and antler bones and ash, indicating a sacrifice. Several naturalistic phallic stones and terracotta and perforated stones (perhaps depicting the female organ) may take the present *Shivalinga* and *Yoni* worship back to the Harappan times. One of the nude male stone torsos from Harappa also appears to be ithyphallic, recalling the *yogisvara* aspect of Shiva, as in later sculptures he is quite often depicted as ithyphallic. Another male statue from Harappa shows a nude male in a dancing pose, reminiscent of Shiva's cosmic dance. All these features indicate that the elements of the latter-day Hindu god Shiva were already there in the Harappa culture. Conical stone objects found in the early excavations at both Mohenjodaro and Harappa have often been referred to as phallic symbols. In the past, these objects were associated with the ring-stones, which were thought to symbolize female reproductive organs. Yet many conical objects appear to have been used as pestles and most ring-stones can be associated with architectural features. Nevertheless, some conical stone pieces, both large and small, may in fact, have been used as phallic symbols. While some may have been gaming pieces, others have a tiny hole in the base, as if they were to be attached or anchored to a base.

The Brahmani bull is associated with Shiva as his *vahana* (mount) and is worshipped even today. Emphasis on the depiction of bulls on seals and terracotta and a scene on a seal where it is carried on shoulders in a procession, can only be explained as being of religious significance. Quite a few small terracotta human figures from Harappa show various postures, identified by some as Yogic exercises.

Mother-goddess

In one of the seals, a deity (?) is shown with a supplicating figure with a sacrificial (?) goat. In the lower row are seven standing figurines, perhaps devotees. Another seal shows an upside-down woman with legs spread apart and a plant coming out of her vagina (Pl. 3-33, upper row). On the other side of the seal is a man holding a scimitar and a seated figure with dishevelled hair (middle row). It has been interpreted as a human sacrifice to a tree-spirit. On another seal, a bull-headed man is attacking a tiger, yet on another, a horned person, recalling the Sumerian mythology of Enkidu and Gilgamesh, has lifted two tigers. The struggle between wild animals and humans is graphically illustrated in a magnificent terracotta tablet discovered in 1995 from Mound ET at Harappa. On one side, the tablet has a narrative motif showing a figure grasping two felines, probably tigers and standing above is an elephant; on the opposite side is a scene depicting the killing of a water buffalo (Kenoyer 1998). Because of the depiction of a clear breast, the figure strangling the tigers must be a female, though the earlier discoveries of this motif on seals from Mohenjodaro definitely show a male figure, which are reminiscent of the carved seals from Mesopotamia that illustrate episodes from the famous Gilgamesh epic. The Mesopotamian motifs show lions being strangled by a hero, whereas the Indus narratives render tigers being strangled by a figure. On the reverse of the same tablet is a narrative scene depicting the killing of a water buffalo. A person, possibly a man, with hair tied in a bun on the back of the head, impales a water buffalo with a barbed spear. The hunter's foot presses down the water buffalo's head as he thrusts the spear into its shoulder. In later Hindu rituals, the water buffalo sacrifice is associated with the worship of the goddess Durga, but on this seal, the sacrifice takes place in the presence of a priest or deity seated in Yogic position. Similar scenes of an individual spearing a water buffalo have been found on other terracotta tablets from both Harappa and Mohenjodaro, but none is associated with the figure strangling two tigers. The seated figure of the hunter wears bangles and a horned and plumed headdress. Above the head of the hunter is a *gharial* (crocodile) that was once common in the Ravi and Indus rivers.

There is an iconic continuity of such traditions. Pupul Jayakar reports that at Jambudvipa in Panchmarhi (Madhya Pradesh) there is a cave-painting depicting a similar subject. Here the hero stands erect, taut with power and majesty, out of his body emerge on either side, two leaping tigers. The rampant tails of the tigers are held taut by the magician-priest. Jayakar questions whether, these are the representatives of ancient magicians, who had special intimacy and control over tigers, the power to summon them their secrets and the capacity to transform themselves into tigers at will? (Pupul Jayakar 1989: 71).

Bhattacharya thinks that the Sumerian mother-goddess whose attributes were later absorbed by Nana of Uruk, Nina of Nineveh, Inanna of Erech, Bau of Lagash, Ninlil of Nippur, Annuit of Akkad, Zarpaint of Babylon, etc., belonged to the same category of the Harappan Magna Mater whose attributes were also specialized by various goddesses of the historic age. Some of the aforesaid deities had evidently an eastward migration in subsequent ages. The goddess Inanna, also known as Nana, Nanai, etc., who was supposed to be the mother of Anaitis and Aphrodite, was able to extend her cult into India through the Scythians and Kusanas in later times. Examples are the Naina Devi of the Kulu valley, Sirmur and Bilaspur, Bibi Nani of Baluchistan, Naini Devi of Nainital, etc. Goddesses of the Ishtar group (Ishtar, Astarte, Astaroth, Atargatis, etc.) might also have contributed something to the later Tantric conception of Tara, as is indicated by the similarity of their names (Bhattacharya 1977: 149-150). It is interesting to note that the most powerful and popular deity of the Himalayas is Nanda, to whom are offered water buffaloes and goats in sacrifice (Agrawal and Kharakwal 1998).

HARP team has found two other broken tablets at Harappa that appear to have been made from the same mould that was used to create the scene of a deity battling two tigers and standing above an elephant. One was found in a room located on the southern slope of Mound ET in 1996 and another example comes from excavations on Mound F in the 1930s. However, the flat obverse of both of these broken tablets does not show the spearing of a buffalo, rather it depicts the more well-known scene showing a tiger looking back over its shoulder at a person sitting on the branch of a tree. Several other flat or twisted rectangular terracotta tablets found at Harappa combine these two narrative scenes of a figure strangling two tigers on one side of a tablet and the tiger looking back over its shoulder at a figure in a tree on the other side.

Both tiger (Pl. 3-5) and pipal are popular motifs on the Harappan seals, imbued with religious significance. Jayakar emphasizes the importance of these symbols in Indian tradition. She relates a Tamil Nadu legend in which Subramaniam, the son of Shiva and the forest mothers, loved an aboriginal virgin, Valli. To win her love he turned himself into a *vengai. Vengai* is the Tamil word for tiger; it is also the name of the neem tree in its male aspect before it flowers. The association of both the male neem tree as well as the tiger with Subramanium is of great interest. Are the Indus valley virgin, the tiger and the neem tree an illustration of an ancient legend, memories of which survive in the Subramaniam story? In ancient magic, the tiger is the guru of initiation. In the great birth seal, he guards the mysteries. In the Indus pictographs, the tiger is never visualized as violent, he never kills. His role is protective. He is in communion with the energy sources of nature. The horned tiger is familiar in Baiga myth. When the Baiga Gunia calls on all the tigers of the world by name, the "horned bagh" is one of them. The tiger is a phallic symbol of wildness and grandeur of the virile, heroic male. The *Atharvaveda* refers to the tiger as the first of all creatures. In Nepal, Bhairava is worshipped in the image of a tiger and in the painting of the Maithili women of Bihar, the tiger mask covers Shiva's loins (Jayakar 1989: 76).

In a seal from Mohenjodaro illustrated by Jayakar (1989: Fig. 7), the woman and the tiger become united, or it is a way of depicting the goddess riding the tiger. Jayakar informs that separated by five thousand years, an amulet worn by primitive people who dwelled on the Narmada river depicts a woman riding a tiger. The body of the tiger and the skirt that covers the body of the goddess are leaf-formed. Plants sprout around the luminous, uprising presence. The arms of the lady are outstretched in the all-including sacred gesture of the goddess. The arms are tendrils, sprouting and extending from the trunk of the body. The fragile nature of the tiger-lady, the interchanging of plant, animal and human, the outstretched arms embracing the cosmos, affirm the mighty roots of the visual tradition. In Indian myth, it is always the lady who rides the tiger (Jayakar 1989: 74).

The semi-nude female terracotta figurines (Pl. 3-23) with their elaborate headdresses have been associated with a mother-goddess cult. In fact, the so-called mother-goddess figures are known from Turkey to Iran starting from the Neolithic times and in India they continue to this day. These figurines could have been associated with the Earth goddess or fertility cults. Mother-goddess cults have been discussed in great detail in a historical perspective by Kosambi (1956, 1962) and Bhattacharya (1977). The act of procreation is a major theme in all ancient religions. Male virility is represented in the nude male figurines, the male animal symbols on seals and stone phallic objects. Kenoyer thinks that female figurines with accentuated breasts and hips represent mother-goddesses and some objects may represent female reproductive organs. Terracotta tablets and inscribed objects show humans engaged in sexual intercourse and others depict animals mating. One of the most controversial seals from Chanhudaro perhaps shows a bull engaged in intercourse with a supine female.

Referring to the Harappan terracotta female figurines and the continuity of the tradition, Jayakar says,

> At the cities of the Indus civilization (2500-1700 BC), the mothers appear with the sacral face of divinity, moulded with deep concern, with the ancient brooding shamanistic face of the seer, elaborate ritual head-dress, serpentine form, long slim legs and slender hips. The ornamentation on ears and neck, the virgin breasts and the girdle that holds the cloth that covers the waist are formed of clay, appliquéd on to the body of the divinity. As the timeless nude Earth Woman, she appears through the centuries headless, sightless, with outstretched arms; the universal gesture of the sacral female in all archaic civilizations. Free of all in essential detail, the awesome lines of her body are tightened and her form abstracted in sacred austerity, as in the early images from the chalcolithic finds of 1200 BC from Nevasa and Bilwali Dhar on the Deccan plateau. She appears with bird, animal or human faces, pinched into shape by hand; with clay pellets applied to eyes, mouth and breasts; with outstretched arms and a hole for the genitals. In later forms, the thighs and breasts of the sacred lady grow rounded and heavy; she becomes synonymous with the vessel of plenty; her heavy girdle accentuates her pubic triangle.... In her manifestation as the Great Mother, creator and destroyer, she is conceived in the northern river valleys as woman with virgin breasts and massive thighs, holding a baby in one hand and a cup of blood to fecundate the Earth in the other. These fired clay images of the Mother date from around 2nd century AD. The conception is monumental. The body is moulded by hand; the texture of the clay is uneven. The massive arms have writhes of clay coiled around them. The body and ornaments are pitted with holes. The face of the mother is a grim mask; the eyes are elongated; the nose is a bird's beak; the breasts are immature; the feet point backwards, indicating links with rituals of death, magic and fertility. In one of the icons from the Farakka barrage, the face of the mother, with her timeless, passionless mask gazing into eternity, has given place to a terror-devoured face with eyes poignant with the knowledge and agony of death. The arms and legs of this image are broken. A strange horseshoe-shaped clay-strip rests over her breast (Jayakar 1989: 168).

Ardeleanu-Jansen says that evidence from Mohenjodaro suggests that the majority of the terracotta figurines were not isolated finds but were usually associated with other terracotta images. Thus the female figurines were found together with animal representations such as bulls, birds and dogs, but also with monkeys, rams and other female or male figurines. Thus the interpretation according to which they are merely to be regarded as idols of the "Great

Mother-goddess" symbolizing the procreative aspects appears to be too simplified. From the results gathered so far, it is apparent that we have to base our interpretation on a combination of two main factors, namely the iconographical diversity of the female figurines themselves and the range of other human and animal terracotta figurines associated with them. Taken together, these factors indicate an ideological sophistication, which goes far beyond the familiar fertility/maternity complex (Ardeleanu-Jansen 1988).

Explaining the use of such female terracotta, Jayakar says,

> Fired or left unbaked, depending on the rituals for which they were intended, these icons of the Mothers, the holders of the secret of the Earth, epitomised magical rites of agriculture, fertility, life and death. At the time of sowing of seed and harvesting and in rituals to dead, icons of the virgin Mothers were made of clay, installed, worshipped and then cast into the waters, or offered to ancient sites of the goddess—to caves, clearings in forests, or to trees or abandoned at village boundaries. By their very nature impermanent, the Earth Mothers could not be kept under a householder's roof except for short ritual purposes (Jayakar 1989: 168).

Ardeleanu-Jansen says that another factor to be considered is that the range of representational subjects and iconographical diversity is complemented by the contemporaneous use of different figurine types. The figurines may have been regarded as substitute symbols for conception in a complex pantheon. We should not forget that a whole cosmos of conceptions regarding divine beings emerged from the subcontinent. Finally, it should also be remembered, that apart from the diversity in the terracotta art from Mohenjodaro, it is still an interesting and perhaps significant point of evidence that no temples or other monumental effigies of a monumentalized ideology have been found so far (Ardeleanu-Jansen 1988).

Quite a few stone statues have been found from Mohenjodaro, which depict a seated male, modelled in a hieratic style (Pl. 3-4). A terracotta head from Kalibangan is also stylistically similar to it. It has been suggested that he represents the priest king.

At Kalibangan and Lothal, however, figurines are conspicuous by their absence despite very extensive excavations at these sites. Seven fire-altars in a row were found on the Citadel at Kalibangan, associated with a sacrificial pit containing animal bones. A small structure outside the settlement housed five such altars. Each house also seems to have had such an altar. At Lothal too several fire-altars are reported, though a little different from those of Kalibangan. No such structures were reported from the main Indus sites. It may be that some sort of fire-worship was in vogue in Rajasthan and Gujarat but no iconic worship seems to be prevalent.

Water Ablution

Concern for cleanliness, bath and ablution is traditional in India. Pious people take bath daily with ice-cold water even in winter and then offer prayers. Elaborate provisions of drains on the Kalibangan platforms and the Great Bath of Mohenjodaro may be the beginning of these ablutionary rituals. Water is essential for life and all societies have a special reverence for the rains. Pure drinking water and the proper disposal of polluted water were important concerns for the Indus cities. At most sites, wells were dug to provide water for the inhabitants. The number ofwells at Mohenjodaro appears to exceed the normal needs of a large urban centre. At Harappa, there are fewer wells, suggesting that there were other sources for water, but at both sites, bathing platforms were found in every block of houses. When considered along with the massive construction known as the Great Bath (Pls. 3-6, -7) at Mohenjodaro, we assume that bathing and the purity of water may have had specific ritual significance in the Indus cities. This high regard for water and bathing is complemented by concern for the removal of polluted water and sewage. The Indus valley civilization is not the only culture with concerns for the purity of water sources, but it is the first urban culture to develop specialized drainage technology throughout the entire urban settlement. Ardeleanu-Jansen says,

> The sheer dimensions of the Great Bath in Mohenjodaro can be taken as proportional to the importance of ritual cleanings in the life of the town. The frequency of bathing platforms in the dwelling-houses of the "Lower Town" would suggest that such ritual cleansings were so inherent to Harappan society that they were likewise primarily the private domestic concern of the inhabitants, the Great Bath being reserved either for more formal, ceremonial occasions or for a particular population group (Ardeleanu-Jansen 1988).

We can now discuss the religious motifs under three main heads: trees, horned deities and other motifs.

Sacred Trees

Of all the religious symbols, pipal seems to be the most popular and potent. It continues to be of special significance at religious places like temples. No temple can afford to be without a pipal tree even today. Cutting a pipal tree or its branches is still a taboo. Kenoyer (1998) in his very interesting book, *Ancient Cities of the Indus Valley Civilization*, giving detailed description of ritualistic objects, becomes poetic in describing the virtues of pipal,

> Deep in the jungle, the pipal tree still provides a natural sanctuary for animals. The red figs sprouting profusely from the trunk and branches attract deer and monkeys. Birds and honeybees live in the protective foliage, while snakes, rodents and a host of insects live in the hollows of its roots and trunk. Two related trees, the pipal (*Ficus religiosa*) with a heart-shaped pipal leaf and the banyan (*Ficus indica*) with a long oval leaf, are found throughout the Indus valley.

Even in the Early Harappan period, heart-shaped pipal leaves, often arranged in groups of three, were commonly painted on small jars and continued into the Harappan phase as elaborate paintings of the pipal tree and its wide, spreading branches on both large storage jars and smaller vessels. In narrative terracotta tablets, human figures with water jars bow before the tree. On other tablets and seals, deities emerge from the centre of a pipal tree or stand under an arch of pipal leaves. Many horned deities wear a distinctive headdress comprising three heart-shaped pipal leaves. As we have not been able to decipher the script so far, the specific meaning of this symbol during the Indus period can only be inferred by examining its meaning in later cultures (Kenoyer 1998).

Let us have a brief look at the myths and traditions associated with pipal and *bata* (*Ficus indica*/banyan) trees.

Both pipal and *bata* (banyan) trees are very important in Indian mythological tradition. Kosambi writes,

> The Pipal (*Ficus religiosa*) has been worshipped throughout India with unbroken continuity from prehistory, long before the Buddha found enlightenment, beneath its boughs. The local name for the god of the Pipal tree is *munjaba*, specially a god of small children before investiture. The Vata (*Ficus bangalensis*) is associated with the devoted Savitri who reclaimed her husband from death, hence becomes the patron deity of all good wives. These two wild fig trees were edible totems, like the tastier and more digestible Udumbara (*Ficus clomerata*) of the same class. We know this from names like *Paippalada* = Pipal eater. *Audumbara* =

descendants of Udumbara marks a well-known historical tribe whose coins bear the mark of that sacred tree (Kosambi 1956: 38).

"Trees are also associated with the *Apsarasas*. In the later *Samhitas* the sphere of the *Apsarasas* extends to the Earth and in particular to trees. They are spoken of as inhabiting banyans (*nyagrodha*) and sacred fig-tree (*asvatha*), in which their cymbals and lutes resound. Elsewhere the same trees as well as other varieties of the fig tree (*udumbara* and *plaksa*) are said to be the house of *Gandharvas* and *Apsarasas*. The *Gandharvas* and *Apsarasas* in such trees are entreated to be propitious to a passing wedding procession" (Macdonell 1995: 134). Regarding tree worship, G.C. Pande writes, "Yaksha worship represents, on the popular level, a continuation of pre-Aryan religion. The Yakshas were spirits, often connected with trees and granted worldly desire, especially progeny and wealth", (Pande 1995: 318).

Kosambi also points to the evil aspects of the tree gods,

> Traders setting out on their travels made animal sacrifices to some deity and vowed to make more if the journey were profitable; the vows were regularly fulfilled. Apparently, such deities were associated with some tree outside the village, sometimes in a grove or the dense jungle. In a Jataka story, men make the sacrifices to the yakkhas (Sanskrit=*Yaksha*) at crossways (*caccara-raccha*) with fish, flesh and wine in bowls or sherds; this resembles the sacrifice to Rudra and the goblins.... King Pasenadi of Kosala is terrified by sixteen ominous dreams in a single night; the Brahmins advise him to make extensive blood sacrifices at every crossway.... In fact, the yakkhas often ate human beings (among them unwary traders) who entered certain localities, which Vessavana as the chief of the demons had assigned, to a particular yakkha or demoness. Many *Jatakas* narrate how the Bodhisattva converted such goblins to a simpler diet and kindlier way of life, which has to be interpreted to mean that human sacrifice went out of general fashion (except among forest tribes) before the time of the Buddha. The specially cruel warrior-king makes sacrifice of ksatriya prisoners to a Nigrodha (*Ficus indica*) tree's deity in another Jataka story in order to take the besieged city of Taxila (Kosambi 1956: 103-104).

Kenoyer remarks, two thousand years after the foundation of the Indus cities, the Lord Buddha attained enlightenment under a banyan or bodhi tree. In Pakistan, even the tombs of Muslim saints are found under the protective branches of a pipal tree.

In a famous seal from Mohenjodaro, the pipal tree is divided into two main branches, each with three leaves and the deity wears a horned headdress with a curved branch emerging from the centre. In front of the deity is a kneeling worshipper also wearing a horned headdress offering perhaps a human head placed on a stool. Behind the figure is a giant ram and along the top is a series of script signs that may identify the ritual for the deity. In the lower register is a procession of seven robed figures. If animal figurines were used as votive offerings substituting for actual animal sacrifice, some human figurines may have served a similar function. Human sacrifice is also indicated by the fragmentary male figurine found in recent excavations at Harappa, which appears to have his arms pressed to the back as if they had been bound. A more common type of figurine shows a seated male with legs together and hands clasped at the knees. This type of figurine has been interpreted as a worshipper, but perhaps it represents a sacrificial victim with hands and feet tied together (Kenoyer 1998).

Such practices, with roots in the Indus religion, continued even in historical times. Bhattacharya (1977: 164) reports, "Self-mutilation was probably a feature of the worship of the goddess during the Pallava and early Chola period, as is evident from several Pallava panels where the devotee is shown to offer his own head. This custom might have some bearing on the later conception of Chinnamasta. A late Pallava inscription upon a slab refers to a warrior who had offered his own head to the goddess and the slab itself contains a relief of that act". Bhattacharya (1977: 65) also refers to such practices in Assam, "When the new temple of Kamakhya was opened, the occasion was celebrated by the immolation of no less than a hundred and forty men, whose heads were offered to the goddess on salvers made of copper".

Kenoyer informs that a recently discovered terracotta tablet from Mound ET at Harappa portrays a deity standing beneath a curved arch of 13 pipal leaves. One other example from Harappa has an arch of 13 leaves; three smaller tablets have seven- and eight-leafed arches. The number of leaves must be significant, especially the number 13, which is generally associated with exceptional power in the subcontinent. There are 13 full moons in a year and in the Vedic literature the 13 sacrifice is considered especially beneficial. Kenoyer suggests that although the rituals depicted on the seals and tablets may have been practised by only the higher classes or priests, they appear to have been carried out in the open under a pipal tree. The purpose of public rituals is often to teach people the power of the deities and to legitimize the power of the rulers who worship the deities. People coming to the larger urban centres to trade and participate in seasonal festivals and rituals, returned to their villages and towns carrying stories about the gods and rulers of the city along with trade goods. The narrative amulets and terracotta figurines may have been commemorative mementos of such events.

Horned Deities (Pl. 3-35)

Male terracotta figurines are usually depicted nude, but wearing turbans or headdresses, neck ornaments and occasionally bangles. Similar postures are represented on seals and moulded tablets, where male figures stand on the ground or in a tree. The standing figure is usually interpreted as a deity, the kneeling figure as a worshipper or priest. A unique posture found only on seals and moulded tablets shows a male with horned headdress seated in a Yogic position, with legs spread wide and heels pressed to the groin. The images of the Buddha and various Hindu deities, including Shiva, are often shown in the famous Yogic posture called *padmasana*. The posture we see on the Indus seals can be correlated with a difficult position of highly advanced Yoga called *mulabandhasana* (Kenoyer 1998).

One of the most common motifs in Indus ritual art is the image of a bearded man wearing a headdress of horns, which has a triple-leafed branch sprouting from the centre. This human-like spirit combined with two of the most fearsome wild animals and the sacred pipal tree produces a complex image that appears for the first time in the Indus cities. Combined together with the tiger, this new motif probably represents a synthesis of various beliefs or perhaps the culmination of a long process of religious development. In fact, the horned deity is a common motif on pottery. Note the horned deity (number 18; Fig. 3-11) that has been on found even in a Kot Dijian pot from the Neolithic site of Burzahom. From Kalibangan a terracotta cake shows a horned deity too (Pl. 3-11).

Some of the horned deities could as well be female, though most horned deities are bearded and therefore, male. One seal from Mohenjodaro shows a bull-horned deity with claw-like hands attacking a horned tiger. The deity has the hindquarters and tail of a bull, but the torso is human, with a prominent pectoral breast in profile. If this is a female deity, it indicates that the horned deity had both male and female aspects. In later Hinduism the male principle, shakta and female principle, shakti, both are important and complementary.

We can identify from the Indus period two distinct horned deities found as terracotta figurines or carved onto seals. Some seated figures with horned headdresses appear to have additional faces carved at the side of the head, suggesting that this deity had three or even four heads, if there was a face at the back of the head. It is tempting to associate this many-faced deity with later Hindu images of Shiva. The human image with bull's horns is generally depicted with bull's tail and hoofed hind legs, but arms with human hands or tiger's claws. On copper tablets from Mohenjodaro, this figure also has a tail and runs with a bow in one hand and arrows in the other. This archer or hunter may represent a deity or simply the common practice of wearing camouflage while stalking game. However, such costumes may also have been worn in ritual dances or processions to represent natural or supernatural powers. The second important horned deity wears a central branch as a headdress in addition to the wide, spreading horns of the water buffalo. The most famous representation of this image is on a seal from Mohenjodaro that shows a male deity seated in Yogic position with erect phallus (Pl. 3-35). The deity is heavily adorned with bangles on both arms and a series of graduated necklaces reaching to his waist. In various contexts and narrative motifs, animals surround the deity: a rhinoceros, a water buffalo, an elephant and a tiger indicate that this deity or different deities depicted in similar manner were the focus of considerable worship and sacrifice. A single line of the undeciphered Indus script (in reverse) is carved along the top of the seal. This seated figure has been referred to as "proto-Shiva" because of its similarity to later iconography of the deity Shiva from the Hindu pantheon. There are similarities in the iconography, but the meaning relayed may have been significantly different. Whereas many later Hindu deities may have had their roots in earlier beliefs of the Indus valley or other indigenous communities living in the subcontinent, any specific connections between the horned figure on the Indus seals and later Hindu deities is difficult to prove (Kenoyer 1998).

From the DK-G area of Mohenjodaro were found two other seals with horned deities wearing bangles and seated in Yogic position. One is a relatively simple figure seated on a throne with legs carved in the shape of bovine hooves (Pl. 3-35). The face is not clear, but there appear to be additional faces on each side, making it a second example of the three-faced deity. The carving of the body shows well-defined pectoral muscles and stylized male genitalia. The headdress has three pipal leaves branching out of the centre and two curving horns on either side. But not all seals or moulded tablets picture this deity with three faces. On one example from Mohenjodaro, the face is shown in profile with a massive braid of hair projecting to the back. A star is carved in the centre of each curving horn and the stylized branch with five leaves curls up from the centre of the headdress. Both arms are covered with bangles; the deity is nude, seated with legs positioned in the standard Yogic pose. On the other seals, the seated deity is witness to the killing or sacrifice of a water buffalo. Almost identical figures are found on other moulded terracotta tablets from Mohenjodaro as well as from Harappa. Two recently discovered tablets from Harappa show this deity on a throne with a reed house or temple at one side. The various contexts and narrative motifs indicate that this deity was predominantly important both for sacrifice and worship.

Most terracotta figurines of the deity are broken, but even these fragmentary pieces give a sense of the powerful beauty of the deity. Many examples of terracotta buffalo horns have been found with holes for attaching them to headdress. Generally these horns are broken, but complete horns may have been from 10 to 20 cm in length. A unique aspect of this

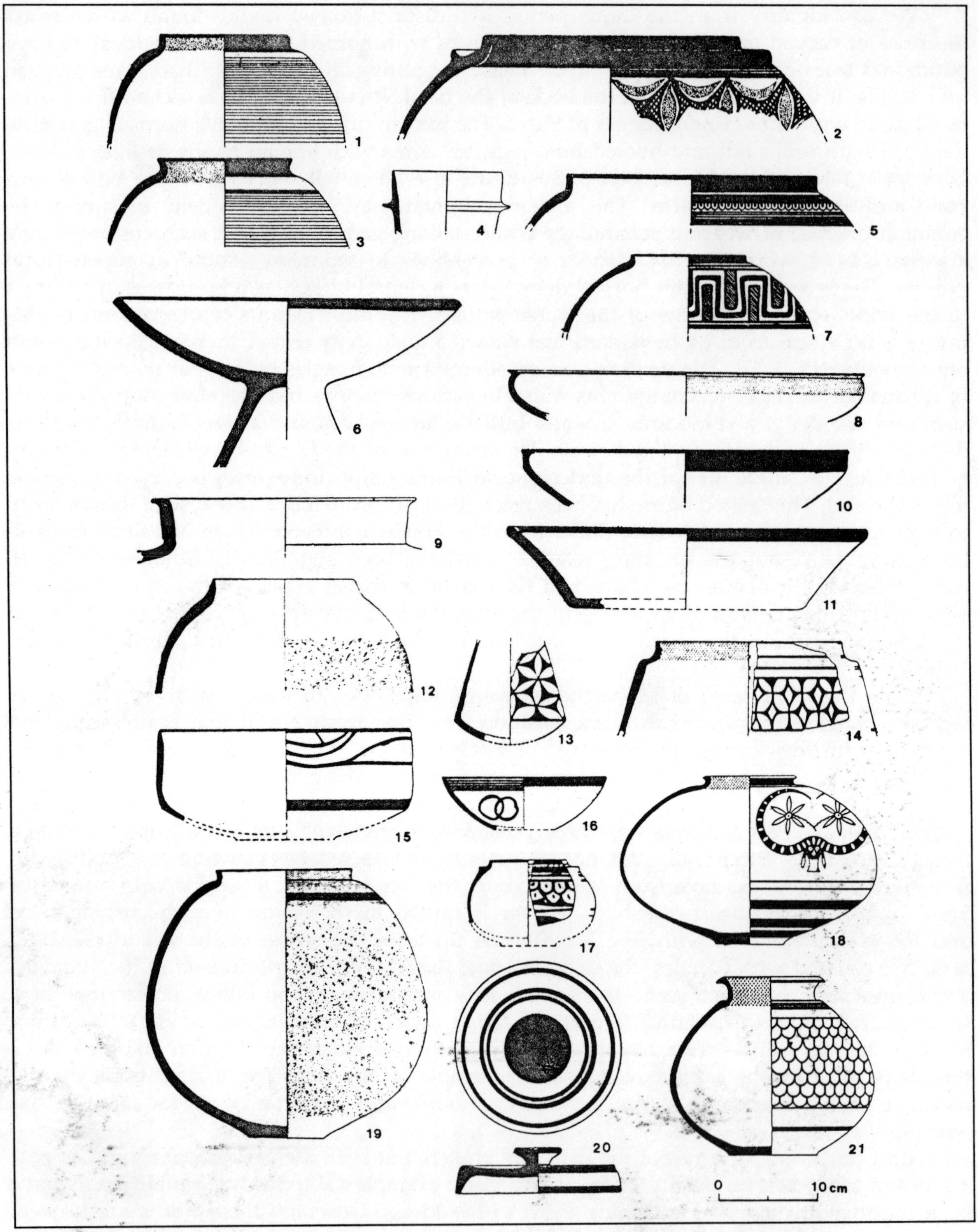

Fig. 3-11. Typical Kot Dijian pottery. Note the horned deity (No. 18).

figurine is the goat-like beard that replaces the normal wide, spreading beard. The goat-like beard may indicate a specific aspect of the deity that is correlated to a myth or cult associated with the wild goat, often depicted on the seals. Such terracotta horns may have been attached to actual headdresses worn by puppets or child performers. Full-sized headdresses may have used actual horns, as is still the practice among the Muria Gond communities in Central India (Kenoyer 1998).

Sacred Motifs and Symbols

No other early civilization used bangles to the extent the Indus people did. Bangles often serve as a symbol of protection or control. A warrior wears bangles to protect the wrist and arm in battle, while a woman wears bangles to protect her family and assure the long life of her husband. The common people probably wore simple circlets of clay, while the more affluent used shell, bronze and gold bangles.

The endless-knot motif (Parpola calls it "Brahma's knot") was found on copper tablets at Mohenjodaro and may have been an important symbol of a specific cult or community. Related designs are found on tablets and seals. Traditional Hindu women continue to paint similar ritual designs to protect and purify the home. In the *rangoli/alpana* paintings this motif is still popular in the Central Himalayas. Swastika is a more common symbol. The intersecting circle, fish-scale design, hatched triangle, checkerboard design and the circle-and-dot motifs are among the more common geometric motifs on pottery. Many of these designs are repeated on seals, in shell inlay or carved on ivory gaming pieces and even on bathtubs or tiles.

Circles and wavy lines are commonly painted on pottery as part of the design, but they also may have had ritual significance as a protective bond. Rings and wavy rings that were not used as body ornaments were made of stone, shell and clay. Many earlier scholars identified these objects as female fertility symbols, but they could have had varied uses and meanings. The shell wavy rings probably decorated the handle of a staff or baton. Larger stone rings were used as column bases at the site of Dholavira and numerous large ring-stones have been found at Mohenjodaro and Harappa. At Harappa, excavators recently found wavy ring-stone fragments near the main gateway at the south-eastern corner of Mound E, possibly parts of massive pillars in the gateway area. The use as a pillar component does not diminish the symbolic significance of these objects, for in prominent contexts such as gateways, they would have been seen by everyone entering or leaving the city.

Human-Animal Deities

Many of the latter-day syncretistic Hindu gods like *Narsingh Avtar*, *Varah Avtar* may have roots in the Indus religion, where human and animal figures occur in various combinations. A tiger with a man's bearded head contrasts with a seated cat-like animal with a woman's head. Some figures have human heads and animal bodies; others have animal heads and human bodies.

Kenoyer mentions another category of human-animal figurines probably used in puppet shows to amuse and teach the public. One of the most famous figures has a dog-like head and a pot-bellied human body with holes for attaching moveable arms. A long penis was once attached under the bulging belly and a broken tail can be seen at the back of the figure. A hole in the base indicates that it was attached to a stick, probably to allow a puppeteer to manipulate the figure while sitting behind a screen. Ithyphallic caricatures, common in most societies, usually attract and keep the crowd's attention in between more serious presentations. More serious figurines that also may have been used as puppets or for special rituals combine several different forms of animals. The two examples of such figurines so far discovered come from the site of Nausharo, Pakistan. Although Nausharo has the only terracotta figurines of multiple animals, multiple-headed animals are found on seals from most of the larger sites. One square seal from Mohenjodaro shows a triple-headed combination of important totemic animals: the bull, the unicorn and the antelope.

A cylindrical seal from the site of Kalibangan, in Rajasthan, depicts two men fighting over a woman, with long braided hair and bangles on each hand, who wears a long skirt. While trying to spear each other, the men grab the woman's hands and their spears form an arch over her head. In the background what may be a female deity with the body of a tiger and the horns of a Markhor goat watches. Kenoyer suggests that since the Indus deities combine the most important totemic and plant motifs, they must be important symbols of Indus religious integration.

Miniature glazed faience figurines of seated rams have a perforation through the body so they could be worn as amulets. The white glazed surface is generally quite thick and well preserved, but it conceals the delicate modelling of the face. These figurines have been found at Mohenjodaro, Harappa and Nausharo. Bull and water buffalo figurines made from terracotta are quite common.

Domestic and wild animals were probably sacrificed for specific Indus rituals, as indicated by narrative scenes on tablets, such as the killing of a water buffalo or the scene of a man grappling with a short-horned and humpless bull. Annually at the end of the rainy season, in Central Himalayas, buffaloes are sacrificed even today to appease Nanda goddess, which Bhattacharya traces from Mesopotamia, as noted above.

Ritual Objects

The most common object is the ritual-offering stand that has been interpreted variously as a sacred filter for making an intoxicating concoction or an incense-burner. Shallow basins or feeding troughs also may have had some ritual significance as a container for food offerings to totemic animals.

Shell ladles and libation vessels may have been used for pouring sacred offerings of water, milk, oil or butter. Another ritual utensil is the libation vessel made from the conch shell *Turbinella pyrum*. Several examples of these distinctive vessels have been found at Mohenjodaro and one example made from another shell specie, *Fasciolaria trapezium*, was found at the nearby site of Chanhudaro. Even today, this type of libation vessel is used throughout the subcontinent for ritual libations and for dispensing medicinal preparations. Trumpets made from horn or shell are used even today on important occasions. An important category of ritual paraphernalia is pottery vessels for holding sacred water or offerings. Another ritual object made from the conch shell *Turbinelia pyrum* is a trumpet that has a mouthpiece chipped at the apex of the shell. This unique example of a conch-shell trumpet was found at Harappa.

Thus we see that, a large number of religious practices and rituals of the present-day have their roots in the Indus civilization.

BURIALS

The normal Harappan burial custom was inhumation in unlined pits, head pointing north, though there is some variation (Pl. 3-36,-37). Only at Ropar the direction is north-west. About 20 pots (sometimes even up to 40) were put as the funerary appendage. Personal ornaments like rings, earrings, necklaces, anklets, bangles and at times copper mirrors were also found with the burials. They were provided with meat and drink for the after-life too as the remains on the pots would have us believe. Of course, in their furnishings, the Harappan graves stand nowhere in comparison to the macabre splendour of the Ur graves.

Very rarely were graves lined with bricks; one such example of each is known from Harappa, Lothal and Kalibangan. This reminds one of the Nal graves of south Baluchistan. A unique example from the Harappan R-37 cemetery has a coffin of rosewood with a lid of deodar (*Cedrus deodara*). Deodar must have been imported from the Himalayas, a few 100 km. away. The lady was provided with 37 pots, but nothing else was lavish about it. The coffin burials may be the standard among elite communities, whereas interpretation of the casual disposal depends on the specific details of preservation and stratigraphy. Some individuals were buried with great care and preparation, wrapped in a shroud and placed in a wooden coffin. But, in some instances, a corpse was thrown into an open pit filled with previously disturbed bones and broken pottery. As mentioned above, Sir Mortimer Wheeler's excavations in 1946 recovered some fragments of wood from a coffin and shroud that were identified as rosewood (*Dalbergia latifolia*) and cedar (*Cedrus deodara*) respectively. In more recent excavations, coffins were visible as dark stains that could be measured, but no traces of wood remained. Most coffins were approximately 0.50 m wide, 1.7 to 1.9 m long and were made of boards that were 2 to 3 cm thick. Traces of a carbonized lid or shroud were found on one individual and another corpse appeared to have been tightly wrapped with cloth, but no traces of the cloth or matting could be recovered.

After the coffin had been interred, the entire pit was filled with earth, covering the burial and pottery offerings. There were no traces of cenotaphs or grave markers, but the cemetery area may have been marked by wooden markers or low mounds of earth. Two mud brick buildings in the cemetery at Harappa may have been used for rituals or bathing the body.

Kalibangan provided other varieties of burial besides the inhumation type. In one case, urns were placed inside circular or oval pits. In the other, there was a rectangular-ovalish pit, with the longer axis directed north-south, containing only pots. No skeletal remains were found in either type of the burial (Pl. 3-13). The grave-goods in all the three types are characteristically Harappan. But the urn burials are confined to an area north of the inhumation graves. One can only guess the sociological import of such differences in the funerary customs. The Harappan cemeteries were away from the settlement, unlike the Chalcolithic cultures of Central India and the Deccan where burials were right below the house floors.

Scattered burials, as well as discrete cemeteries, have been found at sites in each of the major regions, but most cemeteries are small and do not represent all of local inhabitants. It is possible that only certain groups practised burial while others were disposed of by other means. The lack of evidence for differential dietary stress among the individuals buried at Harappa may indicate that the people were healthy and well fed, probably from among the upper classes. However, there are variations in the number of funerary offerings and ornaments with each burial, possibly indicating minor differences in social or ritual status.

At Harappa, the dead were usually buried in deep rectangular graves, sometimes lined with mud bricks. Pottery typical of that used in the home was placed at the bottom of the grave shaft. These vessels may have been filled with food and drink for use in the after-life, but due to the poor preservation of organic material in the tropics, no traces have been preserved inside the vessels. At Harappa where many burials have been excavated, most graves show that the pottery was covered with a layer of soil and then the coffin was placed on top of this partially filled grave shaft. The burials of the Indus people provide the most direct evidence for specific rituals and religious beliefs. Simple grave offerings of pottery suggest a belief in life after death and the inclusion of modest personal ornaments may have served to identify the social and ritual status of the individual in the other world (Pl. 3-14). No seals or inscribed objects have been found with burials and presumably high-value objects such as copper tools and ornaments of gold and long carnelian beads are conspicuously absent.

In the cemetery at Harappa, the skeletons were buried one on top of the other and the later burials often cut through the graves of earlier individuals. Thus the cemetery at Harappa appears to have been used by a limited group, possibly all belonging to a single kinship group or clan. This may suggest that the burial ground itself was treated as a sacred place and that all members of a single group wanted to be buried close together. Later grave diggings disturbed many earlier burials. In some instances, relatively fresh burials were disinterred and partly decomposed corpses were thrown into adjacent pits to make room for new burials. Kenoyer notes that in several of the disturbed female burials, the shell bangles traditionally worn on the left arm of adult women were missing. Unlike the grave robbers of ancient Egypt, who systematically robbed the gold-filled tombs of the wealthy, the meagre grave goods in the Harappan burials (Pl. 3-14) did not leave the grave-diggers much to steal. People of the same kinship group would hardly rob or disturb the burials of their relatives or ancestors, but labourers of a different community might pilfer the disturbed tombs as they dug new ones.

Shell bangles and anklets made of steatite disc beads were commonly buried with adult women. A few beads of lapis lazuli, carnelian or copper have been found with both male and female burials, probably tied around the wrist or on a cord around the waist. Copper rings are found in many burial pits and in one instance a ring was found on the left "ring" finger of what was probably a female burial. The Harappan burials contain very few grave offerings and few ornaments. In South Asia today, ornaments and objects that pertain to marriage, initiations, or protection against magic or illness are seldom passed on to another person, but are broken, burned or buried with the dead. Based on modern analogies we can assume that the ornaments in the Harappan burials were symbolic objects that could not be passed on to the next generation.

The adult females wore a truncated cylindrical amulet, usually made of black stone, but other examples have been found in green serpentine, steatite or faience. The association with adult women suggests that this ornament identified married women or adult women who belonged to a specific cult. A flattened conical ornament with a groove running along the perimeter may have been a variant of this type of amulet and one example from Mohenjodaro was set in a copper frame or pendant. Today typical neck ornaments like *magalsutras* denote marital status of women. A copper/bronze mirror accompanied several adult female burials at Harappa. Because metal mirrors can be recycled and have intrinsic market value, their inclusion with pottery and personal amulets must have some specific ritual significance. Mirrors would have been an essential toiletry item during a woman's life. If the household pottery with food offerings indicates a belief in an after-life, then it is not surprising to find mirrors, which also would have been necessary for everyday grooming in the next life. However, it is also possible that mirrors were used in magical rituals and were buried for superstitious reasons. Whatever the explanation, these copper/bronze mirrors were not passed on to the next generation and were not recycled. Quoting the example of Central Asia and Ladakh, Ratnagar (2000: 76) says that mirrors were used to see the soul of the dead being. As most of the mirrors have been found only in graves, it may have some magical value.

In contrast, generally the male burials have modest funerary offerings, but as an exception two adult men at Harappa were buried with valuable personal ornaments. An adult male was also entombed in a coffin with more than a dozen vessels arranged at the head of the pit and additional vessels along the side. A broken shell bangle was found on his left wrist and near the right hand was a single carnelian bead. An unusual hair ornament was found along the right side at the back of his head, where we would expect to find long hair tied into a double bun like those on the stone sculptures and seals. This ornament was made out of numerous strands of tiny steatite micro-beads twisted together in circlets or bunches, with two or three shell rings and a jasper bead. One older man was wearing a long necklace of 340 graduated steatite beads and three separate pendant beads made of natural stone and three gold beads; he was wrapped in a shroud and entombed in a coffin surrounded by pottery offerings. A single copper bead was found at his waist, though such ornaments may have had some commercial value, they were buried with the owner and not passed on to another individual. The fact that the stone beads were polished and rounded from long use suggests that they may have been worn for a very long time, possibly as amulets. The most prominent pendant bead is made of a rare variety of onyx with natural eye designs in alternating shades of red, white, tan and green. Gold beads framed this important ornament. The other two stone beads were made of banded jasper and turquoise, with a single gold bead at one end of the turquoise bead.

Such micro-bead hair ornaments may have been worn as a crown or ritual headdress during life; it evidently could not be passed on to a surviving relative or clan leader. The value of such steatite bead ornaments can only be appreciated when the techniques of manufacture are considered. Even today, it is difficult to make glass beads of this size and no one has been able to replicate convincingly the techniques used by the ancient Harappans. Each of the thousands of tiny steatite beads is approximately 1 mm in diameter and 1 mm in length. Some scholars suggest that the beads were made individually by delicate drilling and grinding, while others propose that they were made from a steatite paste that was extruded like a hollow noodle and then cut into short segments.

The Harappan burials reflect a very practical attitude towards material wealth and symbols. Precious metals, gold and valuable stone beads were generally kept in circulation among the living, while only the most essential personal objects were buried with the dead: shell bangles, beads with eye designs, steatite disc beads and mirrors. As a whole, the Harappan burial customs further reinforce the importance of ornaments and public symbols to define social and ritual status among the living (Kenoyer 1998).

SCRIPT

The Harappan seals, sealings and pots have legends in a pictographic script comprising some four hundred signs (Pls. 3-18, -32, -33). No evolution in the script throughout the centuries has been reported. Such, a large number of signs preclude the possibility of it being an alphabetic script. But Rao (1973) finds only fifty-two basic signs in the total of the four hundred. He thinks that it is a syllabic-cum-alphabetic script, which was disciplined into an alphabetic one in *c.* 1500 BC. The script does not seem to bear any resemblance either to its contemporary foreign scripts or to the subsequent scripts of India. In the absence of long inscriptions, where recurrent formations could be studied and of bilingual inscriptions, a plethora of claims of decipherment have cropped up and it is not easy to accept one claim or another. The Indus script thus continues to be an enigma even today.

The most comprehensive and systematic study of the Indus script today is Asko Parpola's *Deciphering the Indus Script* (Parpola 1994), though agreement among scholars still eludes us. Tracing the history of the attempts at deciphering the Indus script, Parpola (1994) says that all kinds of answers have been offered to the questions posed by unsolved scripts ever since Graeco-Roman times. Thus in 1580, Goropius Beccanus of Amsterdam tried to prove that the language of the ancient Egyptian was Dutch! In the case of Indus script, connections have been sought with the manuscripts of the Lolos living in southern China and in South-East Asia, dating back to the 16th century AD; with proto-Elamite accounting tablets; with ideograms carved some two centuries ago on easter Island in the south-eastern Pacific Ocean; with Etruscan pot-marks; with the numeral system of primitive Indonesian; with Egyptian, Minoan and Hittite hieroglyphs; with the auspicious symbols carved on a "footprint of the Buddha" in the Maldivian archipelago; and with the glyphs of ancient Central America.

But Parpola does not dismiss them as totally useless and finds a useful idea in them too! To point out clearly how those schemes are mistaken may help to eliminate them from future work on the subject. For example, Sir Alexander Cunningham (1875), considered the first published Indus seal to be a foreign import because the bull carved on it lacked a hump and later (1877) supposed that it might bear "archaic Indian letters of as early an age as Buddha himself". Another example is the "Indo-Sumerian" hypothesis prevalent shortly after the discovery of the Indus civilization. In 1925, it provided a natural starting-point for L.A. Waddell, a Tibetologist, who "read" all the published inscriptions in his book, *The Indo-Sumerian Seals Deciphered*. Waddell read the resulting sequences as "revised forms" of the names of Sumerian and Aryan kings mentioned in the Vedas and in Sanskrit epics. Waddell's method is among those most often used in attempts at decipherment. Transferring the phonetic values of signs in a known script to similar-looking signs in an unknown one is likely to work only if the two scripts are genetically closely related and even then similar signs may have quite different phonetic values.

A favourite approach of many Indian scholars has been to interpret an Indus sign pictorially and then assign it a syllabic value taken from the corresponding word of a chosen language by the principle of acrophony. Nationalistic ideas make it difficult for some North Indians to admit even the possibility of the Indus civilization being pre-Aryan; they deny the very concept of Aryan immigration and insist that the Harappan and Vedic cultures are one and the same. So the language chosen has usually been Sanskrit (Parpola 1994).

On the basis of superficial similarities, Hrozny derived the Indus script from the Hittite hieroglyphs (which actually are a thousand years younger!). Sir John Marshall (1924) was the first to suggest that the Indus civilization was non-Aryan and that its language most probably belonged to the Dravidian family. Dravidian languages are nowadays spoken mainly in South India, where Tamil has a literary history of two Millennia.

Father Heras correctly thought that it would be possible to reconstruct proto-Dravidian by comparing its surviving daughter languages, though his own efforts to do so proved amateurish. Father Heras in his book *Studies in proto-Indo-Mediterranean Culture* (1953), tried to reconstruct it as a proto-Dravidian language. There is no independent means of checking his meanings. Heras characterizes the Indus script as a "pictophonographic" writing system, whose signs "do not stand for syllables and much less for consonant sounds only, but express full words". In practice, however, he entertains quasi-phonological assumptions about the nature of the Indus script, which are in conflict with the established history of writing. His analysis of the signs and his method of determining their phonetic value (from their pictorial shape, or from similar-looking signs in other scripts) has its own logic, but cannot be accepted, because it is not supported by the principles on which known scripts are based.

Thus the Indus script has been deciphered as Indo-Sumerian, Hittite, Indo-Aryan, Dravidian, etc. Meriggi tried to use the Dravidian language of Brahui, spoken in Baluchistan, to decipher the Indus script but later on gave up.

In 1964, the Russian scholar Knorozov and his team launched a more scientific attempt at decipherment. They supposed the Indus script to be Logo-syllabic type rather than syllabic or alphabetic. They did a computer analysis of the Indus signs and considered the high frequency signs as grammatical markers and signs with low frequency as root morphemes, like in the Egyptian. With the help of interval statistics they divided the scripts into blocks of one to five signs corresponding to words of the Indus language. By the structural analysis, the Russian scholars identified the Indus language as belonging to the Dravidian family. Their approach has been criticized for insufficient differentiation between script and language. Kamil Zvelebil (1976: 138) has reviewed the Russian approach in the following words:

> Proof that the readings and translations are correct may be offered only in the following way: (a) either a bilingual inscription or inscriptions will confirm the correctness of the "Dravidian hypothesis"; (b) or, in the absence of a bilingual text, a much greater amount of material must be read, translated and interpreted and this large sum of translated data must form a meaningful, logical and internally consistent corpus of data. Until then, the Dravidian affinity of the proto-Indian language remains only a very attractive and quite plausible hypothesis (Zvelebil in Zide and Zvelebil 1976: 138).

Mahadevan has also interpreted the Indus script as Dravidian. His readings are based on parallels offered by old Tamil descriptions. Parpola thinks that there is nothing inherently improbable in Mahadevan's approach, but his concrete interpretations proposed have failed to produce convincing internal proofs. The attempts by Fairservis have also been called "far-fetched analysis of pictograms".

Thus there are two main groups: one proposing that the Indus script is proto-Dravidian and the other Indo-Aryan. Asko Parpola (1994), Konorozov and others favour a Dravidian affinity, whereas Rao and some others claim it to be an Indo-Aryan language. The arguments and counter-arguments are quite technical and can best be seen in Parpola (1994). To be able to do a systematic decipherment, a comprehensive corpus of concordance has been computer generated by Mahadevan (1977) and the Finnish team (Koskenniemi and Parpola 1979-82). With the publication of *Corpus of Indus Seals and Inscriptions* (Joshi and Parpola 1987), the attempts at deciphering will become easier. In 1992, Franke-Bogte also produced a thorough documentation of the glyptics of Mohenjodaro. M.N. Gupta (pers. comm.) was, however, very critical of these works and has reported many contradictions between the two. He finds about 70 symbols missing from both the works. He severely criticized Mahadevan's "tempered normalized signary" as it has corrupted hundreds of texts beyond recognition. He finds a wasteful repetition of identical texts, at times a single text has been repeated forty times. Despite such reported shortcomings, one feels that such compendia will prove invaluable for research workers.

Parpola (1994) describes the problems of the Indus script as a crossword puzzle. As long as there is no bilingual inscription, we can never be sure. But the probability of correctness increases with the number of interlocking solutions. Though several scholars have been working on the Indus scripts with similar methodology and basic assumptions, there is little consensus on the interpretations. But there are some agreements too between different interpretations and Parpola pleads that they be taken seriously. The debate continues till we have a bilingual or some more compelling evidence to accept a particular reading of the Indus Age scripts.

The direction of the script has now been accepted to be mostly from right to left and not boustrophedon (right to left and then left to right), which is rare. An American comparative historian, Steve Farmer, has recently made a series of startling claims concerning the Harappan "script". At the 2001 Harvard Indology Roundtable, Farmer pointed to a large body of evidence suggesting that Indus inscriptions were not linguistic in nature—and consequently that the Indus valley civilization was not literate, as everyone has assumed since the 1920s.

Paradoxically, Farmer argues that recognition of the non-linguistic nature of Indus inscriptions increases their value, providing us with evidence of a vast ancient society—far larger than Mesopotamia or Egypt—that remained stable for many centuries in preliterate conditions. Many of the striking contrasts between Indus society and their Mesopotamian and Egyptian contemporaries, on this view, make sense as soon as we take literacy out of the picture. Part of Farmer's analysis includes comparison of Indus inscriptions with other non-linguistic symbol systems that served various ritual and political functions outside South Asia.

Farmer's full paper on the inscriptions, including his analysis, their religious-political functions and apparent uses in agricultural rituals, was presented at the 2002 Harvard Indology Roundtable. Below we focus on two central points that Farmer made in his earlier talk:

1. That there were no "lost" Harappan texts of any substantial length written on either durable or perishable materials, as researchers have long argued and
2. That this lack of long texts is explained quite simply by the fact that Indus inscriptions were not linguistic—that for a variety of reasons Indus society was not literate in the usual sense of that term.

Parts of Farmer's arguments arise from comparative history and part from his study of the internal structure of Indus inscriptions. A quick summary of a few of his arguments includes the following; while no single argument proves the case, taken together they seem to provide strong evidence for his views:

1. The "scribal pressures" argument. In all ancient societies that had true scripts and produced genuine manuscript traditions, scribal pressures towards economy in the copying process led to profound transformations in those scripts. In the case of logosyllabic writing systems —the kind usually claimed for the Harappans—this was linked to major changes in writing styles (e.g., to radical simplification of sign shapes and orientations), to a rapid drop in the number of whole-word signs (logograms) and to a major increase in phoneticism as syllable signs replaced those signs. Even when you cannot read a script, markers of these transformations show up in the outward appearance of symbols and in symbol frequencies.

2. Much evidence of "scribal pressures" like this shows up in the cuneiform writing systems developed by the Mesopotamians and in the scripts of the ancient Egyptians, Chinese and Mesoamericans—even when attempts were made to arrest those changes. In contrast, as Marshall, Parpola, Possehl and many others have noted, the Indus symbol system remained remarkably "frozen" in structure over a 700-odd period of history. Recent evidence has emerged of changes of other types in Indus inscriptions, but none that can be remotely compared to the type or scale of the changes noted above. This lack of major change from *c.* 2600-1900 BC is particularly striking when we compare Indus inscriptions with the cuneiform scripts of their trading partners in Mesopotamia, which continued to change dramatically throughout these centuries. The implication is that no "lost" manuscripts on perishable materials were being produced in the background when the Indus seals and other short symbol chains were being engraved on durable materials.
3. Missing longer texts on pottery and potsherds. Every premodern civilization that is known to have produced manuscript traditions also left texts of substantial length behind on pottery or potsherds. This is not the case in Indus inscriptions, where such inscriptions are not longer—and on the average are even shorter—than the brief symbol chains seen on seals and other durable materials, which only average some 4-5 symbols or so long. If the Harappans ever produced long texts on perishable materials, they were the only ancient people—including South Asians in later periods—whoever did so without leaving longer texts behind on pots or potsherds. The implication again is that Indus symbols were not linguistic in nature.
4. Missing longer texts on other durable goods. Every premodern civilization we know that had manuscript traditions also left long texts behind on other kinds of durable goods. Some obvious examples include rock inscriptions, knives, copper and bronze artefacts, architectural inscriptions, stelae and so on. Again, evidence like this is entirely lacking in the Indus valley. The people of the Indus valley left brief chains of symbols behind on copperplates, terracotta cones, ivory plaques, stone balls, earthenware bangles, tools and weapons and similar durable materials. But the longest of these is even shorter than the longest seal inscriptions. As Mahadevan points out, even the giant ten-symbol Dholavira "signboard", made from crystalline rock, resembles nothing so much as a giant seal, in this case created by linking shorter symbol sequences known from other inscriptions together. All this evidence is not consistent with a literate society that created longer texts.
5. Missing pictographic evidence within the inscriptions. Every premodern civilization that had extended written traditions, on perishable materials (including the Maya, Egyptian, Chinese, Assyrian, Babylonian, etc.) also left behind copious pictographic suggestions *within* the script of texts, scribes, or writing materials. The complete lack of such evidence in the Indus valley is particularly remarkable given the fact that the pictographic nature of Indus symbols is unusually high when compared with other ancient scripts, including Egyptian hieroglyphics and (later) Chinese glyphs. Again, if this was a writing system, it is the only ancient one known lacking this kind of internal pictographic evidence.
6. Missing pictorial evidence of texts, scribes, or writing outside the inscriptions. Every premodern civilization known that had extended written traditions, also left evidence behind of texts, scribes, or writing materials outside the scripts (e.g., in paintings,

statues, funerary objects and so on). Despite a few old claims of this sort that have no current adherents, no credible evidence like this exists at all in Indus artefacts. This is again incompatible with every literate ancient society known, including Egypt, China, Mesopotamia and Mesoamerica. Much evidence of this sort is also found in later literate periods in South Asia.

7. Missing evidence of writing instruments. Every premodern literate civilization known—again including China, Mesopotamia, Egypt, Mesoamerica and later South Asia —left clear archaeological evidence behind of writing instruments. No credible evidence of this sort has again ever surfaced in the Indus valley, as mainstream researchers have frequently lamented in recent years. The conclusion here is the same as above.
8. Rapid disappearance of the inscriptions. The fast disappearance after *c.* 1900 BC of Indus inscriptions argues against those inscriptions being part of a true writing system. We know of instances where literate peoples (like the Sumerians or Romans) disappeared and their writing systems were taken over by other peoples; or cases in which one script replaced another (e.g., Brahmi replacing Kharosthi, or Arabic replacing Coptic, or Spanish replacing Mayan) when new literate peoples appeared on the scene. But the disappearance of a mature writing system developed by a major civilization *without* being replaced by another is virtually unknown in history. Potential examples involving the smaller civilizations of the Minoans, Myceneans, or easter Island peoples are hardly relevant when compared with the vast society of the Indus valley, where sharp discontinuities are much more difficult to explain. If this giant society was really literate, the rapid demise of the script becomes one of the biggest unsolved puzzles in history. On the other hand, the quick disappearance of Indus inscriptions is much easier to explain if those inscriptions were part of a non-linguistic system used for limited ritualistic, religious and political purposes, which (unlike a generalized writing system) we can easily imagine being tossed out wholesale by new religious and political forces from within or outside the civilization.
9. Highly anomalous symbol frequencies. Farmer points to, a large number of anomalous symbol frequencies in the Indus symbol system that are incompatible with *any* known writing system—whether logographic, syllabic, logosyllabic (favoured by Parpola, Possehl, Mahadevan, etc.), or quasi-alphabetical (Rao, Kak, etc.). Many of these anomalies have been buried in unreliable statistical analyses by past researchers that have periodically claimed to "prove" that Indus inscriptions were linked to some early version of Dravidian, Indo-Aryan, or some other language. According to Farmer, part of those analyses, in which political motives are often evident, have attempted to "force fit" the inscriptions into linguistic moulds by interpreting extremely high frequency symbols as supposed diacritics, case endings and other grammatical signs. In countering these claims, Farmer points to an amusing number of inscriptions composed *entirely* of such supposed grammatical signs.
10. A large number of Indus symbols are used only once. Strong evidence suggests that a large percentage of Indus symbols were invented for special purposes and never used again—something that is again incompatible with a writing system supposedly used for communication purposes in a civilization as vast as this one. Depending on whose counts of signs you depend, the number of such unique signs

ranges from a low of 27 per cent of all symbols (using a figure cited by Mahadevan 1977 and Parpola 1994) to well over 50 per cent (in Wells 2000)! High as this is, the numbers of symbols used only once rises much higher still if you factor out duplicate inscriptions mass produced in moulds, apparently manufactured for one-time use in religious festivals. Even more revealingly, we find the number of symbols that appear only once continues to rise each year with each season's digs—exactly the reverse of what we would expect if this were a true writing system.

Presentation of a short list of Farmer's arguments without his detailed discussion does not allow one to evaluate his unorthodox claims. But his work gives voice to a previously quiet undercurrent of dissent concerning the "Indus script," evident especially among linguists suspicious of statistical analyses that—in the hands of different researchers—have claimed to "prove" that Indus inscriptions were tied to one language or another differing radically from one another in structure. Farmer suggests that there may be something fundamentally wrong with our approach to what is generally accepted as South Asia's first "literate civilization". The debate heated up sharply once his full study was published in 2002.

DECLINE AND LEGACY: LATE HARAPPAN

The Harappan cultural tradition, with its diversity and uniformity, continued for a long time and probably laid the basic substratum of the present-day Indian civilization. But towards the last quarter of the 3rd millennium BC, a drastic change is writ large all over the Harappan zone. Was it the end of the Indus civilization, a transformation, or merely a change? In the following pages we would address these questions.

Here we would like to quote Mughal who has spent a lifetime chasing the Harappans. His observations do provide a wider perspective to look at the phenomenon of decline and end of the Harappans. He says,

Rangpur IIA to IIB-C and later Period III, or Lothal A to B are to be seen in the context of land and water and in the basic shift from wheat to millet. In that region, the hypotheses for cultural change as suggested for the main Indus river valley are not applicable at all. The settlement pattern during the later (than Rangpur IIA) period, having small size and considerable increase in their numbers, illustrates the effect of diversification of economy as compared to the settlements associated with the preceding Rangpur IIA period.

The above review of the new data demonstrates the need to change our understanding of the geographical extent of the Indus civilization and to correct an erroneous impression created by lumping together all the sites of different phases of the Harappan civilization and thus showing a vast geographical area covered by it. During the Early Harappan period (3400-2600/2500 BC), the populations had no access to the sea but remained confined to the Indus-Hakra river plains, having inter-settlement and inter-regional contacts including the accessible valleys of Baluchistan on the west. In the Mature Harappan period beginning around 2500 BC, a very significant shift towards the seacoast took place stretching at least from Sonmiani Bay near Bala Kot to the Rann of Kachchh. It is in this part of the coastline and its hinterland that Mature Harappan sites are located. The Core Area in the Mature Harappan period consisted most of the Early Harappan Core Area and the seacoast and extended further to cover the Pakistani Makran coast and parts of Saurashtra. The Late Harappan period in the Greater Indus valley on the other hand, was marked by three regional areas, each springing from the Mature Harappan but having distinct assemblages localized in their own areas. The Harappan tradition was retained in each of the three areas for some time until lost completely by about the 1st millennium BC. The limits of these areas are defined by occurrence of similar ceramic types: Cemetery H in the Punjab, Jhukar in Sind which overlapped with Kulli in southern Baluchistan and Rangpur IIB-C and Lothal B in Saurashtra. Interactions between Saurashtra and Sind are indicated but none of these two regions has yet shown contacts with the Late Harappan in the Punjab. The causes of emergence of Late Harappan phenomena in Gujarat were different but for the Punjab and Sindh, frequent river changes may have been the principal reason for change. The end or disappearance of the Late Harappan is not clear and the subject deserves serious research. On the present evidence, at least three geographical areas of the Late Harappan can be distinguished in the Greater Indus valley, which will certainly be modified further as the chronology of this period is reconstructed with precision. Meanwhile, it is proposed to call the Cemetery H related materials as Punjab Late Harappan, Jhukar related as Sindh Late Harappan and Rangpur and Lothal related materials as Gujarat Late Harappan. These are neither intended to be mutually exclusive geographical divisions, nor it is possible to suggest a simultaneous emergence, development and eventual disappearance of the cultural features that characterized the Late Harappan period in the Greater Indus valley. The present review of the available evidence from the vast Harappan territory gives a different perspective of the issues being discussed currently for understanding the nature, causes and consequences of cultural change in the Indus valley starting about the beginning of 2nd millennium BC. The cultural mosaic during the Late Harappan period as suggested at present by the distribution of certain categories of materials mainly in three regions, presents a contrast to an integrated picture of the preceding Mature Harappan period. Admittedly, each region presents a diversity of non-Harappan materials and settlement patterns lasting for more than a millennium. An attempt to reconstruct the sequence of events in the late proto-historic period is equally important. On the present evidence, the Gandhara Grave Culture of northern Pakistan, Pirak and Complex B assemblages of Baluchistan, Painted Grey Wares of the Punjab and Doab, for example, demonstrate a different and unrelated mosaic which spans over another millennium beginning about the last quarter of 2nd millennium BC, suggesting partial contemporaneity with some of the Late Harappan assemblages of western India and the Punjab. These phenomena call for serious attention to examine socio-cultural consequences of environmental changes and adoption of various strategies for human survival in the Greater Indus valley (Mughal 1990: 13-14).

Thus with recent research, it is becoming clearer that new elements were making their appearance in the Harappa region and they are not localized. The Cemetery-H and Jhukar are no more localized aberrations but occupy large areas. In the north, the Phase IV is characterized by Cemetery-H and in the south-west, by Jhukar. At Jhukar, which was excavated by Mughal in 1974, there is a clear cultural overlap and co-mingling of cultures; and in the artefacts new tastes, but perhaps the old artisans, seem evident. At Jhukar now the goblet is painted with Jhukar motifs. So if one is looking for elements in the archaeological record of new people, the Jhukar and Cemetery-H cultures with their larger distribution are now eligible to be claimants for that title.

In the last quarter of the 3rd millennium BC, in the valleys of Saraswati, the population thins down drastically. A bit later, iron starts appearing; so do the grey wares. Rice, pig and buffalo become prominent in the subsistence record. In the Chalcolithic cultures, lentils and leguminous plants appear and assume importance in the diet; they were conspicuous by their absence in the Harappan record. The literate tradition breaks; no script any more. Use of groundwater and wells was given up, besides burnt bricks. No more planned towns; in fact, no more towns. The ones that were there, lost their character and population gradually. It does not mean that populations were decimated, but with lack of control from the metropolitan centres, the provincial towns degenerated and changed. Pande (1987) in a very interesting article points out that cultural items of everyday life of the Mature Harappans disappear in later cultures: antimony rods, terracotta masks, weights and measures, metal pots and pans, even some motifs like knot designs. For the first time, the *lota* and *thali* are introduced in the Indian crockery by the Kayatha culture and continue to this day. Now burials come right into the houses: the dead of the Chalcolithic cultures are buried below the house floors, unlike the Harappan cemeteries located outside settlements.

It is interesting to note here that Meadow has made important observations about early agricultural trends, which are certainly germane to our discussion of break as he has identified two farming transformations in South Asia: one after the Indus civilization declined and the other in the Neolithic times. Meadow (1989) says,

> One of the major unanswered questions of South Asian archaeology is the reason(s) for an apparent "deurbanization" of the Greater Indus valley beginning at about 1900 BC. This phenomenon took place together with the development of distinctly local manifestations of material culture that are particularly striking when compared to the extent of integration evident during the Harappan period. It is possible, even likely, that the degree of diminution in site size and amount of "localization" that actually occurred is overestimated because of gaps in our knowledge and mistakes in our understanding of the archaeological record (e.g., Shaffer 1981, 1986). Yet one cannot escape the impression that significant shifts in settlement did take place if only in the abandonment of certain very large sites, including Mohenjodaro and the establishment of many small sites throughout the region but particularly in east Punjab (Shaffer 1981; Joshi, Bala, and Ram 1984). Some abandonments and realignments can reasonably be attributed to changes in hydrological regimes in Punjab (e.g., Wilhelmy 1969; Mughal 1982; Pal, Sahai, Agrawal 1982; Agrawal and Sood 1982) and in Sind (Flam 1981). Yet there is increasing evidence that it was precisely at this time, in the beginning of the 2nd millennium BC, that a new complex of cereal crops and domestic animals was becoming known in the region.... When viewed on a broad basis, two distinct agricultural revolutions can be identified for the north-western region of South Asia during the pre- and proto-historic period. The first involved the establishment by the 6th millennium BC of a farming complex based principally on the rabi (winter sown, spring harvested) crops of wheat and barley and on certain domestic bovids, including zebu cattle, sheep and goats. The second saw the addition during the early 2nd millennium BC of kharif (summer sown, fall harvested) cereals including sorghum, various millets and rice along with new domestic animals including the camel, horse and donkey.... The proposal explored in this essay is that new agricultural opportunities resulting from the introduction of the summer-sown cereal crops, when combined with the new means of animal-based traction, transport and communication, facilitated widespread settlement in areas previously marginal to food production as well as realignment of settlement in already occupied areas of north-western South Asia. This is by no means a new idea, having been proposed in part by Shaffer (1981: 97) for east Punjab and Possehl (1986) for peninsular South Asia. What Shaffer did not emphasize was the importance of the differences in growing seasons (see Hutchinson 1977 and Costantini 1979, 198 1), while Possehl did not stress the role that such a change could have played in the Greater Indus valley itself. Costantini (1979, 1981), Tosi (1983, but with a broader geographical scope) and Jarrige (1985a), have all underlined the significance of the new food production systems and this essay can be seen only as a distillation of ideas which we have explored together over a number of years.

In his concluding remarks Meadow observes,

> The new crops and animals that came to be widely used in South Asia during the early 2nd millennium BC did not supplant but were exploited together with those that had formed the basis of agriculture for Millennia in the Greater Indus valley. In terms of its subsistence base, the Harappan was very much a Middle eastern civilization, depending principally on wheat, barley, sheep, goats and cattle although with significant distinguishing features including the overwelming importance of cattle, which has continued to characterize South Asia to modern times. The claims of Fentress (1985: 367) that the risks and uncertainties of one-season agriculture led to double-cropping in Sind during the Harappan period in order to "ensure a stable and regular food supply" are unconvincing, as present evidence indicates that the fruit of the date palm is the only significant food source used at that time in the Indus valley that matures in the summer or fall. Summer grown crops such as cotton and grapes were never vital to subsistence, although their cultivation may have developed expertise valuable to farmers who would later plant summer cereals (Meadow 1989).

Summer (kharif) cultivation of the "millets" and rice appears to have begun in areas with significant monsoon rainfall. East and south of the Indus valley where wild forms of some "millets" and rice are likely to have occurred. When and how this took place, however, is still obscure, although there is hope that palaeoethnobotanical investigations will clarify the matter in the not too distant future. The presence of Harappan settlements in these areas may have provided the impetus necessary for local populations to begin to systematically plant the seeds of grasses, which had previously been gathered to feed themselves or their animals (if the keeping of animals is truly earlier than crop-growing east and south of the Indus). The importation of sorghum probably from Arabia into Saurashtra at this time may also have played a role in developing the cultivation of similar grasses.

We also have to note that many of the Harappan items (e.g., burnt bricks, wells, masks, antimony rods, even the knot design, script, of course, a new one) reappear with the second urbanization in the Northern Black Polished Ware times in North India. (Did these artefacts in some way symbolize the state?) There are markers, in diet, in subsistence, in script and literate tradition, in daily items of use, which had suddenly disappeared after the Harappans, obviously conveying the message that the cultural tradition broke down. Perhaps it signifies the advent of new people. The break of tradition is writ large on the evidence.

There were many causes of the Harappan decline: aridification [for which there is now impeccable data from Rajasthan Agrawal 1982b; Wasson *et al.*, 1983. 1984; Cohmap, 1988] and elsewhere from India and globally too (see Chapter 2); tectonic disorganization of perennial rivers like the Sarasvati and their eventual drying up (Agrawal and Sood 1982); the inability of the Harappan culture to cope up with the monsoonal ecology of the Doab; and finally, any culture at some stage has to transform or die out. The process of birth, growth, decay and death governs organisms as well as cultures. But a pressure from the western flank, which was pushing the Harappans to the east and the break of the tradition, as argued above, does suggest a role of new migrants who finally prevailed.

Gordon Childe (1944) in his classical definition of the state and civilization had prescribed many criteria: class stratification; monumental architecture; cities; kingship; full-time craftsmen and smiths; stylized art and architecture; writing; international trade; science and technology, etc. All these criteria show that the subcontinent did not have a civilized state after the collapse of the Indus civilization till the rise of the Ganga civilization in the 1st millennium BC. And therefore, many of the traits, which were lost with the Harappans are revived with the rise of the Ganga civilization. And this explanation may help us understand some traits that vanished but reappeared again in the middle of the 1st millennium BC. This again shows that the period between *c.* 1700 and 600 BC may not have been dark but it certainly was a regression. From the state the society went back to chiefdoms. Between the distinctly organized societies of the Harappans and of the Ganga civilization, the interregnum was perhaps a bit of chaos and disorganization.

Aryans

Sir Mortimer Wheeler (1947b: 78-83), put forward the first coherent "theory" concerning the eclipse of the Harappans; he accused the Aryans for the demise of the Indus civilization. He asked, "What destroyed this firmly-settled civilization? Climatic, economic, political deterioration may have weakened it, but its ultimate extinction is more likely to have been completed by deliberate and large-scale destruction. It may be no mere change that at a late period of Mohenjodaro men, women and children appear to have been massacred there (Mackay 1937-38, vol. 1: 94-95; 116-117, 172). On circumstantial evidence, Indra stands accused".

Possehl (1999b: 13) picks up many holes in Wheeler's dramatic theory and says that no one should assume that the Vedic Aryans were on the scene to be active participants in the transformation process examined here. Also, George Dales (1964) and Kenneth A.R. Kennedy (1994) convincingly argue that the skeletons found in the upper layers of Mohenjodaro are actually hasty interments, not the remains of victims of a massacre.

There are very few takers for the invasion theory now; but migrations of new people cannot be denied. However, we have also to note here that Bisht in a recent article has revived the Aryan invasion theory, though in a totally new form (Bisht 1999).

Recently, Ratnagar has marshalled an array of data, new and old, to understand the end of the Harappa culture. She has given a new life to the Aryan migration theory. It is worth quoting her in detail:

> Scholars inevitably link any discussion of the termination of Bronze Age occupation of north-eastern Iran to the migration of speakers of Indo-Iranian languages. That such a migration occurred has been asserted by historical linguists. Historical linguistics is a discipline, which investigates the histories of languages and their relationships and movements and reconstructs the "proto" or original forms from which similar words of related languages could have been derived. It is also a science of language usage and change and their social context in contemporary life. This discipline, in fact, emerged in the nineteenth century around the common past and interrelated features of a very large group of languages, known as "Indo-European": Greek, Sanskrit, Latin, German, Persian and many others.
>
> These languages are so similar in structure and vocabulary, historical linguists say, that they are all derived from a common parent language, a language they dub "proto-Indo-European (PIE)". On the basis of common words, reconstruction of the cultural context of PIE and Indo-European relationships with other language groups, the ancestral homeland of this parent language is said to have been the vast grasslands or steppes of southern Europe and Central Asia.
>
> Two factors, in particular, are involved in the identification of this homeland. First, there is ample evidence for give and take between Indo-European languages on the one hand and Finno-Ugric or Uralic languages (Hungarian, Finnish, Volgaic, Estonian, etc.) on the other. This means that in their very early history these two language families shared an extensive common border, which provided opportunities for repeated interactions. The Finno-Ugric homeland comprised the fertile forest belt of Europe, which lies north of the drier steppe land. The Finno-Ugric ancestors must have derived their knowledge of agriculture from the Indo-Europeans, as several words like those for grain, grass and goat are derived from Indo-European. There are grammatical affinities as well (Mallory 1989: 147-9).
>
> Second, there is evidence that the ancestral homeland culture involved agriculture and animal herding and simple metallurgy, with great importance being given to the horse. The horse was "embedded in the culture of the early Indo-Europeans" (Mallory 1989: 119) and all the related languages used a term derived from PIE *ekwos*, for "horse". The horse is important in the Rgveda, with tw entire hymns evoted to its praise; it is associated with the Iranian deity Mithra; horse sacrifice was important in ancient India and Rome. This animal, *Equus caballus*, it is certain, was a native of the Eurasian steppes and nowhere else: the wild ancestor from which it was domesticated belongs to these steppes.
>
> For our purposes the relevant question is that of the Indo-Iranian languages (Avestan-Old Persian, Vedic Sanskrit and the language of a few texts from the Mitannian kingdom of northern Syria). They did not each derive singly from the ancestral Indo-European. Instead they are all derived from one branch, an undivided parent, which linguists call Indo-lranian. This branch had split off from Indo-European somewhere in the eastern part of the homeland (probably the north-east Iran-Turkmenia-Bactria steppes) and this split was a separate process from the branching off of Hittite, a language very close to PIE that gained currency in Anatolia between 1600 and 1200 BC. (Between the Vedic, Avestan and Mitannian languages of the Indo-Iranian branch there is little chronological distance.) The horse is evidenced at Tepe Hissar, in Turkmenia in the Namazga VI period, in Bactria and Margiana and in the Kachchhi, generally after 2000 or 1800 BC.
>
> The migration of people is the mechanism by which languages move from one place to another, but archaeological evidence for migrations is rarely self-evident. Moreover, there will always be serious doubt

whether language groupings can be inferred from archaeological patterns. Rarely do we find a clear chronological sequence of related archaeological assemblages over the map; the evidence itself usually comprises a few characteristic items but, a large number of humdrum artefacts remain unobserved and out of purview. Not all the identified characteristic items occur at all the sites marking a reconstructed "route" and similarities in artefacts can themselves be questioned (Ratnagar 1999). Second, the evidence for material culture similarity, which is exceptionally strong over a large region west of the Harappan zone and touching its western and northern frontiers, but this does not necessarily give us the movements/ migrations of specific speech communities. Linguistic groupings are not necessarily co-extensive with material culture groupings. In fact, an archaeological "culture" cannot be assumed to represent one people, or "a tribe". It has often been found that an area with two broad material culture divisions is actually inhabited by 30 recognized-as-separate tribes. Nor does every archaeologically-attested movement out of Central Asia necessarily have to be a migration of Indo-Iranian speaking groups. In the 13th and 14th centuries of our era, for example, it was Turko-Mongolic groups that advanced from the north into eastern and south-eastern Iran.

Third, it is extremely important that the movement of a language into a new homeland certainly requires the movement of native speakers, but this is not tantamount to mass movements of hordes of tribes, much less a sequence of destruction and trails of settlement desertions along the way. Aramaic did not become the *lingua franca* of western Asia due to mass migrations. Even in the case of the Sea Peoples of 1200 BC, it has been stressed that they were groups of marauders and adventurers if not an army. There was no "movement of population" as such (Tritsch 1973). In fact, decades ago Father Heras (1953: 12-17) had asserted that Indo-Aryans came into South Asia in small numbers and intermarried with the natives and that consequently Dravidian speakers became bilingual. Thus, even though Indo-Aryan languages did not originate in South Asia, we cannot suggest that "the Aryans" are "a cause of the end of the Indus valley civilization".

What matters for us, instead, is that the Gurgan valley, as the excavator of Tureng Tepe said in 1932 (quoted by Cleuziou 1986), lies at the junction of the Iranian Plateau, the oases of Turkmenia and the Eurasian steppe land across the Caspian. Tureng Tepe, Yarim Tepe and Hissar occupied a frontier between agriculture and mobile animal rearing, a frontier which, of course, has shifted back and forth through history. Thus, earlier explanations for the desertions of these sites in terms of climatic change and epidemics and cultural decline were soon given up for the "invasion by nomads" theory, especially with Deshayes" discovery of the burned ruins of a monumental structure at Tureng Tepe III C and the subsequent abandonment of that site until about 800 BC. Yet, we should bear in mind the observation of Arne, the excavator of Shah Tepe, that the invaders could as well have been Turks as well as Indo-Europeans!

It is often asked why and how Indo-European languages could have spilled out in so many directions from a single homelnd. Mallory (1989: 147) points out that a similar "spill" was to occur later also. Speakers of Turkic languages, from a 6th century homeland somewhat east of the PIE zone, virtually exploded over an area in excess of 2,50,000 sq. km. by the 9th century AD.

It has been suggested, in addition (Ratnagar 1999), that it was the nature of pastoralism, as it had developed on the steppe by 2000 BC, which gave rise to repeated out-migrations. The herding of several animals, cattle, sheep, goat and also horses was done from horse back. Once the horse could be controlled by a rider, the mounted herder could cover long distances in a day and scout for good pastures and stray animals; this would ensure that flocks moved fast when necessary. This, in-turn, would make the tending of large herds possible and large herds would necessitate more labour and hence a schism between herding and agriculture. In a positive feedback mechanism would arise yet more geographically extensive pastoral circuits and larger flocks. This, coupled with certain geographic factors—such as rainfall variability, scarcity of groundwater and the choking of surface run-off channels by large herds if carelessly moved—would mean a precarious balance between people, animals and the land, necessitating periodic out-migration.

We would, thus, agree with Cleuziou (1986: 246-8) when he argues that the desertions of the Gurgan valley sites reflect less an Indo-Iranian event than the historical pattern of a frontier region: "... gaps in the archaeological record are due to the fluctuations between settled agriculture and steppe pastoralism", he says. We would add that such fluctuations could have been caused by the spilling out of horse-mounted pastoralists from their homeland, as much as by political events or economic factors (Ratnagar 2000: 106-110).

It may be emphasized here that not a single cause but several contributed towards the decline and the disappearance of the mighty Harappan civilization.

In a recent detailed study, Possehl (1999c: 19-33) has delved deeper into the problem of post-Mature Harappan transformations that took place in the north-west of the subcontinent. It places the drastic changes that took place in the beginning of the 2nd millennium in a wider perspective and is therefore, worth quoting in detail. He says that there was an abandonment, or severe depopulation, of the cities and a number of important settlements including Kot Diji, Balakot, Allahdino, Kalibangan, Ropar, Surkotada, Dholavira, Desalpur and Lothal. Long distance trade was reduced and the production of a wide range of special materials, many of which seem to have been luxury items, was curtailed (e.g., long barrel cylinder beads, etched beads, inscribed stamp seals). Sindh and Cholistan were largely abandoned by settled farmers and there was an increase in the number of settlements in the Punjab, Haryana, western Uttar Pradesh and northern Rajasthan, though Gujarat seems to have remained relatively stable. There were shifts in the subsistence regime, with a growth in the population's ability to sustain double-cropping with the use of millets.

The Mature Harappan style in architecture and material culture disappeared, along with the stamp seals and a coherent system of writing. Post-urban times witness a return to a cultural mosaic not unlike the one found during the pre-urban phase. Yet, in spite of these changes, there is a strong line of culture historical continuity throughout the Harappan region.

Ratnagar has also tried to marshal the archaeological evidence of the break of the Harappan tradition and the emergence of new elements. She says:

> The bronze cosmetic flagon known at Hissar, Altyn-depe and in Bactria, also occurs at Chanhudaro as a beautifully fluted piece (Mackay 1943: PI. LXXIII.39), in a probable Jhukar context. Round bronze mirrors with tangs for fitting into wooden handles, as at Hissar, Altyn-depe, Gonur I, Sapalli, Dashly, Shahdad and Khinaman and Mehi—some of them with a handle shaped as a human body—also occur at Harappa (Vats 1940: Plate 29) and Mohenjodaro (Mackay 1938: 477-78). Twelve such mirrors occurred in graves at Harappa (Wheeler 1947-48: 85 ff.) and one in a Kalibangan grave (Rissman 1988: 211-14). Rissman has remarked that in Harappan graves it was mirrors rather than any other bronze item that tended to be deposited (*ibid.*: 214) and that only one such mirror occurs in a Harappan hoarded treasure (*ibid.*: 217).
>
> The beautifully cast socketed adze-axe of Gonur I has counterparts at Hissar, Shahdad, Khinaman and also Mohenjodaro (Mackay 1938: 457-58). Harappa and Chanhudaro each have a single bladed socketed axe (Vats 1940: Plate CXXII.18; Mackay 193: Plate LXXII. 25). Exquisite bronze animal-headed pins or "wands" at Dashly and Hissar (Schmidt 1937: 194-97) have a counterpart in the latest stratum of Harappa (Vats 1940: Plate CXXV. 36, p. 390) in an "antimony stopper rod" surmounted by the figure of a dog biting the ear of a goat; and at Mohenjodaro where a rod is surmounted by an antelope (Piggott 1947-48). There are also compartmented seals whose faces bear raised geometric designs, from Mohenjodaro and the white steatite stepped seal with a stylized eagle from Harappa has Bactrian connections (During Caspers 1997).
>
> The purpose here is not to elaborate on a list of similarities between the regions, for such an exercise often tends to neglect context and co-occurrence and simplistic conclusions are drawn about "trade" or "migrations". The point is, instead, to highlight the relevance of the happenings in this region to the Harappan centres and suggest that there may be some inter-connexion between the series of Harappan settlement desertions and colonizations and events in the western region.
>
> The Kachchhi plain, on the frontier between the Indus valley and Baluchistan, was also affected by group movements. Western contacts reappear at Nausharo after the Harappan period. The famous Neolithic site

of Mehrgarh near Dadhar has a south Cemetery with ordinary graves: "cenotaphs" devoid of human remains but with offerings and grave goods interred in pits. At this cemetery grave goods of international currency include steatite kidney-shaped containers (as in Bactria), a stone sceptre as in sites of the BMAC and eastern Iran, a bronze cosmetic flagon, mirror and pins with double volutes or bird-shaped heads (Santoni 1984: 52-54).... Also in the Kachchhi, near Nausharo, was a small (1 ha) and short-lived settlement, Sibri (*ibid.*). This could have been the settlement of a small group of migrants who came down the Bolan Pass from Central Asia. Among the finds occur a polished stone column, two flat, violin-shaped figurines, compartmented seals, a bronze ornamental pin and a bronze shaft-hole axe-adze. There is also evidence of copper/bronze industry at the site, which is comparatively rich in metal.... Critically important is the fact that Sibri offers not only Central Asian elements but also Harappan ceramic traits and Indus characters on an amulet (Jarrige and Usman Khan 1989: 150), so that the chronological coincidence between the later phase of the Harappan civilization and the momentous happenings to its west are established.... At Pirak, 11 km south of Sibi on a tributary of the Bolan, a 9-ha settlement was founded around 1700 BC (Jarrige and Santoni 1979). The material culture—house forms, hearths, pottery, bone and stone tools and grain storage methods—presents a contrast to the Harappan material culture. Moreover, at Pirak the horse and the two-humped Bactrian camel (probably domesticated, centuries earlier in Turkmenia) are represented by their bones. Among artefacts there are Murghab type stone seals.

Where movements of groups from eastern Iran-Central Asia are concerned, northernmost Pakistan also becomes relevant. From about 1700 BC, cemeteries and villages in Swat (period IV) had a material culture which seems to have been a curious amalgam of elements from South Asia (painted pottery), north-east Iran (grey burnished pottery, violin-shaped figurines, the horse) and China (jade pendants, stone harvesters and ornate bone pins; Tusa 1979, Stacul 1970,1979, 1984). Swat, too, would be receiving steppe elements from Tadjikistan, via north Bactria, according to Kuzmina (1976). As regards connexions with China, it needs to be said that these are visible in Bactria too: in four graves at Sapalli-tepe (2000-1700 BC) there is evidence that the dead were wrapped in silk (Kohl 1984: 155). Was this Chinese silk (see Good 1995)? It is evident that connections with north-eastern Iran-Turkmenia and the BMAC are manifest both at major Harappan centres and on the fringes of the Harappan heartland. While during the Mature Harappan period contacts between the plains of the Indus and the hills of Baluchistan were meagre and there were few villages in the western mountains, pottery of the type found at Pirak and Nausharo now occurs at Ispelanji north of Kalat, at Dabarkot in Loralai and at Sulaimanzai on the Quetta plateau (Jarrige and Santoni 1979: 389-90; Jarrige 1985: 43-5).

Not only were there movements of groups of people, social transformation was also involved. While centres like Altyn-depe with their social stratification, elaborate cult centres and varied metal alloys were clearly urban, the settlement forms in Margiana and Bactria, according to the early excavators (see Lamberg-Karlovsky 1994), are totally different, with each arm of the Murghab settled by an individual tribe or tribal section and, as stated already, separate families occupying each settlement. According to Hiebert and Lamberg-Karlovsky (1992), in fact, the BMAC was a short-lived (say two-century) phenomenon, collapsing between 1900 and 1700 BC and followed by migration to eastern Iran and the Kachchhi (Ratnagar 2000: 113-123).

Environmental Evidence

Let us now look at the environmental evidence. Major evidence for climatic changes has already been discussed in Chapter 2, where we have summarized our work also.

The Indus river in Sindh is a mature stream, which frequently changes its course. Much river training has been done on the Indus in modern times, so these course shifts are not as apparent today as they were through the nineteenth and early twentieth centuries. But they are a powerful part of the history of Sindh. Two other archaeologists have followed Mackay's lead, suggesting that a dramatic shift in the course of the Indus led to the abandonment of Mohenjodaro (Lambrick 1967; Mughal 1990). They have ascribed the abandonment of Mohenjodaro to an avulsion of the Indus river. But the abandonment of

Mohenjodaro alone cannot explain the eclipse of the Indus civilization. A variety of causes played their role.

It was M.R. Sahni who in 1956 first invoked the impounding of the Indus to explain the end of Mohenjodaro. Later on, Raikes and Dales revived the theory with greater force. In brief, they proposed that a tectonically-caused large mud extrusion impounded the Indus causing colossal silting which gradually engulfed Mohenjodaro. Since it was a water permeable barrier, only the silt level kept on rising.

But Lambrick pointed out that such a barrier would result in the shedding off of the silt-load by the river considerably upstream and not on the inner side of the dam. He further asks how such a permeable barrier could stand, at least in the first years, the enormous impact on a narrow front of water arriving at the rate of 2,270,000 litres per second. The Allahbund—a similar mud extrusion caused by the 1819 earthquake—was washed away by the first flood coming down the Nara in 1826. Possehl pointed out that it will require a dam of 250 km length to engulf Mohenjodaro and asked where were the traces of such a bund. He also argued that such a lake would fill vast areas including the lake Manchar region where the discovery of several Harappan sites precludes such a possibility.

Though Raikes and Dales seem to realize the strength of some of the criticism mentioned above, yet they have tried to bring in some new arguments in favour of their theory. Realizing the tremendous force of water coming at 2,270,000 litres/second on a narrow front, they now try to divert part of this discharge through the Nara. They have also raised some objections to the theories of climatic change. We have raised some basic questions. If there was such a vast lake around, how could any crops grow and therefore, provide any surplus to sustain a city. The gallery forests would have perished driving the game away. How could one expect any fish in the shallow waters of a mud lake? How could carts play on muddy roads, if they were living in a quagmire? How did the drains function at all? What happened to the sanitary arrangements? Will not such extreme conditions kill the people in mass before any mud lake engulfed them? Raikes has not been able to answer these questions. Such a developed civilization needed some optimal ecological conditions for its flowering. How could people fighting for sheer survival usher in such a grand urbanization? All these and many other objections make one feel that Raikes" dam does not hold any water (Agrawal 1992).

Possehl asks, is it necessary to believe that just because the Indus river was impounded, the Harappan civilization came to an end? If the Mature Harappan culture succumbed to new and unpredictable riverine forces, the explanation sought by historians and social scientists lies not directly with geomorphological matters but, rather, with the internal structure of the Harappan way of life. The "flaw" that would have led to such catastrophic socio-cultural change is not to be found within the natural world of geomorphology but within the human context of the Harappan civilization, its society and culture, as discussed by Possehl (1967: 37-39).

Having said that, we would hasten to add that the Indus did affect the fortunes of the Harappans in more than one way. Frequent floods were sapping their energy. Their raised platforms and massive bunds indicate the severity of the problem. The Indus river has been raising its flood level, continuously necessitating safeguard measures. The water table could itself rise thus destablizing buildings, causing salinity increase and rendering vast tracts useless for agriculture. The Indus could also leave Mohenjodaro and other cities high and dry by changing its courses drastically.

On the other hand, geomorphological, palynological and archaeological evidence from Rajasthan indicates fluctuations of wet and dry periods. In the present state of knowledge, climatic change for the worse cannot be ruled out. An increasing desiccation may have given the last blow to a people already exhausted by their incessant fight against floods. Progressive degeneration is writ large over the successive levels of Mohenjodaro.

It is relevant to discuss in greater detail the recently discovered evidence of drastic changes in palaeo-channel configurations, especially in Rajasthan. They did affect the Harappans as also the subsequent cultures in the area.

When Ghosh discovered, a large number of Chalcolithic settlements on the now dried-up Ghaggar and the Chautang in Rajasthan, it led to speculations about climatic changes in the area, which caused these rivers to dry up. Our recent work, however, has emphasized the significance of the tectonically-induced environmental changes in north and west Rajasthan. The fluctuations in the palaeo-channel patterns in this area have been noticed since Oldham's times in the nineteenth century. Dikshit has chronicled the various hypotheses in a historical sequence and several others have discussed the evidence of archaeological remains on these dried-up beds. Raikes, without adducing any tangible evidence, even talked of six well-dated diversions of the Yamuna.

The Sutlej once flowed into the Ghaggar following a path east of Ropar, Sirhind, Patiala and Shatrana. The Ghaggar was a mighty river in the past and had on an average 8 km wide bed. The Sutlej, before assuming its present course, braided into a multitude of channels. This event is also recorded in the *Mahabharata* in the form of a legend: when Vashistha threw himself into the Satudri (Sutlej) it broke into hundreds of streams. As the enechlon faults controlled the river course of the Ghaggar, it was prone to drastic changes due to even minor tectonic movements. Both our Landsat imagery derived palaeo-channels and the field data given by Singh support the flowing of the Sutlej into the Ghaggar in the past.

Some major easterly (from the Ghaggar) river of the past was changing its courses more frequently. We have been able to trace three such courses termed Y1, Y2 and Y3. The Y1 channel connected it to the Ghaggar. Later on, it followed the Y2, merging into the Chautang, the latter meeting the Ghaggar near Suratgarh. The third time it flowed further east and south-eastwards, following the Y3 course, finally joining the Ganga probably through the Chambal. When this Y3 river shifted its course further east, it left the various lakes in its course which now lie north of Bharatpur. It is probable that this was the channel, which has now assumed the course of the Yamuna.

Whereas these changes in the courses of the various palaeo-channels are fairly clear and also find support from the published field-data, the terminal course of the Ghaggar is far from clear. Near Anupgarh, the ancient Ghaggar bed bifurcates and both the palaeo-channels come to an abrupt end. The upper one terminates near Marot and the lower one near Beriwala, in Pakistan, into a shallow depression. From the Landsat imagery it looks as if it debauched into the sea here, but obviously to bring the sea so far inland in mid-Holocene is not probable. It is, however, possible that the chain of tectonic events, which diverted the Sutlej and the easterly rivers away from the Ghaggar, caused a depression near Marot into which the Ghaggar, deprived of its major source of water, died into a lake-like depression.

But when the Ghaggar was a perennial river, it is possible that it could have met the Nara and flowed directly into the Rann of Kachchh, without meeting the Indus. The paleo-channels beyond Marot do indicate such a possibility. The legend also says that the Saraswati flowed directly into the sea.

As human settlements were thriving on their banks, when they were alive, it would be easy to date these palaeo-channels. Archaeological explorations have thrown welcome light on these problems. Though a more intensive study of the archaeological remains needs to be carried out, yet broad features can now be recognized. The Ghaggar was alive during the Pre-Harappan and the Harappan times. The Painted Grey Ware (*c.* 1000-400 BC) mounds are located in the river-bed itself, probably indicating a much reduced discharge of the Ghaggar. The Chautang has a large number of Late Harappan sites. The channel Y3 seems to have been a living river during the PGW times. The data on channels Y1 and Y2 are not adequate yet.

Considerable geomorphological and archaeological fieldwork is required to document the vagrancy of these rivers. It has to be supported by chemical/mineralogical analyses of the core profiles from these river-beds to detect the signatures of the different relict rivers. Yet it is obvious that in north and west Rajasthan tectonically-changed palaeo-channel configurations were a major factor which affected the human settlements, perhaps from the Pre-Harappan times onwards. Major diversions cut off the vital tributaries and growing desiccation, on the other hand, dried up the once mighty Saraswati and Drishadvati rivers (see also Possehl 1999a).

The interface between the Cemetery H assemblage and the Painted Grey Ware has not yet been defined in Pakistan. In India, Painted Grey Ware begins at *c.* 1000 BC. The interface between this assemblage and the "Late Harappan" (Fig. 3-12) in the Punjab has been documented at places such as Dadheri and Bhagwanpura (see Joshi 1993).

The relatively high density of the Hakra Ware sites may indicate rather a strong flow in the river, which diminished in the next period, with the Early Harappan (Kot Diji) sites being relatively few in number in this area. The very high number of Mature Harappan settlements suggests a resurgence of the river and a rich well-watered inland delta. Then in the Cemetery H and Painted Grey Ware periods we see the two-step retreat of the river to the east, eventually with insufficient flow to even reach the old Fort Derawar delta. Possehl agrees that the fluvial sequence apparently has little, if anything, to do with broad trends in climatic change but can be explained by tectonics as outlined in Agrawal and Sood (1982). Over what seems to have been the course of the 2nd millennium BC, waters that drained out of the Himalayan watershed were gradually captured by streams that flowed to the east, into the Bay of Bengal, at the expense of the greater Indus system. This process apparently led to the creation of the Yamuna river, a very young stream and the drying up of the Sarasvati and Drishadvati rivers (Possehl 1999b).

Possehl (1999b: 17), however, clarifies his stand,

> This is not to propose that stream capture was the direct cause of the eclipse of the ancient cities of the Indus. A sociocultural cause is sought here, just as with the Raikes-Dales theory of an Indus dam. But, over the course of the third and 2nd Millennia, the Sarasvati that cannot be ignored in a broad consideration of the transformation of the Indus civilization.

Francfort (1986: 98) says of the stream capture:

> This shift would have occurred either in the still badly defined Late Harappan period or in the PGW (Painted Grey Ware) period, or gradually during both since Late Harappan (Cemetery H) and PGW sites in the state of Cholistan in Pakistan are found on one of the palaeo-channels known locally as Hakra. However, the adoption of this "hypothesis" poses an interesting methodological problem. If we accept this hypothesis, we must logically accept as well that another tectonic upheaval would have made the river revert to the Kushan (Rang Mahal) period since sites from the latter are again found in the region.

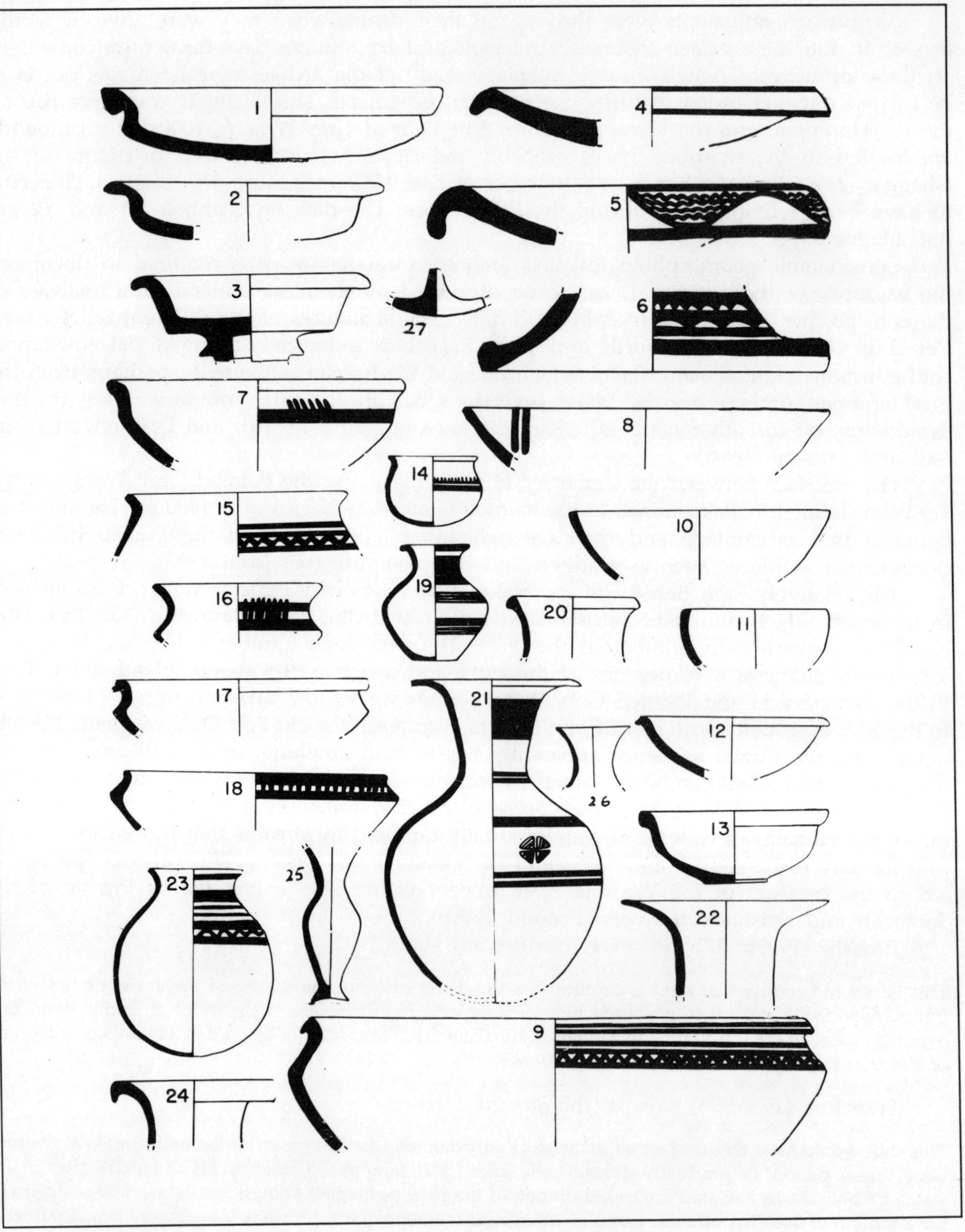

Fig. 3-12. Late Harappan pottery types.

Singh (Singh 1971; Singh *et al.* 1974) on the basis of his palynological studies on the lakes of Sambhar, Didwana and Lunkaransar in Rajasthan proposed that this increase in salinity was due to increased aridity and that this climatic change could have been the root cause for the eclipse of the Indus civilization. But Possehl doubts these inferences, he says,

> The changing salinity of these lakes, which appears to be well documented, need not be due to changes in rainfall. The geology and environment of Rajasthan are coupled. The three lakes investigated are hypersaline today, but there are also freshwater lakes in this same region (Lakes Pushkar and Ganger). This observation leads to the conclusion that, under one climatic regime in Rajasthan, there can be both freshwater and hypersaline lakes, calling into question the Singh hypothesis.... Site counts go up from 218 during the Mature Harappan to 853 in Post-urban times. Although there was a dramatic drop in average site size, down from 13.54 to 3.55 ha, the estimated total settled area remained remarkably stable for both periods. These data do not look like those that one would expect if there had been a severe reduction in rainfall as Singh proposed especially given the fact that it is a dry cropping region (Possehl 1999b: 18).

Possehl doubts the entire notion of an eclipse of the Harappan civilization. He asks, where is the collapse or eclipse in the east? Average site size goes down, but based on the data at hand,there is little change in the total settled area. He admits that the urban paradigm on which the Mature Harappan was founded, with its large, multifunctional settlements, system of writing, weights and measures, long distance trade and contacts with the Gulf, Africa, Mesopotamia and Central Asia was no more a part of the Post-urban Harappan. There is no system of writing in the Post-urban Harappan anywhere, although graffiti from the corpus of Indus signs are found. The cities are no longer functional urban entities. There is an important transformation of Indus life, but there was hardly any collapse.

In Chapter 2 we had discussed that in Rajasthan, it is not only the changing precipitation that affects habitation but also the changing loyalties of the rivers and the sustainability thresholds of semi-arid ecology to allow large sedentary populations for long periods of time. All these trends are superimposed on each other in Rajasthan. The evidence of climatic change from Rajasthan, Gujarat and the Ganga valley is quite definitive and has to be taken into account in discussing their effects on the Harappan culture.

GUJARAT

Discussing the Gujarat Harappan data, Possehl makes an important point that the number of sites drops by one-third and there is a significant drop in the average size of sites. Total settled area, as determined from the settlement surveys, is cut in half. These are robust indicators of deep change in the system of settlement and, probably, subsistence and the socio-cultural system generally. But there is another theme in the transformation process in Saurashtra. At Rojdi the site was expanded and rebuilt just at the time Mohenjodaro was being abandoned and Harappa came to an end as an urban centre. Thus, while we have evidence for fewer and smaller villages, at least some of those that survived have signs of a sound economic base and a population that was able and willing to make significant investments in their community.

Lothal was a gateway settlement of the Sindhi Harappans to gain access to the raw materials of Gujarat. At about 1900 BC, the signs of manufacturing and trade disappeared and Lothal shrank to a squatter's settlement. Possehl argues that the cause of this was not a flood but the collapse of the infrastructure of Sindh.

Around Lothal, the aerial survey carried out by us has indicated an annual pattern of drainage, which points to tectonic disturbances. Either a tectonic uplift or a eustatic fall in sea level was probably responsible for cutting off of the Lothal dockyard from the water channels and eventually from the access to the sea.

Sea level changes also need to be considered. Recent work has shown that the sea level on the west coast did fluctuate between +5 and -100 m in the late Quaternary period compared to the present sea level. At about 5000 BP it was higher by about +5 m and then went down. The coastal-port sites of Sutkagendor, Lothal, etc., are far inland now but may have been connected with the sea in their heyday and perhaps fell out of use due to fall in sea level. How actually did the sea level changes affect the Harappan culture and its prosperity will require a more exhaustive study. There is interesting evidence from Amri. In the Pre-Harappan period 90 per cent snails/molluscs were of marine variety but with the advent of the Harappans, riverine species tended to increase, attaining a parity with the marine species by the end of the Harappan period. This surely must reflect transgression and regression of the sea.

The Harappan trade with West Asia received a tremendous boost in *c.* 2350 BC under Sargon of Agade, as there arose a great demand for luxury articles like carnelian beads, ivory, shell, lapis lazuli and so on. Merchant-traders began to migrate in large numbers to Saurashtra in the 23rd century BC. When Mohenjodaro was threatened by the Indus floods, the number of Harappan migrants swelled. This would explain why most of the Late Mature Phase (*c.* 2200-2000 BC) settlements were located in the fertile river basins of Saurashtra. It was during the Late Mature Phase that the Harappan settlement at Kuntasi was developed into an industrial centre and a port. The structure complex unearthed at Kuntasi is unique and the evidence allows us to identify the Harappan settlement as an industrial centre for manufacturing pottery and a variety of beads as also probably copper artefacts (Possehl 1999b: 22).

At about 1900 BC Kuntasi settlement shrank in size and signs of craft activity and trade were reduced. The Late Harappan occupation at Kuntasi betrays a marked degeneration in the economic activity. People lived in flimsy structures with rubble foundation, mud walls and thatched roofs. Only a few artisans were working. The quality of life had certainly changed for worse, but not the quality of pottery. As already noted, there is not much difference between the pottery of Period I and Period II. But they do not seem to have had enough clientele and after surviving for a couple of centuries, the site was abandoned in *c.* 1700 BC (Dhavalikar 1996: 374-375).

At Dholavira, Periods II and III document a full, Mature Harappan town with the full inventory of Mature Harappan finds. At about 1900 BC, here also the site shrank drastically, with habitation confined to its highest points. There is a good deal of evidence for people destroying earlier architecture and disrupting the old metropolis and also the presence of Jhukar ceramics at the site.

According to Dhavalikar, when the decline begins in West Asia, the Indus civilization also received a setback. Everywhere devastating changes were taking place; one of the causes was a shift in climate, which was becoming more and more arid leading gradually to desiccation and consequent desertification of the once fertile regions in West Asia. This affected the agricultural production adversely as also trade. It is no sheer coincidence that almost simultaneously with West Asia in India too, the great Indus civilization should be on the decline. The prosperity of the Harappans was now a thing of the past and the post-urban phase is marked by rural settlements, which are far too few in number as compared to the Late Mature Phase settlements. Many people seem to have resorted to a nomadic existence and subsisted on hunting-gathering as the evidence from sites like Kanewal and Ratanpura would show (Dhavalikar 1996: 374). But Possehl does not seem to subscribe to this view; he thinks that the Mature Harappan trade with Mesopotamia was never on a scale that could have compromised the integrity of the entire Mature Harappan economic system.

Possehl considers Lothal, Kuntasi and Dholavira as essentially "colonies" of the Sindhi Harappans, which made them vulnerable to severe change at the beginning of the Post-urban Harappan. Rojdi and other places that were farming communities, not deeply involved in the acquisition and processing of materials or in the transport that was part of the commerce, were buffered, protected and insulated from the catastrophic changes in Sindh. But places such as Dholavira, Kuntasi and Lothal succumbed. He therefore, suggests that the tighter the integration the Gujarat or Sorath site had with respect to the Sindhi economy, the greater the impact of the processes of devolution that engulfed Mohenjodaro and other sites in Sindh.

Mughal (1990: 13-14) has visualized some sort of continuity and transition in diverse geographical regions of the Harappan universe, which we have quoted above in detail.

We need to take into account that non-urban Chalcolithic communities were flourishing in Rajasthan, Gujarat, Central India and Deccan around 2nd millennium BC and many of them had regular contacts with the Harappans. Hence it is likely that many of those cultures, discussed in Chapter 4, are also an expression of the decline or transformation of the Harappan society.

PUNJAB AND SINDH

At Mohenjodaro, both the Warehouse and the Bath were abandoned even before the eventual abandonment of the city. In the desertion of these two facilities can be seen the initial outward signs that the Harappan civilization was deeply troubled. Data on settlement that are comparable to those from other regions already presented are given in Table 3.4 (Possehl 1999b: 23).

TABLE 3.4 ESTIMATE OF SETTLED AREA FOR SITES IN SINDH

	Mature Harappan	*Jhukar (Post-urban)*
Total Sites	86	6
Average Site Size in Ha	8.0	5.6
Estimated Total Settled Area in Ha	688	34

The documentation of settlement in Sindh during the Jhukar period, the post-urban there, seems to record significant change. The drop from 86 to 6 sites is important, but so too, is the abandonment, or virtual abandonment, of Mohenjodaro, the premier urban centre.

In Pirak (Jarrige and Santoni 1979; Enault 1979), in the Kachchhi plains, the settlement probably began sometime in the early 2nd millennium. There is cultural continuity at Pirak through to Period III, which is associated with iron. The Pirak assemblage seems to be foreign to the Kachchhi region and lies outside the cultural traditions of the Indus Age. There are four or five other Pirak type sites in Kachchhi.

Settlement data from Baluchistan are also revealing, as shown in Table 3.5 (Possehl 1999b: 24).

TABLE 3.5 ESTIMATE OF SETTLED AREA FOR SITES IN BALUCHISTAN

	Kulli/Quetta Phase 2500-1900 BC	*Post-urban*
Total Sites	129	0
Average Site Size in Ha	5.8	0
Estimated Total Settled Area in Ha	748	0

For the moment it appears that Baluchistan in post-urban times was the most severely affected of the regions that once made up the Harappan civilization. There is no documentation for a Post-urban Harappan in Baluchistan. At some sites, e.g. Mehi (Stein 1931: 153-163), Kulli (Stein 1931: 118-127) and in Quetta City (Jarrige and Hassan 1989) we do have evidence of human activity. These are places where the so-called "Bactria-Margiana Archaeological Complex" (BMAC) has been found (Hiebert 1994). The signs of human activity that are present are not settlements in the conventional sense. One is a cenotaph. The others are stray artefacts and signs of cremation within an uncertain, probably much disturbed, context. The BMAC extends onto the plains in Kachchh at the Sibri Cemetery (Santoni 1984) and Dauda Damb (Jarrige 1994: 295-296). Together, these archaeological signatures seem to reflect the presence of mobile, nomadic peoples of the early 2nd millennium whose home might well have been Bactria and Margiana far to the north (Possehl 1999b: 23).

The settlement patterns around Harappa are not known well enough, but we know that Harappa shrank in size at the beginning of the 2nd millennium. The archaeological assemblage that succeeds the Mature Harappan is the so-called Cemetery H material, now dated to 1730 cal. BC. The distinctive Indus stamp seals, both square and oblong, are no longer made after *c.* 1900 BC. There is a general reduction in artefacts that were primarily intended to carry texts. Writing virtually disappears in Sindh and is at least very much reduced in the Harappan (Cemetery H) region.

TABLE 3.6 A SUMMARY OF THE SUBSTANTIVE DATA COMPARING MATURE HARAPPAN AND POST-URBAN PHASES (after Possehl 1999b)

	Site Count	*Average Site Size in Ha*	*Settled Area in Ha*
Sindh			
Mature Harappan	86	8.0	688
Jhukar	6	5.6	34
Cholistan			
Mature Harappan	174	5.6	974
Cemetery H.	41	5.1	209
Baluchistan			
Kullo-Quetta/Harappan	129	5.8	748
Post-urban	0	0	0
Saurashtra			
Sorath-Harappan	310	5.4	16.74
Late Sorath Harappan	198	4.3	81.5
East			
Mature Harappan	218	13.5	29.43
Post-urban	853	3.5	29.85

Possehl's survey thus indicates that the "eclipse of the Harappan civilization" might hold for Sindh and Baluchistan, but in the east and to a lesser degree in Gujarat, the course of culture change was different. In these areas there were strong lines of continuity through the early centuries of the 2nd millennium, with little, if any, of the "trauma" that affected Sindh.

Here we would like to comment that mid-Holocene climatic amelioration and onset of deterioration from *c.* 2000 BC is well documented globally. It is also clear that habitation is shifting towards wetter areas, as rainfall increases as one moves from Sindh eastwards. One has to concede that in Rajasthan some lakes like Pushkar and Ganger did not show signs of aridity or increase in salinity. But it could be due to climatic change.

It is clear that the Punjab, Haryana, northern Rajasthan and western Uttar Pradesh have produced good evidence for a dramatic increase in human habitation during the opening centuries of the 2nd millennium BC, precisely during the period of the so-called "eclipse" of the Harappan civilization. Possehl finds the evidence going against the climatic deterioration theory on two counts: there is a period of "eclipse" with a growth of human habitation and a proposed "aridity" at a time when archaeological data indicate widespread dry cropping. He does not find any evidence of climatic change in Gujarat either. As mentioned above, Possehl sees few signs of "collapse" or "eclipse" there and at some places, such as Rojdi, they were busy with the expansion and rebuilding of their settlements as Mohenjodaro was being abandoned.

It appears that by Post-urban times, the centre of settlement had shifted to the Punjab, Haryana, northern Rajasthan and western Uttar Pradesh, as well as Gujarat. We think that it simply indicates that the Post-Harappans were seeking greener pastures and were moving to eastern region of higher rainfall, compared to Sindh.

It may be relevant here to discuss the evidence from the Yamuna valley in the wider perspective of the discussions above. All early civilizations – be it on the Nile, or on the Tigris, or on the Indus – were born and thrived in essentially a semi-arid ecology. But the Ganga valley is a monsoonal area, with rainfall increasing from 100 cm/year, as one moves eastwards. The Harappans did not reach the Ganga valley in their prime but only at their declining Late Harappan phase, be it Hulas, Alamgirpur or Mandi. They did cross the Yamuna, but not the Ganga. The Mandi jewellery hoard seems to point to insecure times. In fact, the Harappa culture withered on the fringes of the Doab. It could not have thrived in the monsoon ecology of the Ganga valley, as essentially it was a product of semi-arid ecology. Perhaps it was the dry oscillation, witnessed in the pollen and salinity profiles of the lakes of Rajasthan (discussed above), in the beginning of the 2nd millennium BC, that forced them to move eastwards.

The Jhukar assemblage in Sindh and the CemeteryH assemblage in the Punjab and Cholistan are both poorly understood. The successors to the Kullis in southern Baluchistan have also not yet been identified.

Before we conclude the discussions on the legacy of the Harappans, Ratnagar's perceptive conclusions are worth noting.

Ratnagar finds Wallerstein's (1991: 64-79,135-48) approach useful. According to Wallerstein, it is not "societies" that have been developing over the centuries, but world systems, long-term structures of core and peripheral relationships. Ratnagar says,

> We could thus move conceptually from the Great Tradition we had defined in archaeological terms at the outset, to a more challenging "structural space". Perhaps Harappan urbanization and state development

originated and functioned as a dominant centre in South Asia, conducting unequal exchanges with peripheral tribal or hunting-gathering societies like the metal producers of Rajasthan and Malwa. Perhaps it also developed as a trading partner that carried overseas bulk goods like wood as well as objects of desire like decorated carnelian beads to richer lands abroad. Simultaneously, we have suggested, its economy of production was always dependent on supplies of metal from outside its heartland.

The attempt has been to avoid confusing the evidence (which we can examine again and again) and actual events (which do not recur). There must have been several occurrences, which have left behind no evidence for us to examine. We construct happenings by reasoning about the evidence. The evidence, such as we can gather, gives us a specific kind of decline to explain: it includes the subdivision of houses, scored goblets, secreted treasures, vandalized statues, unconventional burials, destruction levels at sites, one-room huts at some sites, raider/squatter traces at others, reduction in the level of communication on seals and in their artistic qualities, the eclipse of several crafts, together with the important evidence of the end of sea trade and the abandonment of certain sites. These, together, point to breaks in tradition, migrations and a general disintegration or breakdown, not to organic expansion or transformation to a new level, nor a situation in which an elite remained in control.

These specifics enable us to distinguish the symptoms of the collapse from the cause(s). Vegetational change at Lothal is a symptom, probably, of an overextended local ecology. The political strife evidenced by skeletons and the defacement of statuary could have been a symptom of the weakness of the state structure. The depopulation of the Hakra was probably a sign of hydrological change.

We have not constructed a theory out of thirty-six skeletons and three hoarded treasures, so much as realized that in the uppermost levels and debris of sites, very few of the actually secreted treasures and abandoned dead will ever survive for us to find. In other words, it is not the number of skeletons and caches that count, but the fact of their existence.

Having felt dissatisfied with arguments about natural holocausts that brought the Harappan tradition to an end, we shifted attention to political and economic factors. Natural calamities would certainly have occurred: some could have been weathered, others, occurring late in Harappan history, could have hastened the transformation. If recurrent, calamities can provide the background to a collapse.

It has been argued that what declined was a political economy with its institutions of dominance, its economic networks, its interrelationships and dependencies and intellectual norms—in other words, a state system and the cultural circumstances in which it had flowered. What is more, this was a phenomenon of the Bronze Age, which is a unique sort of social formation. It saw technological development dependent on the acquisition of scarce metals like copper, tin and arsenic or the natural copper-arsenic alloy. This was never the pattern in the Iron Age that was to follow. Iron is much more abundantly available than copper and tin...

We can now recapitulate the actual causes. Triggers or immediate causes could have been raids, migrations in the west, or internal dissensions that affected the centres of control and residential stability. In contrast, background conditions or enabling factors could be the shamanistic nature of the religion, the absence of institutionalized temples, tensions in the little communities, an undeveloped division of labour within the villages, absence of village self-sufficiency in a Bronze Age economy, as also the inroads by metal, faience and brick industries into the vegetation cover of the surrounding localities. Ultimate and deep-rooted causes would mainly be the stresses and contradictions of a system which could sustain itself only in its geographic expansion and in which the polity, trade and craft production, all centred on the elite. And elite dominance depended on a paradoxical combination of coercion and the forging of personal ties (this being too early a form of the state to have developed a full-fledged bureaucracy). As Liverani puts it (1987: 69), when there was such great concentration of "all the elements of organization, transformation, exchange",... the physical collapse of the palace was "transformed... into a general disaster for the entire kingdom".

Perhaps the structural strains became too great to override when they were juxtaposed with other independent variables, coincidental occurrences in adjoining regions: the expanding pastoralist mobility in the Eurasian steppe, the emergence of Elam as a dominant power and its possible appropriation of tin supplies after 2000 BC, which in turn could have been connected with group movements and migrations along the western margins of the Harappan world and the possible extension of regional cults.

There were, therefore, internal as well as external factors. No Bronze Age civilization appears to have been able to flourish within its own geographic frontiers. There were systemic stresses but, we would suppose, individual ambition, greed and lack of foresight were also responsible. We do not think any period of transition, violence, or decline can be ascribed to pure abstractions; human beings, surely, have also to bear the blame (Ratnagar 2000: 128-132).

Rulers come and go and the elite changes with new regimes; but the people continue. And so do the local cultural traditions. Despite the break, the Harappan legacy continues.

THE LEGACY

We think we will have to distinguish two types of legacies that the Harappans bequeathed: technological and cultural. There is certainly a change in technology at the end of the Mature Harappa culture, as Ratnagar recounts,

The Harappan civilization was succeeded by cultures we call "chalcolithic": small-scale, usually with small, one- or two-room cottages, very few crafts, a simple stone tool technology supplemented by a few forms of bone tools and not many types of copper/bronze artefacts, often ornaments rather than tools. There were no great storage structures, or distinctive sculptural styles, no fortifications in the true sense, not even wells. There is no evidence of cosmopolitan interaction with other societies. All that we can suggest, following Allchin and Joshi (1970), is that any coastal sailing tradition that continued would have been located in mainland south Gujarat, where Rangpur II B-C and III sites tend to lie near the coast. At the same time, the Chalcolithic cultures exhibited tremendous subsistence diversity in terms of eco-niches utilized, kinds of crops grown, wild foods eaten, animals domesticated and so on. Crafts with large turnovers and steady output (pottery, for example) saw continuous development. But not seal carving or inlaid ivory work or gold ornaments: such crafts would have been dependent on elite demand and state organization of imports of stones and metals. Besides, such crafts required the conscious cultivation of specific skills. Bronze Age economies and technologies, it appears, carried inbuilt structural weaknesses in their dependence on the inflow of materials like copper, tin, gold, lapis lazuli, or carnelian from relatvely few regions, often at appreciable distances from the heartlands of agricultural prosperity and population density. (It was only in the subsequent Iron Age that everyday tools came to be made of a mineral resource that is generously distributed over the world, as in most districts of South Asia.) Trade organized by the state and elite demand meant that crafts like the etched carnelian bead would not survive, let alone thrive (Nissen 1988: 43-44), in non-elite contexts. We may take just one example of Bronze Age technology: the gold granulation technique. Minute spheres of gold were soldered on to the surfaces of ornaments or ceremonial objects. This is said to have been a Mesopotamian invention, though also known in Mycenae, Egypt and the Indus valley. In our century, European jewellers tried to revive this technique but found it particularly difficult to make spheres as small as those on the Bronze Age artefacts and to solder the spheres without spoiling the surface. It took years of trial and error to develop a glue of metallic and organic ingredients that worked on a metal surface (James and Thorpe 1995: 287-89).

Thus the Harappan legacy is not its city life, but rural technologies or peasant science, knowledge that was within the control and experience of the ordinary household or village—elements of culture that had been internalized and passed down generations within the family and the community (Ratnagar 2000: 126-128).

We think that Ratnagar is also referring to the collapse of the Harappan state, hence its cities. The people and the technologies that cater to non-elite populations continued. In a traditional society like ours, hoary traditions continue along with newly acquired fashions and technologies. A closer look clearly shows an old, Harappan substratum, on which the edifice of the present Indian culture stands. Let us recapitulate and re-emphasize some of these cultural traits.

The (Hindu) religion is basically iconic and not animistic as that of the Aryans. The *pasupata, yogisvara, trimukha* aspects of the famous seals have been identified as proto-Shiva, or even proto-Mahisa and to us it appears to be a strong evidence, though Ratnagar thinks that the Harappan religion was shamanistic. The Nandi-bull worship has to be traced to the Harappans and perhaps the sacredness of the cow too. Some of the seals suggest animal sacrifice, so does the terracotta cake from Kalibangan. The linga worship can only be traced to the Harappans, even if the phallus-like objects are only few and some scholars do not believe that the proto-Shiva seal shows an ithyphallic god. The importance of pipal (*Ficus religiosa*), *swastika* and water ablutions in today's religion can be traced back to the Harappan preoccupation with water rituals (the Great Bath, the associated water structures, with the Kalibangan fire-altars, the row of bathing platforms at Lothal, etc.) do suggest a continuity of the religious beliefs. The enigmatic terracotta figures suggest Yoga-like postures.

In a 3rd millennium context, when communication and transport must have been difficult, the credit for unifying the north and west of the subcontinent goes to the Harappans. They were the first to achieve this unification of a society with so much of diversity. The location of their main metropolitan towns in a peculiar network of intersecting circles may have provided impetus for travel to these far-flung areas of the state. In later times, it was achieved by locating the main pilgrimage centres at the farthest points of the country, from Amarnath and Badrinath in the north, Dwarka in the west, Puri in the east, to Rameshwaram in the south.

Even secular objects like the typical Harappan house plan of a central courtyard surrounded by rooms (it has been found by air-conditioning experts to be best suited for Indian climate) seems to have continued from the Harappan times. The binary system of weights of the Harappans followed 1, 2, 4, 8, 16, 32, 64... 128(X), with fractions in one-third. Till recently, the Indian 1 seer = 16 *chattacks* and 1 rupee = 16 *annas* basically followed the same system. Even the *Arthasastra*'s (*angula* 17.86 mm) seems to have been derived from the Harappan measuring unit of 17.7 mm.

What the present Indian culture owes to the Indus civilization will perhaps never be known fully as the intangible heritage that we got from the Harappans can never be traced to their Harappan origins, unless one day one finds long decipherable texts of the Harappans and if they really had a script!

Chapter 4

CHALCOLITHIC CULTURES

Contents:

PREAMBLE

The discovery of Chalcolithic cultures opened up a new chapter in Indian proto-history. In 1950, S.A. Sali identified for the first time a Chalcolithic site at Jorwe in Ahmadnagar district in Maharashtra. It was excavated by the Deccan College, Pune in 1952 (Sankalia and Deo 1955). Following this discovery, hundreds of Chalcolithic settlements (Fig. 4-l) were identified in the Deccan, Central India, Rajasthan and a few in the Ganga doab and Gujarat. These Chalcolithic cultures flourished essentially outside the Harappan universe, between the 3rd and 1st Millennia BC, largely in semi-arid ecologies. They were marked by their distinct painted and wheel-turned ceramic assemblages, a specialized microlithic industry, limited use of copper, subsistence based on farming, stock-raising and hunting. They were all regional and rural in character, perhaps determined by their respective ecological niches. For example, the cultures in the upper and middle Ganga doab were characterized by the Ochre Coloured Pottery (OCP), the lower Ganga valley by the Black-and-Red Ware, north Rajasthan by the Ganeshwar-Jodhpura culture, south-eastern Rajasthan by the Ahar/Banas culture, the Malwa region by the Kayatha and Malwa cultures and the Deccan plateau supported the Savalda, the Malwa and the Jorwe cultures. Many of these cultures, such as Ganeshwar-Jodhpura, Ahar, Kayatha in central and western India and Savalda in the Deccan were part-contemporary to the early/mature/late Harappans. In fact, they can be called early farmers of the respective areas, as their subsistence pattern and tool technologies are analogous. Most of them were living in rectangular or round wattle-and-daub huts, though some cultures like the Aharians

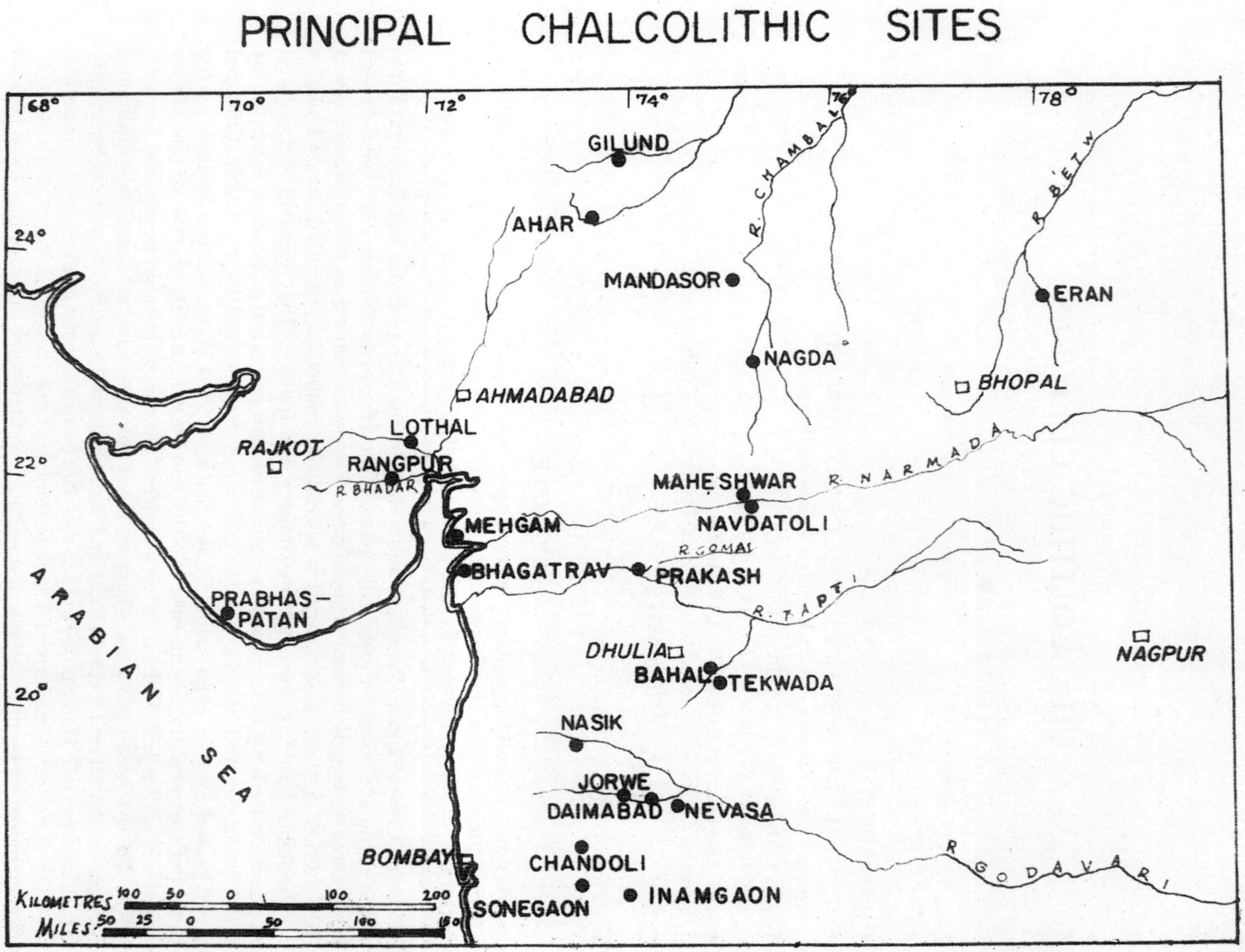

Fig. 4-1. Distribution of main Chalcolithic sites.

did erect large stone structures.

It is generally held that the onset of congenial climate in the Holocene was responsible for the increase in Mesolithic population (Dhavalikar 1988). The population pressure was perhaps responsible for the origin of agriculture (Cohen 1977) in the subcontinent. The discovery of metal objects and pottery at Mesolithic sites like Bagor have led archaeologists to suggest that the Bagorians had a symbiotic relationship (Agrawal 1982a: 65) with the Aharian settled farmers (Luckacs *et al.* 1982) of this region. Hooja (1988) has attempted to understand the interaction between the Mesolithic people of Bagor and the Chalcolithic farmers of Ahar. She also discusses the "Frontier theory" to understand the origin of Ahar culture in Rajasthan. Shinde (2000) suggests that the fertile pockets of black cotton soil attracted the early farmers and that the late Harappans of Gujarat played very important role in the origin and development of the Chalcolithic cultures. The following is the brief description of these cultures.

CENTRAL AND WESTERN INDIAN CHALCOLITHIC CULTURES

Ganeshwar-Jodhpura Culture

Ganeshwar and Jodhpura, both the type sites of this culture, were discovered and excavated in the 1970s by R.C. Agrawala and Vijay Kumar of the Rajasthan State Department of Archaeology and Museums (IAR 1972-73: 29-30; Kumar 1977; Agrawala and Kumar 1993). The Harappan sites in the north, the OCP sites in the east and the Ahar Complex on the south surround this culture-complex.

Jodhpura (27°31' N; 76°5' E), tehsil Kotputali, district Jaipur, is located on the right bank of River Sabi, about 98 km north-east of Jaipur town. The mound is spread over an area of about 8-hectare, the peripheral area of which has been levelled for agriculture. It consists of about 12 m thick habitation deposit and a number of stone and mud brick structures and evidence of smelting is visible on the surface. The well-known Asokan inscriptions of Bhabru and Bairath are also located close to this site. The excavations in the western part of the mound yielded evidence of five cultural periods ranging from Chalcolithic to Sunga-Kushana.

The OCP people were the first inhabitants with a cultural deposit of 1.30 m. Here the wheel-turned OCP is orange to deep red in colour, indicating that it was fired at high temperature, unlike the OCP of doab. The Jodhpura OCP is often treated with a thick coating of red slip and bears a variety of incised decorations, e.g., triangular notches between parallel lines, wavy and rectangular lines or bands. It is represented by bowls, vases, knobbed lids and dishes-on-stand. The Harappan influence is evident in the ceramics. Houses of 4 x 3.5 m size, bricks (size: 18 x 11 x 6 or 30 x 26 x 7 cm), fragments of copper, terracotta and stone beads and bone points have been reported. The evidence of smelting was noticed on the surface, perhaps belonging to a later period.

The subsequent periods at Jodhpura were identified as Black-and-Red Ware (but different from the Ahar variety), PGW, NBPW and Sunga-Kushana respectively.

Ganeshwar (75° 50' E; 27° 40' N) is located about 10 km south-east of Nim-ka-Thana tehsil in district Sikar in the Kantali basin and about 75 km south of Khetri copper deposits. The Ganeshwar region is dotted with hills of the Aravalli ranges and sand-dunes, which form part of the Thar Desert. These hillocks control the drainage of the rivulets originating in this region such as the Kantali, Sota, Sahibi and Dohan. Only the Kantali flows towards north, whereas others flow towards east and north-west. The site, situated to the north-east of the Ganeshwar village, was excavated in 1979 by R.C. Agrawala and has yielded hardly 2 m thick deposit spread over an area about 2 ha. The site has largely been destroyed by agricultural ploughing and by the metalled road.

The following three cultural phases have been identified at Ganeshwar (*IAR* 1987-88):

Phase I: Microliths and large number of animal bones were found in the lower levels, the habitation deposit of which was 30 to 50 cm thick. The geometric tool industry comprises blunted back blades, retouched blades and obliquely blunted blades, pen-knife blades, triangles, points, crescents, trapezes, arrowheads, scrapers and burins.

Phase II: This phase (40-60 cm thick debris) was characterized by introduction of pottery known as Ganeshwar-Jodhpura ware, animal bones, circular huts, floors paved with river pebbles. Use of microliths also continued. Both handmade and wheel-made pottery was found, which is ill-fired and often treated with bright red slip, sometimes decorated with incised designs and represented by globular and bulbous jars, carinated vessels, shallow pans and bowls. A few copper objects like arrowheads, fish-hooks, spearheads and awls were also found in this phase.

Phase III: The last phase was characterized by a profusion of a variety of copper objects (arrowheads, rings, bangles, chisels, balls and celts) and pottery showing Harappan affinity. It is generally decorated with incised designs and the shapes are represented by bowls, beakers, goblets, cylindrical vases, offering stands, basins and jars. Sometimes, black painting was also applied.

As around 1000 copper objects, including a variety of arrowheads (more than 400), 60 flat celts (out of which 58 were discovered from Kulhade-ka-Johad near Ganeshwar), 50 fish-hooks were found in association with the Red Ware pottery identical to what is known as OCP at Jodhpura. Therefore, the excavators have termed this as Ganeshwar-Jodhpura culture. Reserve Slipped pottery has also been reported from Ganeshwar, though details are not available. Since a considerable quantity of microliths were found along with copper tools in the deposit, the excavators report, "though they had developed a metallurgical technology they were still in a hunting stage". The discovery of, a large number of arrowheads and fish-hooks also indicates such a subsistence pattern at Ganeshwar. Considering the evidence of Phases I and II, it seems that they might have begun agriculture on a small scale. It is also possible that they were getting grains in exchange for their copper-bronze objects from the neighbouring Harappans. It appears that they were able to exploit nearby rich copper mines and successfully exploit this local resource as early as the 3rd millennium BC. Ganeshwar area appears to be an industrial site of copper smelting and manufacturing as the evidence of slag deposit and discovery of thousands of copper objects at the site would indicate. The excavator explains that most of the copper artefacts conform to Indus typology and not a single specimen is of the Doab Copper Hoard type.

Ganeshwar Complex Tool Repertory

Agrawala and Kumar (1993) have described some of the Ganeshwar Complex copper tool types as follows:

Arrowheads: Cut from thin copper sheets like those of Indus sites, the Ganeshwar arrowheads are rich and varied in size and shape. Most of them are of the barbed variety. Quite a number have an unusual curved tip. They were probably meant for hunting a flock of birds. One copper arrowhead of this kind was excavated from the Harappan levels at

Banawali. Similar arrowheads from Bagor (district Bhilwara, Rajasthan) (Misra 1970, Fig. 11.3) were provided with two holes each, which allowed them to be tied to the wooden stick. A few of the Ganeshwar variety of copper arrowheads (without holes) were found at Kalibangan, Lothal, Harappa, Mohenjodaro and Chanhudaro (Marshall 1939, Pl. CXLII, no 13; Mackay 1938: Pls. CXXI, CXXVII, CXXXIII; Vats 1940: 383-84 Pl. CXXV, nos. 13-14). Similar arrowheads were also found from Kunal and Dholavira. There are approximately four hundred arrowheads of this style from Ganeshwar alone. K.K. Tripathi of the Geological Survey of India (GSI) has analysed an arrowhead from Ganeshwar and has reported the following composition:

Copper 96.5 per cent, Silver 0.3 per cent, Arsenic 1 per cent, Lead 0.03 per cent, Tin 0.2 per cent, Nickel 0.04 per cent, Zinc 0.25 per cent, Iron 0.2 per cent.

Spearheads: The Ganeshwar copper spearheads are generally very thin. There are, however, a few thick examples too. Comparable objects were also found at Harappa and Mohenjodaro. They were perhaps attached to wooden shafts before actual use.

Fish-Hooks: The Ganeshwar copper fish-hooks, numbering about 50, are usually not provided with a tang. Small fish-hooks were also found at Harappa and Mohenjodaro in the early levels (Mackay 1938: Pls. CXXXII, no. 21 and CXXIV, no 29; Vats 1940: CXXV, no 28). Similar fish-hooks were recovered from Banawali as well.

Spiral Headed Pins: Ganeshwar also yielded a few fragmentary pins of the Harappan type.

Celts: The copper celts from Ganeshwar are 20 to 25 cm in length and weigh between 1 and 1.5 kg. All these flat celts were prepared from moulds by the *cire perdue* technique. Most of them have round indentation marks on the butt portion in groups of 4, 5, 6, 8 and 9, 12 and as many as 15 different combinations of 1 to 3, 4 and 6 dots on one side.

It is perhaps significant to note that the indentation marks on the Ganeshwar celts are near the butt end. The varied permutations and combinations of dots recall somewhat similar marks on the Chalcolithic celts from Navdatoli and Kayatha in Madhya Pradesh where they have been found on the body of the celts, much below the butt end (Ansari and Dhavalikar 1975: 150). At Kayatha these celts were assigned a time bracket of 2000-1800 BC (uncal.); incised pottery was found from these levels. Copper celts with circular impressions have also been reported from the copper hoards of western Uttar Pradesh (Thaplyal and Shukla 1976; Agrawala and Kumar 1993). Though the only analysed copper celt from Ganeshwar does not show any alloying with tin, we should analyse samples from, a large number of sites around Ganeshwar as now the source of tin has also been discovered at Tusham hills, near Bhiwani in Haryana, which is close to Ganeshwar and Khetri region (Kochhar *et al.* 1999). The GSI laboratory at Jaipur has given the following analysis of a typical copper celt from Ganeshwar region:

Analysis of copper celt:

Copper 97 per cent; Silver 0.2 per cent; Lead 1 per cent; Arsenic 0.3 per cent;
Tin 0.01 per cent; Nickel; 10.6 per cent.

Apart from the copper celts, bowls, channel spouts were also discovered at Kurada. The bowls are also important. It was the trade with West Asia which might have induced the Ganeshwar people to prepare copper bowls in imitation of the channel-spouted bowls from Iran, as Sankalia had earlier suggested. It is to be noted that Kurada was situated on a trade route, which runs west via Ganeshwar, Kurada-Pokharan-Phalodi-Jaisalmer-Kot Diji, etc.

Agrawala (1984b) emphasizes that Ganeshwar is ideally situated on the source of one of the streams of the River Kantali. They also discovered dozens of OCP sites along various nullahs and streamlets of the Kanwat and the Khandela, originating from Ganeshwar and discharging into the main Kantali. The pottery from this zone has been called Ganeshwar pottery and is abundant in the Sikar district of Rajasthan. It is to be noted that the ancient Dariba copper mine has also yielded Ganeshwar pottery. The Kantali river is at some places 2-3 km in width and it must have made possible riverine transport from Ganeshwar to Kalibangan and other Indus centres of the west. A number of Kalibangan-type sites along the Drishadwati river, such as Siswal, Sirpura and Sothi are well-known.

The Ganeshwar-Jodhpura complex is spread over an area of about 200,000 sq. km in Sikar, Jhunjhunu, Jaipur districts, which has yielded numerous sites of this culture so far (Hooja and Kumar 1995). As these settlements are located in the richest copper mineral zone of Rajasthan, the discovery of more than 5,000 copper objects from this complex is not surprising. The preliminary results of excavations at Ganeshwar, together with such a large cluster of sites, indicate that they were not itinerant smiths. In fact, settlement pattern of Ganeshwar complex will be clear to us only when the entire dry bed of the Kantali is thoroughly explored right from Ganeshwar to Nohar-Bhadra and further north where the Kanṭali joins the Drishadvati. Copper celts and inverted V-shaped arrowheads are also found in the Pre-Harappan levels at Kalibangan.

Old Workings

The Aravallis are well-known for their base metal (copper-lead-zinc) minerals and the evidence suggests that they have been mined and smelted for several Millennia. The Aravallis and the Delhi group of rocks are dotted with innumerable old workings and slag heaps. The copper mines are mostly along the eastern flank of the Aravallis, extending from Alwar, Khetri, Bharatpur in the north-east to Udaipur and Ambamata. The copper-lead related minerals are mainly chalcopyrite, pyrrhotite, pyrite, pentlandite, sphalerite, galena, bornite, covellite, cubanite with native copper (Radhakrishna 1975: 20-35).

The old workings are reported from Nithahar, Basawar, Hathori, Khan-Khera, Khareri (Bharatpur region), Kho Dariba, Pratapgarh (Alwar region), Singhana and Babai, Madhan, Baleshwar Dariba, Ahirwala (Khetri region), Piplawas, Deogarh and Kankaria (Ajmer region), Delwara, Keroli, Salumber, Dhariawad, Lassadia, Bansda-Bhinder, Udaipur, Kotri Dariba, Rajpur Dariba, Ambamata, Deri in southern Rajasthan.

In north Rajasthan, in Mardan-Kudan section, there is a copper belt of 28 million tonnes with 0.8 per cent copper and in Dariba area there is 0.5 million tonnes ore deposit with 2.5 per cent copper. The mineral found in these areas is chalcopyrite ($CuFe_2S_2$) which is usually disseminated in schists and phyllites (Agrawal 1971: 147)

In our recent survey (Kharakwal, Sharma and Meena, in press), we located ancient smelting sites (Pl. 4-1), e.g., Dokan I, Bhitaro, Bewan Patan, Babai, Kho, Udaipurwati, Thana, Ganeshwar II, Ganeshwar III, Ganeshwar IV, Toda Dariba and Morajawala in Sekhawati region in north Rajasthan. At some sites like Ganeshwar II, Sunari, etc., the evidence of smelting furnaces, tuyeres were also found. All these smelting sites are located within a radius of 15 km from Ganeshwar. Some sites have small heaps of light slag which is brownish, blackish in colour with a glossy surface. Ganeshwar I, Ganeshwar IV, have also yielded Ganeshwar Complex type pottery.

Several ancient copper smelting sites have been reported in and around Ahar, e.g.,

Delwara, Karoli, Anjani, Umra, Matoon, Bhinder, Bhadesar, Bari-Sadari (Agrawala 1984a: 156; Majoomdar and Rajaguru 1962-63: 31). At most of these places malachite stained quartz pieces were discarded. Perhaps superficially stained pieces were discarded and only good quality of copper ore was used. The chief copper bearing minerals extracted from the mining shafts, along the shear zone, are chalcopyrites, sulphides of copper and iron and malachite. They are associated with phyllites and biotite actinolite schist. Most of the ore workings are found in harder geological formations, e.g., quartzite (Majoomdar and Rajaguru 1962-63). It is, therefore, quite likely that these mines supplied copper to the Ahar people.

From the archaeological assemblage of the Bronze Age cultures of Rajasthan, particularly of Ganeshwar and Ahar and the evidence of hundreds of mining and smelting sites, it appears that these non-urban, non-literate rural people were largely involved in craft activity especially copper mining and smithy. The traditional knowledge system did play a positive and significant role in the development of science and technology among these folks as some tribes produce even today high quality rust-free steel and gun-metal quality steel.

It is therefore, quite possible that the Ganeshwar-Jodhpura culture people, like the village-based communities of Thailand (Pigott 1999), carried out extensive mining and smelting and supplied copper/bronze to the contemporary rural and urban societies in the South Asian subcontinent. With such a rich repertoire of copper artefacts and abundant mineral resources, the Ganeshwar Complex, surrounded by a number of important Harappan sites on the north and north-east, seems to have played a pivotal role in supplying copper artefacts and ingots to the Harappans and the Banasians and probably has nothing to do with the Ganga Copper Hoards.

The Harappans did not carry out smelting in their settlements, though evidence of melting is abundant (Chakrabarti and Lahiri 1996; Miller 1999). Rajasthan, Baluchistan, eastern Iran and even far off Oman have been suggested as the important sources of copper for the Harappans. Heather Miller (unpublished thesis) has pointed out that even copper rich prills were discarded at Harappa, which certainly indicates that there was an abundance of metal and that it was not a precious import. Even in the Mesopotamian texts, Meluhha is identified with the Indus and eastern region. We, therefore, suggest that Ganeshwar-Jodhpura Complex may be identified with Meluhha of the Mesopotamian text (Agrawal and Kharakwal 2002).

The ^{14}C dates of Jodhpura place this culture in the early part of 3rd millennium BC, i.e. between about 2900 and 2500 BC (PRL-275, 2926 cal. BC; PRL-278, 2578 BC). These dates are for the later phase of Jodhpura. However, the beginning of this culture may be slightly earlier than 3rd millennium BC.

Ahar or Banas Culture

The Ahar or Banas culture flourished in an undulating topography of gneissic plains in eastern Rajasthan, which supports Khejra (*Prosopis spicigera*), Babul (*Acacia arabica*), Runjra (*Acacia leucophlaea*), Palas (*Butea frondosa*) and date palm (*Phoemix sylvestris*) forest.

About 91 sites of the Ahar/Banas culture have been discovered in south-eastern Rajasthan, traditionally known as the Mewar region. They are located on the banks of the Ahar, Banas, Berach, Gambhiri, Kothari, Khari rivers and their tributaries in the districts of Udaipur, Chittorgarh, Bhilwara, Dungarpur, Ajmer, Bundi and Tonk (Misra 1967; Hooja 1988; Kharakwal in press). This culture is named so because most of the sites have been discovered on the banks of the rivers Ahar and Banas; the former is a tributary of the latter. The first site of this culture was noticed at Ahar (24°35' N, 73° 44' E), locally known as Dhool-kot and located on the bank of the Ahar stream at Udaipur. It is fairly big mound measuring 305 x 270 x 13 m and was excavated in 1950 by Akshay Kirti Vyas of Rajasthan State Department of Archaeology. To ascertain the antiquity of the site, it was again excavated in 1952-53 and 1954-55 by R.C. Agrawala of the same department (IAR 1954-55: 14-15; 1955-56: 11), who identified three different cultures: Prehistoric, Early Historic and Medieval. Finally, horizontal excavations were carried out in 1960-61, jointly by the Deccan College, Pune and Rajasthan State Department of Archaeology under the direction of Sankalia (IAR 1961-62: 45-50; Sankalia *et al.* 1969). And then, for the first time, it was named Ahar culture. Gilund in Rajsamand district is the largest (about 17 ha) known settlement and perhaps a regional cultural centre, located in the valley of Banas and was excavated in 1959-60 by B.B. Lal of Archaeological Survey of India (IAR 1959-60: 41-46). He identified two distinct mounds at Gilund. His limited excavations yielded remains of Ahar/Banas, Early Historic and Medieval cultures. The discovery of a mud brick complex measuring about 30.48 x 24.38 m was significant. As he discovered a number of sites, the cultural material of which he found similar to Gilund, along the valley of Banas, he preferred to call this as Banas culture (Lal 1963). The Aharian and the Banasian denote the same culture.

This Banas culture is characterized by rectangular houses of mud bricks, microliths, copper objects, terracotta figurines, beads of clay, chalcedony, agate and steatite and a variety of pottery including Black-and-Red, Red, Buff, Black Painted Buff Ware, Aharand Grey Wares (Pls. 4-2, -3, -4, -5, -6). The evidence of long parallel walls was one of the enigmatic finds at Gilund. The site is again under excavation after forty years and has been horizontally opened up by Gregory Possehl of Pennsylvania Museum and V. Shinde, Deccan College, Pune. They have also found a similar enigmatic structural complex containing as many as 5 parallel mud brick walls (each about 50 cm thick) runing north-south. These walls are spaced at regular about (one metre) intervals and meet two east-west running walls. They are about 10 metre long and some of them have survived to a height of about one metre. As they are plastered, the excavators think that this complex could be a granary (Shinde pers. comm.). We do not know if this is the same structural complex which B.B. Lal excavated forty years ago. Balathal (IAR 1962-63: 18), another important site of this culture has recently been excavated horizontally by the Deccan College and Institute of Rajasthan Studies, Rajasthan Vidyapeeth, Udaipur under the general direction of V.N. Misra (Misra 1997; Misra *et al.* 1995 and 1997). It is located about 42 km east of Ahar and is a smaller settlement {(135 m NS x 150 m EW x 7 m (height)} compared to Ahar. Sankalia *et al.* (1969) identified three distinct phases of Period I of the Ahar culture at Ahar: Phases A, B and C on the basis of structural remains and ceramic assemblage (Fig. 4-2).

The Jaipur Circle of Archaeological Survey of India has also recently carried out excavations at Ojiyana, located on the bank of the River Khari, a tributary of the Banas in the district Bhilwara (Meena and Tripathi 2000). The site is situated on a gentle hill slope. It is a single culture site (250 m NS x 200 m EW), with a deposit of about 7.5 m. The excavation was carried out on a small scale and three different phases of the Ahar culture have been identified. It appears from the preliminary reports that the Black-and-Red Ware and Bright Red Slipped Wares were predominant at the site. Large number of terracotta bull figurines, beads of agate, steatite, chalcedony and faience; charred grains (wheat), saddle querns and few copper objects such as a minuscule "chopper", a blade, 2 bangle fragments and a ring were found associated with mud brick and stone structures. Ojiyana has also yielded white painted bull figurines, which are very rare in the Chalcolithic cultures.

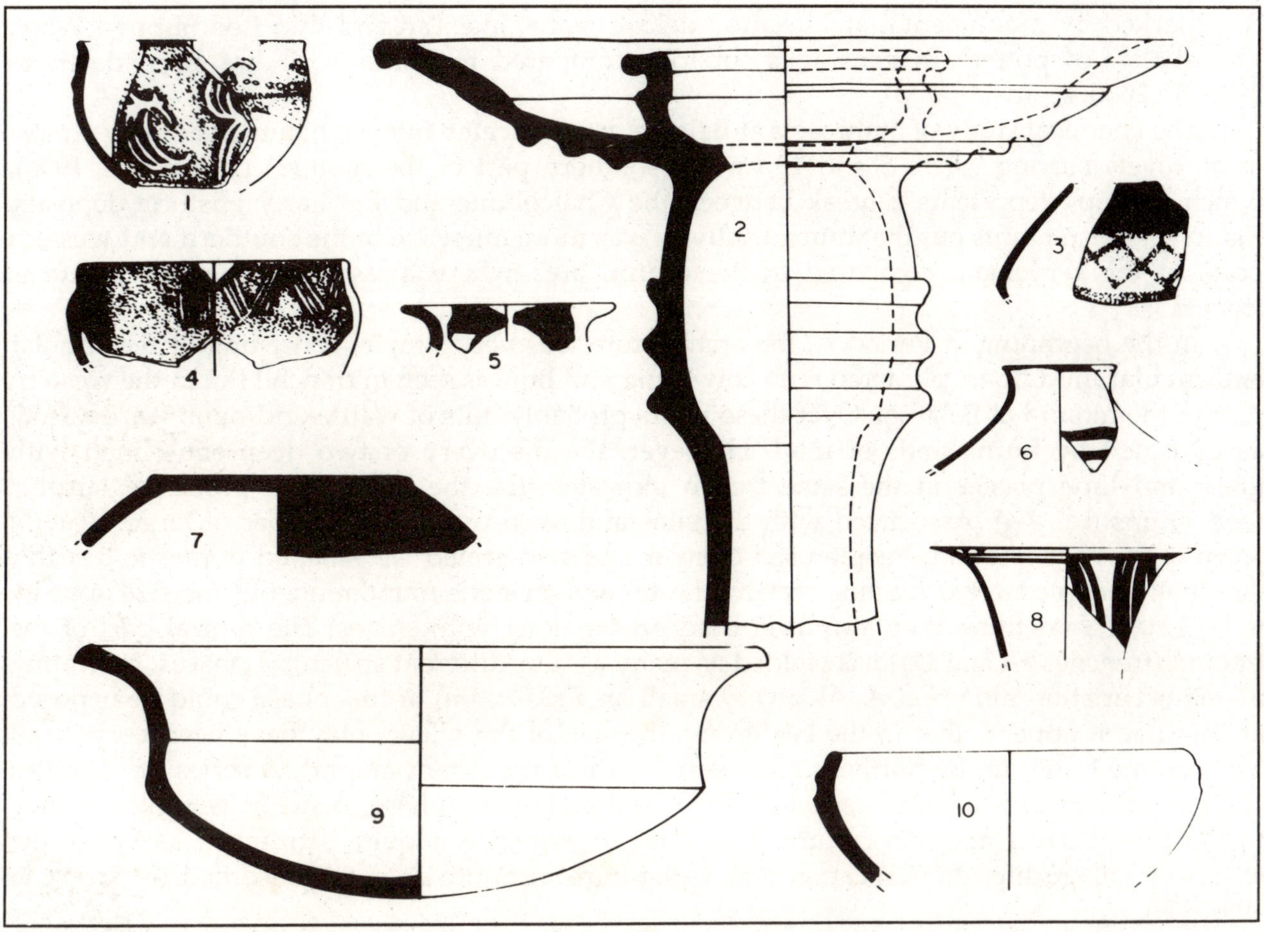

Fig. 4-2. Black-and-Red Ware 1, 4, 7; Tan 2, and Red Wares 9, 10, from Ahar, Rajasthan.

Most of the Ahar settlements are located either on the banks of tributaries of the Banas and the Ahar or close to the perennial water bodies where arable land is easily available. Misra (1967: 196) suggested that the "Sites on the western fringe of the (Ahar) culture zone show earlier wares, while those lying on the eastern edge of the explored area show later features, such as the absence of Tan Slipped and Thin Red Wares, paucity of decorative patterns and the presence of painted red sherds". The results of Purani Marmi (25°06' N; 74°25' E) agree very well with this observation (Mohanty *et al.* 2000). Our recent explorations in southern Rajasthan have also revealed that several Ahar culture sites were reoccupied by the Early Historic people, as the evidence of excavaed and explored sites, e.g., Ahar, Balathal and Gilund and other sites also indicates.

The Ahar culture is characterized by painted Black-and-Red Ware and typical Bright Red slipped Ware. At Ahar, the deposit has been subdivided into three phases A, B and C, whereas at Balathal, two distinct phases A and B have been identified on the basis of stratigraphy, architecture and material culture. A total of 7 m thick cultural deposit was measured out of which less than two metre on top belongs to the Early Historic period (Period II). Balathal Phase A is represented by circular and squarish houses, made of mud and stone. The pottery in this phase is both handmade and wheel-turned, very often with a coarse fabric and incised decorations; also bone tools, steatite and agate beads and copper objects. Phase

B is marked by monumental architecture, deluxe wares like Tan and thin Red Slipped Ware. The quality of pottery in general is superior compared to Phase A. It has been dated to 2900 to 2000 BC (calibrated).

The chemical study of anthrosols at Balathal has indicated intensive human activity almost in all levels barring layers 5 and 13 (in the southern part of the mound) (Kshirsagar 1996), which perhaps represents a break between the Chalcolithic and the Early Historic deposits. Kshirsagar also points out that human activity was more intensive in the southern and western parts of the settlement compared to the central area where massive fortified enclosure is located.

In the beginning of Period A, the architecture was very simple, consisting of rectangular and circular mud floors plastered with cow-dung and lime as seen in trench HX2 in the western part of the mound at Balathal. Over these floors probably huts of wattle-and-daub were raised, as indicated by burnt clods of mud. However, the discovery of two deep silos lined with grass and lime plaster in the same trench indicates that the inhabitants produced surplus food grains (Pl. 4-4). Associated with the silos and even outside, a number of large, heavily worn querns were found. People used circular and two-armed "U"-shaped domestic hearths. Gradually people started erecting rectangular houses on stone foundation, but the size appears to be small. Sometimes they also used mud bricks along with stones. The central part of the mound (trenches E4 and D4) has yielded as many as four different structural phases, indicating a long occupation in Period A. As a very small area (350 sqm) of this phase could be exposed at Balathal, it appears that in the beginning, the size of the village may have been very small and confined only to the northern and central part of the extant mound. A series of ^{14}C dates (calibrated) suggests a time bracket of 2900-2600 BC for this phase, hence it is contemporary to the Pre-/Early Harappan culture. This kind of evidence is quite significant as far as the origin of village life, domestication and agriculture in South Asia is concerned (Misra *et al.* 1997: 58).

These first farmers also introduced pottery in this region, which has been identified as Red, Grey and white painted Black-and-Red, Buff and Reserve Slipped Ware. The Red Ware has two varieties, i.e. fine and coarse. They used both handmade and wheel-turned pottery, however, their raw material was of inferior quality and the firing was not uniform. The course variety of Red Ware, which is named as Thick Bright Red Slip Ware, is treated with a red slip and very rarely decorated with red or white paintings. The discovery of Reserved Slipped Ware right from the beginning at Balathal is certainly quite interesting and important. The common shapes of this assemblage are wide mouthed, deep carinated bowls, dishes-on-stand, basins and jars of various sizes. These wares continued throughout the Chalcolithic period in this region though with slight changes in shape and size.

A gradual development in material culture was observed in cultural Phase B at Balathal. There is a marked change in the size of structures and the materials and techniques used in their construction from the beginning of this phase. The architecture of the phase is marked by extensive use of semi-dressed and undressed stones and mud bricks. The structures of this cultural period are exposed in thecentral, southern, eastern and northern parts of the mound. Like Aharians, the Balathalians were also living in squarish or rectangular houses, invariably oriented north-south. The house-floors at Ahar were prepared by river gravels mixed with clay, whereas at Balathal alternate layers of hard rammed brownish silt and black clay were found. Sometimes the bigger houses/rooms were provided with partition walls.

Four architectural phases have been identified in this cultural phase. Structural Phases

I and IV are represented only by broken walls whereas Phases II and III are better preserved. Out of these, Phase II appears to be the most prosperous as it is best represented by a fortified enclosure and multi-roomed complexes.

Fortified Enclosure

The fortified enclosure is located in the centre of the settlement and surrounded by residential complexes. Except the northern one, all other complexes are largey made of stone. The fortified enclosure is roughly rectangular on plan and flanked by rectangular bastions on all four corners. The western wall (running north-south) is 27.4 m, the northern wall (running east-west) is 38.35 m, whereas the southern wall runs east-west for 16.45 m and then takes a right angle turn to the south. At a distance of 9.5 m, it again turns east and runs for 14.3 m and joins the eastern wall (running north-south), which is 37.65 m long and 6.8 m thick. The walls are made of mud and mud bricks riveted on either side by 1.25 m thick stone courses, set in mud mortar. It is made in a tapering fashion as the average thickness of the wall on top is 4.80 m and gradually broadens to 6.50 m at the base. It has, therefore, survived to a height of 4 m. The structure has enclosed an area of over 500 sq m. Such massive structure may indicate a chiefdom. .

There are three structural complexes to the south of the fortified enclosure located on either side of a 4.8 m wide street running north-south. Out of these, the multi-roomed larger complex made of stones is located on the eastern side, however, other two are on the western side and are made of mud bricks and stones. The latter ones are separated from each other by a 1.6 m wide lane, which opens in the street. The rooms of varied dimensions were used for dwelling, cooking and storage purposes. Traces of similar residential complexes were noticed to the eastern and northern part of the fortified enclosure. Few houses, for example, the complex number 11, represent poor quality of construction. It appears that people living in this complex could not afford stones for their construction, which perhaps suggests a stratified economic and social organization. There is evidence of incipient planning of the settlement. The evidence from the excavated area also suggests that the entire site came under occupation only in the second phase (layers 17 to 9) around 2400 BC. This phase witnessed a remarkable prosperity.

In fact, the Balathalians knew the technique of erecting brick and stone structures right from Phase A, but they did not make large structures in this early phase for some unknown reason. Large monumental and massive structures appear in Period B, possibly due to the remarkable prosperity at the site. To make their houses, theyused undressed, semi-dressed stones, mud, sun-dried bricks and burnt bricks. The burnt bricks were not used everywhere as the excavated sites indicate. At Balathal generally the mud brick walls were found resting on stone foundations. Sometimes they have been used in the walls also. This feature has also been found in the fortified enclosure at Balathal. It seems that everyone could not afford use of dressed stones, therefore, some people made houses of mud walls or mud bricks. These bricks do not have any similarity with Pre-Harappan or Mature Harappan bricks as far as the size is concerned.

At Balathal we have evidence of planned settlement, granaries, stone, brick and mud brick structures and introduction of new pottery types in Balathal Phase B, e.g. Tan Ware identical to the north Gujarat Harappan. Perhaps all these elements suggest a possible Harappan connection with Mewar.

At Balathal, the traces of a sturdy stonewall set in mud mortar were exposed on the eastern margin, which has been suspected as the outer fortification. It was constructed in two phases.

Like architecture, a gradual development in the ceramic assemblage was also seen in this phase. Introduction of a variety of lids with animal figurine handles and pots decorated either with elegant incised patterns or by a thick ledge below the rim are common. The pottery is predominantly wheel-turned and on the basis of quality of clay and surface treatment it can be broadly divided into two categories: fine and coarse wares. The fine variety comprises Thin Red, Black-and-Red and Tan Ware; the coarse variety includes Bright Red Slipped Ware, Plain Red Ware, Burnished Grey and Plain Grey Ware.

The fine variety, made of refined clay, has a thin and highly burnished slip, fired at high temperature and looks very attractive. Dishes dominate this assemblage of bowls, small and medium-size jars. The Thin Red Ware, called the deluxe ware at Balathal, has a highly burnished red slip and is represented by deep convex sided bowls and rarely by small globular vessels with everted rim and narrow opening. It is the principal ware at Balathal and appears profusely right from Layer 18. Often the shoulder portion is decorated with incised design. Though it is found at many sites, at Ahar it appeared only in the last phase. The white painted Black-and-Red Ware is the characteristic pottery of the Ahar culture and it is found right from the beginning. The shapes in this ware are generally a variety of wide-mouthed convex sided bowls and medium-size bulbous jars with narrow opening. The decoration, which includes a band of straight or wavy lines, spirals, dots and circles, appears to be post-firing as it tends to fade. The Tan Ware is named so because of tan colour slip and it is represented by dish and dish-on-stands (Pl. 4-5). Some sherds of this ware are chocolate slipped, which look like the Kayatha ware. This ware is stated to be similar to that of north Gujarat Harappan pottery and appeared at Balathal in cultural Phase B. It may have been the result of contacts with the Hrappans.

The discovery of Reserve Slipped pottery appears to be quite important, as earlier, it was only found from a few Harappan sites. Here at Balathal, two different types, e.g. grey (imported) and red (locally made) are identified. The grey variety is highly burnished and bears beautiful combed decoration on the outer side, whereas the red variety is coarse compared to grey and represented by small bulbous pots and shallow dishes with stand. The decorations include mainly closely spaced horizontal and zigzag sets of lines.

The coarse pottery comprises the Thick Bright Red Slipped or Thick Red and Grey Wares (Pl. 4-6). These wares are made of unrefined clay, generally decorated with incised and appliqué designs and comprise large globular pots of various sizes, possibly some of them, particularly Grey Ware ones, may have been used for storage and cooking purpose. The Red Ware has been treated with thick burnished slip above the shoulder part, whereas the lower portion is rusticated.

Though the structural activity and ceramic tradition continued in structural Phases III and IV, the construction is of poor quality and a gradual decline is also evident in the quality of pottery. Therefore, the last structural phase IV can be interpreted as representing an economic decline.

Burials

Interestingly, Balathal has also yielded an animal and a few human burials. All these burials were found in the fortified enclosure. Stratigraphy inside the fortified enclosure suggests that cow-dung appears to have been thrown from outside at different times. The piling certainly shows various episodes. It was burnt at different temperatures in different areas in multiple episodes over a long period of time. This is clearly attested by the considerable local variation in the composition of layers in respect of colour and compactness of the ash and structure of cow-dung cakes. Barring a few burials, except for bits of potsherds and bones, no other cultural material has been found from the cow-dung. One of the burials (found at the base of dumping) predates the dumping, whereas others were found in the upper horizon of Layer 6. After the burials were put in place in the upper part of Layer 6, no more cow-dung dumping took place. It seems that these burials belong to the last phase of Ahar culture.

The Burial no. 1 was found at the base of this dump, at a depth of 2.70 m from the surface, in trench E3 in the 1997-98 season. It was an adult (35-40 age), buried in a crouching posture with head towards south. Few small stones were found placed at different places beneath the skeleton probably to keep the dead body in position.

Three more burials were found in the 1999-2000 season from Layer 6, which represents the last phase of cow-dung dumping. Burial no 2, oriented east-west, was found from the upper part of Layer 6 in the north-western part of trench E4. The lower portion of the skeleton was missing because it was destroyed by a later pit. It appears to be a secondary burial as folding of arm bones, upside down position of mandible, location of the two scapulae close to each other and position of the ribs to the left of the arm bones suggest. The bones, however, are in a good state of preservation. A small globular Red Ware pot was found associated with the burial, which appears to be an offering as it was placed close to the head. Burial no. 4 was discovered about 2 m south of Burial no. 2 at the same level from trench D4 at a depth of 1.88 m from the surface. This adult man, also oriented east-west, was found in a crouching posture on a compact surface made of burnt cow-dung, with a few small stones placed irregularly. His head was resting on a small flat stone (28 x 20 x 11 cm). Few stones were also placed below the hip and knee portions perhaps to support the body. Most of the bones of this skeleton were perfectly articulated. Two carnelian beads, on the abdomen and a copper pin placed near the right hand were found associated with the skeleton.

Apart from these, Layer 7 also yielded a skeleton of a three-month old calf at a depth of 2.5 m in south-western part of trench E4. This burial pit was dug into the ashy bed of Layer 7, which was sealed by Layer 6. It was buried immediately after death as, according to Thomas, the limb bones are perfectly articulated. The historical levels also yielded an interesting burial (Burial no.3) in the central part of the mound from trench B4. It was found in Layer 5 and sealed by Layer 3. The body was interred in a sitting posture, facing towards north. There were two circular clay rings around the burial. The skull and other bones of the upper part of the body are missing. The arm and leg bones, including the delicate hand and foot bones are, however, very well preserved. It was placed in a Yogic sitting posture. This kind of tradition still persists among the Lingayats and the Giri/Goswami communities (Misra pers. comm.).

Bull Figurines: Several sites, e.g. Kayatha, Ahar, Marmi, Gilund and others have yielded terracotta bull figurines. Misra *et al.* (1993) have identified at least three types of bull figurines: stylized; naturalistic without hump; and naturalistic with hump from the Ahar culture complex. They suggest that some of these figurines were probably votive offerings. However, Dhavalikar (1979) thinks that people may have worn them around the neck. Few white painted bull figurines of naturalistic type with hump have also been found from Ojiyana (Meena and Tripathi 2000). Purani Marmi, a late Ahar culture site (Mohanty *et al.* 2000), located about 30 km north-west of Chittorgarh and close to Gilund, appears to be the production centre of such figurines. One can still pick up hundreds of figurines right from the surface. It is quite likely that these figurines were supplied to all the Ahar sites and may have served some religious purpose, perhaps associated with bull cult. "The earliest evidence of terracotta bull figurines in the subcontinent was found at the site of Mehrgarh in Baluchistan from Period III, dating to 4th millennium BC (Jarrige 1984). Apart from these sites, Kulli (Stein 1931) in Baluchistan and Balakot in Sind (Dales 1974) have also yielded similar bull figurines (Misra *et al.* 1993)". Most of these sites have yielded naturalistic figurines, many of which are decorated. These bull figurines are naturalistic with prominent humps and horns. Naturalistic terracotta bull figurines were also found from Inamgaon (Dhavalikar *et al.* 1988), Daimabad (Sali 1986) and Chandoli (Deo and Ansari 1965).

Copper objects: Though copper was available to the Aharians/Banasians, the microlithic tradition continued at several sites, e.g. Kayatha, Marmi, Gilund, Bedla and others have yielded microliths. Several ancient copper mining and smelting sites have been found in southern ajasthan and some of the mining sites are 40 m deep. Smelting was also carried out at Ahar as the mound is littered with slag.

At Ahar, also known as Tambavati Nagari, five axes, one knife blade, one sheet, a bangle and two rings were found. However, Balathal yielded over a dozen copper-bronze objects comprising choppers, knives, razors and one specimen each of a chisel, a tanged and barbed arrowhead, an ear stud, a bangle, a six-petalled flower-like object (Pl. 4-7) and bits of copper.

Agrawala (1980: 89-91) reports that the thin knife blades which he found from the lowest levels of Ahar are identical to the ones found from Khurdi and Kurada (Rajasthan) and Mitathal (Haryana) and are generally known as *parasu*. The Ahar chopper (*parasu*) is also similar to a curved blade from Pre-Mature Harappan levels at Kalibangan. It seems that this was a multipurpose tool and resembles modern *gandasa*, a common tool in Punjab, Haryana and Uttar Pradesh, used for cutting stalks of wheat, barley and rice plants and long thick grass for animal fodder. From Kurada, district Nagaur, Rajasthan, a hoard of 21 such blades was found, though only four are preserved in the Government Museum at Jodhpur. The thin bladed *parasu* of Ahar is similar to the specimens from the Harappan sites. On the basis of findings at Balathal, it seems obvious that the Harappans had contacts with the Ahar culture (Misra *et al.* 1997).

Though Kayatha, in Madhya Pradesh, has yielded a distinct phase of the Ahar culture, the absence of Ahar type copper objects there is conspicuous. Agrawala is of the view that "the inspiration for copper technology seems to have come from some source other than Ahar" (1984: 158). His suggestion is perhaps based on the fact that the copper celts from Kayatha and Navdatoli in Madhya Pradesh, as well as from Kurada (Agrawala 1979) and Ganeshwar (Agrawala 1978: 123-24) in Rajasthan have round indentation marks, whereas such marks are conspicuous by their absence in the celts both from Ahar and Padaliya. Padaliya is located near Pind, an Ahar culture site in Chittorgarh district.

Bagor, a Mesolithic site in Bhilwara district, has revealed three copper arrowheads with two holes each, from 2800-2000 BC (uncal.) levels and similar specimens have also been found from Kayatha. However, the Balathal example has an impressive tang.

Subsistence Pattern

The Ahar people cultivated, a large number of plants as indicated by the carbonized grains from excavated sites, particularly from Balathal, e.g. wheat (*Triticum* cf *aestivum* Linn.), barley

(*Hordeum vulgare* Linn.), rice (*Oryza sativa* Linn.), Panicum millet (*Panicum sp.*), *Setaria* sp., green gram (*Vigna radiata* (L.) Wilczek), black gram (*Vigna mungo* (L.), pepper, common pea (*Pisum arvense* Linn.), *Trianthema* sp./*Portulaca* sp., Indian jujube (*Zizyphus jujuba* Lamark), Argemone Mexican type, Cucurbitaceae type (*Cucumis sp.*), wild lady's finger type (*Ablemoscheus sp.*) and Italian millet (*Setaria italica*).

The preliminary faunal analysis has revealed 32 species of animals, which include mammals, reptiles, birds and mollusks. The domesticated animals are represented by humped cattle, buffalo, sheep, goat, pig and dog, whereas the wild fauna comprise elephant, gaur, nilgai, black buck, four-horned antelope, chital, sambhar, wild pig, hare, mongoose, rat, pea-fowl, fowl, tortoise, freshwater fish (Thomas and Joglekar 996). Their preliminary analysis has also revealed that, except dog, many of these species were consumed as indicated by the charred and cut-marked bones. Though wild life was plentiful during the Chalcolithic period, their contribution to the subsistence system of Balathalians is not much, as their bones gradually decrease in the upper levels (Thomas and Joglekar 1996). It appears that cattle and sheep-goat pastoralism was probably the main occupation of the inhabitants.

Thus Misra *et al.* (1997: 57) justifiably assert that Balathal "has provided excellent evidence of architecture, suggesting a high degree of economic prosperity among the inhabitants, large quantities of ceramics of high technical quality, vast amount of animal bones, mainly of domesticated animals and plentiful remains of charred seeds of cultivated crops. It is, however, poor in manufactured objects, other than ceramics". Apart from these, few copper bronze objects, terracotta bull figurines and beads, beads of semiprecious stones, numerous stone querns, grinders, hammer stones, small terracotta balls and a few mirco-blades and fluted cores were among the important finds.

Chronology

On the basis of a series of uncal. ^{14}C dates, the Ahar culture at Balathal has now been bracketed between 2900 and 2000 BC (calibrated). The first phase has been tentatively placed between 2900 and 2600 BC (calibrated), which can be equated with the Pre-or Early-Harappan phase. The second phase at Balathal marked by relative prosperity, appears to be contemporary to the Mature and Late Harappan culture. The Early Historic levels at Balathal date from middle of 4th century BC to 2nd century AD, i.e. covering the period from the Mauryans to the Kushans.

Though the horizontal and vertical digs at Balathal have demonstrated evolution of pottery and gradual development of architecture, the issues that need to be further addressed are the origins of the culture, beginning of agriculture, level of contacts with Harappans and other contemporary cultures, settlement pattern, metal technology, relationship with contemporary hunter-gatherers, demography and technological capabilities. At this stage of investigations, it seems that the Ahar people knew the construction of small and large rectangular houses of stone or mud bricks before they came into contact with the Harappans. Perhaps they learnt settlement planning and some varieties of pottery from the Harappans, as the Tan Ware and few other types appear only after their contact were established.

Kayatha Culture

The Malwa region of Madhya Pradesh is a plateau drained by the Narmada, Tapi and Mahi, which debauch into the Arabian Sea and by the Chambal and the Betwa, which join the

Yamuna in the north. This region, largely covered by black cotton soil, receives an average annual rainfall of about 105 cm and nights are cool even during summers. The black cotton soil supports deciduous forests. Some scholars believe that the black cotton soil may have attracted the Chalcolithic people, however, the evidence suggests that the early farmers largely confined themselves to the narrow alluvial strips of rivers and along the main river valleys. Moreover, the main rivers were perhaps often prone to the danger of floods, which may have compelled them to inhabit the alluvial strips of tributaries. Possibly they could not plough the sticky black cotton soil with their meagre copper implements and this kind of ecological constraints did not allow them to produce surplus food. Therefore, they could not attain urbanization despite copper technology.

This culture was identified by V.S. Wakankar in 1964 at Kayatha, located about 25 km to the east of Ujjain, on the right bank of the river Chhoti Kali Sindh, an affluent of the Chambal. This type-site was excavated first by V.S. Wakankar in 1965 and 1966 (Wakankar 1967) and then by Z.D. Ansari and M.K. Dhavalikar (Deccan College) in 1968 in collaboration with Wakankar (Ansari and Dhavalikar 1975) and revealed a fivefold cultural sequence. This culture was found spread over almost the entire Chambal basin where Wakankar discovered as many as 40 sites.

It is characterized by three distinct wheel-thrown ceramic industries, the prominent among which is a thick, sturdy Brown Slipped Ware painted in violet or deep red. It is made of fine levigated clay and treated with pinkish paste. The designs are generally linear, usually painted on the rim and shoulder portion. It is represented by bowls, basins and globular jars and storage jars with concave neck, disc base or ring base. The excavators think that deep bowls with beaded rim, globular jars and ring base recall the Pre-Harappan tradition of Sothi, as far as their surface treatment and fabric are concerned. The Buff Painted Ware, which is of a fine fabric, is another important pottery of Kayatha. Shapes like typical Indian *lota*, medium-size jars with flaring mouth or high concave neck and basins are common. Geometric or linear designs in red pigment were made over buff surface. This ware is similar to the Eran fabric of the Malwa ware; particularly, the *lota*-shaped pots are common in both cultures. The third variety of pottery is known as the Combed ware. It is of fine fabric though usually without slip or wash. It is decorated with multiple zigzag or chevron incised patterns and in some cases with red pigment. Only bowls and basins of this ware have been reported. The excavator has pointed out the similarity of the incised decoration with the Sothi ware.

As the excavations were conducted on a small scale we have no idea of their dwelling structures. However, the Kayatha people appear to be quite well of in copper as two red painted Buff Ware pots yielded 28 copper bangles, 15 in one and 13 in another. They were expert in manufacturing copper-bronze objects, as the discovery of moulded copper celts with punch-marks, similar to the Harappans and Navdatolian examples, indicate. Apart from these, the discovery of two copper axes (Pl. 4-8) with a sharp cutting edge and a lenticular section are the finest examples of the Indian Bronze Age. The axes are cast in a mould unlike the later Chalcolithic specimens, which were just hammered to shape in Central India and Deccan. The repertoire includes two necklaces (each containing 173 and 160 beads), 2 celts, 28 bangles, a chisel and a Bagor type arrowhead. Along with copper objects, 40,000 steatite beads were also found in a rectangular room, which was possibly a storeroom or a vendor's shop. Most of the beads were long barrel shaped and short bicones, made of carnelian, agate and crystal.

The discovery of pots containing bangles and beads was made in a small area of the house floor, which, according to the excavators, suggests a sudden desertion of the site. This may have happened due to some calamity or some sudden attack. It seems that the invaders did not occupy the site, as there is a sterile layer of desertion intervening between the Kayathan and the succeeding Banasian deposits at the site. As the Kayatha culture is dated between 2200 and 1800 BC by uncal. ^{14}C dates, this incident may have happened around 1800 BC. The site remained unoccupied for some time, which is represented by a 15-cm thick sterile layer. And the Ahar or Banas people again occupied it around 1700 BC. Later on, the Malwa culture people also inhabited the site.

No human bones or grains have been reported; however, considering the limited excavation and rich repertoire of copper and stone objects, it is quite likely that their subsistence was largely dependent upon agriculture.

The Ahar levels of the site yielded large number of terracotta bull figurines. They are made of fine clay, fired uniformly at high temperature and can be divided into two categories, e.g. stylized and naturalistic. They have not been treated with slip or wash or any kind of decoration. In the case of stylized ones, conspicuous hump and head with horns are shown whereas the hind part is absent and represented by a rounded stem. The excavators suggest that the stylized bull may have been used as votive offering. (See also Ahar culture.)

Mould cast copper axes (Pl. 4-8) have been reported from Kayatha excavations. These are some of the finest specimens of copper axes in proto-historic South Asia. The Kayathans were also using blades/flakes of fine-grained chalcedony as the discovery of a large number of parallel-sided blades, points, lunates with blunted back and fluted cores indicates.

Malwa Culture

Malwa, in Madhya Pradesh, has two main parts: the northern Vindhyan scarp-land and the Deccan lava plateau in the south. The Vindhyan scarp-land rises from 450 to 580 m. Though the Chambal and its tributaries arise within 30 km of the Narmada, they drain northwards into the Ganga system whereas the Narmada debauches into the Arabian Sea. There is a sharp contrast between the Vindhyan and the Deccan lava landscapes, which is reflected in the present-day settlement pattern also. The Vindhyan country is more rugged, arid and with little soil cover. The vegetation is marked by poor grassland and acacia scrub.

Malwa region is the main seat of the Malwa and the Kayatha cultures; even the Ahar or Banas culture extended to this region. A few sites like Sihoniya, Khudai, Bassaiya, Manoti in the Chambal basin have also yielded late Harappan type ceramic. Though the Late Harappan cultures preceded the Malwa culture, a large part of Central India was first occupied by the Malwa culture people (Shinde 1998).

The Malwa culture is marked by the Malwa Ware (a buff or orange slipped pottery painted in black or dark brown), use of copper and stone tools and wattle-and-daub huts. Barring a few, most of the Malwa settlements are found on the tributaries, because the river Narmada was often subjected to high floods. Even the settlements on the main river are generally 1 or 2 km away, situated in the hinterlands.

The Malwa culture sites have been reported both from Madhya Pradesh and Maharashtra and a few have been excavated such as Navdatoli (Sankalia *et al.* 1971), Eran (U.V. Singh 1962), Kayatha (Ansari and Dhavalikar 1975), Nagda (Banerjee 1986) in Madhya Pradesh or Central India and Inamgaon in Maharashtra. At some sites like Eran and Manoti, traces of a massive mud wall, rampart and moat have also been found. Navdatoli, meaning the village of the boatmen, is situated on the southern bank of the Narmada. On the other side of the river is Maheshwar where also extensive traces of settlements are found. The Chalcolithic habitation extended over four mounds at Navdatoli, though not simultaneously. The horizontal excavations identified four distinct phases of the Chalcolithic culture:

Phase I is marked by the Ahar type Black-and-Red Ware;
Phase II by the Cream-slipped Ware;
Phase III by the Black-on-Red Ware; and
Phase IV is characterized by a Coarse Red Ware in association with the Lustrous Red Ware somewhat similar to that of the Post-Harappan Gujarat cultures. The Malwa Ware however, continues all through these phases.

Navdatoli has a uniquely rich ceramic tradition. Sankalia claims that Navdatoli has the richest repertory of designs (Figs. 4-3, -4, -5) amongst all the Chalcolithic cultures, including the Harappans. There are about 600 painted motifs recorded from Navdatoli. They include geometric designs, naturalistic motifs of animals, birds, human beings and plants. The Malwa Ware is generally buff or cream slipped (Pl. 4-9, -10) and bears painted patterns in dark brown, but the fabric is thick due to the use of chopped husk. A thinner variety of this ware has been called the Eran Fabric. The pottery forms are *lota*, a variety of bowls, dishes and high necked storage jars, channel-spouted cups and pedestalled goblets.

The Malwa people subsisted on agriculture and animal husbandry. Navdatoli has yielded ample evidence regarding the food habits of these early farmers as indicated by the charred grains of wheat (*Triticum vulgare compactum*); barley and rice (*Oryza sativa* L) from Phases II and IV; black gram, green gram, lentil (*Lens culinaris* Medicus), grass pea (*Lathyrus sativus* Linn); linseed, ber (*Zizyphus jujuba* Lamk), amala (*Phyllanthus embellica*), etc. Beef, venison and pork were part of their diet, as the evidence of cut and charred bones of both wild and domestic animals suggests.

They had single to multi-roomed rectangular houses as well as round huts (Pl. 4-11). It has been suggested that some of these round huts might have been the dwelling pits (Dhavalikar 1997: 130) or sunken floor dwellings.

A recent survey in the Narmada valley by the Archaeological Survey of India has brought to light several new settlements in west Nimar and Dhar districts of Madhya Pradesh, most of which were found on the left bank of the Narmada. A few sites such as Pipri, Utawad and Nawarakheri (22°6' N; 75° 13' E) in west Nimar district and Chikhalda (22°5' N, 74°53' E) in Dhar district have been excavated (IAR 1994-95, 1996-97). Several cone shaped dwelling pits (diameter 2.5 and depth 1.9 m) have been found at all these sites. Floors of these pits were generally plastered with lime. Such dwelling pits are well-known from the Neolithic context at Burzahom (IAR 1960-61: 11, 1961-62: 17, 1962-63: 9, 1965-66: 19, 1966-67: 17, 1968-69: 10, 1971-72: 24) and Gufkral (IAR 1962-63: 9) in Kashmir. It seems that pit dwellings were also common among these early farmers of Deccan and Central India. But these pits are not comparable to the Neolithic examples of Kashmir. We do not know if these pits indicate a different class of the society.

A variety of copper objects were found, e.g. flat celts with convex cutting edges, fish-hooks, nail-parers, arrowheads, spearheads, chisels, blades, rings, bangles and a mid-ribbed sword. Agrawal (2000: 117) writes that the mid-ribbed sword must have been cast whereas all other objects were hammered to shape. These early farmers knew cold work and annealing techniques. A comparison of the trace chemical impurity patterns of ores and these artefacts has been carried out to locate the copper mines used. To make bronze, they alloyed tin up to 3 per cent and lead up to 2 per cent.

Pl. 4-1. Smelting furnace, discovered during our exploration at Ganeshwar, District Sikar, Rajasthan.

Pl. 4-2. Painted Buff Ware, Ahar.

Pl. 4-3. Black Painted Buff Ware, Ahar.

Pl. 4-4. Pottery corn bins and fire places at Ahar, Rajasthan.

Pl. 4-5. A dish-on-stand in Tan Ware, Ahar.

Pl. 4-6. A crude Grey Ware dish-on-stand, Ahar.

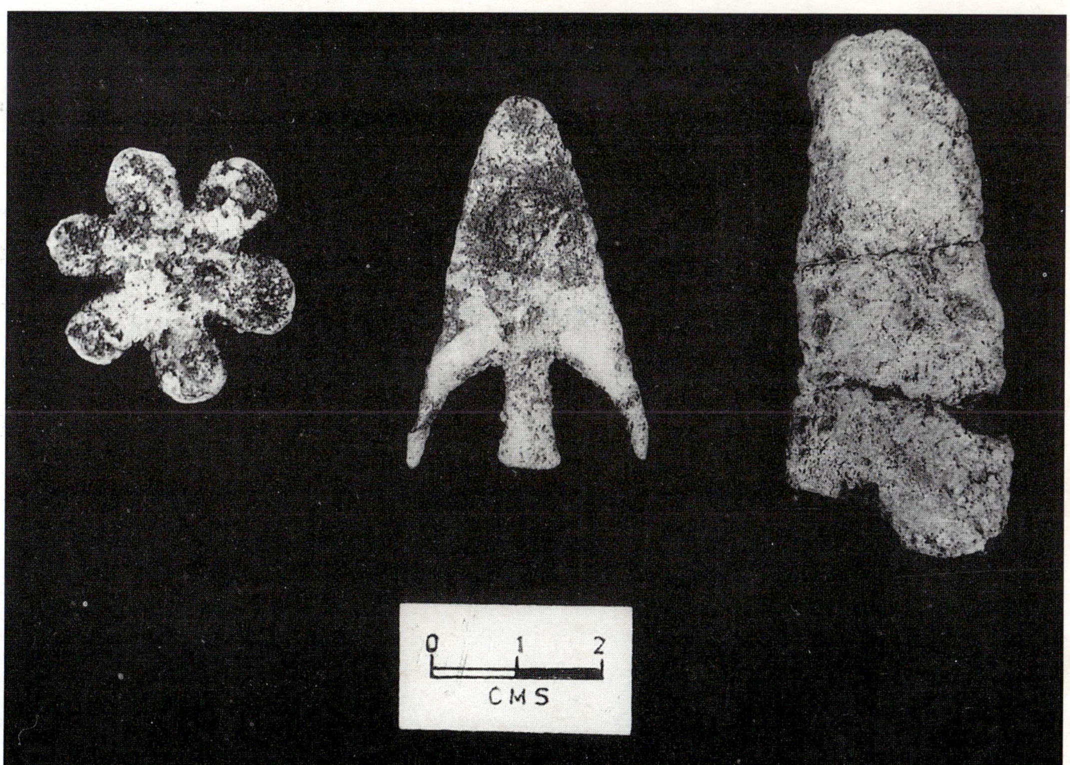

Pl. 4-7. Copper artefacts from Balathal, Rajasthan.

Pl. 4-8. Mould cast copper axes, Kayatha excavations. These are some of the finest specimens of copper axes in protohistoric South Asia.

Pl. 4-9. A Cream Ware bowl, Malwa culture, Navdatoli.

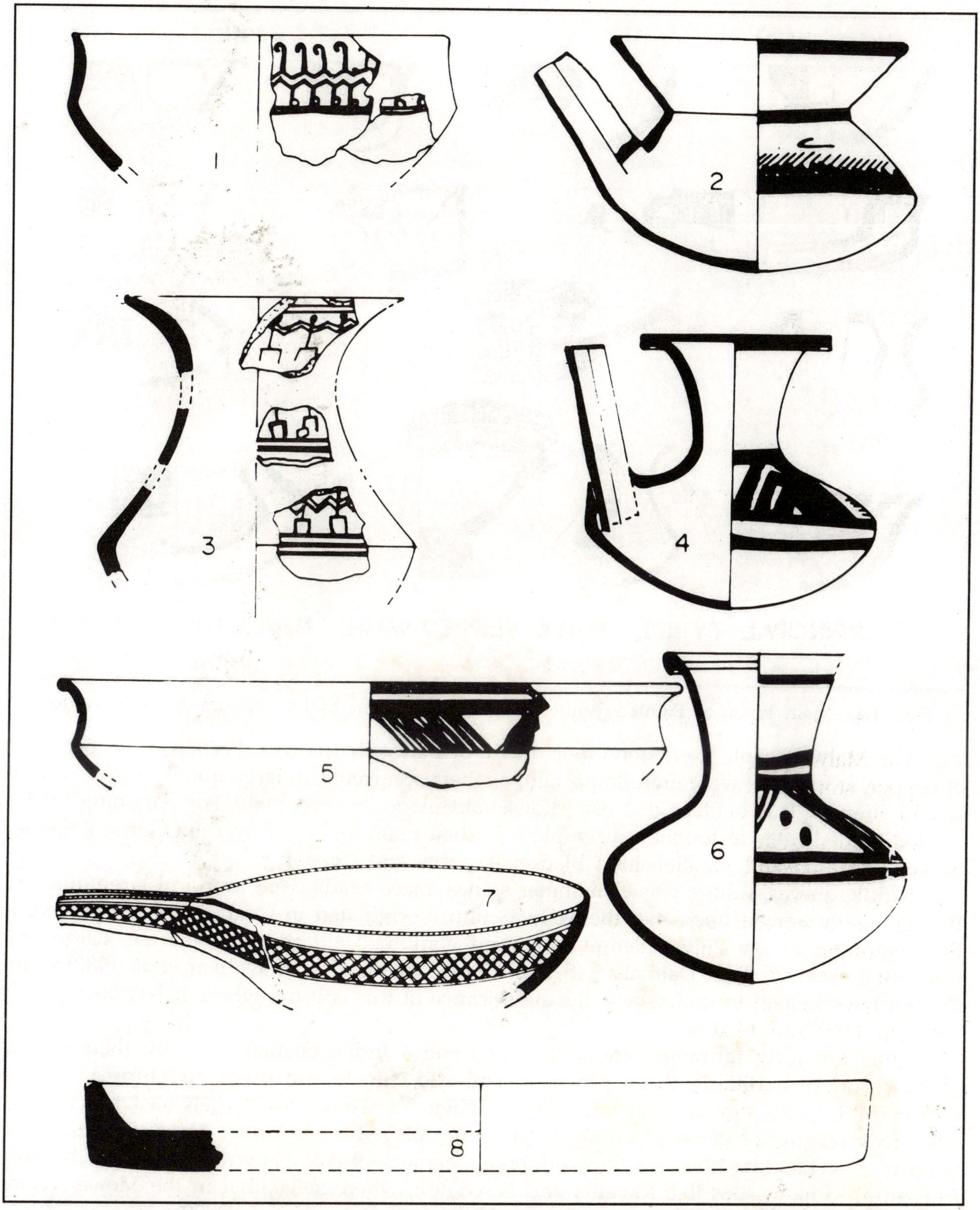

Fig. 4-3. Deccan Chalcolithic pottery. Malwa Ware (Nos. 1, 3, 5, 7, 8) and Jorwe Ware (Nos. 2,4,6) types.

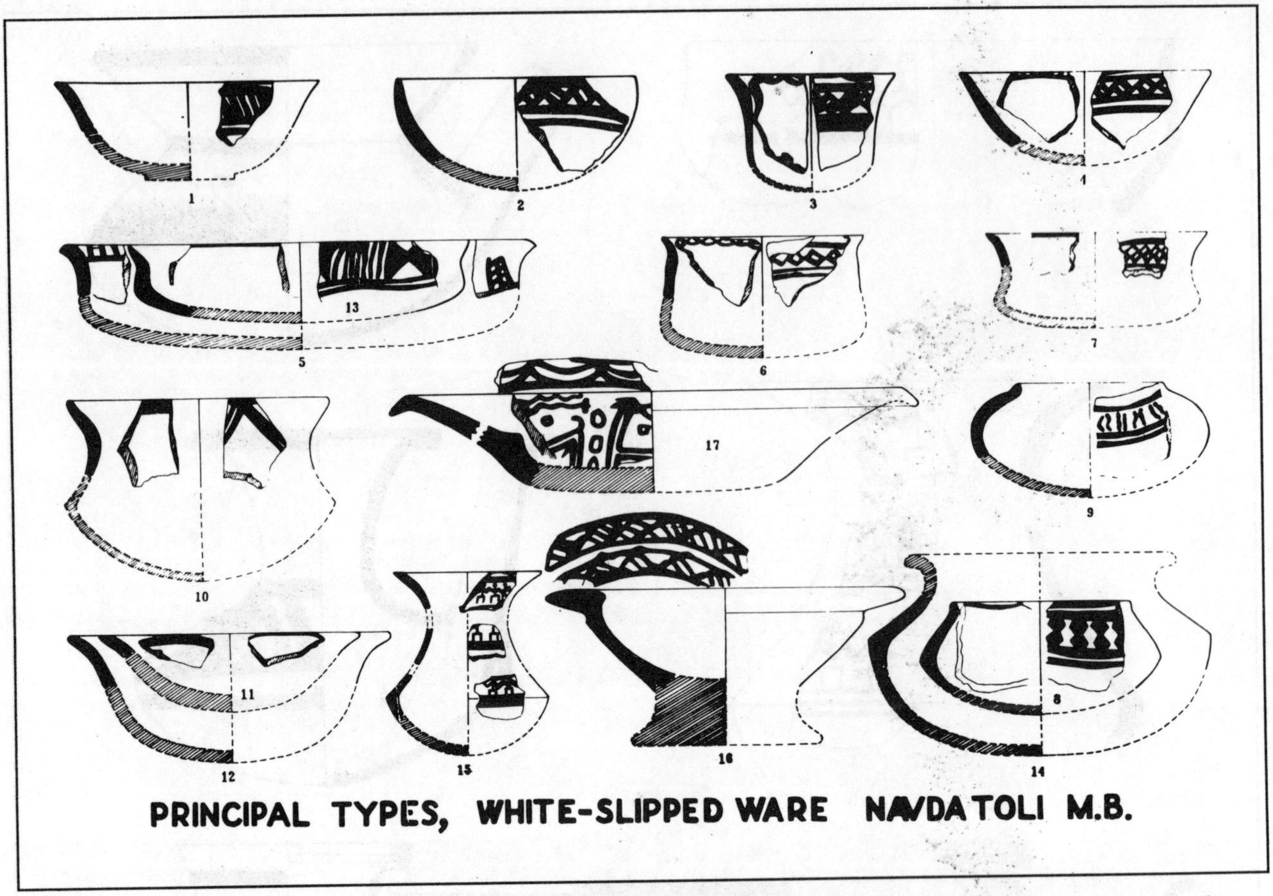

Fig. 4-4. Main types of Painted White Slipped Ware from Malwa culture from Navdatoli.

The Malwa people used stone tools made of milky chalcedony. Perhaps due to paucity of copper, stone tools were more important, as their occurrence in large quantity (over 2,3000) would suggest. It is evident that each household made its own tools. For obtaining blades, crested-guided ridge technique was employed. Their main tool types were penknives, blunted backed, serrated and parallel-sided blades, trapezes and lunates.

Saddle querns, rubber stones, hammer stones, mace-heads were found in large quantity. It is generally agreed upon that the Malwa culture originated in Central India sometime in the beginning of the 2nd millennium BC and continued till the last quarter. Large-scale horizontal excavations at Daimabad (Sali 1986) and Inamgaon (Dhavalikar *et al.* 1988) in the Deccan have helped to understand the significance of this culture, where it has been placed between 1600 and 1400 BC.

Thus the early farming communities of Central India, characterized by their distinct painted pottery traditions, flourished in a semi-arid climate and used microliths as well as copper implements, though limited in number. Their subsistence was largely based on farming and stock raising; of course, hunting might have played a vital role. They were living in circular or rectangular huts. We find sudden appearance of cultures with advance technology in Central India at sites like Kayatha and Navdatoli, whereas Balathal in the Mewar region presents a picture of gradual development of Ahar culture (Shinde 2000).

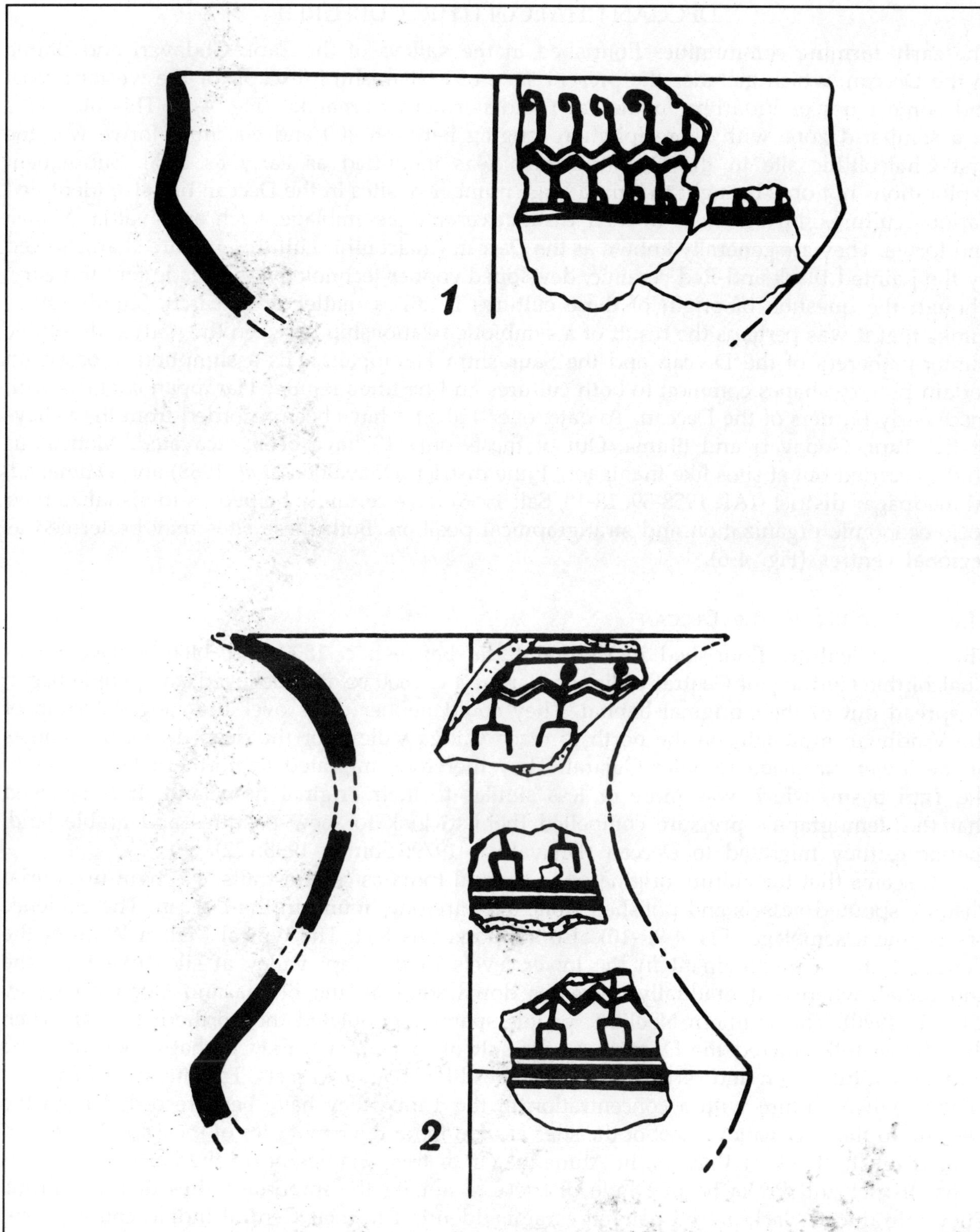

Fig. 4-5. Malwa Ware pots with typical decoration.

DECCAN CHALCOLITHIC CULTURES

The early farming communities flourished in the valleys of the Tapi, Godavari and Bhima in the Deccan, which includes the present state of Maharashtra (except for the western coast and some parts of Vidarbha in the east) and northern Karnataka (Fig. 4-1). This area falls in a semi-arid zone with a precipitation ranging between 400 and 900 mm. Jorwe was the first Chalcolithic site in the Deccan, which was identified as early as 1950. Subsequent explorations not only brought to light a large number of sites in the Deccan but also identified various cultures, on the basis of their distinct ceramic assemblage, such as Savalda, Malwa and Jorwe. They are generally known as the Deccan Chalcolithic cultures and are characterized by the painted Black-and-Red ceramic, developed copper technology and blade tool industry. Though the question of origin of these cultures is still a matter of research, Shinde (1998) thinks that it was perhaps the result of a symbiotic relationship between the native Mesolithic hunter-gatherers of the Deccan and the Saurashtra Harappans. His assumption is based on certain pottery shapes common to both cultures and he finds regular Harappan contacts with these early farmers of the Deccan. To date, over 150 sites have been recorded from the valleys of the Tapi, Godavari and Bhima. Out of these, only 13 have been excavated. Meticulous studies carried out at sites like Inamgaon, Pune district (Dhavalikar *et al.* 1988) and Daimabad, Ahmednagar district (IAR 1958-59: 15-18; Sali 1986) have certainly helped us to visualize their socio-economic organization and stratigraphical position. Both these sites may be termed as regional centres (Fig. 4-6).

Malwa Culture in the Deccan

The Malwa culture flourished in Central India between *c.* 1800 and 1400 BC (see under Chalcolithic Cultures of Central India) and around *c.* 1600 BC, it is believed, the people began to spread out of their original habitat. They could neither cross over the rugged terrain of the Vindhyan mountain on the north to reach Ganga valley nor the deep dangerous gorges of the lower Narmada to enter Gujarat. They therefore, migrated to northern Deccan or to the Tapi basin, which was more or less similar to their original homeland. It is believed that the demographic pressure compelled them to look for new pastures and arable land, therefore, they migrated to Deccan (Dhavalikar 1979; Shinde 1998: 22).

It seems that the culture originated in Central India as certain traits, e.g. twin urn burial custom, spouted vessels and polished stone axes are only found in the Deccan. The evidence of ceramic assemblage (Pls. 4-9, -10) also supports this fact. The typical Malwa Ware of the Central India is predominant in the lower levels in the Tapi valley at sites like Prakashe and Bahal, whereas it gradually decreases down south in the Bhima and Godavari valley (Shinde 1990). The southern Neolithic people sparsely populated the northern Deccan when the Malwa folk entered the Deccan. As a result of this contact, they perhaps took over the traits like inhumation and certain pottery shapes like spouted vessels. To date, over fifty sites of the Malwa culture with a concentration in the Tapi valley have been recorded from the Deccan. In the Tapi valley, most of the sites are found on the tributaries of the Tapi. Daimabad located on the bank of Pravara, in Ahmadnagar district, Inamgaon on the bank of Ghod in Pune district and Prakashe in Dhule district are among the important sites of this culture. They introduced black-on-red painted ceramic, identical to their Central Indian counterparts, in the Deccan, which is found at the lowest level at Inamgaon and assigned to Pd IV at Daimabad. Unlike the Central Indian coarse fabric and paintings on buff or orange slip, the Malwa pottery (Pl. 4-9, -10) in Deccan has a fine fabric, sometimes treated with red or pink

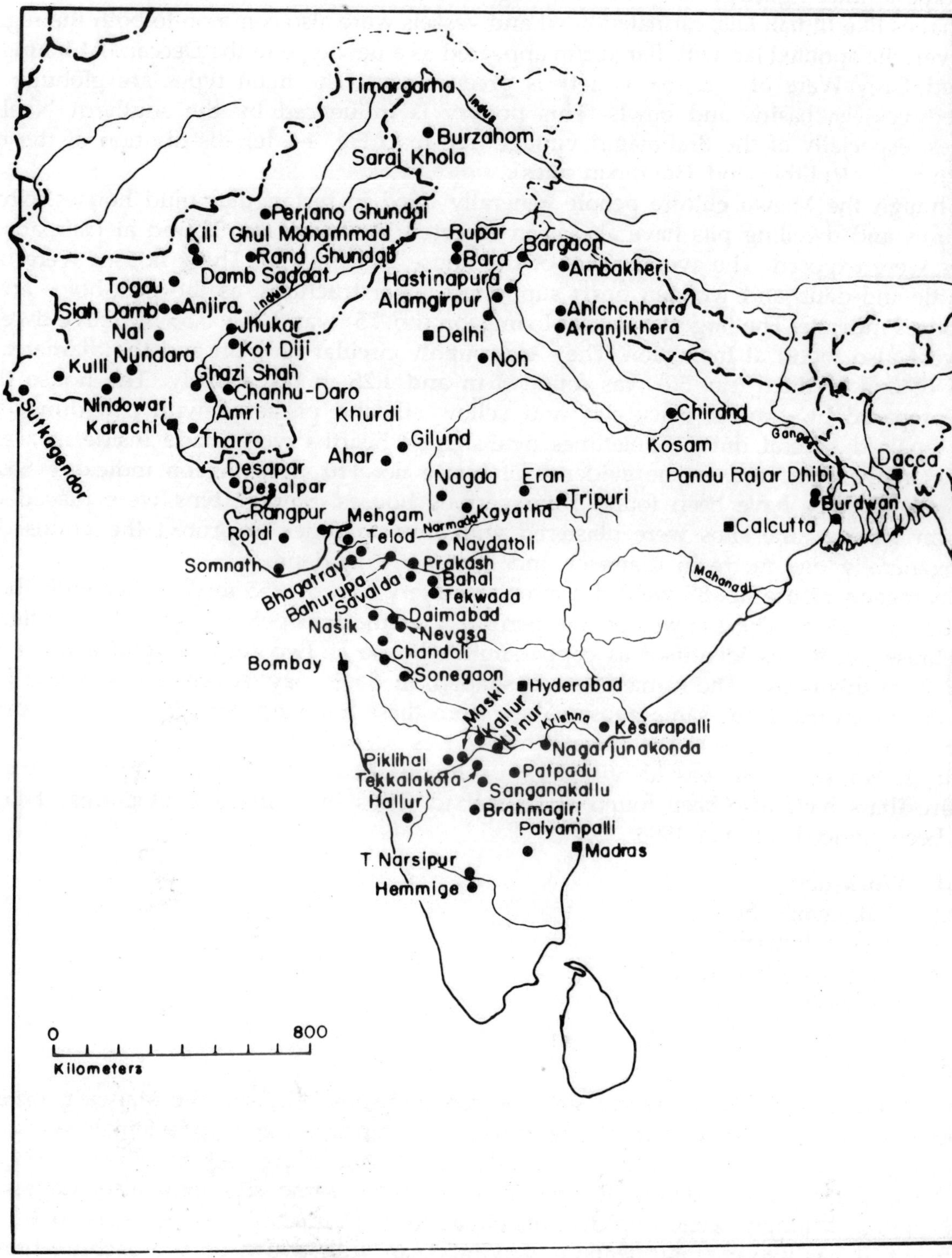

Fig. 4-6. Map of protohistoric sites of South Asia.

wash over which black paintings are made. The decoration of linear and geometric patterns and some animal figurines like bull and dog, which continued (Figs. 4-3, -4, -5) on pottery and shapes like Indian *lota*, carinated bowl and vessels were also common to both the regions. However, the spouted jar, with flared rim appeared as a new type in the Deccan. At Inamgaon, the Red/Grey Ware of a coarse variety is predominant. The main types are globular jars, spouted vessels, basins and bowls. This pottery is influenced by the southern Neolithic cultures, especially of the Brahmagiri vintage (see map Fig. 4-1 for distribution of the main Neolithic, Chalcolithic and Harappan sites).

Though the Malwa culture people generally lived in rectangular mud houses, circular structures and dwelling pits have also been reported. At Inamgaon 32 and at Daimabad 12 houses were exposed. The average size of the house was 8 x 3 m. These houses were made of wattle-and-daub and wooden posts supported superstructures, as the post-holes around the houses indicate. The largest house at Inamgaon (no. 75) was 9.75 x 5.55 m. Three dwelling pits were also found at Inamgaon. They are roughly circular on plan and the diameter and depth of one of them (no. 50) was found 3 m and 1.25 m respectively. The house floors were prepared by gravels, black clay and yellow silt and plastered with cow-dung. They were repaired several times. Sometimes oval-shaped hearths were made inside as well as outside in the courtyard as the evidence of house no. 110 at Inamgaon indicates. Storage bins and pit silos have been found from various houses. Storage bins were placed on a platform whereas the silos were plastered with lime in order to protect the grains. They were generally one metre in diameter and one metre in depth.

Inamgaon House no. 85 yielded a circular pottery kiln of 1.55 m diameter with the fire chamber of 1.86 m. The grooves on the periphery of the kiln perhaps served as outlets for gas. House no. 9 was identified as coppersmith's house as two furnaces and a razor were found from this house. The furnaces are U-shaped, made of clay. A crucible was also found from the courtyard of the same house. Apart from these a stonecutter's house and a priest's house were also identified. The priest's house was identified on the basis of evidence of fire-altars. House no. 37 was identified as a religious house. Similarly an apsidal structure and fire-altars have also been found at Daimabad. Thus five different categories of houses have been noticed (Shinde 1998: 25):

1. Workshop;
2. Craftsman's house;
3. Priest's house;
4. Religious place; and
5. Unclassified types.

Religious Beliefs

Certain artefacts from the excavated sites indicate religious beliefs of the Malwa people. For example, a huge jar from Navdatoli is decorated with appliqué figures of a female worshipper on the right and a lizard on the left of a shrine (?). According to Dhavalilkar (1979), this may be a deity. The evidence of fire-altars from the same site may also suggest fire worshipping. A jungle scene depicted on a pot from Daimabad also appears to be quite significant. It has two compartments: a standing man with two deer approaching him and peacocks in between is shown in the upper one, the lower part depicts three tigers. A mud platform has also been identified as a religious structure at Daimabad.

Burial Customs

The excavations at Inamgaon and Daimabad have revealed 23 and 16 child burials respectively. Generally the body was placed in two urns of coarse Grey Ware facing each other horizontally and was buried in a pit (Pl. 4-12). The body was placed in north-south orientation with head towards north and legs towards south. In a few cases, painted urns were also used. These urns were buried either inside the house or in the courtyard. Often bowls and spouted jars were found in the burials, which possibly contained food and water for the child. The evidence of such burials from the lowest levels at Inamgaon, sunk in the virgin soil, apparently suggest that the Malwa people in the Deccan practised this custom right from beginning. At Inamgaon, out of 23 urn burials, 15 were of twin-urn type, 7 single-urn types and one without bones, possibly representing a symbolic burial. Though similar burials have also been found at Tozilikaya in Turkey and at Alishar Huyuk and other sites in West Asia, they are much older than the Malwa culture.

Subsistence Pattern

The Malwa people harvested crops like wheat (*Triticum* spp.; *Triticum* cf. *sphaerococum* Pers. and *Triticum* cf. *aestivum* Linn.), barley (*Hordeum vulgare* Linn.), lentils (*Lens esculenta*), the common pea (*Pisum arvense* Linn.), the horse gram (*Dolichos biflorus* Linn.), the hyacinth bean (*Dolichos lablab* Linn.), the grass pea (*Lathyrus sativus* Linn.), the Indian jambon (*Eugenia jambolana* Syn.), Indian cherry (*Cordia myxa* Linn.), babul (*Acacia* cf. *nilotica* L), etc. (Kajale 1988). Apart from these, the Malwa people at Daimabad cultivated finger millet (*Eleusine coracana* Garth), beans (*Phaseolus/Vigna sp.*), black gram (*Vigna mungo* Hepper), green gram (*Vigna radiata* Wilezek) (Vishnu Mittre *et al.* 1986).

Agrawal (1982a) thinks that the Chalcolithic people could not cultivate the sticky black cotton soil with their poor metal artefacts and the paucity of large tracts of silty alluvial plains was another ecological constraint for them to attain urbanization. However, Shinde (1990: 58) has suggested that due to the dearth of sufficient alluvial plains, the Malwa people might have cultivated the black cotton soil. As they cultivated both summer as well as winter crops, it is quite likely that they had knowledge of double and mixed cropping. The evidence from the excavations suggests that the subsistence of Malwa people was largely dependant on cultivated cereals. However, wild plants/fruits like *Terminalia belerica* Roxb and *Syzigium cumini* Lamk., which grow in moist deciduous forest, might have also formed important part of their diet.

Both Inamgaon and Daimabad have yielded evidence of wheat, a winter crop, which cannot be grown, at least in Deccan, without irrigation facilities. As there is no such evidence of artificial irrigation at both these sites, at least in the Malwa period, Shinde (1990: 59) suggests that wheat was also possibly obtained from Central India where it was grown on a large-scale (1998).

"The Malwa people depended heavily on their domesticated animals for meat. At Inamgaon cattle are represented by 41.45 per cent, sheep/goat 24.67 per cent and dog 5.40 per cent. These animals alone could have provided about 26,257.50 kg of meat. In addition to this, they also hunted wild animals like the sambar, chital, black buck, mongoose and hare, which contributed nearly 3,713.25 kg. of meat (the estimation of the consumable meat of cattle and sheep/goat is applicable only to the excavated area). Aquatic and avian fauna would have supplemented the food economy. The ratio between domesticated and wild animals is 72.37 per cent and 27.63 per cent respectively" (Thomas 1988). This kind of analysis is done for annual production of meat from the excavated area (Shinde pers. com.). The discovery of a number of artefacts like bangles and beads of conch shell and remains of fish bones is very significant and points to long distance trading activities of the Malwa people. The Saurashtra and Kalyan coast could be possible source of such shells (Shinde 1990: 59), but this has to be studied carefully.

Copper Technology

On the basis of the comparison of trace impurity patterns, it was suggested that Khetri mines may have been the prime source of copper for the western and Central Indian Chalcolithic people (Agrawal 1971: 147). But considering the long distance the excavators of Inamgaon suggested that people may have used pyrite ores that are available around Inamgaon and even the native copper which is found at Rashin in Karjat *taluka* of Ahmednagar district. Lumps of native copper were reported from the excavation. Native copper is easy to use but smelting pyrite ores requires advanced smelting and furnace technology for which there is no evidence so far. Copper objects occur at all the levels at Inamgaon and the remains of smelting (?) furnace, possibly for copper, have also been reported from Period II. It is a boat-shaped structure, built of clay on stone foundation, found near the kiln. The excavators suggest that this structure is similar to the Bronze Age furnaces found in Israel belonging to the middle of the 2nd millennium BC (Dhavalikar *et al.* 1988: 566-571). The furnace was possibly for melting and not smelting.

Inamgaon yielded a variety of copper objects like bangles, pins, discs, rings, crescents, drills, pokers, tranchets, tubes, a pair of tong, fish-hooks, antimony rods, punch, chisel, arrowheads and few small bits of copper. A total number of 205 objects were found out of which Period I yielded 18, Period II, 69, Period III, 103 and 15 objects were found from surface. Beads, bangles and anklets were found in large numbers. The excavator thinks that the spirals or pin-heads are similar to those found from the Harappan sites or West Asian sites (Dhavalikar *et al.* 1988: 553-571). Though Pd II was the most prosperous phase at the site, Period III yielded the maximum number of copper objects perhaps because it was exposed more at Inamgaon. In Period III, possibly gold was obtained from the Hatti mines of Karnataka through the trade contacts with the southern Neolithic people.

Like Inamgaon, Daimabad also yielded a good number of copper objects from the stratified contexts, but most of the specimens were found in a highly corroded state. As most of the objects were in a crumbling state due to encrustations they could not be treated chemically either (Sali 1986). Following is the distribution chart of copper objects found at Daimabad (see Table 4-1).

A hoard of four bronzes (Pl. 4-13, -14, -15) was discovered from an unstratified digging at Daimabad, which has been assigned to Bronze Age by some scholars. The first one is a chariot and bull (0.45 x 0.16 m). It consists of an elaborate chariot yoked to two bulls and driven by a man standing on it. The solid wheels, resting over the light body of the chariot, have a projecting hub on the inner side. The elephant, standing on a platform (27 x 14 cm), is the largest of the three animals in the hoard. This icon is 25 cm high and its large trunk is curved at the lower tip. A similar elephant, of course, female, found from the Deccan area has been assigned to 3rd century AD (Dhavalikar 1993b: 421-426). The third figure is a rhinoceros standing on two horizontal bars over two sets of wheels and it is 25 cm high. The last figure is of a water buffalo, which looks quite naturalistic. It is 31 cm high including the wheels and 25 cm long. It is also shown on a platform like elephant. The front wheels of this figure are smaller compared to the rear ones, i.e. 8 and 10 cm respectively.

TABLE 4.1 COPPER OBJECTS FROM DAIMABAD (after Sali 1986)

Phase Objects	*I*	*II*	*III*	*Overlap III/IV*	*IV*	*Overlap IV/V*	*V*	*Total*
Bangles	2	X	X	X	2	3	8	15
Chisel	X	X	X	X	1	X	X	1
Celt (frg.)	X	1	X	X	X	X	X	1
Spearhead	X	X	X	X	1	X	X	1
M. goddess	X	X	X	X	X	X	2	2
Rect. piece	X	X	X	X	X	X	1	1
Trap. piece	X	X	1	X	1	X	X	2
Razor	X	X	X	X	1	X	X	1
Wire	X	X	X	1	X	X	1	2
Lump	X	1	X	X	X	X	1	2
Slag	X	1	1	X	X	X	X	2
Total	2	3	2	1	6	3	13	30

Dhavalikar (1993b: 425) writes that "It is tempting to identify the person in the chariot as *Pasupati*, "the lord of beasts," for the simple reason that all the animals, save the tiger, which appear on the famous Pasupati seal from Mohenjo-daro, are present in the Daimabad hoard. Marshall's identification of *Pasupati* on the seal was based on comparisons with medieval representations of Shiva (Marshall 1931: I, 52-56; Pl. VII, 4)".

From the repertoire of metal objects from Daimabad excavations, it seems that the Deccan Chalcolithic people were not so rich in copper. None of the metal icons of the Indian Chalcolithic cultures and even of the Harappans, are so big and massive in weight, besides most of the metal was used in utilitarian artefacts, unlike Chinese bronzes, which are massive and ornate. The Daimabad bronzes therefore, do not fit in the proto-historic copper repertoire at all! Dhavalikar (1993b: 421-426), however, writes that "In all probability, the bronzes in the hoard belong to the late Harappan period at Daimabad and that they were probably imported from Harappa, or some smith from Harappa made them locally".

Inamgaon

The site, located about 89 km east of Deccan College, Pune, was excavated horizontally on a large-scale between 1969 and 1982 under the supervision of H.D. Sankalia, M.K. Dhavalikar and Z.D. Ansari. Here the ancient site, 3 km from the modern village, is situated on the right bank of the river Ghod. The site, measuring 550 x 430 m, consists of five mounds. It has yielded three different phases of the Deccan Chalcolithic culture, i.e. Malwa (1600-1400 BC, uncal.), Early Jorwe (1400-1000 BC, uncal.) and Late Jorwe (1000-700 BC, uncal.). Several circular and rectangular structures, a kiln, an embankment and irrigation channel were some of the important features of the excavations. This is a large settlement of the Deccan Chalcolithic culture. Inamgaon has made an important contribution by showing that the Jorwe people continued here till about 700 BC.

Daimabad

Daimabad (19°31' N, 74°42' E), a multicultural site, is spread over 30 ha and is the largest known Chalcolithic site in the Deccan. It is located on the left bank of the Pravara in the Godavari basin and was first excavated by M.N. Deshpande in 1959 (IAR 1958-59: 5-18) and later on by Sali (Sali 1986). The studies at Daimabad have shown that the Savalda people (*c.* 2000-1800 BC, uncal.) were the first Chalcolithic farmers of the Deccan and they were succeeded by the late Harappans (*c.* 1800-1600 BC, uncal.), the Malwa (*c* .1600-1400 BC, uncal.) and finally by the Jorwe culture. The Jorwe culture has been subdivided into two phases: an Early Phase (*c.* 1400-1000 BC, uncal.) and a Late Phase (*c.* 1000-700 BC, uncal.).

Like Daimabad and Inamgaon, Prakashe (21°30"30' N; 74°21"30' E) is also a large settlement (470 x 200 x 19 m) oriented north-south, oblong in shape and situated on the confluence of the Tapi and the Gomati in the Shahada *taluka* in Dhulia district of Maharashtra. The site was excavated by B.K. Thapar in 1955 and yielded four different cultural phases (Thapar 1967: 1-167). Period IA was characterized by the Malwa Ware and microliths. A variety of beads of shell, carnelian and paste, shell bangles, painted toy-carts, wheel and painted terracotta bulls were found. Period IB yielded Jorwe and Lustrous Red Wares. Period II belongs to the Iron Age and yielded a variety of iron objects, e.g. knife blades, nails, clamps along with Black-and-Red Ware and Northern Black Polished Ware. Pd III and IV were represented by Kshatrapa and Early Christian era material remains. There is a thin sterile layer between Periods I and II, which suggests that the site was not occupied for sometime after Period I.

It has been found that the Tapi valley was occupied more extensively (around 103 sites) compared to the Bhima and the Godavari, possibly because of the availability of more arable land and perennial water sources (Shinde 1998). It has also been observed that most of the settlements in the Tapi valley are located either on the banks of its tributaries or away from the banks of the Tapi, perhaps to avoid the danger of the floods in Tapi. In fact, the archaeological importance of the Central Tapi and eventually of the Deccan was realized when Prakashe was excavated and Sali (1965: 207-10) and Shinde (1998) recorded 75 and 28 sites respectively.

Savalda Culture

This culture (*c.* 2000-1800 BC, uncal.) was identified by S.A. Sali as early as 1958 (IAR 1958-59) in Central Tapi basin. The type-site of this culture "Savalda" is located about 20 km north-east of Nandurbar, a *taluka* in Dhule district of Maharashtra. It is characterized by a distinct ceramic tradition, which is coarse in fabric and often with a gritty core. It is made with a slow turn-table and treated with pink, red or chocolate slip. The pottery is decorated with linear and geometric patterns, figures of wild animals and birds, e.g. elephant, wild boar, peacock, cock, snakes and aquatic animals like fish and frogs. Sometimes hunting objects like harpoons, bows, arrows and swords have also been depicted in black pigment on the pottery. The common shapes of this assemblage are globular pots either with high necks and round bottom or with high but narrow neck bowls with featureless rim and convex sides and Indian *lota* type pots. Except Daimabad, all the 27 sites of this culture have so far been discovered in the Tapi basin. Only two large settlements of this culture, Savalda and Bahurupa, have been excavated vertically (IAR 1959-60). The studies carried out at Daimabad (Sali 1985) and Kaothe (Dhavalikar and Shinde 1989) have unfolded various facets of this culture. Considering the concentration of sites, it could be concluded that this culture originated in the Tapi basin.

At Daimabad, the Savalda people were living in rectangular structures as indicated by the exposed 11 houses (Sali 1986). They were built close to each other and had low mud walls above which perhaps wattle-and-daub structures were raised. The floor was made of black soil and yellow silt and plastered with mud. The evidence of post-holes suggests that wooden posts supported the roof of these houses. Inside the houses were found hearths and circular storage pits. One of the structures (no. 11) consisting of three rooms has been identified as village nobleman's house (8.3 x 3.6 m), the floor of which near the hearth was decorated by freshwater shells. Another large house (no 15) has been suggested to belong to a priest, which comprised two rooms and measured 7 x 4.5 m. Inside this house were found five circular hearths and one of them has a phallus of agate (Sali 1986: 87). However, at Kaothe, the people were living in circular pits with average diameter of 1.75 m and depth ranging from 20 to 40 cm. Their walls and base portions were plastered with cow-dung and clay. They made superstructures over these pits, as the evidence of post-holes on the periphery would suggest. Though pit dwellings from the Neolithic phase at Burzahom, Kashmir, are well-known but they are quite deep and cannot be compared with the examples of Kaothe. However, three examples of such pit-dwellings from the Malwa phase at Inamgaon have been found and one of them also had a hearth. The Chalcolithic folks of the Deccan were using both rectangular as well as circular houses. Deep circular pits have also been found recently at several Malwa sites in Madhya Pradesh (IAR 1994-95, 1996-97). It is possible that some of these were used for dwelling purposes, though we do not have any definite evidence of pit dwelling from any site in the Deccan. Such pits could even be used for storage, cooking, etc. (Shinde 1998).

Kaothe has also yielded evidence of five human burials. Two of them are of adults whereas three belong to infants. They were buried in a dug pit in a supine posture, oriented north-south. No burial goods were found. In Daimabad, however, there is evidence of urn burials (Pl. 4-12).

Among the artefacts, parallel-sided blades of chalcedony, semiprecious stone beads are significant.

Thus on the basis of cultural remains, it appears that the Savalda culture had a stratified society.

Jorwe Culture

The Jorwe people succeeded the Malwa culture in the entire Deccan around 1400 BC. In fact, outside the Harappan universe, Jorwe (1400-1000 BC, uncal.) was the first Chalcolithic site, which was discovered as early as 1950, near Sangamner in Ahmednagar district of Maharashtra. The culture is known after the type-site. To date, over eighty sites of this culture have been discovered and only a few sites like Inamgaon, Daimabad, Chandoli, Nevasa, Jorwe, Nasik, Prakashe, Bahal, Tekwada and Walki have been excavated. The horizontal excavations at Inamgaon and Daimabad have contributed largely not only to an understanding of their lifestyle and socio-political organization but also revealed a late phase of this culture, which continued till 700 BC. It is believed that the Jorwe culture is a result of the synthesis of the Malwa culture and the southern Neolithic (Dhavalikar 1970). Later on, Dhavalikar (1973) revised his opinion and stated that it could be the result of the internal development within the Malwa tradition. Shinde (1998) also agrees with Dhavalikar.

Among the Jorwe settlements, three regional centres such as Prakashe in the Tapi valley, Inamgaon in the Bhima basin and Daimabad in the Godavari basin have been identified, as out of 84 known sites, 52 are located in the Tapi, 22 in the Godavari and 10 in the Bhima basins (Shinde 1998: 30).

The Jorwe phase at Inamgaon appears to be the most prosperous as the habitation extended over five hectares area and a defence wall and a moat fortified the settlement. The bastions were made of stone rubble set in mud masonry. A long ditch (195 x 20 m) was revealed by aerial photography. To save their settlement from flood, a long channel (120 x 10 m) was also dug. All this public architecture is assigned to early Jorwe phase (Shinde 1998).

The Jorwe Ware (Fig. 4-7) is the hallmark of this culture, which has a red or orange matt surface painted with geometric designs in black. This wheel-turned ceramic is fired at high temperature and has a fine fabric. It is devoid of any tempering material. It has been treated with light to dark red wash over which black paintings have been depicted. The designs are generally found on the upper half of the pot, which include geometric patterns like vertical and horizontal bands, criss-cross, chevron, diamond patterns. Sometimes cranes, snakes, deer, fish-scale have also been painted. The main types of this ware are the spouted jar with a flaring mouth (Pl. 4-16), the carinated bowl (Pl. 4-17), the *lota* (Pl. 4-18), the high-necked jar with a globular profile and storage jar. Handmade shapes like platters, dough plates and lamps, both in Red and Grey Wares, are common. Some pots are spouted and some zoomorphic (animal-shaped).

A few polished dolerite axes and a prolific blade/flake industry of chalcedony and agate comprises their lithic assemblage. Though they were aware of copper technology, it appears that copper was hardly available to them as only a few implements, e.g. axes, chisels, knives, fish-hooks, bangles and beads have been found. Dhavalikar (1979: 258) thinks that they might have smelted chalcopyrite, as a boat-shaped kiln to smelt copper ores has been identified at Inamgaon. The copper axes were found at Nevasa, Jorwe and Inamgaon. The discovery of a copper punch from Inamgaon is quite significant, which was perhaps used for detaching stone flakes (Dhavalikar *et al.* 1988: 726). It is 6.5 cm long and 1.4 cm thick. Very few artefacts have been chemically analysed. An axe from Jorwe and a chisel from Nevasa show 1.8-2.8 per cent tin alloying.

Beads from Daimabad and ear ornaments from Inamgaon made of gold have been reported. As gold was only available in the Hatti mines of Karnataka, it could have come to Jorwe people through trade contacts with the southern Neolithic people. Apart from these, a large number of ivory beads have also been found from Inamgaon.

The Jorwe people fired their pottery in specially designed kilns as one of them was found at Inamgaon and two at Daimabad. It was circular on plan with a long fire chamber plastered with clay. In case of Inamgaon it was built on stone foundations, like a trough of clay about 1.7 m in diameter. Oval clay cushions with a hole in the centre and grooves on the side were placed over the fire chamber at a depth of 60 cm to provide outlets for hot gases. Air ducts radiated from the centre of the kiln. Though the Harappan kilns were built on similar principles, their design and material were different. The Daimabad kilns were squarish on plan with rounded corners and were certainly larger in size too.

Like the Malwa culture, the Jorwe people also lived in rectangular houses of wattle-and-daub with low mud walls. The average size was found 5 x 3 m. Their house floors were made of rammed clay and often plastered with cow-dung and lime. The chief perhaps occupied a large house containing 5 rooms (covering an area of about 25 x 10 m) in the centre of the settlement. This house yielded a skeleton of a 1.83 m tall male with his ankles and feet intact. The rules of the community of knocking off the feet were not applied to this

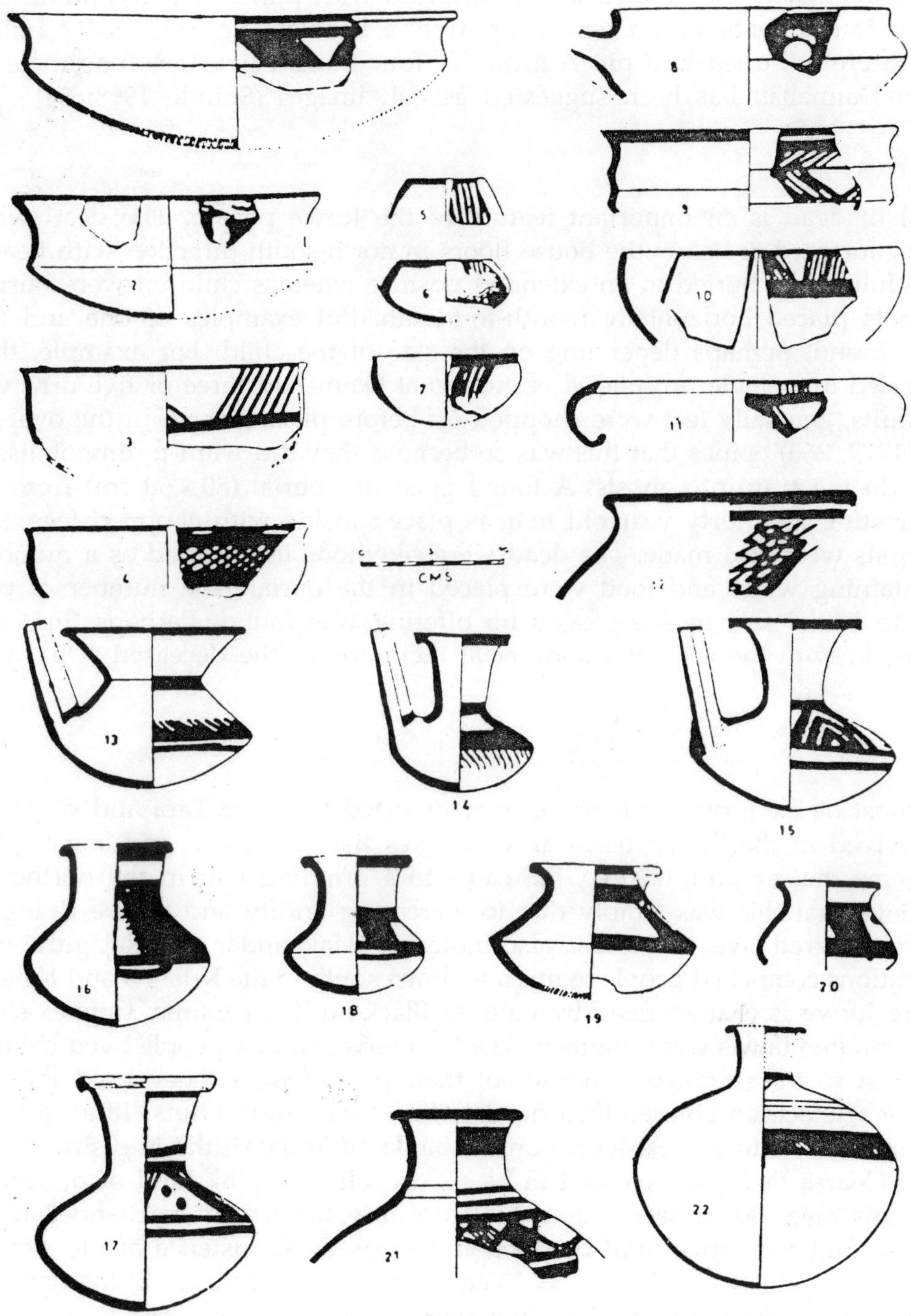

Jorwe ware

Fig. 4-7. Jorwe Ware types with a variety of motifs.

individual, possibly because he was the chief. Spacious courtyards flanked the houses. Perhaps they worshipped both male and female deities as human figurines have been found from various sites. Inamgaon has yielded a few figurines with punctured decoration and a clay box has been found containing a female figurine, a headless figurine and a bull over the box. It was carefully buried in a pit. A group of four human figurines (one male and three female) from Daimabad has been suggested as cult images (Shinde 1998: 34)

Burial Customs

The disposal of dead is an important feature of the Jorwe people. The dead were buried either in the courtyard or below the house floors in north-south direction with head towards north. The adults were buried in an extended posture whereas children were buried in two handmade pots placed horizontally mouth-to-mouth. But examples of one and more than two are also found, perhaps depending on the size of the child. For example, the Nevasa child was buried in a single urn placed vertically; at Daimabad three or five urns were used. In case of adults, generally feet were chopped off before placing them in the oval pit burial. Dhavalikar (1979: 260) opines that this was so because they did want to immobilise the dead so that they do not turn into ghosts! A four legged urn burial (80 x 50 cm) from Inamgaon is quite interesting as a forty year old man is placed inside with chopped legs. Sometimes symbolic burials were also made. The dead were ceremoniously buried as a number of pots possibly containing water and food were placed in the burial. The number of pots varies from burial to burial and in some cases no offering was found. Perhaps this custom has something to do with the economy and social hierarchy of the deceased (Dhavalikar 1979: 260).

Decline

By 1000 BC most of the Jorwe settlements were deserted from the Tapi and Godavari basins but they survived in the Bhima basin at some sites like Inamgaon and some others till *c.* 700 BC. It seems that around 1000 BC, life came to a grinding halt in the northern Deccan. Scholars believe that this was simply due to increasing aridity and severe draughts as the evidence of weathered layer of Nevasa also indicates (Majoomdar and Rajaguru 1965). Such adverse conditions compelled people to migrate down south in the Krishna and Kaveri valleys.

The Late Jorwe is characterized by painted Black-on-Red ceramic. Convex-sided bowls and channel-spouted bowls were common. The Late Jorwe culture people lived in small round huts in contrast to the rectangular houses of their predecessors. They used microliths and limited copper artefacts and buried their dead. Some of their round huts (18 to 28 m diameter) have been found at Theur and Sastevadi on the banks of Mula-Mutha in district Pune. Black-and-Red and Coarse Red Ware painted in black, chocolate or pink kind of pottery has been found from this area. But it seems that due to aridity the irrigation channel at Inamgaon fell into disuse and the agricultural production decreased. Subsistence of life slowly shifted from agricultural products to animal food. Even the dog was consumed at Inamgaon (Thomas 1988). Around 800 BC, the southern Megalithic people reached Deccan and occupied the Jorwe settlements as the evidence at Inamgaon suggests.

Panja (1999) has recently carried out survey in the Bhima basin and has presented an analysis of mobility and subsistence change among the Chalcolithic communities of Inamgaon. She finds that the Bhima basin was occupied by diverse groups of people following different mobility strategies: semi-sedentary, sedentary and nomadic. There was no evidence of settlement change. The larger settlements could only grow in the valley of Tapi and not in the alluvial strips of the tributaries, though the number of sites is large in those areas.

In the Tapi valley, most of the Savalda and Late Harappan settlements were found on its banks, whereas the Malwa and Jorwe settlements were either away from the banks or concentrated along the tributaries. Larger settlements could grow only on the banks of the main river.

Shinde thinks that all these cultures used wheel-turned painted pottery, though each one has distinct painting tradition. All these cultures have many common cultural traits. Hence he suggests that instead of identifying them as different cultures they could be different phases of Deccan Chalcolithic culture.

GUJARAT CHALCOLITHIC CULTURES

The map (Fig. 4-8) shows the distribution of Harappan and other Chalcolithic sites in South Asia. Like Central India and Deccan, the Chalcolithic cultures also flourished in various regions of Gujarat, though their contribution to the development of the Harappan civilization is poorly understood. Thanks to the studies undertaken by M.S. University, Baroda, Archaeological Survey, State Department of Archaeology, Deccan College and Pennsylvenia University Museum in the last few decades, a number of Chalcolithic sites/cultures have been identified in different regions of Gujarat.

It is interesting to note that like Rajasthan, north Gujarat is dotted with Mesolithic sites and at a number of places, e.g. Loteshwar, Datrana, Santhli, Moti Pipli and others, the non-Harappan or Chalcolithic people settled (Fig. 4-8). Chalcolithic sites in Gujarat are right over the Mesolithic deposit. These Chalcolithic sites are termed as "Anarta tradition sites," after the name of the region. They perhaps lived on rammed mud floors and used a variety of pottery, which includes Black-and-Red, Reserve Slip, Fine Red Ware, Buff Ware, Grey Ware, Gritty Red Ware, Burnished Red Ware and Burnished Grey/Black Ware. Large and medium pots, small pots with constricted neck and bulbous body, bowls, basins, dishes and dish-on-stand are some of the common vessel forms of north Gujarat Chalcolithic. Sometimes painted decorations are executed in chocolate or black colour on the pottery. At some sites like Santhli, child as well as adult burials have also been found (Sonawane and Ajithprasad 1994). Recent studies have shown that the Anarta Chalcolithic had independent existence in north Gujarat prior to the Harappan culture, as some of the sites have been dated around middle of 4th millennium BC. The evidence also indicates that even after the penetration of the Harappans in Gujarat, the Chalcolithic people continued flourishing at several sites during the Mature and Post-Harappan times. Ratanpura is an important site in north Gujarat, which has yielded pottery similar to Rangpur Period III and some pottery like Ahar.

Similarly Kachchh and Saurashtra have also yielded evidence of Pre-or Early non-Harappan sites and Post-Harappan sites, which represent indigenous regional Chalcolithic traditions, for example, Padri Ware, Pre-Prabhas Ware, Micaceous Red Ware, Black-and-Red Ware and Lustrous Red Ware. The Lustrous Red Ware, however, found at a number of Harappan sites in Saurashtra has been assigned to the late Harappan phase. On the other hand, Shinde finds a lot of similarity between the Padri Ware of Gujarat and the Savalda Ware of Deccan. The role of these different Chalcolithic traditions should be studied to unravel the regional manifestations of the Harappa culture and also to determine the beginning of agriculture and domestication of animals in Gujarat.

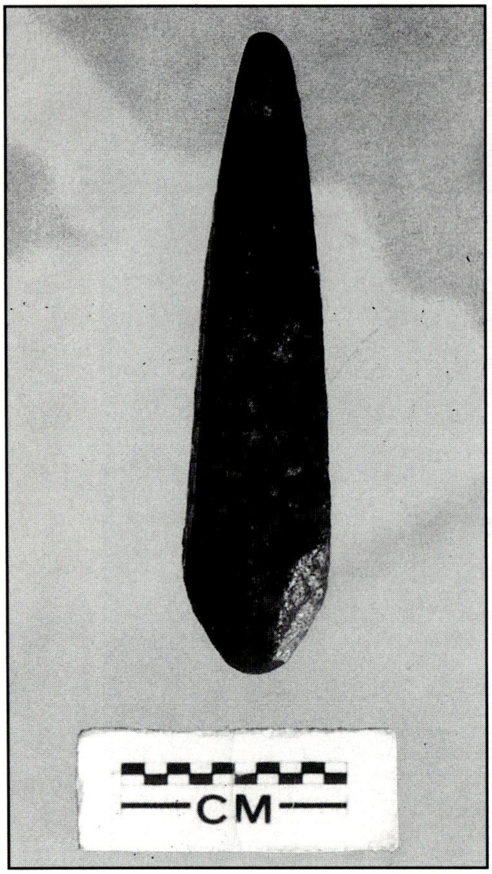

Pl. 4-23. Bronze punch, Datrana, north Gujarat.

Pl. 4-24. Terracotta mother goddess, Nagwada, Gujarat.

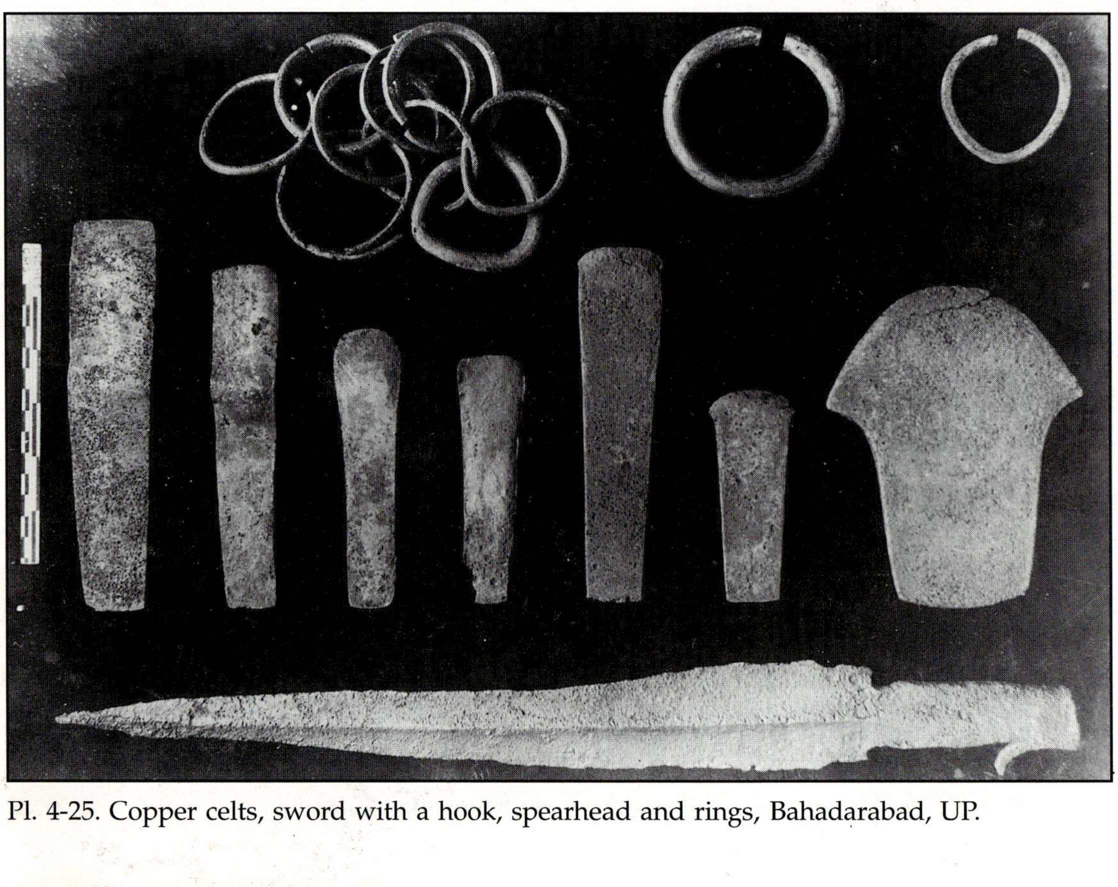

Pl. 4-25. Copper celts, sword with a hook, spearhead and rings, Bahadarabad, UP.

like beads, bangles, pendants and inlays of shell, semiprecious stones and faience (a synthetic vitreous/glaze-like material formed by heating a mixture of powdered quartz with soda and some colouring agent). The excavation has revealed a large quantity of different varieties of semiprecious stones and large shells (shank) stored at different places within the walled area indicating the importance of the above industrial products and their trade in the economy of the site.

The inscribed seal (Pl. 4-19) unearthed from the site could have played a role in authenticating commercial consignments. The seal is a small, 1.8 x 1.8 cm square steatite tablet bearing a two-letter inscription and the figure of a one horned bull, popularly known as the mythical unicorn, engraved on it. In front of this animal, there is also engraving of a small standard-like device. The projected boss at the backside of this seal has a small hole for passing a thread. Several samples of clay lumps bearing stamped impressions of similar seals (Pl. 4-20) have also been recovered from the site.

Another important item possibly connected with trade recovered from the excavation was a few large, pear-shaped, black slipped jars which are believed to have been used by the Harappans for overseas transportation of goods. Some of these vessels bear graffiti in the Harappan script. Similar vessels have been reported from a number of 3rd millennium Bronze Age sites in the Oman peninsula. Clay matching analysis of the black slipped jars found in Oman by French archaeologists has indicated that these jars have their origin in the Indian subcontinent. Hence, the black slipped jar sherds discovered from Bagasra are a sure indicator of the trade contact of the Harappans with overseas Bronze Age settlements of the 3rd millennium BC, especially that of the Oman peninsula. Tapping the rich copper deposits of Oman might have been the major attraction for the Harappan interest in that region. A number of household copper implements and tools including heavy chisels, punch points, knives and a hoard of copper bangles and a small axe in a copper pot (Pl. 4-21) were recovered from the site during excavation. Apart from the trade of industrial products, the economy of the settlement was also dependent upon agriculture, stock-raising and fishing. A good collection of fish remains including otoliths (the stone-like calcium carbonate concretions formed in the internal ear of bony fish) indicate that fish was one of the important food items of the Harappans at Bagasra.

Bagasra is located midway between Kachchh, Saurashtra and north Gujarat regions. This advantageous geographical position has helped the site to act as a conduit for the transportation of materials and movement of communities from one region to the other during the 3rd millennium BC. Therefore, the site was a meeting point for divergent cultural traits from all the three major cultural regions. The excavation has also revealed late survival of the settlement up to about the first half of the 2nd millennium BC (1700 BC) even after the decline of the urban Harappan centres by the end of 3rd millennium (2000 BC).

The description of the following Harappan and Harappan related Chalcolithic sites of Gujarat is based on Sonawane (in press).

North Gujarat was extensively inhabited by the hunters and gatherers of Mesolithic period. At sites like Loteshwar, Datrana, Santhli and Moti Pipli cultural remains of Chalcolithic period representing non-Harappan and Harappan traits have been found in a well-defined strata above the Mesolithic occupation. Even after the emergence of Chalcolithic cultures, Mesolithic people continued to live in this area along with the Chalcolithic communities. Sonawane points out that until recently it was assumed that the earliest settled Chalcolithic communities were associated with the Mature/Urban phase of the Harappa culture (*c.* 2550-

2000 BC). However, recent excavations at Loteshwar in north Gujarat suggest that prior to the coming of the Harappans, this part of Gujarat was already inhabited by the regional non-Harappan Chalcolithic communities. Calibrated radiocarbon dates for this cultural phase from well-defined stratified levels at Loteshwar go back up to the second-half of the 4th millennium BC making them earlier than the Harappans. The region of Kachchh and Saurashtra also revealed sites of a Pre-Urban phase of an indigenous regional Chalcolithic tradition with non-Harappan pottery types such as Padri Ware, pre-Prabhas Ware, Micaceous Red Ware and Black-and-Red Ware. A critical review of this Pre-/Early non-Harappan phase of Gujarat is available in Sonawane and Ajithprasad (1994: 132-36) and Bhan (1994: 77-78). Very little is known about its cultural interaction with the neighbouring regions like Kachchh and Saurashtra and also about the origin and development of these early village farming communities. However, it played a vital role in the regional manifestation of the Harappa culture and refuted earlier claims of the mass migration of Harappans into this region during the Mature/Urban phase (Sonawane in press).

Nagwada and Santhli excavations reveal an early penetration of Harappans in north Gujarat. The burial pottery does not show any similarities with the classical Harappan pottery, rather it resembles the ceramic forms from the Pre-Harappan levels at Kot Diji (Khan 1965), Amri (Casal 1964) and Balakot (Dales 1974). Analogous pottery types have been reported from the cemetery at Surkotada. These too are comparable with Pre-Harappan pottery of Sind and Baluchistan (Joshi 1990; Possehl 1997). Stratigraphically the burials at Nagwada are found buried below the Mature/Urban Harappan levels. However, no distinct habitation deposit of the community who buried their dead is reported from these sites. Moti Pipli, another site in the same region, however, showed a substantial habitation deposit containing similar burial pottery but without burials. Similar pottery is reported from six more sites from the same region during the recent explorations. According to Sonawane, this similarity may signify that the elements of Pre-Harappan culture of Sind and Baluchistan extended southwards as far as north Gujarat when this region was already inhabited by the indigenous Chalcolithic communities.

The settlements of Mature/Urban Harappan phase are few in north Gujarat, Nagwada I being the most important site of this phase showing most of the classic Harappan traits. Other sites like Nagwada IV, Zekhda and Datrana IV can also be included in this category although they incorporate only few type-fossils of the Mature phase. At all these sites, non-Harappan elements dominate compared to the Harappan traits. It appears that the Mature Harappans penetrated north Gujarat basically to exploit the natural resources of the region. This resulted in an amalgamation of the cultural traits. The excavations at Nagwada I, Zekhda and Datrana IV demonstrated that they were also engaged in specialized craft production centres, like Nageswar, Kuntasi, Bagasra and other coastal settlements of Saurashtra. Their location demonstrates that these sites were developed mainly for trade and access to raw material of specific commodities. Apart from these, a large number of sites belong to the Post-Urban phase comparable to Rangpur Periods IIC and III category. Ratanpura and Datrana II are the only excavated sites representing this phase.

Sonawane thinks that, unlike the Indus valley in Sind, none of the rivers in north Gujarat allowed irrigation. Agriculture here is entirely dependent on dry farming techniques. As a result, a complicated picture emerges which shows the inter-related aspects of sedentism, pastoralism, hunting, craft production and many other diversified resource exploitation strategies. Sites in north Gujarat indicate a dispersed type of settlement pattern, in contrast to the linear-dendritic pattern of Saurashtra. While majority of the territorial Saurashtra sites are based on agrarian economy, western part of north Gujarat favoured pastoral activities. The availability of excellent grassland, water, patchy appearance of thin cultural deposits and large frequency of animal bones suggest that the north Gujarat sites may have been seasonal camps involved in pastoral activities (Bhan 1992: 175-79). Thus, the settlement pattern shows a lack of standardization and homogeneity in its material culture during the Post-Urban Harappan phase. There was a decline in the material prosperity transforming the urban way of life into a rural one. As a result, the Post-Urban phase witnessed a process of decentralization and localization, giving rise to regional cultural expressions (Sonawane in press).

With this background, we can now describe the recent excavations of north Gujarat, mainly based upon Sonawane's reports.

LOTESHWAR

Loteshwar (23°36' N and 71°50' E), 17 km north-east of Shankheshwar in Mehsana district, lying half a kilometre east of Loteshwar village on the left bank of the Khari, a tributary of the Rupen, was excavated by the M.S. University of Baroda in 1991. The site measuring 120 x 50 m revealed a habitational deposit of 1.65 m belonging to two cultural periods. Period I representing 1 m thick deposit lying directly on the stabilized sand-dune yielded, a large number of microliths together with sandstone palettes, hammers and grinding stones. The microlithic tools include both geometric and non-geometric types made of chert, chalcedony, jasper, agate and quartz. Besides, small shouldered bone points and few prismatic red and yellow ochre crayons and two human burials constitute important material remains of this period. One of these burials was found placed in an extended inhumation position while the other was placed in a crouching position. A preliminary assessment of the rich collection of faunal remains indicates an abundance of a few wild species. Stratigraphically, the Chalcolithic deposit directly overlies the Mesolithic deposit without any break in the central (highest) part of the mound.

A solitary radiocarbon date on a charred bone sample from Layer 4 of the Mesolithic deposit suggests the beginning of micrlithic tradition at the site to around six millennium BC.

The cultural deposit of Period II spread over a small area of 50 x 30 m is hardly 30 cm thick. These pits have varying dimensions from 0.50 m to 2 m in diameter and 0.50 m to 2 m in depth, filled with ashy soil, containing habitation debris including pottery, animal bones, terracotta lumps, etc. The significance of these pits has not yet been fully understood. The ceramic assemblage shows similarity with the non-Harappan pottery types reported from Nagwada and Surkotada. It represents the regional ceramic types of north Gujarat, termed as "Anarta Tradition" after the traditional name of this region, which is distinct from the Mature and Sorath Harappan pottery. In addition, Black-and-Red Ware was also found at the site. Unlike Nagwada and Surkotada, Harappan pottery, terracotta triangular cakes and other typical Harappan antiquities are significantly absent here. Only a few sherds of Reserved Slip Ware were found. Also found were steatite micro-beads, carnelian beads and crudely made bangles and beads of shell. The settlement appears to be very ephemeral. The faunal analysis has indicated heavy emphasis on the domestication of cattle, indicating a pastoral economy.

Two ^{14}C dates of charcoal obtained from Period II levels date back to around 3500 BC.

Evidently, it suggests that the Anart Chalcolithic had its independent existence in north Gujarat prior to the Harappan culture.

Santhli

Santhli (23°54' N and 71°29' E) is situated about 20 km north-west of Radhanpur in Banaskantha district on a large stabilized sand-dune. It was excavated by the M.S. University of Baroda in 1994. The excavation revealed a total habitation deposit of 40 cm belonging to two distinct cultural periods. Period I belonged to the Mesolithic period. The assemblage includes typical Mesolithic artefacts of both geometric and non-geometric microliths, made on fine siliceous materials, besides, a number of small pieces of flat sandstone slabs or palette-stones, which are generally associated with the Mesolithic assemblage in Gujarat. The meagre collection of finished artefacts and lithic debitage may be due to only seasonal occupation by the Mesolithic hunter-gatherers. The habitation debris, however, yielded a large quantity of skeletal remains of the animals, mainly bovines, hunted by the microlith using community. These bones are found as discrete clusters; the largest of such clusters had four such skulls piled together along with other bones. Therefore, the available evidence suggests that the site might have been used as a butchery and food-processing place by the Mesolithic folk. Apart from these, the other faunal remains included sheep/goat, gazelle, pig and equuid species (*Equus hemiones*?).

Period II has only a patchy Chalcolithic deposit directly overlying the Mesolithic debris. The deposit included a few sherds of pottery and bangles and beads of shell besides some stone objects. The most interesting finds are two extended inhumation burials placed in an east-west orientation with the head towards east. The first one is an extended joint/double burial of two adult individuals interred in the same pit. With the burials were found five pots, similar to the burial pottery at Nagwada (Pl. 4-22). The second is a child burial associated with a few pottery vessels, similar to the first burial. Except pottery vessels, no other burial goods were found in these graves (Sonawane and Ajithprasad 1994: 136).

Moti Pipli

Moti Pipli (23°49' N and 71°32' E) is situated about 10 km west of Radhanpur town of the Banaskantha district on a large stabilized sand-dune. Adjacent to the site, there is a large inter-dunal depression known as Shakatari Talav. The excavation revealed a regular habitation deposit of 90 cm belonging to the Mesolithic, Harappan affiliated Chalcolithic and Historic periods.

Period I had a Mesolithic deposit of about 20 cm which yielded a number of microlithic blade and flake cores along with industrial debitage, besides a few typical Mesolithic tools like lunates, backed blades, points and scrapers. The tools were made of locally available chert, chalcedony, agate and jasper. No pottery was associated with the Mesolithic industry. Faunal remains were fragmentary.

Period II representing Harappan affiliated Chalcolithic culture had a deposit of about 50 cm. There was no evidence of structural remains. A variety of different pottery types like Fine Red Ware, Buff Ware, Grey Ware, Gritty Red Ware, Burnished Red Ware, Burnished Grey/Black Ware, Black-and-Red Ware and Reserved Slip Ware comprised the major ceramic assemblage. Fine Red Ware and Buff Ware form the most important group. Important shapes in this group are large pots, dishes, dish-on-stand, beaker, large beaker-like vases with narrow mouth and bulbous body. A few of the Fine Red Ware pots were treated with a cream or chocolate slip and painted with thick bands of chocolate or black pigments at rim and shoulder. In addition, some of the pots are treated with red pigment generally on a cream background, imparting a polychrome effect. Similar vessels are reported from the Pre-Harappan levels at Kot Diji, Balakot and Amri. It is interesting to note that here they are associated with the habitation levels and not found as part of burials unlike Nagwada and Santhli.

A few typical Harappan Red Ware and Buff Ware types were also recovered from these strata. There is a prominent presence of Reserved Slip Ware. However, the Anarta tradition is more predominant at the site, in the form of Gritty Red Ware and Red Ware. Large and medium pots, small pots with constricted neck and bulbous body, bowls, basins, dishes and dish-on-stand are some of the common vessel forms of these wares. Very often, these are decorated with thick bands and lines of dark chocolate or black colour at the rim, neck and shoulder. Invariably such decorations are executed on a cream background to get a bichrome effect. Similar pots are found in the Burnished Grey/Black Ware and Burnished Red Ware of the same ceramic tradition. The Black-and-Red Ware is another indigenous ceramic tradition of Gujarat. Very few sherds of bowls of this ware were noticed here. All the above types are common at many of the Chalcolithic sites in north Gujarat.

Other important antiquities of this period are a copper/bronze nail, a fish-hook and a folded tip of copper; a number of long parallel-sided chert blades of Rohri origin and ornamental beads of agate, lapis lazuli, steatite and faience. The collection also included shell bangles and beads, biconical and spherical terracotta beads decorated with delicately incised lines or dots, terracotta pellets, two- or four-pinched clay lumps, *mushtikas*, moulded terracotta triangular cakes, spindle whorls and scrapers. Faunal remains include cattle, sheep/goat, deer and pig.

Datrana

Datrana (23°46' N and 71°07' E) is a small village situated about 8 km north-west of Santhalpur town of Banaskantha district. There are 10 distinct clusters of the Harappan affiliated Chalcolithic settlements around Datrana. Datrana was excavated by the M.S. University of Baroda.

Datrana IV is located about 1.5 km on a large crescent shaped fossil sand-dune. The excavated area revealed a total habitational deposit of about 90 cm belonging to two distinct cultural periods.

Period I-Mesolithic. The lithic assemblage includes crudely worked micro-blade cores, sandstone palettes and small backed tools like lunates, triangles, trapeziums, blades, scrapers and points, mainly made on chert. Overlying the Mesolithic deposit is the Chalcolithic (Period II) stone blade industry, though there is no stratigraphic break between the two. The Period II is characterized by long blades, made on fine chalcedony. The assemblage incorporates hundreds of crested ridge blades and cores including different types of backed blades, points, truncated blades, large-size crescents, burins and simple long blades. Some of the blades show a very heavy inverse retouch. In addition to chalcedony, agate, jasper and chert were also used. A few characteristic long parallel-sided chert blades of Rohri origin also make their presence.

A bronze punch-point (Pl. 4-23) was also found, which might have been used for detaching blade flakes from the prepared core. It is a small squarish prism-like tool measuring 2.8 cm in length, having a thickness of 0.5 cm. The broad blunt end might have been used as a working end after hafting it into a socketed wooden handle, like a punch, for removal of blades by indirect pressure flaking method.

A few cylindrical and small disc-like beads rough-outs in carnelian with perforation and a few with tell-tale marks of attempted perforation, small tanged chert drill-bits and sub-cylindrical drill-points in banded agate were also found.

Besides a few sherds of the typical north Gujarat regional pottery types, like Gritty Red Ware, the ceramic assemblage includes a few unique wares like the Burnished Grey Ware and the Burnished Coarse Grey Ware with a thick grey/black slip. These vessels are handmade and show panels of thick, obliquely impressed lines all over the body, set in between two lines of similar character. These incised/impressed lines are drawn on the burnished surface of the pot by using a smooth rod with a blunt, flat end. A few Black-and-Red Ware sherds showing a similar decorative feature at the rim with distinct shapes are also part of this assemblage. There is also a type of Red Ware with a corrugated/ribbed surface. Occasionally, sherds of the burial types recovered from Nagwada and Santhli have also been found associated with them.

These artefacts are found in discrete clusters within the excavated trenches in association with heaps of animal bones. Many of these clusters include unworked nodules, hammer stones, fragments of copper tools and other artefacts. A large number of animal bones, antlers, teeth and fish vertebrae were collected from this deposit. Cattle, sheep/goat, antelope and pig are the important animals identified in the faunal collection.

Datrana V

The Mound V at Datrana is located about 300 metres north-east of Mound IV. Here, the total cultural deposit varies from 70 to 90 cm belonging to two periods: Mesolithic and Chalcolithic.

The Mesolithic assemblage of Period II includes, a large number of geometric and non-geometric tools along with lithic debitage apart from hammer stones, flat sandstone palettes, red ochre crayons with facets and a few fragmentary bones, horn-cores and teeth. The Mesolithic artefacts including the raw material are comparable with the Mesolithic assemblage unearthed from Datrana IV.

The Chalcolithic Period II lies over Mesolithic deposit. It has revealed two large pots, intact up to their body part from the base and also a number of sherds similar to the burial pots from Nagwada and Santhli. Besides these, except long chalcedony blades, no worthwhile artefacts of the Chalcolithic period were unearthed during the excavation.

Datrana II is located about 1 km east of Datrana Mound IV and about half a kilometre south-west of the village. It is a stabilized sand-dune flanked by two inter-dunal depressions covering an area of about 50 x 40 m. However, the evidence of the Chalcolithic occupation at the site is patchy and probably confined to the southern slope of the mound. Interestingly, habitation deposit in all the three clusters is confined to pits of different dimensions. A few of them measure a maximum of 2 m diameter and also depth, while the smaller ones measure hardly half a metre both in diameter and depth. Some of these pits were, in fact, served as pottery kilns. These pits have yielded a rich collection of pottery, most of which belonged to Sorath Harappan pottery of Rojdi A and B type, made of finely elutriated clay and is uniformly well baked, painted with typical bull figures and other usual designs. One of these pits has yielded a number of Lustrous Red Ware bowls, dishes and a neck of a corrugated vessel, typical of the Post-Urban Harappan sites of Saurashtra. While most of the pottery recovered from other pits are of Gritty Red Ware and Fine Red Ware representing the regional Chalcolithic ceramic tradition of north Gujarat.

However, the most interesting find is the discovery of a pottery kiln, stocked with Sorath Harappan pottery types especially pots/jars, basins, bowls and dishes. These features, therefore, suggest that the site might have been a pottery manufacturing centre, although, no evidence of habitation structures was unearthed within the excavated trenches. The pottery types reported from Datrana IV are not found in any of the trenches dug at Datrana II. Therefore, it seems these two mounds are chronologically well separated and the occupation at Datrana IV seems to be much earlier than Datrana II.

NAGWADA

Nagwada (23°20' N and 71°41' E) is an important Mature Harappan settlement situated in Dasada *taluka* of Surendranagar district, close to the eastern margin of the Little Rann of Kachchh. A shallow stream, the Vonkali, drains the area. To its north-east is a large inter-dunal depression that accumulates monsoon run-off, which could have served as a source of potable water. The M.S. University of Baroda excavated the site from 1986 to 1990. The site measuring 140 x 110 m has a 1 m deposit with four structural levels. The single period occupation is divided into two distinctive phases.

Period IA has hardly any substantial deposit. Structural remains are indicated by a few post-holes and rammed mud floors. Four symbolic pot burials and two extended inhumation burials with pots, lying in east-west direction, belong to this phase. Of these, five burials show a close affinity with the pottery found from Pre-Harappan levels at Kot Diji and Nal, while one urn burial reflects the local style. The pottery types of first category are not met within any of the later habitational deposits at the site. One of the symbolic pot burials contained 10 intact pots. The burial ceramics include dish-on-stand, dish, beaker, bowl, disc-based globular jars and short-necked globular medium-sized vessel (Pl. 4-22). It appears that the Pre-/Early Harappan settlements of Sind and Baluchistan extended further south into the north-western part of Gujarat prior to the beginning of the Mature Harappan phase.

The Period IB comprises the upper four layers with artefacts of the Mature Harappa culture. The mud brick sizes show the standard Harappan ratio of 1: 2: 4 (8 x 16 x 32 cm and 7 x 14 x 28 cm). The brick masonry consisted of alternate layers of headers and stretchers (English bond), using mud mortar. The exposed structures are rectangular, except for a semicircular one, with a uniform thickness of 65 cm. One of the independent rubble structures measured roughly 6.6 x 4.4 m, while other brick structures measured 6.6 x 5.1 m.

The ceramic repertoire at Nagwada has both the Harappan and non-Harappan types. Though the classical Mature Harappan types in Fine Red Ware, Buff Ware and Chocolate-Slipped Ware were few, they are represented by the typical painted natural and abstract decorations and standardized vessel forms like the "S" profile jars, perforated jars, beakers, dish-on-stands, large storage jars, medium-sized disc-based vases, bowls, basins and even typical miniature vessels. Gritty Red Ware, dominating the ceramic assemblage and white painted Black-and-Red Ware represent the indigenous non-Harappan wares. Gritty Red Ware is distinctly different, from the Harappan wares, in its form and the use of pigments for decorative design. The ceramic assemblage recovered from the lower levels shows more ornate and intricate patterns. Other pottery types found at the site include Reserved Slip Ware, Coarse Red Ware and incised Grey Ware.

The most significant contribution of the Nagwada excavation is that it clearly demonstrates that a variety of stone beads and shell objects were manufactured here. Although no industrial workshop was found, a variety of evidence indicates that beads were manufactured here. The occurrence of raw materials such as chert, agate and amazonite; fine-grained stone nodules and their bladelets and blades; mostly unretouched variety of bead roughouts and blanks; stone hammers and polishers; disposed defective beads and broken beads; a large number of well polished, finished semiprecious stone beads are definitive indicators of the local lapidary industry. The other indicators of stone bead industry are, a large number of micro drill-bits of chert and a few tubular drills of ernestite. Among the semiprecious stone beads of carnelian, agate, amazonite and lapis lazuli obtained from Nagwada, etched carnelian beads (eye beads of typical Indus origin) are most striking. It seems steatite micro-beads, faience and shell beads were also produced here. The islands of the Little Rann are known for their rich semiprecious stone deposits, especially the Mardak Bet.

Nagwada has also yielded small hemispherical gold caps for covering the ends of the semiprecious stone for use as pendants. The Nagwada jewellers made necklaces using colourful stone beads and gold caps perhaps to cater to the needs of the urban elite of the Harappan towns.

Nagwada was also engaged in the production of shell objects, though it appears that only cutting and polishing of shell objects were carried out at the site. Primary dressing of gastropods was not done here. The most common shell products were the bangles produced from *T. pyrum* gastropods. Finished shell bangle pieces were invariably decorated with the typical chevron motif. Beads and pendants form other shell ornaments. Waste fragments of shell were recycled to produce a variety of tiny, flat, geometric forms as inlay pieces. The most fascinating was the discovery of a spherical object decorated with six sets of concentric circles. *T. pyrum* and *C. ramosus* might have been easily procured from the shallow bays of the Gulf of Kachchh by the Nagwada shell workers.

Other important antiquities recovered from Nagwada include a variety of gold and silver ornaments; copper implements and ornaments like celts, chisel, saw blade, knives, bangles, beads and pendants; cubical weights of agate; inscribed clay sealing; long parallel-sided chert blades of Rohri origin; terracotta female figurine (Pl. 4-24) with embedded steatite beads; triangular cakes; toy-cart frames and wheels and bone points, along with several other household objects. Most of these artefacts show the typical Mature Harappan style.

The domestic animals at the site included cattle, sheep and goat, forming more than 60 per cent of the total faunal assemblage at the site. Wild animals exploited here are represented by 12 different taxa. Among these, sambar, chital, black buck, gazelle and pig are more common while nilgai is rare. The bones of wild ass are also suspected in the faunal collection. Bones of hare, hyena, camel and fowl are also recovered in a small quantity.

Radiocarbon assay of a single charcoal sample collected from the site has given a date of *c.* 2100 BC (calibrated).

Zekhda

Zekhda (23°40' N and 70°20' E) is another important Harappan affiliated Chalcolithic settlement situated about 7 km north of Varahi town of Banaskantha district, spread over an area of about 600 x 200 m with four distinct artefact concentrations. The excavation carried out here by the M.S. University of Baroda in 1978 revealed a habitational deposit varying from 0.5 m to 1.5 m in depth, though the actual mound is 3 to 4 m high from the surrounding ground level. At Zekhda also, Harappan and non-Harappan pottery types were found mixed throughout the habitation strata with Harappan ceramics in a minority. The excavated assemblage compares well with the Nagwada material obtained from Period IB deposit. Though Zekhda revealed most of the diagnostic artefacts of the Mature Harappan phase, unlike Nagwada, it had only simple circular mud hut floors with post-holes. It seems that some portion of the settlement was occupied during the Post-Urban Harappan phase. Zekhda also perhaps was involved in craft production using marine gastropods and semiprecious stones. The most interesting is the discovery of two small clay pots containing approximately 34,000 steatite micro-beads and two gold beads found carefully buried underneath in one of the circular hut floors.

Ratanpura

Ratanpura (23°28' N and 71°48' E), one of the Post-Urban Harappan settlements on the Rupen estuary, is situated about 5 km south of Shankheshwar in Sami *taluka* of Mehsana district. A large depression seen on the eastern side of the mound might have served as the main water source for the settlement. The site was excavated by the M.S. University of Baroda in 1985. The entire mound measuring 500 x 250 m (12.5 hectare) has revealed four distinct localities with two cultural periods.

Locality III with an area of about 90 x 90 m is strewn with exploited faunal remains and lithic materials. The excavation had revealed a thin cultural deposit of 5 cm with a lot of chipped blades, lunates and points together with debitage of the microlithic industry, made of chert, chalcedony, agate and jasper. The faunal remains revealed nearly 60 per cent of domestic species, with a high frequency of sheep/goat followed by cattle and buffalo. Among the wild animals were chital, sambar, black buck, chinkara, nilgai, Indian boar, camel and wild ass. It seems that before the Harappans came here, this portion of the mound was occupied by the Mesolithic hunting/gathering community.

The other three localities were subsequently inhabited during the Post-Urban Harappan period. The lower two strata yielded circular huts marked by post-holes, while the upper one was devoid of such well-laid structures. Mostly circular pits characterized the Locality IV. These pits appear non-religious in their use and were filled with ash, terracotta lumps, charred and uncharred bones, besides the ceramic types of the Post-Urban Harappan phase. The most distinctive types at the site are Lustrous Red Ware, Fine, Medium and Coarse Black-and-Red Ware, Red Ware, Buff Ware and Cream Slipped Ware. The shapes and decorations of the Lustrous Red Ware and Fine Black-and-Red Ware show affinity with the pottery reported from Rangpur Period III. Besides pottery, a number of pestle stones, saddle querns, variety of terracotta objects and ornamental beads of carnelian, steatite, shell and terracotta were recovered. Of these, the most noteworthy finds are stamped clay lumps bearing the intricate circular geometric designs. These enigmatic objects formed a special feature of Ratanpura since none of the Harappan affiliated Chalcolithic culture sites recorded such decorated clay lumps. The occurrence of chocolate coloured Tan Slipped Ware, Buff Ware and Cream Slipped Ware at Ratanpura indicates that the Post-Urban Harappan phase of Gujarat had developed contacts with cultures related to Period IC of Ahar.

The small size of the settlement with thin and patchy cultural deposit and high frequency of animal bones suggest that Ratanpura was a temporary or seasonal campsite involved in pastoral activities.

GANGA DOAB AND EASTERN ZONE

Besides Central India and the Deccan, the Chalcolithic cultures also flourished in the northern and eastern parts of the country, largely confined to the eastern Uttar Pradesh (UP), Bihar, Bengal and Orissa – generally called the middle or lower Ganga region. The Vindhyan sites have more similarity with the middle and upper Ganga sites. Pal (1986: 159-69) observes that the Vindhyan Chalcolithic pottery tradition has elements of Central India, Deccan and of the Upper Ganga valley. A large number of sites across the middle and lower Ganga plains have been assigned to the Chalcolithic phase.

MIDDLE GANGA VALLEY CULTURES

Koldihwa, Onaur, Unchadih, Kosambi Period I, Sringverpura Period I, Puredeojani, Pelkhawar, Bhiwani, Akahua, Nahush ka Tila, Sohgaura Period II, Narhan Period I, Banawarighat, Gularihwaghat, Lahuradewa in Uttar Pradesh and Chirand Period II, Sonpur Period I, Oriup, Antichak, Champa, Buxar and Chechar Kutubpur Period II in Bihar are some of the Chalcolithic sites belonging to the middle Ganga valley. However, in the lower Ganga region, a number of sites, e.g. Pandu Rajar Dhibi, Gangadanga, Mangalkot, Mahisdal, Haripur (Solkhana), Hatikra, Kotasur, Bahiri, Tulsipur, Nanur, Bharatpur, Dihar, etc., have been reported. Though most of these sites have been excavated for one or two seasons, only brief reports are available in *Indian Archaeology—A Review*. The sites of lower Ganga region are characterized by Black-and-Red Ware. Generally the ceramic assemblage consists of black-and red, red/red slipped, black slipped, buff wares. Shapes like dish, or bowl-on-stand, channel-spouted bowls and dishes-on-stand are common and Black-and-Red Ware is predominant. Often Black-and-Red and red slipped wares bear painted decorations. Chakrabarti (1994: 255) suggests that these people could have obtained copper from Singhbhum and Hazaribag-Girdih area. It is believed that Barudih was an industrial site in this region.

The Chalcolithic pottery of Koldihwa compares well with its counterparts of Kakoria (IAR 1962-63: 39-41: 1963-64; 57-58), a Chalcolithic-Megalithic site in the Varanasi district on the one hand and with that of Chirand in Bihar on the other. Prahladpur in Varanasi and Atranjikhera II (Black-and-Red Ware phase) in Etah also offer some analogous types. The Black-and-Red, the black slipped and Red Wares have been found in all these sites. Numerous types like bowls, dishes, basins, medium-sized vases and big sized jars have been found at all these sites. Pedestalled bowl is another type, which links these sites. Like Kakoria, Koldihwa has also yielded funnel-shaped lids both in Black Slipped and Red Wares.

Like Chirand and Prahladpur, Koldihwa has also yielded some painted sherds both in Black-and-Red and Red Wares. Identical bone arrowheads both of socketed and tanged varieties are other common features at Koldihwa, Prahladpur and Atranjikhera in Uttar Pradesh, Chirand in Bihar and Pandu-Rajar-Dhibi in West Bengal.

Some sites like Prahladpur, Rajghat, Kamauli, Takiaper, Rakhat and Belkhara yielded Chalcolithic pottery along with a few microliths and iron implements from the pre-NBP deposit.

Pal (1986) has noted that many pottery traits of the Neolithic phase survived both in the Chalcolithic cultures of the middle and lower Ganga. The slip treatment on the Red Slipped and the Black Slipped wares of the Chalcolithic period evolved out of the Burnished Red Ware and Burnished Black Ware of the Neolithic period respectively. Rustication on the outer surface of Red Ware may also be treated as a survival of the Neolithic Rusticated Ware. Applique decoration is also a Neolithic trait, which continued in the Chalcolithic period. Many of the pottery shapes of Neolithic culture survived in the same or slightly modified form in the Chalcolithic period, though spouted vessels are conspicuous by their absence in the Chalcolithic period.

In the middle Ganga valley, Chirand and Koldihwa are very important sites. Chirand is located on the confluence of the Ganga and the Saryu in the Saran district of Bihar. It was excavated between 1962 and 1965, though on a small scale and the earliest levels were assigned to 1600-1700 BC (uncal.). Here Pd I is represented by the Neolithic culture, Pd II by Chalcolithic and Pd III is marked by the appearance of NBP and iron. The copper artefacts of Pd II include tanged arrowheads, rings, bangles, antimony rods, etc. The Chalcolithic cultures were also equipped with stone tool industry. Though the evidence of copper was found from the top of Pd I, it was available in relative abundance to the people only in Pd II. The polished stone axes appear curiously enough as late as Pd III. The abundance of the bone points gradually increases from Periods I to III.

Though on the basis of fabric and surface treatment, the middle Ganga wares have often been identified as Red, Black Slipped and Black-and-Red Wares yet there are some regional variations, e.g. the Koldihwa pottery is superior in fabric, finish and firing than the Kakoria group. Stray occurrences of corded ware have also been reported from Koldihwa and some other sites. The pottery is largely wheel-turned, made of levigated clay and sometimes tempering material has also been used. Some sherds show rustication on lower outer surface, while on some others the evidence of burnishing is observed. The common shapes of this zone are bowls, dishes, basins, various sizes of jars, funnel shaped lids, vases and troughs. Out of these, the Black-and-Red Ware is represented by bowls, dishes, lipped and plain basins, small vases, straight-sided troughs and funnel shaped lids. However, the Black Slipped Ware is represented by small and medium-size pots, bowls (often pedestalled), basins and funnel shaped lids, possibly indicating tableware. The Red Ware comprises bowls, shallow dishes with convex sides, basins, funnel-shaped lids, medium-size vases, troughs, storage jars and footed and perforated vessels. The Black Slipped Ware also continued into the early historical period as the evidence of transition from Kakoria group of pottery to the early historical pottery has been obtained from the excavation at Munhai in the Adwa valley (Pal 1986).

Though the pottery types like cup-on-stand or button-based goblet, beaker, basin and jar and decorative motifs (ripple designs) show a distant affinity with the late Harappan pottery, they cannot be claimed late Harappan in the true sense of the term. The pottery is often treated with incised, applique or painted decorations. Black horizontal rim bands, single or multiple, vertical or oblique, sometimes emanating from horizontal rim band, zonal design or broad horizontal band, combination of circles and loops, concentric semicircles, fish-scale like motif and filled triangle or trapezoid, on outside as well as on the inner side of the Red Ware pots are the principal motifs. Horizontal, vertical or slanting lines, groups of dots and dashes, pellets or ovals emanating from bands, groups of concentric semicircles are painted in white or creamy white pigment on Black-and-Red and Black Slipped Wares. A few painted sherds in the Black-and-Red Ware group bear paintings in white pigment on the inner surface of the pots and the motifs consist of oblique strokes and dots. It may be pointed out that the painting is confined exclusively to the incised cavities alone. This is a combination of incision and painting. Incised and appliqué patterns are available on the external surface of some of the pots of Black-and-Red and Red Wares. The incised designs consist of rows of dots and strokes, chevrons, wavy, vertical, horizontal or oblique lines, criss-crosses, latticed diamonds and floral designs. Among the applique decorations, mention may be made of thumbnail impressions forming cord, chain or notch patterns on the Red and Black-and-Red Wares. Some sherds of Red Ware are marked with ripple or channel-like decorations. Pal finds Neolithic elements in the surface treatment of the pottery. Almost all the wares, along with most of the shapes and decorative patterns of the Kakoria group, survive in the second group, but some new pottery types are introduced in the second group (Pal 1986). Of the important new types, mention may be made of dish-on-stand (with plain or corrugated stem), pan with strap handle, dish with externally thickened bevelled rim and vessel with elongated conical profile and pointed base. Hence Koldihwa and Kakoria could be the representative sites of Chalcolithic culture in the middle Ganga valley. The Chalcolithic cultures of lower, middle and upper Ganga perhaps represent different stages of the same culture.

Lower Ganga Valley Culture

In the lower Ganga region, Pandu-Rajar-Dhibi in district Burdwan has been extensively excavated. The deposit has been divided into four periods, the first two being Chalcolithic. It appears that Period I occupation ended due to a flood, however, Period II settlement was destroyed by the Iron Age people. The site yielded a handmade Thick Grey Ware, wheel-turned Red Ware and Black-and-Red Ware. Period II was identified at the site by the appearance of Lustrous Red Ware and Channel-spouted bowls. The painting generally shows geometric patterns. The floors were paved with murum and plastered with mud, cow-dung and lime. Storage jars, dishes-on-stand, spouted vases, bowls-on-stand, *lotas*, high necked jars and basins are common shapes at the site. Mahisdal, another important site of this region has also yielded more or less a similar cultural sequence. People used copper arrowheads (tanged), celts, rings, bangles and antimony rods, lithic tools, stone and steatite beads. The discovery of stone weights and a realistic terracotta phallus are interesting finds of the site. People buried their deceased family members in urn burials in east-west direction, with head towards east. But some fractional burials have also been found. The ^{14}C dates bracket the eastern or Lower Ganga Chalcolithic between *c.* 1600 and 800 BC.

A number of sites such as Chirand, Koldihwa, Pandu-Rajar-Dhibi, Mahishdal and others, have indicated that the Chalcolithic people were living in rectangular as well as round wattle-and-daub huts with rammed earth floors as the evidence of post-holes, burnt clay lumps, clay clods with bamboo impressions suggest. One such floor at Koldihwa measured 5.25 x 3.20 m. Circular, squarish and oblong dwelling huts were made. Possibly they plastered the walls of their houses with mud as often burnt-clay clods were also observed on the floor. Like their counterparts in Deccan and Central India, they were also using microliths as various sites have yielded finished tools, cores and flakes of chert and chalcedony. Their tool-kit comprises parallel-sided blades, blunted back blades, points, lunates, scrapers and triangles. Some sites like Koldihwa have even yielded excellent arrowheads (tanged and socketed) of bones. Engraved circlets are a unique feature of the socketed arrowheads as they have also been found at Nagal (IAR 1961-62, Plate XXVII-A) in the Narmada estuary in Gujarat, Atranjikhera (IAR 1963-64, Pl XXXI-B) and Prahladpur (IAR 1962-63, Pl. LXXIV) in Uttar Pradesh, Chirand (IAR 1962-63, Plate XIII) in Bihar and Pandu-Rajar-Dhibi (IAR 1963-64, Pl. XLIV-B) in West Bengal, almost in a similar late Chalcolithic archaeological context.

Their subsistence was based both on agriculture and wild animals. Animal bones, some with cut-marks, have been found in profusion. On preliminary examination, these seem to belong to the Bovid family. Lower Ganga people cultivated paddy as evidence of rice from this zone is common from a number of sites. Apart from cereals (wheat, *moong*, *masur*) and rice, hunting of wild animals like deer, pig, nilgai and aquatic fauna like fish supported the Chalcolithic communities.

In sum, the foregoing analysis of the archaeological evidence amply shows that pottery originated in the late Mesolithic in the Vindhyas and not in the Neolithic as is popularly believed. That this Mesolithic beginning did inspire the Neolithic augmentation of the ceramic tradition can be concluded on the basis of compelling similarities between the two, which cannot be absolutely accidental. This seeding process also continued down to the early historical period through the Chalcolithic. The breakthrough of pottery making initially achieved by the Mesolithic man was not only bequeathed to the people of the succeeding stages of culture in the Vindhyan area, but it was also disseminated and diffused over a vast area covering the whole of upper, middle and lower Ganga valley on the one hand and Central India, Deccan and South India, on the other (Pal 1986: 159-69).

The ^{14}C dates available (4330±185 BC; 5440±240 BC, uncal.) for the beginning of Chalcolithic culture at Koldihwa in Doab appear to be too old to accept as they are even older than the known dates of Neolithic. There is, however, another date, PRL 223, 1440+120 BC (uncal.). All these dates appear inconsistent, but the recent studies at Balathal (Misra *et al.* 1995, 1997 and Misra 1997) have established the beginning of the Ahar culture around 3rd millennium. On the other hand, the excavations conducted at Spirit Cave in northern Thailand have pushed back the beginning of the Corded Ware at the site to 6000 BC (Gorman 1970: 98a). It is not unlikely that the Neolithic culture of Assam and adjoining areas might have a more respectable antiquity than assigned to it so far. In that eventuality, the Neolithic culture of the Belan valley, probably a derivative from the Neolithic complex of Assam with which it shares rounded celts and Corded Ware, may claim a similar high antiquity. This hypothesis, however, needs confirmation.

The use of copper is very restricted and perhaps it was not available to everyone. Therefore, people used microliths at most of the places. The discovery of a flat copper celt with convex cutting edge from Mahisdal is quite significant. Koldihwa also yielded fragmentary copper pieces and beads of terracotta, bone, shell and semiprecious stones. One of the copper pieces is a broken blade with a very thin section. Apart from these, querns and mullers have also been found from various sites. A few stone pieces with grooved surface, probably used as a sharpener, have also been obtained.

Recently Singh *et al.* (1996: 123-129) have attempted to establish that the Chalcolithic people of the middle Ganga, e.g. Senuwar, Chirand, Taradih, Chechar-Kutubpur, Narhan, Maner used Rakha mines of Bihar for copper ore. They claim that there is definite evidence of use of low tin bronzes since 1300 BC in this region and believe that smelting of copper ore may have started as early as 2000 BC, if not earlier.

TABLE 4.2 DATES OF CHALCOLITHIC SITES (PAKISTAN) (after Possehl 1994)

(All BP ages are based on 5568 years half-life of radiocarbon. Calibrated ages are given in BC.)

Site	*Sample No.*	*Date/Half Life*	*Calib. Dates*	*Culture*	*Material*
Sibri	BETA-2691	3220±60 BP	1541 cal. BC	Mehrgarh VIIC or Later	Unknown
Pirak	LY-1641	4080±290 BP	2250,2245, 2652,2647, 2617 cal. BC	Period I	Charcoal
Pirak	TF-1202	2940±80 BP	1159,1142, 1138 cal. BC	Period II	Charcoal
Pirak	LY-1642	3150±150 BP	1428, cal. BC	Period II	Charcoal
Pirak	LY-1640	3410±140 BP	1737,1713, 1706 cal. BC	Period II	Charcoal
Pirak	LY-1643	2970±140 BP	1255,1240, 1221 cal. BC	Period II	Charcoal

TABLE 4.3 DATES OF CHALCOLITHIC SITES (NORTH AND WEST INDIA) (after Possehl 1994)

(All BP ages are based on 5568 years half-life of radiocarbon. Calibrated ages are given in BC.)

Site	*Sample No.*	*5568 Yrs.BP*	*Calib. Dates*	*Culture*	*Material*
Jodhpura	PRL-275	4360±160 BP	3018,3001, 2926 cal. BC	Ganeshwar/Jodhpura culture	Charcoal
Pirak	PRL-278	4060±10 BP	2578 cal. BC	Ganeshwar/Jodhpura culture	Charcoal
Pirak	PRL-277	2610±110 BP	803 cal. BC	Ganeshwar/Jodhpura culture	Charcoal
Oriyo Timbo	PRL-1424	3750±130 BP	2191,2161, 2145 cal. BC	Period II, Lustrous Red Ware	Charcoal
Oriyo Timbo	PRL-1425	5010±170 BP	3706 cal. BC	Period II, Lustrous Red Ware	Charcoal
Oriyo Timbo	PTL-1427	3240±110 BP	1519 cal. BC	Period II, Lustrous Red Ware	Charcoal
Oriyo Timbo	PRL-1426	4250±160 BP	2897 cal. BC	Period II, Lustrous Red Ware	Charcoal
Prabhash Patan	PRL-20	3340±105 BP	1643 cal. BC	Period III, LRW	Charcoal
Prabhash Patan	TF-1287	4280±105 BP	2911 cal. BC	Period I, Pre-Prabhas	Shell
Prabhash Patan	PRL-91	3860±165 BP	2343 cal. BC	Period III, LRW	Charcoal

Cont. Table 4.3

Table 4.3 Cont.

Site	*Sample No.*	*5568 Yrs.* BP	*Calib. Dates*	*Culture*	*Material*
Prabhash Patan	TF-1284	3465±95 BP	1859,1848, 1769 cal. BC	Period II, Prabhas	Charcoal
Prabhash Patan	PRL-90	4240±110 BP	2892 cal. BC	Period I, Pre-Prabhas	Charcoal
Prabhash Patan	PRL-19	3100±160 BP	1406 cal. BC	Period III, LRW	Charcoal
Prabhash Patan	TF-1286	3595±90 BP	1953 cal. BC	Period II, Prabhas	Charcoal
Prabhash Patan	PRL-92	3830±95 BP	2299 cal. BC	Period II, Prabhas	Charcoal
Sanghol	PRL-510	3550±150 BP	1895 cal. BC	Period I, post-urban Bara culture	Charcoal
Sanghol	PRL-511	3740±60 BP	2181,2166, 2142 cal. BC	Period I, post-urban Bara culture	Charcoal
Sanghol	PRL-509	3570±150 BP	1923 cal. BC	Period I, post-urban Bara culture	Charcoal
Sanghol	PRL-513	3540±150 BP	1888 cal. BC	Period I, post-urban Bara culture	Charcoal
Sanghol	PRL-512	3350±110 BP	1673 cal. BC	Period I, post-urban Bara culture	Charcoal

TABLE 4.4 DATES OF CHALCOLITHIC SITES (WESTERN INDIA) (after Possehl 1994)

Site	*Lab No.*	*5568* BP	*5730* BC	*Calib.*	*Cultural Assn.*	*Material*
Ahar	V-54	3835±95 BP	2000±100 BC	2306 Calib. BC	Period IA Lower	Charocal
Ahar	V-57	3975±95 BP	2145±100 BC	2551, 2549,2489 Calib. BC	Period IA Top	Charocal
Ahar	V-56	3715±95 BP	1875±100 BC	2316 BC	Period IA Middle	Charocal
Ahar	TF32	3400±105 BP	1550±110 BC	1733, 1721,1697 Calib. BC	Period IC	Charocal
Ahar	TF18	190±90 BP	1755±95 BC	1669, 1776, 1793, 1947,1953 Calib. BC	Medieval	Charocal
Ahar	TF31	3130±105 BP	1275±110 BC	1420 Calib. BC	Period IC	Charocal
Ahar	V-58	3890±100 BP	2055±105 BC	2455, 2416,2405 Calib. BC	Period IA Bottom,	Charocal
Ahar	TF34	3570±135 BP	1725±140 BC	1925 Calib. BC	Period IB	Charocal
Ahar	V-55	3825±120 BP	1990±125 BC	2293 Calib. BC	Period IA	Decayed Wood

TABLE 4.5 BALATHAL (AHAR CULTURE) WESTERN INDIA (after Stuiver *et al.* 1998)

Site	*Sample No.*	*Radiocarbon age in* BP	*Calib. Date*	*Culture and layer*	*Material*
Balathal	PRL 1834	4220±60	1 sigma cal. BC 2894 (2879) 2701 cal. BP 4844 (4828) 4651 2 sigma cal. BC 2918 (2879) 2601 cal. BP 4868 (4828) 4551	Chalcolithic	Charcoal
Balathal	PRL 1835	3720±60	1 sigma cal. BC 2200 (2137,2076,2071) 1984 cal. BP 4150 (4086, 4025, 4020) 3934 2 sigma cal. BC 2292 (2137, 2076, 2071) 1942 cal. BP 4242 (4086, 4025, 4020) 3892	Chalcolithic	Charcoal
Balathal	PRL 1843	4000±70	1 sigma cal. BC 2617 (2551, 2541, 2491) 2462 cal. BP 4567 (4500, 4490, 4440) 4412 2 sigma cal. BC 2856 (2551, 2541, 2491) 2303 cal. BP 4806 (4500, 4490, 4440) 4253	Chalcolithic	Charcoal
Balathal	PRL 1844	4180±70	1 sigma cal. BC 2883 (2866, 2805, 2781, 2769, 2762, 2717, 2710) 2623 cal. BP 4833 (4815, 4754, 4730, 4718, 4711, 4666, 4659) 4573 2 sigma cal. BC 2912 (2866, 2805, 2781, 2769, 2762, 2717, 2710)2501 cal. BP 4862 (4815, 4754, 4730, 4718, 4711, 4666, 4659) 4451	Chalcolithic	Charcoal
Balathal	PRL 1846	4180±70	1 sigma cal. BC 2883 (2866, 2805, 2781, 2769, 2762, 2717, 2710) 2623 cal. BP 4833 (4815, 4754, 4730, 4718, 4711, 4666, 4659) 4573 2 sigma cal. BC 2912 (2866, 2805, 2781, 2769, 2762, 2717, 2710) 2501 cal. BP 4862 (4815, 4754, 4730, 4718, 4711, 4666, 4659) 4451	Chalcolithic	Charcoal
Balathal	PRL 1930	3650±100	1 sigma cal. BC 2193 (2027, 1992, 1982) 1883 cal. BP 4143 (3976, 3941, 3931) 3833 2 sigma cal. BC 2295 (2027, 1992, 1982) 1742 cal. BP 4245 (3976, 3941, 3931) 3692	Chalcolithic	Charcoal

Cont. Table 4.5

Table 4.5 Cont.

Site	*Sample No.*	*Radiocarbon age in* BP	*Calib. Date*	*Culture and layer*	*Material*
Balathal	PRL 1932	3950±100	1 sigma cal. BC 2576 (2466) 2294 cal. BP 4526 (4415) 4244 2 sigma cal. BC 2859 (2466) 2142 cal. BP 4809 (4415) 4092	Chalcolithic	Charcoal
Balathal	PRL 1935	4270±110	1 sigma cal. BC 3013 (2888) 2701 cal. BP 4963 (4837) 4651 2 sigma cal. BC 3311 (2888) 2504 cal. BP 5261 (4837) 4454	Chalcolithic	Charcoal
Balathal	PRL 1981	2520±80	1 sigma cal. BC 798 (763, 676, 674) 414 cal. BP 2748 (2712, 2625, 2623) 236 2 sigma cal. BC 827 (763, 676, 674) 401 cal. BP 2777 (2712, 2625, 2623) 2351	Chalcolithic	Charcoal
Balathal	PRL 1984	3930±90	1 sigma cal. BC 2564 (2462) 2291 cal. BP 4514 (4411) 4241 2 sigma cal. BC 2830 (2462) 2142 cal. BP 4780 (4411) 4092	Chalcolithic	Charcoal
Balathal	PRL 1985	3740±90	1 sigma cal. BC 2288 (2141) 1982 cal. BP 4238 (4090) 3932 2 sigma cal. BC 2460 (2141) 1885 cal. BP 4410 (4090) 3835	Chalcolithic	Charcoal
Balathal	PRL 1925	3700±170	1 sigma cal. BC 2396 (2129, 2082, 2043) 1831 cal. BP 4346 (4078, 4031, 3992) 3781 2 sigma cal. BC 2572 (2129, 2082, 2043) 1638 cal. BP 4522 (4078, 4031, 3992) 3588	Chalcolithic	Charcoal
Balathal	PRL 1928	4410±170	1 sigma cal. BC 3358 (3078, 3071, 3025) 2881 cal. BP 5308 (5027, 5020, 4974) 4831 2 sigma cal. BC 3626 (3078, 3071, 3025) 2580 cal. BP 5576 (5027, 5020, 4974) 4530	Chalcolithic	Charcoal

Cont. Table 4.5

Table 4.5 Cont.

Site	Sample No.	Radiocarbon age in BP	Calib. Date	Culture and layer	Material
Balathal	PRL 1933	5600±100	1 sigma cal. BC 4537 (4452, 4417, 4404) 4342 cal. BP 6487 (6401, 6366, 6353) 6292 2 sigma cal. BC 4688 (4452, 4417, 4404) 4249 cal. BP 6638 (6401, 6366, 6353) 6199	Chalcolithic	Charcoal
Balathal	PRL 1937	3860±70	1 sigma cal. BC 2462 (2305) 2202 cal. BP 4412 (4254) 4152 2 sigma cal. BC 2552 (2305) 2069 cal. BP 4502 (4254) 4019	Chalcolithic	Charcoal
Balathal	PRL 2039	3990±90	1 sigma cal. BC 2619 (2487, 2481, 2473) 2353 cal. BP 4569 (4436, 4430, 4422) 4303 2 sigma cal. BC 2863 (2487, 2481, 2473) 2205 cal. BP 4813 (4436, 4430, 4422) 4155	Chalcolithic	Charcoal
Balathal	PRL 2041	3860±60	1 sigma cal. BC 2460 (2305) 2203 cal. BP 4410 (4254) 4153 2 sigma cal. BC 2472 (2305) 2140 cal. BP 4422 (4254) 4090	Chalcolithic	Charcoal
Balathal	PRL 2042	2350±90	1 sigma cal. BC 517 (400) 264 cal. BP 2467 (2349) 2214 2 sigma cal. BC 765 (400) 200 cal. BP 2715 (2349) 2150	Early Historic	Charcoal
Balathal	PRL 2043	2170±90	1 sigma cal. BC 377 (200) 61 cal. BP 2327 (2149) 2011 2 sigma cal. BC 400 (200) cal. AD 21 cal. BP 2350 (2149) 1929	Early Historic	Charcoal
Balathal	PRL 1841	2050±60	1 sigma cal. BC 163 (46) cal. AD 21 cal. BP 2113 (1995) 1929 2 sigma cal. BC 201 (46) cal. AD 76	Early Historic	Charcoal

Cont. Table 4.5

Table 4.5 Cont.

Site	*Sample No.*	*Radiocarbon age in* BP	*Calib. Date*	*Culture and layer*	*Material*
Balathal	PRL 1849	2220±70	1 sigma cal. BC 387 (354, 291, 256, 251, 232, 217, 213) 175 cal. BP 2337 (2303, 2240, 2205, 2200, 2181, 2166, 2162) 2125 2 sigma cal. BC 402 (354, 291, 256, 251, 232, 217, 213) 60 cal. BP 2352 (2303, 2240, 2205, 2200, 2181, 2166, 2162) 2010	Early Historic	Charcoal
Balathal	PRL 2040	2330±90	1 sigma cal. BC 479 (397) 260 cal. BP 2429 (2346) 2210 2 sigma cal. BC 762 (397) 175 cal. BP 2712 (2346) 2125	Early Historic	Charcoal
Balathal	PRL 1983	2280±80	1 sigma cal. BC 401 (384) 206 cal. BP 2351 (2333) 2156 2 sigma cal. BC 518 (384) 124 cal. BP 2468 (2333) 2074	Early Historic	Charcoal
Balathal	PRL 1848	1760±60	1 sigma cal. AD 221 (256, 303, 317) 379 cal. BP 1729 (1694, 1647, 1633) 1571 2 sigma cal. AD 95 (256, 303, 317) 419 cal. BP 1855 (1694, 1647, 1633) 1531	Early Historic	Charcoal
Balathal	PRL 1850	3420±70	1 sigma cal. BC 1866 (1737, 1711, 1693) 1628 cal. BP 3816 (3686, 3660, 3642) 3578 2 sigma cal. BC 1889 (1737, 1711, 1693) 1523 cal. BP 3839 (3686, 3660, 3642) 3473	Early Historic	Charcoal
Balathal	PRL 1851	3400±70	1 sigma cal. BC 1767 (1726, 1724, 1689) 1618 cal. BP 3717 (3675, 3673, 3638) 3568 2 sigma cal. BC 1883 (1726, 1724, 1689) 1520 cal. BP 3833 (3675, 3673, 3638) 3470	Early Historic	Charcoal

TABLE 4.6 DATES OF CHALCOLITHIC CULTURES (EAST INDIA) (after Possehl 1994)

(All BP ages are based on 5568 years half-life of radiocarbon. Calibrated ages are given in BC.)

Site	*Sample No.*	*5568 Yrs.* BP	*Calib. Dates*	*Culture*	*Material*
Chirand	TF-1030	3430±110 BP	1740 cal. BC	Period II, Chalcolithic	Charcoal
Chirand	TF-444	2590±105 BP	799 cal. BC	Period II, Chalcolithic	Charcoal
Chirand	TF-1028	3390±90 BP 1689 cal. BC	1730,1729,	Period II, Chalcolithic	Charcoal
Chirand	TF-1029	2915±85 BP	1121,1119, 1104 cal. BC	Period II, Chalcolithic	Wood
Chirand	TF-445	3500±100 BP 1824,1793,	1877,1834, 1787 cal. BC	Period II, Chalcolithic	Wood
Mahisdal	TF-391	3235±105 BP	1517 cal. BC	Early Chalcolithic	Charcoal
Mahisdal	TF-392	2950±105 BP 1165 cal. BC	1211,1180,	Early Chalcolithic	Charcoal
Mahisdal	TF-390	2725±100 BP	894,875, 850 cal. BC	Late Chalcolithic	Charred rice

TABLE 4.7 CHALCOLITHIC DATES (CENTRAL INDIA AND DECCAN) (after Possehl 1994)

(All BP ages are based on 5568 years half-life of radiocarbon. Calibrated ages are given in BC.)

Site	*Sample No.*	*5568 Yrs.* BP	*Calib. Dates*	*Culture*	*Material*
Chandoli	TF-43	2905±100 BP	1096 cal. BC	Jorwe	Charcoal
Chandoli	P-474	3099±1851 BP	140 cal. BC	Jorwe	Charcoal
Chandoli	TF-42	3035±115 BP	131 cal. BC	Jorwe	Charcoal
Chandoli	P-472	3157±68 BP	143 cal. BC	Jorwe	Charcoal
Chandoli	P-473	3184±68 BP	144 cal. BC	Jorwe	Charcoal
Daimabad	PRL-419	2980±110 BP	1258,1235, 1226 cal. BC	Period III, Daimabad Culture	Charcoal
Daimabad	BS-177	3460±100 BP	1851,1850, 1761 cal. BC	Period III, Daimabad Culture	Charcoal
Daimabad	BS-178	2950±100 BP 1165 cal. BC	1211,1180,	Period V, Jorwe	Charcoal
Daimabad	PRL-655	3490±110 BP	1875,1838, 1818,1800, 1782 cal. BC	Period III, Daimabad	Charcoal
Daimabad	PRL-429	3390±150 BP	1730,1729, 1689 cal. BC	Period I, Savalda culture	Charcoal
Daimabad	PRL-428	3400±110 BP 1697 cal. BC	1733,1721,	Period III, Daimabad culture	Charcoal
Daimabad	BS-176	350±90 BP	1947 cal. BC	Period I, Savalda	Charcoal
Daimabad	BS-181	2990±100 BP	1261 cal. BC	Period IV, Malwa	Charcoal
Daimabad	PRL-412	3250±110 BP	1521 cal. BC	Period IV, Malwa	Charcoal

Cont. Table 4.7

Table 4.7 Cont.

Site	*Sample No.*	*5568 Yrs.* BP	*Calib. Dates*	*Culture*	*Material*
Daimabad	BS-179	2970±100 BP 1221 cal. BC	1255,1240,	Period V, Jorwe	Charcoal
Daimabad	PRL-654	3460±100 BP	1851,1850, 1761 cal. BC	Period I, Savalda	Charcoal
Daimabad	PRL-411	3230±100 BP	1561 cal. BC	Period IV/V, Malwa/ Jorwe overlap	Charcoal Daimabad
PRL-656	3050±150 BP	1376,1346,	1318 cal. BC	Period V, Jorwe	Charcoal
Daimabad	BS-182	3130±90 BP	1420 cal. BC culture	Period III, Daimabad	Charcoal
Dangwada	PRL-690	3400±150 BP	1733,1721, 1697 cal. BC	Malwa Period	Charred rice
Dangwada	PRL-686	3110±140 BP	1411 cal. BC	Malwa Period	Charcoal
Dangwada	PRL-687	3810±140 BP	2283 cal. BC	Malwa Period	Charred Grain
Dangwada	PRL-691	3200±120 BP	1506,1475, 1465 cal. BC	Malwa Period	Charcoal
Dangwada	PRL-692	2900±140 BP	1092 cal. BC	Malwa Period	Charred Wheat
Dangwada	PRL-693	3280±100 BP cal. BC	1570,1528,	Malwa Period	Charcoal
Eran	TF-327	3280±100 BP cal. BC	1570,1528,	Period I, Malwa	Charcoal
Eran	P-526	3136±68 BP	1422 cal. BC	Period I, Malwa	Charcoal
Eran	TF-331	3355±90 BP	1675 cal. BC	Period I, Malwa	Charcoal
Eran	TF-324	3130±105 BP	1420 cal. BC	Period I, Malwa	Charcoal
Eran	TF-326	2905±105 BP	1096 cal. BC	Period I, Malwa	Charcoal
Eran	P-528	2878±65 BP	1042 cal. BC	Period I, Malwa	Charcoal
Eran	P-527	2515±58 BP	786 cal. BC	Period II, Iron ?	Charcoal
Eran	TF-330	3220±100 BP	1514 cal. BC	Period I, Malwa	Charcoal
Eran	P-525	3193±69 BP 1455 cal. BC	1496,1485,	Period I, Malwa	Charcoal
Eran	TF-329	3300±105 BP	1607,1554, 1544 cal. BC	Period I, Malwa	Charcoal
Inamgaon	BS-486	3020±100 BP	1299,1276, 1269 cal. BC	Period III, Late Jorwe	Unknown
Inamgaon	BS-489	3020±100 BP	1299,1276, 1269 cal. BC	Period III, Jorwe	Unknown
Inamgaon	BS-463	2980±110 BP	1258,1235, 1226 cal. BC	Period III, Jorwe	Unknown
Inamgaon	BS-277	3078±100 BP	1393,1332, 1328 cal. BC	Period I, Malwa	Unknown
Inamgaon	BS-263	3310±130 BP	1614 cal. BC	Period I, Malwa	Unknown

Cont. Table 4.7

Table 4.7 Cont.

Site	*Sample No.*	*5568 Yrs.* BP	*Calib. Dates*	*Culture*	*Material*
Inamgaon	TF-1085	3295±105 BP	1603,1558, 1538 cal. BC	Period II, Early Jorwe	Charcoal
Inamgaon	PRL-93	3020±105 BP	1299,1276, 1269 cal. BC	Period III, Late Jorwe	Charcoal
Inamgaon	TF-1330	3090±100 BP	1400 cal. BC	Period III, Late Jorwe	Charcoal
Inamgaon	PRL-94	3020±115 BP	1299,1276, 1269 cal. BC	Period III, Late Jorwe	Charcoal
Inamgaon	BS-502	3050±100 BP	1376,1346, 1318 cal. BC	Period III, Late Jorwe	Unknown
Inamgaon	TF-923	2890±170 BP	1057 cal. BC	Period III, Late Jorwe	Charcoal
Khed	PRL-221	3040±90 BP	1314 cal. BC	Jorwe	Charcoal
Khed	PRL-220	2900±160 BP	1092 cal. BC	Jorwe	Charcoal
Navdatoli	P-205	3294±125 BP	1602,1559, 1536 cal. BC	Phase 4, Malwa, Jorwe Coarse red	Burnt Wheat
Navdatoli	P-475	3455±70 BP	1754 cal. BC	Phase I, Malwa, Bichrome, Ahar	Charcoal
Navdatoli	P-476	4125±69 BP	2861,2815, 2733,2729, 2694,2681, 2664,2632, 2681 cal. BC	Phase II, Malwa, Little Jorwe, Bichrome	Charcoal
Navdatoli	P-202	3503±128 BP	1878,1833, 1826,1791, 1789 cal. BC	Phase II, Malwa, Little Jorwe, Bichrone	Charcoal
Navdatoli	P-204	3449±127 BP	1749 cal. BC	Phassse II, Malwa, Jorwe, cream slipped	Charcoal
Navdatoli	TF-59	3380±105 BP	1685 cal. BC	Phase I, Malwa, Biochrome, Ahar	Charcoal
Navdatoli	P-201	3492±128 BP	3032,2962, 2942 cal. BC	Phase I, Malwa, Biochrome, Ahar	Charcoal
Navdatoli	P-200	3457±127 BP	1757 cal. BC	Phase I, Malwa, Biochrome, Ahar	Charcoal
Nevasa	P-181	3106±122 BP	1409 cal. BC	Period III, Jorwe	Charcoal
Nevasa	TF-40	3110±110 BP	1411 cal. BC	Period III, Jorwe	Charcoal
Nevasa	P-184	2545±115 BP	790 cal. BC	Period III, Jorwe	Charcoal
Songaon	TF-384	3415±105 BP	1783 cal. BC	Period I, Blotchy Grey Ware	Charcoal
Songaon	TF-383	3185±100 BP	1448 cal. BC	Period II, Jorwe	Charcoal
Songaon	TF-379	3150±90 BP	1428 cal. BC	Period II, Jorwe	Charred grain
Songaon	TF-380	3230±105 BP	1516 cal. BC	Period II, Jorwe	Charcoal
Songaon	TF-382	3195±100 BP	1499,1482, 1458 cal. BC	Period II, Jorwe	Charred wheat

COPPER HOARDS CULTURE

Backdrop

A variety of copper artefacts, mostly found in caches, are known as Copper Hoards. The first discovery of such an object in India was a copper harpoon from Bithur in Kanpur district as early as 1822. Since then more than 90 sites spread over a large geographical area from Shalozan in north-west Pakistan to Hallur (Karnataka) in the south and Bhagrapir (Orissa) in the east to Khurdi (Rajasthan) in the west, have been found. Except the southern part of the peninsula and north-eastern states, they have been discovered in the whole of the country and most of them have been chance discoveries. The concentration of these caches, however, has been found in Uttar Pradesh, Haryana, Madhya Pradesh and Bihar, particularly in the Ganga doab region. Scholars like Smith (1905 and 1907), Heine-Geldern (1936, 1956), Piggott (1944,1950), Bongard-Levin and Deopik (1957, see in Lal 1972), Lohuizen-de Leeuw (1960, see in Lal 1972), Gupta (1963, 1965), Sharma (1964), Agrawal (1969, 1971, 2000), Agrawal *et al.* (1978), Lal (1951, 986, 1972), Yule (1985, 1989), Joshi (1990) and many others have made important contributions to the understanding of the problem of the Copper Hoards. Besides the Copper Hoards, we have few other metal hoards from ancient sites, e.g. Daimabad Bronzes (weighing over 100 kg), Mandi Hoard (gold and silver ornaments weighing about 12 kg from Uttra Pradesh) and others, but here we are dealing only with the Copper Hoards culture, which is used as a term to denote a particular type of artefact assemblage, found in caches. The Copper Hoards appear to be distributed in four different geographical zones, e.g. Ganga doab, Chota Nagpur or Plateau zone, Madhya Pradesh, Haryana, north Rajasthan and central Himalaya. The Copper Hoards have been found from several sites in South Asia and Europe too. Therefore, scholars have proposed different hypotheses to identify the cultural association of the Copper Hoards, e.g. they represent the traces of Vedic Aryans in India; they were the Harappan refugees; they are the relics of the aboriginal Mundas. Some scholars even believe that they were itinerant smiths. We will discuss this issue in the following pages.

Considering the quantity and size of objects as well as hoards, it appears that the authors of the Copper Hoards were rich in copper compared to the Chalcolithic and even to the Harappa culture people, as for example, at Gungeria (Balaghat, Madhya Pradesh), 424 objects were found in a single hoard weighing about 400 kg! This Hoard also yielded 102 silver objects along with copper ones. The Gungeria Hoard objects are now housed in various museums, e.g. Copenhagen, British Museum, Dublin, Indian Museum, Nagpur and Raipur Museum (Gupta 1997: 233). As the artefacts have been found in hoards, they may give an exaggerated impression of abundance of copper.

Heine-Geldern (1936: 87-88) carried out a typological study of a large number of hoards from widely distributed sites, both in time and space, e.g. Egypt, Sardinia, British Isles, Greece, Transcaucasia and others. He associated the Copper Hoards with the Aryan immigration into India and suggested that: (a) the Trunnion axe came from Transcaucasia via Persia 1200-1000 BC; (b) the axe-adze, originating from Danubian region, also reached via Persia 1200-1000 BC; (c) the Fort Munroe sword came from west Persia around *c.* 1200-1000 BC; and (d) the antennae swords were strongly influenced by the Koban examples datable to 1200-1000 BC. Piggott (1944: 172) also initially associated the Copper Hoards with the Aryan migration, but later on identified them with the Harappan refugees (Piggott 1950).

Lal (1951: 20) presented an excellent analysis of the Indian Copper Hoards and showed that the Trunnion axes, the Fort Munroe sword, the socketed axe and axe-adze never occurred

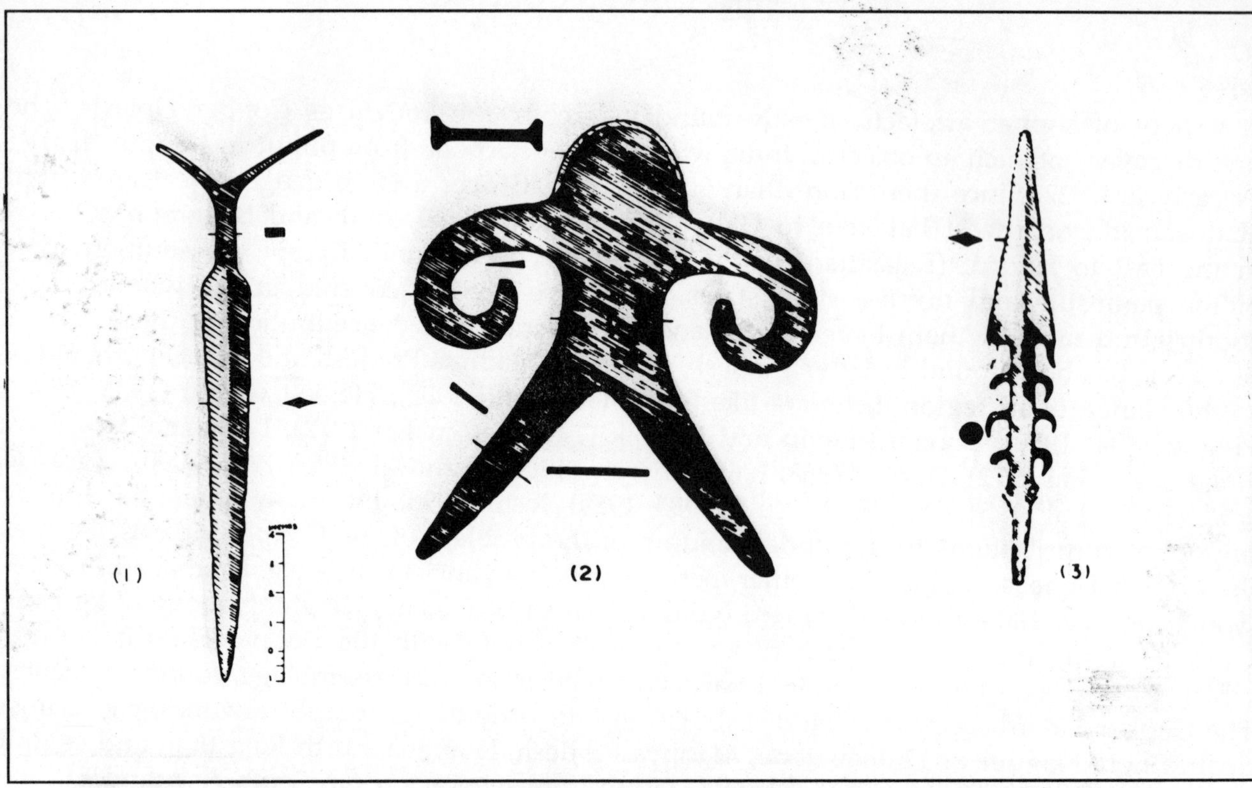

Fig. 4-9. Typical Copper Hoard artefact types: antennae hilted sword, harpoon and anthropomorph.

in the Doab but were confined to the north-western part of the subcontinent. As a corollary, he showed that the harpoons, the bar-celts and the anthropomorphs (Fig. 4-9) of the Doab were cast as a single piece, unlike the Koban specimens. Here it may be pointed out that stray examples of socketed axes and adzes are reported from Chanhudaro, Mohenjodaro and even from Mundigak Period III, from much earlier contexts than 1200-1000 BC as claimed by Heine Geldren. It is therefore obvious that this Aryan-equation is not tenable (Agrawal 2000: 105).

It seems that Heine-Geldern (1956: 151)) does not agree with Lal's conclusions as despite his criticism he found more parallels of mace-head from Chanhudaro in Hissar III and noted similarities in the Koban culture of Caucasus, the Gandsha-Karabagh culture of Transcaucasia, the Luristan culture and the Sialk Cemetries A and B. Heine-Geldern's view is not accepted widely as his conclusions are based only on typological similarity of only a few types.

Agrawal (1971: 196), Gupta (1963: 147) and Lal (1951: 20, 1972: 284) have suggested an indigenous origin of the Copper Hoards as the alleged parallels in certain tool types between the Copper Hoards and the other cultures are superficial and technologically the objects of the Ganga doab region are distinct and unique. Though the Copper Hoards have been found from several sites in India, they are mainly concentrated in Uttar Pradesh, Haryana, Bihar and Madhya Pradesh, perhaps because rich ores of copper are available in northern India. The anthropomorphs, antennae swords, harpoons (Pl. 4-25, -26, -27, -28, -29) and hooked swords (Pl. 4-25) appear to be the specialized tool types of the main Ganga doab. In the eastern area, particularly from Ranchi, Singhbhum, Santhal Parganas, Purulia, Bankura,

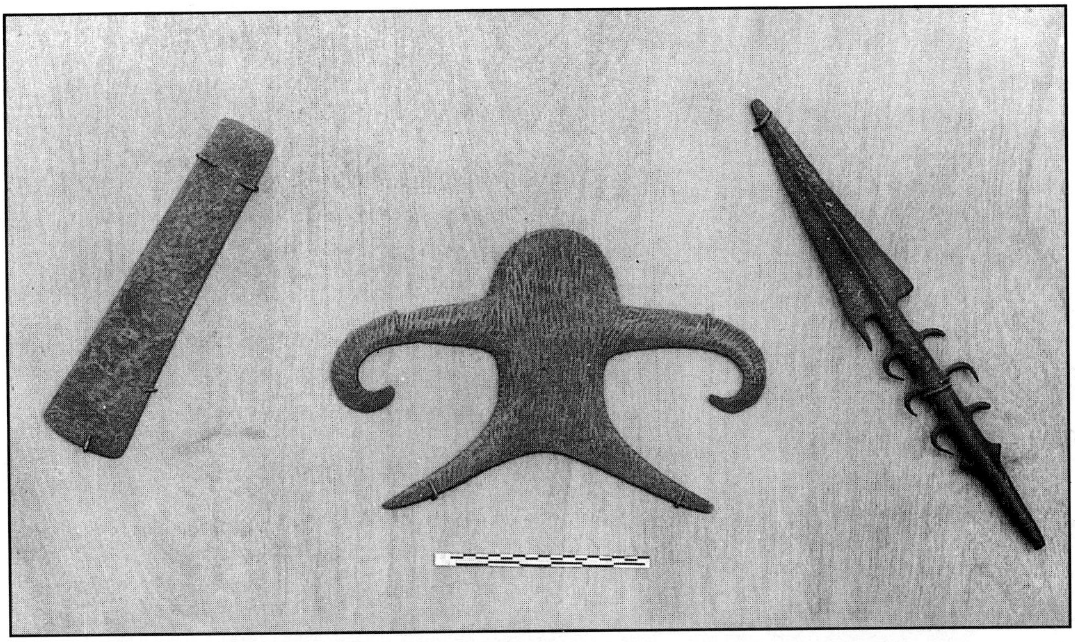

Pl. 4-26. Copper celt, anthropomorph and harpoon, Bisauli, District Badaun, UP.

Pl. 4-27. Copper anthropomorph, Bisauli, District Badaun, UP.

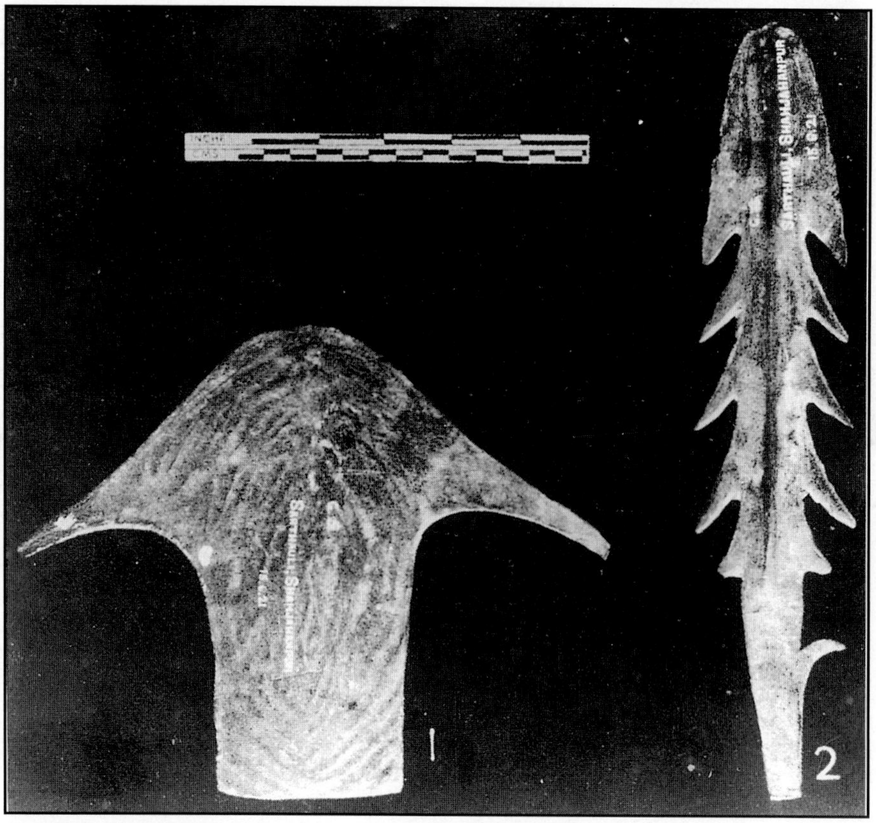

Pl. 4-28. Copper celt and harpoon from Sarthauli.

Pl. 4-29. Copper celts from Itava village, District Varanasi, UP.

Burdwan, Midnapur and Birbhum districts of Bihar and Bengal, a large number of hoards comprising double axes, bar celts, flat celts and shouldered celts, a pick-like object, roughly pointed at the top and tapering towards the edge, ring, discoidal lumps, etc., have been found, though bar celt is the main tool type (Yule 1985; Chakrabarti 1993). The flat and shouldered celts are equally common in this zone but they are rare in the middle Ganga region (Agrawal 1982a: 203-210). Rajasthan too has mostly yielded bar and flat celts. The flat and shouldered celts are found in several regions of the country, therefore, they cannot be taken as the diagnostic types of the Copper Hoards of a particular zone. Therefore, only the anthropomorphs, the harpoons, the hooked sword and the antennae sword are the diagnostic tools of the Copper Hoard. These types are found associated together, e.g. at Bisauli harpoon (Pl. 4-26) and anthropomorphs (Pl. 4-26, -27) occur together. At Bithur antennae sword and harpoons are associated; antennae swords and anthropomorphs were found together at Fatehgarh. The hooked sword was associated with the other three types at Fatehgarh, Sarthauli (Pl. 4-28), Bahadarabad (Pl. 4-29) and Niorai.

Yule (1989: 236-37) suggests that for north Rajasthan, Haryana and middle Ganga doab, the Khetri region may have been the source of metal. He writes that especially for the Doab, the Khetri region may have been a simpler source than the next closest source in the Himalayan mountains. For the Gungeria hoard perhaps the well-known mine of Malanjkhand, located just 35 km away, was perhaps exploited. D.P. Agrawal (1999a: 194-196) has also examined the probable sources of ores for the Copper Hoards of different regions and he suggests that the Singbhum belt of Bihar, which is rich in ore, may have been a source of metal for the Copper Hoards of eastern India. For the middle Ganga valley hoards, he strongly recommends the Central Himalayan region (see chapter 6). He writes,

> Not many trace element analyses are available to compare the impurity patterns of the Copper Hoards with different mines. No lead isotope analyses have been carried out. However, one trait marks the Copper Hoard artefacts of Central Ganga: about 50 per cent of the artefacts analysed so far show a significant arsenic content (1-7 per cent), but no tin whatsoever Agrawal 1982b). Whether arsenic was deliberately added for increasing the hardness of the metal artefacts, or it was an impurity present in the metal used, is difficult to say. As arsenic minerals are rare in India even today, deliberate addition of arsenic seems to be rather a remote possibility. If it was an impurity, the possibility of Kumaun being the source of copper becomes strong as the copper minerals there contain arsenic (Agrawal 2000: 119-120).

The Copper Hoards are a polemical problem in Indian archaeology. Though in recent years Yule (1985 and 1989) has done an extensive work on Indian Copper Hoards with chemical analysis of a few artefacts, it is largely based on typological and physical analysis. It appears that the authors of the Copper Hoards did not share much with the Chalcolithic or the Harappan people for the latter only, though rarely, used arsenic for alloying copper. Unless we conduct exhaustive sampling across the country and undertake chemical studies like trace impurity pattern, lead isotope and spectroscopic analysis and establish ore-artefact co-relationship, we will not be in a position to infer something concrete about the Copper Hoards. Now let us discuss the main tool types of the Copper Hoards.

Yule (1985, 1989) has prepared a catalogue for over 1300 artefacts, however, he thinks that all the recorded artefacts may not be true representatives of the Copper Hoards. About half of these artefacts are in the personal collections of Swami Omanand Saraswati (Haryana) and S.C. Roy (Bihar). Yule (1989: 220-221) has given the following geographical distribution of the artefacts (Table 4.8).

TABLE 4.8 DISTRIBUTION OF COPPER HOARD OBJECTS

1.	Southern Harayana/North Rajasthan	382
2.	Eastern Chota Nagpur	352
3.	Doab	207
4.	Madhya Pradesh	224

Tool Types

The tools types are varied, e.g. rings, a variety of celts, anthropomorphs, antennae swords, double-edged axes, socketed axes, harpoons, etc., have been found in hoards (Lal 1972; Yule 1985; Chakrabarti and Lahiri 1996).

Celts: They are of three types such as flat, shouldered and bar. They have generally a flat or sligtly concave ventral side and a convex dorsal side. The flat and shouldered (Pl. 4-28, -29) celts were probably used for cutting trees. Some flat celts had bull figurines engraved near the butt-ends, which were discovered from Midnapur, district Hardoi by Misra (1976) and weigh about 2 kg. A shouldered celt from Bhaktabandh, Bengal was 4.25 kg. The bar celts are generally heavy and long (sometimes about 60 cm). The bar celts of Chota Nagpur region appear like a long chisel with a crescent edge on one side and a pointed butt on the other and have nearly parallel, though tapering sides (Thapar 1980: 97-99). A large number of such specimens were found from Gungeria and other sites in the east and the edge of these objects was produced by bevelling the upper side. D.P. Agrawal (1971: 198) examined few specimens and thinks that the bar celts were possibly used for mining or digging hard surface as their sturdiness and use marks suggest. Lal (1951) found typological similarity between stone bar celts and the copper ones particularly in the eastern region. He therefore, thought that the copper bar celts were derived from the stone ones. It may, however, be pointed out that the the sites yielding stone specimens have not yielded any Copper Hoard artefacts, e.g. Sitabhanji, Ban Ashuria, Santhal Parganas, Jashpur, Thakurani. The shouldered stone-celt and bar-celt of the eastern and South-East Asian stone tool complexes may not even be very old (Dani 1960: 146, 152), which makes Lal's view untenable.

Harpoons: The harpoons are like mid-ribbed spearheads with oblique or backward curving barbs (length ranges from 17 to 44 cm and weight ranges from 200 to 1000 gm). They are of two types: one, which is cut from a thick sheet and hammered and the other, cast in a double mould. In fact, the first type looks very crude compared to the second. The cast variety demonstrates skill of their smithy and craftsmanship and it seems that they knew closed casting. It has been found in association with OCP at Saipai, Etawah in the doab and at Mitathal with late Harappan material. They may have been used for killing big animals or fish as similar weapons have been depicted in a rock shelter at Sohagighat in Mirzapur.

Swords: Like harpoons, there are two varieties of swords (length ranges between 40 and 77 cm). One is called the antennae sword and the other is the hooked sword. The antennae hilted swords are called so because they have antennae like bifurcations at the hilt-end and are mostly found from the Doab zone. D.P. Agrawal (1971: 199) thinks that the antennae swords could have been used for killing or wounding big game by trapping and writes that they are cast with the antennae as one piece and have long blades with a short hilt, a sharp median ridge and their length varies between 42 and 75 cm. The Chandoli dagger, however, was cast as an ordinary tanged dagger and the hilt cut-split and beaten back, perhaps to prevent a wooden handle from slipping. It is smaller in size and has a diffused ridge and looks very flimsy unlike the sturdy examples of the Doab. The antennae swords of Kallur, district Raichur, have a very short antennae compared to the Doab specimens and are supposed to be of a later date on technical grounds. Four antennae swords were recently reported from Mehsana (Gujarat) but their antennae are beaten flat. The hooked sword, found associated with the diagnostic Doab types, has a median ridge and forked hook on the stem. Such examples have been found at Fatehgarh, Niori, Sarthauli (Pl. 4-28) and Bahadarabad (Pl. 4-25) and other sites. These swords, with sharp median ridge, have a barb (for hafting) near the end of the tang, which was not cast originally but has been chiselled off from the tang itself. Some of the thin flat, long blades from Bahadarabad have sharp-edges on one side and the tip.Agrawal (1971: 202) suspects them to be sickles. The hooked swords have also been reported from the Harappan sites, e.g. Mohenjodaro, where a hole is used for hafting unlike a hook of the Doab examples. The Navdatoli specimens, however, do not have a barb and the median ridge is quite diffused compared to the Copper Hoard examples. The hooked sword has been found associated with the other diagnostic types, e.g. the anthropomorph, the antennae sword and the harpoon at Sarthauli, Bahadarabad, Fatehgarh and Niorai.

Rings: Rings associated with the Copper Hoard have been reported from Bhagrapir (Orissa). As many as 47 rings were discovered from Pondy. Various Harappan as well as Chalcolithic sites in India have also yielded rings but it is often difficult to differentiate rings from bracelets. D.P. Agrawal (1971: 199) suggests that the only criterion for the ring characterizing the Copper Hoards could be their standard weight. They could be convenient units of metal-weight for the itinerant smiths to carry. The number of such rings expended in making a tool would be a useful measure to determine the barter.

Axes: The double axes were made by cutting away almost circular pieces from the sides of an oval sheet. Most of the axes have been reported from Parihati, Bhagrapir and other sites from Orissa and Bengal. These double axes, however, are not associated with any Copper Hoard types. Though typologically similar artefacts were found from the Harappan sites like Lothal and from a Neolithic site at Hallur, they cannot be compared Agrawal 1971: 201). Such specimens are also common at Chalcolithic sites. The only distinctive type in the eastern group is the bar-celt, which is generally absent from the Doab zone.

Anthropomorphic figure: The most distinctive and enigmatic type is the anthropomorphic figure or anthropomorph (Pl. 4-26, -27). In most of the cases the head portion of this human like figure is thickened by hammering from the top, hind limbs are plain and arms are generally incurved and sharpened externally. They appear to have been cut from a plain sheet. Since these heavy artefacts look like human figures, they are often identified as ritualistic objects. Their length varies from 23 to 30 cm and breadth between 30 and 43 cm. Their average weight is 5 kg. Recently a hoard of such anthropomorphs has been discovered at Madarpur in Moradabad district of Uttar Pradesh. They have been hammered and chiselled on either side and the sides are thickened. They are on display at the National Museum at Delhi and it has been claimed that they were found associated with the OCP. In one case, one of the arm is curved upward, which appears to be interesting feature. About the function of these anthropomorphs,Agrawal (1971: 200) writes, "It was perhaps used as missile to kill birds as the sharp arms could cut the bird, the thick head could stun it and the incurved arms could entangle and bring it down.... An experimental model, when thrown, went in a whirling fashion and seemed to make a trajectory which made one suspect a boomerang-like effect. Sankalia, however, thought that such a device would be too complicated to have been used by a simple folk, but then the boomerang was invented by the simple Australian aborigines only!"

An oblong copper object from the Harappan levels of Lothal with a convex end and two broken side-lugs is included by some in the anthropomorph category. It is plain in section and does not have hammered head like the Doab ones. In fact, in the entire Harappan repertoire, this is the only object, which compares with the Copper Hoards.

Copper Hoards of Uttaranchal

The Uttaranchal or the Central Himalayan region appears to have played a very significant role in the metal technology of Ganga valley (see chapter 6) as, a large number of mining and smelting sites have been discovered in this hilly terrain (Agrawal and Kharakwal 1998).

In 1989, a hoard of eight copper anthopomorphs was discovered at Bankot (79°52' E; 29°45' N) in Pithoragarh while digging a dolomite (magnesite) stone quarry, close to the Inter College. They were placed one over other in a tray like stone slab, according to the villagers who discovered them. The Bankot village is located about 91 km east of Almora town in district Pithoragarh. They have an oval-shaped head and their arms are spread horizontally across the body. The lower part of the body, however, is almost flat, slightly widening near the feet. There is a concave depression between the feet. The edges are generally thick and roundish, but in one case both the arms are broken. Typologically these anthropomophs appear to be local in character. They were no doubt buried intentionally, but the reason behind this is unknown. Out of these artefacts, six are in the custody of Sri Chanchal Singh Bankoti and one is in the possession of Govind Ballabh Pant Museum, Almora. They were brought down to the Museum for chemical treatment. Our exploration revealed that there are no traces of ancient mining and smelting activity within 10 km area of the site, but the famous Kharahi mines are located within a distance of 20 km from the site. There are few other copper mines, e.g. Rai-Agar and Sira in Gangoli area and Chinaka-Kali Billar and Khemkhet in eastern Kumaon.

These anthropomorphs contain 98 per cent copper, 1.22 per cent iron and a minor impurity of arsenic (Pant 1991: 41). Our close examination of these artefacts revealed that they were made in an open, single mould, probably made of stone as their measurements show some uniformity in the finishing as well. Copper was identified as the main element along with the presence of iron and arsenic. These were perhaps manufactured by direct melting of copper ore and poured into an open mould. Iron and arsenic remain as an impurity of the ore. Their obverse side shows some gas cavities, which suggest that they were made in an open mould, without green poling and left unfinished. These anthropomorphs with stub-like arms are a bit crude compared to the typical specimens of the Doab. As weights of these Bankot specimens vary between 3.4 + 0.1 and 2.4 + 0.1 kg, they could simply be copper ingots as well (Agrawal and Kharakwal 1998).

According to a local report (*Amar Ujala,* 8 May 1986: 3), an anthropomorph was found in a scrap dealer's shop at Haldwani in Nainital district similar to the ones found at various sites in the Ganga valley (Joshi 1990: 14). Whether it was a local production cannot be said as we could not examine the artefact. Nonetheless it is a significant discovery of the remains of Copper Hoard Culture in the foothills of the Kumaun Himalaya.

According to a recent local report (*Amar Ujala,* 10 October 1999), a hoard of five anthropomorphs (Pl. 6-1) was discovered from an earthen jar buried in the ground at Khuna-Tok in Nainipatal village of Munakot block in Pithoragarh district. The incurved arms are longer than usual and much thinner at the end. These objects do not have the lower "legs" but only a truncated trunk, which has a sharp-edge. Dr. D.N. Tiwari brought them to the

State Museum of Almora where the senior author could examine them. The artefacts were made by hammering a copper sheet. The vertical cross-section is almost rectangular. The head does not show any thickening.

The anthropomorphs of Uttaranchal appear to be quite simple and crude compared to the sophisticated examples of the Doab zone. Therefore, considering the availability of copper ore and simplicity of the artefacts, these anthropomorphs are perhaps prototypes of the Doab ones.

North Rajasthan and Haryana

Though the Ganeshwar-Jodhpura complex of Rajasthan has yielded thousands of copper objects including hunting tools, bar-and flat-celts, fish-hooks and various other objects, these artefacts are generally not included in the Copper Hoards culture. Many of these objects, however, have been found in association with OCP (see above). The typical Copper Hoard artefacts are absent from the Jodhpura Complex, though some harpoons have been reported only from northern part of the state. Celts (flat and bar) have been found from various parts of Rajasthan, e.g. Ganeshwar, Ekalasimgha, Elana, Nandalpura, Kota (Karauli) and other places but they are too general types. The well-known Khurdi or Kurada Hoard of Rajasthan (now in Jodhpur Museum) yielded channel-spouted bowls along with celts (16.5 cm), chisels (19.5 cm), thin blades and rings. The channel-spouted copper bowl is identical to the ceramic bowls of Navdatoli (R.C. Agrawala 1984b: 89). R.C. Agrawala holds that as early as 1934 the then Jodhpur State Government had acquired 103 copper objects from Kurada, which comprised celts 7, chisels 11, bowls 4 (without handle), channel-spouted bowls 5, curved thin blades 21, rings 55. In fact, this is the only Hoard, which yielded some kind of utensils.

We may now note some unique tool types.

1. At Mallah, Haryana (Yule 1989: 222) a new hoard has yielded a unique chisel and a harpoon, which according to Yule neither resembles the types of this region nor of the Ganga doab. An arm spiral is another interesting object he has reported from Rewari, Haryana, which is "similar to those in Europe".
2. It is a long simple copper blade with broad cutting edge. There are three to four examples of this type in the State Museum, Lucknow, although only one is complete, the rest are fragmentary, with tenon broken off. At least two examples of this tool-type were also discovered from Bithur, near Kanpur. A similar tool used even today by the villagers is called *khurpi* and is used primarily in removing unwanted grass from agricultural fields. Although this type of tool has so far been found only from the alluvial plains of the Ganga in Uttar Pradesh, it may occur in other parts too. Yule (1989: 226, 230) has identified fragmentary small, honeycombed, bun-shaped ingots each from Aguibani and Shahabad and a miniature sword from Bithur, which he thinks is similar to the object found from burials in Europe.

Techniques: The Copper Hoards, especially the anthropomorphs, harpoons and the antennae swords are superb examples of craftsmanship, employing techniques of double mould and closed casting of copper. Some of these objects were cut and hammered from thick sheet. They used close moulds for casting, employed cold work and annealing in tool fabrication. Smith (1905) found from the analysis of four copper objects housed in the British Museum that they were alloyed with tin from 3.38 to 13.3 per cent. D.P. Agrawal (1971), Agrawal *et al.* (1974, 1978) and Nautiyal *et al.* (1981) carried out analysis of 41 Copper Hoard objects and found that 46 per cent objects showed arsenic alloying (up to 7 per cent). Agrawal examined celts from the eastern zone at Patna Museum, which show a flat bottom and a slightly convex dorsal side. This could be a result of open-mould casting, though some of the Gungeria flat axes show signs of double mould. Complicated castings of harpoons could only be achieved in a developed closed-mould. Several sites of the eastern region have yielded objects of primitive workmanship, as they were products of single mould technique (Thapar 1980: 97-99).

Bhardwaj (1980) has discussed early copper-arsenic alloys in India, including the raw materials, extraction of arsenic and production of copper-arsenic alloys and their metallurgical and mechanical properties.

Yule (1989: 231) has made the following observations on the surface texture of artefacts in different regions:

1. south Haryana: middle glossy, green-dark green, often with heavy accretions mixed with sand.
2. Doab: middle glossy, light green to dark green.
3. Chota Nagpur: dull, light to dark green; high incidence of flour patina.
4. Madhya Pradesh: dull, dark green, usually dull grainy surface (Gungeria).

Yule thinks that the axes and bar chisels (celts), which have solid unworked castings, could be ingots as they are convenient to store and transport the raw copper (Yule 1985: 72-83, 103).

Hauptmann (1989: 261-267) and Hughes (1989: 267-269) have presented the following results of trace element patterns, metallographic and atomic absorption analyses of a few Copper Hoard artefacts. During the course of the drilling, they found that the metal of many of the implements was quite hard. The presence of hammer-marks on the surfaces of the objects indicates that they were extensively worked subsequent to casting, in order to raise their hardness to a level appropriate to their function.

Hauptmann has analysed 35 samples from Gungeria hoard, which are housed in the British Museum and comprise 23 flat axes, 9 bar chisels and 2 antennae swords and few more from Haryana. He finds that most of the Gungeria hoard objects contain very little tin (0.02–0.27 per cent) and they cannot be regarded as tin bronzes. Two objects from Rewari (Haryana) show remarkable high tin value up to 2 .68 per cent (no. 577, axe: 0.55 per cent; no. 767, axe: 2.68 per cent). Also noteworthy are relatively high lead and silver contents (0.21-2.06 per cent Pb, 150-480ppm Ag).

Generally the content of lead and nickel is very low, hence they cannot be considered as alloys; they may represent impurities in the ores. The amount of arsenic is generally so low as to be regarded as a common impurity in copper. Only few artefacts (2 swords and 2 bangles each from Rewari and Sankarjang show 3-5 per cent arsenic) have high arsenic content and perhaps could be considered as examples of deliberate alloying.

Hauptmann (1989: 265) thinks that out of his 35 analysed samples as many as 25 should come from an oxidic ore source whereas only 10 would have been smelted from sulphidic ores. He found that as many as 5 axes (which he calls axe-ingots) from south Haryana (nos. 540, 668, 714, 750, 796) and a bar celt from the Gungeria hoard (no. 498) consist of highly ferruginous copper with 20-33 per cent Fe, in one case 8 per cent Fe. The iron content results from globules of alpha-iron suspended in a matrix of low iron-containing copper. It could be the result of smelting copper ore under very strongly reducing conditions in the presence of an excess of iron oxide flux. He also claims that finished objects like bangles and other tools do not contain such high percentage of iron and that the iron-rich raw copper can be produced directly in the furnace.

We think that "the identity of the Copper Hoards in the Doab seems to be established beyond doubt. The Bihar variety of copper artefacts are simpler basic types (e.g., flat celts), except for the bar-celt. Keeping in view the proximity of copper ores in Bihar and the simplicity of the tool types, one may claim precedence in time for them. The mid-Doab has its own distinctive and advanced types without parallels in other areas. This uniqueness may reflect a local origin of the culture" (D.P.Agrawal 2000: 106).

TABLE 4.9 PERCENTAGE COMPOSITION OF COPPER HOARD ARTEFACTS FROM NORTH RAJASTHAN AND SOUTH HARYANA (after Hauptmann in Yule 1989)

No	*Find spot*	*Object*	*Cu*	*Fe*	*Pb*	*Ni*	*Sn*	*As*
1.	Hansi	Axe	75.7	23.6	0	0.1	0	0.3
2.	Hansi	Axe	92.7	0.5	0.2	0.1	0.55	1.9
3.	Hansi	Axe	98.9	0	0	0	0	0
4.	Rewari	Axe	66.2	32.9	0	0	0	0
5.	Rewari	Axe	95.8	0.4	0	0	0	2.5
6.	Rewari	Axe	88	8.4	0	0.1	0	0.7
7.	Rewari	Axe	93	0.5	1.2	0	2.68	1.2
8.	Rewari	Axe	99.4	0	0	0	0	0
9.	Rewari	Axe	98	0	0	0	0	1.1
10.	Rewari	Chisel	97.6	0	0	0	0	1.1
11.	Rewari	Sword	97.9	0	0	0	0	0.3
12.	Rewari	Sword	94.7	0.1	2.1	0.2	0.1	3.2
13.	Rewari	Bangle	95.1	0	0	0.2	0	4.9
14.	Rewari	Bangle	99	0	0	0.6	0	0
15.	Rewari	Bangle	88.2	0	0	0	0	3.6
16.	Rewari	Axe	71.8	25.8	0	0	0	0
17.	Rewari	Axe	76.7	20.6	0	0	0	0
18.	Narnaond	Bar	97.5	0	0.1	0	0	1.9
19.	Narnaond	Harpoon	94.6	0	0	0	0	2.4

TABLE 4.10 PERCENTAGE COMPOSITION OF COPPER HOARD ARTEFACTS FROM UPPER GANGA VALLEY

(after Agrawal, Krishnamurthy and Kusumgar 1978; Nautiyal, Agrawal and Krishnamurthy 1981; Hauptmann in Yule 1989.)

No	*Find spot*	*Object*	*Cu*	*Fe*	*Pb*	*Ni*	*Sn*	*As*
1.	(P-76) Bahadarabad	Bangle	Cu	0.086	0	0.0108	0	1.351
2.	(P-77) Bahadarabad	Bangle	Cu	0.0068	0	0	0	0.285
3.	(P-155) Manpur	Celt	Cu	0.0658	0.0148	0.058	0	1.165
4.	(P-156) Hardi	Celt	Cu	0.088	0.0097	0.016	0	0.285
5.	(P-157) Mujahidpur	Celt	Cu	0.1784	0.0057	0.008	0	0.468

Table 4.10 Cont.

Table 4.10 Cont.

No	*Find spot*	*Object*	*Cu*	*Fe*	*Pb*	*Ni*	*Sn*	*As*
6.	(P-158) Sitapur	Celt	Cu	0.1587	0.0117	0.0231	0	0.289
7.	(P-159) Bithur	Celt	Cu	0.037	0.4264	0.1037	0	1.5776
8.	(P-160) Sarthuli	Celt	Cu	0.0045	0.0235	0.005	0	0.7954
9.	(P-161) Sheorajpur	Anthropomorph	Cu	0.0056	0.0046	0.0067	0	0.0794
10.	(P-162) Rajpur	Harpoon	Cu	0.2275	0.9115	0.0636	0	1.5194
11.	(P-163) Nasirpur	Celt	Cu	0.0863	0.0102	0.0435	0	0.8913
12.	(P-164) Nasirpur	Celt	Cu	0.0106	0.0038	0.0137	0	0.2187
13.	(P-165) Nasirpur	Celt	Cu	0.1643	0.013	0.0426	0	1.336
14.	(P-166) Nasirpur	Spearhead	Cu	0.89	0.0224	0.91	0	1.0691
15.	(P-167) Nasirpur	Celt	Cu	0.0685	0.0224	0.0423	0	1.2349
16.	(P-168) Nasirpur	Spearhead	Cu	0.0089	0.0291	0.0492	0	2.0076
17.	(P-169) Nasirpur	Harpoon	Cu	0.0437	0.015	0.0438	0	2.0622
18.	(P-170) Nasirpur	Chisel	Cu	0.0037	0.004	0.0313	0	1.8655
19.	(P-171) Nasirpur	Chisel	Cu	0.0113	0.6744	0.0499	0	3.3148
20.	(P-193) Sadabad	Celt	Cu	0.2489	0.217	0.0407	0	0.7019
21.	(P-194) Sadabad	Scrubbing	Cu	0.3246	0.052	0.016	0	0.8883
22.	(P-195) Sadabad	Outer surface scrubbing	Cu	0.2526	0.291	0.04	0	1.322
23.	(P-196) Sadabad	Outer surface	Cu	0.3363	0.0633	0.016	0	1.5106
24.	(P-197) Sadabad	Sword	Cu	0.0965	2.432	0.055	0	2.4568
25.	P-198) Sadabad	Celt	Cu	0.0331	0.0079	0.0161	0	0.5059
26.	(P-199) Sadabad	Celt	Cu	0.6831	0.0176	0.0176	0	0.6226
27.	(P-200) Sadabad	Celt	Cu	0.0362	0.1764	0.0137	0	0.9651
28.	(P-201) Sadabad	Celt	Cu	0.4683	0.1274	0.453	0	4.053
29.	(P-202) Sadabad	?	Cu	0.1448	0.0115	0.0124	0	0.1361
30.	(P-185) Shanjanpur	—	Cu	—	—	n.d.	n.d.	0.57
31.	(P-214) Bithur	—	Cu	—	—	n.d.	n.d.	1.02
32.	(P-215) Bithur	—	Cu	—	—	n.d.	n.d.	1.94
33.	(P-217) Kiratapur	—	Cu	—	—	n.d.	n.d.	0.14
34.	(P-222) Nasirpur	—	Cu	—	—	n.d.	n.d.	0.12
35.	(P-223) Nasirpur	—	Cu	—	—	n.d.	n.d.	0.23
36.	(P-224) Nasirpur	—	Cu	—	—	n.d.	n.d.	1.88
37.	(P-226) Nasirpur	—	Cu	—	—	n.d.	n.d.	1.16
38.	(P-227) Nasirpur	—	Cu	—	—	n.d.	n.d.	2.34
39.	(P-228) Nasirpur	—	Cu	—	—	n.d.	n.d.	2.13
40.	(P-229) Nasirpur	—	Cu	—	—	n.d.	n.d.	1.95
41.	(P-230) Nasirpur	—	Cu	—	—	n.d.	n.d.	3.38
42.	(P-225) Nasirpur	—	Cu	—	—	n.d.	n.d.	n.d.
43.	(P-183) Shahabad	—	Cu	—	—	0.07	n.d.	0.11
44.	(P-184) Shahabad	—	Cu	—	—	n.d.	n.d.	n.d.
45.	(P-186) Shahabad	—	Cu	—	—	n.d.	n.d.	0.58
46.	(P-68) Shahabad	—	Cu	—	—	0.04	0.2	1.95
47.	Khera Manpur	Spearhead	97.5	—	—	0.6	—	1.7
48.	Resgavaon	Axe	96.9	—	—	—	—	0.2
49.	Bithur	Harpoon	95.8	0.32	—	—	—	1.7
50.	Saipai	Spearhead	96	0.3	1.2	0	0	1.8

(Note: For no 20, Chakrabarti and Lahiri [1996: 88] mention that the proper site name is Resgavaon; the tehsil is Sadabad, cf Yule 1985: 23-24.)

TABLE 4.11 PERCENTAGE COMPOSITION OF COPPER HOARD ARTEFACTS FROM CHOTA NAGPUR

(after Agrawal, Krishnamurthy and Kusumgar 1978; Nautiyal, Agrawal and Krishnamurthy 1981; Hauptmann in Yule 1989.)

No	*Find spot*	*Object*	*Cu*	*Fe*	*Pb*	*Ni*	*Sn*	*As*
1.	Chota Nagpur	Axe	98.7	0		0.3	0	0.3
2.	Bassia P.S.	Axe	98.6	0	0	0	0	0
3.	Manbhum Dt.	Axe	96.8	0	0	0	0	0
4.	Chota Nagpur	Axe	93.6	0	1.3	0	0	0
5.	Chota Nagpur	Axe	93.5	0	0	0	0	0.4
6.	Chota Nagpur	Axe	99.7	0	0.1	0.2	0	0
7.	Chota Nagpur	Axe	96.1	0.3	0	0	0	0
8.	Chota Nagpur	Bar celt	99.2	0	0	0	0	0
9.	Chota Nagpur	Bar celt	93.9	0.18	0	0	0.9	0
10.	Akuldoba	Axe	95.4	0	0	0.2	0	0
11.	Bamanghati Subd	Axe	99.1	0	0	0.1	0	0
12.	Bamanghati Subd	Axe	98.6	0	0	0	0	0
13.	Kesna	Bar	98.5	0.1	0	0.3	0	0
14.	Sankarjang	Bangle	90.6	0	0	0.0108	0	5.7
15.	(P-53)Hami	Axe	Cu	0.086	0	0.0135	0	1.3
16.	(P-54 Hami	Axe	Cu	0.0763	1.78	0	0	7.8
17.	(P-60) Hami	Axe	Cu	0.0572	3.51	0	0	0.57
18.	(P-55)Dhanbad	Axe	Cu	0.133	0	n.d	0	4.6
19.	(P-191) Dhanbad	fragment	Cu	0	0	0	n.d	n.d
20.	(P-190) Kamedra	fragment	Cu	0	0	n.d.	0	0

TABLE 4.12 PERCENTAGE COMPOSITION OF COPPER HOARD ARTEFACTS FROM MADHYA PRADESH

(after Hauptman in Yule 1989.)

No	*Find spot*	*Object*	*Cu*	*Fe*	*Pb*	*Ni*	*Sn*	*As*
1.	Gungeria	Axe	97.9	0	1.3	0	0	0
2.	Gungeria	Bar celt	99.2	0	0	0.1	0	0
3.	Kesli	Axe	98.8	0.3	0	0	0	0.3

TABLE 4.13 PERCENTAGE COMPOSITION OF COPPER HOARD ARTEFACTS FROM MADHYA PRADESH

(after Hauptman in Yule 1989.)

No	*Site*	*Object*	*Cu*	*Fe*	*Pb*	*Ni*	*Sn*	*As*
1.	Gungeria	Axe	99.4	0.12	0.09	0.01	0.06	0.02
2.	Gungeria	Axe	98	0.13	0.08	0.02	0.08	0.01
3.	Gungeria	Axe	98.9	0.49	0.01	0.05	0.06	0
4.	Gungeria	Axe	98.2	0.89	0.13	0.15	0.07	0.27
5.	Gungeria	Axe	97.4	0.31	0.07	0.05	0.06	0.06
6.	Gungeria	Axe	95.4	0.34	0.11	0.05	0.24	0.26
7.	Gungeria	Axe	97.9	0.31	0.27	0.06	0.09	0.43
8.	Gungeria	Axe	94.6	0.04	3.11	0.01	0.18	0
9.	Gungeria	Axe	95.9	0.44	2.24	0.05	0.16	0
10.	Gungeria	Axe	96.5	0.28	2.58	0.03	0.16	0
11.	Gungeria	Axe	96.9	0.58	1.42	0.06	0.18	0
12.	Gungeria	Axe	96.7	0.04	0.36	0.01	0.18	0
13.	Gungeria	Axe	97.1	0.18	1.15	0.01	0.07	0
14.	Gungeria	Axe	98	0.16	1.71	0.01	0.07	0.07
15.	Gungeria	Axe	96.2	0.25	1.66	0.02	0.19	0.02
16.	Gungeria	Axe	96.9	0.24	1.71	0.02	0.13	0.02
17.	Gungeria	Axe	98.7	0.37	0.44	0.04	0.07	0
18.	Gungeria	Axe	98.7	0.09	0.47	0.47	0.05	0.06
19.	Gungeria	Axe	99	0.19	0.37	0.02	0.07	0
20.	Gungeria	Axe	98.2	0.73	0.55	0.1	0.11	0.52
21.	Gungeria	Axe	96.9	0.099	1.44	0.12	0.02	0.01
22.	Gungeria	Axe	99.9	0.28	0.02	0.09	0.04	0.01
23.	Gungeria	Bar-celt	96.5	0.25	0.09	0.08	0.17	0.08
24.	Gungeria	Bar-celt	97	0.12	0.94	0.02	0.17	0.1
25.	Gungeria	Bar-celt	98	0.24	0.17	0.07	0.15	0.66
26.	Gungeria	Bar-celt	98	0.05	0	0.1	0.14	0
27.	Gungeria	Bar-celt	97.6	0.2	0.01	0.04	0.16	0.01
28.	Gungeria	Bar-celt	98.3	0.23	0.42	0.04	0.16	0.01
29.	Gungeria	Bar-celt	97.1	0.31	0.85	0.04	0.16	0
30.	Gungeria	Bar-celt	97.1	0.18	0.35	0.05	0.18	1.15
31.	Gungeria	Bar-celt	69.4	24.87	0.04	0.46	0.27	0.81
32.	Gungeria	Bar-celt	66.9	28.1	0.04	0.4	0	0.73
33.	Kosam	Axe	96.4	1.34	0.04	0.04	0.12	1.19
34.	Unknown	Spearhead	98.7	0.86	0.96	0.07	0.08	0.34
35.	Unknown	Sword	97.7	0.32	0.38	0.06	0.1	0.24
36.	Unknown	Sword	87.7	0.26	—	0.04	0.28	0.05

Ochre Coloured Pottery and Copper Hoards

OCP was identified for the first time in the lower levels of Hastinapur, Rajpur Parsu and Bisauli by B.B. Lal in 1951 (Lal 1954-55). At Hastinapur, the OCP assemblage underlies the Painted Grey Ware (PGW) deposit. Since then about 75 sites of this culture have been discovered in Uttar Pradesh, Haryana, Punjab and Rajasthan, the concentration being in the Ganga doab (Dikshit 1979). Some important sites such as Saipai, district Etawah (Lal 1971-72), Ahichchhatra, district Bareilly (IAR 1963-64: 43-44), Atranjikhera, district Etah (Gaur 1969), Lal Quila, district Bulandshahar (Gaur 1973), Ambkheri, district Saharanpur (IAR 1963-64: 56), Noh, district Bharatpur and Jodhpura, district Jaipur (1972-73: 29-30; R.C. Agrawala and Vijay Kumar 1976) have been subjected to excavation. Most of the settlements, located in the alluvial plain, are very small in size and the habitation deposit varies between 0.60 and 1.50 m. D.P. Agrawal (1982a: 198) writes that, "The OCP occurs in sediments of a few metres thick, brown in colour, sandy and silty in texture and with a detrital appearance. None of them has a character of a normal habitational deposit. These sediments could arise either because of a huge deluge that engulfed the Doab, or due to a prolonged Eolian activity, which deposited these sediments—both views have its proponents. Our recent sedimentological and scanning electron microscopic analysis (SEM) on these sediments suggests that originally these were derived from glacial environments which were subsequently deposited by floods, thus ruling out a wind-born deposition". In the upper Doab region, sites are located at a distance from 4 to 8 km, indicating the density of population.

The concentration of OCP sites appears to be mainly in the Ganga doab, whereas the Copper Hoards are largely concentrated in east Rajasthan, Haryana, Ganga doab and Chota Nagpur plateau. It is quite interesting that a number of OCP sites, e.g. Bahadrabad, Narsipur, Lal Quila, Jhinjhana, Saipai, Nandalpura, Jodhpura and others have also yielded Copper Hoards and scholars have attempted to associate the Copper Hoards with the OCP. R.C. Agrawala and Kumar (1993: 125) claim that they discovered thousands of copper objects in association with OCP from Ganeshwar region, but it is not clear if they bear any kind of relationship or similarity with Copper Hoards. However, on circumstantial ground they have been associated together in the Doab. In fact, we do not know what was the relationship between the Copper Hoard culture (see below) and OCP using people? Considering the technological skill of Copper Hoard people and the contextual evidence from various sites like Saipai, Atranjikhera, etc., Sankalia (1974: 399) writes that "In size (and weight), shape and technique these weapons ...from the Copper Hoards are much finer and better than those seen in the otherwise advanced Indus civilization. On that ground alone, one should have thought twice before crediting them to nomads, hunters and itinerant coppersmiths. The objects might have been made by such roaming smiths, but they were made for a society or people who needed or had developed the art of making such well developed weapons, probably by using local resources.... These people were no nomads but lived in simple mud (as well as brick?) walled houses and had an assemblage of pots and pans, showing varied features as definitely indicated by excavation at Saipai and Atranjikhera". We would even suggest that the Copper Hoards Culture, whatever its origins, could have ushered the Doab into the first incipient urbanization.

Here, a modern parallel is worth recording as it may better explain the relationship of OCP and Copper Hoard culture. The Gadolia Lohars are itinerant ironsmiths, scattered all over Rajasthan and in south-western Haryana. Though a very few Gadolias in southern Rajasthan have now settled permanently, they still live in their carts in all other areas, which they seasonally shift from one region/place to other and supply a variety of iron objects, prepared by themselves, to the villagers and collect grains or money in exchange. They recollect that earlier they obtained the metal (iron) from the local mines but now it is bought from the market. It is, therefore, quite possible that they might have also been involved in mining and smelting in the past, particularly in Rajasthan. Like potters, they are equally important for villagers even today in whole of Rajasthan.

The OCP is often described as ill-fired pottery with porous body, worn, rolled or detrital in appearance. The ware is made of fine clay to which sand was added as tempering material. It has, however, not been fired uniformly at high temperature as the grey core and dull red surface would indicate. At several sites, on rubbing off the surface it leaves an ochreous powder, which is perhaps because of waterlogging or ill firing, or both. It is generally decorated with black paintings on red slip or wash and sites like Lal Quila and others even yielded graffiti on the pottery.

In the Upper Ganga doab, jars with slightly splayed out or beaded rim, dishes-on-stand, basins with undercut rims, bowl or dish with splayed out rims are the characteristic shapes. In the Central Doab region, though with slight variation in shape, a variety of jars, basins with splayed out rims, bowls with internally bevelled rims, incised decorations, dish-on-stands, spouted vessels, handled pots, storage jars are the representative shapes. At Noh and Jodhpura, the pottery is orange to deep red in colour and the shapes include vases, basins and bowls decorated with appliqué and incised designs, somewhat similar to that of Atranjikhera.

As a result of several excavations and explorations, considering the nature of remains and distribution of sites over a large Ganga terrain, it was alleged that certain pottery shapes are analogous to the Harappan ones. Therefore, Dikshit (1971) and Suraj Bhan (1975) suggested two broad categories of the OCP: Zone A (western) comprises sites of eastern Rajasthan, Haryana and western Uttar Pradesh whereas Zone B includes sites of mid- and eastern Uttar Pradesh. In Zone A Jodhpura, Siswal, Mitathal, Bara, Amkheri and Bargaon and in Zone B, Lal Quila, Atranjikhera and Saipai have been subjected to excavation.

In eastern Rajasthan, Haryana and western Uttar Pradesh certain pottery shapes, e.g. vases with out-curved flaring rim or loop handled, basins with beaded rim, dishes-on-stand, channel spouts, tubular spouts, ring stands, bowls with everted rim, storage jar with beaded or horizontally splayed out rim are found and are common and are identical to those found at Harappan sites. It is quite possible that the OCP in these regions may have been influenced by the Harappans. Noh (27°15' N; 77°39' E) in Rajasthan yielded only 90 cm deposit of OCP from the lowest stratum of the mound. It is repesented by vases, basins, bows, handled pots.

Though no structures have been reported, the incised and appliqué decorations, similar to Atranjikhera, are common in the pottery. Similarly, Jodhpura near Jaipur yielded only 1.30 m deposit of the OCP culture. The pottery unlike the Doab region has been fired at high temperature treated with a slip, decorated with a variety of incised patterns and common shapes are bowls, vases, knobbed lid and dish-on-stand (see Ganeshwar-Jodhpura culture above). The excavators have claimed the Harappan influence in the ceramics.

Zone B. On the other hand, the mid- and eastern Uttar Pradesh is marked by the absence of the basin with beaded rim, the dish-on-stand and the flask. Therefore, the problem of origin remains unanswered, as we do not know if all these OCP sites belong to the same culture and whether it was derived from the Harappans or it is an indigenous local ceramic. Is there one or several OCPs? The identity of the OCP still remains undefined. OCP has become an umbrella term under which all sorts of red wares have been included. Nobody knows, which OCP variant was really associated with the Copper Hoards, if at all such an association is warranted. We think that the new discoveries at Madarpur and Uttaranchal will throw more light on this problem.

Copper Hoards, Harappans and the OCP Culture: Some Conjectures

At Lal Quila there is some unique evidence of habitation in the form of floors paved with rammed potsherds, mud bricks, post-holes, burnt pieces of reed and bamboo marked plasters and even a burnt brick. Most of the floors and the house remains appear highly damaged. A large quantity of pottery comprising a Red Ware painted in black or with incised designs was discovered at the site. The shapes include storage jars, vases, basins, bowls, lids, dishes-on-stands (?) and miniature pots. Handled vases are characteristic of both Atranjikhera and Lal Quila. The dish-on-stand is not available as a complete shape but was inferred from fragmentary pieces and is therefore, subject to doubt. Unlike the typical OCP which has an ill-fired, powdery surface, the Lal Quila Red Ware has a slip and does not look like the OCP of Hastinapura or Bahadrabad at all. Gaur finds a great homogeneity in the pottery of Atranjikhera, Saipai and Lal Quila.

Wahal (1971-72: 12) claims that at Saipai, a hooked spearhead was discovered from the trial digging and a harpoon during the regular excavation at the site. The excavators found both types of sherds, those giving off ochreous colour on rubbing and those with a red slip and some with black painted design or incised decoration. Jars with a flaring rim, bowls and basins sometimes with spouts and handles, constitute the main shapes. From some fragments, a dish-on-stand and ring base are also inferred, though the evidence is not conclusive. Rubbers, querns, chert and chalcedony blade, a burnt brick bat, chunks of burnt clay with reed impression and fragments of *Bos indicus* are the other associated finds.

With this inadequate data, it is difficult to work out developmental stages of OCP, but it is important to note here that as far as fabric, shapes and material uses are concerned, the OCP of mid- or central Doab is certainly of inferior quality compared to upper Doab, Haryana or eastern Rajasthan. This might have happened partly because of Harappan ifluence as the Cemetery H pottery types at Ambkheri and incised decoration traits of Bara at several sites would indicate. Therefore, the central or mid-Doab could be the first phase of OCP? As Dikshit (1979: 295) writes that the "upper Doab revealed two groups of sites. There are certain settlements where Harappans were found living with OCP users, whereas there are also sites, which are absolutely free from any Harappan admixture except for some typological similarity in pottery. Thy do not yield anything Harappan as such".

Barring few sites, for example, Bahadarabad, Bisauli, Nasirpur, Saipai, generally the Copper Hoards have not been found in association with any pottery so far, though circumstantially they have been associated with the OCP. In fact, except Saipai, we do not have any other stratigraphic contextual example of the Copper Hoard finds; some scholars even doubt Saipai evidence. The identity of the OCP itself is doubted because it has not been fully understood so far. Except for a harpoon from Mitathal, no Doab types are found in Haryana and Rajasthan. The *parasu* seems to be a type of this area. Gupta (1965) appears to be more logical as he pointed out that the OCP has an individual identity and is non-Harappan. Sankalia suggested West Asiatic influence in the OCP, especially in the handled and spouted pottery of Saipai. D.P. Agrawal (1971: 202) initially suggested an indigenous tribal origin and later (1999) has indicated the Central Himalayan and South-East Asian affiliation. Lal (1951, 1972) associated Copper Hoard with OCP and identifies them with the Mundari-speaking Australoid tribes of the primeval Uttar Pradesh. "The Hoard people might have been the "Mundas" who once expandedfrom Bihar to Garhwal and then again retreated. The presence of "Munda" speech amongst Pahari group of languages and the proto-Australoid people in Doms, Koltas, etc., in the Indo-Aryan population of the cis-Himalayan region amply testifies to this story of migration and return. Grierson and Risley also have supported this theory". It may be added that even today smithy is exclusively a Dom occupation in Kumaun. Joshi (1995-96: 23-31) aptly writes, "It is true that there are many places, for example, Kumaun and Nepal, where anthropomorphs have been found, but not the OCP. Discovery of the anthropomorphs in Kumaun and Nepal leaves no room for doubt that there is a community of the coppersmiths called Tamtas. They are traditional coppersmiths". It is quite possible that the ancestors of the Tamtas may be the authors of the Copper Hoards in Kumaun and in the Doab.

Here we have tried to establish the individuality of the Copper Hoards. However, we do not know what was the relationship between the OCP and the Copper Hoard culture. Therefore, few more OCP sites should be excavated horizontally to establish any kind of relationship. In fact, nothing concrete can be stated unless we open up few OCP sites particularly where Copper Hoards have also been found.

The Doab region was a thick monsoonal forest and a riverine country, forming a distinct ecological unit which could provide plenty of game, freshwater fish and limited agriculture, therefore, tools like harpoons, antennae, sword and anthropomorph, according to D.P. Agrawal, may have been very useful for big game. The Copper Hoard people were perhaps the first inhabitants of the tangled forests of the Ganga doab. The clearance of forests, however, on large-scale was possible perhaps only when the Painted Grey Ware people flourished with their iron tools. D.P. Agrawal emphasizes that they were specialized hunting tools. Since these tools are generally found in caches and not associated with any cultural material, it is often argued that the authors of the Copper Hoard were itinerant smiths or nomadic hunters. In the south-eastern zone, we find only flat and shouldered celts, bar-celts and double-edged axes and none of typical Doab type. It is possible that the authors of the Copper Hoard might have exploited the Mauladib, Rakha mines, Masobani copper ore sites of Singhbhum.

The Copper Hoards people had a developed tool technology and they were rich as far as metal is concerned. Since the objects of these Hoards have a distinct techno-typology, it is quite likely that the authors of these Hoards developed metallurgy independently. The association of Copper Hoard objects with OCP at Saipai, channel-spouted bowls from Kurada, Rajasthan and *khurpi*-like object from Kanpur and their metal technology possibly suggest that the authors of these Hoards were not entirely itinerant smiths. It is quite possible that some of their groups may have been engaged in agriculture also. Agrawal (1999) revised his view about the origin of the Copper Hoards and suggests to examine the South-East Asian origin as the archaeometallurgical tradition in Thailand has now been dated to 3rd millennium BC. With the advancement of arhchaeometallurgical studies, it seems that there may be different centres of origin of archaeometallurgy in South Asia and we do not know which area was largely exploited for ores.

As far as the Hoards of eastern region, i.e. around Chota Nagpur region are concerned, Chakrabarti (1993: 212) holds that the preponderant impression is that very few of these objects could be put to the functional uses suggested by their shapes. For instance, the so-called shouldered celts were too heavy to be used as celts; in some cases, they were irregularly shaped and their cutting edges were rounded. As Yule (1985 : 103-104) puts it, "An interpretation for these often irregularly shaped objects as ingots finds numerous parallels outside of India. Even the double axes with blunt edges could not have a straight functional use; neither do the bar-celts without any use-mark suggest this. If they are ingots we suggest that they belong to a much later period than what is generally assumed. In the case of Parihati we tried to link the local metal-smelting furnaces to the period of the Jaina Tirthankara image in the village, *c.* 13th century at the latest.... If true, this hypothesis will also suggest that the distribution of these "copper hoards" was linked to the movements of itinerant metal craftsmen, the successors of whom still survive as "Dhokra" craftsmen in the same areas of West Bengal even today".

Though we have not dealt with individual discovery in our discussion, we can, however, visualize four distinct zones of tools such as the Ganga doab, eastern Plateau, north Rajasthan and Haryana and Central Himalaya. The Doab is marked by the harpoon, the antennae sword and the anthropomorphs, the eastern Plateau by the bar celts, Rajasthan by the celts and utensils and the Central Himalaya can be characterized by prototypes of the Ganga anthropomorphs. We should also bear in mind that celts of all varieties are ubiquitous. Among all these types the harpoons made by closed pure copper-casting are masterpieces.

Yule (1989: 196) claims that typologically speaking Indian hoard artefacts have prehistoric parallels in prehistoric European hoards particularly from Hungary, Spain, Italy, Scandinavia and others. He finds striking typological similarity of arm spirals, flat axes, axe-ingots and bar celts. The European hoards are, however, generally from burials and settlements. He writes that "Both the regions share a propensity for a deposition in swamps; fields, forests and riverbanks". Unlike European examples the Indian hoards have generally been found away from the settlements and burials. The circumstantial evidence from various OCP sites in the Doab and particularly Saipai has lead archaeologists to believe that they were the first occupants of the monsoonal forests of the Doab. They were perhaps contemporary of the OCP people and preceded the Painted Grey Ware culture. A few TL dates from Nasirpur, Jhinjhana, Lal Quila and Atranjikhera bracket the OCP culture, showing considerable scatter, between 2600 and 1100 BC.

TABLE 4.14 TL AGE RANGE OF SOME OCP DEPOSITS

Site	*TL Age*
Atranjikhera	2280 BC 1250 BC
Lal Qila	1730 BC 2030 BC
Jhinjhana	1570 BC 2650 BC
Nasirpur	1500 BC 1180 BC

Apart from these, two ^{14}C dates from Jodhpura, ranging from 2500-2300 BC (uncal.), also support the early beginning of this culture. If the OCP and the Copper Hoards were contemporary, the latter Hoards could be tentatively assigned to a period around 2nd millennium BC.

Conclusion

We have discussed the nature of archaeological remains of various Bronze Age cultures, which flourished between 3rd and 1st Millennia BC in different regions of South Asia. Barring few areas generally the Mesolithic cultures were succeeded by the Neolithic. However, in Gujarat and Rajasthan, the so-called Neolithic tools are absent and the Chalcolithic material is quite often found directly resting on the Mesolithic remains as the sites belonging to Anart culture in Gujarat would indicate. Though these Chalcolithic cultures appear to be the first farmers in western India, the sedentary lifestyle had started much earlier in the Mesolithic phase. As number of Mesolithic sites across the continent, Bagor in Rajasthan, Baghor, Chopani Mando, Sarai-Nahar-Rai, Warikalan-Damdama, Adamgarh and others in Ganga doab and Central India and Langhnaj in Gujarat and many other sites, have indicated that people had started living in houses and incipient domestication of animals as well as agriculture was also attempted in some areas. Pal (1986) even says that this kind of situation in Doab region could be termed as proto-Neolithic. The palynological studies carried out by Gurdeep Singh and others in Rajasthan found *Cerealia*-type pollen and comminuted pieces of charcoal, perhaps indicating clearance of vegetation for agriculture as early as 7500 BC (8300 cal. BC) (Singh 1971: 185-86). Recent studies carried out at Balathal in the Ahar complex also suggest that subsistence was based mainly on agriculture even in the early levels.

Rajasthan is a polymetallic state like Anatolia and the Aravallis are dotted with, a large number of ancient mining and smelting sites and their antiquity has yet to be worked out, apart from ore artefact corelations particularly for the source of copper/bronze for the Harappans. Though we have yet to find out the exact beginning of metallurgy in Rajasthan, circumstantial evidence of Ahar and Ganeshwar sites suggests that they were equipped with metal tools of Harappan vintage in the early 3rd millennium BC. These Chalcolithic cultures were surrounded on the north, south and on the west by the Harappan sites and recent studies (Misra *et al.* 1995, 1997) have established that the Harappans and Chalcolithic people had regular cultural contacts. It is, therefore, quite likely that the Ganeshwar and Ahar people were engaged in supplying copper ingots/objects to the Harappans. In the Chalcolithic cultures of India, only 17 per cent artefacts are found alloyed with tin. In some areas like in the Ahar complex, pure copper was used for tools. An axe from Jorwe (Deccan Chalcolithic complex) has been found containing 1.7 per cent tin, a chisel from Nevasa has 2.7 per cent tin, at Navdatoli 3.5 per cent tin was found in the objects whereas the heighest 12.8 per cent was found from an axe at Somnath. Lead alloying was more common among the Chalcolithic culture rather than arsenic that was used by the Harappans and Copper Hoard people. The Harappan and Chalcolithic copper-bronze objects are neither massive nor artistic like China and South-East Asia; they are however, purely utilitarian type.

The Ganeshwar-Jodhpura complex is dotted with a variety of sites such as microlithic or Mesolithic, archaeometallurgical and Ganeshwar-Jodhpura type village settlements. A number of sites have all these features, which may or may not be contemporary (Hooja and Kumar 1995). This is certainly good evidence of small bands and tribal or semi-nomadic and agro-pastoral groups, which gradually developed as chiefdoms. Though excavations in Ganeshwar-Jodhpura complex have not given any solid evidence of domestication and agriculture like Ahar, Malwa and Jorwe, considering the number, size and types of sites and the artefacts we suggest that chiefdom must have emerged. Perhaps agriculture and cattle breeding were main occupation initially but later on metallurgy was also included. The subsistence may have been based on agriculture, supported by hunting. It is possible that mining and metallurgy was a family business like Thailand even prior to the emergence of rank society. We do not know how the trade mechanism with the Harappans and the other Chalcolithic people operated. Did camel play any role for transportation of metal to the Harappans and grains in exchange to the metallurgists? Perhaps the ancestors of modern Banjaras of Rajasthan were related to the Bronze Age ethnic groups that were operating hinterland trade related to the Harappans.

At Balathal we have not been able to determine the possible function of the fortified enclosure standing in the centre of the settlement. This kind of monument could have been made by employing organized labour only after the emergence of a chief/king. Hence it is certainly good evidence of public architecture. In the north-eastern area of this enclosure, at the base of cow-dung dumping, the sinking layers abruptly drop (in one metre area) suggesting some empty space beneath. This area could not be exposed much as various structures predating the enclosure had appeared. Except for a floor at the base no other walls, houses, hearth, etc., were found in this enclosure. Either some mysterious (?)/religious (?) activity was going on inside in which perhaps cow-dung was also used! Otherwise why so much pain was taken to dump it inside at different times. Did the enclosure wall (5 m wide on top) provide enough space for all the viewers to walk and see the "ongoing activity"(?) that was performed inside!

Why Balathalians buried only three adults? One of them was buried before this mysterious cow-dung dumping took place and remaining two when the dumping was already burnt, perhaps few generations (if not few hundred years!) later. Were these people very important for the Balathalian society that they were buried inside this monumental structure! Could they be shamans/chiefs/important people of the society? We are looking forward for the analysis of skeletons, cow-dung and floor material to arrive at some conclusion.

Though the Deccan Chalcolithic complex has yielded more burials than other regions they are still very few in number. Both Malwa and Jorwe people practiced this trait as the evidence from Inamgaon, Kaothe, Daimabad, Nevasa and other sites would indicate. But it seems that only important people were offered burial and not everyone. As in some cases the feet were not chopped off, perhaps indicating an important person! Dhavalikar (1979: 260) also thinks that this kind of evidence may have some information about the social hierarchy and the economic status of the deceased.

A few Anarta Tradition sites of north and north-west Gujarat and Chalcolithic sites of the Lower Ganga valley have also yielded evidence of burials. In both these areas too every deceased was not offered a burial. Since not much work has been attempted in this direction it is difficult to claim that all the adults held high position in the society. Though no burials have been reported from the Copper Hoard culture and Ganeshwar-Jodhpura complex sites in most other complexes, the burials are within the habitation or right under the house courtyard or floor. This perhaps indicates a break in Harappan tradition.

In the Deccan Chalcolithic complex, Dhavalikar and others identified different components of chiefdom social organization such as craft specialization, public architecture, residential structures and burials of the chief and others. Like Deccan the mirco settlement studies have not been carried out in Rajasthan, though a number of features such as fortified enclosures, pottery kiln, storage facilities, etc., offer good examples of the evidence of social organization in Ahar complex. Recently, Deshpande (1998-99) has attempted to study the social organization in Central India with special reference to the evidence of Balathal, Rajasthan.

It seems that a number of microlithic bands did exist when the Ahar culture emerged and flourished as a number of Ahar culture sites have also yielded such tools. The Aharians were perhaps living in circular or squarish wattle-and-Doab huts and using coarse pottery (Grey Ware and Red Slipped Ware, Black-and-Red Ware). Gradually they learnt the use of stone, mud and innovated mud bricks for construction. Around mid-3rd millennium BC they were able to construct a massive fortified enclosure, supported by rectangular bastions on all corners, in the central part their settlement at Balathal. We do not know the exact function of this massive structure yet this kind of monument could be made only when there was a central authority or a chiefdom kind of social organization. A number of residential complexes have been found on all sides of this massive enclosure. In south-western and northern complexes, mud bricks have been used for construction, whereas in south-eastern part mud brick are generally absent. Perhaps everyone could not afford stones! The identification of public granary and potter's kiln may certainly be important components of social organization. The evidence of copper objects, lithic tools, beads of terracotta and semiprecious stones, pottery and terracotta animal figurines, etc., not only represent diverse craft activities but also point towards a ranked society. In the Deccan, the chief, the priest, craftsmen (like potter, smith and flint-knapper) and farmers have been identified in the Chalcolithic society; the Aharians and Ganeshwarians may also have more or less similar social stratification. The late Mesolithic people at Bagor and nearby areas were contemporary to the Chalcolithic cultures in Rajasthan. The discovery of copper arrowheads and pottery from Bagor is evidence of symbiotic relationship with Chalcolithic people. Perhaps the Mesolithic people did hunting to supply meat to the settled neighbours. This kind of symbiosis is evident in Rajasthan even today in some form between the semi-nomadic Van Vagris and settled farmers.

Unlike their contemporaries the Aharians lived in permanent squarish houses made of mud bricks, stones or mud with rammed and plastered floors. At Balathal we have found a gradual development in ceramic techniques and structures and in the middle levels the introduction of Tan Ware and massive fortified enclosure are believed to be the result of Harappan contact. They had considerably large settlements like Gilund, currently under excavation, which appears to be a regional centre. It will not be surprising if Gilund emerges as a town. Most of their settlements though are located close to fertile soil patches but still neither the Aharians nor the Ganeshwarians could achieve urbanization perhaps because of ecological limitations.

We thus have remains of hunting-gathering, pastoral, semi-sedentary and sedentary stages in the entire extra peninsular region followed by large village settlements, emergence of chiefdoms and ranked society and finally a state (Harappans). Unfortunately due to lack of multidimensional studies we are not able to illustrate possible exchange between different regions (western and Central India or Central India or Deccan), in various craft activities, in inter-site relationship, in gradual change in lifestyle, social hierarchy, rank societies, comparison of rank societies between two regions and economy of the prehistoric communities like Levy (1998) and others have done in Israel.

Chapter 5

IRON AGE CULTURES

Contents:

In South Asia, the Iron Age bridges the gap between the Bronze Age and the Early Historic Period. The iron technology played a crucial role, along with socio-political institutions, in achieving the first urbanization (second in South Asia) in the Ganga doab, an area of monsoon ecology, in the mid-1st millennium BC. The use of iron minerals (ochre) had begun in the Stone Age and iron metallurgy had started as early as the 3rd millennium BC in Anatolia (modern Turkey) (Wertime and Muhly 1980), but iron became common in the Old World only around 1st millennium BC. Here we are dealing with the South Asian cultures, which were largely dependent on iron technology.

We have several Iron Age cultures in South Asia, e.g. Megalithic culture, Painted Grey Ware culture, Gandhar Grave culture, etc., though we have very little or no evidence of early stages of development of iron technology in South Asia to support Wertime's (1980) diffusion of iron from an eastern Mediterranean source or for a unilinear development. Therefore, we have to consider the possibility that there could be different centres of iron technology, developed independently over time in different geographic regions of the large Indian subcontinent. We do not know whether meteoritic iron was also used along with terrestrial iron as in West Asia. Unlike China and other regions, copper and iron metallurgy were possibly the main engines of the two early urbanizations in South Asia. Nor is it clear if the Bronze Age people introduced iron technology in South Asia, as for example, in Pirak. In the proto-historic cultures of the Malwa region also, scholars argue that except iron there is no change in cultural assemblage in the upper levels of the sites. It is, however, generally agreed that the beginning of the 1st millennium BC saw the advent of iron into India, though Chakrabarti (1992: 68) has argued for a much earlier beginning.

Prakash and Tripathi (1986: 568-569) have divided the Iron Age cultures into five different zones, e.g., Zone A, north-western India, which also includes Pakistan; Zone B, Painted Grey Ware culture of North India; Zone C, Black-and-Red Ware culture of North-East India; Zone

D, Megalithic culture of Central India; Zone E, Megalithic culture of peninsular India. Chakrabarti (1992) also has identified six early iron-using centres in the subcontinent: Baluchistan; the north-west; the Indo-Ganga divide and the upper Ganga valley; eastern India; Malwa and Berar in Central India; and the Megalithic South India. Both these schemes are similar and differ only slightly from each other. Let us first survey these different zones, though we are not strictly adhering to these classifications.

PART – A: ARCHAEOLOGICAL CULTURES

NORTH-WESTERN ZONE

1. Gandhar Grave Culture

This region is categorized by Prakash and Tripathi under Zone A. In the eastern part of ancient Gandhar, a large number of burial complexes have been found in association with habitation sites, which have yielded evidence of the late Bronze and the early Iron Ages. This mountainous region, comprising Swat, Bajaur and other valleys, is located to the north-east of Peshawar between Kunar-Chitral on the west and the Indus on the east. Studies have been carried out in Dir and Chitral districts at Timargarh, Balambat and in the valleys of Bajaur and Swat (Dani and Durrani 1964; Dani 1967; Stacul 1969). This rugged geographical region provides only small strips of plain land along the river valleys for settlements and agriculture. Antonini, Dani and Stacul excavated a number of iron-bearing graves at Aligrama, Butkara II, Loebnar I, Katelai and Birkot Ghundai in the Swat valley (Antonini 1963; Dani 1967; Stacul 1966 a, b and Antonini and Stacul 1972). Periods I and II in this region are assigned to Bronze Age, which have yielded coarse handmade pottery besides burials. Period III is marked by graves with a variety of iron tools, e.g. spearheads, arrowheads, axe (flat and rectangular), forks, nails, finger rings, spoons and horse cheek-bars. The cheek-bars, found from Timargarh grave, have exact parallels in Central Asia and therefore, appear to be quite interesting. Three types of burial are known such as complete inhumation, interment of bones and ashes after cremation and fractional burials. It is interesting to note that the terracotta human figurines associated with these graves have almost exact parallels in the figurines recovered from the Painted Grey Ware (PGW) levels at Jakhera in Uttar Pradesh. The urns with perforations near the neck have parallels in similar pots from the Ahichchhatra PGW levels. Both Dani and Stacul have offered a three phase sequence for this whole region but they differ in the periodization of these Swat sites, e.g. Loebanr, Timargarh in Bajaur, Butkara, Katelai and Ghalighai. Dani divides them into Periods I, II and III, whereas Stacul uses the terms Archaic, Middle and Late and he does not agree to include them under the umbrella term, "Gandharan Grave Culture" (Stacul 1981: 89-91).

Dani (1967: 1) assigns the iron-bearing Period III to *c.* 800-500 BC. Here we have followed Stacul's scheme. According to Stacul's work at the cave site of Ghaligai, the Archaic Phase (Period I) of the proto-historic graveyards of the Swat valley is only Period V of Ghalighai sequence. This Period I has yielded graves made of stone slabs and orthostats, rectangular constructions, wheel and handmade pottery, bone, stone and copper tools. Compared to inhumation, cremation was more dominant in this period. Stacul ascribes Dani's Timargarh graves (numbered 102, 140, 142, 149, 192, 197) to the Ghalighai Period V. According to him the button-base grey wares of Ghalighai V have parallels in Hasanlu Iron Age Period I (Phase V, *c.* 1300-1000 BC) and Ghalighai VI with Hasanlu IV. In Ghalighai VI however, inhumation dominates over cremation. The wheel-turned Grey Ware is represented by a variety of shapes and the chalice type is most common. Pots are generally decorated with incised motifs. Only copper is reported; no iron in any grave. Iron artefacts, of course very few, appear in the upper levels of Period VI whereas Period VII (3rd and last phase of the grave complex) is characterized by a fine wheel-made Red Ware, terracotta human figurines and abundance of iron artefacts recovered from the graves (Stacul 1981: 90). Stacul compares Ghalighai VII with Hasanlu IIIA.

Stacul draws attention to various important features of Swat, corresponding to Period VII of Ghalighai, in a recent paper (1995: 341-342) and finds that:

a. There was an increase in settlements and graveyards in various locations in Swat valley, e.g. at Loebnar II, Kalako-deray, etc. and in Chitral area. All these highland areas were registering new occupation.
b. The archaeological remains, e.g. large saddle querns used for long periods indicate increase in agricultural production.
c. Period VII has yielded a large amount of iron objects (weapons) particularly from graves along with pottery, which suggests that perhaps warriors and the elite flourished, indicating a more class-stratified society.
d. From Period V to Period VII, covering a time span of nearly one thousand years, the graveyards show superimposition of graves of different periods. "With all the changes and innovations, the use of the same graveyards in subsequent times suggests a process of integration and fusion, in spite of the evidence of a break or a gap recorded at some settlement sites" (Stacul 1995: 342).
e. He finds a well-defined change in burial customs at the end of Period VII possibly due to the spread of new ideologies/religion as at Butkara II, in Swat, the structural remains of a Buddhistic monument, overlapping some proto-historic graves, suggest similar events.
f. The grey pottery of Period VI was largely replaced by wheel-turned red shapes in Period VII and is represented by shapes like carinated bowls, stemmed bowls, cylindrical-conical vessels and beakers, handled jugs and a large variety of bottles. Some of these varieties like carinated bowls, bottles and jugs frequently occur in the same grave.

Thus the continuity and transition in cultural equipment are observed in the form of change in ceramics and continuity in burial practice from the Late Bronze Age to the Early Iron Age in this rugged mountainous region. Therefore, the first appearance of iron in the Swat area can be assigned to *c.* 1000 BC (Agrawal and Kusumgar 1974, see table 5.2).

At Saraikhola, Period II (phase 2nd) is also represented by Iron Age graves and has been assigned to the first half of 1st millennium BC. A variety of iron objects such as rings, rods and bracelets are found from these graves. Apart from these, there are three sites, Balamb, Bhir Mound and Charsada, which have yielded a variety of iron objects datable to 5th–6th centuries BC (Dani 1967).

Baluchistan Region

Hundreds of cairn burials are known from the region between Persia (Fars) and Zhob-Loralai region of north-east Baluchistan. A majority of them are located in Baluchistan and Makran area.

A variety of barbed and leaf-shaped arrowheads, daggers, knives and thick iron hooks were found from the cairns of Mughal Ghundai and Jiwanri respectively (Piggott 1950). These burials have yielded green glazed and whitish wheel-turned pottery, the shapes of which were represented by squat, spouted and lugged flask. The handmade variety is very crude. However, the southern region has yielded the Londo ware, which is characterized by a continuous spiral motif in black over a red slip. On the basis of some similarities of these cairn-assemblages with Sialk Necropole B, Piggott assigned them a bracket of *c.* 1100-750 BC. Though some scholars related the beginning of iron in India to the authors of these cairns (Gordon 1950), Chakrabarti is against even including the cairn burials among the Early Iron Age cultures (1976: 114). He (1992: 36-46) has discussed this issue at length and finds that several burial groups at Mughal Ghundai, Zangian, Jiwanri, Gatti, Nasirabad, etc., associated with Londo ware can be assigned to the early centuries of Christian era.

PIRAK

Pirak is a unique site in the Kachchhi plains of Baluchistan and it was discovered by Robert Raikes as early as 1963. He attempted to compare the Pirak pottery (bichrome and grey) with the Samarran levels of Iraq, Nineveh III and Arpachiyah, thus assigning Pirak to *c.* 5000 BC. Casal and Jarrige, who were part of the French Archaeological Mission, excavated the site between 1968 and 1974 (Jarrige and Santoni 1979; Enault 1979) and identified three different cultural periods. Period I has yielded Pirak pottery (i.e. a handmade bichrome-on-cream or buff slip with the motifs of multiple triangles, intricate lattices, etc. and a wheel-turned Grey or Black Ware) and multi roomed well-built houses besides stray sherds of Wet Ware, Faiz Mohammad Grey Ware and few others indicating the continuity from the Bronze Age of Baluchistan. Possehl and Gullapalli (1999: 157) write that the subsistence was mainly based upon rice and millets, which is perhaps one of the earliest evidence of rice in the north-western region. The site is rich in terracottas: double-humped Bactrian camels, naturalistic horses and humans are represented. Bone tools particularly indicate that industry was well developed and copper-bronze artefacts were also recorded (Possehl and Gullapalli 1999: 157). Apart from this kind of archaeological artefacts, the site also yielded large number of compartmented seals. Though Period II has continuity with Period I, some new shapes and fabrics were introduced in this period. Period III is characterized by the evidence of iron production. Though iron appeared in level 6, it became common in levels 4 and 3. The main tool types are winged arrowheads and bars. Even the use of stone blades continued in these levels. The artefacts also include crucibles, iron slag, copper/bronze, lead, silver and gold objects. There is no discontinuity between the iron-free lower levels and the upper ones with iron. The appearance of a new Grey Ware or black pottery seems to be important. The common shapes are bowls and dishes. It is wheel-turned and often bears burnishing.

It is interesting that in this long cultural sequence at Pirak, iron appeared only in Period III. There are more than a dozen consistent ^{14}C dates available for Pirak, which suggest that the beginning of iron at Pirak can be assigned to around 900 BC (Agrawal 1982: 250; Possehl and Gullapalli 1999: 157) and not between 1200 and 1300 BC as the excavators suggested (Jarrige and Santoni 1979). A number of sites, e.g. Pirak, Chashma Murad, Durkhan Malazai, Pathani Damb II, Sulaimanzai others have been identified as belonging to Pirak culture.

TABLE 5.1 LATE CHALCOLITHIC AND EARLY IRON AGE DATES FROM PAKISTAN (after Possehl 1994)

(All BP ages are based on 5568 years half-life of radiocarbon. Calibrated ages are given in BC.)

Site	*Sample No.*	*Date/Half Life*	*Calib. Dates*	*Culture*	*Material*
Pirak	PRL-388	2730±110 BP	897 cal. BC	Chalcolithic	Charcoal
Pirak	PRL-390	2730±100 BP	897 cal. BC	Chalcolithic	Charcoal
Pirak	PRL-389	2590±100 BP	799 cal. BC	Chalcolithic	Charcoal
Pirak	PRL-391	2730±100 BP	897 cal. BC	Chalcolithic	Charcoal
Pirak	LY-1643	2970±140 BP	1255,1240, 1221 cal. BC	Period II	Charcoal

TABLE 5.2 GANDHAR GRAVE CULTURE

(after Possehl and Gullapalli 1999: 166)

Site and Period	*Lab. No.*	*Calibrated Date* BC *(Calib-3 Programme)*
Swat Valley Period V	PRL-243	1259 (1045) 916
Late Bronze Age	PRL-244	916 (810) 768
	PRL-246	1516 (1381, 1342, 1321) 1063
Katelai	R-476	1527 (1414) 1220
	R-477	1121 (1009) 926
	R-477A	923 (897, 870) 826
Loebanr I	BM-196	1257 (999) 827
	BM-195	1405 (1251, 1248, 1205) 943
Early Iron Age		
Barama I	R-196	812 (794) 569
Swat Valley Period IV (Early Iron Age)	R-195	400 (391) 374
Butkhara II	R-194	752 (472, 467, 417) 404
Katelai	R-279	192 (157, 137, 125) 53
	R-479	385 (365, 275, 264) 201
Loebanr I	R-278	481 (403) 393
	R-276	763 (750, 746, 526)
	R-474	751 (405) 391
Timargarh Period III	H-XXY	1007 (924) 852

PAINTED GREY WARE AND NORTHERN BLACK POLISHED WARE CULTURES

In South Asia, the first urbanization was achieved by the Bronze Age people in a semi-arid ecology. However, the second urbanization was realized in the monsoon ecology of the Ganga doab, in the mid-1st millennium BC with the advent of iron technology. The Ganga doab receives high rainfall (100–150 cm/per year) and the first colonizers of this region had to

Pl. 5-2. General view of excavations, Taxila, Sirkap.

Pl. 5-3. Megalithic excavations, Brahmagiri.

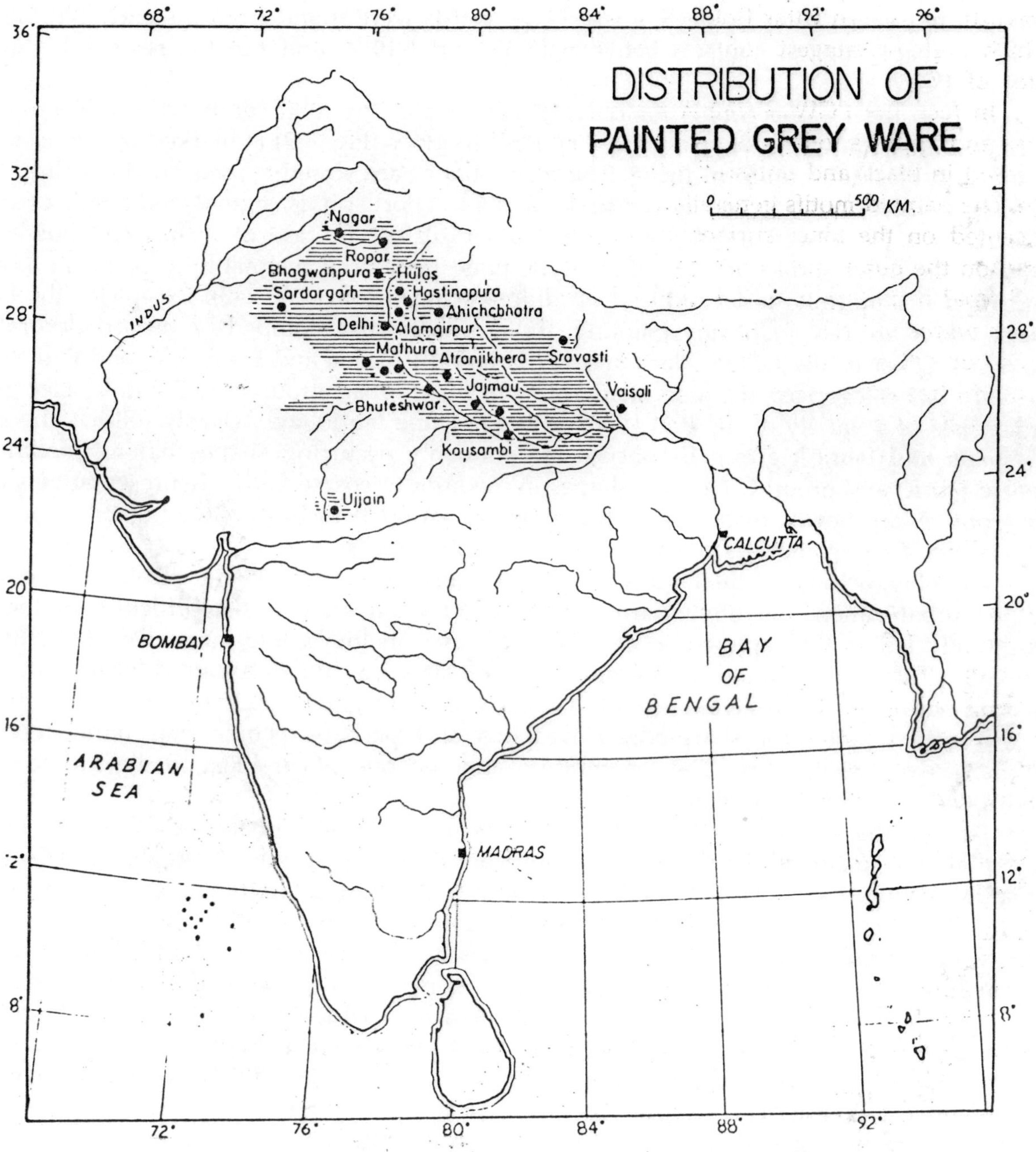

Fig. 5-1. Distribution map of Painted Grey Ware sites.

Most of the PGW sites are small ranging between 1 and 2 ha, however, Mughal (1984: 501) has reported relatively a large site at Satwadi, spread over an area about 13 ha.

In the second-half of the last century, a large number of PGW sites were excavated, e.g. Noh, Jodhpura and Sardargarh in Rajasthan; Khalaua, Bateswar, Ahichchhatra, Hastinapur, Allahpur, Atranjikhera, Jakhera, Mathura and many others in Uttar Pradesh. At Sravasti, in eastern Uttar Pradesh, a few PGW sherds were found from the early NBP levels, which perhaps suggest contacts between PGW and NBPW and not the regular habitation sites of PGW.

In fact, the PGW accounts for only 10 per cent of the total ceramic assemblage at the sites and appears to be a deluxe ware. The PGW pottery (Fig. 5-2) is marked by a thin fabric, painted in black and uniform firing. The main shapes are straight-sided bowls, dishes, *lotas,* etc. The painted motifs generally comprise *swastikas*, short spirals, sigmas and bands of stroke executed on the inner surface and vertical outer surface in case of dishes and bowls and only on the outer surface in case of *lota*-type pots. They used magnetite to paint the pottery and fired it uniformly under reduced conditions (Ghosh 1989: 240-243). Except for the PGW, other wares are devoid of any painting, though occasional stamped or incised decorations do occur. Other wares include Black-and-Red, Black Burnished and Plain Grey and Red Wares. Tripathi has categorized the associated wares in three broad groups: A, B and C. Her group A consists of a variety of the Red Ware which has fine fabric and "closely follows the PGW in shape and fabric"; group B consists of commonly occurring shapes having medium to coarse fabric; and group C has rare shapes in medium to coarse fabric. Representative shapes of group A are bowls, dishes and *thalis* whereas group B includes storage jars, basins and bowls. Group C comprises a variety of miniature vessels.

Probably, because of the large-scale clearance of forests in the Ganga doab and the needs of the urbanization, the limited iron resources of Kumaun and the difficulty of logistics eventually led to the exploitation of river-sands rich in low grade magnetite (Tripathi and Tripathi 1994: 241-52). In the Mediterranean region also, sea-sands were used for the extraction of iron since several Millennia. In the Ganga valley, magnetite rich iron ore was smelted, which suited better for sharp-edged weapons and perhaps people had understood the properties of specific ores. The temperature and the rate of air blast to the furnace were controlled accordingly (Prakash 1991).

Barring the sites of north-eastern Rajasthan and Central Himalayas, others are located in the alluvial plains of the doab zone away from iron ore deposits. A number of PGW sites despite such distance have yielded evidence of iron smelting, e.g. Atranjikhera, Hulas, Jakhera in the doab zone. A number of sites of the same culture, located relatively closer to the source of iron ore, at Jodhpura, Bairath, Aguchha in Rajasthan have also yielded remarkable evidence of smelting. At Jodhpura and Aguchha, fragments of crucibles, ore and slag were recorded. Perhaps crucible-shaped furnaces were used for direct reduction of ore; bloom was heated in an open furnace and was forged on an adjacent platform. The Aravallis were good source of iron ore for the PGW people in Rajasthan as a large number of old workings have been recorded on the eastern margin of Aravallis. As the old workings at Bania ka Bas, Morija, Rampura contain high grade ore and are close to Jodhpura, they could have been a source of the ore. In case of the upper Ganga doab sites, source of ore was perhaps the Central Himalayan region where we have located a large number of old workings (Agrawal and Kharakwal 1998).

Vibha Tripathi (1976) classifies the iron repertory in three categories. Spearheads,

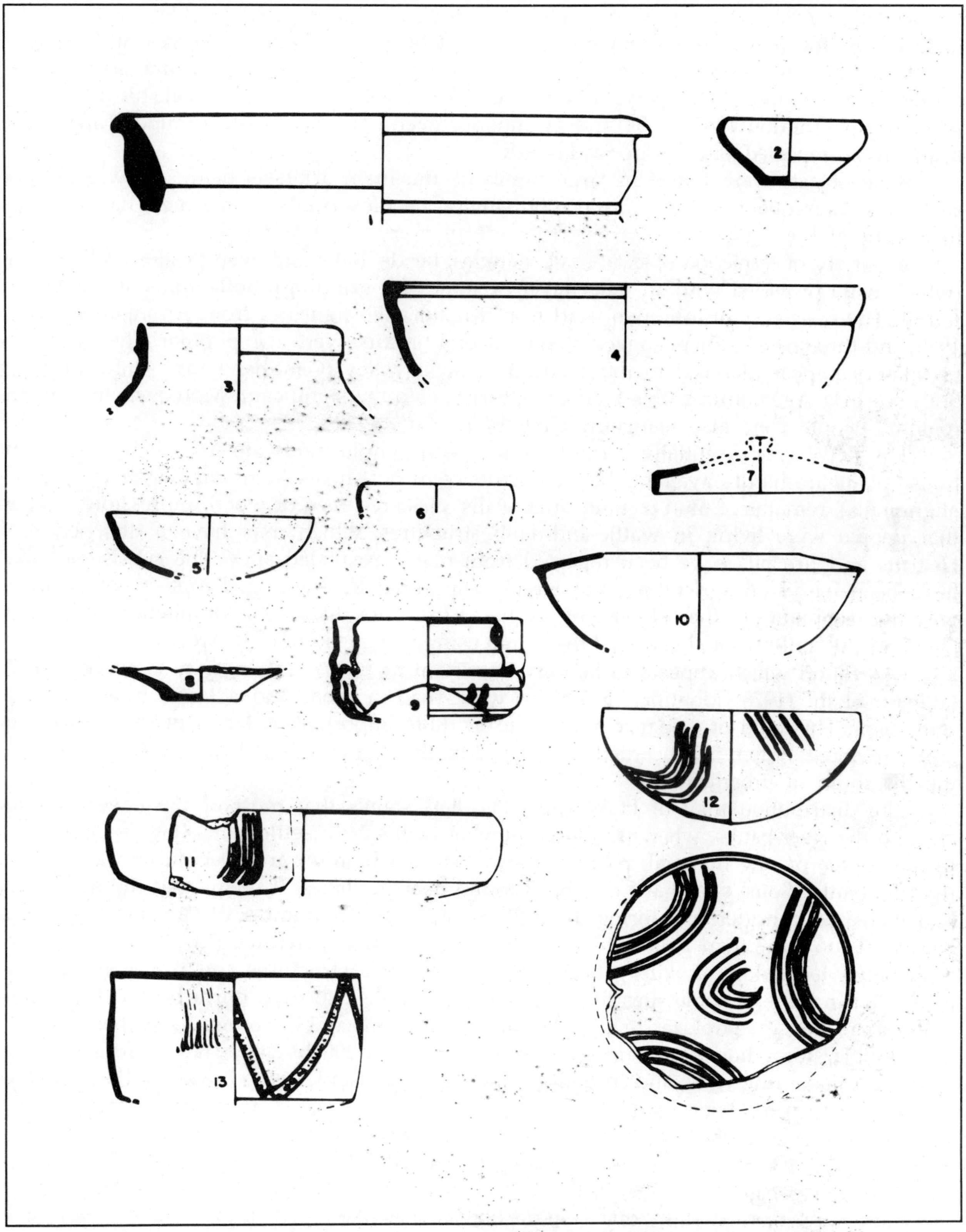

Fig. 5-2. Red Ware (Nos. 1-8) and Painted Grey Ware (Nos. 9-13), Hastinapur, U.P.

arrowheads, socketed tangs, blades, etc., constitute the hunting kit; sickles and axes are included in the agricultural category and the kitchenware comprises knives and tongs.

Beads of various shapes were made of a variety of materials, e.g. terracotta, jasper, agate, carnelian, bone and chalcedony. In the late PGW levels of Allahpur (Dikshit 1973: 148), Alamgirpur (Tandon 1967-68: 54) and Hastinapur even glass beads were found. Lapis lazuli beads were reported only from Sardargarh.

Bone objects were found in large numbers, the main artefacts being arrowheads and sockets. Less frequent is the occurrence of bangles, needles, combs, gamesmen, hairpins, etc., made out of bone. Rare are the objects made of ivory, shell and horn.

A variety of terracotta objects: seals, bangles, beads, balls and even pestles and grinders (which were provided with an outer layer of stones for grinding), bulls, rams and birds are found. The discovery of a human head from Khalua, two figurines from Atranjikhera (Gaur 1983) and three from Jakhera suggest that terracotta figurine were also popular. The terracottas of Jakhera appear identical to those found in Swat valley (Gandhar Grave Culture). Since both are Iron Age cultures, this kind of similarity is quite significant. Moreover, in both the regions, people were also using the Grey Ware.

The PGW was essentially a rural culture with simple moderate-sized habitations. The house plans are hardly available but the evidence of post-holes (with circular or rectangular alignments), remains of mud or mud brick walls, plastered reed or wood impressions suggest that people were living in wattle-and-daub structures, which may have a thatched roof. Hearths and fire pits have been reported from many excavated sites. The subsistence may have been based on agriculture, but largely supported by hunting. People were aware of weaving techniques as the evidence of potsherds from sites like Noh, Atranjikhera and others have indicated. It is quite likely that they were using woven clothes. At Atranjikhera, a pottery kiln was found which appears to be very important as far as craft activity is concerned. At Jakhera, Shahi (1978) identified a 4.25 m wide road, a moat and a bund from the large settlement. This kind of evidence appears to be quite important as far as public architecture and settlement system is concerned. This could be the first evidence of the PGW approaching the threshold of urbanization.

The distribution map of PGW sites (Fig. 5-1) shows that most of them were located close to the river-banks, whereas, a large number of the NBP settlements (Fig. 5-4,) are close to the source of raw material, particularly in Madhya Pradesh and Deccan and away from the riverbanks. Some sites have also been found near the lakes. It seems that the population had increased considerably during the NBP as not only the number of sites increased from 700 (PGW) to more than 2,000 settlements but also the size increased. People were equipped with better technological skills. Though wattle-and-daub structures and use of mud bricks continued in NBP, at some sites like Atranjikhera people also used burnt bricks. They could make large house complexes, e.g. at Hastinapur and Kosambi. Kosambi also has evidence of a double storey house measuring 8.4″ x 4.5″ (Tripathi 2001b: 240). They were able to dig wells and make ring wells and irrigation canals. In large settlements brick-lined and unlined drainage system has been found. At Rajghat the evidence of a 33.10 cm thick road prepared by rammed potsherds, gravel and mud clods is certainly a remarkable discovery of archaeological artefacts, of course, belonging to the late NBP phase (Tripathi 2001b: 228-243).

The archaeological artefacts also include a variety of terracotta, glass, semiprecious stone, ivory and copper ornaments. Some semiprecious stones like topaz and crystal may have been obtained by trade with neighboring areas. Copper ornaments comprise pins, pendants, bangles

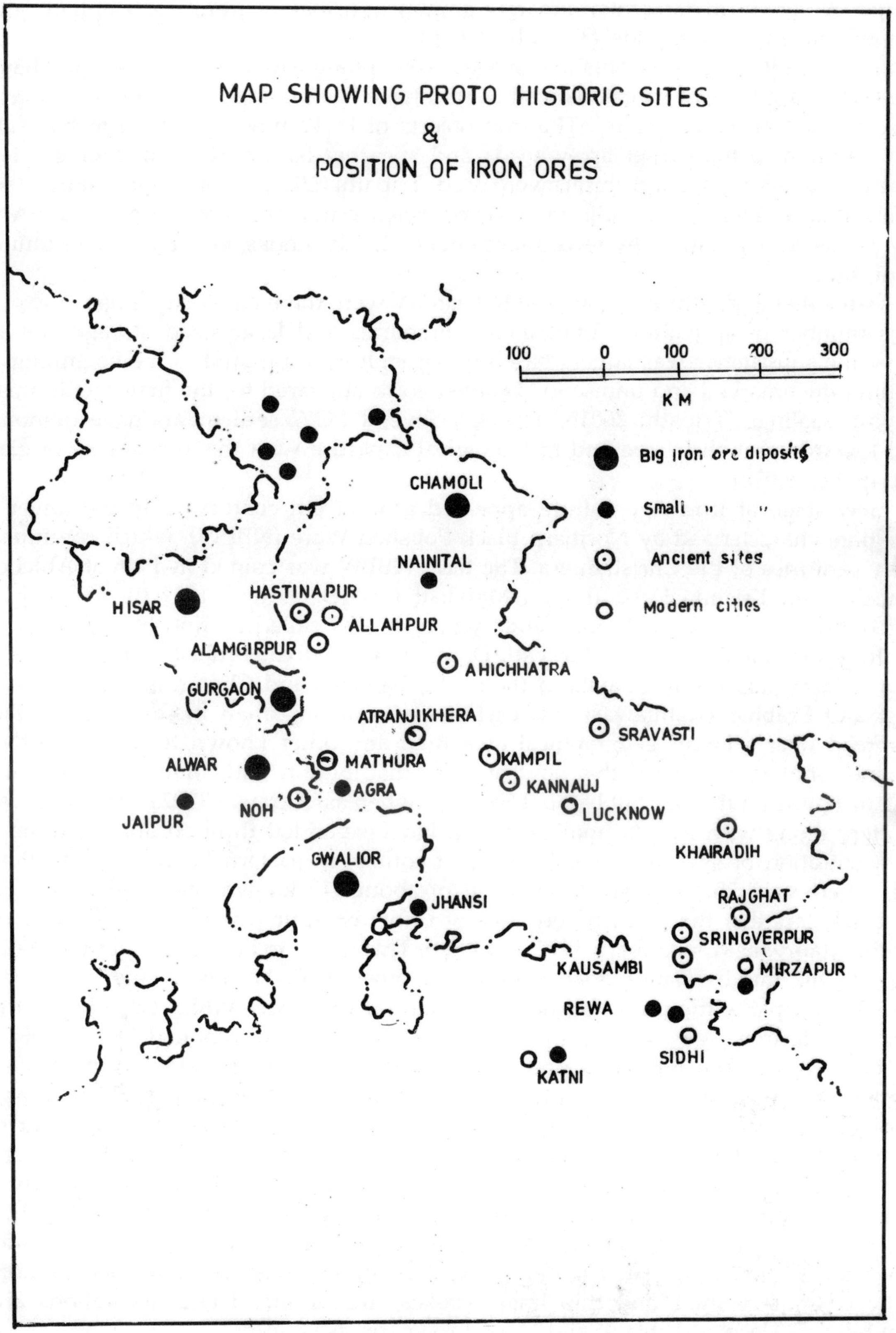

Fig. 5-3. Map showing protohistoric sites and main iron ore sites.

and rings. A variety of terracotta and few animal figurines of iron, e.g. elephant and goat are among the important finds (Tripathi 2001b).

Some agricultural implements like sickles, axes, ploughshare, spades and hoe have been reported. Hunting tools of copper as well as iron have been found. The iron objects gradually increase and are of better quality. The iron objects of PGW type continued in NBP also but now in addition to the earlier arrowheads and spearheads, a variety of double- or single-tang spears, dagger blades and chisels were used. Tripathi (2001b) points out that the discovery of chisels almost at every site indicates their proficiency in carpentry and masonry. A variety of copper objects, e.g. antimony rods, nail pairers, chisels, hooks, etc., have been found from different sites.

It seems that agriculture and animal husbandry were the main occupations. The evidence of large number of agricultural implements, granaries and large-sized storage jars suggest that now the subsistence was largely based on agriculture compared to the beginning of Iron Age. Both punchmarked and uninscribed copper coins appeared for the first time in this phase along with sealings (Tripathi 2001b: 228-243). Several PGW settlements have demonstrated a trend towards growth in size and technological expertise with the appearance of glass and iron (Tripathi 2001b).

A new stage of Iron Age culture appeared around 6th century BC in the lower Ganga doab region, characterized by Northern Black Polished Ware (NBPW), which continued until the early centuries of the Christian era. The term NBPW was coined in 1946 at Ahichchhatra by Wheeler and Krishna Deva though Marshall (1904-5: 59 and 1909-10: 40) had already identified this ware at Sarnath and Bhita, where it was called as fine black lustrous ware. This culture extended as far as Amravati, Dharanikota and Chebrolu (Andhra) in the south, areas of Swat, Charsada and Taxila in the north, Bangarh and Chandraketugarh (Bengal) in the east and Prabhas (Kathiawar) and eastern parts of Rajasthan in the west. In fact, this ware spread over a larger geographical area than any other known Iron Age pottery (Fig. 5-4). Some scholars associated this kind of wide distribution with Mauryan imperialism, or Buddhism (Ghosh 1973: 15; Subbarao 1958: 46), whereas Agrawal (1971: 244) suggests that this pottery along with iron technology might have expanded through ancient trade routes. The concentration of sites of this culture is, of course, in eastern Uttar Pradesh, Bihar and Bengal, where over 292 sites are located out of about 415 known ones. It has been argued by some scholars that the rich iron ore area of Chota Nagpur was neither exploited by NBP nor by the Mauryans (Chakrabarti 1992; Lal 1986). This needs to be confirmed by metallurgical analysis. In the middle Ganga doab region, a number of PGW settlements were succeeded by the NBP people without any break in the cultural sequence. Vibha Tripathi (2001b) calls this as "Middle Iron Age". In fact, the NBP shapes (dishes) are typologically largely similar to the PGW types. The NBPW is one of the best ceramic of the old world. At few sites this pottery has been divided in two types, monochrome and bichrome. Both types are made of well-levigated clay, fired at high temperature, have a thin fabric and black-grey or reddish core. The surface colour of the monochrome type is generally either blackish grey or bluish black, though deep red, violet, steel blue have also been found. Some pots have glossy surface and metallic sound; it is difficult to scratch their surface even with a knife. The bichrome or deluxe variety of NBP is remarkable as polished surface of the pots gives combination of two colours. Sometimes such pottery is also decorated with designs such as horizontal or vertical bands of thick and thin lines, strokes, arches, etc. These decorations are done in steel-blue or deep red, black and dark brown or ashy grey.

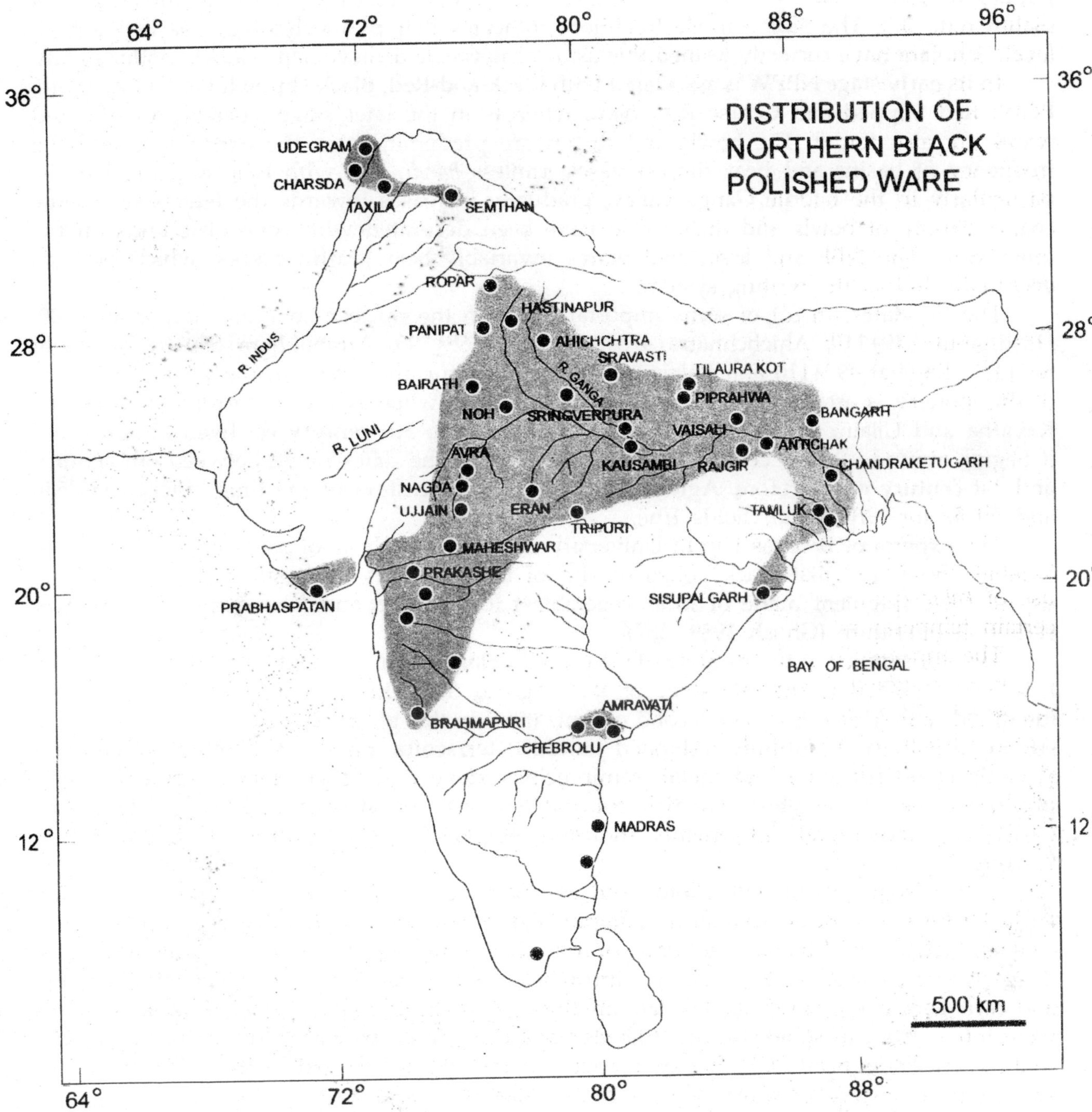

Fig. 5-4. Distribution of Northern Black Polished Ware sites.

The common shapes are dishes with inverted or straight sides, bowls with straight, convex, corrugated or tapering sides and carinated *handis*. Such shapes are found even in contemporary Black-and-Red Ware and PGW. The NBPW was certainly a deluxe kind of pottery of South Asia as broken fragments were refitted with copper rivets, fillets or pins (Sahni n.d.: 37). The NBP surface treatment indicates that pyrotechnology reached a high level. Scholars have correctly termed this as a "remarkable achievement" in the potter's craft.

In its early stage NBPW is associated with Black-and-Red, Black-slipped, Plain Grey Ware, PGW, Red Slipped and Coarse Red Ware whereas in the later stage, coarse grey and red wares are also found. The bowls and dishes are predominant in the early stage and the frequency of basins and pear shaped vases, rimless *handi*, pan with loop and lug handle, particularly in the middle Ganga valley, gradually increases towards the later stage. Some coarse variety of bowls and dishes also have been decorated with concentric bnds on the inner wall. The NBP and associated wares invariably bear graffiti marks, which perhaps eventually led to the writing system.

The ^{14}C dates (in BC) of some important sites in the nuclear zone are: Ropar 485$\pm$100; Hastinapur 340$\pm$110; Ahichchhatra 475$\pm$105; Noh 685$\pm$105; Atranjikhera 530$\pm$85; Kosambi 500$\pm$110; Rajghat 490+110 and Rajgir 265$\pm$105. At Sonpur and Chirand, the earliest evidence of this pottery is assigned to 7th and 8th centuries BC, whereas in the peripheral areas like Kayatha and Ujjain, the beginning has been assigned to 5th century BC. Even at Amravati, it begins around 4th–3rd centuries BC. In fact, most of the dates range between 6th century and 1st century BC, therefore, Agrawal's (1971: 102) suggestion of the time bracket, i.e. 550 and 50 BC for NBPW still holds true.

The experts of Banaras Hindu University conducted analysis of some NBP sherds from Rajghat and found that black polish or slip of the NBPW is the result of reduced firing, use of *kabiz* (pigment made of local vegetables) for the slip and iron oxide and firing at certain temperature (Ghosh 1989: 257).

The appearance of towns at Taxila, Kosambi, Hastinapur, Atranjikhera and other places has been assigned to the late stage of Iron Age by Tripathi, a period which is generally identified with *Mahajanpadas* or second urbanization. In this phase, according to her, intensive structural activity, beautifully fashioned moulded terracotta, pottery and other objects tend towards standardization and metal, semiprecious stone and other archaeological artefacts proliferate, hence the sites have rich cultural remains indicating an urbanized stage. The variety of agricultural implements indicates emphasis on agriculture (Tripathi 2001b: Chapter 7).

A few fragments of NBP sherds and associated Grey Ware were also found from the Early Historic deposit at Balathal in Udaipur, Rajasthan, which may have been due to trade contacts with Central India. Thousands of iron objects, which include adzes, nails, hoe, bells, daggers, swords, sickles, clamps, hooks, arrowheads, knives, sockets, bowl fragments, furnaces and carnelian, glass, terracotta, crystal, amethyst, lapis lazuli, ivory, copper, iron, gold, shell, were found from these levels. These levels have been dated between 3rd century BC to 2nd century AD. Though no PGW has been found at the site, bowls and dishes with vertical or slightly pronounced sides, featureless rim and flat base were made in fine grey fabric. The shapes have also been copied in Red Ware. They bear a stamp design on the inner side in the centre and invariably bear fine surface treatment reminding PGW and NBP traditions.

We thus see that the PGW people, characterized by a simple subsistence and use of mud houses, appear as the first large-scale colonizers of the forested country of the doab.

They were still in a village economy, without any coinage or writing system. They had a limited number of iron and copper tools, but were approaching urbanization as indicated by the Jakhera settlement. More than 700 PGW sites are reported which is indicative of a fair density of population. The NBP by and large appears to be the continuation of the same tradition with advancement of technique in each walk of life.

To date, a large number of ^{14}C dates are available for the PGW sites (Agrawal and Yadav 1995). Except for Atranjikhera (TF-191, 1057+110), all other dates from other sites provide a bracket of *c.* 1000-400 BC (uncal.) for the PGW. The NBP sites are generally bracketed between 6th century BC and 1st century BC.

From the above data, Tripathi (2001b: 228-247) has suggested the following three different stages of gradual development of iron technology as well cultures in South Asia:

Stage I: During this early stage, generally objects such as spearheads, arrowheads and occasionally knives, nails, hooks and chisels (found from PGW levels) made of wrought iron were in use. This stage is largely represented by Painted Grey Ware culture people and the subsistence was based on hunting, animal husbandry and some farming as the lack of agricultural implements suggests a low level agricultural production. Some sites like Atranjikhera have yielded remains of wheat, barley and rice. People also used copper tools (arrowheads, toiletries) and they introduced glass ornaments. The house plans are rarely available but post-holes and plastered reeds suggest that wattle-and-daub circular and rectangular structures were prevalent and possibly they had thatched roofs.

Stage II: This stage is represented by the NBP Ware culture and Megalithic culture. The former was concentrated in the middle and lower Ganga doab whereas the latter was in the peninsular India. People had started making mild steel at some sites and iron objects became more profuse and of better quality. Agricultural implements like ploughshare, spades, hoe, sickle and axes, etc., gradually increase. In addition to these, arrowheads and spearheads, spears, dagger blades, etc., were in use. Chisels have been reported from almost every site indicating thereby a proficiency in carpentry and masonry. It seems that besides craftsmanship subsistence on agriculture increased as we find evidence of double-cropping, pulses and remains of large-size storage bins and granaries at Atranjikhera and other sites. Pulses like black gram appear for the first time at Atranjikhera. Evidence of millet, black gram, green gram, peas, *khesari, sesame, ber* and *anwala* were found at Narhan. The size of houses, settlement and use of burnt bricks increased, glass ornaments became common, large quantity of semiprecious stones beads, use of ivory and coins (punch-marked and uninscribed cast types) appeared and there is evidence of making irrigation canals. During this phase, pyrotechnology reached its zenith as deluxe variety of NBP, which characterizes this stage, was used. Copper continued to be used for hunting tools, as also for hooks, chisels, borers, antimony rods, toiletries like nai pairers, ornaments, pins, pendants, bangles, rings, etc.

Stage III (200 BC onwards): Urban centres like Taxila (Pl. 5-2, Sirkap exacavations at Taxila), Kosambi, Hastinapur, Atranjikhera and many others flourished. Some of them were capitals of *Mahajanpadas* too. Typological proliferation of iron objects particularly agricultural and war weapons increased, iron became common and the smiths used carburization technique as specimens from Taxila contained 1.3 per cent to 1.5 per cent carbon with higher Brinnel hardness. The agricultural tools like spade, ploughshare, hoe, etc., become common in most of the sites. Potter's art at this level tends towards standardization. Moulded terracotta were fashioned beautifully. Luxury goods like beads of semiprecious stone and other archaeological artefacts proliferate. Literary evidence also suggests knowledge of quenching and larger-scale production of iron.

Upadhyaya (2000: 239-246) has carried out typological study of iron objects belonging to different stages of Iron Age and he found that the percentage of hunting tools remains the same during the PGW and NBP but the tools belonging to agriculture and different kinds of craft increased largely during the NBP.

We understand that the urbanization of the Ganga valley was not only the result of iron technology and agricultural surplus but also several social, political and economic factors contributed to this process (Chakrabarti 1973). The emergence of monarchical system was perhaps the synthesis of diverse socio-economic factors due to considerable prosperity in the Iron Age society, which not only controlled and canalized the surplus but also paved the way to urbanization. In fact, the credit largely goes to the PGW people (Thapar 1978: 91).

TABLE 5.4 DATES OF PAINTED GREY WARE SITES (after Possehl 1994)

(All BP ages are based on 5568 years half-life of radiocarbon. Calibrated ages are given in BC/AD. After Possehl 1994.)

Site	*Sample No.*	*5568 Yrs.* BP	*Calib. Dates*	*Culture*	*Material*
Hastinapur	TF-90	2270±110 BP	383 cal. BC	Uppermost Painted Grey Ware, Period II	Charcoal
Hastinapur	TF-112	2260±95 BP	379 cal. BC	Uppermost Painted Grey Ware, Period II	Charcoal
Hastinapur	UCLA-684	1800±100 BP	227 cal. AD	Painted Grey Ware Period II, probably an intrusive burial ?	Bone Collagen
Hastinapur	TF-85	2385±125 BP	406 cal. BC	Late Painted Grey Ware, Period II	Charcoal
Hastinapur	TF-83	2220±110 BP	362,282,258 cal. BC	Uppermost Painted Grey Ware, Period II	Charcoal
Hastinapur	TF-91	2450±120 BP	752,709,530 cal. BC	Late Painted Grey Ware, Period II	Charcoal
Hulas	PRL-HLS-TL-1	2300	TL Date	Period II, Painted Grey Ware, late phase	Soils in association with Period II
Khalua	PRL-67	2450±155 BP	752,709,530 cal. BC	Painted Grey Ware	Charcoal
Khalua	TF-1228	2420±95 BP	484,437,424 cal. BC	Painted Grey Ware	Charcoal
Khalua	PRL-68	2370±170 BP	403 cal. BC	Painted Grey Ware	Charcoal
Noh	TF-1144	2370±85 BP	403 cal. BC	Painted Grey Ware	Charcoal
Noh	TF-994	2560±100 BP	793 cal. BC	Painted Grey Ware	Charcoal

Cont. Table 5.4

Table 5.4 Cont.

Site	*Sample No.*	*5568 Yrs.* BP	*Calib. Dates*	*Culture*	*Material*
Noh	UCLA-703A	2480±250 BP	760,684,656 638,592,586 550 cal. BC	Painted Grey Ware	Charcoal
Noh	UCLA-703B	2690±220 BP	833 cal. BC	Painted Grey Ware	Charcoal
Noh	TF-993	2600±145 BP	801 cal. BC	Painted Grey Ware	Charcoal
Sonkh mound Mathura	I-6277	2570±85 BP	795 cal. BC	Painted Grey Ware	Charcoal
Sonpur	TF-376	2510±105 BP	767 cal. BC	Pre-NBP	Charred Rice
Thapali	PRL-732	2070±120 BP	101 cal. BC	PGW	Charcoal
Thapali	PRL-731	2030±140 BP	43 cal. BC	PGW	Charcoal
Tilaurakot	TF-737	2235±95 BP	368,273,268 cal. BC	PGW	Charcoal
Jodhpura	PRL-212	2270±100 BP	383 cal. BC	Black-and-Red Ware/ Painted Grey Ware overlap	Charcoal

TABLE 5.5 EARLY IRON AGE DATES FROM RAJA-NAL-KA-TILA, UTTAR PRADESH

Site	*Sample no.*	*Date*	*Calib. Dates*	*Layer*
Raja-Nal-ka-Tila	PRL 2045	3260±90 BP	1 SIGMA: 1622 BC...1426 BC 2 SIGMA: 1772 BC... 1378 BC 1348 BC... 1316 BC	10
Raja-Nal-ka-Tila	PRL 2046	3100±90	1 SIGMA: 1500 BC... 1490 BC 1448 BC... 1256 BC 1240 BC... 1214 BC 2 SIGMA: 1524 BC... 1112 BC 1098 BC... 1056 BC	9
Raja-Nal-ka-Tila	PRL 2047	2890±80 BP	1 SIGMA: 1196 BC... 1188 BC 1164 BC... .1143 BC 1132 BC... 976 BC 970 BC... .930 BC 2 SIGMA: 1304 BC... 1284 BC 1268 BC...894 BC 882 BC... 846 BC	6

Cont. Table 5.5

Table 5.5 Cont.

Site	*Sample no.*	*Date*	*Calib. Dates*	*Layer*
Raja-Nal-ka-Tila	PRL 2049	3050±90 BP	1 SIGMA: 1406 BC... .1198 BC 1186 BC... 1164 BC 1143 BC... 1132 BC 2 SIGMA: 1508 BC... 1482 BC 1456 BC... 1024 BC	7

TABLE 5.6 NORTHERN BLACK POLISHED WARE AND EARLY IRON AGE SITES (INDIA AND PAKISTAN)

(All BP ages are based on 5568 years half-life of radiocarbon. Calibrated ages are given in BC/AD. After Possehl 1994.)

Site	*Sample No.*	*5568 Yrs.* BP	*Calib. Dates*	*Culture*	*Material*
Atranji-khera	TF-283	2150±105 BP	192 cal. BC	Northern Black Polished Ware, Period IV	Charcoal
Atranji-khera	BM-193	2040±150 BP	50 cal. BC	Painted Grey Ware/ Northern Black Polished Ware overlap	Charcoal
Atranji-khera	TF-415	2450±200 BP	752,709,530 cal. BC	Period II, Black and Red Ware	Charcoal
Atranji-khera	TF-289	2550±105 BP	791 cal. BC	Period II, Black and Red Ware	Charcoal
Atranji-khera	TF-194	2410±85 BP	410 cal. BC	Painted Grey Ware, Period III	Charcoal
Atranji-khera	TF-291	2415±100 BP	512 cal. BC	Painted Grey Ware, Period III	Charcoal
Atranji-khera	BM-194	2420±150 BP	484,437,424 cal. BC	Painted Grey Ware/ Northern Black Polished Ware overlap	Charcoal
Atranji-khera	TF-191	2890±105 BP	1057 cal. BC	Painted Grey Ware, Period III	Charcoal
Atranji-khera	TF-287	1605±95 BP	427 cal. BC	Painted Grey Ware, Period III	Charcoal
Atranji-khera	TF-284	2180±95 BP	340,322,203 cal. BC	Northern Black Polished Ware, Period IV	Charcoal
Atranji-khera	TF-195	1845±95 BP	137 cal. BC	Post-Northern Black Polished Ware, Period IV	Charcoal
Atranji-khera	UW-XXXX	2407±150 BP	489 cal. BC	Painted Grey Ware/ Northern Black Polished Ware overlap	Unknown

Cont. Table 5.6

Table 5.6 Cont.

Site	*Sample No.*	*5568 Yrs.* BP	*Calib. Dates*	*Culture*	*Material*
Atranji-khera	Oxford-TL-111-C1	2280 BC	None	Ochre Coloured Pottery, Period I	Pottery
Atranji-khera	Oxford-TL-111-B4	1670 BC	None	Ochre Coloured Pottery, Period I	Pottery
Atranji-khera	Oxford-TL-111-B5	1170 BC	None	Ochre Coloured Pottery, Period I	Pottery
Atranji-khera	Oxford-TL-111-C2	1250 BC	None	Ochre Coloured Pottery, Period I	Pottery
Atranji-khera	Oxford-TL-111-C3	2130 BC	None	Ochre Coloured Pottery, Period I	Pottery
Hastinapur	TF-88	2225±110 BP	340±115 BC 364,279,261 cal. BC		Lowest NBP Ware, Period III
Hastinapur	TF-80/82	1940±110 BP	50±115 BC	66 cal. AD	Upper-most NBP Ware, Period III
Hastinapur	TF-81	2015±95 BP	125±100 BC	32 cal. BC	Upper-most NBP Ware, Period III
Hetimpur	TF-176	2000±100 BP	110±105 BC	1 cal. BC	NBP Period
Hetimpur	TF-177	1820±100 BP	75±105 AD	214 cal. AD	NBP Period
Kausambi	TF-225	2285±105 BP	405±110 BC	390 cal. BC	Mid-level, Mid-NBP Ware, Period III
Kausambi	TF-105	2220±110 BP	335±115 BC	362,282,258 cal. BC	Late-level Mid-NBP Ware, Period III
Kausambi	TF-103	2295±105 BP	415±110 BC	391 cal. BC	Mid-level, Late NBP Ware, Period III
Kausambi	TF-219	2325±100 BP	445±105 BC	396 cal. BC	Mid-level, Mid-NBP Ware, Period III
Kausambi	TF-221	2385±100 BP	505±105 BC	406 cal. BC	Early-level Mid-NBP Period III
Kausambi	TF-226	2110±95 BP	225±100 BC	160,138,124 cal. BC	Late level Mid-NBP Rampart II

Cont. Table 5.6

Table 5.6 Cont.

Site	*Sample No.*	*5568 Yrs.* BP	*Calib. Dates*	*Culture*	*Material*
Kausambi	TF-100	2160±95 BP	275±100 BC	196 cal. BC	Mid-level, Mid-NBP Period III
Kausambi	TF-104	2150±105 BP	265±100 BC	192 cal. BC	Late level, Mid-NBP Period III
Kayatha	TF-674	2350±95 BP	470±100 BC	400 cal. BC	NBP
Kayatha	TF-394	2380±95 BP	500±100 BC	405 cal. BC	NBP with some PGW
Khairadih	PRL-1050	2060±150 BP	170±150 BC	96 cal. BC	NBP
Manjhi	PRL-980	1930±140 BP	37±145 AD	72 cal. AD	Late NBP Period
Manjhi	PRL-983	2350±140 BP	470±145 AD	400 cal. AD	Early NBP
Mathura	PRL-343	2150±100 BP	265±105 BC	192 cal. BC	Late NBP
Mathura	PRL0340	2390±150 BP	510±155 BC	407 cal. BC	PGW/NBP overlap
Mathura	PRL-333	2490±140 BP	615±145 BC	762,678,662 627,600 cal. BC	Late NBP
Mathura	TF-338	2280±100 BP	400±105 BC	387 cal. BC	Late NBP
Mathura	TF-342	2180±160 BP	295±165 BC	340,322,203 cal. BC	Early NBP overlap
Mathura	TF-339	2380±100 BP	500±105 BC	405 cal. BC	Post-NBP
Mathura	TF-337	2340±100 BP	460±105 BC	399 cal. BC	Mid-NBP
Mathura	TF-336	2540±90 BP	665±95 BC	786 cal. BC	Mid-NBP
Mathura	TF-334	2600±150 BP	730±155 BC	801 cal. BC	Early NBP
Narhan	BS-563	2240±100 BP	355±105 BC	370 cal. BC	NBP, Period III
Narhan	BS-564	2200±100 BP	315±105 BC	353,306,236 cal. BC	NBP, Period III
Narhan	BS-581	2100±100 BP	215±105 BC	151,149,11 cal. BC	NBP, Period III
Rajghat	TF-293	2370±105 BP	490±110 BC	403 cal. BC	NBP, Period
Ropar	TF-209	2365±100 BP	485±105 BC	403 cal. BC	NBP Period
Ropar	TF-213	2275±100 BP	395±105 BC	385 cal. BC	NBP Period
Semthan	PRL-946	1880±120 BP	15±125 AD	118 cal. AD	NBP, Period II
Semthan	PRL-945	2280±110 BP	400±115 BC	387 cal. BC	NBP, Period II
Semthan	PRL-941	2200±140 BP	315±145 BC	353,306,236 cal. BC	NBP, Period II
Sohgaura	PRL-182A	2130±90 BP	245±95 BC	177 cal. BC	NBP, Period III
Sohgaura	PRL-183	2466±105 BP	590±110 BC	756,692,541 cal. BC	NBP, Period III
Sohgaura	PRL-182B	2290±400 BP	410±410 BC	391 cal. BC	NBP, Period III
Pirak	LY-1643	2970±140 BP	1110±145 BC 1221 cal. BC	1255,1240,	Period II

TABLE 5.7 DATES OF BLACK-AND-RED WARE SITES

(All BP ages are based on 5568 years half-life of radiocarbon. Calibrated ages are given in BC/AD. After Possehl 1994.)

Site	*Sample No.*	*5568 Yrs.* BP	*Calib. Dates*	*Culture*	*Material*
Chirand	TF-336	2640±95 BP	809 cal. BC	Black-and-Red Ware Period Iron	Charcoal
Khairadih	PRL-1049	2890±150 BP	484,437,424 cal. BC	Black-and-Red Ware	Charcoal
Kilayur	TF-207	2200±100 BP	353,306,236 cal. BC	Black-and-Red Ware	Wood
Mahisdal	TF-389	2565±105 BP	794 cal. BC	Early Iron Age	Charcoal
Rajghat	TF-294	2190±85 BP	348,316,207 cal. BC	Black-and-Red Ware	Charcoal
Rajghat	TF-292	2350±95 BP	400 cal. BC	Black Slipped Ware	Charcoal
Sohgaura	PRL-178	3190±110 BP	1491,1489, 1451 cal. BC	Black-and-Red Ware Chalcolithic	Charcoal
Sohgaura	PRL-179	3090±130 BP	1400 cal. BC	Black-and-Red Ware Chalcolithic	Charcoal
Sringa-verpura	PRL-669	2620±130 BP	805 cal. BC	Black-and-Red Ware	Charcoal
Ujjain	TF-407	1990±100 BP	8 cal. AD	Black-and-Red Ware	Charcoal

MEGALITHIC CULTURE

The Megaliths have a widespread distribution both in Europe and Asia including Japan, Korea, China, Indonesia, Malaysia, Gulf countries (south-eastern Arabia), Sind (near Karachi) in Pakistan, India and the northern parts of Sri Lanka. We do not know why there is such a striking similarity in the use of Megaliths over such a wide geographical area. The European Megaliths are generally much older than the Asian ones as they have been assigned a broad time bracket from 5000 to 2000 BC and quite often are associated with early farming cultures. However, in the Indian subcontinent the Megaliths are generally not older than the 1st millennium BC, barring a few examples such as a cist burial in the Central Himalayas has been dated back to middle of 3rd millennium (Agrawal *et al.* 1995; Kharakwal 1994), the Megaliths of Kashmir have been assigned to mid-2nd millennium BC, the Chalcolithic Megaliths of southern Uttar Pradesh are placed in the second-half of 2nd millennium BC and also at Hallur, Karmanhalli in Karnataka they appear slightly older than the 1st millennium BC. Though voluminous literature has been produced on the Megaliths they still present many enigmas.

In the Indian subcontinent, the Megalithic burials (Fig. 5-5) have been found from Kashmir, Central Himalayas, the Vindhyas, Vidarbha, Deccan and from southern India. In peninsular India, particularly in the states of Kerala, Tamil Nadu, Karnataka and Andhra, the Iron Age is represented by the Megalithic remains and, in fact, this entire region appears to be dotted with Megaliths. In this region we do not have the Chalcolthic phase; the Neolithic

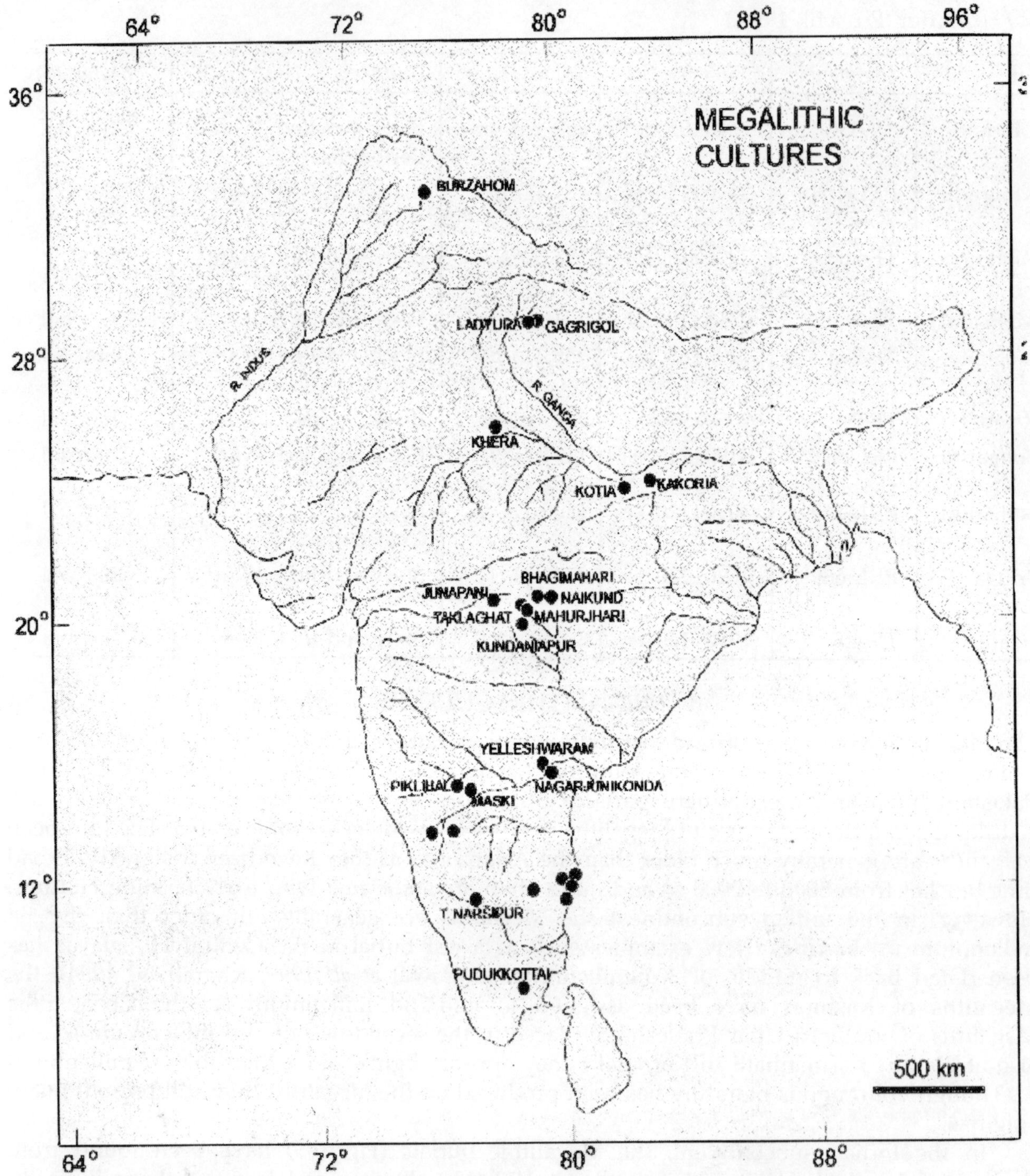

Fig. 5-5. Map showing the main Megalithic sites.

culture is succeeded directly by the Iron Age (Megalithic) remains. It is interesting to learn that some Megalithic traits are still in vogue among some tribal groups in Orissa, Bastar, Chota Nagpur and among the Nagas and Khasis of the north-eastern region of India. It appears to be a sheer coincidence that most of these tribal groups, e.g. Gadaba and Bondos (Orissa), Aka and Apa Tani in the north-eastern India and others use Megalithic burials and cultivate rice (Tiziana and Baldizzone nd: 18). The relationship of these groups has not been worked out so far, though Breeks, as early as 1873, attempted to correlate customs of some of the tribal groups of Nilgiri hills of Tamil Nadu with the Megalithic culture.

Babington (1823: 324-30) was the pioneer to record *pandukulis* as Megalithic monuments in northern Kerala. Subsequently, Taylor (1851, 1862), Henwood (1856: 204-206), Fergusson (1872), Carnac (1877, 1879), Breeks (1873), Foote (1901) and Rea (1915) and others brought to light Megalithic monuments from various parts of South Asia. In this early stage, a large number of "burials were ransacked for archaeological artefacts" (Wheeler 1948: 181) but many scholars attempted to work out the chronology and origin of the Megalithic culture. A large number of sites had come to light by the first quarter of last century and an entire volume of *Man* (a research journal, number 30), was brought out addressing various facets of the Megalithic culture. It was Wheeler (1948: 181-185) who for the first time, after excavating Brahmgiri and Chandravalli in Karnataka in 1944, provided a chronological framework for the Megalithic culture. Soon after this, Krishnaswami (1949) carried out exhaustive explorations in the Chingleput district and discovered over 200 sites. He recorded a variety of monuments and meticulously presented a scientific classification of the then known Megalithic monuments and burials. Even at this early stage, some scholars studied the mortuary practices of various tribal groups, e.g. the Todas (Breeks 1873), Khasis (Gurdon 1914), Gadabas and Bondos (Hutton 1922; Furer Haimendorf 1943).

In the last five decades, considerable research has been carried out across the Indian subcontinent and some important publications like Gordon (1950), Banerjee (1965), Allchin and Allchin (1968), Dikshit (1968) Ramchandran (1971), Leshnik (1974), Sundara (1975), Gururaja Rao (1972), Agrawal (1982: 257-61), Rami Reddi (1992), Moorti (1994), Mohanty and Walimbe (1993 and 1996) and many others have appeared (see for details Mohanty and Selvakumar 2000). Deo (1985) and Mohanty and Selvakumar (2000) have presented an up-to-date review and history of the Megalithic research. The word megalith or Megalithic has invariably been used in literature for burials sites and other structures associated with or without Black-and-Red pottery belonging to the Megalithic culture of Iron Age. According to Deo (1985: 89) there are over 1,400 sites in South Asia, out of which 1,116 are located in peninsular India, whereas Moorti (1994) claims 2000 sites in South India alone. Though there may be many more sites to be added to this preliminary list, the existing number of sites certainly indicates considerably large population. Mohanty and Selvakumar (2000) report that around 100 sites have so far been excavated in the entire subcontinent, which certainly have helped to understand various facets of the culture.

DISTRIBUTION AND TYPOLOGY

Megalithic sites have been found from almost all over the Indian subcontinent. Maharashtra has alone yielded over 300 burials (Carnac 1879). In the north-west zone, a large number of cairns (Piggott 1950) have been found from Pirak, Zhob and Loralai regions whereas Swat and Central Himalayas are marked by rectangular box-like cist burials (Agrawal *et al.* 1991, 1995; Khanduri *et al.* 1998-99; Kharakwal 1992, 1994; Kharakwal and Harbola 1996; Kharakwal *et al.* 1993). Stacul (1987) has compared some of the Swat burial complexes with those of Kashmir. Malari (Garhwal) has yielded crouched horse burials. In fact, such tradition of human burials containing animal skeletons can be traced up to Neolithic southern China and inner Mongolia. In a recent survey, a child burial has been found containing bones of goat, besides a dozen terrocatta pots and a bronze bowl from Malari by Garhwal University. Madhya Pradesh, Maharashtra and Karnataka too have yielded large number of cairns, stone circles and menhirs. In southern Uttar Pradesh, particularly in the Vindhyan hills (G.R. Sharma 1985), a large number of burials have been found. Singh (1985) has identified three different groups, which comprise a variety of cairns with or without stone circles. Jungal Mahal, Mirzapur, Banda, Kakoria and Kotia in Belan valley are some of the important sites. The Chandrabhaga basin in Varanasi district has yielded orthostats, capstones with or without cairn circles. Microliths, bones, pottery and in one case a gold bangle have been found, but no human remains. At Kakoria also, they are associated with Chalcolithic remains, therefore, this group has bee placed between mid-2nd millennium and 3rd century BC (Misra 1977). An iron yielding grave from Kotia, Allahabad has given a ^{14}C date, TF-319, 270 ± 105 BC (uncal.). In the eastern and north-eastern India, Megalithism is still practised (Binodini Devi 1993; O.K. Singh 1985). In Maharashtra cairns and stone circles are predominant whereas Karnataka has the distinction of passage graves and stone alignments. The rock-cut burials and *topikkal*, umbrella types are found in Kerala. Compared to thousands of burials, there are very few habitation sites of this culture and very limited excavations have been carried out in Maharashtra, Karnataka and Andhra Pradesh to understand their lifestyle, e.g. at Bhagimohari, Naikund, Maski, Takalghat.

Over the years, a number of scholars have attempted classification (Agrawal 1982: 257-261; Allchin 1956; Allchin and Allchin 1982: 331-333; Dikshit 1969; K.J. John 1985; Krishnaswami 1949; Moorti 1994; Gururaja Rao 1972; K.P. Rao 1988; Sundara 1979) of the Megalithic burials, but because of space limitations it is not possible here to give each classification. Mohanty and Selvakumar (2000) write that the geographical features as well as cultural choice played a vital role in shaping the architecture of the burials, though they do not illustrate these facts with examples. Following are the only common types. We are not discussing here various sub-types as many regions have more than one type with a lot of variation in material culture as well as in architecture. Unless such features are recorded at micro level in each region, a holistic understanding of the Megalithic culture would not be possible.

Stone Circles: The body was first excarnated and then interred. Grave goods include pots and iron artefacts. Single or double stone circles are made around the pit and sometimes, triple concentric circles have also been found in Vidarbha region andhra and in north Arcot district of Tamil Nadu. Very often cairn fillings have also been found in these circles, hence we are not calling cairns as one more sub-type. A large number of cairn burials are found in the north-western part of the subcontinent and are termed Zangian and Jiwanri type.

Cists: These graves have a variety of forms, e.g. dolmenoid, port-hole, rectangular box-like structure, oblong chambers, etc. They are common in Andhra-Karnataka, Kerala, southern Uttar Pradesh and Uttaranchal and are made out of large slabs with one or more capstones. And they are either entirely buried, partially buried or sometimes made right on the surface. They may contain single or multiple burials. Generally in South India a single or multiple stone circle surrounds the cists.

Rock-cut chambers: Rock-cut pits and passage chambers and rock-cut caves used for burials are found in Malabar region of Kerala. The Megalithic people cut these chambers in the laterite rocks.

Sarcophagus: The sarcophagus urns of burnt clay are either boat-shaped with separate lid or at times have animal(ram)-shaped heads. They have been found from Andhra, Karnataka and other areas in South India. Apart from human skeletal remains, sometime pottery and iron objects have also been found in them.

Urns: The practice of burying excarnated bones in urns seems to be a Neolithic trait. They are generally marked by cap-stones or stone circles and have been found in large number on the eastern coast in Tamil Nadu and Kerala.

Menhir and Alignments: Menhirs (known as Nadukal in Kerala) were perhaps erected in the memoy of the dead and are found in Kerala andhra Pradesh, Karnataka, Chhatisgarh, Kashmir and in the north-eastern region. In Gulbarga district of Karnataka and south of Hyderabad, a large number of erected stones (height ranging from 2 to 6 m) are arranged in squares or diagonals. In Kashmir, menhirs are however, arranged in a semicircle. Some such tradition of menhir is still alive in the north-east, particularly in Manipur (O.K. Singh 1985). The Megalithic memorials are erected either inside or outside the village by the Mao Naga people. One can erect such Megalithic memorial in his name only after performing a sequence of feasts of merit. This kind of tradition obviously suggests that perhaps Megaliths were not only erected for funerary but also to commemorate various ritualistic purposes and feast of merit, etc.

There has been a strong tradition across South Asia to erect memorial stone or hero-stones for various regions, e.g. saving their community, crops, animals, etc. Such hero-stones are known by different names such as Birsthambh, Birkhambh, Veerakkal, etc. In Kerala literary references are available for such stones right from the early centuries of the Christian era (John 1985: 487)., a large number of such stones have been recorded in Central Himalayas (Kharakwal 1993), Pali district of Rajasthan, Nepal (Dilli Sharma 1997); Tim Harvard (Pers. Comm.), Maharashtra (Setter and Sontheimer 1982). The huge memorial stone erected at Shakti Sthal, Delhi in the memory of late Prime Minister Indira Gandhi could be taken as the latest example of this tradition.

Kodakkal: It is a mushroom-shaped monument found only in Kerala. They have a capstone resting on four dressed laterite orthostats, each with a pronounced external surface and flat internal surface and conical in shape. These orthostats are placed in squarish or rectangular fashion sheltering an urn burial. A huge hemispherical (looks like mushroom or umbrella) capstone was placed on top of these orthostats. They have been found in Palghat, Trichur, Malappuram, Calicut and Cannanore districts of Kerala.

Toppikkal: Toppikkals are, in fact, a kind of urn burials. They have been generally found close to Kodakkals in Kerala only. The capstone is convex on top and with a flat base. They are placed to cover a sunken pit containing a pot. Human bones are found inside the pot.

Moorti (1994) has grouped all these types under two broad categories, i.e. sepulchral (pit, chamber, legged and unlegged burials) and non-sepulchral (either commemorative or memorial in nature). According to his broad classification, the Indian Megalithic burials and monuments are largely sepulchral in character. The antiquity of burial practice in South Asia dates back to the Mesolithic period and this tradition continued down to the Neolithic, Chalcolithic and Iron Age periods. It seems that this tradition became popular only during the Iron Age, as during this period, for the first time, the Megalithic burials were reported from almost all the regions, barring few pockets, e.g. upper and middle Ganga doab.

Though one finds several types of burials, as explained above and elaborate architecture too, in most cases the burials are fractional and the preservation is very poor hence very few complete skeletons have been reported. Various scholars have undertaken studies of skeletal remains in different regions in the last century (Kennedy 1975, 1984; Walimbe 1992). Initially such studies were focused on racial affinities to find out the authors of the Megaliths. In recent years, with advancement of methodology, a number of facets such as pathological aspects, sex determination, trauma, food habits, etc., have also been studied and it has been suggested that the Iron Age society was not homogeneous. No solid evidence of immigration of new people from outside is available as suggested by Gururaja Rao (1972). Mohanty and Walimbe (1993) made a bold suggestion for the Vidarbha Megaliths that burials were not constructed for everyone in the society, perhaps by and large people were cremated as evidence of cremation has also been cited from Kaniyathirtham and other sites (Mohanty and Selvakumar 2000).

Various scholars have attempted to study literary references, found in Vedic and Sangam literature and mortuary traditions prevalent among several tribal groups in India (Gupta 1969; Arokiaswamy 1952; Srinivasan 1946). Srinivasan studied the Sangam texts and concluded that the Megalithic traditions gradually disappeared from South India after 300 BC due to the "impact of Aryan ideas". Pant (1985: 482-83) also draws attention to references of burial traditions in Vedic literature. He finds the description of *Satpatha Brahmana* very close to the cairns of Jangal Mahal. According to the reference, the body was first cremated and the remains collected in a pot and buried. He writes that, "After a long time the pot was unearthed and contents reburied according to the rules prescribed". It seems that this kind of interpretation does not hold true for the cairns across the country.

In the Vidarbha region, the burials are marked by an abundance of iron tools and Black-and-Red pottery, which Prakash and Tripathi (1986) have categorized as Zone D. All these burials are no more inside habitations, as was the practice in the Neolithic times. Mohanty and Walimbe (1993, 1996) have done anthropological and demographic studies of Megaliths in Vidarbha area and they conclude that the child burial practice was common in peninsular region during the Neolithic and Chalcolithic periods, however, such burials are rarely found in the Megalithic complexes. They also conclude that burials were not made for everyone as most of them, irrespective of sex, belong to the age group ranging between 18 and 35, who met a traumatic, accidental or untimely death. Soil analysis has been undertaken for various sites, e.g. Burzahom, Mahurjhari, Naikund, Raipur, Sanana-Baseri and others to examine organic carbon, phosphate and various activities (Joshi *et al.* 1982; Deotare 1984; Kshirsagar 1992; Farswan and Nautiyal 1997) and it was found that in Maharashtra the pots and copper utensils served a symbolic purpose. The Kumauni (Uttaranchal) burials are rich in phosphorous content, indicating the presence of decomposed skeletal remains.

In the Vidarbha region, near Nagpur, Megalithic graves have been excavated at Takalaghat-Khapa, Junapani and Mahurjhari. These Megaliths comprise stone circles with pits in which are interred fragmentary excarnated bones, occasionally accompanied by horse bones. The interesting discovery of this region is the furnace at Naikund, complete with tuyeres and slag flowing from its holes. Deo has pointed out several similarities in ceramics, iron tools, etched carnelian beads and graffiti marks on potsherds between the Vidarbha and the peninsular Megalithic cultures. The iron objects of this region appear more sophisticated as the assemblage includes a variety of war-like weapons too, e.g. sword, spearhead, ladle, knife, arrowhead, chisel, axe, spike along with fish-hook, bangle, horse bit, cauldron, etc. (Deo 1970).

Mahurjhari iron has 0.9 per cent carbon, comparable to the rust-free Delhi iron pillar of *c.* AD 400. From western India, Hegde has reconstructed the iron technology of Early Historic cultures (Hegde 1973: 416).

In fact, the Iron Age in South India is almost wholly known only from the burials, Prakash and Tripathi (1986) have termed this region as Zone E. The peninsular India has emerged as the nuclear area of the Megalithic burials and in recent years some of them, e.g. at Tadkanhalli, Hallur, etc., have been assigned to 1200 BC date (see review paper Mohanty and Selvakumar 2000). It appears that there was an abrupt change from the Neolithic stage into the Iron Age, without any significant intermediate Chalcolithic stage. At Hallur in Karnataka, there are a couple of layers termed transitional between the Neolithic and the Iron Age (Nagraja Rao 1971). However, the Neolithic blade industry ends abruptly in Hallur Period I and does not continue into Period II (Iron Age). Even iron appears only in the middle levels of Period II. The Iron Age habitations are not adequately explored and the sites so far known have flimsy deposits and therefore, the evidence is confined to the Megaliths only.

CERAMICS

Most of the Megalithic complexes are characterized by the presence of Black-and-Red Ware though few other wares were also found, e.g. Micaceous Red Ware, Red Ware, Black Ware Russet Coated and Painted, grey or earthenware in different regions. Micaceous Red Ware has been generally found in Vidarbha region, Russet Coated and Painted Ware is associated with the remains in Kerala, Grey Ware or Earthenware and Black Ware have been found from Central Himalayan cists. The Black-and-Red Ware, which is either plain or white painted, has surprising uniformity all over the peninsula. Since the Black-and-Red Ware is also found with many other antecedent Bronze Age as well as contemporary Iron Age cultures, it could give us a good clue to study symbiosis between cultures in different areas, especially in South India and cultural continuity across the terrain. We should try to find out "Why this particular ceramic type was shared by many regional cultures? This may also help to understand the origin and development of Megalithic tradition. In general, the pottery shapes are conical or looped lids, carinated vases, bulbous or globular pots, a variety of bowls with convex or pronounced or tapering sides, flat base and projecting rim or featureless rim and pedestalled bowls, spouted dishes. Leshnik (1974) and McIntosh (1985) have done typological study of ceramics with an aim to provide a chronological sequence to the burial complexes. Krishnan (1997) has carried out technical analysis of slip, fabric and firing temperature.

In peninsular India, a number of sites, e.g. Kodumandal and others have yielded graffiti marks and *Brahmi* letters on pottery. Lal (1960) finds some similarity between the graffiti marks of the Harappan and Megalithic pottery. Some scholars believe that they may be potter's marks (Rajan 1994: 116-22).

SUBSISTENCE

The number of known habitation sites is still exceptionally low compared to the burials, which may be due to the lack of our systematic approach/intensive explorations to locate the habitation sites in different regions. The Megalithic people were perhaps agro-pastoralists and certainly engaged in agricultural activity as a large number of habitation sites as well as burials have yielded plant remains, e.g. Maski and Hallur (Vishnu-Mittre 1971), Naikund (Kajale 1982), Bhagimohari (Kajale 1989) and others. Coupled with this kind of evidence is the fact that a number of sites have also yielded agricultural implements. They cultivated rice, barley, wheat, kodo, millet, job's tear, common pea, lentil, grass pea, horse gram, red gram, etc.

Archaeolozoological studies have been carried out at a large number of sites, e.g., Maski, Brahmagiri, T. Narshipur, Mahurjhari, Bhagimohari, Naikund, Sangankallu, Raipur and others by various scholars to understand the economy and subsistence (see for details Thomas and Joglekar 1994; Mohanty and Selvakumar 2000). Domestic animals like cattle, buffalo, sheep, goat, pig, ass, dog, horse have been identified in addition to a variety of wild animals, which were perhaps consumed. At several sites in Maharashtra such as Naikund, Raipur and Mahurjari, Sanur and other sites, animal bones, e.g. cattle, sheep, goat, domestic fowl and horse have been found from burials. In the case of Raipur, Thomas (1992: 77-8) thinks that stallions of 3.5 to 6 years were sacrificed. In fact, horse bones are more common in burials than other animals. Even charred bones of horse have also been found from Naikund and Bhagimohari, which indicate that the animal was also consumed. At Bhagimohari among the faunal remains birds account for 19.89 per cent and Thomas (1993) thinks that bird hunting could have been one of the major subsistence at the site. The dental pathology indicates a mixed food habit. The discovery of large number of bone tools have also been interpreted as the result of scarcity of metal at Bhagimohari and other sites.

ART

Few Megalithic sites particularly in South India have yielded engravings on the Megaliths of the burials or paintings in the nearby shelters particularly at Navilthirtha in the Malprabha basin in Karnataka (Sundara 1985), Perumukkal, Tamil Nadu (Rajan 1996), Kerala (Mohanty and Selvakumar 2000: 321). In recent years, a large number of cupules and cup-marks have also been found from Megalithic contexts from Vidarbha, Karnataka and Central Himalayan and other regions. Some burials have even been found marked by anthropomorphic figures (Narsimhiah 1980). The evidence of art objects has also been found from the excavations. The menhirs in Central Indian area have also been stated to represent nude human figures.

ORIGIN

Initial studies of skeletal remains suggested that the Megalithic people belong to the proto-Australoid, Negroid and Mediterranean groups (Sarcar 1960, 1972; Gupta and Dutta 1962). The peninsular Indian and Sri Lankan Megaliths appear to belong to the same stock of people. Gupta (1970-71) found close parallels of Indian Megaliths, as far as architecture is concerned, in Oman and hence suggested that origin of the Indian Megalithic culture may have been affected by foreign elements. In the Perumal hills, Madura district, Aiyyapan excavated two graves, the pottery and horse bits from which have close parallels in Sialk Necropole B. Loofs-Wissowa (1985) has attempted to find relationship between South Indian and Thailand's Megaliths. The tradition of making relic chamber in U-Thong of Lawa, belonging to the Mon-Khmer linguistic group, is identical to the ones found in stupas. Hence there is a possibility of South-East Asian elements in the South Asian burials.

About the Caucasian affinities of the Indian Megalithis, Parpola (1998) writes,

> The nearest large group of port-hole Megaliths are the cemeteries in the Kuban region east of the Black Sea and in the Caucasus, dated to the early centuries of the 1st millennium BC. These two groups are linked by port-hole Megaliths at the Sialk B necropolis (*c.* 1000-800 BC) in north-western Iran and at Las Bela in

south Baluchistan have been compared with Sialk B, which is supposed to reflect the coming of Iranian tribes from the steppes north of the Caucasus. Bands of Cinnerians are known to have come from the Kuban area over the Caucasus to Iran around 800 BC (Jettmar 1967: 23-25,48-50). Thus the Megalithic culture may have been brought into India by horse-riding and warring nomads, probably speaking a west Aryan/Old Iranian language. In India, the Megalithic invaders were comparatively few in relation to the earlier inhabitants and are likely to have quickly become linguistically assimilated to the local Dravidian speakers (Parpola 1994: 171f)…. In North India, the Megalithic invasion may be the historical reality behind the white-skinned Pandavas, who, coming from Rajasthan (Virata), conquered the Kuru lands. Herodotus (1,216) described their polyandrous customs. The Pandavas are first mentioned in Late Vedic texts and their association with Mathura (Krishna) also places them into the later phase of the PGW (from *c.* 800 BC).

It is not easy to trace the Megaliths to one source as they seem to have incorporated diverse elements. The cist graves have parallels in the southern Arabian coast and the Levant also. Sarcophagi are common in Bahrain, Failaka and Mesopotamia.

Kennedy and Levisky (1985) have undertaken analysis of a large number of skeletal remains from various Megalithic sites and conclude that the "Indian Iron Age populations were relatively heterogeneous and not representative of a single homogeneous racial element" (1985: 461).

We would like to suggest that unless we have an exhaustive study of skeletal material from South Asia, we must be careful in crediting the origin of Megalithic culture to the foreign elements, as the analysis carried out by Caldwell and Kennedy (1995) at Karamanhalli also does not indicate any alien elements in skeletal remains. In South Asia, the burial tradition had begun since the Mesolithic period, if not earlier and the Harappans and the Neolithic folks also buried their dead, but they were simple in architecture. It is only during the Iron Age, the Megalithic people innovated elaborate burials. May be different types of burials belong to different groups of people and in course of time their diverse styles became common in wide geographic regions, e.g. Oman to South Asia, South-East Asia and to the Far East.

CHRONOLOGY

After his excavations at Brahmagiri (Pl 5-3) and Chandravalli in Karnataka, Wheeler (1948) placed the Megalithic culture between 2nd century BC and 1st century AD. His time bracket was tentative as it was based on stratigraphic position and relative dating. In the course of time, a large number of sites have been dated by radiocarbon and thermoluminescence (TL) methods (Agrawal and Yadav 1995) and most sites have been bracketed between the end of 2nd millennium BC and early centuries of the Christian era. Most of the absolute dates belong to the habitation sites.

The ^{14}C dates suggest that the Megalithic culture of Karnataka and Andhra Pradesh had an earlier beginning than those of Kerala. In fact, the earliest dates for iron come from Hallur (1100 BC), Karnataka where Neolithic-Megalithic overlap has been found. Nagaraja Rao (1985) undertook excavation of some graves at Tadakanhalli in Karnataka and finds that the painted Black-and-Red Ware and iron tools are identical to the ones found from Period II at Hallur and hence he proposes Tadakanhalli as one of the earliest grave sites. The TL dates (PRL TL-47, 1290+90 BC; PRL TL-50, 1270+170 BC) from Kumaranhalli also strongly support the early beginning of Iron Age in Karnataka. In Karnataka, Tamil Nadu and Kerala, the Megalithic traits continued in the early centuries of the Christian era (Mohanty and Selvakumar 2000; Possehl and Gullapalli 1999: 158). The Megaliths of Vidarbha generally fall between *c.* 600 BC and 200 BC.

In the Vindhyan region, however, the so-called "Chalcolithic-Megaliths" (pre-Iron Age) have been assigned a bracket of 1500 to 1000 BC, whereas the Iron Age Megaliths in this very region have been generally dated between 8th and 3rd century BC (P. Singh 1985: 475; Sharma 1985: 480). Moving further north in the Central Himalayas, the evidence of iron smelting has been dated close to 1st millennium BC, whereas a cist burial at Gagrigol was found beneath a soil horizon dated to mid-3rd millennium BC (Agrawal *et al.* 1995). At Gufkral in Kashmir, the Megalithic remains belonging to Pd II, have been dated to mid-2nd millennium BC (A.K. Sharma 1982). Tentatively it can be suggested that the Iron Age cultures had appeared in South Asia as early as mid-2nd millennium BC. But iron as a commodity became available only in the 1st millennium BC.

TABLE 5.8 DATES OF MEGALITHIC SITES (SOUTH INDIA) (after Possehl 1994)

(All BP ages are based on 5568 years half-life of radiocarbon. Calibrated ages are given in BC/AD.)

Site	*Sample No.*	*5568 Yrs.* BP	*Calib. Dates*	*Culture*	*Material*
Halingali	TF-685	1970±95 BP	22 cal. BC	Megalithic, Neolithic	Charcoal
Hallur	TF-570	2970±105 BP	1255,1240, 1221 cal. BC	Period II, Neolithic/ Iron Age Overlap	Charcoal
Hallur	TF-573	2820±100 BP	993 cal. BC	Period II, Neolithic/ Iron Age Overlap	Charcoal
Hathinia Hill	TF-109	30 ± 90 BP	1955 cal. BC	Megalithic	Charcoal
Korkai	TF-987	2680±90 BP	828 cal. BC	Megalithic, Ancient port	Wood
Naikund	BS-94	2495±105 BP	763,675,665 620,604 cal. BC	Megalithic	Charcoal
Naikund	BS-92	2455±100 BP	753,704,533 cal. BC	Megalithic	Charcoal
Paiyampalli	TF-828	2100±95 BP	151,149,117 cal. BC	Megalithic	Charcoal
Paiyampalli	TF-824	785±90 BP	1256 cal. BC	Megalithic	Charcoal
Paiyampalli grain	TF-823	2515±100 BP	786 cal. BC	Megalithic	Charred
Paiyampalli	TF-825	695±95 BP	1280 cal. AD	Megalithic?	Charcoal
T. Narsipur	TF-414	220±90 BP	1660 cal. AD	Megalithic	Charcoal
Togara Palli	PRL-134	2180±100 BP	340,322,203 cal. BC	Megalithic	Charcoal
Togara Palli	PRL-135	2150±110 BP	192 cal. BC	Megalithic	Charcoal
Veerapuram	PRL-727	2090±140 BP	110 cal. BC	Megalithic	Charcoal
Veerapuram	PRL-730	3150±140 BP	1428 cal. BC	Megalithic	Charcoal
Veerapuram	PRL-725	1780±140 BP	239 cal. AD	Megalithic	Charcoal
Veerapuram	PRL-728	2870±140 BP	1035 cal. BC	Megalithic	Charcoal

TABLE 5.9 DATES OF MEGALITHIC SITES (GANGA DOAB) (after Possehl 1994.)

(All BP ages are based on 5568 years half-life of radiocarbon. Calibrated ages are given in BC.)

Site	*Sample No.*	*5568 Yrs.* BP	*Calib. Dates*	*Culture*	*Material*
Kakoria	TF-183	200±95	1666, 1790, 1949, 1952 AD	Megalithic	Charcoal
Kakoria	TF-179	195±90	1668, 1783, 1791, 1948, 1953 AD	Megalithic	Charcoal
Kotia	TF-319	2135±100	182 cal. BC	Megalithic	Charcoal

IRON AND OTHER METAL TOOLS

A variety of metal objects such as iron, copper-bronze and gold have been found from Megalithic burials and sites. Of course, the bronze and gold artefacts represent a meagre percentage in the repertoire. Of the iron implements, the main types are axes with crossed straps, sickles, tripods, tridents, spearheads, swords, lamp hangers, arrowheads and lamps. Bronze artefacts ike horse-harness, bits, bangles, rings, bowls and bells are also common (Wheeler 1947-48: 180; Deo 1985). An iron dagger with copper handle is an important discovery from Chandoli, Maharashtra, as far as metallurgical development is concerned. The gold ornaments were found from Arippa, Kerala, Mahurjhari and other sites in peninsular area. It is quite likely that the Hutti gold mines of Karnataka were exploited by the Megalithic people of Maski (Thapar 1957). Occasionally, beads of etched carnelian, gold ornaments and sundry objects of copper or stone are also associated with the Megaliths (Sundara 1975).

PART B: IRON TECHNOLOGY AND ASSOCIATED ISSUES

HISTORY OF IRON AGE STUDIES

In South Asia, unlike the studies on the Bronze and Stone Ages, research on ancient iron technology and associated cultures has been limited. Chakrabarti (1976 and 1992) delineates different stages of research on Indian iron, deals with the beginning of iron technology and gives a detailed account of pre-industrial iron working. Here we would like to give only a summary.

According to Chakrabarti, the first phase (*c.* AD 1795-1850) was marked by a scientific interest in understanding the properties and the manufacturing process of pre-industrial Indian steel, which came to be known in Europe as wootz. This word was derived from the Kannada term *ukku,* meaning steel. That pre-industrial Indian steel had a reputation in contemporary Europe is exemplified by its sale in Hamburg in the 18th century as Indian steel and also was referred to by Remour in 1722 in his memoirs. The first significant publication on the subjectwas by George Pearson in (1795: 322-46 cited from Chakrabarti 1992), following which Chakrabarti (1992) mentions various reports, which described the extent, distribution and methods of pre-industrial iron-smelting particularly in eastern India by the Kol tribe. Among the early scholars, the writings of J.M. Heath (1839: 390-7) are of great interest as far as the antiquity and origin of iron is concerned. He writes, "The antiquity of the Indian process is no less astonishing than its ingenuity.... One can hardly doubt that the tools with which the Egyptians covered their obelisks and temples of porphyry and syenite with hieroglyphs were made of Indian steel". In this context Heath referred to the classical writers, who mentioned an Indian gift of steel to Alexander.

In the second phase (1850-1930), according to Chakrabarti (1992), the earlier metallurgical interest continued as a number of scholars contributed studies on the pre-industrial metallurgy, distribution of ores and geological context, contemporary iron smelting practices among various tribal groups. Besides these, origin and antiquity of iron and steel from very early period in India and the relevance of literary data were emphasized. In 1914, Neogi attempted to analyse the whole range of data systematically. Writings based on archaeological data, without much attention given to origin and expansion of iron technology, mark the next phase (1930 to mid-1980s). D.H. Gordon (1950) and Banerjee (1965) were concerned about the beginning of Iron Age and attempted to explain the development with a diffusionist viewpoint.

Finally, Chakrabarti claims that the current phase (1976 onwards) deals with a definitive study of the problem. A band of scholars like Hegde (1973, 1991), Bharadwaj (1979), Gogte (1982), Chakrabarti (1992), Sahi (1976), Tripathi (1984-85, 1990), Prakash (1984, 1991), Narayan (1990 cited from Vibha Tripathi 1994), Chattopadyaya and De (1984), Agrawal *et al.* (1995) have contributed to archaeometallurgy and addressed various other issues related to Iron Age cultures. Agrawal (2000) has dealt with the beginning of iron technology in South Asia in a global perspective. Chakrabarti has identified six early iron-using centres in the subcontinent: Baluchistan; the north-west; the Indo-Ganga divide and the upper Ganga valley; eastern India; Malwa and Berar in Central India; and the Megalithic South India. This scheme, however, slightly differs from Prakash and Tripathi (1986). A look at the list of iron ore occurrences shows that all these early centres overlap. The evidence of pre-industrial smelting also comes from almost all these areas and indicates an apparent continuity between the early and the contemporary (pre-industrial) traditions of iron metallurgy in India.

Ore Bearing Regions and Iron Ores

Chakrabarti (1976: 116-117) has worked out a long list of iron ore bearing regions of South Asia, on the basis of the various geological reports (Ball 1881; Dunn 1942; Krishnan 1951, 1954; Krishnan and Aiyengar 1954; Roy Chowdhury 1955; Roy 1959; Hunday and Banerjee 1967). He gives the following list:

Sind: Ranikot area (magnetite, red and brown hematite).

Baluchistan: Bolan area (clay iron-stone).

north-west Frontier zone: Bajaur (black magnetic iron sand), Bannu (earthy hematite), Hazara (magnetite and hematite) and Waziri hills (limonite); evidence of pre-industrial smelting.

Kashmir: different parts of the state (magnetite, hematite, limonite and other sedimentary ores); pre-industrial smelting.

Salt Range and Kot Kerana hills: earthy hematite.

Punjab and Uttar Pradesh Himalayas (now known as Uttaranchal), Kangra (magnetic and micaceous), Shele near Simla (magnetic and micaceous), Mandi (magnetic and hematite, micaceous schists), Sirmur (magnetite, probably mixed with specular ore), Kulu, Nainital, Almora, Garhwal (red and brown hematite); pre-industrial smelting.

Patiala: brown hematite and magnetite; pre-industrial smelting.

Rajasthan: Alwar, Jaipur, Udaipur, Ajmer, Bharatpur, Bundi, Jodhpur, Kota (hematite, magnetite, limonite); pre-industrial smelting.

Gujarat: Surat, Panchmahals, Rewa Kantha, Abmedabad, Kachchh, Kathiwar (lateritic ore in Kachchh-Kathiawar; pre-industrial smelting.

Central India: Bhilsa (lateritic ore), Ujjain, Shajapur, Shivpuri, Mandasore; the ore of the Vindhyan system principally in Mandasore and that of the Gwalior series in Gwalior; the ore of the Bijawar series in Indore, Jhahua and Dhar; also, hematite in Lalitpur, Hoshangabad, Narsinghpur, Nimar; important deposits in Bastar, Chanda, Durg; Jabalpur, Bilaspur, Banda, Mandla, Rewa, Bundelkhand; re-industrial smelting and traces of mining. The iron ore bearing region between Agra and Gwalior appear to be popular as the inustry of Gwalior has also been mentioned by Abul Fazal in his *Ain-i-Akbari* (ed. Blochman, p. 47). Some scholars propose this area as one of the important sources of iron for the Ganga valley people (Makhan Lal 1986).

Maharashtra: Konkan laterite; Ratnagiri, Kolhapur, Mahabaleshwar, Goa; pre-industrial smelting.

Mysore: Laterite of south Konkan; hematite-quartzites and titaniferous ores; magnetic sand; Tumkur, Mysore, Chitaldurg, Kadur, Kolar, Shimoga; pre-industrial smelting.

Kerala: Magnetite and laterite, also black magnetic sand; Malabar and Travancore; pre-industrial smelting.

Madras: Magnetite, hematite, laterite, specular ores; Tinnevelly, Madura, Salem, Trichinopoly, Coimbattur, Nilgiris, Pudukottai, Chingleput, north and south Arcots; pre-industrial smelting.

Andhra: Magnetite, hematite, limonite, etc.; Cuddapah-Kurnool, Guntur, Bellary, Nellore, west Godavari, Krishna, Vizagapatanam, Hyderabad; pre-industrial smelting.

Orissa: Laterite outside the delta; magnetite, hematite of Bonai-Keonjhar, Talcher, Sambalpur, Mayurbhanj; pre-industrial smelting.

West Bengal: different ore-types including the magnetic sand in the western and northern parts of the state; pre-industrial smelting.

Assam: Clay iron-stone and an impure limonite in upper Assam; titaniferous magnetic iron sand in the Khasi Jaintia hills; pre-industrial smelting.

Bihar: various ore-types in the entire Chota Nagpur block; pre-industrial smelting.

Uttar Pradesh: Magnetite and magnetic sand in Mirzapur.

Scores of pre-industrial iron mining and smelting sites (to name a few, Lukhani, Uleni, Agar, Raulkuri, Chhani, Lob, etc., in Kumaun and Lohariya, Ghatol, Iswal, Aguchha, Anjani, Nathara ki Pal, Kikwawas, Chhipikhera, Devgarh, Udaipur, etc., in Rajasthan) have been located by us in recent years (Agrawal and Kharakwal 1998; Kharakwal in press). It is apparent from the above list that except for alluvial tracts of the Indo-Ganga doab, iron ore has been reported from all the regions and pre-industrial smelting has also been found in several areas attesting to the awareness of the quality of iron (Chakrabarti 1976).

Following main iron bearing minerals are found in different regions of India:

Magnetite: a black magnetic stone; Mhos hardness 5.5 to 6.5. Specific gravity 5.4; containing 72.4 per cent iron when pure; it is Fe_3O_4.

Hematite: a sesquioxide of iron, with about 70 per cent iron when pure. Specific gravity 5; Mhos hardness 5 to 5.5; chemically it is Fe_2O_3.

Limonite: hydrated iron oxide; hardness 4 to 5.5; specific gravity 2.7 to 4.3.

Goethite: it occurs in lateritic soils; specific gravity 3.3 to 4.3.

Siderite or Chalybite: Chemically it is $FeC0_3$; with only 48.3 per cent iron when pure.

Pyrite: Chemically FeS_2; with only 46.5 per cent iron.

Gossan: it is the multi-mineral red iron cap on an exposed sulphide deposit whose Chalcopyrite ($CuFeS_2$) has oxidized and iron leached out.

Ethnography and Ethnoarchaeological Data

As it is clear from the above list, the pre-industrial iron working was prevalent almost in all iron ore-bearing regions of South Asia. There are various communities, itinerant smiths and tribal groups who still practice traditional ironsmithy and have kept the technology alive. It seems that iron was manufactured in ancient India by non-urban guilds, which were called as *kammagramas* in *Arthasastra*. They were outside the state control and therefore, there were complaints about them. In recent decades, some scholars have carried out ethnographic and ethnoarchaeological studies to understand the ancient iron technology (Agrawal and Kharakwal 1998; Misra 1996-97; Tripathi and Tripathi 1994; and Tripathi and Mishra 1997: 59-68). The evidence from China and West Asia also seems to show a similar pattern as self-sufficient iron making communities played a significant role during the Han dynasty in China for iron production (Wagner 1992). It therefore appears that though metal technology was conducive to urbanization processes, it was essentially a contribution of the non-urban communities (Agrawal 2000).

The contribution of Vibha Tripathi and her colleagues, who have largely worked in the Ganga doab sites and Central India, has proved very useful to understand the ancient techniques. Tripathi (2001a), Tripathi and Tripathi (1994) and Tripathi and Misra (1997) have reported their ethnoarchaeological studies based on Chhattisgarh area in Central India, where they found that the pre-industrial iron workers generally live close to the mieral deposits. They did not need to dig deeper to reach the desired ore, as it was available on the surface. In one trip they could cover about 15-20 km and collect about 45-60 kg of ores, which they could smelt within 3-4 days. Several families of the village are involved in this kind of search. In some areas they found that iron produced by traditional smelters is preferred by the local people because of its high durability, ductility and capacity to provide a better cutting edge. Some scholars think that the pre-industrial smelting was wasteful and low yielding as only 4-5 kg of iron was produced from about 15-20 kg of ore. Tripathi and Misra (1997), however, argue that using high percentage of charcoal in traditional working was rewarding as it produced steely iron, as it carburizes and hardens iron, making it malleable and providing the object with a sharper and longer lasting working edge. They found that the Chhattisgarh smelters use about 30-40 kg of charcoal for 15-20 kg ore, i.e. more than double the amount. Earlier, Hughes (1873) also reported similar observations from Central Provinces.

The processes of ore dressing (hand-picking, crushing, winnowing, density separation), smelting techniques in different parts of India and steel production are very important and certainly useful for understanding ancient iron working (Tripathi and Tripathi 1994). They think that pre-industrial iron working was like a cottage industry to meet limited demand of people. The smiths were completely aware of the properties of the ore and produced desired quality of iron. They knew how to control temperature of furnace and produce steel based on their close observation and long experience. Generally "a ritualistic aroma prevailed the workplace and technique and prayers were offered for a successful process" (Elvin 1942). "Technology spread must have been painfully slow and difficult due to the secretive attitude... thus confined the technology in the hands of a few families in a village". It is surprising enough that the smiths of Pariah (South India) and crucible steel-makers of Salem were ignorant of each other (Holland 1892). This kind of ethnographic data strongly suggest that there may have been various centres of independent iron origin and working in ancient India, as Holland (1892) also thought about a century ago (Tripathi and Tripathi 1994).

Tripathi and Mishra (1997: 59-68) mention the following special features of pre-industrial metallurgy:

1. The size of the furnace is very small, barring a few exceptions. The height of the furnace varies between 0.6 and 1.2 m and diameter at the base 0.25 m-0.5 m.
2. In Central India (Chhattisgarh), the tribals are very particular about the type of wood (sal or teak) they use to make charcoal for fuel, the clay, the time and the spot chosen for smelting (as external humidity supposedly affects their working) and the ores that they use. The fuel used is supposed to be lower in sulphur and phosphorous contents. Generally no flux is used, even when lime, which removes sulphur from the products, is easily available. Several such groups, perhaps due to its better workability, use the magnetite bearing sand from rivers as ore. And they do not want to take the risk of experimenting with other ores. The temperature in the furnace is not uniform. It is around 600°C in the upper portion, going up to 1300°-1400°C or sometimes nearly as high as 1500°C near the tuyere. The traditional smelter is constrained by the low temperature in the furnace and the process is fine-tuned to his requirements, otherwise any rise in the slag melting temperature can ruin the product, hence the temperature control is very important.
3. The smelters were capable of producing a variety of iron similar to wootz steel of South India. Ingots of this steel have been analysed. It is a high quality steely iron with a homogeneous structure. They inform that white iron or *chakra loha* was obtained from magnetitic sand in Sarguja district, Madhya Pradesh and the Mahuli Agarias are good artisans of this product, which is alo used for making weapons. Even gun-barrels are clandestinely made from this iron or steel because of its superior quality.
4. They suggest that the ethnographic data of pre-industrial iron working technology tallies closely with the archaeological evidence. As the small pits (20-25 cm), filled with ash, charcoal and bits of slag occasionally found in association with finished iron objects from Painted Grey Ware, Black-and-Red Ware or Megalithic cultures, perhaps using the bloomery process of smelting, represent the remains of ancient smelting/forging activity. Some efforts have been made to reconstruct these iron working processes by Gogte (1982) for the Naikund site, Hegde (1973, 1991) for Dhatwa, Tripathi and Tripathi (1997) for Khairadih, Uttar Pradesh.

Tripathi and Tripathi (1994) have illustrated different stages of iron mining, smelting and production of pre-industrial iron working. Tylecote suggested that the ancient people preferred low-grade ores like magnetite as it was easier to crush and smelt them than ores with higher iron content. Some Central Indian tribes also use river-sand as ore. Tripathi and Tripathi (1994) however, could only be partially correct while generalising the inferences in a pan-Indian context that iron deposits are easily available on the surface, therefore very little mining was required. However, in most of the areas of Kumaun (Lukhani, Asurchula, Agar), Rajasthan (Ghatol, Loharia, Iswal, Aguchha and others), eastern Madhya Pradesh (Agaria belt) and many other areas, small shafts (measuring 1 to 2 m) and more deeper mining pits (ranging from 1 to 10 m) have been dug obviously to obtain better quality of ore.

Misra (1996-97) has also carried out ethnographic study in Bastar district in Central India and reports that the Muria tribe people still practice traditional metallurgy. They smelt the ore, which they mine from Bailadilla range, in close furnaces and employ air blast by a pair of foot-operated bellows. To obtain 1 kg of iron, about 8-9 kg of ore is consumed. The whole process of smelting takes about 15 hours.

Agrawal (2000: 202) writes that there are large number of iron smelters and itinerant smiths in various parts of South Asia still surviving despite the most adverse conditions, perhaps because:

- There was an old tradition of such crafts
- These artisans were full-time iron workers
- They have been able to make a livelihood out of this craft
- The quality of their product is still in demand even when compared with more cheaply available factory-made iron. In fact, the quality of iron is closely interlinked with the demand and larger production. It is quite likely that only full-time workers could have produced good quality iron that was in demand in ancient India. This is the strength of traditional iron working.

Central Himalayas: Possible Source of Iron for Ganga Valley PGW

The Khasas

The Khasas, who were perhaps of Central Asian origin, came to India through the north-west like the Sakas and the Kusanas. At the time of their movement, they might have been scattered over almost all the hilly regions of northern India, i.e. Kashgar, Kashmir, Kangra, Kumaun, Kulu, Nepal, even up to Tibet. Though in strength and numbers they might have been stronger than other groups, they were probably only a nomadic-pastoral tribe. In the course of time, the social peculiarities (Joshi 1929) of the Khasas were more or less dissolved in the larger society of the hills.

Now the role of the Caucasoids in spreading iron technology into China is also being recognized. As An Zhimin (in Pigott 1996: 90) states that metal and its technology could have travelled along the Silk Route and that the technology could have developed in the Qijia culture (2000-1600 BC) of north-western China, a culture which was well ahead of the central plains in its use of copper/bronze. This could also apply to iron technology, with the discovery of the cemeteries in the Tarim basin, Xinjiang province, that contained more than 100 mummified individuals who were clearly Caucasian (Mair 1995), datable to 2000-1000 BC and with the presence of iron in west China in 10th century BC. Could the same people have been responsible for both PGW and iron in the central Ganga valley? Could they have been related to the Khasas?

Elsewhere we have discussed the problem of origin of iron in India (Agrawal and Kharakwal 2002). Here it seems germane to note Parpola's comments. He has connected the Tarim basin mummies with the Indo-Aryans basing on the evidence of *Ephedra*, identified with Soma. And Hemphill (1998) finds craniometric affinities between Tarim and Timargarh skeletal material. These new data have a crucial bearing on the advent of iron technology in India and have to be properly understood. Parpola says,

> The Soma cult may actually have its origin in the Afanas"evo culture of southern Siberia and Xinjiang (*c.* 3000–1800 BC), which, with good reasons, has been identified with the proto-Tocharians (cf. Mallory 1989: 56-63, 223-26; the Tocharian texts of the 6th to 8th centuries AD come from the Tarim Basin). Small parcels containing twigs of *Ephedra* have in several instances been found on the chests of bodies buried in shaft

pit graves of the Afanas"evo/early Andronovo-related Gumugou I culture in the Loprïor region of the middle Tarim basin in Xinjiang (*c.* 2000-1550 BC; Chen and Hiebert 1995, quoting the excavator Wang Binghua).... Therefore, it may well be in Xinjiang that the Andronovians, here assumed to be ancestors of the Rgvedic Aryans, adopted the Soma cult and the same applies to the Saka Haumavarga, who in 500 BC occupied the area around Ferghana. (Parpola: 1998).

Parpola writes that the authors of Megaliths in the east of the Black Sea and in the Caucasus, dated to the early centuries of the 1st millennium BC, are linked by port-hole Megaliths at the Sialk B necropolis (*c.* 1000-800 BC) in north-western Iran and at Las Bela in south Baluchistan. This suggests movement of people from Caucasus to Iran around 800 BC (Jettmar 1967). He thinks that the Megalithic culture may have been brought into India by horse-riding and warring nomads, probably speaking a west Aryan/Old Iranian language (see under Origin of Megalithic culture in this chapter). Thus Parpola's interesting equations, based on archaeological and linguistic evidence, about the movements of the Indo-Aryan and the Megalithic people have a crucial bearing on the advent of iron technology in India and have to be pursued further.

Now let us again turn towards Central Himalayas where, a large number of cist burials and other graves have een found from various parts (Agrawal *et al.* 1991, Agrawal *et al.* 1995; Kharakwal 1992) and typologically appear quite similar to the Gandhar graves of Swat valley (Dani 1967). The parallels in grave architecture and ceramics besides the dates between the Swat valley and the Kumauni cists are striking indeed. The authors of the Swat valley (Tusa 1981; Stacul 1987) graves used iron and grey ware so also Central Himalayan authors (Agrawal *et al.* 1995). Let us also mention here that a Gagrigol cist burial (near Bageshwar, Central Himalayas) is now dated (PRL-1592, 2666-2562 cal. BC) older than middle of 3rd millennium BC (Agrawal *et al.* 1995). Stacul (1987) has compared some of the Swat burial complexes with those of Kashmir. From Malari (Central Himalayas), crouched burials, comparable to Burzahom (Kashmir), have been reported. The main common tool type is the rectangular stone sickle. In fact, such (animal with human) burial tradition could be traced up to the middle reaches of the Yangtze (Yasuda 2000) and inner Mongolia (Zhao Fangzhi 1996: 38) also. Linguists (Sankrityayana 1958; Vaishnava 1977) have found affinities between the words Khash, Kasha, Kassite, Kashmir, Kashgar, etc.; the warrior class of Kumaun is still called *Khas* or *Khasia*. They are supposed to be pre-Vedic Indo-Europeans. If these linguistic equations are correct, some of these burial complexes may belong to early Indo-European migrations into the western and Central Himalayan regions. It may be mentioned here that Rahul Sankrityayan (1958) and other early writers have traced the Khasa people of Kumaun back to the Kassites of Mesopotamia. The people of Kashmir, Kasgar, etc., are all supposed to be related to the Khasas. These were the tribes who preceded the Vedic Aryans and were looked down upon by them.

On the other hand, the iron metallurgical tradition in Kumaun is very old and has become part of the folklore. Like Bihar and Central India, in Kumaun also, folklore attributes early iron working sites to the *Asuras* (Agrawal and Kharakwal 1998). The folklore also attributes a fort near Lohaghat in Pithoragarh district to Banasur (is it a corrupt form of the Assyrian king's name, Asur-bani-pal?). However, we do not have any archaeological evidence to prove an Assyrian association with the early iron technology in this region. Generally, the ancient iron working sites in the Central Himalayas are either associated with the name *Asura*, e.g., Asurchula (the hearth of the Asuras) or with *Agar* (mine) (e.g., Rai-Agar, Banagar) or with the word *lu* (the Kumaun word for iron), e.g., Lukhani, Lohaghat. *Agar* means mine/storage and the ironsmith communities even today are called *Agaris or Agarias* (Dom people). We are emphasizing the folklore tradition, because it points to the antiquity of this craft in Kumaun.

In Kumaun, the *shilpkars* are supposed to be Kols, speakers of Munda dialects (D.D. Sharma 1988). Munda and MonKhmer dialects are two branches of the Austro-Asiatic family. There are many Austro-Asiatic aboriginal languages still spoken in Thailand (Bayard 1996). Elsewhere we have discussed (Agrawal and Kharakwal 1998) that the Kols are said to be the first ethnic people of Kumaun, which had descended from the Munda-speaking group and were related to the Austro-Asiatic sub-group. The modern *shilpkars* (earlier called Dom), dark complexioned and perhaps representing the Austro-Asiatic features (Agrawal and Kharakwal in press), are perhaps the modern representatives of the Kols (Atkinson 1980-81: 370) in Kumaun. Some of them are called Agarias and practise traditional blacksmithy. They also claim to have been in Kumaun before the Khasiya or the immigrants from the plains arrived. In eastern India, the Kol tribe was largely involved in pre-industrial iron working (Chakrabarti 1992).

A number of PGW sites have been found from the mountainous region as well as from the adjoining terai region of the Central Himalayas (Uttaranchal). Some of them like Thapli, Purola and others have been studied by Garhwal University in the recent decades (Nautiyal *et al.* 1978-79; Khanduri *et al.* 1998-99). Also they have found a proto-PGW type pottery and evidence of iron from cist burials in western Ramganga valley.

In recent years we have explored a number of mining and smelting sites with iron ores, mining shafts, slags, kilns, etc. High grade ores have been reported and analysed from some sites, e.g., Lukhani, Asurchula, Agar, Lob and others (Agrawal and Kharakwal 1998, Chapter 4 and Kharakwal in press). The large production of iron is also evident from the pre-indutrial iron working reports. The British even tried to start an iron industry in Kumaun in the nineteenth century. There was a strong local ironsmithy tradition until recent times. Lohaghat, Pithoragarh district was known for a rust-resistant iron made of the local ores.

The iron ores found in Kumaun belong to either of the two varieties, the rhombohedral or the prismatic. The first is a peroxide of iron cntaining in its best defined type 70 per cent iron and 30 per cent oxygen (Atkinson 1980-81: 287). Scaly iron ore was mined at Ramgarh and Dhaniyakot on the Koshi. Both yielded good quality iron. During the British period, Lusgani, Nathuakhan, Gulla and Satbunga were the principal mines in the Nainital district. For the first 18 years of British rule, these mines were leased to the headmen of the Agarias at a nominal tax (Atkinson *ibid.*) (Agrawal and Kharakwal 1998, Chapter 4).

Uleni, located in the catchment area of the western Ramganga river and about 8 km north-west of Dwarahat in Almora district, has turned out be an important iron smelting site. A large heap of slag was noticed on one of the agricultural terraces and the slag is littered around. Though traces of any kind of furnace could not be found on the surface, our close examination yielded slag deposit and charcoal in the rock shelter nearby which was dated to the early 1st millennium BC (PRL-1648: 2770+90 BP; calibrated range-1022 to 826 BC). Such early date certainly supports the antiquity of the folk tradition. From this area we have also collected iron slág, which has been analysed and found to be mainly iron silicate, with no traces of copper.

As the Ganga valley is essentially a foredeep caused by the Miocene orogeny of the Himalayas, now filled with alluvium, it has no mineral outcrops. Then from where the PGW people obtained minerals? Elsewhere we have suggested that the Central Himalayan region could be a possible source. As we have shown above, folklore, historical tradition, the early 1st millennium ^{14}C date of Uleni, XRD analyses of magnetite, goethite, pyrites, discovery of proto-PGW type pottery when all taken together, provide circumstantial evidence that Central Himalayan iron and iron ores could have been used by the PGW people of the Ganga valley (see for details Agrawal and Kharakwal 1998, Chapter 8). Perhaps the Central Himalayan region played a vital role in the diffusion of metal technologies and agriculture.

Tripathi and Misra (1997) have pointed out that in Central India most of the pre industrial ironsmiths lived close to the sources of ores. We have found that this holds true in Kumaun and other areas too. In Central Himalayas we have found cist burials, PGW and iron smelting sites. On the basis of the circumstantial evidence discussed above, we would propose to associate the cists and PGW sites with the Khasas, a pre-Vedic Indo-Aryan group, the iron smelting sites with Agaris (Dom or Kol people), the first ethnic stock of this region! Perhaps the early date of Uleni also supports this fact. Khasas or Khasias still have a strong presence in the Central Himalayan region. This kind of evidence, only suggestive so far, tends to link up the Swat valley (Pirak), Central Himalayan cist burials, Khasa tribes, the Chinese Caucasoid connections, early ^{14}C dates and ancient iron smelting tradition into a consistent pattern which indicates Kumaun to be the probable source of early iron for northern India.

Furnaces

Although hundreds of mining and smelting sites and thousands of iron objects have been found in the subcontinent, unfortunately the reports of smelting furnaces have been scarce. To trace the origin and development of iron technology, we need to understand the smelting and manufacturing techniques. Like PGW, a number of Megalithic sites, e.g., Naikund (Gogte 1982), Kodumanal (Rajan 1994), Banahalli (IAR 1984-85: 44) and many others have also yielded evidence of iron smelting. Moorti (1994: 38-42) claims that at least 108 sites have evidence of metallurgy. But unfortunately intact furnaces have not been found anywhere. Some scholars attribute such scarcity of remains of furnaces to the destructive technique of iron working. In fact, quite often circular pits filled with ash or associated with slag or iron objects have been reported and they perhaps represent the earliest furnaces (1100/1000 to 800 BC). The best example of furnace and smelting operation is known from Naikund, Maharashtra and Gogte suggests that they must be obtaining 3 to 3.2 kg iron by smelting around 10 to 12 kg of ore in a single operation (1982: 59). We discuss below some of the main sites from where smelting furnaces have been reported.

Malhar

Malhar, located in Chandauli district, Uttar Pradesh, is an early Iron Age site, which has been excavated recently by the State Department of Archaeology. A cylindrical clay furnace was found in Period II, the diameter of which measures 1.38 m. It has survived to a height of about 35 cm. Slag was found sticking on the inner burnt wall. A few Red, Grey and Black Slipped ware potsherds were found associated with the furnace.

Pandu Rajar Dhibi

At Pandu Rajar Dhibi (1045±55 BC to 920±50 BC, uncal.) in district Burdwan, West Bengal, which is a Chalcolithic site, slag and iron objects associated with ash pits have been identified as iron smelting furnaces. De and Chattopadhyay (1984) have carried out analysis of artefacts and slag and they conclude that the smelting was conducted at a low temperature (below 1100°C) and suggest a very primitive technological level. Tripathi and Tripathi (1994: 241) write that "A combination of factors, such as low temperature, the absence of tuyeres and the use of very shallow pit would indicate that iron smelting was attempted in furnaces of the type previously used by coppersmiths for copper smelting".

Naikund

Naikund is a Megalithic habitation and burial site located about 42 km north- north-east of Nagpur in the Vidarbha region of Maharashtra (Deo and Jamkhedkar 1982; Gogte 1982) and dated from the 6th to the 4th centuries BC. The furnace was discovered with the help of resistivity recording probe. The site is reported to have 73 stone circles, a majority of them undisturbed, with two habitational mounds, all surrounded by Megalithic circles and situated on the left bank of the river Pench. About 200 m eastwards of Mound II and 130 m south of Mound I were located the remains of a smelting workshop designated as Mound III. At a depth of 1.25 m was exposed an iron smelting furnace, which was built of circular clay bricks of a thickness of 4 cm. The diameter of the furnace was about 30 cm and height about 25 cm. The bottom of the furnace was paved with bricks and was fused with slag and cinders. There were holes to pump air into the furnace with bellows. Besides these, a large quantity of iron slag was found. According to Gogte's observation, the Naikund Megalith folk used about 10 to 12 kg iron ore for a single smelting operation producing 3.0 to 4.2 kg of pure iron. It has been stated that Naikund is the first Megalithic site to have given evidence of an iron smelting furnace (Gogte 1982: 52-59).

The habitational deposits and burials were rich in iron artefacts at Naikund. The artefacts were composed of a wide range of dishes, ladles or lamps, daggers, knife blades, adzes, hoes, axes, chisels, clangs and hooks. The iron found was of a very pure quality, devoid of any other intrusions except carbon, which qualified it to be designated as steel. The local iron ore was utilized by them.

Kodumnal

Chakrabarti refers to the Megalithic site of Kodumnal in the Periyar district of Tamil Nadu, where the Megalithic levels have been dated to *c.* 250 BC. "A large oval-shaped furnace surrounded by a number of small furnaces was exposed in the bottom-most level. Vitrified crucibles were collected here which appear to be *in situ* and may suggest that the large furnace was used to stack up a number of crucibles containing iron and carbon to produce steel by prolonged heating".

Atranjikhera

At Atranjikhera, Uttar Pradesh, Gaur (1983: 129) identified remains of a possible furnace (oval pit) from the PGW level (Period II). A fire pit was also located close to this and besides a pair of tongs and some charred bones. Inside the pits were found rounded tapering clay lumps and finished iron tools. He also points out openings for bellows. He also found similar evidence in the upper levels associated with NBPW culture (Period IV) but with iron slag. It seems that both these pits were shallow like Pandu Rajar Dhibi and very elementary technique for smelting was used as at many other early sites, though Gaur does not discuss smelting.

Noh and Jodhpura

Noh and Jodhpura, both in Rajasthan, yielded good evidence of iron smelting as the sites are littered with slag. Ash pits have been reported from both sites from the PGW levels. Perhaps there were openings for bellows, but no details are available. Iron objects have been found from these levels.

Ujjain

Ujjain, located in western Madhya Pradesh, has yielded evidence of iron smelting from post-PGW levels. A very small squarish feature was identified as smelting furnace from the NBPW culture levels (Banerjee 1965), though it looks like a forge.

Khairadih

Khairadih (1100-200 BC), district Ballia, Uttar Pradesh has yielded interesting evidence of iron smelting (Tripathi 1991), which has been assigned to 2nd century BC. She has identified three furnaces in a row, with partially underground pits with flat bases. The diameter of the pits below floor level was 20 cm and they were approximately 40 cm deep. She notes that the pit was lined with clay paste and a superstructure was raised above the ground with curved or tapering walls to take the shape of a shaft furnace. This was again shaped with clay mixed with straw or sand. Bamboo, plastered with thick layers of clay may have served as tuyeres, which have been found *in situ* at the floor level, on the side of the furnace. A channel was perhaps provided for tapping of slag, which flowed out of the furnace and fell at a lower level as drippings. She found a large amount of iron slag and a variety of finished iron objects.

Balathal

At Balathal, in south-eastern Rajasthan, the Iron Age deposit (1.50 m), overlying the Chalcolithic remains, is located in the central part of the mound, which is hardly spread over an area of 70 square metres. The Iron Age deposit is resting directly on a 15-20 cm thick uniform layer of ash and is characterized by Red, Grey, Fine Grey (shapes identical to PGW dishes) and few NBP sherds and associated Grey Ware fragments. The site has yielded several hundred iron objects which include adzes, nails, clamps, rods, lumps, daggers, blades, swords, bell, arrowheads, rings, sockets, animal figurines, hoes, chisels, knives, sickles, etc., from the Early Historic deposit which has been bracketed between 300 BC and AD 200. Most of these objects are in a corroded state and encrusted with soil. The site is located in the Aravallis, which are rich in iron ore. There are various large ancient mining and smelting sites recently identified in this region, e.g., Karanpur, Kikawas, Chhipikhera, Iswal, Nathara ki Pal, Devgarh, Lohariya and others. Iswal, located about 20 km north of Udaipur town, has yielded evidence of furnaces, bellows, large quantity of slag and habitation deposit (stone structures and Red and Grey Wares). The site is being excavated by Lalit Pandey of Institute of Rajasthan Studies, Rajasthan Vidyapeeth, Udaipur (pers. com.).

An iron smelting furnace, made of burnt bricks and stone slabs, was discovered in the north-western corner of trench B, the base of which rests on layer (2) and it is datable to 2nd century BC. Barring the northern part of the furnace, which is made of vertically placed stone slabs, all other sides are made of bricks arranged vertically and supported by horizontally placed bricks. The furnace flares at the bottom, the inner diameter is 44 cm whereas the outer one measures 79 cm (including the walls) in the central part. It has a roughly circular opening with a diameter of 39 cm. It is 53 cm high and inside the furnace were found layers of ash, charcoal pieces and highly burnt clay lumps. It is hardly 15 cm below the surface.

Another possible furnace (fire pit) was found in the south-eastern part of trench A in layer (2), which was roughly oblong on plan and measured 48 cm (N-S) and 30 cm (E-W). It is 50 cm deep. This pit contained ash, lumps of burnt clay, charcoal. Large number of iron artefacts and few lumps of slag were found from this level. The iron smelting (?)/ melting activity was perhaps confined only to the central part of the existing mound. A small platform (1.50 x 1 m), paved with flat stones, was found to the north of this fire pit. Few cylindrical clay lumps embedded with quartz fragments and slag fragments were found close to this platform, which may have been used to retain the heat in the furnace. From the base of layer (3), still further from the northern part, two circular (about 30 cm diameter) bases of furnaces were discovered, one of which was resting right on the Chalcolithic fortified enclosure, whereas the other one was found resting on layer (5). The base contains some portion of slag with cinder. It seems that Balathalians were not smelting iron ore but were melting and producing artefacts perhaps to supply to other sites. This activity is associated with the lower level of the Early Historic deposit, which has been dated to 3rd century BC.

FURNACE TYPES

Shrivastava (1999) has examined various types of furnaces, which have been reported from Iron Age sites and classified them into the following three types:

Bowl furnace: The bowl furnaces, perhaps reminiscent of copper working, are simple pits covered with fuel mixed with dome-shaped superstructure with a tuyere inserted at the bottom. The examples of Pandu-Rajar-Dhibi (Bengal), Jodhpura (Rajasthan) may be classified under this category.

Dome-shaped furnace: Shrivastava (1999: 40) writes that the dome-shaped furnace is different and better than the bowl-shaped furnace as in this type there is provision for tapping slag from the pit. In these furnaces, a cylindrical cavity was made. There are two openings at the bottom facing each other and tuyeres were inserted in one of them. Such a provision was quite useful for maintaining reducing conditions. It also had provisions for intermittent feeding of fuel and ore and could generate temperatures up to 1200°C with the help of bellows! The examples of this type could be cited from Atranjikhera and Noh.

Shaft furnace: Shrivastava (1999: 40) has described two sub-types of shaft furnaces, i.e. (a) furnace with a channel for slag tapping, (b) slag pit furnace. The furnaces at Naikund, Khairadih, Netarhat Plateau and the types used by the Agaria's in Sarguja district, Madhya Pradesh are shaft-type furnace with channels. Such furnaces are supposed to be more efficient than simple bowl- or dome-shaped ones. The furnaces have two holes: one for bellows; and the other for tapping the molten metal. Some such furnaces are still in use in Netrahat Plateau and in Bastar region. In one operation, 18-20 kg of charcoal along with 15-18 kg of iron ore are used and within two-three hours around 5-6 kg of iron is obtained. The slag pit furnaces, however, do not have a channel; they have straight or tapering walls and slag along with the bloom gets deposited at the base and the superstructure is broken to retrieve the bloom. Chakrabarti (1988: 119) also writes that furnace slag could not be separated from the bloom in the pre-industrial working, which had to be broken to pick up pieces of pure metal.

Iron-silica and calcium carbonate (along with soda) were closely interconnected in furnace operations at temperatures that stayed consistently above the melting point of copper (1100° C). Although the kilns or furnaces may have come from widely separated sources (the pottery kiln from the cooking hearth and the lime kiln from the fire setting of stone, for example), what emerged during the Bronze Age were four major interwoven pyrotechnologic products: terracotta, iron, glass and cement (Wertime 1980).

METALLURGY

Compared to bronze objects, not really much has been done to understand the metallography of ancient Indian iron. In order to understand the metallurgical techniques, chronological sequence and gradual development of early Iron Age, a number of scholars, e.g. Agrawal (1983), Agrawal *et al.* (1983, 1990), Bhardwaj (1973), Biswas and Biswas (1996: 225-33), De and Chattopadhyay (1991), Ghosh *et al.* (1987-88), Gogte (1982), Gururaja Rao (1970), Hegde (1991), Joshi (1973), Leshnik (1974), Munshi and Sarin (1970), Prakash and Tripathi (1986) have attempted typological and metallurgical and metallogaphic analysis of artefacts from different regions. We do not know if carburization, quenching and lamination had become common in each region in the 1st millennium BC. Do we have good evidence of hardening and tempering with consistency? Metallurgical and metallographic analyses would certainly help us to understand various relationships of metallurgical traditions among different regions. In fact, in most of the cases, our analyses were aimed at composition and determination of steeling as Possehl and Gullapalli (2000) also point out.

The metallurgical and metallographic results of few iron artefacts from Kumaranhalli (1200-1100 BC) and Tadakanahalli (ca. 1000 BC), both Megalithic sites in Karnataka, have yielded evidence of carburization (both ferrite and pearlite), quenching and lamination technique (Agrawal *et al.* 1983), though evidence for hardening was not found. Bhardwaj (1973) carried out metallographic analysis of four iron objects from NBP levels at Rajghat (600 BC) and found the evidence of carburization, though not consistent. The PGW levels at Atranjikhera (900 BC) also revealed evidence of wrought iron and mild steel (O.P. Agrawal 1983). Since very few samples were analysed, we do not know if carburization was consistent and done for most of the objects.

A very few iron objects from the Megalithic complex of Vidarbha region, e.g. Mahurjhari (Joshi 1973), Khapa (Munshi and Sarin 1970), Naikund were subjected to chemical and metallogaphic studies. The iron axe from Mahurjhari was found to contain 99.1 per cent Fe, 0.9 per cent C and traces of chromium, whereas the spear from Megalith 7 at Khapa contained 99.6 per cent Fe and some sites also yielded high percentage (1.5) of carbon. Gogte (1982) shows that the iron pieces of plain medium carbon steel were forged in high temperature. They perhaps employed quenching, tempering and lamination techniques.

It has been found that the bronze artefacts associated with Megaliths in different regions have varying proportions of tin, e.g. Mahurjhari 8.5 per cent, Bhagimohari 15.8 per cent, Raipur 21 per cent and Nilgiri hills 29.89 per cent (Deo 1985: 92) perhaps suggesting different sources of origin. Srinivasan (1994) has analysed various copper-bronze objects from Megalithic context as also the medieval one's too and finds similarity in technique (Mohanty and Selvakumar 2000).

From eastern India also, a few artefacts have been subjected to metallographic and chemical examinations, e.g., Hatigra (1000 BC), Dhuliapur and Kankrajhar and other sites in West Bengal (De and Chattopadhyay 1991; Ghosh *et al.* 1987-88; Ghosh and Chattopadhyay 1982). Some of them yielded evidence of low carbon steel in early 1st millennium BC. According to Chattopadhyay (1990) in eastern India the first or early stage of iron technology is characterized by wrought iron (900 BC), second stage {what he likes to call as the beginning of Iron Age) is characterized by the introduction of carburization (e.g. a dagger from Hatgira of 900 BC) and a sickle from Barudih (850 BC) yielded pearlite, ferrite and evidence of low carbon steel, thoroughly forged and slow cooling. In the following stage, introduction of quenching and tempering has been found around 3rd century BC.

Possehl and Gullapalli (2000: 162) write that this lamination technique continued as revealed by analysis of later artefacts, e.g. from Jajamau (600-300 BC, NBP phase). During the NBP stage we certainly have widespread evidence of low and medium steel, quenching and tempering.

Upadhyaya (2000) has surveyed the metal implements right from the early stages of Bronze Age in South Asia down to the early centuries of Christian era. He has prepared an exhaustive list of most of the known artefact types from different sites, contexts, measurements, etc. He has also taken care of all the iron artefacts reported from different parts of the country. He finds (2000: 239-246) that 47.9 per cent PGW artefacts were for household use, 35.1 for hunting, 11.1 per cent for craft and 4.8 per cent for agricultural purpose. In the case of NBP, agricultural implements account for 10 per cent, hunting 35.5 per cent and craft 18 per cent. However, the hunting objects of Megalithic culture (43.85 per cent) outnumber all others, household artefacts were found hardly 20, agricultural 18.5 per cent and various crafts 18 per cent. All these were rural cultures and represent early stage of iron. It seems that hunting was a major subsistence for life whereas agriculture gradually increased and offered subsistence to life as the percentage of agricultural tools suggests. From the metallurgical analysis, it seems that in many areas, people had become aware of carburization, quenching, lamination techniques but they used these techniques only to manufacture tools for special purposes, e.g. hunting, etc. The evidence of high and low carbon steel is certainly very important to understand the gradual development of the early iron technology. Possehl and Gullapalli (2000: 163) point out that more technical studies would be very useful in understanding social, political and economic processes.

The iron pillar at Delhi belonging to 4th century AD was a wrought iron pillar manufactured by forge-welding and the entire pillar was rounded off with forge hammering and cold working (Chakrabarti 1988: 119). It has been called the "rustless wonder" by some scholars.

Wootz

The term "wootz" was derived from the Kannada (Canarese) word *wooku* (ukku), which eans steel and came to be known in Europe as wootz. Pre-industrial Andhra Pradesh, Karnataka and Tamil Nadu were the world famous centres for the ancient wootz (steel) production. Tripathi and Tripathi (1994) write that steel was manufactured by two techniques: by carburization of wrought iron fragments in small crucibles; and by decarburization of white cast iron. They have illustrated the following process of these techniques, based on the reports of Heath (1839) and Holland (1892):

> Iron was refined by repeated heating and hammering and eventually formed into bars measuring about 12 x 1.5 x 1.5 inches (Heath 1839). These were cut into small pieces and divided into batches weighing one to two pounds. The small pieces of iron were packed closely in a crucible, together with a tenth part by weight of dried wood chopped small. The hole was then covered over with one or two green leaves and the mouth of the crucible was filled up with tempered clay, rammed in close. As soon as the clay

was dry, from twenty to twenty-four crucibles were built up, in the form of an arch, in small furnace, which was lighted and the blast kept up for about 2½ hours. The crucibles were then removed, allowed to cool, broken and the steel ingots, which had the form of the bottom of the crucible, were taken out. If the fusion of the metal has been achieved, the top of the ingot is covered with striae radiating from the center. The ingots were subsequently heated for several hours at a temperature just below their melting point and turned over in the current of air from the bellows. The objective of this treatment was probably to eliminate, by oxidation, the excess of carbon which the ingots contained and to which they owe their comparatively low fusing point. When this operation was completed, the ingots were hammered out into short stout bars, in which state the steel is solid. The crucibles were formed of a refractory "red loam", mixed with a large proportion of charred rice-husk. The wood used was of the *Cassia auriculata* and the leaves of the *Asclepias gigantea* or, if these are not available, of *Convolvulus laurifolia*.

Steel making through de-carburization

This method as described by Holland (1892) of the manufacture of steel is based on the principle of partial de-carburization of the cast iron, as opposed to carburization of wrought iron in wootz steel. During the manufacture of wrought iron, certain easily fusible beads of iron were produced and melted off as shot. These were actually highly carburised particles, or cast iron and it is from these, that the steel was made. The shots were first pounded in a stone mortar with a wooden pole guarded with an iron ring called the olakai, generally used for pounding rice. This operation served to remove the particles of slag adhering to the shots and the cast iron received an imperfect polish. The powered slag was separated by sifting in a shallow basket. Subsequently, a hole about one foot deep and one foot in diameter was dug into the ground. At one side, a semicircular groove was excavated from surface to the bottom of the pit. A large cake of soft clay served to divide this small excavation from the other part of the pit. This smaller chamber served as the finery in which the steel is made. The bottom of this was first covered with a layer of dirty quartz obtained from sifting of the crushed ore during the ore dressing process. On this heap of quartz, an ignited coal was placed and the small chamber was filled with charcoal. A tuyere, previously built in with the clay portion pointed down at an angle of 45° and received the nozzles of two goat skin bellows. The shots were first wet and then thrown upon the charcoal. The amount used was governed by experience and the blast was kept up for about thirty minutes. After the end of this period the blast was withdrawn and the clay portion was broken for recovering the steel-cake, which was first cooled by a dash of water and then hammered to remove the casing of slag which had formed around it (Tripathi and Tripathi 1994: 248-249).

The Indian ironmasters had realized the effect of addition of carbon to iron and the excellent cuffing edges formed on carbon steels. The medieval alchemical text *Rasaratnasamuchchaya* reveals three kinds of iron : *mundam* (wrought iron), *kantam* and *tikshnam* (cast, carburized or steel). Lowe (1990) carried out study of iron smelting and crucible steel production sites (between 1987-1989) in Andhra Pradesh and identified over a dozen wootz production sites and a few dozen iron smelting ones and says that wootz steel was exported to Europe even as early as 400 BC. The trade was carried through Damascus where this steel was used for the manufacture of swords and hence it was also known as Damascus steel. The processes of forge welding, hardening, tempering and probably carburizing were well developed by the end of AD 300.

Iron from Copper Technology

The beginning of iron technology in India appears to have a respectable antiquity. The geological, archaeological and ethnographic studies clearly show that iron ores are abundant in many regions of India and it is believed that the easy availability of ore may have enhanced technological innovation (Chakrabarti 1977: 168-171).

At Bhagwanpura, Katpalan, Dadheri, Nagar and other sites (Joshi 1978: 98-101) found the interlocking of the PGW with the Late Harappans. Though iron is absent from these levels yet this kind of evidence may be useful in finding out the continuity and transition from Bronze Age to Iron Age culture.

Eastern Uttar Pradesh, Bihar and Bengal are devoid of the PGW but in the earliest Iron Age levels Black-and-Red Ware (often painted in white) continues from Chalcolithic phase, of course, with new features. Prakash and Tripathi call this as Zone C in their classification. Kosambi, Prahladpur, Rajghat and Sohgaura in eastern Uttar Pradesh, Sonepur and Chirand in Bihar and Pandu Rajar Dhibi and Mahisdal in Bengal are some of the important sites. In most of these sites, there is a Chalcolithic level with a lithic industry which seems to merge almost imperceptibly into the Iron Age; even microliths continue into the early Iron Age. Pandu Rajar Dhibi and Mahisdal provide a clear evidence of local iron-smelting. Mahisdal also produced iron arrowheads, spearheads, chisels and nails. They all appear to be small village settlements. The ^{14}C dates from Sonpur (TF-376 635+110 BC) and Mahisdal (TF-389 690+105 BC) suggest the beginning of Iron Age around 700 BC.

Several Chalcolithic sites in Madhya Pradesh, e.g. Eran, Kayatha, Nagda and Bahal, Prakash and Inamgaon in Maharashtra have Iron Age occupations at the top. At most of these sites, the Black-and-Red Ware characterizes the Iron Age and continues from the Chalcolithic cultures to the Iron Age, of course, with new features. Similar situation also occurs in Pirak. Does this really mark a cultural change? Except for the use of iron (see Possehl and Gullapalli 1999: 165), the assemblage seems to be the same. Even Chakrabarti has questioned this. On the other hand, he clinches this kind of evidence with Lothal to push back the beginning of iron into mid-2nd millennium BC (Chakrabarti 1992). At Inamgaon, a late phase of Jorwe culture appears to reach the threshold of the Iron Age. At Nagda there is a substantial Iron Age deposit yielding double-edged daggers, axe-sockets, knives, arrowheads, spearheads and sickles. A continuity of tradition between the Chalcolithic and the Iron Age levels indicates an early beginning of iron here (Banerjee 1965). There are no ^{14}C dates for the early Iron Age of Central India, except for Eran (Singh 1967: 29). There is, however, some confusion about the ^{14}C dates from Eran, which may be cleared when and if, the full report on the site is published. The Black-and-Red Ware has a distinct character in each region and the Black & Red wares of Bihar and eastern Uttar Pradesh are technologically as well as typologically closer to each other than that of Madhya Pradesh.

It is now generally held that in a well-developed bronze technology, iron can be produced while smelting copper (Cooke and Aschenbrenner 1975; Charles 1980; Gale 1990; Moorey 1994: 279; Pigott 1981). If we use iron oxide (hematite, limonite or magnetite) as flux or we smelt iron-rich copper ore to obtain copper, we may produce some pure iron. It is likely that this kind of result may have provided clues to bronze metallurgists to initiate iron technology. This kind of transitional stage of metallurgy is available in the Middle east, but we are not aware of this kind of evidence in South Asia. Possehl and Gullapalli (2000: 158-162) however, have compiled evidence of iron from over half a dozen Bronze Age sites. In fact, such a convincing stage at several Chalcolithic sites in the subcontinent may certainly facilitate the transition to iron technology, which we have yet to come across.

From Mundigak (Afghanistan) Period IV (2600-2100 BC), five iron objects such as a copper/bronze bell with an iron clapper (Casal 1961: 242, Fig. 138, no. 17); a fragment of a copper/bronze rod with two iron "buttons" affixed to it (Casal 1961: 249, Fig. 139, no. 14); an iron button affixed to a copper/bronze mirror (Casal 1961: 250, Fig. 140, no. 21);

two indistinct lumps of "carbonates of iron" weighing 1 and 3 kg respectively (Casal 1961: 237-238) were found. At Said Qala Tepe, located in southern Afghanistan, 24 ferrous lumps in pre-Iron Age levels (Periods II and III, contemporary to Munidgak IV) were identified as hammer stones by Shaffer (1984). They were not made or smelted iron ore. Shaffer has made the important observation as he finds that people were perhaps aware of the hardness of iron. Louis Dupree (1963: 99) also found a nodule of magnetite at Deh Morasi Ghundai, which was associated with the so-called Shrine Complex and perhaps contemporary with Mundigak IV (Shaffer 1984: 48). Katelai in Swat valley (Period V 1500-800 BC) has also yielded an iron object, which has been described to be in a highly corroded state (Stacul 1979: 341). From Mohenjodaro, lollingite (an arsenic-and iron-bearing mineral) was found (Marshall 1931: 32, 485, 690), which Possehl and Gullapalli (2000) think that it may have been used in the smelting of arsenical copper or preparation of arsenic. A leaf-shaped iron arrowhead (?) has been found from Chanhudaro (Mackay 1943: Pl. LXXII, no. 24) just below the surface, which raises doubt about its context. A metal fragment found at Lothal, Gujarat has yielded interesting results as it contains 66.10 per cent iron and 9.30 per cent copper (Lal 1985: 658; Table XXVIII, no.11). Though it is not clear whether it comes from Lothal A or B, it will be older than 1800 BC. At Ahar, located in south-eastern Rajasthan (Sankalia *et al.* 1969), 1 tanged iron arrowhead and a ring from Period Ib (2150-1950 BC), 5 iron arrowheads, 2 chisels, 2 nails and a tube or socket were found from Period Ic (1950-1500 BC). The dates of these periods are based on Possehl and Rissman (1992). There has been considerable debate about the discovery of these objects in Bronze Age context (Sahi 1979; Lal 1987-88). Sankalia (1979) had made it clear that since there were several pits at the site hence there is a strong possibility of the later material (iron objects) getting mixed up with the earlier. But scholars did not give much attention to his comments. Iron artefacts have also been found in Chalcolithic levels from various sites in West Bengal (Datta 1998). Even Chattopadhyay (1991) termed their occurrence in the Chalcolithic levels at Pandurajar Dhibi and Mangalkot as "ferro-chalcolithic".

Except for the five objects from Mundigak and one from Lothal, we cannot rely much on other objects cited from different sites. Possehl and Gullapalli (2000) also admit the fact that except for the awareness of their hardness at some sites, neither these artefacts have been analysed to understand their properties nor do we know whether they were made of meteoritic or terrestrial iron. We do not have strong evidence of smelted iron either. We cannot give too much of credit only to awareness of mineral form to the Bronze Age people as various iron minerals were being used by the Stone Age man for Millennia. But unfortunately scholars have generally ignored Sankalia's (1979) comment and keep digging the excavation reports religiously to establish the antiquity of iron. Currently, a large number of neem and *Acacia* trees and other bushy plants are growing on the mounds at Ahar and one can see a number of rat and fox holes in the exposed sections besides thick and long roots. Since the site is located right in the Udaipur town and next to the old village, we cannot ignore the local disturbance either. The second author (JSK) who works at Udaipur has examined the mound thoroughly and has picked up Iron Age pottery from Chalcolithic levels. At Balathal, an Ahar culture site located about 42 km east of Ahar, the upper portion in the southern part of the mound was dug away and levelled by local farmers for agriculture. Despite this, a number of Early Historic iron artefacts were recovered from middle and lower levels of the mound. All these factors discussed above were certainly responsible for the occurrence of artefacts in the Chalcolithic levels. Hence there is a strong possibility of iron objects and pottery percolating down to the late levels of Chalcolithic culture.

In Karnataka, in South India, the early radiocarbon dates of the Neolithic-Megalithic transition at Hallur are now supported by the TL dates from the relevant context of a neighbouring site. This is an important development and clearly strengthens the case of a pre-1000 BC beginning of iron in South India. Both in the upper Ganga valley and eastern India, the use of iron began unmistakably around 1000 BC (Chakrabarti 1992). This kind of evidence of iron from Central and South India is earlier than the iron in the north-western periphery and the early Indian iron tool-types also do not significantly correspond to the iron tool-types known in West Asia. On the basis of these points, he argues that India was a separate and possibly independent centre of manufacture of early iron (Chakrabarti 1976, 1992).

Agrawal (2000), however, suggests that pushing back the beginning of iron to mid-2nd millennium BC is really not warranted by evidence. Accidental smelting of iron from copper pyrites is very ancient indeed, as has been pointed out by Muhly for Anatolia. In fact, some TL dates for South Indian Megalithic sites seem to go beyond 1400 BC. But the TL dates have large errors and uncertainties. Nowhere in the world iron use on a regular basis has begun before 1200 BC. Claiming it for India alone will be a bit anomalous. Even Chakrabarti agrees that by the time of *Satapatha Brahmana* (*c.* 800/700 BC), iron was a common metal to be associated with the ordinary people.

LITERARY EVIDENCE

In ancient Indian literature, the terms like *ayas, syama and krisnayasa* generally denote iron. Chakrabarti (1992: 96-124) has surveyed a large body of literary evidence of iron right from the Vedic phase and says that *ayas* appears to be a generic term in Rigveda and may have also been used for copper and bronze apart from iron. References occur in the later *Vedas*: *Taittiriya Samhita, Kathak Samhita, Atharvaveda;* **Brahmanas**: *Aitareya, Kausitaki, Taittiriya, Satpath Brahmana;* ***Upanishads***: *Chhandogya, Maitri;* ***Kalpsutras*** : *Baudhayana Srauta Sutra*; Panini's *Asthadhyayi;* Patanjali's *Mahabhasya;* **Epics**: *Mahabharata* (*Drona parva), Ramayana* (*Aranyakanda);* Kautilya's *Arthasastra, Amarakosa;* Varahmihir's *Brihatsamhita, Rasaratnasamuchchaya* (13th-15th centuries AD); **Buddhist Canons**: *Anguttaaranikaya, Samyuttanikaya, Suttanipata, Mahavagga, Dhammapada; Ther-gatha;* ***Jatakas***: *Chhadanta Dhamma, Nimi* and others; **Jain Canons** (6th century AD): *Uttaradhyana Sutra* and Greek and Roman accounts. Chakrabarti (1992: 167) concludes from literary evidence that in the upper Ganga valley, iron tools were associated with agriculture as early as 800-700 BC whereas in the middle Ganga doab around 500 BC. The archaeological evidence is, however, older than these dates in the respective regions.

Kosambi (1963: 318) has quoted an early reference from Buddhist canon, which not only confirms the use of iron in the 1st millennium BC but also is a good evidence of metallurgical technique. He says,

> For the iron-ore country, however, we have one ancient record well worth consideration, the Pali *Suttanipata*.... The language is the most archaic of any work in the whole Buddhist canon; the style too is simple and direct. There is no question but that the work is pre-Asokan and contains the oldest of Buddhist traditions.... The fourth discourse in the collection is of "Farmer Bharadvaja" (*Kasi-Bharadvaja-sutta*), a Brahmin who farmed land at Dakkhinagiri in Magadha. This is the portion of Mirzapore district along the southern bank of the Ganges. The word *phala* for ploughshare occurs in both the prose and the metrical portions of the discourse. The simile runs: "like a *phala* heated for a whole day and plunged suddenly into water... ". Bronze treated like this would become brittle and useless, apart from being much too costly

for ploughshares. Iron reduced from ores by any primitive method comes out as a spongy mass, which has to be heated and forged repeatedly as well as hardened by sudden chilling before it is of any use for tools.... *Milindapanho* also gives the reference for quenching practice.

Besides these, the Ayurvedic medicinal system was well developed in ancient India and according to Sushruta, an Ayurvedic physician, iron and steel were well-known as early as 7th century BC. Jha *et al.* (1989) have pointed out from Ayurveda that the Ayurvedic physicians were very selective in the choice of metallic source used for the production of iron *bhasma* (oxide or other compounds) such as use of biotite instead of hematite or other minerals of iron. By experience they had learnt the conditions for optimum extraction of iron from biotite and convert it into *bhasma* (oxide) for medicinal use. The description also informs that surgical instruments made of steel were used by Sushruta in 700 BC (Jha *et al.* 1989).

Lal carried out explorations and excavations at a number of sites mentioned in the *Mahabharata*, e.g. Hastinapur, Indraprastha and others and he found PGW and iron from all such sites (Lal 1954-55). He therefore, concluded that *Mahabharata* episode could be associated with PGW culture, though this identification has not been widely accepted by scholars. Kochar (2000) has critically analysed the archaeological data and literary evidence of *Puranas, Mahabharata, Zenda Avesta* in order to work out the date of *Mahabharata*. He concludes that 900 BC would be reasonably correct date for *Mahabharata*, which certainly supports Prof. Lal's identification.

DISCUSSION

Like in the Middle east, we do not have a clear transitional/experimental stage from copper to iron where iron was invariably smelted while copper smelting and tools were also made. Except for Mundigak's copper rods with iron button and Chandoli's copper dagger with an iron tang, we do not have an ornamental stage of iron like in Iran. The copper fragment of Lothal containing extremely high percentage of iron is also of some interest. We should carefully scrutinise the evidence of Pirak (Pakistan), Noh and Jodhpura in Rajasthan, Black-and-Red Ware levels in Bihar and Bengal, e.g. at Chirand and Mahishdal, Pandu Rajar Dhibi and Central Indian sites like Nagda, Eran, Dangwada and others for the early evidence of iron as well as experimental stages, if there are any. Though these examples do not set a stage for iron technology, they certainly give us clues to look for a possible transitional stage. We need to find a polymetallic stage of iron and should work out its socio-economic impacts too.

The archaeological evidence from Malhar and Raja-Nal-ka-Tila (1200 BC AMS, see Table 5.5), Atranjikhera (1100 BC), Uleni (1022 to 826 BC calibrated range) in North India and Hallur, Tadakanhalli, Kumaranhalli in South India (1300 BC) do suggest an early beginning of iron. We, however, should not rely too much on the early TL date of Hallur and others, which scholars have often quoted, because TL has a large range of error. In addition to Ahar, a few more sites have been studied in south-eastern Rajasthan, in recent years but nowhere the date of iron is older than 500 BC. The occurrence of iron objects in Chalcolithic levels may merely be the result of local disturbance as later on Sankalia also mentioned. Therefore, we should not dig any more the excavation reports. It has also been argued that at some sites in Central India, there is no significant time gap or cultural break between Bronze and Iron Age cultures. They should be re-examined whether the Chalcolithic cultures continued (like late Jorwe at Inamgaon) for few more centuries or the Iron Age had really an early beginning as has been argued by Chakrabarti. If the latter is the case, where are the consistent dates? The Gandhar Grave Culture sites, Pirak, PGW complex of northern India, Black-and-Red Ware level of eastern India and Megalithic sites of peninsular India all register a variety of utilitarian type iron objects, which suggest that iron had become common around 800 BC. The literary evidence of *Satpath Brahmana* and other sources also support this date. As other metal objects, of course, with functional types, also continue with iron, though very few in number, we cannot draw a straight line between the Bronze and Iron Ages in South Asia to illustrate the stage when iron replaced copper entirely.

The urbanization ushered in only by the mid-1st millennium BC in the Ganga valley when iron technology was well established as an industry, though agriculture had begun Millennia earlier in the doab. Iron was useful for draining out the swamps, clearing off the forests and cultivating the hard kankary soil of the Ganga doab, though some scholars have ruled out such use of early tools (Lal 1986).

We have discussed multidisciplinary evidence from Central Himalayan region and shown that there may be a relationship among the authors of the burials in Central Himalayas, Kashmir, Swat and Caucasus, which also may have contributed in the diffusion of metallurgy.

In Central Himalayas the blacksmithy, however, is associated with Asuras/Agaris or Kols (Austro-Asiatic speaking). Perhaps they were mining, smelting and manufacturing and supplying to the Khasas—the nomads and warriers! The availability of high grade iron minerals in the Central Himalayas, evidence of smelting in the early 1st millennium BC, cist burials and proto-PGW pottery all suggest a strong possibility of iron being supplied to the PGW people of the Ganga plains because the Doab was an alluvial fill and there were no mineral outcrops. At a later stage, the abundantly available river-sands rich in magnetite, though of a low grade, were also used.

Tripathi and Tripathi (1994: 250) draw attention to an interesting ethnographic example of wootz-making people at Pariah, who remained ignorant about the technique employed by people at Salem in the same region of South India. They also write that the spread of technology in the Old World must have been painfully slow and difficult due to secretive attitude of the smiths. Based on their ethnographic studies, Tripathi and Misra (1997) suggest that the growth of technology was not a unilinear process in India and simple techniques gradually led to more complex ones. They suggest that different techniques were learnt and applied simultaneously as required by the tool to be fabricated.

They argue for independent and multicentered origin of iron technology in India. Chakrabarti (1992), however, attempts to push back the beginning to around mid-2nd millennium BC taking into account the evidence from Hallur, Ahar and Lothal. He also thinks that the Central Indian Iron Age cultures begin well before 1st millennium BC.

Vibha Tripathi (2001a) while tracing the origin of Iron in India discusses the Indo-European philology and refers to the Boghaz-Keui inscription of 1365/80 BC in Asia Minor. She writes,

> Varuna, Mitra, Indra and Nasatya (Asvini) are mentioned in a treatise of Mitanni-Hittites agreement and finds similarities among the names of Mitanni kings and the Indo-Aryans. Quoting the work of Parpola and Witzel she argues that Mitannis were connected to the Indo-Aryan group. She says, "Movements of certain migrants...have been identified through parts of central Asia, western Iran, Afghanistan by the presence of Grey Ware, cemeteries, their grave goods and also iron.... Weapons, model chariot, mortars, pestles, open spouted pots...horse burials along with prestige objects.... Such items are significant because of their association with Vedic funerary beliefs. It may also be taken as a testimony of association of the Rgvedic people (Indo-Aryans) with the Indo-Europeans and Indo-Iranians. That the Indo-Aryans moved eastwards may be indicated in such material remains" (Tripathi 2001a: 27-28).

However, Shaffer (1989) has pointed out that the Black-and-Red Ware and associated cultural traits, common in the Iron Age complexes in South Asia, were unknown to the west of the Indus valley. The early Iranian iron objects are ornamental, perhaps ceremonial and status-linked objects as they are mostly found from burials, besides the Grey Ware. Such a stage is entirely absent in South Asia. Hence there seems to be a sharp difference in the context of functional nature of South Asian and south West Asian objects. This observation also supports the idea of indigenous development of iron technology.

Recent studies (Tripathi and Misra 1997) indicate that in the first half of 1st millennium BC, hunting tools were used more and most of the objects were made of wrought iron. This does not indicate a lack of knowledge of metallurgical processes or carburization as we have seen the evidence of carburization from various sites. Perhaps smiths exercised a deliberate and conscious choice and manufactured only what was required. For example, the techniques necessary for the manufacture of sharp-edged weapons or longer lasting, sharp-edged craftsmen's implements did not have to be the same as those for household items, utensils, etc. The ethnographic studies of the Asur-Birjia, the Mahuli Agarias (producing white iron) or the Parsa group of Agarias in Central India and the Kamis in Darjeeling (iron-makers for weapons like swords and gun) suggest that the ancient workers had deliberate choice of ore, technique and product. The Pali texts (6th century BC) also inform that quenching was done especially for ploughshares to make them sharp-edged, durable and malleable. The variety of iron samples—*kant loha, tikshna loha, munda loha,* being soft iron, carbon-steel and cast iron respectively—have also been mentioned in literary sources. The detailed and intricate process of manufacturing such divergent types of iron have been elaborately described in the early medieval alchemy texts like the *Ras Ratna Samuchchaya.* People engaged in full-time smithy perhaps lived in *kammar-gama* (artisans" settlements), which are mentioned in Pali literature and the *Arthasastra* and they were perhaps outside the state control.

Subsequently the smiths mastered iron technology and developed purification technique of iron and produced wootz, which became world famous as Damascus steel. As the archaeological evidence suggests, iron became common close to the beginning of 1st millennium BC. In course of time, the subsistence became largely based on agriculture as the increased number of agricultural tools and more evidence of carburization would also indicate. Though carburization had begun in early 1st millennium BC yet not many objects were processed. By AD 300 they had mastered casting. The occurrence of iron ores, evidence of ancient smelting sites, pre-industrial sites and Iron Age cultures, barring the doab zone, appear to overlap in various regions of South Asia.

CONCLUSIONS

The foregoing discussion shows that there is circumstantial evidence of diffusion of iron technology from Caucasus to north-wesern region and Himalayan region. The iron technology could have travelled in early 1st millennium BC down to the Ganga valley. Iron is widely referred in ancient literature. Parpola seems to give credit of the introduction of the Megalithic culture of south to the horse-riding and warring nomads, probably speaking a west Aryan/ Iranian language. On the other hand, a large number of pre-industrial workings, ethnographic data and some recent archaeological evidence is suggestive of various centres of development of iron technology even before the 1st millennium BC (as at Raja-Karna-ka Kila and Malhar in UP). Iron certainly appeared in various parts of South Asia around 1st millennium BC, perhaps even earlier, though its role in the urbanization of the Ganga doab is noticeable only by mid-1st millennium BC. It may not have appeared everywhere at the same time and it is quite possible that the older cultures/cultural traits continued in the so-called Iron Age. We need a lot more systematic research to have a better understanding in a pan-Asian context. We do not know why cast iron was so late in India and the exact antiquity and various stages of wootz making have also to be worked out. Chakrabarti rightly points outs that it is difficult to find the beginning of iron technology in ancient literature but we need to study the Sangam literature also for metallurgical techniques of wootz and iron.

Chapter 6

ROLE OF CENTRAL HIMALAYAS

Contents:

- PREAMBLE
- EARLY AGRICULTURE
- GENETIC DATA
- ARCHAEOLOGICAL EVIDENCE
- LINGUISTIC DATA
- METAL TECHNOLOGY
- CONCLUSIONS

PREAMBLE

The new state of Uttaranchal in North India, in the Central Himalayas (Fig. 6-1), comprises the major divisions of Almora, Nainital, Garhwal and Pithoragarh (Fig. 6-3). Recent years have seen fairly extensive archaeological research in this region, thanks to the efforts of the Kumaun and Garhwal universities and the Uttar Pradesh State Department of Archaeology, besides our own modest efforts (Agrawal and Kharakwal 1998).

The Central Himalayas provide a mini-example for understanding the Indian civilizational processes. Through the Millennia, different tribes and people—Protoaustroloids, Mundas, Kiratas, Mongoloids, Indo-Aryans, Khasas, Sakas and others—have been pouring into this cultural cauldron and leaving their signatures and producing a mosaic of cultures, which got integrated in the course of time. For long years, this region of Central Himalayas was considered a *cul-de-sac*. But now it is becoming clear that this region has provided a corridor for cultural interactions. We have briefly indicated the role of the Central Himalayas in the introduction of copper and iron technology and the urbanization processes of the Ganga valley (Chapter 5). The new evidence requires a paradigm shift in our thinking.

It is very interesting to note that in this region, the local deities are more powerful than the Brahmanical gods. The antiquity of the local deities goes back to prehistoric times. Even Badrinath, which has been regarded a Vaishnav deity is, in fact, a local god. Nanda is essentially a local goddess but later on appropriated as a consort of Shiva. In the Central Himalayas, one can also study how people create deities (and not vice versa!). Often historical personages have been deified as powerful gods like Goll Devata. He was in fact, a court judge of the local kings less than a thousand years back. There are several shrines in this region devoted to him. Thus we see that the process of apotheosis of making gods of historical persons can be seen in a very concrete form here. Brijendra Lal Shah ("Lala") has brought

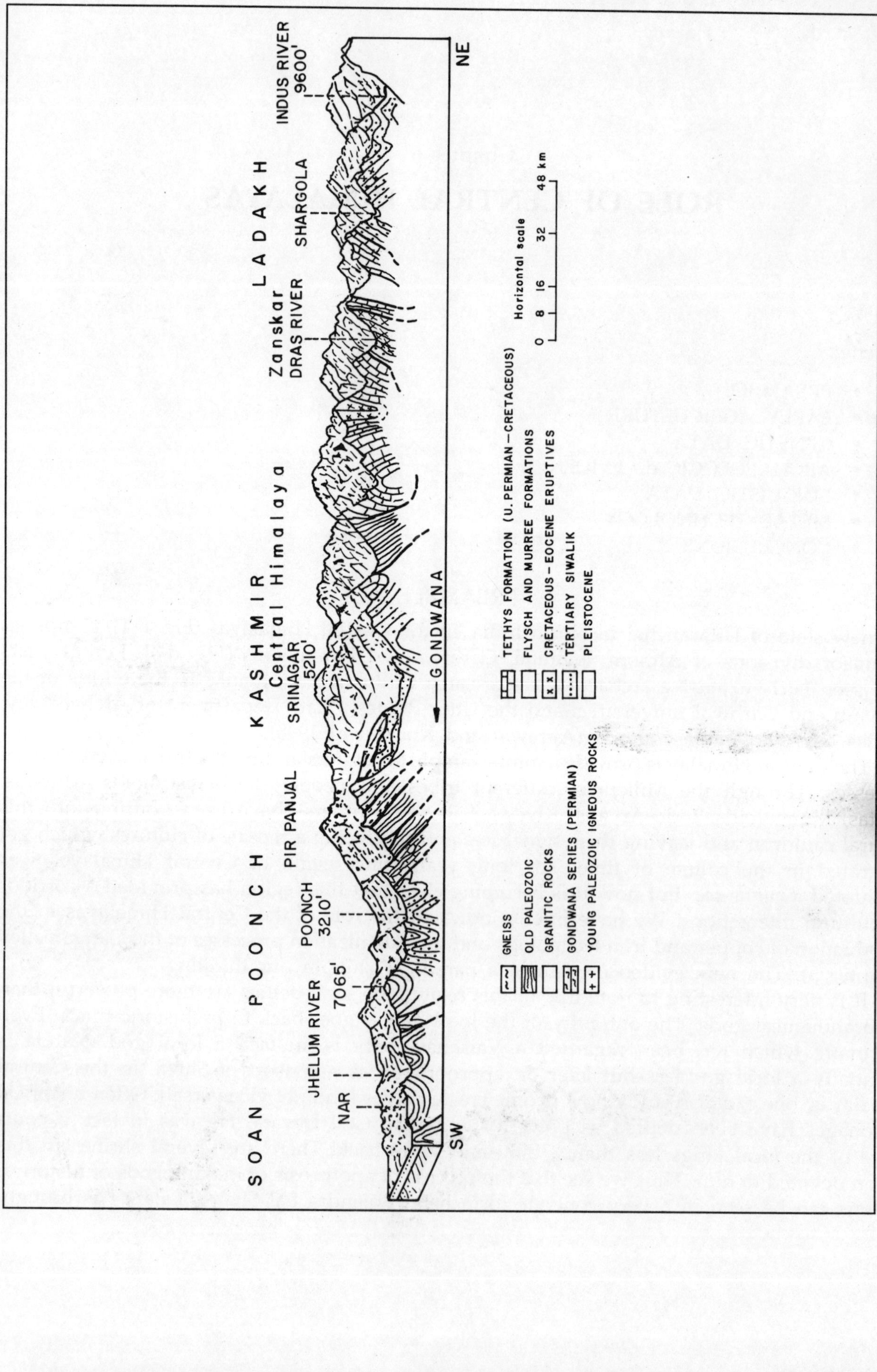

Fig. 6-1. Block diagrammatical sketch of the north-western Himalayas.

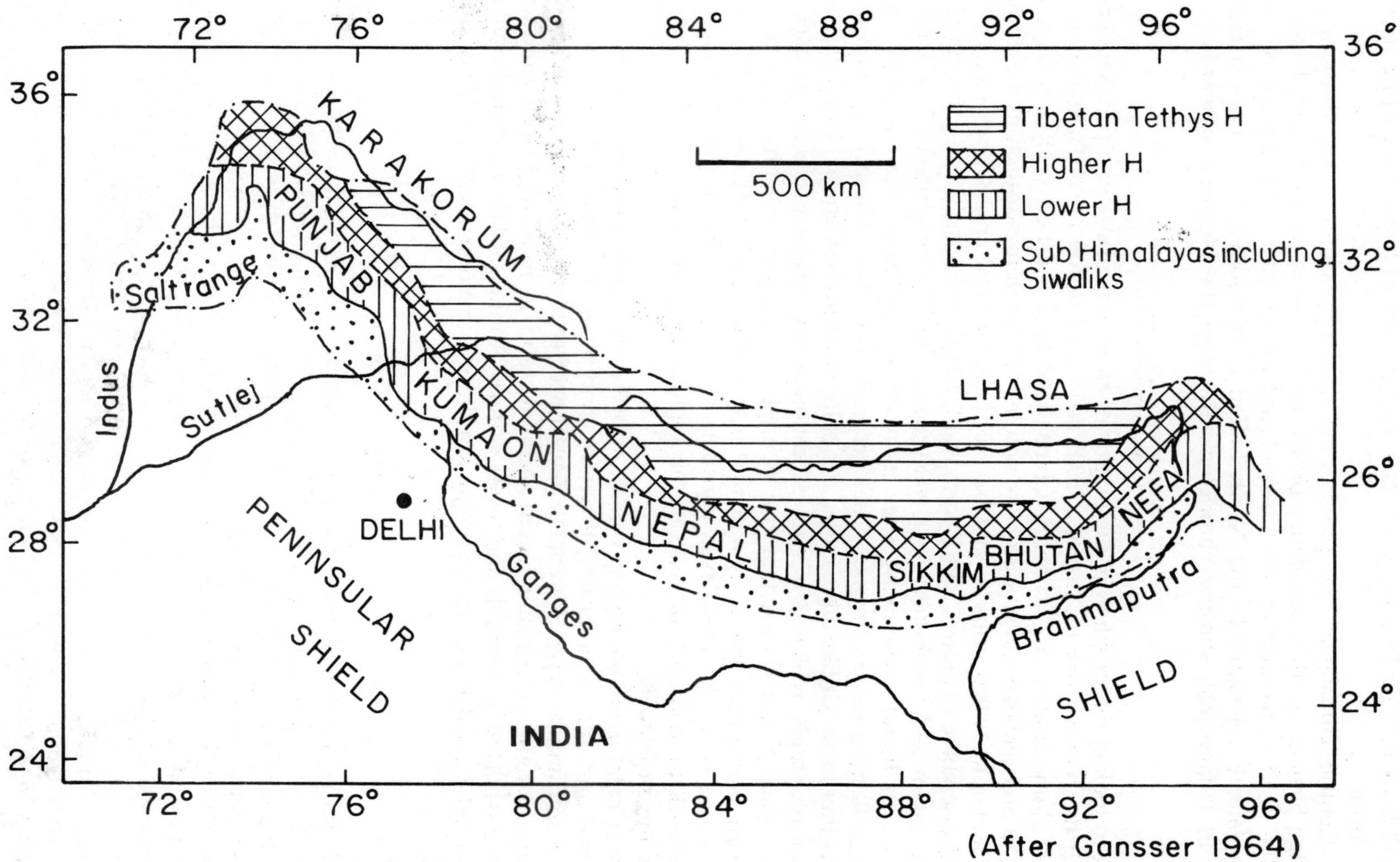

Fig. 6-2. Map of Himalayas showing higher, lower and sub-Himalayas, and Tibetan Tethys Himalayas.

out a small book on Goll Devata, which is in fact, a piece of historical writing though written in verse form.

The Central Himalayas also provide excellent opportunities for studying Traditional Knowledge Systems as they are better preserved here than in the plains. These systems of knowledge need to be studied, documented and preserved for the benefit of human kind. To appreciate its relevance to the North Indian archaeology, let us have a closer look at the past of Uttaranchal, starting chronologically from the Neolithic onwards.

EARLY AGRICULTURE

We have to look at the problem of the origins of early agriculture in a pan-Asian perspective.

With the recent work of Yasuda (2000: 1-4) and Gordon (1999 Field Report), the dates of earliest domesticated rice in south China have been pushed back considerably. Recent progress in archaeobotanical studies have pointed to rice domestication in the middle reaches of the Yangtze to 10,000 years BC and beyond (see Agrawal and Kharakwal 2002). We have discussed elsewhere (Agrawal and Kharakwal 2002) that the early rice growing communities of China, Japan and South-East Asia were using Cord Ware pottery. This kind of pottery has been also found from many sites in north-eastern India, Ganga valley and Central Himalayas. Barring the last region, it has generally been found associated with the evidence of rice in other areas. Unlike other crops, rice cultivation in the Central Himalayas, is associated with a lot of rituals, which is a sure indication of its antiquity. Recent archaeological and linguistic research has shown that rice domestication in south China goes back to 15,000 years. There is evidence that early agriculture spread to South-East Asia and to Brahmaputra valley, as also along the Himalayan corridors. We will not be surprised if the antiquity of rice goes back to thousands of years in this region. Linguistic evidence also sheds some new light on the problem.

Rice (*Oryza*) is unique among cereals in being an aquatic crop, which can vary between a perennial and annual according to water conditions. The wild *Oryza rufipogon* has both perennial and annual types. Perennials have lower seed productivity, lower self-pollination, long anther length and greater height. Annuals tend to have high seed productivity, self-pollination, short anther length and lesser stature. Annuals adapt to more heavily disturbed conditions like pond edges and drought conditions, making them the likely domestic rice ancestor.

GENETIC DATA

A significant proportion of the South-East Asian human populations possess the 9-BP "non-deletion" allele on Ddel (10394)-Alul (10397) +/+ or +/-backgrounds. In fact, the two classes of haplotypes observed in South-East Asian populations, one of which is completely absent in Indian populations, leads one to believe that they were derived from two sources; one from India and the other possibly from central or southern China. It may be noted that the 9-BP deletion is present in high frequencies among Tharus and Japanese populations that are postulated to have arisen from human migrations originating from southern China (Roychoudhury *et al.* 2000: 1182-1192). Tharus now live in the foothills of the Central Himalayas. Another tribe, called Raji-Raut, is also suspected to be original speakers of MonKhmer language. It may be essential to determine if there is genetic evidence also of the south China populations having come through the Central Himalayas corridors.

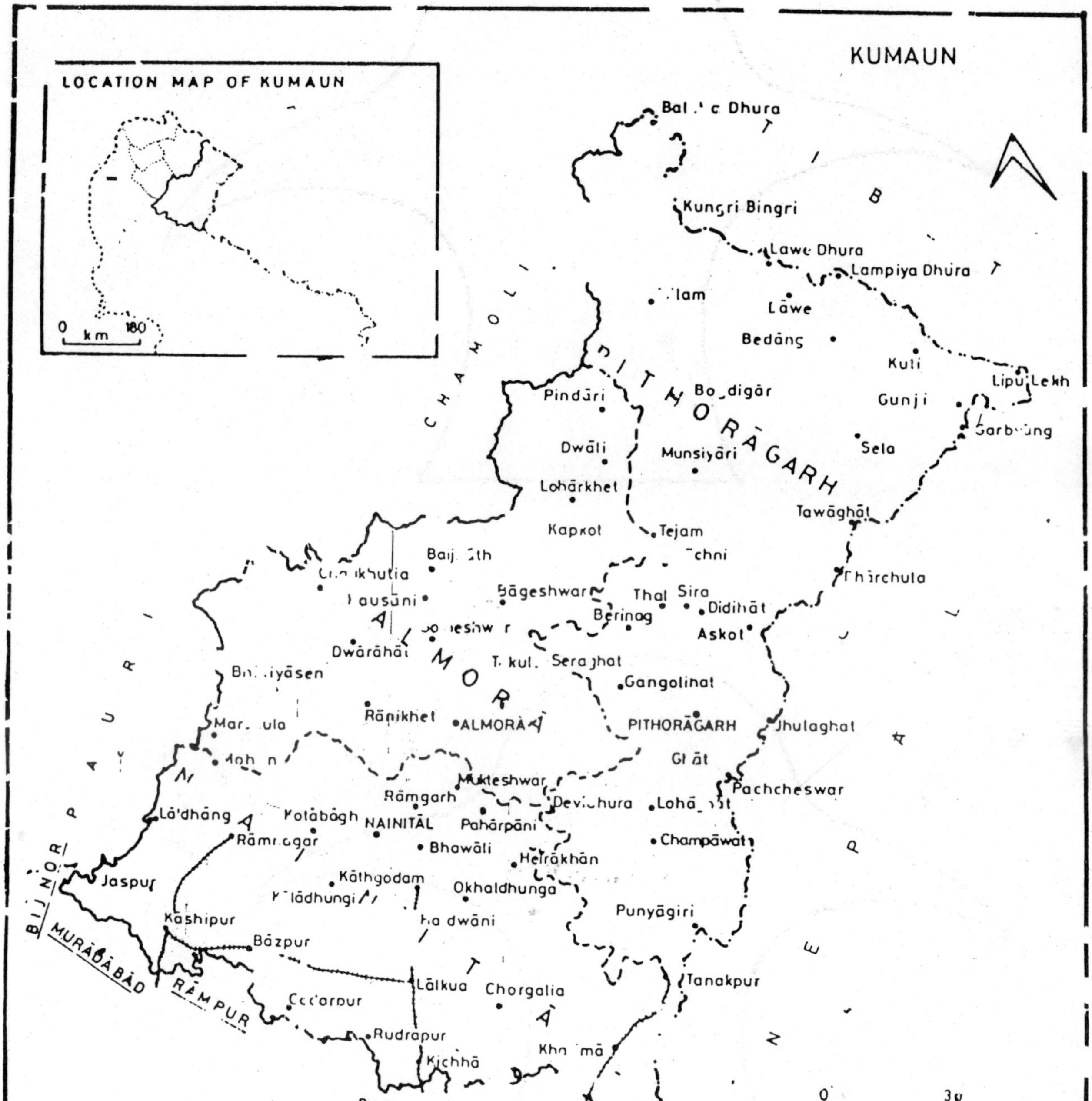

Fig. 6-3. Map of Kumaun showing main sites.

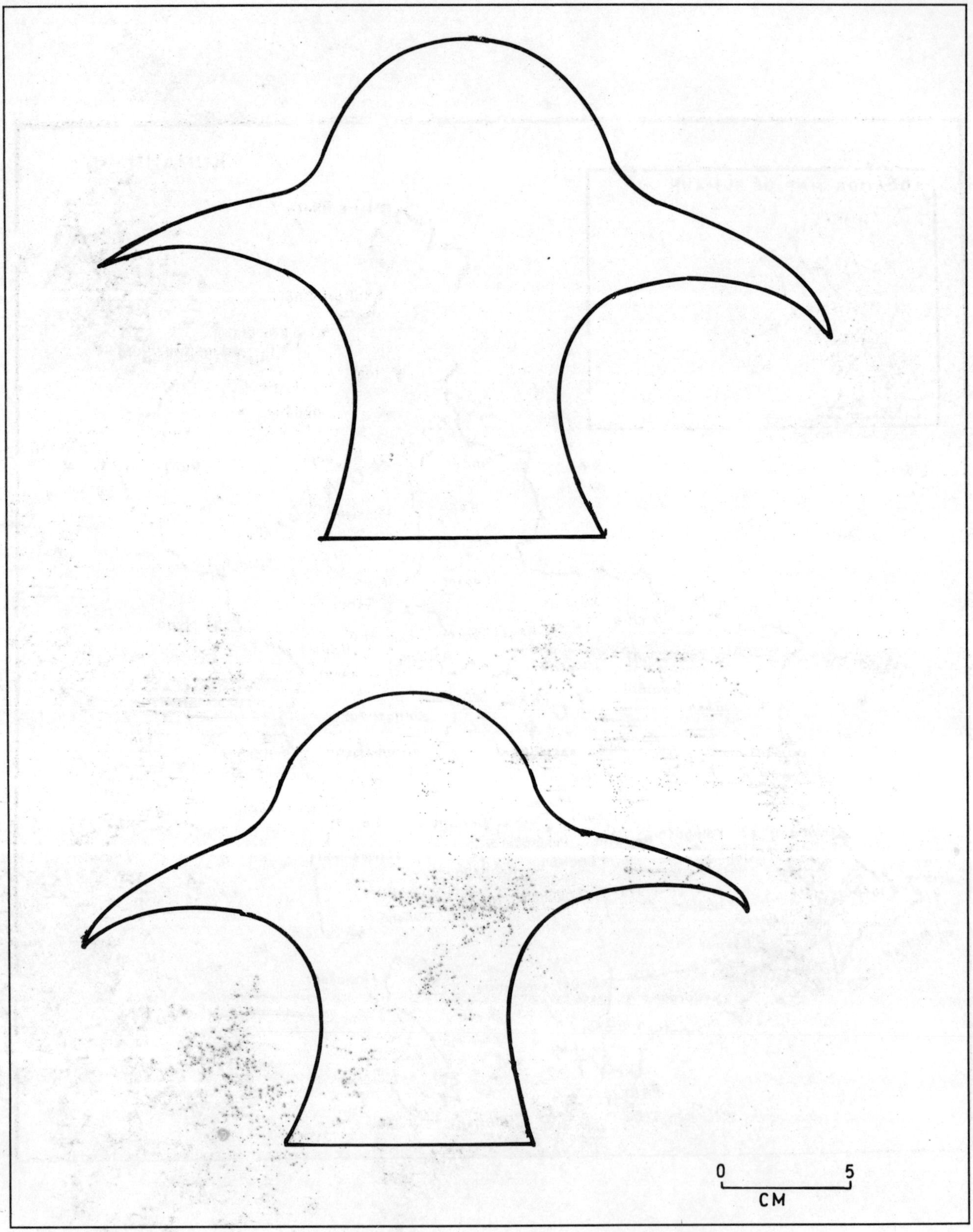

Fig. 6-4. Copper anthropomorph from District Pithoragarh.

Chinese wild rice *japonica* carries specific isozyme alleles and neucleo- and cyto-types at high frequency. Carrying this further, DNA analyst Sato (1996) showed that *indica* and *japonica* differentiated before domestication. As the main domesticated rice in China is *japonica,* we should look for circumstances surrounding its transition from wild *rufipogon*. The same should be studied for the Indian varieties also. This transition can be estimated with multivariate analysis of wild vs domesticated rice phytoliths, but important environmental data may be found using pollen and insects from the same samples.

ARCHAEOLOGICAL EVIDENCE

In the Ganga valley, several sites have yielded rice impressions on clay, e.g. Koldihwa, Mahagara, Chapani Mando and others. Though abundant use of domesticated rice in the subcontinent comes from Pirak, which begins around *c.* 1800 BC whereas in the Ganga valley sites it has been assigned to 7-6th millennium BC (Sharma *et al.* 1980: 23). There are four radiocarbon determinations for the Mahagara Neolithic phase with calibrated dates ranging between *c.* 1700 and 1200 BC, concordant with the chronology of Pirak I. It should be noted that an uncal. ^{14}C date for the pre-Neolithic Mahagara is 8080+115 BC (Sharma *et al.* 1980: 3). We, however, think that rice domestication in this area should go to early Holocene period. Though some of the dates go back to 7000 BP, there is considerable controversy both about chronology and proof of domestication. Rice (*Oryza sativa*) is the most popular cereal in South Asia today. Wild rice, *Oryza rufipogon* is pan-tropical in distribution and found generally in the Ganga valley, Indus river system and in Gujarat. The archaeological record in India suggests that hunting and gathering communities used the wild form. We have, however, yet to make some serious effort to find out when exactly rice came under cultivation in the Ganga valley and in Central Himalayas. We thus see that rice technology has a high probability to reach Central Himalayas and then on to Ganga valley from south China. But this has to be confirmed through a multidisciplinary study as suggested above.

LINGUISTIC DATA

Grierson (1967-68) in his linguistic survey of the Himalayas had identified some residue of MonKhmer words in the Kumauni dialects. MonKhmer is part of the Austro-Asiatic language group (Bayard 1996). With the new ^{14}C AMS dates from Thailand, the copper metallurgy there can be pushed back to 2nd-3rd Millennia BC. White (1997) reports, "The earliest evidence of bronze at Ban Chiang appears by Early Period II/III in both burial and non-burial contexts. The calibrated results… indicate an early 2nd millennium BC date for this part of the sequence". White further says, "The 3 KUM dating and pollen evidence is broadly consistent with Blust's (1996) linguistic arguments for the expansion of rice-cultivating, MonKhmer speaking societies down the Mekong from south-western China beginning by the late 6th millennium BC". The dates quoted by White from 3 KUM come from a sediment core. The evidence is consistent with land clearance in the early 5th millennium BC. Such a date seems to accord well with the linguistic argument of Blust (1996). Our experience from the Rajasthan lakes has also been similar: the advent of *Cerealia* type pollen is accompanied (*c.* 7000 BP) by finely comminuted charcoal, which has been interpreted as clearance for agriculture (Singh *et al.* 1990: 351-358). White argues for a 6th millennium BC beginning of agriculture accompanied by the expansion of the MonKhmer family of languages, as argued by Blust (1996) and a substantial time gap between the advent of agriculture and metallurgy. Higham, on the other hand, thinks that this gap could be only a few hundred years.

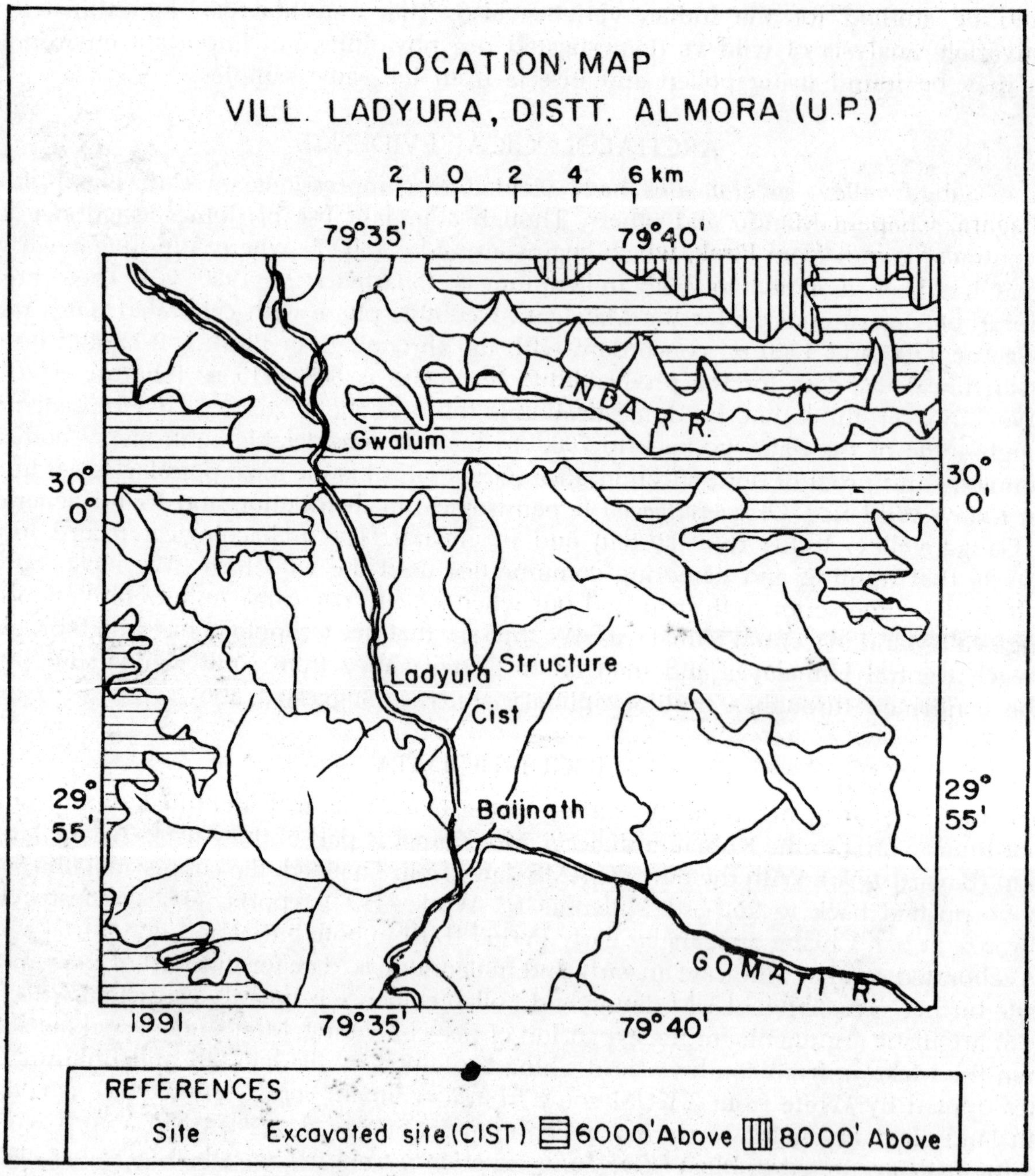

Fig. 6-5. Location map of the Megalithic site, Ladyura, District Almora.

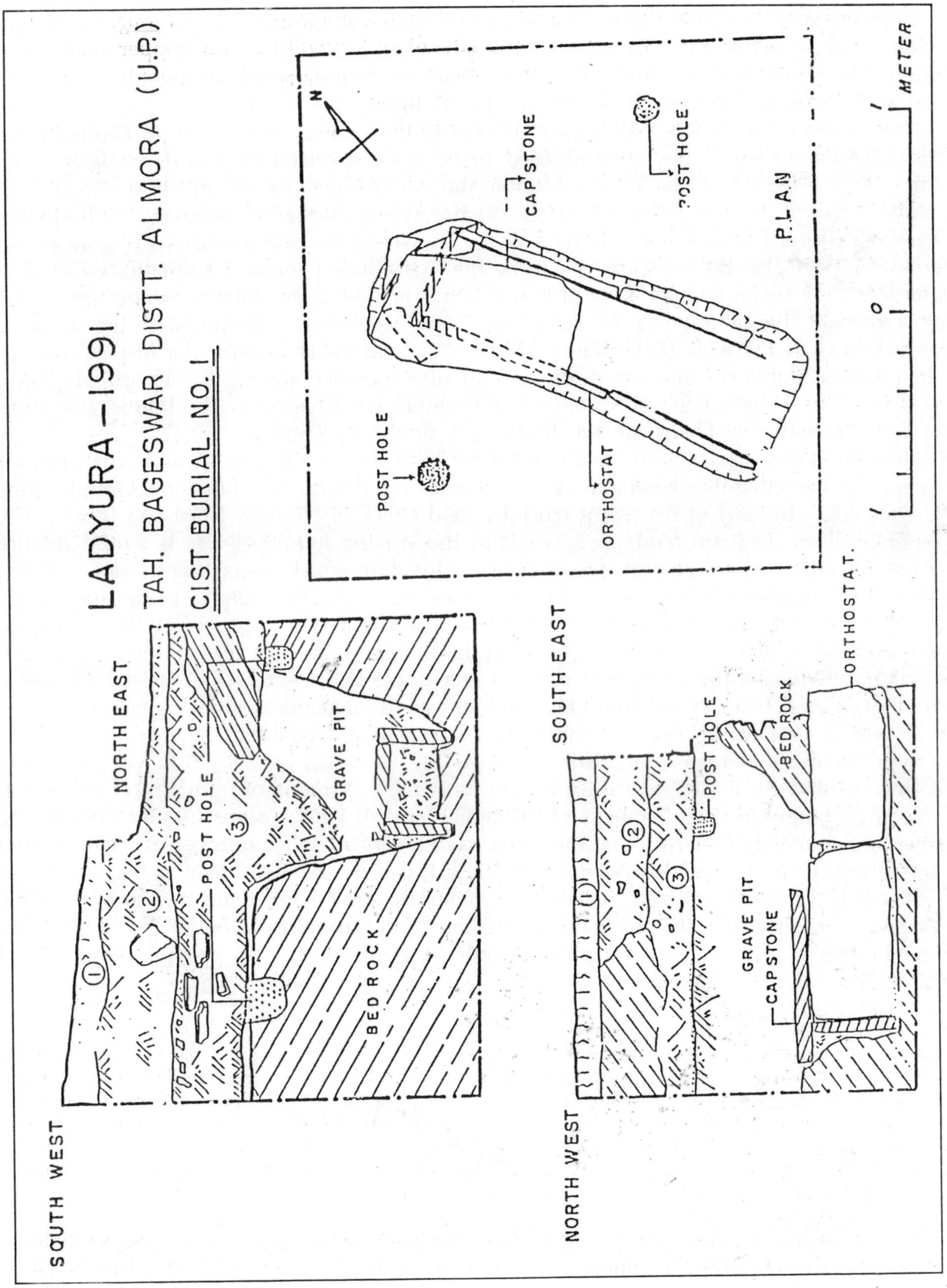

Fig. 6-6. Plan of excavated cists and post-holes, Ladyura, District Almora.

Unfortunately in India, the north-east is still archaeologically a *terra incognita*. It will be interesting to define the gap between the advent of agriculture and copper metallurgy through the Himalayan corridor. The movement of Munda-speaking people along the Himalayan corridor, however, is generally agreed upon.

Now let us see how this evidence is relevant to the Central Himalayas. In Kumaun, the *shilpkars*, earlier called Doms, are supposed to be Kols, speakers of Munda dialects (D.D. Sharma 1988, 1989,1990,1994a, 1994b). Munda and MonKhmer dialects are two branches of the Austro-Asiatic family. There are many Austro-Asiatic aboriginal languages still spoken in Thailand (Bayard Pers. Comm.; Bayard 1996). Elsewhere we have discussed (Agrawal and Kharakwal, 1998) that the Kols are said to be the first ethnic people of Kumaun, which had descended from the Munda-speaking group, which is related to the Austro-Asiatic sub-group. They represent the aborigines of Kumaun. Doms (*ṣhilpkars*) are perhaps the modern representatives of the Kols (Atkinson 1980-81: 370), who today occupy the lowest rung in the hierarchical status in Kumauni society and are now included among the Scheduled Castes. They also claim to have been in Kumaun before either the Khasiya or the immigrants from the plains arrived. The Doms are the traditional smiths in Kumaun.

Higham (1996) discusses the relationship between the Austro-Asiatic and Austronesian languages and whether they belong to a common ancestral Austric phylum and its implications for archaeology. In view of the recent work by Reid (1993, in Higham 1996) and Blust (1993, in Higham 1996), Higham tends to agree with the Austric hypothesis as it would require only one Neolithic expansion and spread of rice cultivation which, according to him, is better supported by archaeological evidence. He describes the SE Asian rivers as being like spokes in a wheel, "with the hub in the eastern foothills of the Himalayas.... In a westward direction, ancestors of the Munda moved, perhaps down the Brahmaputra into eastern India" (Higham 1996: 115). Obviously, the movement did not stop there but went further westward to the Central Himalayas. This type of South-East and westward movements probably better explains the expansion first of the rice cultivation and later on of metallurgy.

Synthesizing the archaeo-linguistic evidence Bayard (1996) agrees, "It is very tempting to correlate this with the westward expansion, under the stimulus of agriculture, of Austro-Asiatic (AA) language from Nanhailand through Vietnam, Laos, Cambodia and Thailand to Burma and ultimately eastern India. Linguists have reconstructed a number of terms related to agriculture in proto-Munda and some of these (husked rice, rice husking pestle) appear to go back to proto-AA as well. It has been generally agreed for some time now that the prehistoric and Early Historic inhabitants of Thailand and Burma spoke languages in the Mon-Khmer branch of AA. Such an expansion would account neatly in a general sense for the distribution of the AA languages".

Bayard further says,

> Based on morphological evidence such as that presented by Reid (1988: 31-32, in Bayard 1996), Blust is convinced that Schmidt's Austric hypothesis is correct and postulates an Austric homeland in the eastern Himalayan foothills in the area of the converging Valleys of the Salween, Mekong and Yangtze rivers. From this homeland, one group of rice cultivating people moved down into the middle Yangtze valley to give rise to the AT superfamily of languages ca. 6500-6000 BC. Somewhat later the now-proto-AA speakers remaining in the homeland began to move down the Valleys of the Salween and Mekong (proto-Mon-Khmer), with pre-Munda speakers moving westward down the Brahmaputra...

We admit that considerable miscegenation has been going on in the Central Himalayas for several millennia and the concept of race is now defunct. Yet in the relative isolation

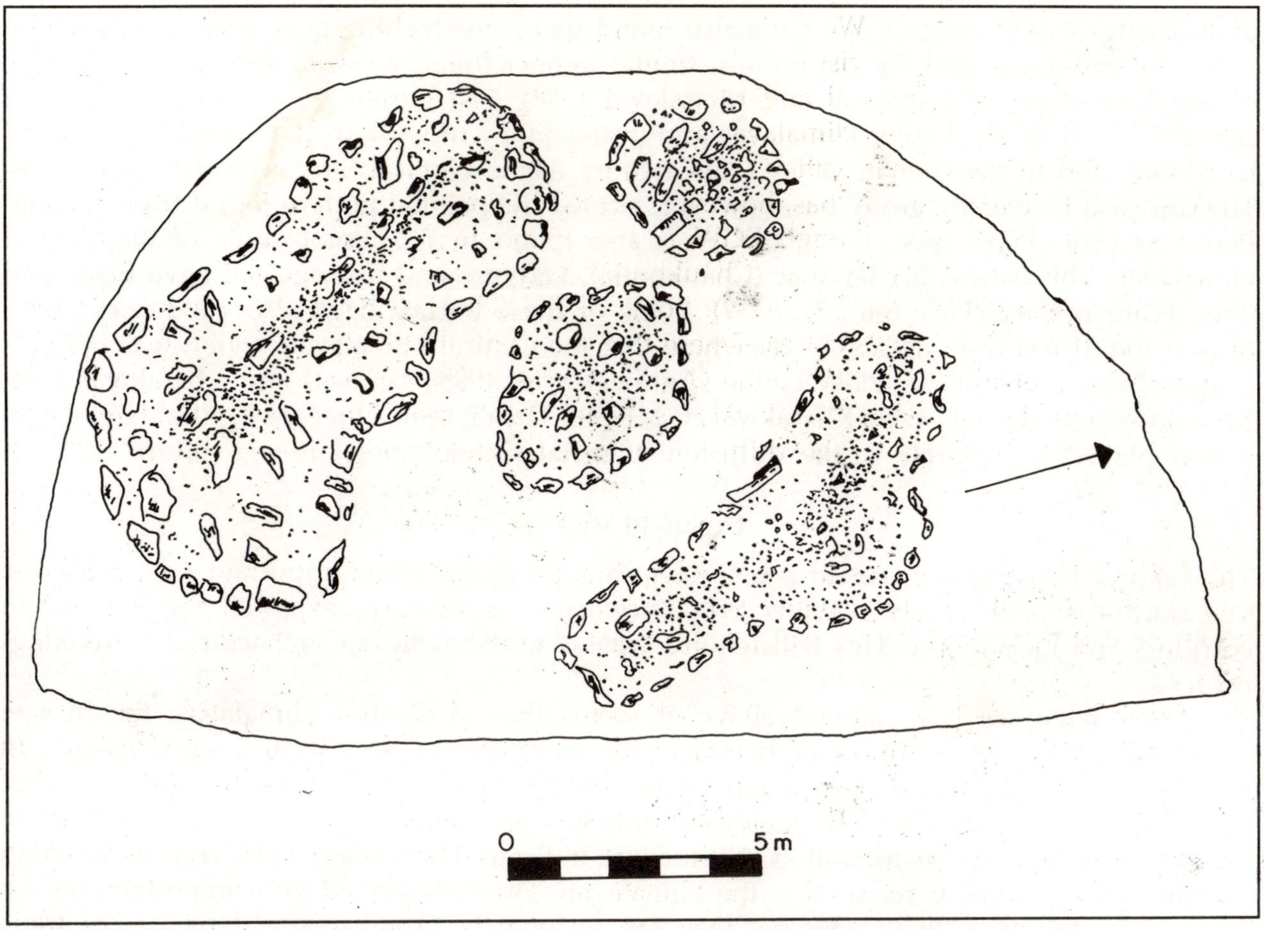

Fig. 6-9. Cairn burials near the cup-marks site Odyari, District Almora.

(compared to the Ganga doab) of Central Himalayas, one can still observe that the Brahmins and Kshatriyas have sharp features and fair complexion. The Bhotiyas and the descendants of the Kiratas bear unmistakable Mongoloid features. The Doms, who practise blacksmithy as a traditional craft, are typically short-statured, dark complexioned and answer to Austro-Asiatic features.

METAL TECHNOLOGY

Let us briefly look at the possibility of contacts between Central Himalayas and Ganga valley in early metal technology and metals.

The Copper Hoards of the Ganga valley are by and large made of arsenical copper, the source of which was perhaps Central Himalays (Agrawal 2000). In recent years, copper hoards have also been found from many sites in the Central Himalayan region, which are technologically crude compared to the Doab examples. A hoard of five anthropomorphs (Pl. 6-1) was discovered from an earthen jar buried in the ground at Khuna-Tok in Nainipatal village of Munakot block in Pithoragarh district (Fig. 6-4). We have discussed this evidence in Chapter 4. We examined these artefacts at the Government Museum Almora. It is quite likely that they preceded the Ganga specimens. There has been a strong tradition of ancient copper and iron mining and smelting in Kumaun region as the discovery of, a large number of such sites would suggest. We have also found that iron smelting goes back in this region to 1st millennium BC and the cist burials, similar to ones found in Swat, appear to be equally ol (Agrawal *et al.* 195; Agrawal and Kharakwal 1998). Cist burials were exposed at Malari (Pls. 6-2, -3 -4), in the higher Himalayas and in the valley of western Ramganga by Garhwal University and in the Gomati valley (Figs. 6-5) by Archaeological Survey in the early 1990s. The Garhwal University group has, however, termed the painted pottery found from Sanana-Baseri as proto-PGW type, though PGW is also found in the remote hills of the Central Himalayas. The cists at Bechandhar (Chaukhutia), Ladyura and Gagrigol all have Black and Grey Ware pottery (Figs. 6-6, -7, -8, -9). Some of these burials have also yielded evidence of iron too. It has been discussed elsewhere that the Central Himalayan region was perhaps a prime source of iron for PGW cultue (Agrawal *et al.* 1995; Agrawal and Kharakwal 1998; Kharakwal and Harbola 1996; Kharakwal *et al.* 1993). Thus it seems that the Central Himalayan region played a vital role in the diffusion of metal technologies and agriculture.

CONCLUSIONS

The Central Himalayas in recent years, have thus produced some important new evidence. The north-east still largely remains *terra incognita*. It is time we explored the Himalayan corridors and looked east. This will require a paradigm shift in our archaeological thinking-no less.

From what we have argued above, it seems that in Central Himalayas, the human occupation is as old as any other region of the subcontinent despite its rugged terrain. In fact, this region, endowed with a rare scenic beauty, may not have been a *cul-de-sac* but involved in the dynamics of technological diffusion as the evidence of, a large number of archeaometallurgical sites as well as rich folklore indicate. The folklore even records different human immigrations. It seems that the Himalayan corridors played very important role in trade and agriculture of this region. One can fortunately visualize the dynamics of trade to date across the Himalayas as now Gunji, an important corridor, is opened. These considerations justify the inclusion of this small chapter in the archaeology of North India.

Chapter 7

CONCLUSIONS

South Asian archaeology still seems to be preoccupied with only artefacts and material remains, without any serious efforts to look beyond—to humans and their society, which created them. When the French Annales Schools (Braudel 1972; Bintliff 1991) are providing new ideas and insights for archaeological reconstructions, we in South Asia seem to have stuck up most of the time with morphological descriptions of artefacts. In contrast is the book, *The Archaeology of Society in the Holy Land* (Levy 1998), in which the very title emphasizes that it is archaeology of society, not merely of artefacts. There are excellent reconstructions in the book: not flights of fancy–but logical inferences based on multidisciplinary data.

We have done some interdisciplinary studies to reconstruct the past environment. The most exhaustive studies have been done in Kashmir, Rajasthan and Gujarat. In other areas, the evidence is still sketchy. In marginal areas, like Rajasthan and Kashmir, a little change in precipitation or temperature forces the humans to seek out greener pastures. The mid-Holocene climatic amelioration is a global phenomenon and it has had its impact on the Neolithic and Bronze Age cultures in India too. The turn of the 2nd millennium BC, was followed by severe aridity, which had a marked impact on the decline of the Harappans; and at the beginning of the 1st millennium BC, on the Chalcolithic cultures of the Deccan. We have quoted a long passage from Diamond's *Guns, Germs and Steel* in Chapter 2 to emphasize that the environmental changes do affect humans, as they did in the past, as well as do today. We need to study the Bronze and Iron Age cultures in a holistic perspective, which takes into account resources, technology and environmental change. This is one of the directions in which we have to move. In Chapter 2, we have discussed the evidence of environmental change and what needs to be done.

We have discussed elsewhere (Agrawal and Kharakwal 2002) that the roots of plant and animal domestication and agriculture could be traced to the Transitional Cultures (Upper Palaeolithic and Mesolithic), which in fact, paved the way for revolutionary changes in the society. We have discussed the beginning of village life and cultivation of various cereals, millets, maize, rice, etc. Agricultural surplus and new metal technologies led to urbanization of the Bronze Age.

Thanks to decades of painstaking and meticulous work of the French team in Mehrgarh and Nausharo area, led by Catherine and J.F. Jarrige and with no less significant contributions from Richard Meadow, now we can trace a continuous history of humans—from the late Stone Age to the flowering of the Great Indus civilization. Their researches have finally demonstrated that the Indus civilization, a glorious chapter of South Asian history, was first written in Baluchistan and not in the Sarasvati valley, as some scholars have claimed. Their explorations also finally settled the controversy whether the Indus civilization was a West Asian implant. It has turned out to be a flowering of purely the South Asian genius. We have discussed the Indus civilization, or Harappa culture, in Chapter 3.

The Great Indus civilization was a gigantic phenomenon both temporally and spatially. It begins in the 3rd millennium BC and shows signs of withering away at the turn of the 2nd millennium BC. It spread from Baluchistan-Makran in the west to Alamgirpur in the east; from Jammu in the north, to south Gujarat in the south – an area more than a million sq km; more than the area of present-day Pakistan. The first discovery of the Indus civilization at Harappa, gave a big boost to the nationalist freedom movement. It showed that the British masters were still barbarians, when their colonies had developed into highly planned towns. Somehow, the large Harappan towns attracted the excavators more and as a result our knowledge of the Indus civilization is a bit skewed. We know so little about its rural component, or the role played by the neighbouring village-based societies and the hunter-gatherer tribes. We have highlighted the role of Jodhpura Complex in supplying metal artefacts and ingots to the Harappans and also of the hunter-gatherers in supplying minerals, conch shells, precious stones, etc., for the Harappan artisans. We have ventured to identify the Jodhpura Complex sites with the Meluhha of the Mesopotamian texts. It is interesting to note that even in the 3rd millennium BC, the affluent Harappan state did not allow the polluting smelting furnaces in their towns, but used the poor village based societies to do this dirty job for them, very much as it is done today by the rich nations who dump their dirty chemical and even nuclear waste on the Third World countries!

Thus we see that unlike the usual belief, smelting was mainly an industry looked after by the village-based societies or tribes. The tribal people did not only practise iron technology, they kept it alive despite the export of cheap iron by the British to their colonies.

In a way, the Indus civilization depicts the concept of Indian civilization, which always had unity in diversity, a concept under attack these days by overzealous jingoists. The Indus civilization shows uniformity in weights, measures, planning, industries, etc.; but the regional beliefs were not interfered with. Some regions practised mother-goddess cults, others used fire-altars for worship; there was considerable variation in burial customs also; even in items of daily use, there was variation in detail. Each Harappan town seems to represent not only an economic interest, but also a system of beliefs and language. Harappa which controlled the hilly trade in timber and minerals eventually developed into a centre of Punjabi language and culture; Mohenjodaro which supervised sea trade became the centre for the Sindhi culture and language; Rakhigarhi which perhaps controlled the copper mineral wealth in its hinterland, eventually developed into a Hindi-speaking group of people and so on.

Despite the domination of studies in the Harappan phase, no definite criteria for identifying domestication of various animals have been scientifically standardized. One glaring example is of horse bones. Though there are large collections of bones from various sites like Kalibangan, Banawali, Dholavira, etc., they have not been systematically studied to solve this problem of horse in the Harappan sites. We need to study some rich collections from a place like British Museum and establish the diagnostic criteria. Of course, there are some honourable exceptions. Deccan College Research Institute has done some pioneering studies in these fields, but it cannot cover the whole of the continent.

For some time, Indus civilization was taken to be a sort of storm in the cup: it appeared out of the blue and vanished without a trace. But now we know that it was a gradual cultural development from hunter-gathering subsistence to full-fledged urbanism. Nor did it vanish into thin air. It continues to be the solid substrate of the Indian civilization. The traditions of water ablution, mother-goddess cults, phallic symbols, basic architectural styles, Yoga, tree worship, etc., can all be traced back to the Indus civilization. Now there is evidence to show that it did not simply collapse but gradually transformed into non-urban cultures.

There is a difference of opinion about the causes of its decline.

Obviously, it was not one single cause, which put an end to this grand chapter of Indian history. After the mid-Holocene climatic amelioration, for which we have ample evidence from Rajasthan, Gujarat, Kashmir and even the Ganga doab, the turn of the 2nd millennium BC saw a climatic deterioration. As one moves eastwards from arid Sindh, precipitation increases and the onset of aridity seems to have pushed the Harappans to greener pastures. But by the time they reached the fringes of the Doab, the Harappans seem to have withered away. Perhaps the monsoon ecology of the Doab was too much for them to cope up with, used as they were to semi-arid environment. There is evidence of disturbed times as large gold and silver hoards have been found from western Uttar Pradesh. It is estimated that Mandi, in Muzaffarnagar district, alone yielded 30-40 kg. of jewellery! If there were large migrations from the west, they could have hastened the demise. One is not talking of Aryan invasion here, as there is no concrete evidence of that. But there is a cultural break, the Indus script is forgotten forever and the urban centres vanished till we witness them again in the mid-1st millennium BC. Even the internal dynamics of cultures is such that they have all to go through a life cycle of birth, growth and death. In the riverine areas of Sindh, there is evidence of rise of water table and salt efflorescence rendering vast tracts of land infertile.

It may perhaps help to seek parallels from the Holy Land. *The Archaeology of Society in the Holy Land* (Levy 1998) offers very rational yet stimulating models to understand the social phenomena the Levant witnessed during its Bronze Age.

Denver says,

> The pattern of alternating phases of low-level and higher-level organization, a pattern of socio-political complexity spiralling upwards and downwards around the "domestic mode of production", is the essential characteristic of social evolution in the southern Levant. When modelling other periods and in cross-culture comparisons, these alternating patterns must be taken into account and individual episodes reassessed on that basis...
>
> The most fecund approach to understanding such short-term cycles of cultural complexity and changes as EB IV is probably that of "collapse", as several scholars have recently developed that notion (Yoffee and Cowgill 1988; Tainter 1988). In Palestine in EB IV, the centralized political institutions that regulated the flow of goods and services in the urban EB II-III era have broken down. Socio-economic structure collapsed down to a lower level of integration, where diversified but largely rural and pastoral nomadic strategies will enable the society to survive for more than three centuries, until the urban renaissance in Palestine begins with the Middle Bronze Age, *ca.* 2,000 BC. With that, the "Dark Age" ends. Perhaps the "darkness" was less an aspect of reality than of archaeological myopia. If so, it may be dispelled by more focused, sophisticated and disciplined fieldwork and research in the generation to come (in Levy 1998: 294-295).

To repeat Denver's quote, "In Palestine in EB IV, the centralized political institutions that regulated the flow of goods and services in the urban EB II-III era have broken down. Socio-economic structure collapsed down to a lower level of integration, where diversified but largely rural and pastoral nomadic strategies will enable the society to survive for more than three centuries... " Does this model also explain the fate of the Indus civilization? The main difference is that this devolution in South Asia continued for more than a millennium, when Iron Age urbanization revived higher-level integration of society.

The catastrophic change in the north-west of the subcontinent is writ large but has to be investigated further to understand its implications.

The glamour of archaeology of the rich Indus civilization, led to neglect of less prosperous cultures. Transition from Mesolithic to village-based agricultural societies to urban centres was not an exclusive Indus valley phenomenon, but a universal process, which is now traceable in Gujarat, Rajasthan, etc. At Balathal in Rajasthan, we encounter large houses and fortifications and signs of modest prosperity. So also in Gujarat, Mesolithic cultures were gradually using copper and increasing the size of their settlements and also population, as has been explained elsewhere (Agrawal and Kharakwal 2002). Some of the Chalcolithic cultures had some sort of symbiotic relationship with the Harappans.

There were many causes of the Harappan decline: aridification (for which there is now impeccable data from Rajasthn) (Agrawal 1982b; Wasson *et al.* 1983, 1984; COHMAP 1988) and elsewhere from India and globally too; waterlogging in the Indus; tectonic disorganization of perennial rivers like the Sarasvati and their eventual drying up (Agrawal and Sood 1982); the inability of the Harappan culture to cope up with the monsoon ecology of the Doab; and finally, any culture at some ripe stage has to die out. The process of birth, growth, decay and death governs organisms as well as cultures.

The beauty of the Chalcolithic cultures (Chapter 4) lies in their infinite variety and aesthetic rendering of even items of daily use, unlike the Harappans where a dull uniformity marks even the ceramics. Perhaps the Chalcolithic cultures had to contend with deteriorating climate, small alluvial strips, inadequacy of technology and dearth of tools to generate agricultural surplus that prevented them to reach the peaks of urbanism. In the Deccan, black cotton soil is rich and fertile and ubiquitous too but such a sticky soil required heavy ploughshares, which only the Iron Age could provide. Detailed demographic studies, keeping in view the ecological and technological constraints, can alone give us a richer picture of the Chalcolithic society.

The Copper Hoards culture is another enigma. A hoard from Gungeria, in Madhya Pradesh, weighed about 400 kg! The hoards give a false impression of abundance of copper, though the artefacts exhibit high technology of closed casting. Presence of arsenic, though common, does not appear deliberate but perhaps is an artefact of ore-impurities. The Copper Hoards have been circumstantially associated with the OCP, but as the hoards are themselves accidental finds, any definite association at this stage can only be conjectural. Besides, some waterlogged potsherds of Red Ware were termed Ochre Coloured Ware. The identities of different claimants of the term OCP have yet to be defined. Nor can the Copper Hoards be dated unless they are found from stratified digs with datable material, though there seems to be a general consensus that they can be assigned to 2nd millennium BC.

The problem of the Copper Hoards culture is quite challenging, not only for dating but to identify their authors too. Most of the Copper Hoards are accidental finds, so the first requirement is that we find them in stratified contexts. The evidence of Saipai is not too convincing. Their main types – antennae sword, harpoon and even the anthropomorphs – appear to be denoting a hunting economy. But the advanced technology of closed casting and the apparent abundance cannot totally rule out an urban economy. Should we expect to find towns created by the Copper Hoards culture in the Ganga valley? Can we hope to locate them in the thickly populated Ganga valley with vast layers of flood alluvia covering the sites? Though this is highly speculative at this stage, we would not be surprised if future research brings out such startling evidence. The new evidence from Pithoragarh and Madarpur, does indicate the role of the Central Himalayas in providing the arsenic laden copper for the tools. In any case, Copper Hoards do provide one of the most challenging problems (Chapter 4) of South Asian archaeology.

Iron brings us down to the historical era (Chapter 5). Now we do not have to depend exclusively on the archaeological data; literary evidence is also becomes available. The iron and ceramic technologies bring in their wake new ideas and materialistic philosophies of Charvak and the Lokayat schools. Atheistic theories claimed that after death the body decomposed and merged with the elements. Buddhism represented the new agricultural and trading classes and it was essentially a revolt against the old order of the Brahmanical rituals and nomadic pastoralism. Ceramic technology gave us the deluxe ware of the Northern Black Polished Ware. Iron was not necessarily a harder metal than bronze; its real strength lay in its abundance: it became a tool of the masses. The tangled forests and also its swamps required massive abundance of iron axes and ploughshares to colonize the Ganga valley. It is interesting to note here that the tribal people, against the onslaught of the cheap British industrial iron, preserved the traditional iron technology. Even in the Early Historical times, the non-urban tribal people produced iron and they were always beyond the pale of the state control. In China also the tribal people who were beyond the state control carried out iron production. We noticed in the Bronze Age also that the village-based societies of the Jodhpura Complex supplied copper artefacts and metal to the Harappans. They too were beyond the control of the Harappan state.

In Anatolia even smelted iron goes back to early 3rd millennium BC. As iron is generally a constituent of copper minerals like Chalcopyrite ($Cu_2SFe_2S_3$), Bornite (Cu_2FeSO_4) etc., it can be produced accidentally. Moorey (1994: 279) also explains that "it is possible under certain conditions to produce iron when smelting copper, it is increasingly thought likely that a significant proportion of the iron current in the Near east, at least before the Late Bronze Age, might have been produced in the process of smelting copper, or possibly lead". There is evidence of iron from very few Harappan sites, but that is not enough to establish the early stage.

There is some archaeological evidence, which suggests that iron technology was brought by the Indo-Aryans, as suggested by Parpola (1998). "Small parcels containing twigs of *Ephedra* have in several instances been found on the chests of bodies buried in shaft pit graves of the Afanas"evo/early Andronovo-related Gumugou I culture in the Lopnor region of the middle Tarim basin in Xinjiang (*c.* 2000-1550 BC).... Therefore, it may well be in Xinjiang that the Andronovians, here assumed to be ancestors of the Rigvedic Aryans, adopted the Soma cult...(Parpola 1998)" His suggestion that Indo-Aryans speaking people brought both iron and Megalithic burial custom with port-holes gets support by the discovery of port-hole cists datable to 900 BC, as also the iron slag bearing sites in Uttaranchal datable to the sam age (Agrawal *et al.* 1995).

On the other hand, in the course of the survey, various early Iron Age sites have been discovered, e.g. Raja-Karan-ka-Tila and Malhar, which seem to go back to the last quarter of the 2nd millennium BC. Considering literary, ethnographic and archaeological evidence, it seems that there has been a very strong tradition of iron making in India, which is still practiced in some regions. Unlike West Asia, we have not been able to locate the ornamental stage of the use of iron when it was as precious as silver. Use of meteoritic iron has also not been recorded so far. All these problems are unresolved mainly because we have not been able to carry out proper metallurgical investigations. There is urgent need to carry out such investigations.

The Ganga valley is a monsoon area with high rainfall and was full of swamps and dense forests. It therefore, required abundance of iron to colonize. We think that it was mainly the abundance of iron, which was responsible for the second urbanization of the 1st millennium BC. Large-scale agriculture and trade led to city states and class stratification. Agriculture and trade replaced the earlier economical order based on animal husbandry and Brahmanical rituals and sacrifices. Buddha and Mahavir were essentially leaders of the new order against the old Brahmanical system and emphasized non-violence.

Chapter 6 is a bit of a digression, though relevant and necessary. Archaeological, linguistic and also genetic studies seem to indicate that rice technology was perhaps introduced from south China, via South-East Asia, Brahmaputra valley and the Himalayan corridors to North India. It has now been found that the *japonica* rice originated in the mid-Yangtze region, but the origin of *indica* is still a mystery. Since rice is in high esteem in South Asian society as it is believed to have a soul, it is worshipped and symbolizes the beauty and prosperity, it may be no surprise if we find that the *indica* variety originated in India. On the other hand, we also need to examine the possibility of the MonKhmer speaking people bringing rice technology with them. This would require a paradigm shift in our thinking, hence the need of interpolating this chapter, which deals with the role of the Central Himalayas in the archaeology of North India. We have tried to demonstrate that the Central Himalayas were not *cul-de-sacs* as is often assumed, but were responsible for diffusion of technology and trade – from rice, to copper to iron.

Our conclusions thus seem to be more like an inventory of unfinished tasks in South Asian archaeology, which need to be addressed. That does not, however, belittle the tremendous strides that have been made in all the periods of Indian prehistory. Though archaeological research in the government organizations is on the wane, the mushrooming of departments of archaeology in various universities has more than compensated it.

Like liberalizing the economy, perhaps opening up of archaeological research to other countries may bring in some fresh air and more emphasis on interpretation, on the humans and their society and not only on the morphology of the artefacts.

Bibliography

Agrawal, D.P. 1966. Harappan chronology: A re-examination of the evidence. In *Studies in Prehistory* (Robert Bruce Foote Memorial Volume), (Eds.) D. Sen and A.K. Ghosh. Calcutta: Firma K.L. Mukhopadhyay. Pp. 139-148.

——. 1969. The copper hoards problem: A technological angle. *Asian Perspectives* 12: 113-119.

——. 1969-70. The metal technology of the Indian protohistoric cultures: Its archaeological implications. *Puratattva* 3: 15-22.

——. 1970. Metal technology of the Harappan culture and its socio-economic implications. *Indian Journal of History of Science* 5(2): 238-252.

——. 1971. *The Copper Bronze in India.* Delhi: Munshiram Manoharlal Publishers Pvt. Ltd.

——. 1972-73. Genesis of Harappa culture. *Puratattva* 6: 37-41.

——. 1976. Problems of protohistoric copper artefacts and their ore correlations. In *Archaeological Congress and Seminar: 1972* (Ed.) U.V. Singh. Kurukshetra: Kurukshetra University. Pp. 35-89.

——. 1979. The relevance of archaeology today. *Society and Science* 2(1): 1-15.

——. 1981. The technology of the Indus civilization. In *Indian Archaeology: New Perspectives.* (Ed.) R.K. Sharma. New Delhi: Agam Kala Prakashan. Pp. 83-112.

——. 1982a. *The Archaeology of India.* London: Curzon Press.

——. 1982b. The Indian Bronze Age cultures and their metal technology. In *Advances in World Archaeology.* (Eds.) F. Wendorf and A.E. Close. New York: Academic Press. 1: 213-264.

——. 1984. Metal technology of the Harappans. In *Frontiers of Indus Civilization.* (Eds.) B.B. Lal, S.P. Gupta and S. Asthana. New Delhi: Books & Books. Pp. 163-168.

——. 1992. *Man and Environment in India Through the Ages.* New Delhi: Books & Books.

——. 1993. The Harappan legacy: Break and continuity. In *Harappan Civilization : A Recent Perspective* (Second Revised Edition). (Ed.) Gregory L. Possehl. New Delhi: Oxford & IBH Publishing Co. Pp. 450-453.

——. 1999a. The role of Central Himalayas in Indian archaeometallurgy. In *Metals in Antiquity.* (Eds.) M.M. Suzanne, A. Young, P. Budd, A.M. Pollard and Rob Ixer. Oxford: Archaeopress. Pp. 193-199.

——. 1999b. Early Indian iron technology: Himalayan contacts and Gangetic urbanisation. In *Proceedings of Fourth International Conference on the Beginning of the Use on Metals and Alloys (BUMA-IV).* Matsue, Japan: The Japan Institute of Metals. Pp. 53-58.

——. 2000. *Ancient Metal Technology and Archaeology of South Asia.* New Delhi: Aryan Books International.

——. 2001. Prehistoric copper technology in India: A review: Part I – Our Metallurgical Heritage. In *Metallurgical Studies in India: A Retrospective.* (Ed.) P. Ramachandra Rao and N.G. Goswami. New Delhi: India International Publisher. Pp. 143-162.

Agrawal, D.P., R.K. Avasia and S. Guzder. 1973. A multidisciplinary approach to the quaternary problems in Maharashtra. In *Radiocarbon and Indian Archaeology.* (Eds.) D.P. Agrawal and A. Ghosh. Bombay: Tata Institute of Fundamental Research. Pp. 3-17.

Agrawal, D.P., Diwa Bhatt, S. Malaiya and J.S. Kharakwal. 1991. Archaeology of Kumaun: Problems and Prospects. *Man and Environment* 16(1): 59-63.

Agrawal, D.P. and D.K. Chakrabarti (Eds.). 1979. *Essays in Indian Protohistory.* New Delhi: B.R. Publishing Corporation.

Agrawal, D.P., Rekha Dodia and Mala Seth. 1990. South Asian climate and environment at *c.* 18000 BP. In *The World at 18000 BP.* Vol. II. (Eds.) O. Soffer and Clive Gamble. London: Unwin and Hyman. Pp. 231-235.

Agrawal, D.P. and A. Ghosh (Eds.). 1973. *Radiocarbon and Indian Archaeology.* Bombay: Tata Institute of Fundamental Research.

Agrawal, D.P., S.K. Gupta and P. Sharma (Eds.). 1988. *Palaeoclimatic and Palaeoenvironmental Changes in Asia.* New Delhi: Indian National Science Academy.

Agrawal, D.P. and S. Guzder. 1972. Quaternary studies on the western coast of India: Preliminary observations. *Palaeobotanist* 21(2): 216-222.

Agrawal, D.P. and J.S. Kharakwal. 1998. *Central Himalayas: An Archaeological, Linguistic and Cultural Synthesis.* New Delhi: Aryan Books International.

——. In press. Jodhpura-Ganeshwar complex, Meluhha and sociology of metallurgy. Paper presented at the Annual Conference of *Indian Society for Prehistoric and Quaternary Studies,* held at Deccan College, Pune, 27th to 30th December, 1999.

——. 2002a. *South Asian Prehistory: A Multidisciplinary Study.* New Delhi: Aryan Books International.

——. 2002b. Outstanding problems of early Iron Age in India. In *Tradition and Innovation in the History of Iron Making* (Eds.) Girija Pande and Jan af Geijerstam. Nainital: PAHAR. Pp. 3-20.

Agrawal, D.P., J.S. Kharakwal, S. Kusumgar and M.G. Yadava. 1995. Cist burials of the Kumaun Himalayas. *Antiquity* 69(264): 550-554.

Agrawal, D.P., B.S. Kotlia, P. Sharma and S.K. Gupta. 1988. Environmental magnetism of lake sedimentation in Kumaon Himalayas. *Proceeding of Indian National Science Academy* 54(4): 595-604.

Agrawal, D.P. and R.V. Krishnamurthy. 1981. Some new analysis on the protohistoric copper artefacts. *Man and Environment* 5: 48-51.

Agrawal, D.P., R.V. Krishnamurthy and S. Kusumgar. 1978. New data on the copper hoards and the Diamabad Bronzes. *Man and Environment* 2: 41-46.

——. 1979. On the affiliation of the Daimabad Bronzes: Some fresh data. (Ed.) I. Scollar. *International Symposium on Archaeometry and Archaeological Prospection.* Bonn. Pp. 8-13.

——. 1981a. Arsenical coppers in the Indian Bronze Age. In *Recent Indian Researches in Archaeology and Art History.* (Ed.) M.S. Nagaraja Rao. New Delhi: Agam Kala Prakashan. Pp. 9-18.

——. 1981b. Some new analysis on the protohistoric copper artefacts. *Man and Environment* 5: 48-51.

——. (Eds.). 1985. *Climate and Geology of Kashmir and Central India: The Last 4 Million Years.* New Delhi: T.T. Publishers.

Agrawal, D.P., R.V. Krishnamurthy, S. Kusumgar, L.A. Narain and M.N. Sarin. 1974. Alloying in the copper hoards. *Bulletin of the Museum and Archaeology* 14: 14-18.

Agrawal, D.P. and S. Kusumgar. 1974. *Prehistoric Chronology and Radiocarbon Dating in India.* Delhi: Munshiram Manoharlal Publishers Pvt. Ltd.

Agrawal, D.P., S. Kusumgar, R.D. Deshpande, R. Ramesh, C. Sharma and M.G. Yadava. 1994. A comparative study of monsoon and non-monsoon Himalayan lakes, India. Presented at 15th *International Radiocarbon Conference* held at Glasgow, 15th to 19th August.

Agrawal, D.P., S. Kusumgar and P. Sharma. 1989. Radiocarbon chronology and magnetic susceptibility variation in Kumaon lake sediments. *Radiocarbon* 31(3): 957-964.

Agrawal, D.P., S. Kusumgar, M.G. Yadav, V.D. Gogte, J.S. Kharakwal and M. Pant. 1995. Was Kumaon the source of early iron in North India? *Man and Environment* 20(1): 81-85.

Agrawal, D.P., C. Margabandhu and N.C. Shekhar. 1976. Ancient copper workings: Some new ^{14}C dates. *Indian Journal of History of Science* 11(2): 133-136.

Agrawal, D.P. and B.M. Pande (Eds.). 1977. *Ecology and Archaeology of Western India.* New Delhi: Concept Publishers.

Agrawal, D.P. and R.K. Sood. 1982. Ecological factors and the Harappan civilization. In *Harappan Civilization,* (Eds.) G.L. Possehl. New Delhi: Oxford & IBH Publishing Co.

Agrawal, D.P. and M.G. Yadava. 1995. *Dating the Human Past.* Pune: Indian Society for Prehistoric and Quaternary Studies.

——. 1998. A comparison of proxy climatic data from Tibet and Kashmir. *Himalayan Geology* 19(2): 55-59.

Agrawal, O.P. 1983. Scientific and technological examination. In *Excavations at Atranjikhera* (Ed.) R.C. Gaur. Delhi: Motilal Banarasidass and Aligarh Muslim University. Pp. 487-498.

Agrawal, O.P., Harinarayan and S.K. Bhatia. 1983. Technical studies of iron implements from the Megalithic sites, Tadakanhalli. *Puratattva* 12: 97-100.

Agrawal, O.P., Harinarayan, J. Prakash and S.K. Bhatia. 1990. Lamination technique in iron from artefacts in ancient India. *Journal of the Historical Metallurgy Society* 24(1): 12-26.

Agrawala, R.C. 1978. Copper celts and an Indus arrowhead from Khulhade-ka Johad, Dist. Sikar, Rajasthan. *Man and Environment* 2: 123-124.

——. 1979a. More copper finds from Rajasthan. *Man and Environment* 3: 91-92.

——. 1979b. Three copper objects from Ganeshwar, Rajasthan. *Journal of the Oriental Institute* Baroda (and plate): 159-160.

——. 1980. Khurdi copper hoard from Rajasthan. *Man and Environment* 4: 89-92.

——. 1984a. Aravalli, the major source of copper for the Indus civilization and Indus related cultures. In *Frontiers of the Indus Civilization* (Eds.) B.B. Lal, S.P. Gupta and S. Asthana. New Delhi: Books & Books. Pp. 157-162.

——. 1984b. Ganeshwar culture—A review. *Journal of the Oriental Institute, Baroda* 34(1-2): 89-95.

Agrawala, R.C. and Vijay Kumar. 1976. The problem of PGW and iron in Northeastern Rajasthan. In *Mahabharat: Myth and Reality—Differing Views* (Eds.) S.P.Gupta and K.S. Ramchandran. New Delhi: B.R. Publishing Corporation. Pp. 241-244.

——. 1993. Ganeshwar-Jodhpura Culture: New traits in Indian archaeology. In *Harappan Civilization* (Ed.) G.L. Possehl. New Delhi: Oxford & IBH Publishing Co. Pp. 125-135.

Allchin, B. and F.R. Allchin. 1968. *The Birth of Indian Civilization.* Harmondsworth: Pelican.

——. 1982. *The Rise of Civilization in India and Pakistan.* Cambridge World Archaeology Series. Cambridge: Cambridge University Press.

Allchin, F.R. 1956. The stone alignments of Hyderabad. *Man* 56: 133-56.

Ansari, Z.D. and M.K. Dhawalikar. 1975. *Excavations at Kayatha.* Pune: Deccan College.

Antonini, C.S. 1963. Preliminary notes on the excavation of the necropolises found in Western Pakistan. *East and West* 14: 13-26.

Antonini, C.S. and G. Stacul. 1972. *The Protohistoric Graveyard of Swat (Pakistan).* 2 vols. Rome.

Ardeleanu-Jansen, Alexandra. 1988. The terracotta figurines from Mohenjo-daro: Considerations on tradition, craft and ideology in the Harappa culture (*c.* 2400-1800 BC). *Lahore Museum Bulletin* 1 (2): 18-20.

Arokiaswamy, M. 1952. Dolmens in the Pudukottai region. *Tamil Culture* 1 (1): 73-83.

Asthana, Shashi. 1985. *Pre-Harappan Cultures of India and the Borderlands.* New Delhi: Books & Books.

Atkinson, E.T. 1980-81. *The Himalayan Gazetteer.* Vols. 1,2,3. New Delhi: Cosmo Publication. (First published in 1884).

Babington, J. 1823. Description of Pandoo coolies in Malabar. *Transactions of the Literary Society of Bombay* 3: 324-30.

Balasubramaniam, R. 2001. New insights on the corrosion resistant Delhi iron pillar: Part I – Our Metallurgical Heritage. In *Metallurgical Studies in India: A Retrospective.* (Eds.) P. Ramachandra Rao and N.G. Goswami. New Delhi: India International Publisher. Pp. 104-133.

Ball, V. 1869. On the ancient copper miners of Singhbhum. *Proceedings of the Asiatic Society of Bengal.* Pp. 170-175.

Ball, V. 1881. *A Manual of the Geology of India, Part III, Economic Geology*. Calcutta: Geological Survey of India.

Banerjee, N.R. 1965. *The Iron Age in India*. Delhi: Munshiram Manoharlal Publishers Pvt. Ltd.

——. 1986. *Nagda*. New Delhi: Archaeological Survey of India.

Bayard, D.T. 1970. Excavation at Non Nok Tha, Northeastern Thailand. *Asian Perspectives* 13: 110-143.

——. 1996. Linguistics, archaeologists and Austronesian origins: Comparative and socio-linguistic aspects of the Meacham-Bellwood debate. *Bulletin of Indo-Pacific Prehistory Association* 15(2) : 71-86.

Bayard, D.T., P. Charoenwongsa and S. Rutnin. 1986. Excavations at Non Chai, Northeastern Thailand. *Asian Perspectives* 25(1): 13-62.

Bhan K.K. 1989: Late Harappan settlements of Western India with specific reference to Gujarat. In *Old Problems and New Perspectives in the Archaeology of South Asia*. Wisconsin Archaeological Report, Vol. 2. (Ed.) J.M. Kenoyer. Madison: University of Wisconsin. Pp. 219-242.

——. 1992. Late Harappan Gujarat. *The Eastern Anthropologist* 45: (1-2): 173-92.

——. 1994. Cultural development of the prehistoric period in North Gujarat with reference to Western India. *South Asian Archaeology* 10: 71-90.

——. In press. In the sand dunes of North Gujarat. *Marg* (Special Issue).

Bhan K.K. and J.M. Kenoyer. 1984. Nageshwar: A mature Harappan site on the Gulf of Kutch. *Journal of Oriental Institute of Baroda* 34: 67-80.

Bhan, K.K., M. Vidale and J.M. Kenoyer. 1994. Harappan technology: Theoretical and methodological issues. *Man and Environment* 19: 141-157.

Bhan, Suraj. 1975. *Excavation at Mitathal (1968) and Other Explorations in the Sutlej-Yamuna Divide*. Kurukshetra: Kurukshetra University.

Bharadwaj, H.C. 1973. Aspects of early iron technology in India. In *Radiocarbon and Indian Archaeology*. (Eds.) D.P. Agrawal and A. Ghosh. Bombay: Tata Institute of Fundamental Research. Pp. 391-399.

——. 1979. *Aspects of Ancient Indian Technology*. Delhi: Motilal Banarasidass.

Bhatt, R.C. and K.P. Nautiyal. 1987-88. Trans-Himalayan burials vis-à-vis Malari: An assesment. *JOSHARD* 11&12: 95-101.

Bhattacharya, N.N. 1977. *The Indian Mother Goddess*. New Delhi: Manohar Publication.

Binodini Devi, P. 1993. Studies on Megalithic remains of Manipur. Ph.D. dissertation. Gauhati: Gauhati University.

Bintliff, J. (Ed.). 1991. *The Annales School and Archaeology*. London: Leicestor University Press.

Bisht, R.S. 1984. Structural remains and town-planning of Banawali. In *Frontiers of the Indus Civilization*. (Eds.) B.B. Lal, S.P. Gupta and S. Asthana. New Delhi: Books & Books. Pp. 89-97.

——. 1989a. A new model of the Harappan town planning as revealed at Dholavira in Kutch: A surface study of its plan and architecture. In *History and Archaeology* (Prof. H.D. Sankalia Felicitation Volume). (Ed.) Bhaskar Chatterjee. Delhi: Ramanand Vidya Bhawan. Pp. 397-408.

——. 1989b. The Harappan colonisation of Kutch: An ergonomic study with reference to Dholavira and Surkotada. In *History and Art*. (Eds.) Krishan Deva and Lallanji Gopal. Delhi: Ramanand Vidya Bhawan. Pp. 265-72.

——. 1991. Dholavira: New horizons of the Indus civilization. *Puratattva* 20: 71-82.

——. 1993. Excavations at Banawali: 1974-77. In *Harappan Civilization*. (Ed.) G.L. Possehl. New Delhi: Oxford & IBH Publishing Co. Pp. 113-124.

——. 1994. Urban planning at Dholavira: A Harappan city. Presented at the seminar on *The City and the Stars: Cosmic Urban Geometries of India*. New Delhi: Indira Gandhi National Centre for the Arts.

——. 1998-99. Dholavira and Banawali: Two different paradigms of the Harappan *urbis forma*. *Puratattva* 29: 14-37.

——. 1999. Harappans and the Rgveda: Points of convergence. In *Dawn of Indian Civilization*. (Ed.) G.C. Pande. New Delhi: Centre for Studies in Civilizations. Pp. 393-442.

Biswas, A.K. 1991. Archaeo-materials in India: Some residual problems and future prospects. *National Seminar on Indian Archaeology*, 2nd to 4th October. Banaras Hindu University: Department of Ancient Indian History and Archaeology.

——. 2001. Minerals and their exploitation in ancient and pre-modern India: Part I – Our Metallurgical Heritage. In *Metallurgical Studies in India: A Retrospective.* (Eds.) P. Ramachandra Rao and N.G. Goswami. New Delhi: India International Publisher. Pp. 1-24.

Biswas, A.K. and S. Biswas 1996. *Minerals and Metals in Ancient India* (Vol. 1: Archaeological Evidence). New Delhi: D.K. Printworld.

Blackman, M.J. and M. Vidale. 1992. The production and distribution of stoneware bangles at Mohenjo-daro and Harappa by chemical characterization studies. In *South Asian Archaeology 1989.* (Ed.) C. Jarrige. Madison: Wisconsin Prehistory Press.

Blust, R. 1996. Beyond the Austronesian homeland: The Austric hypothesis and its implications for archaeology. In *Prehistoric Settlement of the Pacific*. Transactions of the American Philosophical Society. (Ed.) W. Goodenough. Philadelphia. 86(5): 117-140.

Bondioli, L., M. Tosi and M. Vidale. 1984. Craft activity areas and surface survey at Mohenjo-daro. In *Interim Reports.* (Eds.) M. Jansen and G. Urban. Aachen: RWTH 1: 9-37.

Bopardikar, B.P. 1972. Prehistoric investigations in Daphabum. *Archaeological Congress and Seminar Papers.* Nagpur: 1-8.

Braudel, F. 1972. *The Mediterranean and the Mediterranean World in the Age of Phillip II.* London: Collins.

Breeks, J.W. 1873. Cairns and Chromlechs. In *An Account of the Primitive Tribes and Monuments of the Nilgiris.* Delhi: Cultural Publishing House (1983 Reprint).

Brooke, J.C. 1864. The mines of Khetri in Rajputana. *Journal of the Asiatic Society of Bengal* 33: 419-29.

Bryson, Reid A. 1988. What the climatic past tells us about the environmental future. In *Earth 88: Changing Geographic Perspectives.* Proceedings of the Centennial Symposium. Washington D.C. : National Geographic Society. Pp. 230-247.

Budd, Paul and Timothy Taylor. 1995. The faerie smith meets the bronze industry: Magic versus science in the interpretation of prehistoric metal-making. *World Archaeology* 27(1): 133-143.

Caldwell, J.R. 1966. *Tal-i-Iblis: The Kerman Range and the Beginnings of Smelting.* Illinois State Museum Preliminary Reports 7. Springfield: Illinois State Museum.

Caldwell, P.C. and K.A.R. Kennedy. 1995. Human skeletal remains from Tadkanhalli and Komaranahalli. In *Sri Nagabhinandanam.* (Eds.) L.K. Srinivasan and S. Nagaraju. Bangalore: M.S. Nagaraja Rao Felicitation Committee. Pp. 35-70.

Cambell, A. 1916. Note on the occurrence of copper celts in Manbhum. *Journal of the Bihar and Orissa Research Society* 2: 85-86.

Casal, J.M. 1961. *Fouilles d" Mundigak.* Paris: Librairie C. Klincksieck.

——. 1964. Fresh digging at Amri. *Pakistan Archaeology* 1: 57-65.

——. 1966. Nindowari: A Chalcolitic site in South Baluchistan. *Pakistan Archaeology* 3: 10-21.

Chakrabarti, D.K. 1973. Concept of urban revolution and the Indian context. *Puratattva* 6: 27-32.

——. 1976. The beginning of iron in India. *Antiquity* 50: 114-24.

——. 1977. Distribution of iron ores and the archaeological evidence of early iron in India. *Journal of the Economic and Social History of the Orient* 20: 168-171.

——. 1986. The pre-industrial mines of India. *Puratattva* 16: 65-72.

——. 1988. The old copper mines of Eastern India. In *The Beginning of the Use of Metals and Alloys.* (Ed.) R. Maddin. Boston: MIT. Pp. 230-244.

——. 1990. *The External Trade of the Indus Civilization.* Delhi: Munshiram Manoharlal Publishers Pvt. Ltd.

——. 1992. *The Early Use of Iron in India.* Madras: Oxford University Press.

——. 1993. *Archaeology of Eastern India : Chota Nagpur Plateau and West Bengal.* Delhi: Munshiram Manoharlal Publishers Pvt. Ltd.

Chakrabarti, D.K. and P.K. Chattopadhyay. 1985. A preliminary report on the archaeology of Singhbhum with notes on the old mines of the district. *Man and Environment* 9: 128-150.

Chakrabarti, D.K. and P.K. Chattopadhyay. 1983. Parihati: A medieval smelting site in Midnapur District. *Puratattva* 12: 161-63.

Chakrabarti, D.K. and Nayanjot Lahiri. 1994. The Iron Age in India: The beginning and consequences. *Purattava* 24: 12-32.

——. 1996. *Copper and its Alloys in Ancient India.* Delhi: Munshiram Manoharlal Publishers Pvt. Ltd.

Charles, J.A. 1967. Early arsenical bronzes : A metallurgical view. *American Journal of Archaeology* 61: 351-365.

——. 1980. The coming of copper and copper base alloys and iron: A metallurgical sequence. In *The Coming of the Age of Iron.* (Eds.) T.A. Wertime and J.D. Muhly. New Haven: Yale University Press. Pp. 1512-81.

Chattopadhyay, P.K. 1984. Archaeometallurgical studies in Indian subcontinent: A survey of metallurgy of iron objects. *Indian Journal of History of Science* 16(4): 361-365.

Chattopadhyaya, U.C. 1990. A study of subsistence and settlement patterns during the late prehistory of North-central India. Unpublished Thesis. Cambridge: University of Cambridge.

Childe, V.G. 1944. Archaeological ages as technological stages. *Journal of the Royal Anthropological Institute of Great Britain and Ireland* 74: 7-24.

——. 1950. The urban revolution. *Town Planning Review* 21: 3-17.

Cleuziou, S. 1984. Oman peninsula and its relations eastwards during the 3rd millennium. In *Frontiers of the Indus Civilization.* (Eds.) B.B. Lal, S.P. Gupta and S. Asthana New Delhi: Books & Books. Pp. 371-394.

——. 1986. Dilmun and Makkan during the 3rd and early 2nd millennia BC. In *Bahrain Through the Ages: The Archaeology.* (Eds.) Shaikha Haya Ali Al Khalifa and Michael Rice. New York: KPI Ltd. Pp. 143-158.

——. 1989. The chronology of protohistoric Oman as seen from Hili. In *Oman Studies.* (Eds.) P.M. Costa and M. Tosi. Rome: Serie Orientale. Vol. 63. Pp. 47-78.

——. 1992. The Oman peninsula and the Indus civilization: A reassessment. *Man and Environment* 17(2): 93-103.

Coggin Brown, J. 1915. Notes on a copper celt found in the Palamau district. *Journal of Bihar and Orissa Research Society.* Pp. 125-126.

——. 1916. Further relics of the Copper Age. *Journal of Bihar and Orissa Research Society.* Pp. 386-387.

Cohen, M.N. 1977. *The Food Crisis in Prehistory: Over Population and the Origins of Agriculture.* London: New Haven.

Cohmap. 1988. Climatic changes of the last 18,000 years: Observations and model simulations. *Science* 241: 1043-1052.

Cooke, S.B. and S.E. Aschenbrenner. 1975. The occurrence of metallic iron in ancient copper. *Journal of Field Archaeology* 2(3): 251-266.

Costantini, L. 1979. Plant remains from Pirak. In *Foullies de Pirak.* 2 Vols. (Eds.) Jean-Francois Jarrige and Marielle Santono. Paris: Publications de la commission des Foulles Archaeologique, Fouilles de Pakistan No 2: 326-33.

——. 1981. Palaeoethnobotany at Pirak: A contribution to the 2nd millennium BC agriculture of the Sibi-Kachi Plain, Pakistan. In *South Asian Archaeology 1979.* (Ed.) H. Hartel. Berlin: Dietrich Reimer Verlag. Pp. 271-77.

——. 1984. The beginning of agriculture in the Kachi plain: The evidence of Mehrgarh. In *South Asian Archaeology 1981.* (Ed.) B. Allchin. Cambridge: Cambridge University Press. Pp. 29-33.

Craddock, P.T., I.C. Freestone, K.T.M. Hegde, L.K. Gurjar and V.H. Sonawane. 1985. Early zinc production in India. *Mining Magazine,* January. Pp. 45-51.

Cunningham, A. 1864-65. *Archaeological Survey of India Report III.* Delhi: Govt. of India.

——. 1875. Harappa. *Annual Report of the Archaeological Survey of India* 5: 105-08.

——. 1871. *Ancient Geography of India.* London: Tribune.

Dales, G.F. 1962a. Harappan outpost on the Makran coast. *Antiquity* 36: 86-92.

——. 1962b. A search of ancient seaports. *Expedition* 4(2): 2-10.

Dales, G.F. 1964. The University of Pennsylvania expedition to Makran. *Pakistan Archaeology* 1: 36-7.
——. 1965. New investigations at Mohenjo-daro. *Archaeology* 18: 145-150.
——. 1974. Excavations at Balakot, Pakistan. 1973. *Journal of Field Archaeology* 1(1-2): 3-22.
——. 1979. The Balakot project: Summary of four years of excavations in Pakistan. *Man and Environment* 3: 45-53.
——. 1990. Excavation at Harappa-1988. *Pakistan Archaeology* 24: 68-176.
Dani, A.H. (Ed.) 1967. Timargarh and the Gandhar grave culture. *Ancient Pakistan* No. 3 (special number).
——. 1971. Excavations in the Gomal valley. *Ancient Pakistan* 5: 1-177.
Dani, A.H. and F.A. Durrani. 1964. A new grave complex in West Pakistan. *Asian Perspectives* 8: 164-165.
Datta, A. 1998. Iron technology at the Chalcolithic phase of West Bengal. In *Archaeometallurgy in India.* (Ed.) Vibha Tripathi. Delhi: Sharda Publishing. Pp. 36-43.
Datta, A. and P.K. Chattopadhyay. 1986. The problems of copper hoards in West Bengal—A reappraisal in the light of metallographic and chemical analysis. *Indian Museum Bulletin* 11: 61-67.
De, S. and P.K. Chattopadhayay. 1984. Archaeometallurgical sites in Indian subcontinent: A survey on metallography of iron objects. *Indian Journal of History of Science* 19(4): 361-365.
——. 1989. Iron objects from Pandurajar Dhibi: Archaeometallurgical studies. *Steel India* 12(1): 33-41.
——. 1991. Archaeometallurgical studies at Kankarjhor and Dhuliapur. *Puratattva* 20: 115-117.
Deo, S.B. 1970. *Excavations at Takalghat and Khapa—1968-69.* Nagpur: Nagpur University.
——. 1985a. The Megalithic problem: A review. In *Recent Advances in Indo-Pacific Prehistory.* (Eds.) V.N. Misra and P. Bellwood. New Delhi: Oxford University Press. Pp. 447-53.
——. 1985b. The Megaliths: Their culture, ecology, economy and technology. In *Recent Advances in Indian Archaeology.* (Eds.) S.B. Deo and K. Paddayya. Pune: Deccan College. Pp. 89-99.
Deo, S.B. and Z.A. Ansari. 1965. *Chalcolithic Chandoli.* Pune: Deccan College.
Deo, S.B. and A.P. Jamkhedkar 1982. *Excavation at Naikund 1978-80.* Maharashtra: State Department of Archaeology and Museums.
Deo, S.B. and K. Paddayya. 1985. *Recent Advances in Indian Archaeology.* Pune: Deccan College.
Deotare, B.C. 1984. Phosphate spot test of Megalithic settlement site of Bhagimohari, district Nagpur, Maharashtra state. *Bulletin of Deccan College and Research Institute* 43: 37-42.
Deshpande, Shweta Sinha. 1998-99. Chalcolithic social organisation in central India: A case study of Balathal.
Dhavalikar, M.K. 1969. Daimabad: A rediscovery. *Puratattva* 3: 34-43.
——. 1970a. Kayatha: A new Chalcolithic culture. *Indica* 7(2): 85-93.
——. 1970b. Genesis of Jorwe culture. In *Studies in Indian Archaeology.* (Eds.) S.B. Deo and M.K. Dhavalikar (Prof. H.D. Sankalia Felicitation Volume) *Indian Antiquary* 4: 32-41.
——. 1970c. Some aspects of the Chalcolithic cultures of central India. *Puratattva* 4: 24-30.
——. 1973. Development and decline of the Deccan Chalcolithic. In *Radiocarbon and Indian Archaeology.* (Eds.) D.P. Agrawal and A. Ghosh. Bombay: Tata Institute of Fundamental Research. Pp. 138-47.
——. 1976. Settlement archaeology of Inamgaon. *Puratattva* 8: 44-54.
——. 1979a. Early farming cultures of the Deccan. In *Essays in Indian Protohistory.* (Eds.) D.P. Agrawal and D.K. Chakrabarti. New Delhi: B.R. Publishing Corporation. Pp. 247-265.
——. 1979b. Early farming cultures of central India. In *Essays in Indian Protohistory.* (Eds.) D.P. Agrawal and D.K. Chakrabarti. New Delhi: B.R. Publishing Corporation. Pp. 229-45.
——. 1988. *First Farmers of the Deccan.* Pune: Ravish Publishers.
——. 1992. Kuntasi: A Harappan port in Western India. In *South Asian Archaeology 1989.* (Ed.) C. Jarrige. Madison: Prehistory Press. Pp. 73-82.
——. 1993a. Harappans in Saurashtra: The mercantile enterprise as seen from recent excavation of Kuntasi. In *Harappan Civilization.* (Ed.) G.L. Possehl. New Delhi: Oxford & IBH Publishing Co. Pp. 555-570.

Dhavalikar, M.K. 1993b. Daimabad Bronzes. In *Harappan Civilization.* (Ed.) G.L. Possehl. New Delhi: Oxford & IBH Publishing Co. Pp. 421-426.

——. 1997. *Indian Protohistory.* New Delhi: Books & Books.

Dhavalikar, M.K., M.R. Raval and Y.M. Chitalwala. 1996. *Kuntasi: A Harappan Emporium on West Coast.* Pune: Deccan College.

Dhavalikar, M.K., H.D. Sankalia and Z.D. Ansari. 1988. *Excavations at Inamgaon.* Vol. 1. Pune: Deccan College.

Dhavalikar, M.K., V. Shinde and S. Atre. 1990. *Excavations at Kaothe in Central Tapi Basin.* Pune: Deccan College.

Diamond, Jared. 1997. *Guns, Germs and Steel.* London: V.W. Norton & Company.

Dikshit, K.N. 1968. The copper hoards in the light of recent discoveries. *Bulletin of Ancient Indian History and Archaeology,* University of Saugar. 2: 43-50.

——. 1969. Megalithic tools typology and chronology: A restatement. In *Sanskirti : Dr. Addityanath Jha Felicitation Volume.* (Ed.) G. Kaviraj. Delhi: A. Jha Abhinandan Granth Samayojan Samiti. Pp. 85-89.

——. 1971. Harappa culture in Western Uttar Pradesh. *Bulletin of National Museum* 2: 21-38.

——. 1973. The Allahpur evidence and the PGW chronology. In *Radiocarbon and Indian Archaeology.* (Eds.) D.P. Agrawal and A. Ghosh. Pp. 148-57. Bombay : Tata Institute of Fundamental Research.

——. 1979. The Ochre Coloured Ware settlements in Ganga-Yamuna doab. In *Essays in Indian Protohistory.* (Eds.) D.P. Agrawal and A. Ghosh. New Delhi: B.R. Publishing Corporation. Pp. 285-299.

——. 1981. The excavation at Hulas and further explorations of the upper Ganga-Yamuna doab. *Man and Environment* 5: 70-76.

——. 1982. Hulas and the late Harappan complex in Western Uttar Pradesh. In *Harappan Civilization: A Contemporay Perspective.* (Ed.) G.L. Possehl. New Delhi: Oxford & IBH Publishing Co. Pp. 339-351.

Dubey, S.K. and Manju Pant. 1997. Copper anthropomorphic figures of Bankot in Kumaon (U.P.)— Analysis and conservation. In *Facets of Indian Civilization—Recent Perspectives.* Vol. 1 (Essays in honour of Prof. B.B. Lal). (Eds.) J.P. Joshi, D.K. Sinha, S.C. Saran, C.B. Misra and G.S. Gaur. New Delhi: Aryan Books International. Pp. 259-263.

Dunn, J.A. 1942. *The Economic Geology and Mineral Resources of Bihar Province.* Calcutta.

Dupree, L. 1963. Deh Morasi Ghundai: A Chalcolithic site in south-central Afghanistan. *Anthropological Papers of the American Museum of Natural History* 50: 59-135.

During Caspers, E. 1984. Sumerian trading communities residing in Harappan society. In *Frontiers of the Indus Civilization.* (Eds.) B.B. Lal, S.P. Gupta and S. Asthana New Delhi: Books & Books. Pp. 363-370.

Elwin, V. 1942. *The Agarias.* Calcutta.

Enault, Jean-Francois. 1979. *Fouilles de Pirak.* 2 vols. Paris: Publications de la Commission des Fouoilles Archaeologiques.

Fairservis, W.A. 1967. The origin, character and decline of an early civilization. *Novitates* (New York: American Museum of Natural History) No. 2302.

——. 1983. The script of the Indus valley civilization. *Scientific American* 248(3): 58-66.

Farooqui, A. and G.G. Vaz. 2000. Holocene sea level and climatic fluctuations: Pulicat lake — A case study. *Current Science* 79(10): 1184-1188.

Farswan, Y.S. and Vinod Nautiyal. 1997. Investigation of phosphorus enrichment in the burial soil of Kumaon, mid-Central Himalayas, India. *Journal of Archaeological Science* 24: 251-58.

Father Heras. 1953. *Studies in ProtoIndo-Mediterranean Culture.* Bombay: Historical Research Society.

Fentress, M.A. 1977. *Resource Access, Exchange Systems and Regional Interaction in the Indus Valley: An Investigation of Archaeological Variability at Harappa and Mohenjo-Daro.* Ph.D. dissertation, University of Pennsylvania. Ann Arbor, MI: University microfilms 77-10, 163.

Fergusson, J. 1872. *Rude Stone Monuments in All Countries: Their Age and Use.* London: John Murray.

Flam, L. 1981. Towards the ecological analysis of prehistoric settlement patterns in Sind, Pakistan. *Man and Environment* 5: 52-58.

——. 1993. Excavations at Ghazi Shah, Sindh, Pakistan. In *Harappan Civilization: A Recent Perspective*, 2nd revised edition. (Ed.) G.L. Possehl. New Delhi: Oxford & IBH Publishing Co. Pp. 457-468.

Foote, R.B. 1901. *Catalogue of Prehistoric Objects in the Madras Museum*. Madras.

Fujiwara, H., M.R. Mughal, A. Sasaki and T. Matano. 1992. Rice and ragi at Harappa: Preliminary results by plant opal analysis. *Pakistan Archaeology* 27: 129-42.

Furer-Haimendorf, C. von. 1943. Megalithic ritual among the Gadabas and Bondos of Orissa. *Journal of Royal Asiatic Society of Bengal* 9(1): 149-78.

Gale, W.K.V. 1990. Ferrous metals. In *An Encyclopaedia of Technology*. (Ed.) Ian McNeil. London: Routledge. Pp. 146-59.

Gaur, R.C. 1969. The Ochre Coloured pottery from Atranjikhera and its significance. In *Potteries in Ancient India*. (Ed.) B.P. Sinha. Patna. Pp. 95-101.

——. 1973. Lal Quila excavation and the OCP problem. In *Radiocarbon and Indian Archaeology*. (Eds.) D.P. Agrawal and A. Ghosh. Bombay: Tata Institute of Fundamental Research. Pp. 154-162.

——. 1983. *Excavation at Atranjikhera: Early Civilization of the Upper Ganga Basin*. Delhi: Motilal Banarasidass and Aligarh Muslim University.

Ghosh, A. 1965. The Indus civilization: Its origin, authors, extent and chronology. In *Indian Prehistory*. (Eds.) V.N. Misra and M.S. Mate. Pune: Deccan College.

——. 1989. *An Encyclopaedia of Indian Archaeology*. Delhi: Munshiram Manoharlal Publishers Pvt. Ltd.

Ghosh, A.K. and P.K. Chattopadhyay 1982. An early steel implement from Barudih, Bihar province, India. *Metallurgical Studies, MASCA Journal*. Pennsylvania: University of Pennsylvania 2(2): 63-64.

Ghosh, N.C., Arun K. Nag and P.K. Chattopadhyay. 1987-88. The archaeological background and iron sample from Hatigra. *Puratattva* 18: 21-27.

Gogte, V.D. 1982. Megalithic iron smelting at Naikund. In *Naikund Excavations—1978-80*. (Eds.) S.B. Deo and A.P. Jamkhedkar. Bombay: Govt. of Maharashtra. Pp. 52-59.

Gordon, D.H. 1950. The early use of metals in India and Pakistan. *Journal of the Royal Anthropological Institute*. Pp. 55-78.

Goswami, M.C. and T.C. Sharma. 1963. Further report on the investigations into prehistoric archaeology of north Cachar hills, Assam. *Journal of the University of Gauhati* 14(2): 45-47.

Gradener, P. 1980. Laxicostatistics and Dravidian differentiation *in situ*. *Indian Linguistics* 41: 17-180.

Grierson, G.A. 1967-68. *The Linguistic Survey of India*. Vol. 1(1) and Vol. 9(4). Calcutta: Central Publication Branch. Govt. of India.

Gupta, H.P. 1876. Holocene palynology from Meander Lake in the Ganga valley, dist. Pratapgarh, UP. *The Paleobotanist* 2: 109-19.

Gupta, P.L. 1997. Gungeria copper hoard. In *Facets of Indian Civilization—Recent Perspectives*. Vol. 1 (Essays in honour of Prof. B.B. Lal). (Eds.) J.P. Joshi, D.K. Sinha, S.C. Saran, C.B. Misra and G.S. Gaur. New Delhi: Aryan Books International. Pp. 233-358.

Gupta, P. and P.C. Dutta. 1962. Human remains excavated from Megaliths at Yalleswaram (Andhra Pradesh). *Man in India* 42: 19-34.

Gupta, S.K., P. Sharma, N. Juyal and D.P. Agrawal. 1991. Loess-palaeosol sequence in Kashmir: Correlation of mineral magnetic stratigraphy with the marine palaeoclimatic records. *Journal of Quarternary Science* 6(1): 3-12.

Gupta, S.P. 1963. Indian copper hoards: The problems of homogeneity, stages of development, origin, authorship and dating. *Journal of the Bihar Research Society* 49: 147-66.

——. 1965. Further copper hoards: A reassessment in the light of new evidence. *Journal of the Bihar Research Society* 51: 1-7.

——. 1969. Sociology of burial practices and its bearing on the problem of Megaliths. In *Seminar Papers on the Problem of Megaliths in India*. (Ed.) A.K. Narayan. Varanasi: Memoirs of the Department of Ancient History, Culture and Archaeology 3. Pp. 99-106.

Gupta, S.P. 1970-71. Gulf of Oman: The original home of Indian Megaliths. *Puratattva* 4: 4-18.

——. 1979. *Archaeology of Soviet Central Asia and the Indian Boderland.* 2 Vols. New Delhi: B.R. Publishing Corporation.

Gurdon, P.R.T. 1914. *The Khasis.* London: Macmillan & Co.

Gururaja Rao, B.K. 1970. Development of technology during the Iron Age in South India (*c.* 1000 BC to the beginning of Historical times). *Indian Journal of Historical Sciences* 5(2): 253-71

——. 1972. *Megalithic Culture of South India.* Mysore: University of Mysore.

Halim, M.A. 1970-71. Excavation at Sarai Khola (Part 1). *Pakistan Archaeology* 7: 23-80.

——. 1972. Excavation at Sarai Khola (Part 2). *Pakistan Archaeology* 8: 1-112.

Handa, D. 1968. Harappans, Ochre Ware and the copper hoards. *East and West.* New series 18(1-2): 147-50.

Hargreaves, H. 1929. *Excavations in Baluchistan.* 1925. Memoirs of the Archaeological Survey of India. No. 35. Calcutta: Government of India Press.

Harlan, J.R. and D. Zohary. 1966. Distribution of wild wheat and barley. *Science* 153: 1074-1080.

Hauptmann, A. 1989. Chemical analyses of prehistoric metal artefacts from the Indian subcontinent. See in Paul Yule 1989 (*The Copper Hoards of the Indian Subcontinent Preliminaries for an Interpretation)* as appendix 1. Jahrgang: Sonderdruck aus Johrbuch Des Romisch-Germanischen Zentral Museums Mainz.

Hauptmann, A., G.P. Weisgeiber and H.G. Bachmann. 1988. Early copper metallurgy in Oman. In *The Beginning of the Use of Metals and Alloys.* (Ed.) R. Maddin. Massachusetts. Pp. 34-51.

Heath, J.M. 1839. On Indian iron and steel. *Journal of Royal Asiatic Society.* Pp. 390-97.

Hegde, K.T.M. 1965. Studies in copper objects recovered from Chalcolithic levels at Chandoli. In *Chalcolithic Chandoli.* (Eds.) S.B. Deo and Z.D. Ansari. Pune: Deccan College. P. 185.

——. 1969. Appendix I: Technical studies in copper artefacts excavated from Ahar. In *Excavations at Ahar (Tambavati) 1961-62.*

——. 1971. The metal objects of Navdatoli. In *Chalcolithic Navdatoli.* (Eds.) H.D. Sankalia, S.B. Deo and Z.D. Ansari. Pune: Deccan College. Pp. 449-456.

——. 1973. Early stages of metallurgy in India. In *Radiocarbon and Indian Archaeology.* (Eds.) D.P. Agrawal and A. Ghosh. Bombay: Tata Institute of Fundamental Research. Pp. 401-5

——. 1991. Ancient iron metallurgy. *Man and Environment* 16 (1): 1-3.

Hegde, K.T.M. and J.E. Ericson. 1985. Ancient Indian copper smelting furnaces. In *Furnaces and Smelting Technology in Antiquity.* (Eds.) P.T. Craddock and M.J. Hughes. British Museum Occasional Paper No. 48. London: British Museum Research Laboratory. Pp. 59-70.

Hegde, K.T.M., K.K. Bhan,V.H. Sonawane, K. Krishana and D.R. Shah. 1991. *Excavations at Nageshwar: A Shell Working Site on the Gulf of Kachchh.* Baroda: M.S. University Archaeological Series 18.

Hegde, K.T.M., S.N. Pande. 1972. Chemical analysis of Mitathal copper objects. *Studies in Museology* 30-35.

Hegde, K.T.M., V.H. Sonawane, D.R. Shah, K.K. Bhan, Ajit Prasad, K. Krishnan and S. Pratapa Chandran. 1988. Excavation at Nagwada-1986 and 1987: A preliminary report. *Man and Environment* 12: 55-66.

Heine-Geldern, R.V. 1936. Archaeological traces of Vedic Aryans. *Journal of Indian Society of Oriental Arts* 4: 87-88.

——. 1956. The coming of the Aryans and the end of the Harappa civilization. *Man* 56: 136-40.

Hemphill, B.E., J.R. Lukacs and K.A.R. Kennedy. 1991. Biological adaptations and affinities of Bronze Age Harappans. In *Harappa Excavations 1986-1990.* (Ed.) R.H. Meadow. Madison: Prehistory Press. Pp. 137-182.

Henwood, W.J. 1856. Notice of the rock basins at Devidhoora near Almora in upper India. New *Philosophical Journal.* New Series 4: 204-06.

Hiebert, F.T. 1994. *Origins of the Bronze Age Oasis Civilization in Central Asia.* Peabody Museum of Archaeology and Ethnology, American School of Prehistoric Research. Bulletin No. 42. Cambridge.

Higham, C.F.W. 1989. *The Archaeology of Mainland South-East Asia*. Cambridge: Cambridge University Press.

——. 1996. Archaeology and linguistics in South-East Asia: Implications of the Austric hypothesis. *Indo-Pacific Prehistory Association Bulletin* 14(1): 71-86.

Holland, T.H. 1892. Mineralogical and metallurgical characters of the iron ores of the Salem district. *Records of Geological Survey of India* 25: 136-159.

Hooja, R. 1988. *The Ahar Culture and Beyond: Settlements and Frontiers of "Mesolithic" and Early Agricultural Sites in South-Eastern Rajasthan c. 3rd-2nd Millennia* BC. BAR International Series 412. Oxford: British Archaeological Reports.

Hooja, R. and V. Kumar. 1997. Aspects of the early copper age in Rajasthan. In *South Asian Archaeology 1995*. (Eds.) Raymond Allchin and Bridget Allchin. New Delhi: Oxford & IBH Publishing Co. Pp. 323-339.

Hughes, M.J. 1989. Atomic absorption analysis of Indian copper hoard implements in the British Museum collections. See in Paul Yule 1989 (*The Copper Hoards of the Indian Subcontinent Preliminaries for an Interpretation)* as appendix 2. Jahrgang: Sonderdruck aus Johrbuch Des Romisch-Germanischen Zentral Museums Mainz.

Hughes, T.W.H. 1873. Notes on some of the iron deposits of Chanda Central Province. *Records of Geological Survey of India.* Part 4.

Hunday, A. and S. Banerjee. 1967. *Geology and Mineral Resources of West Bengal*. Calcutta.

Hutchinson, Sir Joseph. 1974. *Evolutionary Studies in World Crops: Diversity and Change in the Indian Subcontinent*. Cambridge: Cambridge University Press.

——. 1977. India: Local and introduced crops. In *The Early History of Agriculture.* (Eds.) J.G.D. Clark, E.M. Jope and R. Riley. Oxford: Oxford University Press. Pp. 129-38.

Hutton, J.H. 1922. The meaning and method of erection of monolithis of the Naga tribes. *Journal of the Royal Anthropological Institute* 52: 55-70.

IAR. *Indian Archaeology—A Review*. Annual publication of the Archaeological Survey of India, New Delhi.

Jacobson, J. 1985. The Harappan civilization: An early state. In *Studies in the Archeology of India and Pakistan.* (Ed.) J. Jacobson. New Delhi: Oxford & IBH Publishing Co. Pp. 137-174.

James, P. and N. Thorpe. 1995. *Ancient Inventions.* London: M.O"Mara.

Jansen, M., M. Mulloy and G. Urban. 1996. *Forgotten Cities on the Indus: Early Civilizations in Pakistan from the 8th to the 2nd millennium* BC. New York: Oxford University Press.

Jansen, M. and G. Urban 1983. *Interim Reports on Field Work Carried Out at Mohenjo-daro: Pakistan 1982-83*. Roma: IsMEO-Aachen-University Mission. Vols. 1 & 2.

Jarrige, C., J.-F. Jarrige, R.H. Meadow and G. Quivron. 1995. *Mehrgarh Field Reports 1974-1985.* Karachi: Govt. of Sindh.

Jarrige, J.-F. 1984. Chronology of the earlier periods of the Greater Indus as seen from Mehrgarh, Pakistan. In *South Asian Archaeology 1981.* (Ed.) B. Allchin. Cambridge: Cambridge University press. Pp. 21-28.

——. 1985a. A propos d"un foret a tige hélicoïdale en cuivre de Mundigak. In *De l"Indus aux Balkans, Recueil Jean Deshayes* (Eds.) J.-L. Huot, M.Yon and Y. Calvet. Paris: Éditions Recherche sur les Civilizations. Pp. 281-292.

——. 1985b. Continuity and change in the north Kachi plain (Baluchistan, Pakistan) at the beginning of the 2nd millennium BC. In *South Asian Archaeology 1983.* (Eds.) J. Shotsmans and M. Taddei. Naples: Istituto Universitario Orientale. Pp. 35-68.

——. 1986. Excavation at Mehrgarh-Nausharo. *Pakistan Archaeology* 10-22: 62-131.

——. 1990. Excavation at Nausharo 1988-89. *Pakistan Archaeology* 25: 193-240.

——. 1993. Excavations at Mehrgarh: Their significance for understanding the background of the Harappan civilization. In *Harappan Civilization.* (Ed.) G.L. Possehl. New Delhi: Oxford & IBH Publishing Co. Pp. 79-84.

Jarrige, J.-F. 1994. The final phase of the Indus occupation at Nausharo and its connection with the following cultural complex of Mehrgarh VIII. In *South Asian Archaeology 1993.* (Eds.) A. Parpola and P. Koskikallio. Helsinki: Suomalainen Tiedeakatemia. Pp. 295-314.

Jarrige, J.-F. and Usman Hassan. 1989. Funerary complexes in Baluchistan at the end of the 3rd millennium. In *South Asian Archaeology 1989.* (Eds.) K. Friefelt and P. Sorenson. London : Curzon Press. Pp. 150: 166.

Jarrige, J.-F. and R.H. Meadow. 1980. The antecedents of civilization in the Indus valley. *Scientific American* 243(2): 122-133.

Jarrige, J.-F. and M. Santoni. 1979. *Fouilles de Pirak.* Paris: Diffusion de Boccard.

Jarrige, J.-F. and M. Tosi. 1981. The natural resources of Mundigak. In *South Asian Archaeology 1979.* (Ed.) H. Härtel. Berlin: Dietrich Reimer. Pp. 115-142.

Jarrige, J.-F. *et al.* 1995. *Excavations at Mehergarh—Nausharo 16th to 20th Seasons (1990-94).* Report submitted to the Director-General of Archaeology and Museums, Govt. of Pakistan (unpublished, but privately circulated).

Jaykar, Pupul. 1989. *The Earth Mother.* Delhi: Pelican.

Jettmar, Karl. 1967. An iron cheek-piece of a snaffle found at Timargarha. *Ancient Pakistan* 3: 203-209.

——. 1987. *Between Gandhara and Silk Roads Rock Carvings Along the Karakorum Highway.* London: The Royal Geographic Society.

Jha, C., B.D. Joshi and B. Prakash. 1989. Metal extraction : An Ayurvedic system of medicine. *Bulletin of Metals Museum* 14: 17-26.

John, K.J. 1985. The Megalithic culture of Kerala. In *Recent Advances in Indo-Pacific Prehistory.* (Eds.) V.N. Misra and P. Bellwood. New Delhi: Oxford & IBH Publishing Co. Pp. 485-9.

Joshi, A.P. 1973. Analysis of copper and iron objects. In *Mahurjhari Excavations 1970-72.* (Ed.) S.B. Deo. Nagpur: Nagpur University. Pp. 77.

Joshi, J.P. 1972. Exploration in Kachchh and excavation at Surkotada and new light on Harappan migration. *Journal of the Oriental Institute* 22(1-2): 137-143.

——. 1987. Interlocking of Late Harappan culture and Painted Grey Ware culture in the light of recent excavations. *Man and Environment* 2: 98-101.

——. 1990. *Excavation at Surkotada 1971-72 and Exploration in Kachchh.* New Delhi: Archaeological Survey of India.

——. 1993. *Excavations at Bhagwanpura 1975-76 and Other Explorations and Excavations 1975-81 in Haryana, Jammu-Kashmir and Punjab.* New Delhi: Memoirs of Archaeological Survey of India. No. 89.

Joshi, J.P., Madhu Bala and Jassu Ram. 1984. The Indus civilization: A reconsideration on the basis of distribution maps. In *Frontiers of the Indus Civilization* (Eds.) B.B. Lal, S.P. Gupta and S. Asthana. New Delhi: Books & Books. Pp. 511-530.

Joshi, J.P. and A. Parpola. 1987. *Corpus of Indus Seals and Inscriptions 1: Collections in India.* Helsinki: Suomalainen Tiedeakatemia.

Joshi, L.D. 1929. *The Khasa Family Law,* Allahabad: Government Press.

Joshi, M.P. 1987. Perspectives in the social history of Kumaun. In *Archaeology and History.* (Eds.) B.M. Pande and B.D. Chatopadhayaya. New Delhi: Agam Kala Prakashan. Pp. 709-726.

——. 1990. *Uttaranchal Kumaon Garhwal Himalaya.* Almora: Shree Almora Book Depot.

——. 1995-96. The anthropomorphs in the copper hoard culture of the Ganga valley. *Puratattva* 26: 23-31.

Joshi, R.V., B.C. Deotare and A.A. Kshirsagar. 1982. Chemical analysis of soils from Megalithic Naikund. In *Excavations at Naikund 1978-80.* (Eds.) S.B. Deo and A.P. Jamkhedkar. Pune: Deccan College. Pp. 65-69.

Kajale, M.D. 1974. Ancient grains from India. *Bulletin of Deccan College Postgraduate and Research Institute* 34(1-4): 55-74.

——. 1982. First records of ancient grains at Naikund. In *Excavations at Naikund 1978-80.* (Eds.) S.B. Deo and A.P. Jamkhedkar. Pune: Deccan College.

Kajale, M.D. 1989. Archaeobotanical investigation on Megalithic Bhagimohari and its significance for ancient Indian agricultural system. *Man and Environment* 13: 87-100.

Kalyanaraman, S. 1999. Saraswati: River, goddess and civilization. *Memoir Geological Society of India* 42: 25-33.

Kennedy, K.A.R. 1975. *The Physical Anthropology of the Megalithic Builders of South India and Sri-Lanka.* Canberra: Australian National University Press.

——. 1982. Skulls, Aryans and flowing drains: The interface of archaeology and skeletal biology in the Harappan civilization. In *Harappan Civilization.* (Ed.) G.L. Possehl. New Delhi: Oxford & IBH Publishing Co. Pp. 289-95.

——. 1984. Growth, nutrition and pathology in changing palaeodemographic settings in South Asia. In *Palaeopathology at the Origin of Agriculture.* (Eds.) M.N. Cohen and G.J. Armelagos. Orlando: Academic Press. Pp. 169-92.

——. 1994. Evolution of South Asian Pleistocene hominids: Demic displacement or regional continuity. In *South Asian Archaeology 1993.* (Eds.) A. Parpola and P. Koskikallio. Vol. I. Pp. 337-344.

——. 1995. South-East Asia: Biological anthropology and concepts of ancient races. In *The Indo-Aryans of Ancient South-East Asia : Language, Material Culture and Ethnicity.* (Ed.) George Erdosy. Berlin: Walter De Gruyter. Pp. 32-66.

Kennedy, K.A.R. and J. Levisky 1985. The element of racial biology in Indian Megalithism: A multivariate appproach. In *Recent Advances in Indo-Pacific Prehistory,* (Eds.) V.N. Misra and P. Bellwood. New Delhi: Oxford & IBH Publishing Co. Pp. 455-64.

Kenoyer, J.M. 1998. *Ancient Cities of the Indus Valley Civilization.* Oxford: Oxford University Press. Pp. 1-262.

——. 1999. Wealth and socio-economic hierarchies of the Indus valley civilization. In *Order, Legitimacy and Wealth in Early States.* (Eds.) J. Richards and M.van Buren. Cambridge: Cambridge University Press. Pp. 90-112.

Kenoyer, J.M. and Heather M.-L. Miller. 1999. Metal technologies of the Indus valley tradition in Pakistan and Western India. In *The Archaeometallurgy of the Asian Old World.* (Ed.) Vincent C. Pigott. University of Pennsylvania Museum Monograph 89. Philadelphia: University Museum Publications. Pp. 107-151.

Khan, F.A. 1965. Excavations at Kot Diji. *Pakistan Archaeology* 2: 13-85.

Khanduri, B.M., K.P. Nautiyal, V. Nautiyal, R.C. Bhatt, Pradeep Saklani and Y.S. Farswan. 1998-99. Excavations of burial complexes in Ramganga valley, Kumaon Himalaya. *Puratattva* 29: 68-71.

Kharakwal, J.S. 1992. Mahasmiya Sanskriti ke Avses (in Hindi) *PAHAR* 5-6: 16-17.

——. 1994. *Archaeological Explorations in Kumaon Himalaya.* Unpublished Ph.D dissertation. University of Pune: Deccan College.

Kharakwal, J.S. and Deep Harbola 1996. Kumaon mai mahapasankalain savagar parampara (In Hindi). *Pragdhara* 6: 169-76.

Kharakwal, J.S. and Anita Rane. 1997. Cup-marks and Gaychole game. In *Himkanti.* (Eds.) B.M. Khanduri and V. Nautiyal. Delhi: Book India Publishing Co. Pp. 155-160.

Kharakwal, J.S., D. Bhatt and M. Pant. 1993. Madhya Himalaye kshetra Kumaon: Puratattva aur paramparain (In Hindi). *Sodh Patrika* 44: 64-77.

Kharakwal, J.S, M.L. Sharma, Madan Meena (In press) Ancient mining and smelting sites in Nim ka Thana tehsil, Sikar, Rajasthan. *Sodh Patrika.*

Khatri, J.S. and M. Acharya. 1994-95. Kunal: A new Indus-Saraswati site. *Puratattva* 25: 84-86.

Kochar, Rajesh. 2000. *The Vedic People: Their History and Geography.* Hyderabad: Orient Longman.

Kochhar, N., R. Kochhar and D.K. Chakrabarti. 1999. A new source of primary tin ore in the Indus civilization. *South Asian Studies* 15: 115-118.

Kohl, P.L. 1984. *Central Asia: Palaeolithic Beginning to the Iron Age.* Paris: Centre de la Recherche Scientifique, Editions Recherche sur les Civilizations, Synthese, No. 14.

Koskenniemi, K. and A. Parpola. 1979. *Corpus of Texts in the Indus Script.* Helsinki: University of Helsinki.

Kosambi, D.D. 1956. *An Introduction to the Study of Indian History.* Bombay: Popular Prakashan.

Kosambi, D.D. 1962. *Myth and Reality: Studies in the Formation of Indian Culture*. Bombay: Popular Prakashan.

——. 1963. The beginning of the Iron Age in India. *Journal of Economic and Social History of the Orient* 6(3): 309-318.

Krishna, Deva and R.E.M. Wheeler. 1946. Note on the Painted Grey Wares at Ahichchhatra. *Ancient India* 1: 58-59.

Krishnan, K. 1997. Scientific analysis of pottery. In *Ancient Ceramics: Historical Enquiries Scientific Approaches*. (Eds.) P.C. Pant and V. Jayaswal. New Delhi: Agam Kala Prakashan. Pp. 177-96.

Krishnan, M.S. 1951. *Mineral Resources of Madras*. Calcutta.

——. 1954. *Iron Ore, Iron and Steel*. Calcutta.

Krishnan, M.S. and N.K.N. Aiyanger 1954. *The Ion-Ore Deposit of Parts of Salem and Trichinopoly Districts*. Calcutta.

Krishnaswami, V.D. 1949. Megalithic types of South India. *Ancient India* 5: 35-45.

Kshirsagar, A. 1992. Chemical analysis of soils from Raipur. In *Megalithic Raipur 1985-1990*. (Eds.) G.B. Deglurkar and G. Lad. Pune: Deccan College. P. 123.

——. 1996. Anthrosols from Balathal: A chemical study. *Man and Environment* 21 (1): 111-116.

Kukla, G. 1989. Long continental records of climate—An introduction. *Palaeogeography, Palaeoclimatology and Palaeoecology* 72: 1-9.

Kumar, Sudhir, B. Prakash, M.L. Manchanda, A.K. Singhvi and Pankaj Srivastava. 1996. Holocene landform and soil evolution of the western Gangetic plains : Implications of neotectonics and climate. *Z. Geomorph. N.F. Suppl-Bd*. 103: 283-312.

Kumar, Tuk-Tuk. 1988. *History of Rice in India: Mythology, Culture and Agriculture*. Delhi: Gian Publishing House.

Kumar, V. 1977. Excavation at Jodhpura. *Journal of the Rajasthan Institute of Historical Research* 15(1): 28-33.

——. 1986. Excavations at Ganeshwar, district Sikar. *Indian Archaeology : A Review* 1983-84: 71-72.

Kusumgar, Sheela, N. Bhandari and D.P. Agrawal. 1985. Fission track ages of the Romushi Lower Karewas, Kashmir. India. In *Climate and Geology of Kashmir and Central Asia*. (Eds.) D.P. Agrawal, S. Kusumgar and R.V. Krishnamurthy. Delhi: T.T. Publishers. Pp. 245-247.

Kuzmina, E.E. 1976. The Bactrian mirage and the archaeological reality. *East and West* 26: 111-131.

Lahiri, N. 1993. Some ethnographic aspects of the ancient copper-bronze tradition in India. *Journal of the Royal Asiatic Society Series* 3(2): 219-231.

Lal. B.B. 1951. Further copper hoards from the Ganga valley and a review of the problems. *Ancient India* 7: 20-39.

——. 1954-55. Excavations at Hastinapur and other explorations. *Ancient India* 10-11: 5-151.

——. 1960. From the Megalithic to the Harappa : Tracing back the graffiti on the pottery. *Ancient India* 16: 4-24.

——. 1963. A picture emerges—An assessment of the Carbon-14 dating of the protohistoric cultures of the Indo-Pakistan subcontinent. *Ancient India* 18-19: 208-21.

——. 1968. A deluge? Which deluge? Yet another facet of the problem of the Copper Hoard culture. *American Anthropologist* 70: 857-63.

——. 1972. The Copper Hoard culture of the Ganga valley. *Antiquity* 46: 232-87.

——. 1985. Report on the chemical analysis and examination of metallic and other objects from Lothal. In *Lothal: A Harappan Port Town (1955-62) Vol.* 2. (Ed.) S.R. Rao. New Delhi: Memoirs of the Archaeological Survey of India. No. 78. Pp. 651-666.

Lal, B.B., S.P. Gupta and S. Asthana. 1984. (Eds.) *Frontiers of Indus Civilization*. New Delhi: Books & Books.

Lal, Makhan. 1979. New copper hoards from Bithur, Kanpur district, Uttar Pradesh. *Archaeological Studies* 4: 34-37.

——. 1984. Summary of four seasons of explorations in Kanpur district, Uttar Pradesh. *Man and Environment* 8: 61-80.

Lal, Makhan. 1986. Iron tools, forest clearance and urbanisation in the Gangetic plains. *Man and Environment* 10: 83-90.

——. 1987-88. Iron at Ahar: A comment. *Puratattva* 18: 109-112.

Lamberg-Karlovsky, C.C. 1993. Reflections on the Central Asian Bronze Age. In *International Association for the Study of the Cultures of Central Asia Information Bulletin* 19, Moscow: Nauka

——. 1994. The Bronze Age Khanates of Central Asia. *Antiquity* 68: 398-405.

——. 2001. Converting currencies in the Old World. *Nature* 411: 437.

Lambrick, H.T. 1967. The Indus flood plain and the Indus civilization. *The Geographical Journal* 133: 483-494.

Lechevallier, M. 1984. Flint industry of Mehrgarh. In *South Asian Archaeology 1981.* (Ed.) B. Allchin. Cambridge: Cambridge University Press. Pp. 41-51.

Leshnik, L.S. 1974. *South Indian Megalithic Burials: The Pandukal Complex.* Weisbaden: Franz Steiner Verlag.

Levy, E. Thomas (Ed.). 1998. *The Archaeology of Society in the Holy Land.* London: Leicester University Press.

Liverani, M. 1987. The collapse of the neareast regional system at the end of the Bronze Age: The case of Syria. In *Centre and Periphery in the Ancient World.* (Eds.) M. Rowlands, M. Larsen and K. Kristiansen. Cambridge: Cambridge University Press. Pp. 66-73

Loofs-Wissowa, H.H.E. 1985. Traces of South Indian Megalithic in Thailand: A dolmen in a Chedi in U-Thong. In *Recent Advances in Indo-Pacific Prehistory.* (Eds.) V.N. Misra and P. Bellwood. New Delhi: Oxford & IBH Publishing Co. Pp. 497-500.

Lowe, Thelma L. 1990. Refractories in high carbon iron processing: A preliminary study of the Deccan wootz making crucibles. In *Cross Craft and Cross Cultural Interactions in Ceramics.* Vol. IV. (Eds.) P.E. Mcgovern, M.D. Notis and W.D. Kingery. Westerville (USA): The American Ceramic Society. Pp. 237-251.

Lukacs, J.R., V.N. Misra and K.A.R. Kennedy. 1982. *Bagor and Tilwara: Late Mesolithic Cultures of North-West India, the Human Skeletal Remains.* Pune: Deccan College.

Macdonell, A. 1995. *Vedic Mythology.* Delhi: Motilal Banarasidass.

Mackay, E.J.H. 1931. Technique and description of metal vessels, tools, implements and other objects. In *Mohenjo-daro and the Indus Civilization.* (Ed.) J. Marshall. London: A. Probsthain. Pp. 488-508.

Mackay, E.J.H. 1937-38. *Further Excavations at Mohenjo-daro.* Vol. I Text, Vol. II. Plates. Delhi: Government of India Press.

——. 1943. *Chanhu-Daro Excavations 1935-36.* New Haven, CN: American Oriental Society.

——. 1948. *Early Indus Civilization.* 2nd edition revised and enlarged by Dorothy Mackay. London: Luzac and Co. Ltd.

Maddin, R. 1998. Early metallurgy: The tin mystery. In *Proceedings of Fourth International Conference on the Beginning of the Use on Metals and Alloys (BUMA-IV).* Matsue (Japan): The Japan Institute of Metals. Pp. 1-14.

Mahadevan, I. 1977. *The Indus Script: Texts, Concordance and Tables.* In *Memoirs of Archaeological Survey of India No. 77.* Delhi: Archaeological Survey of India.

Mair, V.H. 1995. Mummies of the Tarim basin. *Archaeology* 48(2): 28-35.

Majoomdar, G.C and S.N. Rajaguru. 1962-63. Early mining and metallurgy in Rajasthan, copper around Udaipur. *Bulletin of the Deccan College Postgraduate and Research Institute* 23: 31-33.

——. 1965. Comments on soils as environmental and chronological tool. In *Indian Prehistory.* (Eds.) V.N. Misra and M.S. Mate. Pune: Decccan College. Pp. 248-53.

Majumdar, R.C. and A.D. Pusalkar. 1952. *The Vedic Age.* London: George Allen and Unwin. Pp. 565.

Mallory, J.P. 1989. *In Search of the Indo-Europeans: Language, Archaeology and Myth.* New York: Thames and Hudson.

Marshall, Sir John. 1904-05. A new type of pottery from Baluchistan. *Annual Report of the Archaeological Survey of India* 1918-19: 22.

Marshall, Sir John. 1923-24. Exploration and research : Harappa and Mohenjo-daro. Delhi: *Annual Report of the Archaeological Survey of India* Pp. 47-51.

——. 1924. First light on a long forgotton civilization. *Illustrated London News*, 20th September : 528-32.

Marshall, Sir John. 1931. *Mohenjo-daro and the Indus Civilization*. Vols. I & II Text, Vol. III Plates. London: A. Probsthain.

Masson, V.M. 1988. *Altyn Tepe*. Philadelphia: University Museum.

McIntosh, J.R. 2002. *A Peaceful Realm : The Rise and Fall of the Indus Civilization*. Colorado: Westview Press.

McNeil Ian (Ed). 1990. *An Encyclopaedia of the History of Technology*. London : Routledge

Meadow, Richard H. 1989. Continuity and change in the agriculture of the greater Indus valley: The palaeoethnobotanical and zooarchaeological evidence. *Wisconsin Archaeology Review*: 1-16.

——. 1991. *Harappa Excavations 1986-1990*. Madison Wisconsin: Prehistory Press.

Meadow, R.H. and J.M. Kenoyer. 1994. Excavations at Harappa 1993: The city walls and inscribed materials. In *South Asian Archaeology*. (Eds.) Asko Parpola and P Koskikallio. Helsinki: Suomalainen Tiedeakatemia 2: 451-70.

Meadow, R.H. and J.M. Kenoyer. 1997. Excavations at Harappa 1994-1995: New perspectives on the Indus script, craft activities and city organization. In *South Asian Archaeology 1995*. (Ed.) Bridget Allchin. New Delhi: Oxford & IBH Publishing Co. Vol. 1. Pp. 139-172.

Meena, B.R. and A. Tripathi. 2000. *Recent Excavations in Rajasthan*. Jaipur: Jaipur Circle, Archaeological Survey of India.

Miller, Heather M.-L. 1985. Metals. In *Archaeological Excavations in the Area of the Long Row Building, 1984 Season*. (Ed.) Helen Haskell. Texas Antiquities Permit 402. Austin: Texas State Archaeology Department.

——. 1994. Metal processing at Harappa and Mohenjo-daro: Information from non-metal remains. In *South Asian Archaeology 1993*. (Eds.) A. Parpola and P. Koskikallio. Annales Academiae Scientiarum Fennicae; Series B. Helsinki: Suomalainen Tiedeakatemia. Vol. 271. Pp. 497-510.

——. 1997a. Locating ancient manufacturing areas: High-temperature manufacturing debris from surface surveys at Harappa, Pakistan. In *South Asian Archaeology 1995*. (Eds.) Raymond and Bridget Allchin. New Delhi: Oxford & IBH Publishing Co. Pp. 939-946.

——. 1999. Reassessing the urban structure of Harappa: Evidence from craft production distribution. In *South Asian Archaeology 1997*. (Ed.) Maurizio Taddei. Rome: Istituto Italian per l"Africa e l"Oriente (IsIAO) & Istituto Universitario Orientale, Naples.

Miller, H.M-L. and Vidale Massimo. 1997. On the development of Indus technical virtuosity and its relation to social structure. In *South Asian Archaeology 1997*. (Ed.) M. Tadderi. Rome. Pp. 1-15.

Misra, A.K. 1996-97. The iron technology in the Bastar region: An ethnoarchaeological study. *Pragdhara* 7: 187-92.

Misra, V.D. 1977. *Some Aspects of Indian Archaeology*. Allahabad: Prabhat Prakashan.

——. 1999. Agriculture, domestication of animals and ceramic and other industries in prehistoric India: Mesolithic and Neolithic. In *The Dawn of Indian Civilization*. Vol. 1. Part I (Ed.) G.C. Pande. New Delhi: Centre for Studies in Civilizations. Pp. 233-252.

Misra, V.N. 1967. *Pre- and Protohistory of the Berach Basin, South Rajasthan*. Pune: Deccan College.

——. 1970a. Evidence for a new Chalcolithic culture in South Rajasthan. *Indian Antiquary NS, (Festschrift Sankalia)*. Pp. 85-95.

——. 1970b. Cultural significance of three copper arrowheads from Rajasthan, India. *Journal of Near Eastern Studies* 29(4): 221-232.

——. 1971. Two microlithic sites in Rajasthan : A preliminary investigation. *The East Anthropologist* 24(3): 237-288.

——. 1976a. New copper hoards from Midnapur, district Hardoi. Paper presented at annual conference of *Indian Archaeological Society* held at Jaipur.

Misra, V.N. 1976b. Ecological adaptation during the terminal Stone Age in western and central India. In *Ecological Background of South Asian Prehistory.* (Eds.) K.A.R. Kennedy and G.L.Possehl. Ithaca: Cornell University. No. 4: 28-51.

——. 1997. Balathal: A Chalcolithic settlement in Mewar, Rajasthan, India: Results of first three seasons excavations. *South Asian Archaeology (Journal of the Society for South Asian Studies)* 13: 251-273.

Misra, V.N., V.S. Shinde, R.K. Mohanty and Lalit Pandey. 1993. Terracotta bull figurines from Marmi: A Chalcolithic settlement in Chittorgarh district, Rajasthan. *Man and Environment* 18(2): 149-152.

Misra, V.N., V.S. Shinde, R.K. Mohanty, Kurush Dalal, Anup Mishra, Lalit Pandey and J.S. Kharakwal. 1995. Excavations at Balathal: Their contribution to the Chalcolithic and Iron Age cultures of Mewar, Rajasthan. *Man and Environment* 20(1): 57-80.

Misra, V.N., V.S. Shinde, R.K. Mohanty, Lalit Pandey and J.S. Kharakwal. 1997. Excavations at Balathal, district Udaipur, Rajasthan (1995-97), with special reference to Chalcolithic architecture. *Man and Environment* 22(2): 35-59.

Mohanty, R. and S.R. Walimbe 1993. A demographic approach to the Vidarbha Megalithic culture. *Man and Environment* 23 (2): 93-103.

——. 1996. An investigation into mortuary practices of Vidarbha Megalithic cultures. In *Spectrum of Indian Culture.* (Eds.) C. Margbandhu and K.S. Ramchandran. New Delhi: Agam Kala Prakashan. Pp. 157-69.

Mohanty, R.K., A. Mishra, P.P. Joglekar, P.K. Thomas, J.S. Kharakwal and T. Panda. 2000. Purani Marmi: A late Ahar culture settlement in Chittorgarh district, Rajasthan. *Puratattva* 30: 132-141.

Mohanty, R.K., S.B. Ota and M.D. Kajale 1998-99. Chalcolithic pit dwellers of central Narmada valley with special reference to Chikhalda, district Dhar, Madhya Pradesh. *Bulletin of the Deccan College Postgraduate and Research Institute* 58-59: 105-115.

Mohanty, R. and V. Selvakumar. 2000. The archaeology of the Megaliths in India. In S. Setter and R. Korisetter (Ed.) *Indian Archaeology in Retrospect.* Vol. I. Pp. 313-351. Delhi: Manohar Publisher.

Mohanty, R. and S.R. Walimbe. 1993. A demographic approach to the Vidarbha Megalithic culture. *Man and Environment* 18(2): 93-103.

Moorey, P.R.S. 1985. *Materials and Manufacture in Ancient Mesopotamia: The Evidence of Archaeology and Art.* BAR International Series No. S237. Oxford: British Archaeological Reports.

Moorey, P.R.S. 1994. *Ancient Mesopotamian Materials and Industries.* Oxford: Clarendon Press.

Moorti, U.S. 1994. *Megalithic Culture of South India: Socio-Economic Perspectives.* Varanasi: Ganga Kaveri Publishing House.

Mughal, M.R. 1980. New archaeological evidence from Bahawalpur. *Man and Environment* 4: 93-98.

——. 1982. Recent archaeological research in the Cholistan Desert. In *Harappan Civilization: A Contemporary Perspective.* (Ed.) G.L. Possehl. New Delhi: Oxford & IBH Publishing Co. Pp. 86-95.

——. 1984. The Post-Harappan phase in Bahawalpur district, Pakistan. In *Frontiers of the Indus Civilization.* (Eds.) B.B. Lal, S.P. Gupta and S. Asthana New Delhi: Books & Books. Pp. 499-503.

——. 1990a. Further evidence of the early Harappan culture in the greater Indus valley: 1971-1990. *South Asian Studies* 6: 76-199.

——. 1990b. The decline of the Indus civilization and the Late Harappan period in the Indus valley. *Lahore Museum Bulletin* 3(2): 13-14.

——. 1997. *Ancient Cholistan: Archaeology and Architecture.* Lahore: Ferozsons. Pp. 1-170.

Muhly, James D. 1980. The bronze age setting. In *The Coming of the Age of Iron.* (Eds.) A.T.Wertime and J.D. Muhly. New Haven: Yale University. Pp. 25-68.

Munshi, K.N. and R. Sarin. 1970. Analysis of copper and iron objects from Taklaghat and Khapa. In *Excavations at Taklaghat and Khapa 1968-69.* (Ed.) S.B. Deo Nagpur: Nagpur University. Pp. 78-79.

Murty, M.L.K. 1981. Hunter-gatherer ecosystems and archaeological patterns of subsistence behaviour on southeast coast of India : An ethnographic model. *World Archaeology* 13(1) : 47-58.

Nag, A.K. and Dilip Chakrabarti. 1977-78. Copper Hoards from West Bengal. *Puratattava* 9: 97-100.

Nagaraja Rao, M.S. 1971. *Protohistoric Cultures of Tungabhadra Valley : A Report on Hallur Excavations.* Dharwad, Karnataka.

——. 1985. The earliest Iron Age graves in Karnataka. In *Recent Advances in Indo-Pacific Prehistory.* (Eds.) V.N. Misra and Peter Bellwood. New Delhi: Oxford & IBH Publishing Co. Pp. 469-70.

Narsimhaiah, B. 1980. *Neolithic and Megalithic Cultures of Tamil Nadu.* New Delhi: Sandeep Prakashan.

Naswa, Sumedha. 2001. *Tribes of Uttar Pradesh and Uttaranchal.* Delhi: Mittal Publications.

Nautiyal, V., D.P. Agrawal and R.V. Krishnamurthy 1981. Some new analysis on the protohistorical copper artefacts. *Man and Environment* 5: 48-51.

Nautiyal, K.P., B.M. Khanduri, V. Nautiyal and D.L. Rajput. 1978-79. Thapli: A Painted Grey Ware site in Garhwal. *Puratattva* 10: 94-95.

Negi, B.S. 1980-81. Distribution of Painted Grey Ware sites in Bharatpur, Rajasthan. *Puratattva* 12: 120-132.

Neogi, P. 1914. *Iron in Ancient India.* Calcutta.

Nissen, Hans J. 1983. Report on the preliminary archaeological reconnisance in Northwest Sind. Berlin : Free University Press.

Ottaway B.S. 1975. Aspects of early copper smelting. *Journal of the Historical Metallurgy Society* 9(1): 30-31.

Pal, J.N. 1986. *Archaeology of Southern Uttar Pradesh.* Allahabad: Swabha Prakashan.

Pande, B.M. 1987. Missing cultural components between Harappan and Early Historical periods: Some observations based on microstudy. In *Archaeology and History.* Vols. I & II. (Eds.) B.M. Pande and B.D. Chattopadhyaya. New Delhi: Agam Kala Prakashan. Pp. 241-246.

Pande, G.C. (Ed.). 1999. *The Dawn of Indian Civilization Upto 600 BC.* Vol. I, Part 1. New Delhi: Centre for Studies in Civilization.

Panja, S. 1999. Mobility and subsistence strategies: A case study of Inamgaon, a Chalcolithic site in Western India. *Asian Perspectives* 38(2): 154-185.

Pant, C.C. 1988. Mineral wealth of Kumaun: Prospects and problems. In *Kumaun: Land and People.* (Ed.) K.S. Valdia. Naini Tal: Gyanodaya. Pp. 213-222.

Pant, Manju. 1991. Conservation problem and analysis of copper anthropomorphic figures of Bankot in Kumaun. Paper presented in 19th annual conference of *Indian Society for Prehistoric and Quaternary Studies.* Bhopal 16-18th December.

Pant, P.C. 1985. The Megaliths of Jangal Mahal and Vedic tradition. In *Recent Advances in Indo-Pacific Prehistory.* (Eds.) V.N. Misra and Peter Bellwood. New Delhi: Oxford & IBH Publishing Co. Pp. 481-3

Parpola, A. 1984. Interpreting the Indus script. In *Frontiers of the Indus Civilization.* (Ed.) B.B. Lal, S.P. Gupta and S. Asthana New Delhi: Books & Books. Pp. 179-91.

——. 1994. *Deciphering the Indus Script.* Cambridge: Cambridge University Press.

——. 1998. The formation of the Aryan Branch of Indo-European. In *Combining Archaeological and Linguistic Aspects of the Past* (Eds.) Roger Blench and Mathew Spriggs. World Archaeology and Archaeology and Language Series No. 34. London: Routledge. Pp. 180-207.

Patel, Ajita. 1997. The pastoral economy of Dholavira: A first look at animals and urban life in 3rd millennium Kutch. In *South Asian Archaeology-1995.* (Eds.) Raymond Allchin and Bridget Allchin. Pp. 101-114..

Piggott, S. 1944. Prehistoric copper hoards in the Ganges basin. *Antiquity* 18: 173-82.

——. 1948. Notes on certain metal pins and a macehead in the Harappa culture. *Ancient India* 4: 26-40.

——. 1950. *Prehistoric India.* Harmondsworth: Penguin Books.

Pigott V.C. 1981. *The Adoption of Iron in Western Iran in the Early First millennium BC: An Archaeometallurgical Study.* Ph. D. dissertation, Department of Anthropology, University of Pennsylvania.

Pigott V.C. 1984. The Thailand archaeometallurgy project 1984: Survey of base metal resource exploitation in Loei province, Northeastern Thailand. In *South-East Asian Studies Newsletter.* (Ed.) John Villiers. (Thailand: British Institute in South-East Asia, 566 Soi, Somprasong 5, Petchburi Road, Bangkok 10400) 17: 1-5.

——. 1985. Pre-industrial mineral exploitation and metal production in Thailand. *MASCA Journal* 3: 170-175

——. 1996. The study of ancient metallurgical technology: A review. *Asian Perspectives* 35 (1): 89-97.

——. 1999. Reconstructing the copper production process as practised among prehistoric mining/ metallurgical communities in the Khao Wong Prachan Valley of central Thailand. In *Metals in Antiquity.* (Eds.) M.M. Suzanne, A. Young, Mark Pollard, Paul Budd and R.A. Ixer. England: British Archaeological Reports. Pp. 10-21

Possehl, G.L. 1967. The Mohenjo-daro floods: A reply. *American Anthropologist* 69 (1): 32-40.

——. 1979a. *Indus Civilization in Saurashtra.* New Delhi: B.R. Publishing Corporation.

——. 1979b. *Ancient Cities of the Indus.* New Delhi: Vikas Publishing House Pvt. Ltd.

——. 1986a. *Kulli: An Exploration of Ancient Civilization in South Asia.* Durham : Carolina Academic Press.

——. 1986b. African millets in South Asian prehistory. In *Studies in the Archaeology of India and Pakistan.* (Ed.) Jerome Jacobson. New Delhi: Oxford & IBH Publishing Co. Pp. 237-56.

——. 1992. The Harappan civilization in Gujarat : The Sorath and Sindhi Harappan. *The Eastern Anthropologist* 45(1-2): 117-145.

——. (Ed.). 1993. *Harappan Civilization.* New Delhi: Oxford & IBH Publishing Co.

——. 1994. *Radiometric Dates for South Asian Archaeology.* Philadelphia: University of Pennsylvania Museum.

——. 1997. Seafaring merchants of Meluhha. In *South Asian Archaeology-1995.* (Eds.) B. Allchin and R. Allchin. New Delhi: Oxford & IBH Publishing Co. Pp. 87-97.

——. 1999a An Harappan outpost on the Amu Darya: Shortughai. Why was it there? *Indologica Taurinensia* 23-24: 57-70.

——. 1999b Prehistoric population and settlement in Sindh. In *The Indus River: Biodiversity, Resources, Humankind.* (Eds.) A. Meadows and P.S. Meadows. Karachi: Oxford University Press. Pp. 393-409.

——. 1999c *Indus Age: The Beginnings.* New Delhi & Calcutta: Oxford & IBH Publishing Co.

Possehl, G.L. and Gullapalli, Praveena. 1999 The early iron age in South Asia. In *The Archaeometallurgy of the Asian Old World.* (Ed.) V. Pigott. Philadelphia: The University Museum Monograph 89, MASCA Research Papers in Science and Archaeology. Volume 16: 153-175.

Possehl, G.L. and M.H. Raval. 1989. *Harappan Civilization and Rojdi.* New Delhi: Oxford & IBH Publishing Co.

Possehl, G.L. and P.C. Rissman 1992. The chronology of prehistoric India: From earliest times to the Iron Age. In *Chronologies in the Old World Archaeology.* 3rd ed. 2nd vol. (Ed.) R.W. Ehrich. Chicago: University of Chicago Press. Pp. 465-490 and 447-474.

Prakash, B. 1991. Metallurgy of iron and steel making blacksmithy in ancient India. *Indian Journal of History of Science* 26(4): 351-371.

——. 2001. Ferrous metallurgy in ancient India: Part I – Our Metallurgical Heritage. In *Metallurgical Studies in India: A Retrospective.* (Ed.) P. Ramachandra Rao and N.G. Goswami. New Delhi: India International Publisher. Pp. 52-91.

Prakash, B. and V. Tripathi. 1986. Iron technology in ancient India. *Historical Metallurgy* (September issue). Pp. 568-579.

Prasad, Sushma, S. Kusumgar and S.K. Gupta. 1997. A mid to late Holocene record of palaeoclimatic changes from Nal Sarovar: A palaeodesert margin lake in Western India. *Journal of Quaternary Science* 12(2): 153-159.

von Rad, Ulrich, M. Schaaf, K.H. Michels, H. Schultz, W.H. Berger and F. Sirocko. 1999. A 5000-yr record of climatic change in varved sediments from the oxygen minimum zone of Pakistan, Northeastern Arabian Sea. *Quaternary Research* 51: 39-53.

Radhakrishana, B.P. (Ed.). 1975. *The Development of Base Metal (copper-lead-zinc) Deposits in Rajasthan and Gujarat* (suppliment to the *Journal of the Geological Survey of India*, Vol. 16). Bangalore: Geological Survey of India.

Raghunandan, K.R., Shruva B.K. Rao and M.L. Singhal. 1981. Exploration for copper, lead and zinc ores in India. *Bulletin of Geological Survey of India, Series A—Economic Geology* No. 47. Calcutta.

Rajan, K. 1994. *Archaeology of Tamil Nadu (Kongu Country).* Delhi: Book India Publishing.

Ramchandran, K.S. 1971. A bibliography of Indian Megaliths. Madras: State Department of Archaeology.

Rami Reddi. 1992. Megaliths in India : Past and present. In *New Trends in Indian Arts and Archaeology.* (Eds.) B.U. Nayak and N.C. Ghosh. New Delhi: Aditya Prakashan. Pp. 37-44.

Rao, K.P. 1988. *The Deccan Megaliths.* New Delhi: Sandeep Prakashan.

Rao, Ramachandra P. 2001. Iron and steel heritage of India: Contributions from the National Metallurgical Laboratory: Part I – Our Metallurgical Heritage. In *Metallurgical Studies in India: A Retrospective.* (Eds.) P. Ramachandra Rao and N.G. Goswami. New Delhi: India International Publisher. Pp. 182-193.

Rao, S.R. 1963. Excavations at Rangpur and other explorations in Gujarat. *Ancient India* 18-19: 5-207.

——. 1973. *Lothal and the Indus Civilization.* Bombay: Asia Publishing House.

——. 1987. Mining and metallurgy of copper in ancient India. In *Archaeology and History.* Vol. I. (Eds.) B.M. Pande and B.D. Chattopadhyaya. New Delhi: Agam Kala Prakashan. Pp. 383-398.

Rapp, G. 1982. Native copper and the beginnings of smelting: Chemical studies. In *Early Metallurgy in Cyprus, 4000-500* BC (Eds.) J.D. Muhly, R. Maddin and V. Karageorghis. Nicosia: Pierides Foundation. Pp. 33-40.

Ratnagar, Shereen. 1981. *Encounters: The Westerly Trade of the Harappan Civilization.* New Delhi: Oxford University Press.

——. 1995. Harappan trade in its "world" context. *Man and Environment* 19: 115-127.

——. 1999. Does archaeology hold the answer? In *Aryans and Non-Aryans in South Asia.* (Eds.) J. Bronkhorst and M.M. Deshpande. Cambridge: Harvard Oriental Series. Pp. 2207-38.

——. 2000. *The End of the Great Harappan Tradition.* Delhi: Manohar Publisher.

Rea, A. 1902-03. Prehistoric antiquities in Tinnevelly. *Annual Report of the Archaeological Survey of India* Pp. 114-40.

——. 1915. *Catalogue of the Prehistoric Antiquities from Adichanallur and Perumbair.* Madras: Government Press.

Reedy, C.L. 1992. The materials and technology of Gandhara and related copper-based sculptures. In *The Crossroads of Asia* (Eds.) E.Errington, J.Cribb and M. Claringbull. Cambridge: Pp. 241-55.

Reid, L.A. 1988. Benedict's Austro-Tai hypothesis—An evaluation. *Asian Perspectives* 26(1): 19-34.

Renfrew, Colin. 1984. *Approaches to Social Archaeology.* Ediburgh: Ediburgh University Press. P. 106.

——. 1997. *Archaeology and Language : The Puzzle of Indo-European Origins.* London: Pimlico.

Rissman, Paul. 1986. Seasonal aspects of man/cattle interaction in Bronze Age Western India. *Journal of Ethnobiology* 6(2): 257-277.

Rivett-Carnac, J.H. 1877. Rough notes on some ancient sculptures on rock in Kumon similar to those found in monoliths and rock in Europe. *Journal of Asiatic Society of Bengal* XLVI (1): 1-15.

——. 1879. Prehistoric remains in central India. *Journal of Asiatic Society of Bengal* 48: 1-16.

Roaf, M. 1982. Weights of the Dilmun standard. *Iraq* 44: 137-141.

Roy, B.C. 1959. *The Economic Geology and Mineral Resources of Rajasthan and Ajmer.* Calcutta.

Roy Chowdhury, M.K. 1955. Economic geology and mineral resources of Madhya Bharat. *Bulletin of the Geological Survey of India Series.* Calcutta.

Roychoudhury, S., S. Roy, B. Dey, M. Chakraborty, M. Roy, B. Roy, A. Ramesh, N. Prabhakaran, M.V.U. Rani, H. Vishwanathan, M. Mitra, S. K. Sil and P.P. Majumdar. 2000. Fundamental genomic unity of ethnic India as revealed by analysis of mitochondrial DNA. *Current Science* 79(9): 1182-1192.

Sahi, M.D.N. 1978. New light on the life of the Painted Grey Ware people as revealed from excavations at Jakhera (district Etah). *Man and Environment* 2: 101-103.

——. 1979. Iron at Ahar. In *Essays in Indian Protohistory*. (Eds.) D.P. Agrawal and D.K. Chakrabarti. New Delhi: B.R. Publishing Corporation. Pp. 365-66.

Sahni, D.R. n.d. *Archaeological Remains and Excavations at Bairath, Jaipur*. Delhi: Archaeological Survey of India.

Sali, S.A. 1965. A new ceramic of the Chalcolithic from Dhule district, Maharashtra. *Journal of the Asiatic Society of Bombay* 38: 207-210.

——. 1986. *Daimabad 1976-79*. Memoirs of the Archaeological Survey of India No. 83. New Delhi: Archaeological Survey of India.

Sankalia, H.D., 1965. *Excavations at Langhnaj: 1944-63*. Pune: Deccan College.

——. 1969. Kot Diji and Hissar III. *Antiquity* 43: 142-44.

——. 1971. *Chalcolithic Navdatoli: The Excavations*. Pune: Deccan College.

——. 1974a. *The Pre-and Protohistory of India and Pakistan*. Pune: Deccan College.

——. 1974b. Functional significance of the OCP and PGW shapes. *Puratattva* 7: 47-52.

——. 1979. Review of *Essays in Indian Protohistory*. (Eds.) D.P. Agrawal and D.K. Chakrabarti 1979. *Commerce* (Aug.) : 1-2. (quoted from Possehl 1999c)

Sankalia H.D. and S.B. Deo. 1955. *Report on the Excavations at Nasik and Jorwe*. Pune: Deccan College.

——. 1958. *Excavation at Maheshwar and Navdatoli 1953-53*. Pune: Deccan College.

Sankalia, H.D. S.B. Deo and Z.D. Ansari. Pune: Deccan College. Pp. 225-228.

——. 1960. *From History to Pre-History at Nevasa: 1954-56*. Pune: Deccan College.

——. 1969. *Excavations at Ahar (Tambavati)-1962*. Pune: Deccan College.

——. 1971. *Chalcolithic Navdatoli*. Pune: Deccan College.

Sankalia, H.D., G.G. Majumdar and K.T.M. Hegde. 1965. *Archaeology*: *Excavations at Langhnaj: 1944-6*. Part II Pune: Deccan College.

Sankrityayana, Rahul 1958. *Kumaun* (In Hindi). Varanasi: Jnanmandal.

Santoni, M. 1984. Sibri and the south cemetry of Mehrgarh: 3rd millennium connections between the Northern Karachi plain (Pakistan) and Central Asia. In *South Asian Archaeology 1981*. (Ed.) B. Allchin. Cambridge: Cambridge University Press. Pp. 52-60.

Sarkar, S.S. 1960. Human skeletal remains from Brahmagiri. *Bulletin of Dept. of Anthropology, Calcutta* 1: 5-25.

——. 1972. *Ancient Races of the Deccan*. Delhi: Munshiram Manoharlal Publishers Pvt. Ltd.

Sasisekaran, B. and B. Raghunatha Rao. 2001. Iron in ancient Tamil Nadu. Part I. Our Metallurgical Heritage. In *Metallurgical Studies in India: A Retrospective*. (Eds.) P. Ramachandra Rao and N.G. Goswami. New Delhi: India International Publisher. Pp. 92-103.

Sato, Yo-Ichiro. 1996. *Origin of Rice and Rice Cultivation Based on DNA Analysis*. Tokyo: NHK Books.

Seshadri, R. 1992. The composition and smithery techniques of copper artefacts from Nagwada-preliminary study. *Man and Environment* 17: 7-12.

Setter, S. and G.D. Sontheimer (Eds.). 1982. *The Hero Cult in Memorial Stones*. Dharwad : Institute of Indian Art History, Karnataka University. Jim G. Shaffer. 1981. The prehistoric periods in the Eastern Punjab: A preliminary assesment. In *Indus Civilization: New Perspective*. (Ed.) A.H. Dani. Islamabad: Quid-i-Azam University. Pp. 65-102.

Shaffer, J.G. 1984. Bronze age iron from Afghanistan: Its implications for South Asian protohistory. In *Studies in the Archaeology and Palaeoanthropology of South Asia*. (Eds.) K.A.R. Kennedy and G.L. Possehl. New Delhi: Oxford & IBH Publishing Co. Pp. 41-62.

——. 1986. Cultural development in the Eastern Punjab. In (Ed.) J. Jacobson *Studies in the Archaeology of India and Pakistan*. New Delhi: Oxford & IBH Publishing Co. Pp. 195-235.

Shaffer, J.G. 1989. Mathura: A protohistoric perspective. In *Mathura the Cultural Heritage.* (Ed.) D.M. Srinivasan. Delhi. Pp. 171-180.

——. 1992. The Indus valley, Baluchistan and Helmand traditions: Neolithic through Bronze Age. In *Chronologies in Old World Archaeology* (3rd edition) (Ed.) R. Ehrich. Chicago: University of Chicago Press 1: 41-464.

Sharma, A.K. 1998. *Prehistoric Burials of Kashmir*. Delhi: Agam Kala Prakashan.

Sharma, D.D. 1988. Kumauni language and dialects. In *Kumaun Land and People,* (Ed.) K.S. Valdiya. Naini Tal: Gyanodaya. Pp. 120-136.

——. 1989. *Tibeto-Himalayan Languages of Uttarakhand.* Part 1. Delhi: Mittal Publications.

——. 1990. *Tibeto-Himalayan Languages of Uttarakhand.* Part 2. Delhi: Mittal Publications.

——. 1994a. *A Comparative Grammar of Tibeto-Himalayan Languages.* Delhi: Mittal Publications.

——. 1994b. *Linguistic Geography of Kumaun Himalayas.* Delhi: Mittal Publications.

Sharma, Dilli. 1997. Vir Khambha of Western Nepal. *Contributions to Nepalese Studies,* Tribhuwan University 24(1): 57-70.

Sharma, D.P. and M. Sharma. 1991. Two unique lugged shouldered axes of copper hoard in National Museum collection. Varanasi: *National Seminar on Indian Archaeometallurgy.*

Sharma, D.V., V.N. Prabhakar, R. Tewari and R.K. Srivastava. 1999-2000. Harappan jewellery hoard from Mandi. *Puratattva* 30: 36-41.

Sharma, G.R. 1985. Megalithic cultures of northern Vindhyas. In *Recent Advances in Indo-Pacific Prehistory.* (Eds.) V.N. Misra and P. Bellwood. New Delhi: Oxford & IBH Publishing Co. Pp. 477-80.

Sharma, G.R., V.D. Misra, D. Mandal, B.B. Misra and J.N. Pal. 1980. *Beginnings of Agriculture.* Allahabad: Avinash Prakashan.

Sharma, T.C. 1966. *Pre-historic Archaeology of Assam.* Ph.D dissertation (unpublished), London University.

Sharma, Y.D. 1964. Protohistoric remains. In *Archaeological Remains Monuments & Museums.* Pt. 1. (Ed.) A. Ghosh. New Delhi: Archaeological Survey of India. Pp. 1-42.

——. 1964. Remains of early historical cities. In *Archaeological Remains Monuments & Museums.* Pt. 1. (Ed.) A. Ghosh. New Delhi: Archaeological Survey of India. Pp. 43-84.

Sherratt, A. 1994. Core, periphery and margin: Perspectives on the Bronze Age. In *Development and Decline in the Mediterranean Bronze Age.* (Eds.) C. Mathers and S. Stoddart. Sheffield: Sheffield Academic. Pp. 335-45.

Shinde, V.S. 1990. The Malwa culture in Maharashtra: A study of settlement and subsistence patterns. *Man and Environment* 15(2): 53-59.

——. 1992. Padri and the Indus civilization. *South Asian Studies* 8: 55-66.

——. 1998. *Early Settlements in the Central Tapi Basin.* Delhi: Munshiram Manoharlal Publishers Pvt. Ltd.

——. 2000. The origin and development of the Chalcolithic in central India. *Indo-Pacific Prehistory Association Bulletin* 19-3: 125-135.

Shinde, V.S. and Elizabeth Thomas. 1993. A unique Harappan copper fish-hook from Padri, Gujarat. *Man and Environment* 18: 145-147.

Shrivastava, Rina. 1999. Smelting furnaces in ancient India. *Indian Journal of History of Science* 34 (1): 33-45

Singh, Gurdip. 1971. The Indus valley culture: Seen in the context of post-glacial climate and ecological studies in Northwest India. *Archaeology & Physical Anthropology in Oceania* 6(2): 177-189.

Singh, Gurdip and D.P. Agrawal. 1976. Radiocarbon evidence for deglaciation in north-western Himalaya, India. *Nature* 260(5548): 232.

Singh, G., S.K. Chopra and A.B. Singh. 1973. Pollen-rain from vegetation of North-West India. *New Phytology* 72:191-206.

Singh, G., R.D. Joshi, S.K. Chopra and A.B. Singh. 1974. Late quaternary history of vegetation and climate of the Rajasthan desert, India. *Philosophical Transactions of the Royal Society of London.* B, Biological Sciences, 267 (889): 467-501.

Singh, G., R.J. Wasson and D.P. Agrawal. 1990. Vegetational and seasonal climatic changes since last full glacial in the Thar Desert. *Review of Palaeobotany and Palynology* 64: 351-358.

Singh, O.K. 1985. A live Megalithic culture in Manipur. In *Recent Advances in Indo-Pacific Prehistory.* (Eds.) V.N. Misra and P. Bellwood. New Delhi: Oxford & IBH Publishing Co. Pp. 491-96.

Singh, P. 1985. Megalithic remains in the Vindhyas. In *Recent Advances in Indo-Pacific Prehistory.* (Eds.) V.N. Misra and Peter Bellwood. New Delhi: Oxford & IBH Publishing Co. Pp. 473-76.

Singh, Purushottam. 1999. Rise of cultures in Eastern India. In *The Dawn of Indian Civilization Upto 600 BC.* Vol. I, Part 1. (Ed.) G.C. Pande. New Delhi: Centre for Studies in Civilization. Pp. 509-529.

Singh, R., J.F. Merkel and A.K. Singh. 1996. SEM and EPMA analysis of copper objects from Narhan. *Pragdhara* 7:123-129.

Singh, U.V. 1962. Excavation at Eran. *Journal of the Madhya Pradesh Itihas Parishad* 4: 41-44.

Smith, V.A. 1905. Copper Age and prehistoric Bronze implements of India. *Indian Antiquary* 5: 229-44.

——. 1907. The copper age and prehistoric implements of India: A supplement. *Indian Antiquary* 34: 229-244.

Sonawane, V.H. 1992. Fresh light on the specialized crafts of the Harappans of Gujarat. *The Eastern Anthropologist* 45(1-2): 155-72.

——. 1994-95: Harappan settlement of Rupen estuary, Gujarat. *Pragdhara* 5: 1-11.

——. 2000. Early farming communities of Gujarat, India. Indo-Pacific Prehistory: The Melaka Papers. *Bulletin of the Indo-Pacific Prehistory Association* 19(3): 137-146.

——. (in press). Harappan and Harappan affiliated Chalcolithic settlements of Rupen, Saraswati and Banas river valleys of North Gujarat. *National Seminar on River Valley Cultures* IGMRS-BHOPAL Theme 2: Cultural History and Rivers. Pp. 1-23.

Sonawane, V.H. and P. Ajitprasad. 1994. Harappan culture and Gujarat. *Man and Environment* 19(1-2): 129-39.

Srinivasan, K.R. 1946. The Megalithic burials and Urn-fields of South India in the light of Tamil literature and tradition. *Ancient India* 2: 9-16.

Srinivasan, Sharada. 1997. Present and past of Southern Indian crafts for making mirrors, lamps, bells, vessels, cymbals and gongs: Links with pre-historic high tin bronzes from Mohenjo-daro Taxila, South Indian Megaliths and later finds. *South Asian Studies* 13: 209-225.

Stacul, G. 1966a. Preliminary report on the pre-Buddhist necropolis in Swat (W. Pakistan). *East and West* 16: 37-79.

——. 1966b. Notes on the discovery of a necropolis near Kherai in the Gorband valley (Swat-West Pakistan). *East and West* 16(3-4): 261-74.

——. 1969. Discovery of protohistoric cemetries in the Chitral valley (West Pakistan). *East and West* 19: 92-99.

——. 1970. The Grey pottery in the Swat valley and the Indo-Iranian connections (*ca.* 1500-1300 BC). *East and West* 20: 92-102.

——. 1975. The fractional burial customs in the Swat valley and some connected problems. *East and West* 25(3-4): 323-333

——. 1979. The sequence and protohistorical periods at Aligrama (Swat, Pakistan). In *South Asian Archaeology* 1975. (Ed.) E. van Lohuizen-de Leeuw. Leiden: E.J. Brill. Pp. 88-90.

——. 1981. On periods and cultures in the Swat valley and beyond. *Puratattva* 10: 89-91.

——. 1984. Cultural Change in the Swat valley beyond 3000-1400 BC. In *South Asian Archaeology 1981.* (Ed.) B. Allchin. Cambridge: Cambridge University Press. Pp. 205-212.

——. 1987. *Prehistoric and Protohistoric Swat, Pakistan.* Rome: IsMEO.

——. 1995. Early Iron Age in Swat: Development or intrusion? In *South Asian Archaeology.* (Eds.) R. Allchin and B. Allchin. New Delhi: Oxford & IBH Publishing Co. Pp. 341-348.

Stein, Sir Aurel. 1931. *An Archaeological Tour in Gedrosia.* Delhi: Memoirs of Archaeological Survey of India No. 43.

Stuiver, M., P.J. Reimer and T.F. Braziunas. 1998. *Radiocarbon* 40: 1127-1151.

Sundara, A. 1975. *The Early Chamber Tombs of South India: A Study of Iron Age Megalithic Monuments of North Karnataka*. New Delhi: University Publishers.

——. 1979. Typology of Megaliths. In *Essays in Indian Protohistory*. (Eds.) D.P. Agrawal and D.K. Chakrabarti. New Delhi: B.R. Publishing Corporation. Pp. 331-340.

——. 1985. Cultural ecology of the Neolithic in India. In *Recent Advances in Indian Archaeology*. (Eds.) S.B. Deo and K. Padayya. Pune: Deccan College. Pp. 39-57.

Tandon, O.P. 1967-68. Alamgirpur and the Iron Age in India. *Puratattva* 1: 54-60.

Taylor, M. 1841. *Megalithic Tombs and Other Ancient Remains in the Deccan*. Hyderabad: Archaeological Department of Hyderabad State.

——. 1851. Ancient remains at the village of Jiwargi, near Ferozabad on the Bhima. *Journal of the Bombay Branch of the Royal Asiatic Society* 3(2):179-83.

——. 1862. Descriptions of Cairns, Cromlechs, Kistvaens and other Celtic, Druidical or Scythian monuments in Dekkan. *Transactions of the Royal Irish Academy, Antiquity* 24(3): 329-62.

Thakur, V.K. 2001. Iron technology and social change in early India 350 BC-200 BC: Part I – Our Metallurgical Heritage. In *Metallurgy in India: A Retrospective*. (Eds.) P. Ramachandra Rao and N.G. Goswami. New Delhi: India International Publisher. Pp. 134-142.

Thapar, B.K. 1957. Maski 1954: A Chalcolithic site in the Tapti valley. *Ancient India* 13: 1-167.

——. 1965. Neolithic problem in India. In *Indian Prehistory:1964* (Eds.) V.N. Misra and M.S. Mate. Pune: Deccan College. Pp. 87-112.

——. 1964-65. Prakashe 1955: A Chalcolithic site in the Tapi valley. *Ancient India* 20-21: 5-167.

——. 1975. Kalibangan: A Harappan metropolis beyond the Indus valley. *Expedition* 17(2): 19-32.

——. 1979. Excavations at Kalibangan. In. *Ancient Cities of the Indus*. (Ed.) G.L. Possehl. New Delhi: Vikas Publishing House Pvt. Ltd.

——. 1985. *Recent Archaeological Discoveries in India*. Tokyo: Centre for East Asian Culture Studies.

Thapar, R. 1975. A possible identification of Meluhha, Dilmun and Makan. *Journal of Economic and Social History of Orient* 18(1):1-42.

——. 1978. Puranic lineages and archaeological cultures. *Puratattva* 8: 86-98.

Thaplyal, K.K. and S.P. Shukla. 1976. Copper celts with circular depressions: Some observations. In *Archaeological Congress and Seminar Papers*. (Ed.) U.V. Singh. Kurukshetra: Kurukshetra University. Pp. 98-101.

Thomas, P.K. 1988. Faunal assemblage. In *Excavations at Inamgaon*. Vol. I. (Eds.) M.K. Dhavalikar, H.D. Sankalia and Z.D. Ansari. Pune: Deccan College. Pp. 823-962.

——. 1992. Faunal background of Iron Age culture in Maharashtra. *Man and Environment* 17(2): 75-79.

——. 1993. Faunal remains from the Megalithic habitation site at Bhagimohari, Maharashtra. *Man and Environment* 18(2):105-118

Thomas, P.K. and P.P. Joglekar. 1994. Holocene faunal studies in India. *Man & Environment* 19 (1-2): 179-204.

——. 1996. Faunal remains from Balathal, Rajasthan: A preliminary analysis. *Man and Environment* 21(1): 91-97.

Tiwari, R.K. and N.K. Kavdia. 1984. Ancient mining activity around Aguncha village, Bhilwara district, Rajastan. *Man and Environment* 8: 81-87.

Tiwari, Rakesh and R.K. Srivastava. 1997-98. Excavation at Raja-Nal-ka-Tila (1996-97), district Sonabhadra (U.P.) *Pragadhara* 8: 90-106.

Tiziana and Baldizzone, Gianni. nd. *Tribes of India*. Delhi: Bookwise Pvt. Ltd.

Tosi, M. 1982. A possible Harappan seaport in Eastern Arabia: Ras'al-Junayz in the Sultanate of Oman. Paper presented at the First International Conference on Pakistan Archaeology (Peshawar, 1st to 4th March).

——. 1986. Early maritime cultures of the Arabian Gulf and the Indian Ocean. In *Bahrain Through the Ages*. (Eds.) S.H. Ali Al Khalifa and M. Rice. London. Pp. 94-107.

Tripathi, V. 1976. *Painted Grey Ware: An Iron Age Culture of Northern India.* Delhi: Concept Publishing Company.

——. 1984-85. From copper to iron. *Puratattva* 15: 75-79.

——. 1990. Origin and development of iron in India and its economic implications. In *History of Science and Technology 6.* (Eds.) G. Kuppuram and K. Kumudani. New Delhi.

——. 1991. Iron working in ancient India with special reference to excavations at Khairadih. Paper presented in the Annual Congress of the *ISPQS,* Bhopal.

——. 2001a. Emergence of iron in India: Archaeological perspective. Part I – Our Metallurgical Heritage. In *Metallurgical Studies in India: A Retrospective.* (Eds.) P. Ramachandra Rao and N.G. Goswami. New Delhi: India International Publisher. Pp. 25-51.

——. 2001b. *The Age of Iron in South Asia.* New Delhi: Aryan Books International.

Tripathi, V. and Arun K. Mishra. 1997. Understanding iron technology: An ethnographic model. *Man & Environment* 22(1): 59-66.

Tripathi, V. and Amit Tripathi. 1994. Iron working in ancient India: An ethnographic study. In *From Sumer to Meluhha.* (Ed.) J.M. Kenoyer. Wisconsin Archaeological Reports. Vol. 3. Pp. 241-251

Tritsch, F.J. 1973. The sackers of cities and the movements of populations. In *Bronze Age Migrations in the Aegean.* London: Duckworth. Pp. 233-239.

Tusa, S. 1979. The Swat valley in the 2nd and 1st millennium BC: A question of marginality. *South Asian Archaeology 1977.* (Ed.) M. Taddei. Naples: Istitutio Universitario Orientale. Pp. 675-695.

——. 1981. Notes on some protohistoric finds in the Swat valley (Pakistan). *East and West 31*(1-4): 99-120.

Upadhyaya, J.P. 2000. *Metal Implements in Ancient India* (from earliest times to 2nd century BC). Delhi: Pratibha Prakashan.

Vaishnav, A.K. 1977. *Kumaun ka Itihas* (in Hindi). Nainital: Gyanodaya.

Vanzetti, A. and Massimo Vidale. 1994. Formation processes of beads: Defining different levels of craft skill among early bead-makers of Mehrgarh. In *South Asian Archaeology 1993.* (Eds.) A. Parpola and P. Koskikallio. Helsinki: Suomalainen Tiedeakatemia. Pp. 763-776.

Vats, M.S. 1940. *Excavations at Harappa.* 2 Vols. Delhi: Govt. of India.

Vidale, Massimo. 1989. Specialized producers and urban elites : On the role of craft industries in mature Harappan urban contexts. In *Old Problems and New Perspectives in the Archaeology of South Asia.* (Ed.) J.M. Kenoyer. Madison (Wisconsin): UW-Madison Department of Anthropology 2: 171-182.

——. 2000. *The Archaeology of Indus Crafts: Indus Crafts-People and Why We Study Them.* Rome: Instituto Italiano Per L"Africa E L"oriente.

Vishnu Mittre. 1971. Ancient plant economy at Hallur. In *Protohistoric Cultures of Tungabhadra Valley: A Report on Hallur Excavations* by M.S. Nagaraja Rao. Dharwad: Karnataka University. Pp. 125-33.

——. 1974. The beginning of agriculture, palaeobotanical evidence in India. In *Evolutionary Studies in World Crops – Diversity and Change in the Indian Subcontinent.* (Ed.) J. Hutchinson. Cambridge. Pp. 3-33.

——. 1985. The uses of wild plants and the process of domestication in the subcontinent. In *Recent Advances in Indo-Pacific Prehistory.* (Eds.) V.N. Misra and Peter Bellwood. New Delhi: Oxford & IBH Publishing Co. Pp. 281-291.

Vishnu Mittre and R. Savithri. 1973. Supposed remains of rice (*Oryza sp.*) in the terracotta cakes and pai at Kalibangan, Rajasthan. *The Palaeobotanist* 22(2):124-26.

——. 1982. Food economy of the Harappans. In *Harappan Civilization: A Contemporary Perspective.* (Ed.) G.L. Possehl. New Delhi: Oxford & IBH Publishing Co.

Vishnu Mittre, A. Sharma and Chanchala. 1986. Ancient plant economy at Daimabad. In *Daimabad 1976-79* (*MASI* 83). (Ed.) S.A. Sali. Delhi: Archaeological Survey of India. Pp. 588-623.

Wagner, D.B. 1992. *Iron and Steel in Ancient China.* Leiden: E.J. Brill.

Wahal, L.M. 1971-72. Session on OCP, comment on Saipai. *Puratattva* 5:12.

Wakankar, V.S. 1967. Kayatha excavation. *Journal of Vikram University* 1-52.

Waldbaum, Jane C. 1980. The first archaeological appearance of iron and the transition to the Iron Age. In *The Coming of the Age of Iron*. (Eds.) Theodore A. Wertime and James D. Muhly. New Haven & London: Yale University Press. Pp. 69-98.

Wallerstein, I. 1991. *Unthinking Social Science*. Cambridge: Polity Press.

Walimbe, S.R. 1992. Human skeletal remains. In *Megalithic Raipur*. (Eds.) G.B. Deglurkar and Gauri Lad. Pune: Deccan College. Pp. 125-132.

Walimbe, S.R. and A. Tavers. 1992. A biological study of man in India. *Man and Environment* 17(2): 81-91.

Wasson, R.J., D.P. Agrawal, S.N. Rajguru, V.N.Misra, R.P. Dhir, A.K. Singhvi, K. Kameshwar Rao. 1993. Geomorphology, late quaternary stratigraphy and paleoclimatology of the Thar dune filed. *Z. Geomprph. Supple.* 45: 117-151.

Weber, S.A. 1997. Harappan archaeobotany: A model for subsistence. In *South Asian Archaeology 1995*. Vol. I. (Eds.) R. Allchin and B. Allchin. New Delhi: Oxford & IBH Publishing Co. Pp. 115-118.

——. 1998. Out of Africa: The initial impact of millets in South Asia. *Current Anthropology* 39(2): 267-274.

Weisgerber, G. 1984. Makkan and Meluhha: 3rd millennium BC copper production in Oman and the evidence of contact with the Indus valley. In *South Asian Archaeology 1981*. (Ed.) B. Allchin. Cambridge: Cambridge University Press. Pp. 196-201.

Wertime, Theodore A. 1980. The pyrotechnologic background. In *The Coming of the Age of Iron*. (Eds.) A.T. Wertime and J.D. Muhly. New Haven & London: Yale University Press. Pp. 1-24.

Wertime, Theodore A. and J.D. Muhly (Eds.). 1980. *The Coming of the Age of Iron*. New Haven & London: Yale University Press.

Wheeler, R.E.M. 1947. Harappa 1946: The defences and cemetery R37. *Ancient India* 3: 58-130.

——. 1948. Brahmagiri and Chandravalli 1947: Megalithic and other cultures in Mysore state. *Ancient India* 4: 180-310.

——. 1960. *The Indus Civilization*, (2nd ed.). Cambridge: Cambridge University Press.

——. 1968. *The Indus Civilization* (3rd ed.). Cambridge: Cambridge University Press.

Wilhelmy, H. 1969. Urstromtal am ostrand der indusebene und der Sarasvati-problem. *Glazialmorphologie. Zeitschrift Fur Geomorphologie, Supplementband* 8: 76-93.

Willies, L., P.T. Cradock, L.J. Gurjar and K.T.M. Hegde. 1984. Ancient lead and zinc mining in Rajasthan (India). *World Archaeology* 16(1): 222-233.

Wood, Bernard. 1997. The oldest whodunnit in the world. *Nature* 385: 292-293.

Yasuda, Y. 1999. Recent archaeological discoveries in the middle Yangtze basin, China. *YRCP Newsletter* 2 (1): 1-2.

——. 2000. The oldest remains of a Chinese circular walled fortification with a ritual earth mound related to rice cultivation. *YRCP Newsletter* 3(1): 1-4.

——. (Ed.). 2002. *The Origins of Pottery and Agriculture*. New Delhi: Roli Books.

Yule, P. 1985. Metalwork of the Bronze Age in India. *Prehistorishe Bronzefunde*, Abteilung XX, Band 8, Munich: C.H. Beck'sche Verlagsbuchhandlung.

——. 1989. *The Copper Hoards of the Indian Subcontinent: Preliminaries for an Interpretation* (with appendix I by Hauptmann and II by Hughes). Jahrgang: Sonderdruck aus Johrbuch Des Romisch-Germanischen Zentral Museums Mainz.

Zhao Fangzh (Ed.). 1996. *Culture of the Plains* (in Chinese). Shanghai: Yuandong

Zide, Arlene R.K. and Kamil V. Zvelebil (Eds.). 1976. *The Soviet Decipherment of the Indus Valley Script: Translation and Critique*. The Hague: Janua linguarum, Series Practica (156).

INDEX